The Global Trading System

Kym Anderson is Professor of Economics and Executive Director of the Centre for International Economic Studies at the University of Adelaide, Australia. He was a WTO Dispute Settlement Panelist during 1996–2000.

Bernard Hoekman leads the International Trade Group at the World Bank in Washington, DC.

The editors worked together in the Economic Research and Analysis Division of the GATT Secretariat in Geneva during the latter years of the Uruguay Round. Both have authored and edited several books on trade policy and the global trading system.

Tauris Guides to Global Economic Issues

International Debt
S.E. Corbridge
ISBN 1 86064 274 8

The Global Trading System
K. Anderson and B. Hoekman
ISBN 1 86064 058 3

Global Transport Issues
R. Tolley and B. Turton
ISBN 1 86064 564 X

The Global Trading System

Edited by

Kym Anderson

Professor of Economics and Director, Centre for International Economic Studies, University of Adelaide

and

Bernard Hoekman

Senior Economist, International Trade Group, World Bank

Volume 3:
Exceptions to the core rules

I.B.Tauris *Publishers*
LONDON • NEW YORK

Published in 2002 by I.B.Tauris & Co. Ltd
6 Salem Road, London W2 4BU
175 Fifth Avenue, New York NY 10010

In the United States of America and in Canada distributed by
St Martin's Press, 175 Fifth Avenue, New York NY 10010

A full CIP record for this book is available from the British Library
A full CIP record for this book is available from the Library of Congress

ISBN 1 86064 058 3

Library of Congress catalog card number: available

Typeset by I.T.S., Edinburgh
Printed and bound in Great Britain by MPG Books Ltd, Bodmin, Cornwall

Contents

Introduction to Volume 3: Exceptions to the Core Rules

Kym Anderson and Bernard Hoekman

Trading has been going on ever since humankind began seeking to improve well-being. It involves exchanging either endowments or the goods and services produced with them, including through specialization in production: between individuals within households or tribes, between households or tribes located within walking distance of each other, between rural and urban areas within nation states, between nation states and, for more than half a millennium, between continents. The Silk Road provided the first major inter-continental trade link, between Europe and Asia, but it was not until the expeditions of European mariners to the Americas, the Far East and Australasia from the middle of the past millennium that truly global trade began.

Anyone familiar with the history of international trade prior to the mid-twentieth century is acutely aware of its unruliness. Indeed it often took a war between nations before leaders would get together to develop a trade agreement. Even then it would typically be a limited bilateral agreement which, if it hurt other economies, could exacerbate tensions elsewhere. The recent popular history of the spice trade from 1553 to 1667 by Milton (1999) is a reminder of the brutal lawlessness with which international trade was conducted in centuries past. Certainly trade relations were relatively tranquil in the five decades to World War I, but they became unruly again in the interwar period.

When viewed from this historical perspective, the development of the modern global trading system since World War II has been both extremely rapid and far more successful than its planners dared hope for. The modern, legally binding, rules-based global trading system originated with the 1947 General Agreement on Tariffs and Trade (GATT). This was encapsulated in the World Trade Organization (WTO) that came into being in 1995 following the successful completion of the Uruguay Round of multilateral trade negotiations. Over that half-century international trade rose rapidly: more than one-fifth of global output is now exported, double the proportion of the 1950s. The GATT was a major contributor to that growth, as it proved to be a powerful vehicle through which nations were able to overcome domestic resistance to trade liberalization. GATT rules outlawing quantitative restrictions on trade, and successive GATT rounds of negotiations that resulted in cuts in bound tariffs on imports of manufactures by industrial countries led to tariffs coming down to 'nuisance' levels for many products. Manufacturing tariffs of OECD countries now average less than 4 per cent, compared with more than 40 per cent when the GATT was first signed in

1947 by the original 23 contracting parties (who at that time accounted for four-fifths of world trade). That membership, incidentally, has since grown to more than 140, with another 30 in the process of joining. Once the largest traders in that latter group accede, which include China and Taiwan (whose accession is imminent), as well as Russia, the WTO membership will account for more than 95 per cent of global international trade.

Appreciating the differences between the trading environment pre-GATT and today's system is an essential precursor to evaluating the latter. The GATT and now the WTO provide not only a set of multilateral rules and disciplines but also a forum to negotiate tariff reductions and rules changes, plus a legal mechanism to settle trade disputes that is recognized as an integral part of the world's body of international law. The WTO has added three other contributions to those of the earlier GATT: to monitor and report on trade and trade-related policy developments on a regular basis, thereby adding to policy transparency; to facilitate the fuller integration of developing and transition economies into the global trading system; and to improve cohesion between the WTO and other international economic agencies such as the World Bank and International Monetary Fund.

Superior though it is, the current system nonetheless still has plenty of room for improvement. Indeed much attention has been directed in recent years at its shortcomings. Among the issues that have focused attention are globalization, regional integration, noisy trade disputes across the North Atlantic and elsewhere, a perception by some that the system is unfair to developing countries, linkages between trade and other policy areas such as foreign investment or competition policy, and concerns about possible adverse impacts of trade on such things as inequality, poverty, the environment, labour standards, and food safety and security. These concerns were voiced loudly at the third WTO trade ministerial meeting in Seattle in late 1999, contributing to the postponing of the first comprehensive round of multilateral trade negotiations under WTO auspices.

There is thus a need for more-accessible information, knowledge and understanding of what the global trading system is about, how it evolved, how it works, why the world needs it, and what more it can, should, or should not try to do to make the world a more peaceful and prosperous place. These needs were accentuated at Seattle (and subsequently at other economic meetings of world leaders) where it was clear that many of the protesting groups knew little about the WTO and the workings of the rules-based global trading system, nor about what the world might be like without that institution and its rules and procedures.

There are a number of books on the GATT/WTO rules-based global trading system that are readily available.[1] The present set of readings is designed to complement those books with less-readily available journal articles and chapters from edited volumes. They come from the core trade disciplines of economics, law, and political science, but with an emphasis on the editors' profession of economics.[2] Our objective was to collect papers that have been cited often, provide a pertinent historical perspective, and/or address current and future issues that confront the trading system. Because of space constraints, quantitative ex ante and ex post assessments of the economic effects of trade reforms are explicitly excluded.[3] The selection is based on responses to a survey of around one hundred of our colleagues, whom we sincerely thank (with apologies for not being able to include more of their papers!). We also thank the original publishers of the included papers for permission to reproduce them in this collection. A list of the full set of papers in the four volumes, together with their original source, is provided in the Acknowledgements.

The present four-volume set has been prepared around the following topics: the genesis of the GATT; the rules and procedures embodied in the GATT (and, since its inception in 1995, the General Agreement on Trade in Services, or GATS); the exceptions to those rules; and the 'new' issues that confront the WTO membership in the twenty-first century as internationalization progresses further (the lowering of the transactions costs of doing business across national borders). Within each of the four volumes the readings appear in alphabetical order, since that makes them easier to find than if they were ordered chronologically or by sub-topics.

The rest of this chapter provides an introduction to the readings in the current volume, which cover the key exceptions to the core rules and procedures of the GATT (national treatment, MFN). The exceptions relate to coverage in three dimensions: products, countries, and policy instruments. In terms of products, the pre-WTO GATT failed to impact very much on three important and highly distorted sectors: agriculture, textiles and clothing, and services. In principle the first two were subject to GATT rules, but were largely excluded because of protectionist forces in powerful OECD countries (see readings 6 by Finger and 7 by Goldstein in Volume 1 of this set). Services were excluded from the coverage of the GATT from the very start, largely reflecting the fact that services were difficult to trade, especially at that time. In terms of country coverage, the most important exceptions to the rules applied to countries that were also signatories to preferential trading agreements (free trade areas or customs unions), were classed as developing countries, or were centrally planned (now mostly so-called economies in transition). And in terms of policy instruments, administrative protection has been given exceptional treatment under the GATT and WTO. Included among those instruments are safeguards (the escape clause), and anti-dumping and countervailing duties (and hence subsidies). Consider each of these in turn

AGRICULTURE

For millennia, agricultural trade has been subject to government regulation. In pre-industrial societies it was common for countries to restrict or ban food exports so as to ensure adequate supplies in the domestic market. Once industrialization began the political economy would change and, if the country began to lose comparative advantage in farm products, the government often would be called on to intervene so as to ease that structural adjustment pressure. In Britain it took the form of import restrictions until 1846, when the Corn Laws were repealed. When steam engines lowered international grain prices in the middle of the nineteenth century, Britain remained open but several other European countries chose to raise agricultural tariffs (see reading 12 in Volume 1 by

Kindleberger). Japan also imposed a tariff on rice in the early twentieth century as its infant industrialization began to flourish and overshadow agriculture; and Korea and Taiwan followed suit from the late 1960s. So it is not surprising that agricultural liberalization has always been contentious. The first four rounds of GATT-based multilateral trade negotiations virtually ignored the sector and the next three had eventually to drop it too.

What kept it on the agenda of the Uruguay Round of negotiations? Agricultural protection had grown so extreme in Western Europe that surpluses of farm products were accumulating to the point they needed to be disposed of with the help of large export subsidies, to which North America countered with its own export subsidies. This drove down real international prices of farm products by 1986 to below those of the Great Depression. It also raised agricultural protection rates in Europe and Northeast Asia to more than ten times those for the manufacturing sector. Hence even though this sector accounted for less than one-twentieth of their GDP and employment and less than one-tenth of world trade, it was responsible for a large proportion of the remaining distortions to merchandise trade. That fact, and the fact that the low international food prices were hurting the majority of the world's producers who are farmers, stimulated the formation of a coalition of non-subsidizing, food-exporting countries known as the Cairns Group (named after the Australian city where the group first met in 1986). The Cairns Group remained focused on the single issue of ensuring an agreement was reached to stem the cancer-like growth of agricultural protection. As reading 5 by Higgott and Cooper shows, it was extraordinarily successful in achieving its aim, and provides a striking example of how even small and middle powers can, through coalition formation, alter the international economic order.

What in fact was achieved by way of liberalization under the Uruguay Round Agreement on Agriculture (URAA)? Some caps were put on production and export subsidies, non-tariff barriers (NTBs) to imports were converted to tariffs that were bound, and guarantees of low-tariff access up to recent import levels were provided. Their net effect was more a case of standstill than rollback of protectionism but, as Anderson stresses in reading 1, the Agreement at least provides a firm basis on which to continue the process of reform in subsequent negotiating rounds. High on the next round's agenda for the Cairns Group will be to lower substantially the bound tariff rates on farm products, since many countries engaged in 'dirty' tariffication: the setting of bound rates at well above the tariff equivalent of the NTBs they replaced (see reading 7 by Ingco).

Agriculture in the WTO remains exceptional in at least three senses: in that it has a special agreement, rather than being subject to the normal GATT rules on goods; in that export subsidies are formally tolerated in the URAA whereas they are banned for non-agricultural trade; and in that a type of import quota has been legalized for farm products whereas they are disallowed for other products.[4] There is also a positive sense in which agriculture is exceptional, namely, that the URAA brings explicit commitments in addition to general discipline to trade-related subsidies.

TEXTILES AND CLOTHING

Textiles and clothing also have an infamous history within the GATT. Like agriculture, this sector is one of the first to come under pressure to decline as a country's industrialization and economic growth proceed. Being intensive in the use of unskilled labour, standard clothing is one of the first things produced for export by densely populated developing countries as they begin to diversify beyond primary production. When Japan first started to flood international textile markets in the 1930s, the USA sought limitations on the trade. After World War II the flood resumed, but by then the USA was a contracting party to the GATT and strongly committed to the most-favoured-nation principle. Nonetheless, it persuaded Japan to restrain exports to the USA in the mid-1950s. That was not enough though, because other developing countries started to export these products. The United Kingdom also sought export restraints, in its case from Hong Kong and former colonies such as India and Pakistan. But three things were becoming clear: first, these measures were like a finger in the dyke; second, the alternative of formal import quotas would be illegal under GATT and, even if their exceptional use was tolerated, protectionists would demand their use in other sectors; and third, even the use of 'voluntary' export restraints (VERs) would need to be adopted more widely if the flood of import competition were to be stemmed. The solution to this problem was to go outside the GATT mainstream and sign a side agreement in 1961 called the Short-Term Arrangement Regarding International Trade in Cotton Textiles. Within a year this was superseded by a Long-Term Arrangement, but then came synthetic fibres. So in 1974 the Multifibre Arrangement (MFA) came into force.

Ostensibly the MFA and its predecessors were designed to avoid market disruption by providing for managed trade expansion. That necessarily required VERs, since import quotas were GATT-illegal. But such was the extent of industrialization in developing countries from the 1960s that the VERs became increasingly protective and therefore ever more valuable over time. It meant that not only import-competing producers in high-wage countries but also licence-holding exporters in VER-restrained countries had a vested interest in continuing the restrictive trade regime.

As with agriculture, by the 1980s exasperation with the MFA was being felt by developing countries. The Uruguay Round provided them with an opportunity: if advanced economies were going to demand greater access to services sectors and make other demands on developing countries, they could in turn demand greater access to agricultural and textiles markets. Several approaches to reform were considered during the Uruguay Round (see reading 15 by Wolf). In the end an Agreement on Textiles and Clothing was signed as part of the Uruguay Round package. It involves a prolonged phase out over ten years of the MFA. By 2005, all quantitative restrictions on textiles and clothing are to be removed and a GATT-consistent tariff-only regime is to operate. But again as with agriculture, the devil is in the details. Specifically, there is a great deal of back-loading of liberalization: as much as half of the reform can be delayed until the end of 2004. If China joins the WTO before then, as is expected, even though its restraints will continue until at least 2008 it will add further pressure for structural adjustment in advanced economies. As Anderson notes in reading 1, the challenge for developing countries is to ensure that the USA and EU do not employ WTO loopholes allowing for the use of administered protection to prolong their adjustment.

The sobering lesson from this exceptional treatment of textiles and clothing is that the use of VERs and similar instruments has dragged out the liberalization of trade in these sectors over a period of five decades. It is sobering because the tariff quotas introduced for farm products through the URAA share with VERs the feature that those lucky enough to hold in-quota licences develop a vested interest in continuing the system of quantitative restraints. Might the URAA have given birth to a process of phasing out agricultural protection that will also take half a century?

SERVICES

The third group of products neglected by the GATT, in this case entirely, involves services. Declines in international transport and communication costs, together with growth in per capita incomes and the opening up of economies to international investment, have meant that trade in services has been growing faster than trade in goods over recent decades. Even so, the share of global output that is traded internationally is far lower for services than for goods. One reason for that is that services remain more difficult to trade than goods. Another reason is that governmental barriers to services trade are far more pervasive than barriers to trade in goods (with the possible exceptions of agricultural and textile products).

The opportunities perceived by advanced economies for growth in services trade, especially if restrictions on that trade were to be lowered, prompted the USA and EU to insist on services reform being included in the Uruguay Round. Developing countries tolerated this on the condition that agriculture and textiles trade would be liberalized and eventually returned to normal GATT disciplines. The challenges of adding multilateral disciplines on services policies to the trading system were non-trivial. Clearly goods trade is not the same as services trade, not least because the latter often involves factors rather than final products moving across national borders (e.g., foreign investment funds or guest workers).

In 1985, Sampson and Snape provided a concise classification of the different types of services (reading 11), one that was ultimately taken up by Uruguay Round negotiators. A great deal of learning had to go on as the negotiations progressed, both conceptually and empirically. In particular, it was not clear how to measure the extent of barriers to services trade, so new types of commitments had to be invented. Unlike in GATT negotiations, where the emphasis is on identification, quantification and reduction of trade barriers, in services the focus has tended to be on rule-making and absolute sectoral reciprocity.

In the Uruguay Round a new General Agreement on Trade in Services (GATS) was negotiated. The GATS consists of two main elements: general concepts, principles and rules that apply across the board to measures affecting trade in services, and commitments on national treatment and market access. The core

GATT principles of non-discrimination (MFN and national treatment) apply also in GATS, with one big difference. GATT has a 'negative-list approach' whereby non-discrimination applies generally, except in instances where explicit allowance is made for their violation (as for example in preferential trade agreements). That is true only for MFN under GATS, and not for national treatment. GATS adopts a positive-list approach to determine the coverage of the national treatment rule: it only applies to services listed in a country's schedule of commitments, and then only insofar as measures that would violate the principle are not exempted. GATS also introduces a commitment not found in GATT: a market access obligation. This also applies on a positive list basis to each member. Government services are excluded, further narrowing the extent of GATS coverage.

As with the URAA, the main contribution of the GATS was to bring services into the trading system alongside goods. Thus, in future WTO negotiating rounds there will be more scope for cross-sector and cross-issue tradeoffs. Minimal services liberalization commitments were made in the Uruguay Round, the sectoral coverage is far from complete, and the use of positive rather than negative listings is unfortunate (see reading 6 by Hoekman). But more is being learnt all the time about the nature and extent of services trade barriers in member countries, not least through the WTO's Trade Policy Review Mechanism. And new methods of measuring the extent and effects of distortions to services trade are actively being explored. The hope is that over time services, like agriculture and textiles, will become ever less exceptional within the WTO.

REGIONAL/PREFERENTIAL TRADING ARRANGEMENTS

A major exception to the unconditional MFN principle enshrined in GATT Article I is explicitly included elsewhere in the GATT, namely in Article XXIV. That provision allows WTO member countries to enter into free trade agreements or customs unions (or even deeper economic and monetary unions such as the EU), even though such arrangements necessarily introduce discrimination as between WTO members included vs. those excluded. As Snape explains in reading 13, this exception to Article I of GATT can be rationalized as reasonable in the case of a complete customs union, for that is no different from the formation of a federation or the political integration of two or more previously separate countries. Indeed since the GATT contracting parties are customs territories rather than countries, complete customs unions are really not exceptions. The reasonableness of the Article XXIV exception to MFN diminishes to the extent a customs union is less than complete, and is certainly less in the case of a free trade area (FTA) or preferential agreement where members retain their differing external tariff structures. Hence it is not surprising that the USA objected to British preferences and FTAs when the GATT was first being negotiated. In the event preferences were grandfathered and FTAs slipped in at the last moment.

Article XXIV contains the vague phrase 'substantially all trade' in referring to the extent to which trade should be free within a customs union or FTA. The vagueness and its slack application were necessary because the EC-6 probably would otherwise have left the GATT. As it happens no other customs union or FTA has yet been declared in breach of Article XXIV either.

There has been a further exception to the MFN principle in the so-called Enabling Clause negotiated in the Tokyo Round of multilateral trade negotiations. This allows developing countries to do more or less whatever they want with respect to trade preferences for each other, unconstrained by Articles I and XXIV.

Have these exceptions been helpful or harmful to the objective of freeing global trade? This question is addressed in reading 14 by Winters. While his answer in short is that neither theory nor empirical analysis can yet tell us, his survey of the recent explosions of economic analyses addressing this question is nonetheless fascinating and underscores the complexity of the issue.

DEVELOPING COUNTRIES

Many have argued that developing countries have been served badly by the GATT because markets for agricultural and textile products – in which many developing countries have a comparative advantage – became increasingly protected while trade in other merchandise was liberalized over the past half century. On the other hand, the Enabling Clause mentioned in the previous section is but one of myriad exceptions in the GATT and now WTO that have been made for and at the request of developing countries. While it is true that this group of countries would have benefited from earlier cuts in farm and textile protectionism, is it also true that the exceptions provided for them in the GATT helped their economies? As Finger points out in reading 2, the answer is almost certainly no, and the rest of the world also is harmed by those exceptions. He surveys what empirically-supported development economics theory suggests is good trade policy practice for developing countries, and then contrasts that with the exceptional provisions in the GATT.

The exceptions provided for developing countries were easy to give, but once the principle was enshrined in the GATT that the provision of legal freedom to those countries constitutes 'help', there was always the temptation subsequently for industrial countries to give more such 'help' whenever other types of assistance were considered inadequate. This did not matter as much to the economies of rich countries while the developing countries were a small part of the global economy. But it matters increasingly now as those countries grow relative to OECD economies.

Least-developed countries (as classified by the United Nations) have been granted even more exceptional treatment. This is understandable given the political logic in the previous paragraph, but may be even more undesirable economically than the general exceptions for developing countries.

The fact that developing countries in the past have found it relatively easy to obtain special and differential treatment in the GATT does not mean that they have been actively engaged in GATT affairs. On the contrary, the opposite is true. In fact the majority of developing country members – the low- and lower-middle income countries — find it very difficult to become actively involved in

WTO affairs. This is primarily because they are inadequately equipped technically and financially and lack negotiating power (see reading 10 by Michalopoulos). One of the solutions to both problems is coalition formation. While the Cairns Group is a spectacularly successful example of that (see reading 5 by Higgott and Cooper), there are many issues for which it has proven difficult for developing countries to build workable coalitions so as to argue their point of view effectively (see reading 8 by Kahler and Odell). The developing country exceptions relate to a wide range of areas within GATT. Importantly in the early years were the special 'light' procedures for accession to GATT for newly independent countries. In the 1960s, 31 developing countries joined GATT, and only eight of them did not make use of those more lenient provisions. In this as in so many of the exceptions for them, developing countries were allowed to pursue almost any trade policy they wished. That absence of restraint on policy choices has not served developing countries well. As Finger and Winters point out in reading 4, the exceptions have provided governments with less capacity to resist domestic political pressures for protection. It is therefore not a bad thing, economically at least, that the accession process is tougher these days.

The emphasis since the formation of the WTO in special and differential treatment of developing countries has shifted to measures of technical assistance and extended periods of transition. That seems appropriate for low-income/least-developed economies, but there needs to be a system of graduation for higher-income developing countries. The encouragement to developed countries to provide preferential access to exports from least-developed countries, however, not only is inconsistent with the fundamental GATT principle of non-discrimination (it may hurt other developing countries more than it helps the least-developed) but also is detrimental to the process of coalition formation within the developing country group. Far more appropriate would be lower MFN tariffs on all imports of items of export importance to low-income countries, most notably agricultural and textile products.

ECONOMIES IN TRANSITION

Centrally planned economies did not fit into the GATT rules-based trading system, because their producing firms and state trading corporations were not subject to market pricing. They instead formed their own trading system, which was incorporated in the Council of Mutual Economic Assistance (CMEA). Much of the trade within CMEA was transacted on a barter basis, so incentives were unclear and often differed between trades. When the CMEA broke down in the late 1980s, many firms in the socialist economies were uncompetitive internationally while many with a natural comparative advantage had yet to form. The intense intra-CMEA trade also diminished. But it was not just the composition and direction of trade that changed for these countries from the late 1980s; also different for them were the rules of the game. Other socialist countries, including China and North Korea, also chose for decades to be virtually closed to trade with GATT contracting parties. China began opening at the end of the 1970s, and since 1986 has been negotiating its re-admission to the GATT club. Its membership of WTO, and therefore Taiwan's, look imminent at the time of writing (mid-2001).

Only when all the major socialist economies of Eastern Europe and the former Soviet Union (plus a few in the Middle East) join the WTO can the trading system over which WTO rules apply be considered truly global. A few were GATT contracting partners and hence founding members of WTO, others have become WTO members during the past five years, yet others are close to completing their accession, and the residual have a long way to go in terms of trade policy reform before they would be accepted.

There also need to be some changes by WTO members as and when these former socialist economies join. The USA and the EU especially need to review their policies regarding so-called non-market economies as they relate to anti-dumping and, in the case of the EU, safeguards. To date those policies have been subject to even more transparent and arbitrary procedures than those associated with regular administrative protection (see below). As has been argued by several writers (e.g. Michalopoulos, 1999) any country jumping the WTO accession hurdles should be considered a 'market' economy and therefore no longer subject to the stricter 'non-market' provisions of US and EU policies.

ADMINISTRATIVE PROTECTION

A number of situations are allowed for in GATT/WTO rules whereby a member can renege on its market access obligations. Some involve national security or the realization of domestic policy objectives (e.g., Articles XX and XXI of GATT). Others allow trade policies to be used in the context of balance of payments problems. The latter has been invoked often by developing countries—see reading 2 by Finger. The most important exceptions invoked by developed countries, in addition to GATT Article XXIV allowing for regional integration, have been those that allow for action to be taken when imports from another member cause injury (actual or threatened) to import-competing domestic producers of similar products. Three provisions of this type exist in the GATT. One is GATT Article XIX and the Uruguay Round Agreement on Safeguards. These provide for emergency action in situations when unforeseen developments and the effect of obligations result in an import surge. A second is GATT Article VI and the associated Uruguay Round Agreement on its implementation. This provides for action in situations when dumping of imports causes material injury. And third, a number of GATT Articles and the Uruguay Round Agreement on Subsidies and Countervailing Measures allow for countervailing duties to be applied on imports when these have benefited from subsidies.

All three provisions provide plenty of scope for administrators to introduce what is often arbitrary and discriminatory protection. Readings 3 and 9, by Finger et al. and Messerlin, analyse past practices by the USA and EU particularly in the anti-dumping area. Both are among the first rigorous empirical analyses of the use of anti-dumping, which became the instrument of choice in the 1980s and 1990s. Reading 12 by Snape critically assesses GATT rules on subsidies and the use of countervailing duties. There is much scope for tightening multilateral disciplines on administered or contingent protection. The Uruguay Round Agreements in these areas attempted to do that, with at most modest success. It needs to be kept in mind, however, that member governments are likely to be less willing to engage in future tariff cuts if these escape vents are shut. Hence it is not surprising that these exceptions to the more fundamental GATT rules remain.

NOTES

1. See, for example, Diebold (1952), Curzon (1965), Jackson (1969, 1997), Dam (1970), Hudec (1975, 1987, 1993), Tumlir (1985), Winham (1992), Davey, Jackson and Sykes (1995), Hoekman and Kostecki (2001), and Trebilcock and Howse (1999). A new one by economic theorists is due shortly (Bagwell and Staiger, 2002). The legal texts of the GATT/WTO rules are collected in WTO (1995a), while GATT legal case history is summarized in WTO (1995b). Detailed negotiating histories of the Uruguay Round can be found in Stewart (1993, 1999) and Croome (1998).
2. A lawyer's collection is available in Howse (1997).
3. See, for example, Deardorff and Stern (1981) on the Tokyo Round and Martin and Winters (1996) on the Uruguay Round of GATT negotiations.
4. These are called tariff quotas, and they differ from normal import quotas in that in-quota trade is subject to a low or zero tariff while out-of-quota trade is permitted but at a higher tariff; but the 'dirty' tariffication was such as to ensure that little or no trade has taken place out of quota so far.

REFERENCES

BAGWELL, KYLE AND ROBERT W. STAIGER (2002), *The Economics of the World Trading System*, Cambridge, Massachussetts: MIT Press (forthcoming).

CROOME, JOHN (1998), *Reshaping the World Trading System: A History of the Uruguay Round* (revised edition), Geneva: World Trade Organization.

CURZON, GERARD (1965), *Multilateral Commercial Diplomacy*, London: Michael Joseph.

DAM, KENNETH W. (1970), *The GATT: Law and International Economic Relations*, Chicago: University of Chicago Press.

DAVEY, WILLIAM, JOHN H. JACKSON AND ALAN SYKES (1995), *Legal Problems of International Economic Relations*, St. Paul: West Publishing Co.

DEARDORFF, ALLAN V. AND ROBERT STERN (1981), 'A Disaggregated Model of World Production and Trade: An Estimate of the Impact of the Tokyo Round', *Journal of Policy Modeling* 3(2): 127–52.

HOEKMAN, BERNARD AND MICHEL KOSTECKI (2001), *The Political Economy of the World Trading System: The WTO and Beyond*, London and New York: Oxford University Press.

HOWSE, ROBERT (ed.) (1997), *The World Trading System* (4 vols of readings), London: Routledge.

HUDEC, ROBERT E. (1975), *The GATT Legal System and World Trade Diplomacy (2nd edition)*, Salem, New Hampshire: Butterworth.

HUDEC, ROBERT E. (1987), *GATT and the Developing Countries*, Aldershot: Gower for the Trade Policy Research Centre.

HUDEC, ROBERT E. (1993), *Enforcing International Trade Law: The Evolution of the Modern GATT Legal System*, Salem, New Hampshire: Butterworth.

Jackson, John H. (1969), *World Trade and the Law of GATT*, Indianapolis, Indiana: Bobbs-Merrill.
Jackson, John H. (1997), *The World Trading System: Law and Policy of International Economic Relations (2nd edition)*, Cambridge, Massachussetts: MIT Press.
Martin, Will and L. Alan Winters (eds.) (1996), *The Uruguay Round and the Developing Countries*, Cambridge and New York: Cambridge University Press.
Michalopoulos, Constantine (1999), 'The Integration of Transition Economies into the World Trading System' Policy Research Working Paper 2182, Washington, D.C.: The World Bank, June.
Milton, Giles (1999), *Nathaniel's Nutmeg*, London: Sceptre (Hodder and Stoughton).
Stewart, Terence (1993), *The GATT Uruguay Round, A Negotiating History (1986–1992)*, Volumes I to III.
Stewart, Terence (1999), *The GATT Uruguay Round, A Negotiating History (1986–1992)*, Volume IV.
Trebilcock, Michael J. and Robert Howse (1999), *The Regulation of International Trade (2nd edition)*, London and New York: Routledge.
Tumlir, Jan (1985), *Protectionism: Trade Policy in Democratic Societies*, Washington D.C.: American Enterprise Institute.
Winham, Gilbert R. (1992), *The Evolution of International Trade Agreements*, Toronto: University of Toronto Press.
WTO (1995a), *The Results of the Uruguay Round of Multilateral Trade Negotiations: The Legal Texts*, Geneva: World Trade Organization.
WTO (1995b), *Analytical Index: Guide to GATT Law and Practice*, Vols. I and II, Geneva: World Trade Organization.

Acknowledgements

The publishers and editors are grateful for permission to use copyright material.

VOLUME 1: GENESIS OF THE GATT

1. Bagwell, Kyle and Robert W. Staiger (1999), 'An Economic Theory of GATT', *American Economic Review* 89(1): 215–48, March. Nashville, Tennessee: American Economic Association
2. Corden, W. Max (1987), 'On Making Rules for the International Trading System', Ch. 10 in Robert Stern (ed.), *U.S. Trade Policies in a Changing World Economy*, pp. 413–26. Cambridge, Massachusetts: MIT Press.
3. Deardorff, Alan V. (1996), 'An Economist's Overview of the World Trade Organization', in Gordon Flake and Florence Myeong-Hwa Lowe-Lee (eds), *The Emerging WTO System and Perspectives From East Asia*, Washington, D.C.: Korea Economic Institute of America.
4. Diebold, William, Jr. (1952), *The End of the ITO*, Essays in International Finance No. 16, pp.1–37. Princeton, New Jersey: International Finance Section, Department of Economics and Social Institutions, Princeton University Press.
5. Eichengreen, Barry and Marc Uzan (1993), 'The 1933 World Economic Conference as an Instance of Failed International Cooperation', Ch. 6 in Peter Evans, Harold Jacobson and Robert Putnam (eds), *Double-Edged Diplomacy: International Bargaining and Domestic Politics*, pp. 171–206. Berkeley: University of California Press.
6. Finger, J. Michael (1991), 'The GATT as an International Discipline Over Trade Restrictions: A Public Choice Approach', Ch. 7 in Roland Vaubel and Thomas Willett (eds), *The Political Economy of International Organizations: A Public Choice Approach*, pp. 125–41. Boulder, Colorado: Westview Press.
7. Goldstein, Judith (1993), 'Creating the GATT Rules: Politics, Institutions and American Policy', Ch. 6 in J. Ruggie (ed.), *Multilateralism Matters: The Theory and Praxis of an Institutional Form*, pp.201–32. New York: Columbia University Press.
8. Hungerford, Thomas L. (1991), 'GATT: A Cooperative Equilibrium in a Noncooperative Trading Regime?' *Journal of International Economics* 31: 357–69. Elsevier Science Publishers.
9. Irwin, Douglas A. (1993), 'Multilateral and Bilateral Trade Policies in the

World Trading System: An Historical Perspective', Ch. 4 in Jaime De Melo and Arvind Panagariya (eds), *New Dimensions in Regional Integration*, pp.90–119. Cambridge and New York: Cambridge University Press.

10. Irwin, Douglas A. (1995), 'The GATT in Historical Perspective', *American Economic Review* 85(2): 323–8, May. Nashville, Tennessee: American Economic Association.
11. Johnson, Harry G. (1965), 'An Economic Theory of Protectionism, Tariff Bargaining and the Formation of Customs Unions', *Journal of Political Economy* 73(3): 256–83, June. Chicago: University of Chicago Press.
12. Kindleberger, Charles P. (1951), 'Group Behaviour and International Trade', *Journal of Political Economy* 59(1): 30–46, February. Chicago: University of Chicago Press.
13. Kindleberger, Charles P. (1989), 'Commercial Policy Between the Wars', Ch. 2 in Peter Mathias and Sidney Pollard (eds), *The Cambridge Economic History of Europe, Vol. 8*, pp. 161–96. Cambridge: Cambridge University Press.
14. Meade, James (1942), 'A Proposal for an International Commercial Union', British War Cabinet paper reproduced in *The World Economy* 10: 399–407, 1987, and in Susan Meade (ed.), *The Collected Papers of James Meade, Volume III: International Economics*, London: Unwin Hyman, 1988.
15. Staiger, Robert and Guido Tabellini (1999), 'Do GATT Rules Help Governments Make Domestic Commitments?' *Economics and Politics* 11(2): 109–44, July. Oxford: Blackwell.
16. United States Tariff Commission (1919), *Reciprocity and Commercial Treaties*, pp.17–48 & 9–14. Washington, D.C.: Government Printing Office.
17. Viner, Jacob (1924), "The Most-Favored-Nation Clause in American Commercial Treaties', *Journal of Political Economy* 32(1), February, pp.17–39. University of Chicago Press. (Reprinted as Ch. 1 in his *International Economics: Studies by Jacob Viner*, Glencoe, Illinois: The Free Press.)

VOLUME 2: CORE RULES AND PROCEDURES

1. Baldwin, Robert (1986), 'Toward More Efficient Procedures for Multilateral Trade Negotiations', *Aussenwirtschaft* 41: 379–94. *The Swiss Review of International Economic Relations.* Swiss Institute for Research in International Economics, University of St Gallen, Switzerland.
2. Baldwin, Robert E. and Richard N. Clarke (1988), 'Game-Modeling Multilateral Trade Negotiations', *Journal of Policy Modeling* 9: 257–84. Elsevier.© Society for Policy Modeling 1987.
3. Caplin, A. and Karla Krishna (1988), 'Tariffs and the Most-Favored-Nation Clause: A Game Theoretic Approach', *Seoul Journal of Economics* 1(3): 267–89.
4. Conybeare, H.A.C. (1988), 'Managing International Trade Conflicts: Explanations and Prescription', *Journal of International Affairs* 42(1): 75–91.© Trustees of Columbia University in the City of New York.
5. Finger, J. Michael (1974), 'GATT Tariff Concessions and the Exports of Developing Countries – United States Concessions at the Dillon Round', *Economic Journal* 84(335): 566–75, September. Oxford: Blackwell.

6. Hillman, Arye and Peter Moser (1995), 'Trade Liberalization as Politically Optimal Exchange of Market Access', in M. Canzoneri, Wilfred Ethier and Vittorio Grilli (eds), *The New Transatlantic Economy*, Cambridge and New York: Cambridge University Press.
7. Jackson, John H. (1998), 'Designing and Implementing Effective Dispute Settlement Procedures: WTO Dispute Settlement, Appraisal and Prospects', Ch. 5 in Anne O. Krueger (ed.), *The WTO as an International Organization*, pp.161–80. Chicago: University of Chicago Press.
8. Kovenock, Dan and Marie Thursby (1992), 'GATT, Dispute Settlement and Cooperation', *Economics and Politics* 4(2): 151–70, July. Oxford: Blackwell.
9. Laird, Sam (1999), 'The WTO's Trade Policy Review Mechanism – From Through the Looking Glass', *The World Economy* 22(6): 741–64, August. Oxford: Blackwell.
10. Ludema, Rodney D. (1991), 'International Trade Bargaining and the Most-Favored-Nation Clause', *Economics and Politics* 3(1): 1–20, March. Oxford: Blackwell.
11. McMillan, John (1989), 'A Game-Theoretic View of International Trade Negotiations: Implications for the Developing Countries', Ch. 2 in John Whalley (ed.), *Rules, Power and Credibility*, pp. 26–44. London: University of Western Ontario.
12. Rhodes, Carolyn (1989), 'Reciprocity in Trade: The Utility of a Bargaining Strategy', *International Organization* 43(2): 273–99. ©1989 World Peace Foundation and the Massachusetts Institute of Technology.
13. Schwartz, Warren F. and Alan O. Sykes (1996), 'Toward a Positive Theory of the Most-Favored-Nation Obligation and Its Exceptions in the WTO/GATT System', *International Review of Law and Economics* 16(1): 27–51, March. Elsevier Science.
14. Stern, Robert M. (1976), 'Evaluating Alternative Formulae for Reducing Industrial Tariffs', *Journal of World Trade Law* 10(1): 50–64.
15. Viner, Jacob (1931), 'The Most-Favored-Nation Clause', *Index 6*, pp.94–108. Stockholm: Svenska Handelsbanken, January. (Reprinted as Ch. 5 in his *International Economics: Studies by Jacob Viner*, Glencoe IL: The Free Press.)
16. Winters, L. Alan (1987), 'Negotiating the Abolition of Non-Tariff Barriers', *Oxford Economic Papers* 39: 465–80. Oxford: Oxford University Press.
17. Winters, L. Alan (1987), 'Reciprocity', Ch. 7 in J. Michael Finger, and Andrzej Olechowski (eds), *The Uruguay Round: A Handbook on the Multilateral Trade Negotiations*, pp. 45–51. Washington, D.C.: The World Bank.
18. Wolf, Martin (1984), 'Two-Edged Sword: Demands of Developing Countries and the Trading System', Ch. 9 in Jagdish Bhagwati and John Gerard Ruggie (eds), *Power, Passions, and Purpose: Prospects for North-South Negotiations*, pp. 201–29. Cambridge, Massachussetts: MIT Press.

VOLUME 3: EXCEPTIONS TO THE CORE RULES

1. Anderson, Kym (2001), 'Bringing Discipline to Agricultural Policy via

WTO', Ch. 3 in Bernard Hoekman and Will Martin (eds), *Developing Countries and the WTO: A Pro-active Agenda*, Oxford: Blackwell.

2. FINGER, J. MICHAEL (1991), 'Development Economics and the General Agreement on Tariffs and Trade', Ch. 13 in Jaime De Melo and Andre Sapir (eds), *Trade Theory and Economic Reform: North, South, and East: Essays in Honor of Bela Balassa*, pp. 203–23. Oxford: Blackwell.
3. FINGER, J. MICHAEL, H. KEITH HALL AND DOUGLAS R. NELSON (1982), 'The Political Economy of Administered Protection', *American Economic Review* 72(3): 452–66, June. Nashville, Tennessee: American Economic Association.
4. FINGER, J. MICHAEL AND L. ALAN WINTERS (1998), 'What Can the WTO Do for Developing Countries?' Ch. 14 in Anne O. Krueger (ed.), *The WTO as an International Organization*, pp. 365–93. Chicago: University of Chicago Press.
5. HIGGOTT, RICHARD A. AND ANDREW F. COOPER (1990), 'Middle Power Leadership and Coalition Building: Australia, the Cairns Group and the Uruguay Round of Trade Negotiations', *International Organization* 44(4): 589–632, Autumn. ©1990 World Peace Foundation and the Massachusetts Institute of Technology.
6. HOEKMAN, BERNARD (1996), 'Assessing the General Agreement on Trade in Services', Ch. 4 in Will Martin and L. Alan Winters (eds), *The Uruguay Round and the Developing Countries*, pp. 88–123. Cambridge and New York: Cambridge University Press.
7. INGCO, MERLINDA D. (1996), 'Tariffication in the Uruguay Round: How Much Liberalisation?' *The World Economy* 19(4): 425–46, July. Oxford: Blackwell.
8. KAHLER, MILES AND JOHN ODELL (1988), 'Developing Country Coalition-Building and International Trade Negotiations', Ch. 8 in John Whalley (ed.), *Rules, Power and Credibility*, pp.149–67. London: University of Western Ontario.
9. MESSERLIN, PATRICK A. (1989), 'The EC Antidumping Regulations: A First Economic Appraisal, 1980–85', *Weltwirtschaftliches Archiv*, 125(3): 563–87.
10. MICHALOPOULOS, CONSTANTINE (1999), 'The Developing Countries' Participation in the WTO', *The World Economy*, 22(1): 117–43, January. Oxford: Blackwell.
11. SAMPSON, GARY AND RICHARD H. SNAPE (1985), 'Identifying the Issues in Trade in Services', *The World Economy*, 8: 171–81. Oxford: Blackwell.
12. SNAPE, RICHARD H. (1991), 'International Regulation of Subsidies', *The World Economy,* 14: 139–64. Oxford: Blackwell.
13. SNAPE, RICHARD H. (1992), 'History and Economics of GATT's Article XXIV', Ch. 12 in Kym Anderson and Richard Blackhurst (eds), *Regional Integration and the Global Trading System*, pp.273–91. London: Harvester Wheatsheaf and New York: St Martin's Press.
14. WINTERS, L. ALAN (1998), 'Regionalism versus Multilateralism', in Richard Baldwin, David Cole, Andre Sapir and Anthony Venables (eds), *Regional Integration*, pp. 1–39. Cambridge and New York: Cambridge University Press.

15. WOLF, MARTIN (1990), 'How to Cut the Textile Knot: Alternative Paths to Liberalization of the MFA', Ch. 9 in Carl Hamilton (ed.), *Textiles Trade and the Developing Countries: Elimination of the MFA in the 1990s*, pp. 215–37. Washington, D.C.: World Bank.

VOLUME 4: 'NEW' ISSUES FOR THE WTO

1. ANDERSON, KYM (1998), 'Environmental and Labor Standards: What Role for the WTO?' Ch. 8 in Anne O. Krueger (ed.), *The WTO as an International Organization*, pp. 231–55. Chicago: University of Chicago Press.
2. BHAGWATI, JAGDISH N. (1994), 'Fair Trade, Reciprocity and Harmonization: The New Challenge to the Theory and Policy of Free Trade', Ch. 13 in Alan V. Deardorff and Robert M. Stern (eds), *Analytical and Negotiating Issues in the Global Trading System*, pp.547–61. Ann Arbor: University of Michigan Press.
3. BHAGWATI, JAGDISH N. AND T.N. SRINIVASAN (1996), 'Trade and the Environment: Does Environmental Diversity Detract from the Case for Free Trade?' Ch. 4 in Jagdish N. Bhagwati and Robert E. Hudec (eds), *Fair Trade and Harmonization: Prerequisites for Free Trade? Vol. 1: Economic Analysis*, pp. 159–99. Cambridge, Massachusetts: MIT Press.
4. BROWN, DRUSILLA K., ALAN V. DEARDORFF AND ROBERT M. STERN (1996), 'International Labor Standards and Trade: A Theoretical Analysis', Ch. 5 in Jagdish N. Bhagwati and Robert E. Hudec (eds), *Fair Trade and Harmonization: Prerequisites for Free Trade? Vol. 1: Economic Analysis*, pp. 227–80. Cambridge, Massachusetts: MIT Press.
5. DAVIDOW, JOEL (1981), 'The Seeking of a World Competition Code: Quixotic Quest?' pp. 361–403 in Oscar Schachter and Robert Hellawell (eds), *Competition in International Business*, New York: Columbia University Press.
6. DEARDORFF, ALAN V. (1992), 'Welfare Effects of Global Patent Protection', *Economica* 59: 35–51, February. Oxford: Blackwell.
7. HAMILTON, BOB AND JOHN WHALLEY (1984), 'Efficiency and Distributional Implications of Global Restrictions on Labour Mobility', *Journal of Development Economics* 14: 61–75. Elsevier Science Publishers.
8. HOEKMAN, BERNARD (1997), 'Competition Policy and the Global Trading System', *The World Economy* 20(4): 383–406, July. Oxford: Blackwell.
9. MCCULLOCH, RACHEL AND ROBERT OWEN (1983), 'Linking Negotiations on Trade and Foreign Direct Investment', Ch. 14 in Charles Kindleberger and David Audretsch (eds), *The Multinational Corporation in the 1980s*, pp. 334–58. Cambridge, Massachusetts: MIT Press.
10. NOGUES, JULIO (1990), 'Patents and Pharmaceutical Drugs: Understanding the Pressures on Developing Countries', *Journal of World Trade* 24(6): 81–104.
11. PALMETER, DAVID (1999), 'National Sovereignty and the World Trade Organization', *Journal of World Intellectual Property* 2(1): 77–91. Geneva, Switzerland: Werner Publishing Company.
12. SYKES, ALAN O. (1999), 'Regulatory Protectionism and the Law of

International Trade', *University of Chicago Law Review* 66(1): 1–46, Winter. ©1999 University of Chicago.

13. Tussie, Diana (1994), 'The Policy Harmonization Debate: What Can Developing Countries Gain From Multilateral Negotiations?' *UNCTAD Review* 5: 1–8. Geneva and New York: United Nations.
14. Vogel, David (1997), 'Trouble for Us and Trouble for Them: Social Regulations as Trade Barriers', Ch. 3 in Pietro Nivola (ed.), *Comparative Disadvantages: Social Regulations and the Global Economy*, pp. 98–145. Washington, D.C.: Brookings Institution.
15. Williamson, Jeffrey G. (1998), 'Globalization, Labor Markets and Policy Backlash', *Journal of Economic Perspectives* 12(4): 51–72, Fall. Nashville, Tennessee: American Economic Association.

1. Bringing Discipline to Agricultural Policy via WTO

K. Anderson

Many perceive one of the great achievements of the Uruguay Round (UR) to be the start to bringing agricultural policies under GATT discipline.[1] Following the signing of the UR accord in 1994, non-tariff barriers to agricultural imports are required to be tariffied and bound and those bound tariffs are scheduled for phased reductions. As well, farm production and export subsidies also are to be reduced, mostly between 1995 and 2000 (with developing countries having an extra four or more years). That UR Agreement on Agriculture (URAA), together with the SPS Agreement (to limit the use of quarantine import restrictions to cases that can be justified scientifically) and the Dispute Settlement Agreement (which has greatly improved the process of resolving trade conflicts), ensure that agricultural trade will be less chaotic in future than prior to the formation in 1995 of the new World Trade Organization (WTO).

Much remains to be done, however, before agricultural trade is as fully disciplined or as free as world trade in manufactures. This paper first explains why agricultural policies need to be disciplined under the WTO (Section 1). It then examines what has been achieved through implementation of the URAA (Section 2), evaluates its impacts on developing countries (Section 3), explores what remains to be tackled as WTO members come back to the negotiating table in 2000, as was agreed in the URAA (Section 4), and reviews ways developing countries can seek to ensure that the process of reform by them and others continues as we move into the next millennium (Section 5).

1. WHY AGRICULTURAL POLICIES NEED TO BE DISCIPLINED UNDER THE GATT/WTO

The history of industrial and post-industrial development has been overlaid with a history of agricultural protection growth. Poor agrarian economies tend to tax agriculture relative to other tradeables sectors, but as nations industrialize their policy regimes tend to gradually change from negatively to positively assisting farmers relative to other producers (and conversely from subsidizing to taxing food consumers). The period since the 1950s has seen substantial growth in agricultural protectionism in the advanced industrial economies and its spread to newly industrializing economies, and those tendencies accelerated in the 1980s (Anderson and Hayami 1986; Anderson 1994, 1995; Lindert 1991).

Given this history, the attempt in the Uruguay Round to reduce farm price supports was seen as both exciting and daunting: exciting, because a successful liberalization would reduce the huge and growing waste of resources that would be associated with the continuation of past trends in farm policies; and daunting, because the history of those policy trends across many countries and over a long period suggests major counter-acting of domestic political forces would be needed for a multilateral agreement to be reached and then implemented.

It seems almost incredible that the Uruguay Round could have been prolonged for years by a farm trade dispute affecting products that account for less than one-tenth of world trade and less than one-twentieth of GDP and employment in the main countries seeking exceptional treatment for agriculture. It seems all the more amazing given that the economies hurt most by these policies are those of the protecting countries themselves. The protectionist policies are wasteful in terms of raising consumer prices for food; requiring ever-larger treasury outlays to farmers; redistributing welfare with increasing inefficiency (not only because it costs consumers and taxpayers much more than one dollar for every dollar received by farmers, but also because the largest producers receive the lion's share of the benefits); making non-agricultural producers less competitive in so far as farm programs retain resources in agriculture; and damaging the natural environment, not least because these price-support policies typically encourage excessive use of farm chemicals (Tyers and Anderson 1992).

Why has agreement on farm trade reform been so difficult to reach? The issue involves two groups of countries. On the one hand, there are the traditionally lightly protected, food-exporting countries, involving not only the members of the Cairns Group[2] but also numerous other developing countries; and on the other hand, there are industrial countries of Western Europe, Japan and Korea that are highly protective of their farmers. Both groups have felt strongly about their positions for a long time. Indeed it is *because* those policies are so contentious that (a) the first four rounds of GATT-based multilateral trade negotiations virtually ignored them and the next three eventually had to drop them, and (b) many minilateral (regional and other preferential) trade agreements also largely exclude farm products. We should therefore not be surprised that the inclusion of farm policies in the Uruguay Round caused problems. Their inclusion was considered necessary, however, because they had become extremely distortionary by the 1980s, both absolutely and relative to non-farm trade policies, and because there was every indication that agricultural protection growth would continue to spread, cancer-like, unless explicitly checked.

The growth of agricultural protectionism in industrializing countries has contributed to the long-term downward trend in the international price of farm products relative to that for industrial products (Figure 1). What is striking about Figure 1 is not only the extent of decline of the relative price of food but also the increase in its coefficient of variation during the past two decades. That, together with the EC's provision from the latter 1970s of export subsidies to dispose of its induced surpluses, stimulated the US to defend its export markets by subsidizing US farm exports as well – a move that contributed to international food prices falling by 1987 to their lowest level this century in real terms. The export subsidies under the US Export Enhancement Program have been very

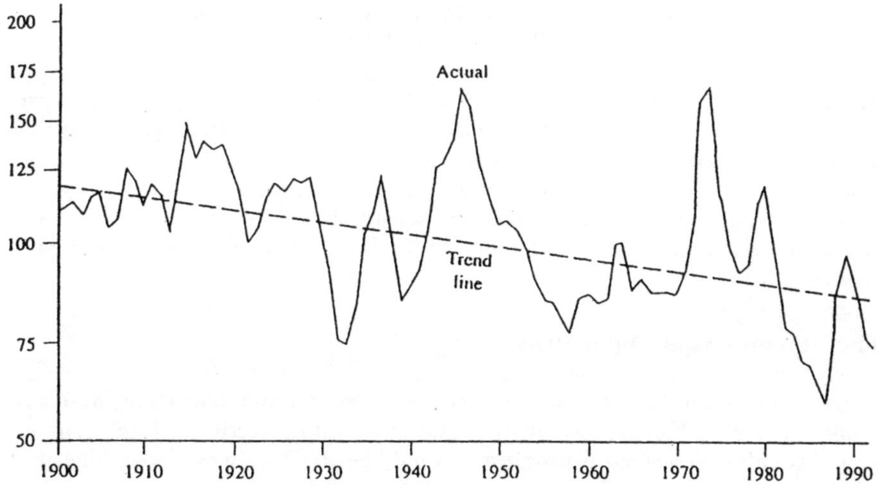

FIGURE 1 Real international food prices, 1900 to 1992 (1977–79 = 100)

Source: Updated from Grilli and Yang (1988), showing an index of export prices in US dollars for cereals, meats, dairy products and sugar, deflated by the US producer price index (primarily for industrial products), with weights based on the importance of each product in global exports in the 1977–79 base period.

costly to the US, have added only very modestly in proportional terms to the EC budgetary cost of the Common Agricultural Policy, and have imposed large costs on other actual or would-be agricultural-exporting countries.

As a consequence of these policy developments (reasons for which are analysed in Anderson 1995), the deadweight welfare losses in those protecting countries from distorting their food markets more than doubled over the 1980s, while the benefits to their farmers as a group increased by about 50 per cent. According to one set of estimates from a multicommonly model of world food markets, the annual benefits of these policies to farmers of Western Europe, the United States and Japan rose from $94 to $141 billion over the 1980s (in 1985 US dollars), while the cost to consumers in those countries rose from $120 to $216 billion. That study estimates the direct global loss of economic welfare because of industrial country food policies to have trebled in the 1980s, rising from $16 billion to $50 billion (Tyres and Anderson 1992, Tables 6.5, 6.6). And that does not include the costs of lobbying for and administering the policies, nor the collection and by-product distortion costs of raising the government revenue needed to finance the subsidies, let alone the indirect cost these policies imposed in terms of holding up the Uruguay Round's conclusion.

2. THE URUGUAY ROUND ACHIEVEMENTS AFFECTING AGRICULTURE

Agriculture benefited in several important ways from the Uruguay Round. Apart from the Agreement on Agriculture itself, there were agreements relating to SPS provisions (quarantine) and to textiles and clothing trade (which will boost net food imports of newly industrializing countries), requirements to notify and review all trade-related policy developments which will boost transparency, and major improvements in dispute settlement producers. Each of these is considered in turn.

The Agreement on Agriculture

In the light of the long history of agricultural protection growth in industrial countries, even achieving a standstill in agricultural protection via the Uruguay Round could be described as progress. It would be an advance over what otherwise might have been the case in part because it would reduce the risk of newly industrializing countries following the more advanced ones down the agricultural protection growth path. As it turned out, though, only a little more than a standstill was agreed to.

The Uruguay Round's Agreement on Agriculture has three main components: reductions in farm export subsidies, increases in import market access, and cuts in domestic producer subsidies. The fact that (often discriminatory) farm export subsidies are still to be tolerated continues to distinguish agricultural from industrial goods in the GATT, a distinction that stems from the addition in 1955 of paragraphs to GATT Article XVI when the United States insisted on primary products being exempted from the new prohibition of export subsidies. Moreover, even by the year 2000 farm export subsidies need be only about one fifth lower than they were in the late 1980s to comply with the agreement. True, the budgetary expenditure on export subsidies is to be lowered by 26 per cent from the base period, but for some commodities it may be only the agreed cut in the *volume* of subsidized exports (21 per cent for industrial countries, 14 per cent for developing countries) that bites because international food prices in the latter 1990s were higher than in the base period, so exportable surpluses have been able to be disposed of with lower subsidy outlays.

A second distinguishing feature of the agricultural agreement is that it requires nontariffs import barriers to be converted to tariffs. Those tariffs are now bound and those bindings are to be reduced over the implementation period. However, the extent of bound tariff reduction by the end of the century will be even more modest than for export subsidies: the *unweighted* average tariff cut must be 36 per cent (24 per cent for developing countries), but it could be less than one sixth as a *weighted* average, since each tariff item need be reduced by only 15 per cent of the claimed 1986–88 tariff equivalents (10 per cent for developing countries).

Moreover, the claimed tariff equivalents for the base period 1986–88, and hence the initial tariff bindings, are in many cases far higher than the actual tariff equivalents of the time. The European Union, for example, has set them on

TABLE 1 *Uruguay Round tariff bindings and actual tariff equivalents of agricultural protection, European Union and United States, 1986 to 2000*

	Actual tariff equivalent (%), 1989–93	Tariff binding Final period 2000(%)	Tariff binding Proportional reduction by 2000(%)	'Dirty' tariff-ication,[a] 1986–88	Binding 2000/ actual tariff equivalent, 1989–93
European Union					
Wheat	68	109	36	1.60	1.60
Coarse grains	89	121	36	1.42	1.36
Rice	103	231	36	2.36	2.24
Beef and veal	97	87	10	1.00	0.90
Other meat	27	34	36	1.32	1.26
Dairy products	147	205	29	1.63	1.39
Sugar	144	279	6	1.27	1.94
ALL AGRIC.					
Unweighted av.	**45**	**73**		**1.61**	**1.63**
std. deviation	**57**	**96**		**1.58**	**1.68**
United States					
Wheat	20	4	36	0.30	0.20
Coarse grains	2	2	74	2.00	1.00
Rice	2	3	36	5.00	1.50
Beef and veal	2	26	15	10.33	13.00
Other meat	1	3	36	0.67	3.00
Dairy products	46	93	15	1.09	2.02
Sugar	67	91	15	1.50	1.36
ALL AGRIC.					
Unweighted av.	**13**	**23**		**1.44**	**1.77**
std. deviation	**22**	**35**		**1.20**	**1.59**

[a]Announced base tariff rate as ratio of actual tariff equivalent in the base period.
Source: Ingco (1995).

average at about 60 per cent above the actual tariff equivalents of the CAP in recent years, while the United States has set theirs about 45 per cent above recent rates. This 'dirty' tariffication is shown in column 4 of Table 1 for the US and EU to be considerable. Nor is it confined to industrial countries. On the contrary, developing countries are even more involved in the practice. This is possible because they were allowed to convert unbound tariffs into 'ceiling bindings' unrelated to previous actual rates of protection. Many developing countries have chosen to bind their tariffs on agricultural imports at more than 50 per cent and some as high as 150 per cent – far above the tariff equivalents of restrictions actually in place in the 1980s/early 1990s (Ingco 1996). Josling (1998b, Table 1) calculates that the unweighted average bound tariffs by 2000 for a sample of 20 major countries will be between 42 and 49 per cent for each of grains, oilseeds, sugar and livestock products, and 35 per cent for fruit and vegetables.

'Dirty' tariffication has two consequences. One is that actual tariffs may provide no less protection by 2000 than did the non-tariff import barriers of the late 1980s/early 1990s. Indeed in the case of the EU the final rates for the year 2000 are almost two-thirds above the actual tariff equivalent for 1989–93, and for the United States they are more than three-quarters above (final column of Table 1). The other consequence of binding tariffs at such a high level is that it allows countries to set the actual tariff below that but to vary it so as to stabilize the domestic market in much the same way as the EU has done in the past with its system of variable import levies and export subsidies. This means there will be little of the reduction in fluctuations in international food markets this decade that tariffication was expected to deliver.

It is true that some countries have agreed also to provide a minimum market access opportunity, such that the share of imports in domestic consumption for products subject to import restrictions rises to at least 5 per cent by the year 2000 under a tariff quota (less in the case of developing countries). But that access is subject to special safeguard provisions, so it only offers potential rather than actual access (another form of contingent protection). As well, there is scope to minimize the impact of those imports on the domestic market. Furthermore, market access rules formally introduce scope for discriminating in the allocation of import quotas between countries, where within-quota imports attract a much lower tariff than above-quota imports. Perhaps even more importantly, the administration of such quotas tends to legitimize a role for state trading agencies. When such agencies have selling rights on the domestic market in addition to a monopoly on imports of farm products, they can charge excessive mark-ups and thereby distort domestic prices easily and relatively covertly – just as such agencies can hide export subsidies if they are given that monopoly. There are thus elements of quantitative management of both export and import trade in farm products now legitimized under the WTO, including scope for discriminatory distortions to trade volumes as well as prices.

The third main component of the agriculture agreement is that the aggregate level of domestic support (AMS) for industrial-country farmers is to be reduced to four-fifths of its 1986–88 level by the turn of the century. That too will require only modest reform in most industrial countries because much of the decline in the AMS had already occurred by the mid-1990s. Furthermore, there are many forms of support that need not be included in the calculation of the AMS. Perhaps the most important are direct payments under production-limiting programs of the sort adopted by the US and EU, which are classified as 'blue box' exemptions. A risk that needs to be curtailed is that the use of such 'blue box' and 'green box' instruments may spread to other developed countries and other commodities as farm income support via trade and domestic price support measures becomes less available and in some cases eventually WTO-illegal.

In short, implementing the agricultural reforms agreed to in the Uruguay Round will involve only very modest liberalization by 2000, with plenty of room for disputes over compliance during the implementation period and for further reductions in the new millennium (see column 2 of Table 1). Only a small number

TABLE 2 *Estimated impact of implementing the Uruguay Round on international prices of farm products relative to prices of manufactured exports from industrial countries*

(per cent)

	If there had been no 'dirty' tariffication	With 'dirty' tariffication
Wheat	10	1
Rice	4	–1
Coarse grain	5	0
Sugar	11	–1
Beef and veal	6	0
Other meat	2	–1
Dairy products	12	–1
Vegetable oils	5	–1
Coffee	–1	–2
Cocoa	0	–1
Tea	1	–2
Other foods	–1	–1
Cotton	1	–1
Other agriculture	3	–1

Source: Goldin and Mensbrugghe (1996)

of import price reductions can be expected from the Round through the implementation period, especially among developing countries. At best that will do no more than slow the decline in real prices for farm products in international markets, rather than reverse it. 'Dirty' tariffication in particular means that the real price of farm products in international markets will be barely above what it otherwise would be (see the modelling results reported in Table 2) – and it will do little this decade at least to reduce price fluctuations around that long-run trend. The Round will accelerate agriculture's relative decline and loss of farm jobs in heavily-protected industrial countries, but only slightly. And it will boost gradually the competitiveness of farmers in countries where the international price rises are transmitted to the domestic market for farm products, although again the improvements will be only slight over the remainder of this decade.

But at least agriculture is now in the mainstream of the WTO (which allowed the other agreements in the Uruguay Round to be concluded), and the agreement has been honoured. Moreover, the requirement to tarrify nontariff import barriers, to quantify the Aggregate Measure of Support, and to notify all subsequent policy changes to the WTO's Committee on Agriculture are major contributions to transparency that in themselves limit the worst excesses. The new rules and obligations eventually will constrain further farm protection growth in both advanced and newly industrialized countries, thereby promising greater certainty and stability to international food markets next century. Furthermore, there has been considerable reduction in the degree of tariff escalation affecting markets for tropical export products. In the cases of rubber, jute, oilseeds, spices, tobacco and wood, for example, tariffs on the primary and semi-processed products have been lower than on the final manufactured products but the latter are to be reduced much more than the former thanks to the Uruguay Round (ESCAP 1995, pp. 128–30). All these developments will encourage developing countries with a natural comparative advantage in farm products to exploit the new market opportunities, not least through seeking reductions in their own country's direct and indirect policy discrimination against agriculture.

The SPS Agreement

Because of the concern among agricultural exporters that the hard-won benefits to them from the UR agriculture agreement could be reduced by current farm protectionist measures being replaced by alternative measures such as quarantine restrictions, an agreement on Sanitary (human and animal health) and Phytosanitary (plant health) measures was also negotiated. The SPS Agreement seeks to ensure that any such SPS import restricts are imposed only to the extent necessary to ensure food safety and animal and plant health on the basis of scientific information, and are the least trade-restrictive measures available to achieve the risk reduction desired. Although there is sufficient vagueness in the wording to ensure that the protectionist abuse of SPS measures is still possible, consultations between WTO members are leading to conflict resolution in numerous cases and, in other cases that go on to form a panel, the dispute settlement evidence to date shows that exporting countries can succeed in getting WTO panels to rule against the most excessive cases (Roberts 1998).

The Agreement on Textiles and Clothing

Another major achievement of the Uruguay Round of indirect but none the less significant importance for agricultural-trading countries was the bringing of highly protected textiles and clothing back into the mainstream of GATT/WTO activities. Since the early 1960s their protection in advanced economies from import competition from newly industrializing countries had grown enormously, contrary to the policy trend for most other manufacturing industries. That had been most unfortunate for (especially densely populated) developing countries seeking to industrialize and export their way out of poverty. In turn it meant those economies' emergence as net food importers has been delayed.

When the Uruguay Round was due to be launched, developing country members of GATT made it clear they would not participate actively in the Round unless, like farm policies, textile and clothing trade policies were high on the agenda for liberalization. That was taken seriously in the Uruguay Round, unlike in previous rounds, because advanced economies were keen to improve their access to services and capital markets, and protection of their intellectual property, in developing countries.

What was achieved in terms of commitments under the Uruguay Round to dismantle textile and clothing protection? As with agriculture, not a lot in absolute terms but a great deal relative to the past and to what might otherwise have been the case. More specifically, the MFA and its 'voluntary' export restraints (VERs) on textiles and clothing are to be dismantled so as to return textiles and clothing to the full discipline of the GATT by 2005. During the transition, quotas on trade volumes are to grow faster than in the past and eventually are to be replaced entirely by tariffs as the only restraint on trade. Those tariffs will be bound and gradually reduced. For advanced economies as a whole, the average tariff on these goods is scheduled to fall from 15.5 per cent in 1995 to 12.1 per cent by 2005. But, again as with agriculture, the devil is in the details. According to Hertel et al. (1996), by 2005 the quotas will have increased by only about half the amount necessary for them to become redundant, in which case full tariffication would require the other half of the increase to occur at the end of the ten-year transition period, which seems unlikely. It is also possible that US and EU will use the special safeguards and/or other forms of contingent protection such as anti-dumping duties as that time approaches.

Furthermore, while China, Taiwan and Vietnam remain outside the WTO, they are likely to enjoy little if any extra growth in their access to EU and US textile and clothing markets as those liberalizing countries are pressured to honour commitments to developing country members of WTO. Should China – the world's largest clothing exporter – be admitted to the WTO before the MFA phaseout is completed in 2005, that could add substantially to structural adjustment pressures for these declining industries in advanced economies, and reduce the quota rents to other developing country suppliers. The least-competitive firms and workers in both sets of countries are unhappy about that prospect, and may use China's accession as an excuse for not completing the phase-out of the MFA by 2005 and/or demand that China continue to restrain its exports of textile products well beyond 2005. Should that happen, a great deal of the potential economic benefits from both the Uruguay Round and China's WTO accession, particularly for food-exporting countries, would be foregone or at least postponed (Anderson et al. 1997).

In short, the bringing of textiles and clothing back into the mainstream of GATT disciplines is a major coup for newly industrializing countries and therefore to agricultural-exporting countries in so far as the former become ever-larger net food importers. But equally clearly, the implementation of this agreement will have to be monitored carefully, in the hope both of minimizing any slippage (particularly if/when China joins the WTO) and of making sure further progress is made in the next round of multilateral trade negotiations as it affects this still-highly protected group of manufactures.

Monitoring Trade-related Policies and Providing Information

One of the reasons protectionist trade policies persist is that the losers from those policies are poorly informed about the nature and extent of their loss. In so far as they underestimate the loss, so they under-invest in lobbying against such distortionary policies. In these circumstances there is an economic return to society from supplying more information on the effects of interventionist policies. Yet many governments choose to under-supply such information, presumably at the request of those interest groups gaining from incomplete transparency (Rattigan and Carmichael 1996).

The shortfall in national transparency agencies can be offset somewhat at least by the WTO Secretariat providing that service. It now does so, in the form both of comprehensive annual notification requirements (to the Committee on Agriculture in the case of farm policies) and of the Trade Policy Review Mechanism (TPRM). Notices of all changes in trade and trade-related policies must be published by each country and made accessible to its trading partners, as well as sent to the WTO Secretariat. The Secretariat now makes those notifications public, including through the WTO's internet website.[3] As well, the WTO's TPRM reviews each country's policies on a regular basis[4] and publishes its findings.

The WTO's Expanded Role in Dispute Resolution

A further Uruguay Round achievement is that the GATT's role in resolving trade disputes has been strengthened very substantially under the WTO. Each case is to be completed in less than nine months. If an appeal is lodged, the new WTO Appellate Body will hear and rule on any claim of legal error within 60 days. Rulings are automatically adopted unless the WTO membership decides by consensus to do so, unlike under the old GATT where the party under review effectively had the power of veto. In its first two years about 100 cases have been brought, compared with the mere 300 cases in the total 48-year history of the GATT. Moreover, the panel reports are causing countries to implement significant policy changes, unlike many of the GATT dispute reports. A prominent trade law professor believes that establishment of the Dispute Settlement Body in the WTO "is likely to be seen in the future as one of the most important, and perhaps even watershed, developments of international economic relations in the twentieth century" (Jackson 1997, p. 176).

This development is of particular significance to agriculture because farm trade is so contentious. From the late 1940s to the mid-1990s, more than 43 per cent of GATT dispute settlement cases were agricultural (Hudec 1998, p. 38), and even since the WTO came into force the share has been about 30 per cent – several times agriculture's share of world trade.[5] The fact that the share has dropped since 1994, despite there being a backlog of claims that were held over until the Round was completed, suggests the Uruguay Round's agricultural and SPS agreements may well have lessened confrontation in farm trade. And the fact that the new dispute settlement procedures are faster, more automatic, and binding once the case is finished means much more satisfactory outcomes are expected in the future than resulted pre-1995 (although the EU's inadequate responses to the banana and beef hormone cases brought against it in the late 1990s have greatly disappointed the complaining parties so far).

3. IMPACT OF THE URUGUAY ROUND AGREEMENTS ON DEVELOPING COUNTRIES

What Determines the Impact on a Developing Country?

The Uruguay Round was not only about agriculture of course. But it together with the many other UR agreements will boost global economic welfare substantially. Whether and to what extent a particular country shares in that welfare gain depends largely on how much (a) its trading partners lower barriers to its exports, (b) its competitors lower their trade barriers, and especially (c) how much the country concerned lowers its own trade barriers. Since the Uruguay Round involved so much more than just agriculture, and since this freeing up of global trade and the associated boost to economic growth is going to alter countries' comparative advantages, it is only possible to think about the impact of the Round on a country from a global, economy-wide perspective. In particular, will the Uruguay Round improve the country's terms of trade and, if not, will its own policy reform commitments be sufficient to ensure its citizens are nonetheless better off from the Round's implementation? And how will the country's agricultural sector and food security be affected? We address these questions in turn for larger economies, before focusing on the smaller and least-developed countries.

Overview of Recent Findings for the Larger Developing Economies

Earlier GATT Secretariat estimates put the economic benefit of the Round as a whole at between US$200 and $500 billion per year (Nordstrom, McDonald and Francois 1994). More recent studies provide lower estimates of global welfare gains, primarily because of the more modest agricultural reforms that are now expected thanks to 'dirty' tariffication and on the fact that agricultural protection has decreased since the Round began (the effects of which were not captured in earlier studies).[6] All such empirical studies grossly underestimate the total benefits from the Uruguay Round, however, because they under-represent or ignore a number of important effects of the agreements that are difficult to quantify. One is in strengthening the multilateral trading system (including the bringing of services, TRIPs and TRIMs under GATT/WTO discipline) and thereby in boosting investor confidence, employment and productivity growth. Another is the encouragement that greater openness abroad gives to accelerating the unilateral reform programs of individual (especially developing) countries beyond their Uruguay Round commitments. These studies also assume the alternative scenario is the status quo, whereas the alternative may well have involved more protectionism, higher barriers around regional blocs, and sporadic trade wars in farm products, autos, etc. with few if any winners.

Bearing those points in mind, much can still be learnt from available quantitative modelling exercises. Hertel et al. (1996) estimate a global welfare gain from agricultural and manufacturing trade liberalization of US$260 billion per year by 2005 (in 1992 prices), or 0.4 per cent of expected global GDP. Much of that estimated benefit of the Round will accrue to developing countries, especially the more open ones and those making the largest liberalization commitments. The estimated gain to East Asia's developing economies, for example, is a 4.7 per cent boost, primarily because of large gains from (a) textile and clothing import liberalization by industrial countries and (b) their own reforms.

Three important implications of these results are worth stressing. One of the consequences of expanded manufacturing export opportunities is that agricultural production growth in Asian developing economies other than China and South Asia is slowed – despite farm trade liberalization in developed countries – as more resources are attracted to textiles and clothing. This can be seen from Table 3, which shows the projected percentage changes in output between 1992 and 2005 for each sector with and without the Round, as estimated by Hertel et al. (1996).

A second important point to note from Table 3 is the absence of negative numbers in row 1. That is, even in the countries reducing their agricultural protection most (the EU, Japan and South Korea), their agricultural sectors are projected to be larger in 2005 than in 1992 – the UR reforms simply slow the expansion of their farm output.

The third point, though, is that the expansion of agriculture outside Western Europe and Northeast Asia is only slightly faster than it would have been without the Uruguay Round, because the benefits from reducing agricultural protection are so widespread and the liberalizations expected to come from the UR are very modest. And it is enough only to slow the relative decline in agriculture in middle- and upper-income countries, not to reverse it.

Francois et al. (1996) estimate the annual gain from the Round to be up to $215 billion in 1992 prices, but their model is calibrated to 1992 rather than 2005 so that gain represents up to 1 per cent of global GDP. That estimate assumes increasing returns to scale and imperfect competition for the industrial sector; when constant returns to scale are instead assumed, the gain is estimated to be only 0.45 per cent. The latter is close to the 0.42 per cent gain estimated by Hertel et al.'s constant returns to scale model – the difference underscoring the point that market structure assumptions are critical in such modelling work. Of that global welfare gain of $215 billion, only one-thirtieth is attributable to agriculture post-1992, compared with one-fifteenth for other primary product reform, half for textiles and clothing, and the rest for other manufactures. For Australasia, however, 60 per cent of the estimated gain is due to agriculture. Again Asian developing economies are projected to gain proportionately much more than other regions from the Uruguay Round Agreements (a GDP boost for China of 4.0 per cent, for other developing East Asia of 3.2 per cent, and for South Asia of 3.1 per cent per year).

What impact will the Round have on international food prices? Estimates prior to the conclusion of the Round were quite optimistic. Tyers and Anderson (1992), for example, estimated that if all industrial countries were to tarrify all their support programs cleanly and then halve those tariffs by 2000, real international food prices would be 8 per cent by the turn of the century and the volatility of those prices would be almost halved. A one-fifth reduction in protection, therefore, might lead one to expect a rise in prices of temperate foods in

TABLE 3 *Projected percentage change in sectoral output between 1992 and 2005 without (upper entry) and with (lower entry) Uruguay Round liberalization*
(per cent)

(a) East Asian developing countries

	S. Korea	Taiwan	China	Indonesia	Malaysia	Philippines	Thailand
Primary agriculture	65 43	76 79	121 125	71 66	102 69	60 19	95 77
Processed food	92 109	94 114	194 180	111 110	156 441	73 118	149 140
Other Primary	134 128	143 142	246 238	79 73	119 98	79 67	104 91
Textiles	91 221	178 181	250 262	126 227	169 217	74 136	171 205
Clothing	67 146	74 89	225 327	114 639	196 262	88 285	168 338
Other light manufacturing	147 167	170 168	285 278	157 142	215 166	71 53	218 108
Transport, machinery and equipment	117 98	89 83	237 220	146 130	132 92	33 30	152 168
Other heavy Manufacturing	141 143	188 182	315 301	177 163	154 262	78 64	194 195

(b) Industrial and other countries

	South Asia	Japan	North America	European Union	Latin America	Sub-Saharan Africa	Rest of world
Primary agriculture	63 67	30 13	23 27	12 5	44 44	76 75	14 15
Processed food	94 108	28 21	21 21	8 5	48 47	81 78	24 19
Other Primary	115 103	60 62	42 43	24 24	76 78	43 46	18 18
Textiles	116 138	23 25	30 7	11 3	53 46	75 58	24 9
Clothing	114 241	8 1	22 –41	–12 –60	53 42	111 30	17 –11
Other light manufacturing	130 129	38 40	31 30	15 15	51 51	59 63	31 34
Transport, machinery and equipment	126 86	30 29	60 62	46 48	23 22	13 16	27 31
Other heavy manufacturing	131 102	42 43	42 41	19 19	50 50	51 52	28 29

Source: Hertel et al. (1996, Table 14).

international markets to average perhaps 3 per cent. But that would ignore three important factors: dirty tariffication is causing the reduction in protection levels to be even less than one-fifth; tropical agricultural products trade has been liberalized even less than temperate farm trade; and non-agricultural trade also is being liberalized, so that food prices relative to manufactured goods prices can be expected to be raised even less or even to be below what they would have been without the Uruguay Round.

All the latter three influences are evident in more recent results from Goldin and Mensbrugghe's (1996) economy-wide model, summarized above in Table 2. The first column shows the change in the relative price of agricultural products that could be expected if there had been no 'dirt' in the tariffication of agricultural nontariff import barriers: temperate food prices would increase between 5 and 12 per cent, while tropical goods prices would barely change at all, relative to prices of manufactures. By comparing that first column with the second column, the impact of dirty tariffication is apparent: agricultural prices are expected to hardly change at all relative to manufactured goods prices. This result is consistent with an even more recent study by Anderson et al. (1997), which finds the Uruguay Round to raise only very slightly agricultural prices relative to prices of manufactures (less than 2 per cent) and to slightly lower the relative price of processed foods, again relative to what would have been the case without the Uruguay Round being implemented.

How can these findings be reconciled with the FAO's projection of the effect of the Round? The FAO suggested international food prices would be 5 to 10 per cent higher in the year 2000 because of the Round. The model used to generate the FAO's results does not include non-farm sectors, however, and so does not measure the change also in prices for non-farm products as a result of the Round. It is the *relative* price change that matters in terms of its effect in altering production and consumption decisions, not just the change in the absolute price of food in each country. More importantly, the FAO study effectively ignores the fact that agricultural tariffications were 'dirty'. It therefore overstates substantially the decrease in farm protection and hence the impact of the Round on international food prices (see Sharma, Konandreas and Greenfield (1996) for a careful and balanced discussion of these reasons for the FAO's higher price projections).

In all the above-mentioned studies of the Round, the big welfare gains for Asia's developing countries are based on the assumption that China (hence Taiwan) does not join the WTO. If/when China (including Taiwan) accede to the World Trade Organization, global welfare will expand substantially but some developing countries competing with China in OECD markets for labour-intensive manufactures could see their benefits from the Uruguay Round diminish by China's accession. The extent of that change depends heavily on how much China would be allowed to share in the expanded access to textile and clothing markets resulting from the Uruguay Round agreement to dismantle the Multifibre Arrangement. Anderson et al. (1997) provides results under the extreme assumption that China and Taiwan are completely denied expanded market access until they join the WTO, after which they are assumed to get the same access as current WTO members without further delay. In those circumstances, global economic welfare from the Round is estimated to be £50 billion per year higher once China is allowed into the WTO, but because of China's export expansion the gain from the Round is diminished somewhat for South and Southeast Asian countries (compare columns 1 and 2 of Table 6).

How is grain self-sufficiency affected by the Round? Contrary to the many concerns expressed during the negotiations, the effects on the larger economies are likely to be quite minor – not least because the UR reforms in agriculture are now expected to be only modest. The second pair of columns of Table 4 provides one set of estimates. Malaysia and the Philippines are seen to become less import dependent and Thailand to export more rice, but otherwise the changes are no more than a percentage point or two away from what they are projected to be without the Uruguay Round being implemented.

What about the Smaller and Least-developed Countries?

In addition to the special and differential treatment given to developing countries in the UR Agreement on Agriculture that is noted in Section 2 above, there are additional provisions for the least-developed countries (LDCs). They include a recognition of their special interests, fewer obligations, longer implementation periods for commitments, and technical assistance provisions (see WTO (1995) for a full list). In the case of the Agreement on Agriculture, for example, Article 15.2 exempts LDCs from having to make commitments in all three areas of domestic support, market access, and export subsidies. There is as well provision for assisting LDCs and net food-importing developing countries to cope with the effects of implementing the Round's agricultural agreement on international food prices and on reduced subsidies on exports from industrial countries. There might also be assistance provided where there has been an erosion of preference margins, as in the case of ACP countries receiving the domestic price in the European Union for their exports. Specifically, in-kind aid in the form of food, short-term financial assistance to import food, and technical assistance to improve agricultural productivity and infrastructure are provided for in this Decision.

If anything, in-kind food aid has fallen rather than increased since the Uruguay Round was completed, with the depletion of discretionary grain stocks held by governments. Assuming governments choose to hold only modest stocks in future now that there is to be less domestic price support, the cost of official food aid will be higher than under previous farm policy regimes. Hence there will be domestic political pressure for food aid to be confined more to short-term emergency and humanitarian relief and to be used less as a substitute for commercial imports by LDCs.

There is already a loan facility at the IMF to help LDC's finance cereal imports during periods of price spikes or foreign exchange shortfalls. It has been used very little in the past, perhaps because the loan carries with it conditions of the type attached to regular structural adjustment loans from the IMF and/or because of the availability up until now of food aid and subsidized exports from industrial countries. Whether it will be used more under conditions of tighter grain markets and less food aid remains to be seen.

TABLE 4 *Impact of the Uruguay Round on economic welfare and on grain self-sufficiency, various countries, 2005*

(US$ billion and per cent)

	Welfare Effects of UR		Grain Self-sufficiency (%)	
	Without China joining WTO	With China joining WTO	Without Uruguay Round	With Uruguay Round (incl. China in WTO)
China, mainland	2.1	44.2	95	96
China, Taiwan	3.5	5.7	64	65
Hong Kong+Sing	–0.5	3.6	–	–
Korea, Rep.	9.5	9.3	79	78
Indonesia	11.1	4.5	97	97
Malaysia	10.4	8.2	63	65
Philippines	1.4	0.1	82	89
Thailand	6.5	2.1	115	135
India	5.9	1.7	100	101
Japan	19.9	25.9	84	81
Australia+NZ	1.9	1.9	187	204
North America	31.8	37.7	132	139
Western Europe	38.6	48.8	111	99
Rest of World	20.9	19.6	92	95
WORLD	163.0	213.5	100	100

Source: Anderson et al. (1997).

As for technical assistance to improve LDCs' agricultural productivity and infrastructure, that too if anything declined in the 1990s. Both bilateral aid agencies and multilateral institutions, such as the international agricultural research institutes and their former key funders such as the Ford and Rockefeller Foundations, have reduced the proportions of their funds targeted at agricultural aid projects. And aid in aggregate has been growing slower as well, as industrial governments respond to demands for downsizing and for providing less funding to international agencies.

Hence there is little evidence that the LDCs and net food-importing developing countries have been assisted significantly more since the implementation of the Round's Agreement on Agriculture began.

Whether this matters depends in part on whether smaller and least-developed countries are likely to suffer disproportionately from that agreement. To help assess that, consider Table 5. It shows the extent to which the LDCs and smaller economies of Asia and the Pacific have been dependent on food imports. Column 1 indicates that in most cases food accounts for well below one-fifth of all merchandise imports (the unweighted average for the countries shown is one-

TABLE 5 *Food trade specialization of smaller and least-developed economies of Asia and the Pacific, 1990–93*

	Gross food imports as a % of all merchandise imports	Food imports net of food exports as a % of all merchandise imports
ASIA		
Afghanistan	14	7
Bangladesh	17	17
Bhutan	10	2
Cambodia	8	7
India	3	–2
Korea, DPR	11	11
Laos	6	–2
Maldives	12	12
Mongolia	10	1
Myanmar	13	–15
Nepal	10	3
Pakistan	12	6
Sri Lanka	13	10
Viet Nam	4	–14
PACIFIC		
Fiji	12	–15
Kiribati	22	16
Micronesia	15	15
New Caledonia	10	10
Papua New Guinea	13	4
Samoa	17	11
Solomon Islands	13	–4
Tonga	21	5
Tuvalu	20	20
Vanuatu	14	–0

Source: FAO (1997)

eighth), and hence an even smaller share of all goods and services imports by these countries. But as many as one-quarter of these countries were actually net food exporters in 1990–93 (column 2) – notwithstanding the fact that some of them (India, Laos) are still classified by the United Nations as net food-importing countries. Of the other three-quarters, net food imports amount on average to only 9 per cent of all their merchandise imports. A one or two per cent change in international food prices would therefore amount to an increase of less than 0.2 per cent of these countries' import bills. This is insignificant when compared with normal year-to-year fluctuations in international food prices.

To go beyond such casual empiricism, Ingco (1996) has used the model and results reported in Table 2 above to estimate more precisely the impact of the Round's effect on international prices for agricultural products for a large number of LDCs. Predictably, though, the results show the impact on both the food import bill and GDP to be extremely small, especially when it is borne in mind that the Round's implementation period is 6–10 years.[7] Certainly it would be swamped by fluctuations in their trade balances due to other economic events, and more or less offset by the normal pressures for a slight long-term decline in the real international price of food depicted in Figure 1.

Of course these policy reforms will tend to help developing countries that are net exporters of farm products and those that are so close to being food self-sufficient that they would be net exporters once food prices rise following implementation of the Round. They also are likely to help those countries that would be net food exporters but for their own distortionary policies that discriminate against farmers (Anderson and Tyres 1993). Even in those developing countries that would remain significant food importers even after the Round is implemented, many rural households, as net sellers of food or of farm labour, would benefit from a rise in food prices.

This suggests a general conclusion that even these poor countries are unlikely to have been harmed very much by the Round's implementation, especially if they took advantage of the now-more-open markets abroad (including through reduced tariff escallataion) by liberalizing their own economies. However, three caveats are in order.

First, countries that enjoyed a disproportionately large share of world food aid supplied out of subsidy-generated surpluses in Western Europe or the United States may be harmed significantly in so far as they now have to purchase such imports at closer to commercial rates.

Second, countries that in the past were able to purchase a large proportion of their food imports at discounted prices financed by the export subsidies of the EU or US have found themselves less able to do so as export subsidies were cut.

And third, ACP and other developing countries benefiting from preferential or duty-free access to EU and other markets under, for example, the Lomé Convention or the Generalized System of Preferences will enjoy that privilege less. This is because the domestic prices in developed countries will be closer to international levels as their agricultural protection is reduced. However, while that reduction in the preferential margin may be large in proportional terms, it is rather minor in absolute terms. Table 6 suggests that the loss of margin in the United States amounts to about 2 percentage points, in the European Union to 4 points, and in Japan to 2 points for tropical products and 6 points for temperate farm products.

For countries adversely affected by one or more of these three phenomena (reductions in food aid, in OECD food export subsidies, and in preferential access to OECD markets), there is even more reason for them not to be seduced by the special and differential treatment clauses of the Uruguay Round but instead to reform and structurally adjust their own economies to take full advantage of the new opportunities arising from the Round.

TABLE 6 *Erosion of tariff preferences for agricultural imports by industrial countries from the world's least-developed countries*

(percentage points)

	Temperate agricultural products	Tropical agricultural products
European Union		
Margin pre-UR	13.3	9.3
Margin post-UR	9.5	5.1
Margin loss	3.9	4.2
(loss in %)	(29)	(45)
Japan		
Margin pre-UR	9.4	6.5
Margin post-UR	3.5	4.2
Margin loss	5.9	2.3
(loss in %)	(63)	(35)
United States		
Margin pre-UR	3.2	5.5
Margin post-UR	1.5	3.3
Margin loss	1.7	2.2
(loss in %)	(54)	(39)

Source: UNCTAD (1995)

4. LOOKING FORWARD TO THE NEXT WTO ROUND

Pathbreaking though the Uruguay Round achievements have been for agriculture, much remains to be done before world agricultural trade is as fully disciplined or as free as world trade in manufactures. Being aware of this at the end of the Uruguay Round, it was agreed that there would be a return to the negotiating table by 2000. That is unlikely to be very productive, however, unless it is part of another comprehensive round of multilateral trade negotiations whereby inter-sectoral and cross-issue tradeoffs are possible. Since services negotiations also began again in 2000, a strong case can be made for the new agricultural and services negotiations to be part of a bigger package. Among other things, that would open up the possibility for broader scrutiny of progress in reforming textiles trade which, for the reasons given above, would be especially worthwhile once China becomes a member of the WTO.

What should be on the Agenda for the Agricultural Negotiations?

In terms of farm export subsidies, nothing less than a ban is needed to bring agriculture into line with non-farm products under the GATT. They are, after all, almost exclusively a Western European phenomenon apart from sporadic US involvement: five-sixths of all export subsidies in the mid-1990s were granted by the EU, and all but 2 per cent of the rest were accounted for by the US, Norway and Switzerland (Tangermann and Josling 1999, p. 16).

With respect to domestic subsidies, gradual reform of policies of the US and EU, in particular the further de-coupling of farm income support measures from production as with America's FAIR Act of 1996, may allow removal of the 'blue box' in the next round of talks. It was an anomaly introduced into the UR negotiations in 1992 simply to satisfy just two members so the negotiations could proceed. Also, efforts to tighten the 'green box' criteria could be made, so as to reduce the loopholes they provide for continuing output-increasing subsidies, and to further reduce the Aggregate Measure of Support.

But the most important area requiring attention has to do with import market access. Tariffication appeared to be a great step forward. However, the combination of dirty tariffication by developed economies (setting bound rates well above applied rates) and the adoption of very high ceiling bindings by developing economies allows many countries still to vary their protection as they wish in response to changes in domestic or international food markets. Reducing bound tariffs from 50–150+ per cent to the 0–15 per cent range of tariff rates for manufactures is one of the major challenges ahead. If the steady rates of reduction of the past are used, it will be several decades before that gap is closed – and some time even before many of those bound tariffs reach current applied rates.

At least three options for reducing bound tariffs present themselves. One is a large across-the-board tariff cut. Even if as much as a 50 per cent cut were to be agreed, however, many very high bound tariffs would still remain. A second option is the 'Swiss formula' used for manufactures in the Tokyo Round, whereby the rate of reduction for each item is higher the greater the item's tariff level. This has the additional economic advantage of reducing the dispersion in rates that was introduced or exacerbated during the Uruguay Round. In particular, it would reduce many of the tariff peaks and the extent of tariff escalation that bothers developing countries. And a third option is the one used successfully in the information technology negotiations, namely, the 'zero-for-zero' approach whereby, for selected products, tariffs are eliminated altogether. In contrast to the second option, this third option would increase the dispersion of tariffs across products, increasing the risk that resources will be wastefully diverted from low-cost to higher-cost activities. While that might appeal as a way of allowing attention to then focus on the politically difficult items such as dairy and sugar, the manufacturing sector experience with long-delayed reductions in protection of textiles and cars makes it difficult to view this third option optimistically as a quick solution.

The just-mentioned tariff reductions refer to above-quota imports. There is also a pressing need to focus on in-quota imports, that is, those that meet the minimum access requirements in the UR Agreement on Agriculture (generally 5 per cent of domestic sales by 2000 for developed economies). Those so-called tariff rate quotas (TRQs) were introduced ostensibly to guarantee traditional exporters a minimum level of market access, equal at least to what was available before tariffication, given that tariffs have been bound at rates greatly above applied rates. As many as 36 WTO member countries listed TRQs in their

Uruguay Round schedules, of which at least half actively use them. But this system ensures that agricultural trade policies continue to be very complex. In particular, the existence of TRQs reduces the extent to which future tariff cuts will lead to actual import growth in the medium term, and it is worrying that quotas have on average been barely two-thirds filled according to the count of notifications to the WTO Committee on Agriculture during 19945 and 1996 at least (Tangermann and Josling 1999, p. 26).

Agricultural-exporting countries are understandably reluctant to suggest TRQs be removed, because TRQs provide at least some market access at low or zero tariffs. Nor would allowing TRQs to be auctioned be seen by all as a solution, because that would be like imposing the out-of-quota tariff on quota-restricted trade that the TRQ was designed to avoid. If banning TRQs is not yet possible, the next-best alternative to is to expand them, so as to simultaneously reduce their importance, increase competition, and lessen the impact of high above-quota tariffs.

One can imagine an outcome from TRQ expansion that is either optimistic or pessimistic from a reformer's viewpoint. On the one hand, optimists may say: if the TRQs were to be increased by, say, the equivalent of one per cent of domestic consumption per year, it would not be very long in most cases before the quota became non-binding. Expanding the TRQ could thereby be potentially much more liberalizing in the medium term than reducing the very high above-quota tariffs. Such an approach may require binding within-quota tariffs at a reasonable level (such as that for manufactures).

On the other hand, negotiators familiar with the tortuous efforts to reform the quota arrangements for textiles and clothing trade see the agricultural TRQs as a way of re-cycling the acronym MFA before it disappears in 2004 when the last of the textile quota are scheduled to be removed. In this case it would stand for a 'multilateral food arrangement' (Francois 1999a). Since the first inception of textile quotas was around 1960, it looks like it will take fifty years or so before they are finally abolished. Is that the expected lifetime of agricultural TRQs?

Those with this more pessimistic view may put the case for a more radical approach to the next round of agricultural negotiations, namely to bring agriculture much more quickly into line with the treatment of non-agricultural goods in the WTO. For example, they might call for the total elimination of agricultural TRQs (along with export subsidies and export credits) and a major reduction in bound (out-of-quota) tariffs. To soften the blow of that request, their quid pro quo could be to put less emphasis on trying to discipline farm domestic measures other than direct output-increasing subsidies. As Summer (2000) has shown, many forms of domestic support are infra-marginal and contribute little to net exports. The almost infinite scope for re-instrumentation of domestic price-support measures makes disciplining them very difficult anyway. And, as Snape (1987) has pointed out, tightening constraints on border measures would ensure an increasing proportion of the cost of support programs would be exposed via the budget and thereby subjected to regular domestic political scrutiny.

Agriculture and 'New' Trade Issues

Inclusion of new trade agenda issues in the next round is considered by some developing country negotiators as undesirable because it would distract attention from the market access issues that are deemed to be of greater importance to them. However, their inclusion could have the advantage that more OECD non-agricultural groups would take part in the round which, depending on the issue, could counter-balance forces favouring agricultural (and other sectoral) protection. As well, better rules on some of those new issues would reduce the risk of farm trade measures being replaced or made ineffective by domestic agricultural measures and technical barriers to trade that may be almost as trade-distorting – a risk that has grown considerably in the past year or so.

Such issues as competition policy and investment policy are as relevant for developing country agriculture as for other groups. However, since they may not be included in the millennium round, and their implications for agriculture are in any case discussed well elsewhere (e.g., Tangermann and Josling 1999), attention in the rest of this section is focused on the interests of developing countries in two emerging issues that very directly affect agriculture. They are the issues surrounding (a) technical standards, including SPS and food safety in the wake of the new biotechnologies, and (b) agriculture's so-called multifunctionality.

Technical standards, including SPS and Food Safety Measures

The inability of the Standards Code that came out of the Tokyo Round to adequately address sanitary and phytosanitary (SPS) issues, plus the desire to reduce the risk of reinstrumentation of agricultural support to SPS measures in response to the reforms committed to under the URAA, gave birth to the SPS Agreement during the UR. That agreement defined new criteria that had to be met if a country chose to impose regulations more onerous than those agreed in international standards-setting bodies. It, together with the UR's strengthening of the dispute settlement procedures at the WTO, was bound to raise the profile of SPS matters. That profile has been raised even more dramatically, especially in Europe, with the emergence of several food safety issues: 'mad-cow' disease, beef hormones, and transgenic food products or genetically modified organisms (GMOs).

Developing countries have a complex set of interests in these developments. One is that the SPS Agreement requires a WTO member to provide scientific justification for any measure that is more trade-restricting than the appropriate international standard would be, and to assess formally the risks involved. At least some technical assistance to help developing countries meet these requirements has been provided, but more may be needed.

A second interest is in maintaining and increasing access to other members' markets that are protected by SPS measures. Again some technical assistance in meeting those importers' standards is helpful. However, numerous countries use very blunt quarantine instruments that excessively restrict imports well beyond what is necessary for protecting the health of their plants and animals, or their citizens in the case of food safety concerns. For example, there are outright bans on imports of many products, including into agricultural-exporting countries seeking to preserve a disease-free image. The levels of protection involved are in some cases equivalent to tariffs of more than 100 per cent. Without some form of notification requirement on WTO members that forces members to disclose the degree to which trade is restricted by such measures, reform in this area is likely to be confined to the very small proportion of those cases that are brought before the WTO's dispute settlement body (DSB). The resource requirements of such legal proceedings ensure the pace of reform by that means alone would be glacial, and would be skewed towards concerns of those richer WTO members able to afford to bring such cases to the DSB.

Who gains and who loses from an SPS measure varies from case to case, depending on how widespread are the externalities affecting production and/or consumption. In the straightforward situation where the import restriction is aimed simply to prevent the rise in the cost of disease control for domestic farmers, the latter group gains at the expense of domestic consumers and overseas producers. James and Anderson (1998) provide an example where the cost to consumers is likely to have outweighed any possible benefit to producers, resulting in a net national loss (not to mention the loss to potential overseas suppliers) from apparently excessive protection in that case where broader externalities appeared to be absent.

Those domestic consumers are unlikely to be a source of pressure for liberalization of quarantine barriers, however, and not just for the usual reasons (poor information, high costs of collective action because of free riding, etc.). As well, citizens are often concerned about possible risks to the natural environment from importing exotic diseases and/or about the safety of imported food. And their demands for higher quality, safer food and for environmental protection are going to continue to rise with their pet capita incomes.

However, perceptions about the safety of different foods and food production and processing methods, and conformity assessment procedures, differ greatly – even between countries with similar income levels. The WTO Dispute Settlement case, brought by the US/Canada against the EU over its ban on imports of beef that had been produced with the help of growth hormones, shows that standards differences across countries are difficult to resolve even with a great deal of scientific advice. So too does the controversy over the banning of intra-EU beef trade over the 'mad-cow' disease scare. How much more, then, are trade disputes likely to arise over issues in which the scientific evidence is far less complete? Thus not having consumers' concerns represented in the SPS Agreement has been a two-edged sword: on the one hand it has meant the absence of a voice arguing that domestic consumers should have better access to lower-priced imported food currently excluded by excessive quarantine regulations; but on the other hand it has kept out of the SPS debate such issues as the consumers' 'right to know' via, for example, labeling. That latter concern is not going to disappear though. On the contrary, it is likely to show up in dispute settlement cases under the WTO's Agreement on Technical Barriers to Trade (TBT).[8]

Whether or not wealthy consumers are irrational and hyper-risk averse when it comes to food safety issues is not really the point. Providing them with more scientific information, and improving the reputation of national, regional and international standards-setting bodies, may be valuable initiatives but they may do little to alter consumer opinions in the medium term, and in any case such information is scarce on new issues (Mahe and Ortalo-Magne 1998, Henson 1998).

In the case of policy dialogues surrounding GMOs, far more heat than light has been generated so far. Attempts to promote science-based assessment of the risks involved have met with extreme versions of the precautionary principle, manifest in the form of complete bans on their production, importation and/or sale in numerous markets. Proposed solutions such as segregating GMO products and identifying them via labels on affected food items have been rejected by many consumer groups; they have also been resisted by the major producing countries in North and Latin America, who claim that 'like' products are involved and so no costly GMO labeling is warranted. The fact that the production of some GMO products is less damaging to the environment than is the production of traditional farm products has done little to dissuade civil society groups of their opposition to GMOs.

How are developing countries affected by this issue? Two ways in particular are worth noting: one is via the impact of the new technology in so far as it is lowering costs of food production; the other is via any food trade barriers that may be erected in response to consumer concerns in (mostly OECD) countries. The former would benefit those food-exporting developing countries able to attract the new technology, which places a premium on them having in place sound intellectual property law and enforcement (because seed companies would otherwise be wary of selling into or producing in such countries). If they cannot make productive use of the new biotechnologies, however, their competitiveness on international markets may be eroded as international food prices come down. Net food-importing developing countries could benefit from that price fall, and perhaps even more so if OECD countries ban imports of GMO products. The likely impact is clouded, however, by the fact that a premium might be attached to GMO-free products in international trade. This is clearly an area requiring more empirical economic research.[9]

While such agricultural issues will arise increasingly under the Uruguay Round's SPS and TBT agreements, they will also arise in other, non-agricultural-related contexts. As with state-trading, subsidies, and competition policies, there is a strong case for developing common disciplines for all types of products, whether agricultural or not. In the case of TBT, there is nothing special about food as compared with, say, dangerous chemicals or heavy metals involved in the production or disposal of manufactured goods. A key advantage of having a common set of rules for risk analysis and risk management is that inconsistencies in current arrangements, and the problems that will keep causing for dispute settlement, would be reduced.

Agriculture's so-called Multifunctionality

Considerable attention has been given in some OECD countries to the term 'non-trade concerns', which appears in Article 20(c) of the URAA. WTO members agreed that, in negotiating the continuation of the agricultural policy reform process after 1999, 'non-trade concerns' would be taken into account. While not spelt out in any detail, the preamble to the URAA defines those concerns to include security of food supplies and protection of the environment. A third concern is the viability of rural areas. The governments discussing these three items are characterizing them as positive externalities and in some cases public goods that are jointly produced along with food and fibre. Hence their use of the word 'multifunctionality' to describe these features of agricultural production.

So-called 'non-trade' concerns are becoming an issue in the WTO in numerous areas, not just with respect to agriculture. They are a direct consequence of the lowering or outlawing of trade barriers: with less natural and governmental protection from import competition, domestic policies are becoming relatively more important as determinants of the international competitiveness of certain industries. Despite their 'non-trade' adjective, these concerns need to be dealt with in the WTO because they certainly can affect trade. Ideally they should be handled in the same way for all sectors (for example, under an expanded Agreement on Subsidies and Countervailing Measures), but until that is done they cannot be ignored in the up-coming agricultural negotiations.

These concerns are not really new, but they are being packaged a little differently than in the past. A key question is: do they require exceptional treatment, or are WTO provisions sufficient to cater for them, for example via the URAA's 'green box'? The short answer appears to be that WTO provisions are adequate (Anderson 1998b). The answers to more-specific questions also seem to suggest no special case for trade measures. For example, does agriculture deserve more price support and import protection than other sectors because of the non-marketed externalities/public goods it produces jointly in the process of producing marketable food and fibre? That is, do these unrewarded positive externalities exceed the negative externalities from farming by more than the net positive externalities produced by other sectors? And even if they did, to what extent if any are those farmer-produced externalities under-supplied? The current farm support programs may more than adequately encourage their supply. And where there is under-provision, what are the most efficient ways to boost their production to the socially optimal levels? Certainly trade measures are a long way from first-best.

CONCLUSIONS AND OPTIONS FOR DEVELOPING COUNTRIES

The WTO's millennium round offers probably the best prospects ever for developing countries in general – and their rural communities in particular – to secure growth-enhancing reforms. Traditional agricultural market access liberalization should be the key priority issue in the next WTO round of multilateral trade negotiations, given the enormous potential for global and developing country welfare gains from reducing agricultural protection. Assurances are also needed that the EU and US will honour fully the spirit of their commitment to gradually expand market access for textiles and clothing, and not simply replace the remaining half of the quantitative restraints on trade in those products, expected to be still there at the end of 2001, with 'safeguard' measures by the end of the phaseout scheme three years later. Substantial progress in freeing up more trade in both these sectors is essential if the next round is to be a genuine development round.

Such reform could boost enormously the earnings of the world's poor, the vast majority of whom are in rural households and developing countries. Rural households would benefit even in newly industrializing economies that take advantage of expanding opportunities to export textile products, for example through some of their household members moving to new jobs in nearby clothing factories.

From an agricultural development perspective, attention should focus also on reducing protection granted to other manufacturing and services industries. Protection in those sectors still bestows a significant anti-agricultural bias in many developing countries, making it more difficult for them to benefit from the agricultural and textile trade reforms of OECD countries. Those reforms can be done unilaterally, but the next WTO round offers an opportunity to obtain a quid pro quo, and can be a useful instrument through which to lock in such reforms domestically.

This next round will, however, be conducted in an environment in which globalization forces (including ever-faster development and international transfers of information, ideas, capital, skills and new technologies) will, by having ever-stronger impacts on domestic markets, simultaneously trigger insulationist policy reactions. For example, further reductions in traditional measures of farm protection will meet significant resistance in numerous OECD countries, as farm groups join with food safety and environmental groups to argue for new forms of agricultural protection. In these circumstances the mercantilist nature of trade negotiations may require that the agenda of the next WTO round include not only other sectors but also some 'new trade agenda' items so as to provide the potential for beneficial issue linkages and tradeoffs.

Given the apparent good will towards making this next WTO round a development round, and given that many developing countries have embraced major reforms unilaterally during the past decade or so (Michaelopoulos 1999), perhaps developing countries should adopt a quite different approach from the past this time. Consideration might be given, for example, to exchanging more MFN market access with OECD countries rather than seeking special and differential (S&D) treatment and tariff preferences. S&D simply allows developing country governments to continue to keep shooting their economies in the foot by delaying beneficial reforms; and tariff preferences tend to divide developing countries into sub-groups, thereby weakening their individual and collective bargaining strength.

A striking example of the latter has been exposed in the prolonged and extremely costly dispute over access to the EU market for bananas. The EU policy regime involves layers of preferences that have divided developing countries into 'we' and 'they' groups and thereby weakened their chances of securing a better deal for all.

Another illustration of how preferential treatment has reduced the resolve of developing countries to push for OECD farm policy reform has to do with their food imports from the protectionist countries. Food export subsidies, export credits and non-emergency food aid are all by-products of OECD farm support programs. Without those programs most developing countries would be better off through expanded trade opportunities, and those that would not could be compensated with expanded access to OECD markets for tropical products and/ or direct financial aid (which would be a far more efficient way of transferring resources to developing countries than doing it in kind as a way of disposing of surpluses).

With these examples in mind, would developing countries' interests be served by the proposal for OECD countries to provide preferential access to exports of least-developed countries? If the things that matter (such as agricultural and textile products) were to be effectively excluded from such a deal, little of substance would be gained by the least-developed countries, and yet those countries would then feel less able to join other developing countries in seeking lower MFN tariffs on products of export interest to all developing countries. Meanwhile, OECD countries could use this initiative as an excuse for not reforming as much in the key areas.

All this suggests a potentially high payoff for developing countries acting collectively to push hard for greater market access for farm and textile products, and for technical and economic assistance to aid their reform processes, in return for providing more access to developing country markets for goods and services. The political price of the latter offer is, after all, now much lower than it used to be: the forces of globalization are such that economies are now rewarded more, via inflows of foreign capital, for good domestic economic governance, but they are also penalized more if poor policy choices are not corrected. Two such corrections that would at the same time help the cause of reducing agricultural protection abroad would be for developing countries to commit to not using taxes or other restraints on agricultural exports, and to reduce their (often very high) ceiling bindings on their own import tariffs on farm products.

Finally, what else should developing countries do to help their own reform processes complement those abroad? One obvious thing is to direct new economic and technical assistance funds towards reducing the under-investments in rural infrastructure (human as well as physical), agricultural research and development, and agricultural technology transfer. Liberalizing foreign investment rules and improving intellectual property law enforcement would enhance the prospects for both transfers of new biotechnologies and their further development locally. And removing domestic disincentives to farmers in the form of agricultural export taxes, manufacturing protection, and over-valued exchange rates remain essential.

NOTES

1 On the long history of exceptional treatment of agriculture in the GATT, see Josling, Tangermann and Warley (1996).

2 The Cairns Group by 1999 comprised 15 members: Australia, Argentina, Brazil, Canada, Chile, Colombia, Fiji, Indonesia, Malaysia, New Zealand, Paraguay, Philippines, South Africa, Thailand and Uruguay. Originally it involved 14 countries excluding Paraguay and South Africa but including Hungary. During 1999 three more joined: Bolivia, Costa Rica and Guatemala. The group is named after the Australian

city where they first met in August 1986. The Group's sole purpose was to ensure that agricultural trade liberalization remained high on the agenda of the Uruguay Round.

3 See the website at http://www.wto.org/wto/online/dff1.htm. WTO members' commitments under the Uruguay Round Agreement on Agriculture are available on the website of the US Department of Agriculture at http://ffas.usda.gov/scriptsw/wtopdf/wtopdf_lout.idc while applied tariffs for APEC countries can be found at the APEC website at http://www.apectariff.org.

4 Once every two years in the case of the EU, the US, Japan and Canada, every four years for the next 16 biggest traders, and every six years in the case of others except for the smallest and poorest developing countries where the internal may be longer.

5 For a list of all the WTO Dispute Settlement cases to early 1998 involving agricultural products, see OECD (1998b, pp. 145–48).

6 See, for example, Brown, Deardorff and Stern (1996), Francois, McDonald and Nordstrom (1996), Goldin and Mennsbrugghe (1996), Harrison, Rutherford and Tarr (1996), and Hertel et al. (1996).

7 This is consistent with recent results reported by the FAO (in ESCAP 1995, pp. 267–74) which show that there would be virtually no change in food consumption or food sufficiency among Asia's low-income food-deficit countries as a result of the Uruguay Round. Specifically, by the year 2000 that country group's self sufficiency in meat is projected to be lowered from 103 to 100 per cent, but its grain self-sufficiency is projected to be raised marginally from 95.7 to 96.0 per cent because of the Round.

8 Indeed one paper has already been posted on the Internet advocating activists to argue under the TBT Agreement for the right of WTO member governments to require compulsory labeling of products containing GMOs sold in their markets (Stillwell and Van Dyke 1999).

9 Early attempts to examine this GMO issue empirically are reported in Nelson et al. (1999) and Nielsen and Anderson (2000).

REFERENCES

Anderson, K. (1994), 'Food Price Policy in East Asia', *Asian-Pacific Economic Literature* 8(2): 15–30, November.

Anderson, K. (1995), 'Lobbying Incentives and the Pattern of Protection in Rich and Poor Countries', *Economic Development and Cultural Change* 43(2): 401–23, January.

Anderson, K. (1998a), 'Agriculture, WTO, and the Next Round of Multilateral Trade Negotiations', paper included on the World Bank/WTO website on the next WTO Round (www.itd.org), November.

Anderson, K. (1998b), 'Domestic Agricultural Policy Objectives and Trade Liberalization: Synergies and Trade-offs', COM/AGR/CA/TD/WS(98)101, in Proceedings of the OECD Workshop on Emerging Trade Issues in Agriculture, Paris, 25–26 October, published on the internet at http://www.oecd.org/agr/trade/. (A revised version is to appear in the *Australian Journal of Agricultural and Resource Economics* 44(3), September 2000.)

Anderson, K., B. Dimaranan, T. Hertel and W. Martin (1997), 'Asia-Pacific Food Markets and Trade in 2005: A Global, Economy-Wide Perspective', *Australian Journal of Agricultural and Resource Economics* 41(1): 19–44, March.

Anderson, K. Y. Hayami et al. (1986), *The Political Economy of Agricultural Protection*, Boston, London and Sydney: Allen and Unwin.

Anderson, K. and R. Tyers (1993), 'More on Welfare Gains to Developing Countries from Liberalizing World Food Markets', *Journal of Agricultural Economics* 44(2): 189–204, May.

Brown, D. K., A. V. Deardorff, A. K. Fox and R. M. Tern (1996), 'Computational Analysis of Goods and Services Liberalization in the Uruguay Round', Ch. 11 in *The Uruguay Round and the Developing Countries*, edited by W. Martin and L. A. Winters, Cambridge and New York: Cambridge University Press.

ESCAP (1995), *Benefits and Challenges Facing Asia-Pacific Agricultural Trading Countries in the Post-Uruguay Round Period*, Studies in Trade and Investment 11, Bangkok: United Nations.

FAO (1997), *FAOSTAT Files*, Rome: Food and Agriculture Organisation.

Francois, J. F. (1999), 'Market Access Liberalization in the WTO 2000 Negotiations', paper to be presented at the WTO/World Bank conference on Agriculture and the New Trade Agenda from a Development Perspective, Geneva, 1–2 October.

Francois, J. F., B. McDonald and H. Nordstrom (1996), 'Assessing the Uruguay Round', Ch. 6 in *The Uruguay Round and the Developing Countries*, edited by W. Martin and L. A. Winters, Cambridge and New York: Cambridge University Press.

Goldin, I. and D. van der Mennsbrugghe (1996), 'The Uruguay Round: An Assessment of Economywide and Agricultural Reforms', Ch. 2 in *The Uruguay Round and the Developing Countries*, edited by W. Martin and L. A. Winters, Cambridge and New York: Cambridge University Press.

Grilli, E. R. and M. C. Yang (1988), 'Primary Commodity Prices, Manufactured Goods Prices, and the Terms of Trade of Developing Countries: What the Long Run Shows', *World Bank Economic Review* 2(1): 1–48, January.

Harrison, G. W., T. F. Rutherford and D. G. Tarr (1995), 'Quantifying the Uruguay Round', Ch. 7 in *The Uruguay Round and the Developing Countries*, edited by W. Martin and L. A. Winters, Cambridge and New York: Cambridge University Press.

Henson, S. (1998), 'Regulating the Trade Effects of National Food Safety Standards', COM/AGR/CA/TD/TC/WS(98)123, in Proceedings of the OECD Workshop on Emerging Trade Issues in Agriculture, Paris, 25–26 October, published on the internet at http://www.oecd.org/agr/trade/.

Hertel, T. W., W. Martin, K. Yanagishima and B. Dimaranan (1996), 'Liberalizing Manufactures Trade in a Changing World Economy', Ch. 7 in *The Uruguay Round and the Developing Countries*, edited by W. Martin and L. A. Winters, Cambridge and New York: Cambridge University Press.

Hudec, R. E. (1998), 'Does the Agreement on Agriculture Work? Agricultural Disputes After the Uruguay Round', IATRC Working Paper #98–2, Department of Applied Economics, University of Minnesota, April.

Ingco, M. (1995), 'Agricultural Trade Liberalization in the Uruguay Round: One Step Forward, One Step Back?' Supplementary paper prepared for a World Bank Conference on *The Uruguay Round and the Developing Countries*, Washington, D.C., 26–27 January.

Ingco, M. (1996), 'The Uruguay Round and the Least-Developed Low-Income Food-Deficit Countries', paper presented to the Inter-Agency Meeting of the World Food Situation and Net Food-Importing Countries, the World Bank, Washington, D.C., 18–19 December.

Jackson, J. H. (1997), *The World Trading System: Law and Policy of International Economic Relations* (second edition), Cambridge MA: MIT Press.

James, S. and K. Anderson (1998), 'On the Need for More Economic Assessment of Quarantine Policies', *Australian Journal of Agricultural and Resources Economics* 41(4): 525–44, December.

Josling, T. (1998), 'The Uruguay Round Agreement on Agriculture: A Forward Looking Assessment', COM/AGR/CA/TD/WS(98)100, in Proceedings of the OECD Workshop on Emerging Trade Issues in Agriculture, Paris, 25–26 October, published on the internet at http://www.oecd.org/agr/trade/.

Josling, R., S. Tangermann and T. K. Warley (1996), *Agriculture in the GATT*, London and New York: Houndmills.

Lindert, P. H. (1991), 'Historical Patterns of Agricultural Policy', in *Agriculture and the State: Growth, Employment and Poverty*, edited by C. P. Timmer, Ithaca: Cornell University Press.

Mahe, L. P. and F. Ortalo-Magne (1998), 'International Co-operation in the Regulation of Food Quality and Safety Attributes', COM/AGR/CA/TD/TC/WS(98)102, in Proceedings of the OECD Workshop on Emerging Trade Issues in Agriculture, Paris, 25–26 October, published on the internet at http://www.oecd.org/agr/trade/.

Michaelopoulos, C. (1999), 'The Integration of Developing Countries into the Multilateral Trading System', mimeo, World Bank and WTO Secretariat.

Nelson, Gerald C., Timothy Josling, David Bullock, Laurian Unnevehr, Mark Rosegrant and Lowell Hill (1999), *The Economics and Politics of Genetically Modified Organisms: Implications for WTO 2000*, with Julie Babinard, Carrie Cunningham, Alessandro De Pinto and Elisavet I. Nitsi. Bulletin 809. College of Agricultural, Consumer and Environmental Sciences, University of Illinois at Urbana-Champaign, November.

Neilsen, C. P. and K. Anderson (2000), 'GMOs, Trade Policy, and Welfare in Rich and Poor Countries', paper prepared for the World Bank Workshop on Standards, Regulation and Trade, Washington, D.C. 27 April.

Nordstrom, H. B. McDonald and J. F. Francois (1994), 'The Uruguay Round: A Global General Equilibrium Assessment', CEPR Discussion Paper No. 1067, London: Centre for Economic Policy Research, November.

Rattingan, G. A. and W. G. Carmichael (1996), *Trade Liberalization: A Domestic Challenge for Industrial Nations*, Canberra: National Centre for Development Studies, ANU.

Roberts, D. (1998), 'Implementation of the WTO Agreement on the Application of Sanitary and Phytosanitary Measures: The First Two Years', Working Paper #98–4, Department of Applied Economics, University of Minnesota, May.

Sharma, R., P. Konandreas and J. Greenfield (1996), 'An Overview of the Impact of the Uruguay Round on Agricultural Prices and Incomes', *Food Policy* 21(4), August.

Snape, R. H. (1987), 'The Importance of Frontier Barriers', Ch. 15 in *Protection and Competition in International Trade: Essays in Honour of W. M. Cordon*, edited by H. Kierzkowski, Oxford: Basil Blackwell.

Stillwell, M. and B. Van Dyke (1999), 'An Activist's Handbook on Genetically Modified Organisms and the WTO', Center for International Environmental Law, Washington, D.C. and Geneva, March (www.consumerscouncil/org/ccc/policyhandbk399.htm).

Summer, D. (2000), 'Domestic Support and the WTO Negotiations', *Australian Journal of Agricultural and Resource Economics* 44(3), September 2000 (forthcoming).

Tangermann, S. and T. Josling (1999), 'The Interests of Developing Countries in the Next Round of WTO Agricultural Negotiations', paper presented at the UNCTAD workshop on Developing a Proactive and Coherent Agenda for African Countries in Support of their Participation in International Trade Negotiations, Pretoria, 29 June to 2 July.

Tyers, R. and K. Anderson (1992), *Disarray in World Food Markets: A Quantitative Assessment*, Cambridge and New York: Cambridge University Press.

UNCTAD (1995), 'Translating Uruguay Round Special Provisions for Least-Developed Countries into Concrete Action: Issues and Policy Requirements' TD/B/WG.8/3, Geneva: UNCTAD, 21 June.

WTO (1995), 'Provisions Related to Least-Developed Countries in the Uruguay Round Agreements, Legal Instruments and Ministerial Decisions', paper presented by the WTO Secretariat to a brainstorming meeting, UNCTAD, Geneva 18–19 May.

2. Development Economics and the General Agreement on Tariffs and Trade

J. M. Finger

WHAT TRADE POLICIES BEST SUPPORT economic development? Over the past forty years, developing countries have tried many different approaches and recorded many different outcomes. Their experiences have been analyzed for policy lessons by many scholars, among whom Béla Balassa has been one of the leaders. Also, the international community has developed a system of rules, the General Agreement on Tariffs and Trade (the GATT) that attempts to guide countries toward certain policy choices and away from others. One might presume that the parts of the GATT relating to developing countries reflect the knowledge these scholars have sorted out of experience. That presumption would be incorrect, however. The process of rules making or institution building, it seems, has a momentum quite separate from the emergence of knowledge about what works. Nobel laureate James M. Buchanan (1984, 5) makes the point as follows: "Institutions do matter – over the long run perhaps far more than the adoption of this or that policy option or the election of this or that politician or party."

In this essay, I compare the evolution of GATT rules about what policy choices a developing country should take with the growth of knowledge about what trade policies are effective. The first section, which reviews this growth of knowledge, is brief because its content is familiar. Balassa's and others' studies of developing countries' actual experiences tended to show that countries did well when they followed what classical economies would prescribe as reasonable trade and exchange rate policies. The thrust of the GATT toward developing countries, a less familiar matter, occupies the next three sections. In these sections, I explain how the GATT has come to institutionalize a set of economic presumptions shown to be inappropriate by the work reviewed in the first section.

The institutional structure, having been established without incorporating the "new" ideas and facts about trade and development, now serves to keep these concepts out. Developing countries, although very active at the Uruguay Round, have been reluctant to bring forward proposals based on economic concepts other than those embodied in the present rules. Thus proposals based on the experiences of the successful developing countries are excluded from consideration. This neglect is a significant loss to the international community. The experiences of successful developing countries have considerable potential to guide the improvement of international rules – rules that could not only pass the lessons of experience from one developing country to another but could also help *developed* country governments resist growing internal pressures for import restrictions. Such matters are taken up in the fifth section of this essay.

THE GROWTH OF KNOWLEDGE: DEVELOPING COUNTRIES' EXPERIENCES AS VALIDATION OF CLASSICAL ECONOMICS

Perhaps the problem was a simple matter of timing. The important decisions that determined the economics of the GATT were made in the 1950s and 1960s, whereas the "new" research on the role of trade in development gained momentum later – its arrival perhaps best signaled by the almost simultaneous publication in 1970–71 of Balassa's *The Structure of Protection in Developing Countries* and of Little, Scitovsky, and Scott's *Industry and Trade in Some Developing Countries.*

I have put the word "new" in quotation marks because even in the 1950s there were strong and clear applications of classical economics to the problems of development, particularly by Jacob Viner (1953) and Gottfried Haberler (1959)[1] – applications arguing that developing countries should avoid direct trade controls and impose at most a modest tariff. Although the "new" economics came wrapped in a new technology, these ideas are close to its central policy conclusions. In essence, what Viner and Haberler took as postulates the new research formulated and tested as hypotheses, then presented as conclusions.

Such thinking was, however, a long way from mainstream development thinking in the 1950s. Ian Little refers to Haberler and Viner as "rebels," and adds that "their opponents would have referred to them as orthodox neoclassicists" (Little 1982, 75). But, Little explains, they were not "orthodox" in the sense that their views coincided with those of policymakers or even with those of economists who wrote mostly about development. "Certainly, United Nations officials were not in this camp, and almost no developing country policymakers would have endorsed such views" (p. 75).

It is interesting to see the orthodox view of development through the eyes of one of the rebels. Viner, in the third of his National University of Brazil lectures of 1950, stated:

> *All that I find in Prebisch's study and in the other literature along similar lines emanating from the United Nations and elsewhere is the dogmatic identification of agriculture with poverty, and the explanation of agricultural poverty by inherent natural historical laws by virtue of which agricultural products tend to exchange on ever-deteriorating terms for manufactures, technological progress tends to confine its blessings to manufacturing industry, and agricultural populations do not get the benefit of technological progress in manufactures even as purchasers, because the prices of manufactured products do not fall with the decline in their real costs (1953, 44)*

Popular developing thinking separated itself not only from conventional economic thinking but from conventional economic history as well. Compare, for example, the following two statements. The first is from Viner:

> *No country except the United States has attained a high level of per capita income which has not maintained a high ratio of imports to total national product, and no*

> *country, except possibly Russia, can in this respect make the United States its model without courting perpetual poverty. The high degree of self-sufficiency of the United States was due in part to a deliberate national policy of high tariff protection. But it was the continental character of the United States . . . as well as the technical skills of its people, which enabled the American [economy] to dispense with foreign products . . . [and] to achieve economic prosperity despite its commercial policy and its low ratio of foreign to domestic trade (1953, 116–17).*

The second is from Prebisch:

> *Development [in the nineteenth century and the initial decades of the twentieth] in the periphery was a spontaneous phenomenon of limited scope and social depth; it came about under the dynamic influence of a unique combination of external factors which have since ceased to exist (1964, 6).*

History and economic theory were irrelevant, and thus everything had to be *planned* anew. Little (1982, chapters 3 and 4) explains that "planning" was an important element of popular development thinking in the 1950s. This belief was complementary to several other precepts. One was the presumption that "industrialization" and "development" were the same thing. Manufacturing made for good jobs and rich countries; agriculture provided bad jobs and kept countries poor. To raise wages, a less developed country had to establish the industries that had the higher wages in the industrial countries. And, because commodity earnings would inexorably decline and capital goods imports would inexorably be required, less developed countries would have a persistent tendency toward balance of payments problems. There was "the absolute necessity of building up trade in industrial exports" (Prebisch 1964, 20).

Every industrial sector was presumed to be linked to every other one in an "external" way – thus, for example, the ceramics industry could not be world class unless the steel industry was likewise world class. But nothing was linked through profits or prices. Price movements created "monopoly" if prices went up and "poverty" if they went down, but they did not provide "resource allocation" or "efficiency." Efficiency had to be planned in, and because industrialization had to change everything simultaneously if it were to succeed, planning, particularly investment planning, had to be based on the shadow prices that would prevail *after* the plan was achieved. The importance of "structural" rather than price links meant that all-at-one-time or "big bang" changes were necessary. A less developed country could be competitive in manufactured goods *across the board* or not at all. The planned-for big bang would transform a country from an exporter of materials and importer of manufactures to the opposite.

What changed? First Japan changed into an industrial power. Then other Asian-Pacific countries that followed Japan's policy experience began to register similar successes. At the level of public perception, this was the beginning of what Staffan Burenstam Linder calls the "demonstration effect," which eventually engendered among the Asian newly industrialized countries a rising regional confidence in their own development model. A scholarly look could perceive across countries varying degrees of mix of import-substitution versus open trade policies, and for a trained observer, the existence of "varying degrees of" allows identification of "the effects of." In 1970–71 came the Little, Scitovsky, and Scott study and the initial World Bank studies, in which Béla Balassa was the leading researcher (Balassa and associates 1971). These were followed by studies at the Kiel Institute led by Jurgen Donges (1976); the 1978 Bhagwati and Krueger studies for the National Bureau of Economic Research; and, eventually, many others.[2]

Balassa also played a leading role in two related lines of research. For one, his research on the European Economic Community showed that the effects of removing trade barriers was to a large degree an expansion of *intraindustry* trade. There were no major displacements of industries in one country by exports from another. Comparative costs, in general, were not so different, and competition tended to be on a product-variety rather than industry basis. This work (Balassa 1963, 1966) helped to put aside the "big bang" presumption of the 1950s that trade in industrial goods was an "all or nothing" proposition.

Second, Balassa initiated work after the 1974 oil shock to investigate how well developing countries had coped with such external shocks.[3] This work compared again the performances of countries with import-substitution strategies and countries that had export-oriented or open-trade strategies or had shifted significantly toward open-trade strategies when hit by severe external stocks. Balassa found that countries that continued or shifted to open-trade strategies were significantly more successful in maintaining investment and growth. The popular presumption that less developed countries are hit by relatively large terms of trade shocks was found to be correct. But the research showed that forced import substitution was not the best policy response. The absence of policies to *force* import substitution did not mean that there would be no import substitution, however. Balassa's work showed that neutral policies that allowed relative price changes to work through the economy would induce significant substitution of domestic production for imports of products whose relative prices had increased.

Perhaps the key shift in development thinking came with the realization that less developed countries *could* export manufactured goods and that they could move into such export production a bit at a time. At the level of the mechanics of development thinking, this change involved (or allowed) two significant simplifications. First, observable world prices, not almost-impossible-to-calculate shadow prices, are the relevant measure of alternatives. "For the individual country, world prices are the pivot on which all scarcities turn" (Bell 1987, 824). Second, the project replaces the plan as an intrinsic unit of analysis. These changes did not make enemies of the technocrats. Indeed, the technocrats saw them as a new challenge: finding ways to see, through the mess of country policies, incentives, and disincentives, how far the signals that influenced domestic decisions were from the real scarcities that lay below.

The content of this change of thinking is well-reviewed elsewhere (see, especially, Little 1982), so I will not extend this discussion. In closing this section, however, I want to note the timing of that change. Almost all of the rest of the "new" empirical research on trade and development was published in 1970 or later. As I explain below, the economics of the GATT was mostly in place by 1970.

THE INITIAL GATT NEGOTIATIONS

Kenneth W. Dam, in his well-known study on the GATT, describes it as "a product of U.S. planning and a reflection of certain views that dominated the thinking on trade matters of U.S. diplomats in the 1940s" (1970). Freedom of international commerce had been the third of President Woodrow Wilson's Fourteen Points. To Cordell Hull, Secretary of State for President Franklin D. Roosevelt, the link was straightforward: "[U]nhampered trade dovetailed with peace; high tariffs, trade barriers and unfair economic competition with war."[4] Keeping trade unrestricted was, in the bigger scheme of things, a means to maintain global peace and stability.

As to *how*, the U.S. proposal came down to asking each member country to accept three basic obligations: that it use only approved instrument of trade control, that is, tariffs only; that it apply these instruments in a nondiscriminatory way; and that it submit them to a long-term process of binding and reduction through multilateral negotiation (Hudec 1987, 133).

The mechanics were drawn from the U.S. Reciprocal Trade Agreements Program. Under the Reciprocal Trade Agreements Act of 1934 and its extensions, the United States by 1947 had negotiated and implemented thirty trade-liberalizing agreements, sixteen of them with a developing country. Each agreement contained a provision for a reciprocal exchange of tariff reductions and a framework of other obligations to protect the commercial value of the tariff reductions. There were some specific exceptions from the general framework of obligations, but there was no pattern of special exceptions for developing countries. Indeed, Hudec reports, "the sixteen developing country agreements . . . tended to contain fewer special derogations than did the agreements with developed countries" (1987, 7). The United States, in its presentations to the International Trade Organization negotiations in 1946–47, actively opposed special commercial policy conditions for developing countries. The United States held that development was primarily a matter of private capital investment and that special measures to deal with this belonged elsewhere, not in the commercial policy rules of the international system.

Neither the United Kingdom nor France fully supported this position. Both wanted to retain preferential tariff regimes of the traditional "metropol versus former colony" sort, and both wanted to retain the power to protect their own economies from imports in order to promote the reconstruction and eventual growth of their economies. Also behind their reluctance to accept nondiscrimination as a universal principle was the worry that they would never catch up to the United States as exporters of industrial goods. And both of these countries accepted to a much greater degree than did the United States that infant industry protection was an effective way to promote industrialization.

Developing countries argued that import quotas were essential to implementation of other development plans and that preferences for developing countries (that is, discrimination against imports from developed countries) were necessary to promote their now industrialization. At the level of principle, they wanted the international community to recognize explicitly that protection in developing countries would, in the long run, increase trade (Little 1982, 60, 61).

Developing country proposals at the International Trade Organization negotiations displayed two major concerns: the desire for a commitment from the developed countries to provide significant resource transfers and the desire for freedom from the general idea of discipline that the arrangement was trying to impose among the other members. Behind developing countries' unwillingness to accept any international discipline over their trade policies, Little sees the following presumptions:

> * First, and this was a grave mistake, they never expected to be able to export manufactures to the industrialized countries; but they might export a little to their [ethnic and geographic] neighbors . . .
> * Second, they assumed that the industrialized countries would not protect against raw materials.
> * Third, on competing farm products (sugar being the most important) the case was probably lost anyway, for the United States itself proposed to exempt farm products from the ban on quotas (1982, 61).

At a more direct level of concern, developing countries wanted to preserve the manufacturing firms that had grown up during World War II.

As no doubt the reader knows, agreement was never reached on the International Trade Organization. The international rules for commercial policy that were agreed are contained in the GATT. The International Trade Organization draft charter had more tightly circumscribed exceptions for developing than for developed countries. In the GATT, the opposite is true. The draft International Trade Organization charter recognized the right of a country to provide infant industry protection by raising bound tariffs or imposing quotas, but prior approval of the organization was necessary (Hudec, 1987, 14). In contrast, no prior approval was required for what might be described as developed country exceptions, such as import restrictions for balance of payments or safeguards reasons.

Article XVIII was the principal provision of the original GATT dealing with the trade problems of developing countries. According to Dam, "The theory of the article is quite simply that less developed countries should be freer than developed countries to impose quantitative and other restrictions in order to protect infant industries and to combat payments imbalances" (1970, 227). Section A of Article XVIII allows protection "to promote the establishment of a particular industry" (para. 7a). Section B allows a developing country to establish restrictions "to safeguard its external financial position and to ensure a level of reserves adequate for . . . development" (para. 9). Section B of Article XVIII parallels Article XII, which allows balance of payments restrictions by developed countries, but the Article XVIII criteria are less stringent. For example, consultations are required of developing countries only every second year rather than every year.[5] In sum, the GATT exceptions for developing countries were circumscribed by procedural requirements, but the international community, in ratifying the GATT, explicitly acknowledged that the special position of developing countries justified some dispensation from the legal discipline other countries must accept (Hudec 187, 15).

Why, at the time of organizing the GATT, did the United States allow the position it had negotiated into the draft International Trade Organization charter to be significantly compromised? A major reason seems to be the nature of the negotiations themselves. The overall structure of the negotiations was that the community of nations would agree to a program of discipline on the behavior of individual countries. The underlying conceptualization recognized this discipline as a "cost" to an individual country, but a cost that would be borne in pursuit of a common good. So the acceptance of *individual costs* for the *common good* was the basic trade-off each participant was asked to make – the basic form of the negotiations. In such a context, it is very difficult to ask the weaker members of the community to make the same sacrifice as the stronger. Protestations that commercial policy rules are not the appropriate way to provide for the less fortunate sound like excuses for greed.

Hudec, in his interpretation of the role of developing countries in the GATT, brings out this factor – what one might describe as the influence of Max Corden's conservative social welfare function on relations between rich and poor states. "It is very difficult to convene an enterprise involving rich and poor without having some welfare dimension to the work . . . [The] inability to resist this need to give 'something' has been a constant factor in the dynamics of GATT legal policy" (1987, 16).

A second factor pushing toward U.S. agreement on exceptions for developing countries was its desire for some exceptions of its own: for its restrictions on agriculture, its existing safeguards, and antidumping and countervailing duty laws. A third reason was that the United States had no clearly articulated economic argument for the economic benefits each country would receive by participating in an open economic system.[6] The articulated "pro" arguments tended to be political arguments based on strategic considerations and the idea of building a political relationship among the free world countries.

Another point against imposing equal discipline on developing countries was that once these countries had taken a position of asking for this kind of "benefit," granting it began to have immediate political value but no immediate economic or budgetary cost. And finally, the GATT itself was not the forum in which the rules of the international trading game were negotiated. The initial GATT was merely the paperwork used to quickly put in place an already agreed round of tariff cuts. If the agreed tariff cuts were not implemented quickly, pressures to renegotiate would build. Besides, everything but the tariff cuts was considered "provisional" and was expected to be superseded by the International Trade Organization. From the U.S. perspective, the GATT was the bird in the hand of trade liberalization for which it might perhaps be worth letting go a few birds in the bush of exceptions – compromises to the idea of discipline. A nice pragmatic solution – get what you most want now and fix the problems that come with it later.

In the conclusion to the first chapter, Hudec provides a less pragmatic interpretation – indeed, an ominous one:

> *Once it had been conceded, as a matter of principle, that legal freedom constitutes "help" to developing countries, the future was virtually fixed. . . . When other kinds of "help" were not enough there was always the possibility of doing something more on the legal side. Granting legal freedom to other countries is an easy concession to give, for it requires*

neither domestic legislation nor the use of other legal powers by the grantor countries. It is possible to "give" merely by doing nothing (1987, 18).

THE HABERLER REPORT AND THE GATT ACTION PROGRAM

For the first seven or eight years, the GATT system operated more or less by the book.[7] The GATT became, in use, the legal code that the International Trade Organization charter had been intended (at least by the United States) to be. The "contracting parties" (the official GATT language for "member" is "contracting party") overcame the absence of an institutional existence by referring to themselves as the CONTRACTING PARTIES (all in capital letters) when they acted collectively and officially – for example, to determine whether the agreed code had been violated. There were tight reviews of exceptions to the general idea of discipline against import restrictions. "Resort to the infant industry exception in Article XVIII was limited, but what activity there was was treated with some importance. . . . Balance of payments reviews were carried out with careful scrutiny" (Hudec 1987, 26). In practice, conditions were imposed on the development exceptions, and when developing countries acceded to the GATT they were required to make substantial tariff concessions.

The period of 1954–60 saw a considerable shift in the momentum of the GATT. Developing countries pressed for more freedom for infant industry measures and for less reciprocity in the trade-liberalization negotiations. The United States became more concerned with strategic-bloc issues: the Cold War made the building of a political relationship more important and the United States therefore more willing to give ground on the details of the economic relationship. Consequently, at the 1954–55 review, the GATT was modified to include in its text a statement that the infant industry argument was consistent with its principles.

From that point, the infant industry justification for protection was written in as consistent with the GATT rather than being treated as an excuse for an exception to the GATT. "In the same spirit, the draftsmen deleted a tough-minded sentence in the original text warning that unwise use of such measures would harm both the applicant country and others" (Hudec 1987, 27). In sum, the review session presented an almost enthusiastic endorsement of the principle that freedom from the sort of constraints that the GATT attempted to impose on individual country behavior *helped* the developing countries. So the GATT in the late 1950s was rapidly losing interest in the enforcement of legal discipline on developing countries (although a formalistic compliance was maintained) and was developing an enthusiasm for an infant industry ideology of growth.

At the same time, the trade performance of developing countries began to worry the international community. The trade of developing countries was expanding less rapidly than the trade of the industrial countries, and the industrial countries were also posting better overall economic growth rates. This lagging economic performance of the developing countries spurred the CONTRACTING PARTIES in November 1957 to ask a Panel of Experts to study the matter. The panel was made up of Roberto de Oliveira Campos, Gottfried

Haberler (Chairman), James Meade, and Jan Tinbergen. The panel's report, commonly called 'the Haberler Report," is described by Kenneth Dam as "perhaps the turning point in the GATT's relations with less-developed countries" (1970, 228).

The terms of reference of the panel begin with an expression of concern "regarding certain trends in international trade, in particular the failure of the trade of less developed countries to develop as rapidly as that of industrialized countries, excessive short-term fluctuations in prices of primary products, and widespread resort to agricultural protection." The panel is charged to provide "an expert examination of past and current international trade trends and their implications, with special reference to the factors referred to above; [and] an assessment of medium-term prospects for international trade in the light of the facts and trends as [the panel] sees them" (Campos et al. 1958, 1).

The report is concerned mostly with trade in primary products and with policies relating to this trade. Of the fifty-seven summary points listed in the first chapter, only one is about manufactured exports. Some twenty concern fluctuations in export earnings or commodity stabilization policies; some twenty more are about the agricultural policies of the industrial countries, including the formation of the European Economic Community (EEC). If the reader interprets as realities the concerns the report expresses about what EEC agricultural policies might become, the discussion of agricultural policies sounds very much like a 1989, rather than a 1957, review.[8]

The report provides a comprehensive response to its terms of reference and does so mostly within the (then) mainstream of development thinking implicit in the terms of reference. For example (the numbers preceding these statements are the paragraph numbers in the report):

> 22. *It is possible, upon the evidence now available, to conclude whether or not there has been an increase in agricultural protection in industrial countries in recent years.*
> 24. *The terms of trade in the post-war period were more favorable to non-industrial countries than in 1938, but recently turned against them . . .*
> 25. *The import requirements of the non-industrial countries are likely to increase more quickly than the rest of world trade . . .*
> 26. *The exports of the non-industrial countries are very sensitive to internal policies of industrial countries . . .*
> 44. *A number of underdeveloped countries are now exporting low-priced manufactures, the markets for which depend upon moderation in industrial protectionism in the highly industrialized countries.*

The report's conclusions, however, as summarized in the first chapter, demonstrate much broader thinking:

> 61. *The issues which we have considered in detail in our report affect primarily the policies of the highly industrialized countries; but we consider that they, as well as the primary producing countries, would gain by the proposed changes.*
> 62. *We think that there is some substance in the feeling of disquiet among primary producing countries that the present rules and conventions about commercial policies are relatively unfavorable to them.*

63. *While the underdeveloped primary producing countries have valid reasons for making a rather freer use of trade controls than the highly industrialized countries, in a number of cases protective policies have been carried too far by these countries; and these countries also have used for the protection of their industries a number of special weapons which are not normally the subject of negotiation with other countries. We have not examined in any detail these problems of protectionism in the non-industrial countries.*
64. *Further progress depends upon the willingness of the industrial and the non-industrial countries to negotiate on a wide range of their economic and financial policies.*

Thus the report concludes that existing arrangements are relatively unfavorable to primary producing countries. While it also concludes that there are valid economic reasons for a developing country to restrict imports, it points out that they have done so to excess and that progress depends on both developed and developing countries reducing their restrictions.[9] The conclusion the report puts first is the crux of the classical economic view of trade policy: a country's import policy reform will have a positive effect on its own economy, not just on the economies of exporting trade partners.

To the diplomatic community, the Haberler report made one point: it verified that developing countries were losing ground under the GATT. Hudec (1975, 209) captures the tone well: "[T]he Haberler Report exploded a good deal of the developed country righteousness by showing that the developing country trade was actually losing ground under GATT." Kenneth Dam, another legal scholar not known for taking a soft line on the matter of GATT discipline for developing countries, argues that "The substance of the report was that the predicament of the underdeveloped countries was due to no small measure to the trade policies of the developed countries" (1970, 229). Thus, in the political world the report's warning about developing countries' own policies was ignored.[10] In effect, the international community overlooked the report's analysis and conclusions.

The thinking implicit in the report's terms of reference, not the thinking explicit in its conclusions, became the basis for policy actions. The CONTRACTING PARTIES responded with a resolution "to initiate immediate consideration of a coordinated program of action" to embrace three topics: a new tariff round, nontariff protection of agriculture, and other obstacles, particularly to the expansion of developing country exports. "Committee III," which was created to take up the third topic, prepared a number of tabulations of developed countries' import restrictions on a long list of "products of export interest" to developing countries. Later, the CONTRACTING PARTIES created an Action Committee to examine submissions by developed countries of such information and to consult the developed countries "with a view to removing" these trade barriers.

The international community saw the matter as a direct one: developing country exports are lagging; therefore, developed country restrictions are the cause.[11] Only a few maverick intellectuals considered the possibility that the lagging trade performance of developing countries might be explained in significant part by their own policies.

The Haberler Report, the Action Program, and the Action Committee added a new *affirmative action* dimension to the developed-developing country relationship within the GATT. Beyond the developed countries' obligation to exempt developing countries from GATT's normal discipline – that is, to allow them to impose trade restrictions – the developed countries also had an obligation to unilaterally remove their import restrictions on products of export interest to the developing countries. In other words, developed countries were to extend the concessions they agreed to at any further tariff rounds beyond the scope of products traded principally among themselves.

Several other factors also contributed to the changes within the GATT that weakened the belief in the need for policy discipline for developing countries and strengthened the belief that developed countries had an obligation to do something for them. One was a simple matter of numbers. From 1960 until 1970, GATT membership increased from twenty-one developed and sixteen developing countries to twenty-five developed and fifty-two developing countries. Twenty-eight of the thirty-six new developing country members came in under special procedures for newly independent territories; only eight got in by negotiating tariff concessions (Hudec 1987, 24).

Another factor was the competition between the U.N. Conference on Trade and Development (UNCTAD) and GATT to be the institution through which relations between developing and developed countries were managed. That rivalry is the topic of the next section.

THE GATT–UNCTAD RIVALRY

What is the best trade policy for development? One alternative is the harsh "tariffs only" conclusion derived from classical economics, as explained, say, in Haberler's Cairo Lectures (Haberler 1959). The idea of "GATT discipline" as it prevailed in the period 1947–54 is the institutional representation of this viewpoint. But the alternative to which the international community turned in the late 1950s and in the 1960s suggested a kinder, gentler attitude toward developing countries. As the poorer members of the trading community, developing countries ought not to be asked to assume the same burden of discipline as the richer members. And, since the facts showed that they were slipping further behind, a kinder, gentler attitude should include an affirmative action program by the richer members, to create new opportunities for the poorer countries to export to the richer. The rivalry between GATT and UNCTAD to "staff out" this concern to promote developing country exports became, in the 1960s, an important influence on the economics of the GATT. Within this rivalry, UNCTAD achieved three significant victories.

First, the UNCTAD view captured the facts: not only the lagging trade performance of developing countries, but also the growing awareness that all was not well with import-substitution policies. As Prebisch phrased it, "Industrialization encounters growing difficulties in the countries where it is pursued furthest" (1964, 9). Extreme capital intensity and very high costs were becoming apparent. The problem, Prebisch explained, is another "vicious circle."[12] Costs are high because exports are low (economies of scale are not achieved), and exports are low because costs are high (1964, 22). Developed countries must therefore provide the needed export opportunities – the developing world requires affirmative action from the developed. UNCTAD's particular twist on the matter was that this access should be preferential, that developing country exporters should not be required to compete with, say, established German exporters for sales in the United States.

The political attractiveness of preferences for developing countries acted synergistically with two technical victories of UNCTAD. These technical victories allowed UNCTAD's concepts rather than the GATT's to provide the scale used by the international community to "keep score" on the amount of affirmative action provided.

One of these victories concerned the attachment of negative connotations to the way in which the normal GATT mode of reducing trade barriers would provide improved access for developing country exporters – even when the improved access was granted unilaterally. Let me give an example. In negotiations with each other through the GATT, Australia and New Zealand agree that each will reduce its tariff on $1000 of imports from the other and that each will also reduce its tariff on $500 of imports from a developing country. The latter action is obviously a unilateral extension of access to the developing country.[13] The case is much the same if Australia and New Zealand exchange concessions on products that each imports two-thirds from the other, one-third from a developing country. In both cases each developed country (Australia and New Zealand) has reduced its tariff on $500 of imports from a developing country, and has done so without receiving a reciprocal concession.

Yet, as UNCTAD taught the world to keep score, Australia and New Zealand would receive no credit for affirmative action. UNCTAD's calculations compared the amount of developed country exports covered by the agreed concessions ($2000 in the example) with the amount of developing country exports covered ($1000 in the example).

Are Australia and New Zealand therefore "good citizens" because the $1000 is something, or "bad citizens" because the $1000 is less than the $2000? UNCTAD's evaluation of the Kennedy Round used the second standard; for example, "the products in which the developing countries had expressed particular interest, and in which they have already established some trade, received on average significantly smaller tariff reductions than did other products. This result reflects the fact that those product groups for which industrialized countries are the main suppliers received deeper and more widespread cuts" (UNCTAD 1968, 4).

By emphasizing that developed countries reduced tariffs on a larger share of their imports from each other than from developing countries, UNCTAD suppressed the idea that such tariff cuts provided a unilateral concession and assigned guilt to the developed countries because the concessions they exchanged among themselves were larger than those they provided without compensation to the developing countries. In so doing, UNCTAD detached the traditional GATT mode of going at trade liberalization – reciprocal most-favored nation concessions – from the earning of any affirmative action credits.[14] The international community (even the GATT, as the following paragraphs show) accepted the UNCTAD way of evaluating the morality of tariff reductions.

The other UNCTAD tactical victory was to build up the idea that tariff preferences (particularly the Generalized System of Preferences, which UNCTAD administered) were the only true indicator of a country's affirmative action.

A concern for expressing the growing belief that developed countries had positive obligations toward the developing countries led also to the adoption in 1965 of Part IV of the GATT. Part IV uses the "shall" language of legal obligation but then adds other specific langauge that undercuts the sense of *legal* obligation. For example, Article XXXVII, titled "Commitments," begins: "The developed contracting parties shall to the fullest extent possible – that is, except when compelling reasons, which may include legal reasons, make it impossible. . . ."

The strength of the old test of good faith – exempting developing countries from normal GATT discipline – did not wane as that of the new test – affirmative action – ascended. Consider, for example, a pamphlet published in 1964 by the GATT Secretariat titled *The Role of GATT in Relation to Trade and Development.* According to Hudec's review, the pamphlet accurately described the GATT's legal discipline for developing countries. "What was interesting was its effort to portray the absence of legal obligations as a virtue. This is perhaps the clearest demonstration . . . of the link during this time between the GATT legal policy towards developing countries and its very strong desire to attract and hold developing country members" (1987, 60).

As this analysis implies, the GATT rules were being shaped by an our-organization-versus-their-organization competition for membership, and not by any concern to guide or push countries to choose the most effective trade policies. UNCTAD for its part was doing the same. Raul Prebisch, UNCTAD's first Secretary-General in 1961, actively recruited developed and developing countries' loyalty to UNCTAD:

> *[GATT represents] the classic pattern of exchanging manufactured goods for primary commodities* (Prebisch 1964, 7).
>
> *GATT has brought about considerable reductions in . . . tariffs and other restrictions [but they] . . . have been of benefit mainly to the industrial countries* (p. 27).
>
> *[in GATT,] problems of international trade are dealt with in a fragmentary fashion, and not as part of a general problem of development . . . GATT has not proved effective in coping with trade between the developing and the industrial countries nor has it promoted trade relations among the developing countries themselves* (p. 99).

By the time of the Tokyo Round of negotiations, the developed countries had returned (at least in form) to the idea of discipline. The focus was shifting from tariffs to nontariff trade restrictions, and the Tokyo Round codes attempted to expand and interpret agreed rules about the use of such restrictions. However, each code included a provision for special and differential treatment of developing countries. Only the United States went so far as to threaten to limit extension of the codes' privileges to developing countries that accepted the codes' disciplines, although it pulled back from its threat whenever practical politics intervened.[5]

At the end of the Tokyo Round, the GATT Secretariat prepared a report on the outcome of the round. Hudec interprets the report as follows:

> *It was written quickly (but very thoroughly) in order to preempt the kind of negative evaluation that UNCTAD had made after the Kennedy Round . . . It celebrated all the "victories" achieved by the Group of 77 . . . [A] central element of the "victories" was all the new legal freedoms developing countries had won, especially those which involved discriminatory special and differential treatment . . . The year was 1979. Here was the GATT, still thoroughly preoccupied with holding the allegiance of developing countries and still making a virtue of the fact that GATT rules do not apply to developing countries (1987, 91).*

If the Kennedy and Tokyo Rounds were the two halves of a GATT–UNCTAD soccer match, we would say that the score was UNCTAD 2, GATT 0, the second goal being an "own-goal." Put another way, the GATT church pretty much took on the theological position of UNCTAD concerning developing-developed country relations and the role of trade in economic development.

Neither the score nor the theology has changed. The subtitle of Hudec's chapter on developments in the 1980s is "form without substance," and this seems to be the mainstream interpretation of developing countries' obligations under the GATT. Another noted legal scholar, John H. Jackson, concludes that "many developing countries are able to take advantage of either explicit or implicit exceptions in the GATT so as to pursue almost at will any form of trade policy they wish" (1989, 277).

If "individual sacrifice for the common good" accurately reflected the economics of the GATT and if the GATT were supposed to serve a social welfare function, then the position of developing countries in GATT might be considered appropriate. But if we look at GATT from a public choice perspective – as an institution designed to nudge countries toward the best choice of trade policy – then we would give it a lower score.

THE URUGUAY ROUND

That things in the GATT have not changed in the 1980s does not mean that things have not changed. Concern is growing about the increased use of trade restrictions by developed countries. While some of these restrictions are GATT-questionable, a significant fraction of them, including antidumping and countervailing duty measures, are arguably GATT-legal.[16] Another matter of concern is that major movements by the developed countries to remove trade restrictions have been bilateral or regional, for example, the Australia–New Zealand and Canada–United States trade agreements and the European Community's "1992" program.

Trade policy changes in developing countries have been equally significant. There have been major reforms in some countries – Chile and Mexico are examples – and continuing liberalization in many others, particularly Korea and other newly industrialized countries in Asia. There have been some new restrictions as well.[17]

Several developing countries took an active role in getting the Uruguay Round under way. In early 1986, achieving agreement to undertake the Round seemed impossible. Preparations were stuck, and agendas for the Punta del Este meeting were reviewed several times without progress. Quietly, however, officials from a group of middle-size developing and developed countries began to discuss matters among themselves. They shaped perspectives, forged operational ideas, and calculated relevant balances. Much more, they discussed ideas with other delegations, patiently modifying and extending their proposals as they went along. One of the positive effects of this behind-the-scenes leadership was the sense of the value of the GATT system that it conveyed to smaller countries and the development of a perspective that gave expression to their concerns.

The contribution of the developing countries to the politics of getting the new GATT Round under way raised hopes that these countries would make an equally important contribution to GATT's economics. Most decisions by developing countries to remove trade restrictions have been unilateral decisions, based on an appreciation of the own-country benefits of such reforms versus the costs.

For developed countries, the removal of trade restrictions has been shaped by a strong vision of an open international trading system and of that system's collective benefits to the community nations. A concern to promote and maintain peace and stability through economic means has perhaps been a clearer objective than have the economic benefits likely to accrue to a particular nation. The focus has been systemic and the approach multilateral. This systemic focus has characterized not just the GATT, but other important vehicles for the reduction of developed countries' trade barriers as well, such as negotiations to remove trade and exchange restrictions in Europe and to form the European Economic Community and the European Free Trade Association. Within the multilateral approach, trade liberalization means an exchange of concessions. Reductions of import restrictions increase the imports of the country granting the concessions and are viewed as a cost. But in the multilateral process, such costs buy increased exports and help build the system from which all will benefit.

For developing countries, the perspective on trade policy reform has been different. The focus has been national and the approach unilateral. This perspective may underestimate the value and fragility of a coherent international trading system, but it includes a fuller appreciation of the classical perspective, particularly of benefits that openness to international competition can convey to an individual economy. Like the multilateral decisions of the developed countries, unilateral decisions for reform reflect an appreciation of the economic benefits that export expansion allows. High-cost inputs are a burden to exports, and lower restrictions on imported inputs are a stimulus to export expansion.

Export expansion is a valid reason for import liberalization, but not the only one. Many developing countries have built on the other reasons. They recognize that economic developing requires the improvement of human resources and the acquisition of modern technology. They also recognize that close communication with other economies, through the competitive process, is an important stimulus to the upgrading of domestic resources and domestic forms of economic organization.[18] The experience of these countries provides many lessons on how an individual economy can benefit from the removal of restrictions that isolate it from the international economy.

Looking at increased international trade from the perspective of the gains to an individual economy offers many possibilities, particularly for controlling the spread of new trade restrictions. The current GATT technology attempts to limit the use of import restrictions by specifying when a country may impose them. A country is not asked to weigh the domestic gains when a country may impose them. A country is not asked to weigh the domestic gains from an instance of import competition against the domestic costs. The GATT technology looks only at the domestic costs and authorizes import restrictions when these costs take a certain form or reach a certain degree. By so doing, the GATT system reinforces the idea that the importer bears the costs of trade while the exporter enjoys the gains.

Despite the promise of a new perspective on the benefits of trade, things seem to have gone the wrong way. The urge to get more exports and suffer fewer imports has dulled the developed countries' sense of the value of the system. Asking developing countries to examine trade liberalization in a multilateral context brings them to the instinctive view that exports are the gains from trade and imports the costs. At GATT, things are done the GATT way.

My pessimism that the potential discussed above will not be realized is based on two observations. The first concerns the developing countries' positions and proposals at the Uruguay Round. At the highest level of visibility, the developing country position is the Brazil–India position, which is the traditional GATT position of developing countries: against any compromise of developing country freedom from stated GATT obligations and for unilateral affirmative actions by the developed countries to help the developing countries. The implicit definition of what will "help" is (as always) the mercantilist one. At a lower level of visibility, developing countries have offered technical suggestions to limit the scope of allowable trade restrictions, for example, on the determination of "dumping" or "injury." These are, *in the traditional GATT sense*, good and responsible proposals. But (and I have emphasized "in the traditional GATT sense" for this reason) the traditional GATT sense of how to discipline the use of trade restrictions no longer works very well.

The other reason for my pessimism comes from the responses I have received when I have challenged researchers and academics on these matters. For example, at a symposium in South America I suggested that the developing countries had missed a chance to contribute to the international community from their own experiences. I asked: What did the government of Mexico or Chile take into account when it decided on its own trade reforms? What is there in such thought processes that might contribute to the Uruguay Round?

I offered two suggestions: (1) a proposal in the safeguards negotiations to give the costs of protection equal standing with the gains; perhaps even introduction of a "reverse safeguards" procedure through which a domestic interest could petition for removal of a trade restriction that caused it harm (for example, machinery producers for removal of restrictions on steel imports); and (2) a proposal to make the "protection balance sheet" (a concept elaborated in the GATT "Wise Men's Report" of 1985) the focus of the trade policy review mechanism.

There were three responses to my suggestion that developing countries prepare and present nonmercantilist proposals: (1) the United States would not accept nonmercantilist proposals, so it would be futile to make them; (2) the current GATT builds on mercantilist economics, and since developing countries want to improve the GATT not overthrow it, they must work within its mercantilist confines; (3) within the mecantilist conception of access to foreign markets as a country's right and discipline over its own use of import restrictions as the obligation, it is easy to define special and differential treatment for developing countries – unrequited access and less discipline. If this perception of costs and benefits is put aside, it is not immediately clear how special and differential treatment for developing countries might be defined.

There is perhaps a reply to each of these objections, but a reply is not my point. My point is this: 'We think about the GATT only in the GATT way.

CONCLUSIONS

At the beginning of this essay, I posited rhetorically that the institutionalized bad economics of the GATT might be just a matter of bad timing: the rules were written one day, but the appropriate economics were not uncovered until the next. It is time to take the question on directly: Is the problem simply a matter of unfortunate timing?

The answer is "no".

The work of Haberler and Viner shows that the "new" ideas about trade and development were around from the beginning. The supporting evidence reviewed at the beginning of this essay came later, but its emergence did overlap some of the events that shaped the GATT's perspective on trade and development, such as the UNCTAD–GATT rivalry throughout the 1970s and the GATT's Tokyo Round report, which was published in 1979. Finally, at no time did more of the evidence favor the economics that was built into the GATT than favored the economics that was left out.

In any case, given the way the choices were made, such evidence was irrelevant. The formative decisions came out of an adversarial process that focused first the emotions and then the intellect on the issue of more versus less of whatever sense of discipline the rules happened to contain.[19] The evidence is relevant mostly to the issue of determining what is the most effective form of discipline. But as the decision process came into being, that was not the focal issue.

As the Uruguay Round unfolds, it is becoming even clearer that the institutional structure of the GATT, having initially left out the "new" ideas and evidence about trade and development, now serves to keep them out. Building the "old" economics into the institutional decision structure of the GATT preserved a developed-developing country division that would have disappeared had the only influence been a strictly intellectual one.

In summary, my conclusions are these three:

* There is a GATT way of thinking about the role of trade in development.
* The economics of the GATT way is different from what is considered good economics by much of the profession.

* When we – policymakers and academics alike – put on our "GATT hats," we tend to put on our "GATT minds" as well.

NOTES

1 Both Viner and Haberler refer to their work as applications of "classical" economics. Haberler, in his exposition, often talks about what the "old-fashioned economist" would conclude.

2 The World Bank's *World Development Report* 1987 reviews and extends what has been learned about the topic "industrialization and foreign trade." It also provides an extensive bibliography.

3 See, for example, Balassa (1981, 1985, part II). Balassa's method became the basis for a significant part of the World Bank's *World Development Report 1981*.

4 Quoted by Cooper (1987, 299) from Cordell Hull's *Memoirs*. Cooper provides similar quotations from Presidents Franklin D. Roosevelt and Harry S. Truman.

5 Dam (1970, 227ff) provides a more extensive comparison.

6 As explained in the first section above, there was no trade and development literature on which to draw.

7 Hudec (1975) provides a useful history and analysis.

8 The other summary points concern capital flows, monetary reserves, and macro-economic stabilization policies.

9 The statement quoted above includes the words "to negotiate" but the text of the report (p. 127) is more specific: "a negotiated settlement involving a gradual shift away from undesirable policies on both sides."

10 Less than a year later, Haberler (1959), in his Fiftieth Anniversary Commemoration Lectures at the National Bank of Egypt, elaborated on these points: "My overall conclusion is that international trade has made a tremendous contribution to the development of less-developed countries in the 19th and 20th centuries and can be expected to make an equally big contribution in the future, if it is allowed to proceed freely" (p. 5). "[D]evelopment policies should be such as to work through and with the help of the powerful forces of the price mechanism instead of opposing and counteracting the market forces" (p. 36). Haberler accepted the infant industry argument and suggested a uniform tariff of 20–30 percent as the only allowable interference with free trade. But he added, "I am fully aware of the fact that practically all underdeveloped countries (and developed countries for that matter) pursue policies that are almost the exact opposite of those sketched above [highly differentiated tariffs, exchange controls, and the like]. It is my contention that this type of policy hurts the underdeveloped countries" (p. 36).

11 Had the community been trained to see the matter as an application of effective protection or domestic resource cost concepts, things might have been different. But such concepts were yet to come in popular usage.

12 Little (1982, chapters 3 and 4) points out that during the period 1943–60, "vicious circles" were a popular form of explanation among development theories of why poverty persists. "Big push" was the complementary concept in policy advice.

13 The concessions are extended on a most-favored nation basis. We assume, for simplicity, that each good is imported only from the country with which the concession was negotiated or only from the developing country.

14 My own work contributed a footnote on this matter. In 1971, while on the UNCTAD staff, I set out to examine the effect of the GATT Rounds on developing country exports. My intent was to demonstrate the need for preference. My hypothesis was

that with most-favored nation tariff cuts, even when they covered developing country exports, developing country exporters were left at the starting gate. I found the opposite to be the case. Where the Dillon and Kennedy Round cuts had touched developing country exports, the response was much faster growth of developing than of developed country exports. These findings are published in Finger (1974 and 1976). Like many of the relevant facts, these were dug out long after decisions had institutionalized the wrong economics.

15 In the 1980s, Section 301 of the U.S. Trade Act has emerged as an important policy instrument of the United States. Section 301 borrows some of the external features of legalism, but its application of a unilateral interpretation of what is legal and its availability to any U.S. interest that argues that its foreign competition is "unreasonable" (though not necessarily "illegal") suggest that it is grounded not in "legalism" but in old-fashioned mercantilism. Section 301 is not reviewed here.

16 Finger and Messerlin (1989) provide a review of these restrictions.

17 World Bank (1988) and Whalley (1989) provide lists of countries in both categories – those implementing new trade restrictions and those removing old ones.

18 The "old-fashioned" or classical view of Viner (1953), Haberler (1959), and Keesing (1976) emphasized the importance of the market process as communication.

19 I have taken this idea so much to heart that I am no longer willing to ask if it is Robert Hudec's idea or mine.

REFERENCES

Balassa, B. 1963. "European Integration: Problems and Issues." *American Economic Review Papers and Proceedings* 53 (May): 175–84.

Balassa, B. 1966. "Tariff Reductions and Trade in Manufactures Among Industrial Countries." *American Economic Review Papers and Proceedings* 56 (June): 466–73.

Balassa, B. 1981. "Policy Response to External Shocks in Selected Latin American Countries." In M. Gillis and W. Baer, eds, *Export Diversification and the New Protectionism*. urbana: University of Illinois Press for the National Bureau of Economic Research.

Balassa, B. 1985. *Change and Challenge in the World Economy*. London: Macmillan.

Balassa, B., and associates. 1971. *The Structure of Protection in Developing Countries*. Baltimore, Md.: Johns Hopkins University Press.

Bell, C. 1987. "Development Economics." In J. Eatwell, M. Milgate, and P. Newman, eds, *The New Palgrave, A Dictionary of Economics*. London: Macmillan; New York: Stockton; Tokyo; Maruzen.

Bhagwati, J. 1978. *Anatomy and Consequences of Exchange Control Regimes*. Cambridge, Mass.: Ballinger.

Buchanan, J. M. 1984. "Alternative Perspectives on Economics and Public Policy." (Cato Institute) *Policy Report* 6: 1–5.

Burenstam Linder, S. 1986. *The Pacific Century: Economic and Political Consequences of Asia-Pacific Dynamism*. Stanford, Calif.: Stanford University Press.

Campos, R. de Oliveira, G. Haberler, J. Meade, and J. Tinbergen. 1958. *Trends in International Trade*. Geneva: GATT.

Cooper, R. N. 1987. "Trade Policy as Foreign Policy." In Robert M. Stern, ed., *U.S. Trade Policies in a Changing World Economy*. Cambridge, Mass.: MIT Press.

Dam, K. 1970, *The GATT: Law and International Economic Organization*. Chicago: University of Chicago Press. (Midway Reprint 1977).

Donges, J. B. 1976. "A Comparative Survey of Industrialization Policies in Fifteen Semi-Industrial Countries." *Weltwirtschaftliches Archiv*. Band 112 (Heft 4): 626–59.

Finger, J. M. 1974. "GATT Tariff Concessions and the Exports of Developing Countries." *Economic Journal* 84 (September): 566–75.

Finger, J. M. 1976. "Effects of the Kennedy Round Tariff Concessions on the Exports of Developing Countries." *Economic Journal* 86 (March): 87–95.

Finger, J. M., and P. A. Messerlin. 1989. *The Effects of Industrial Countries' Policies on Developing Countries.* Policy and Research Series No. 3. Washington, D.C.: World Bank.

GATT. 1979. *The Tokyo Round of Multilateral Trade Negotiations.* Geneva.

GATT. 1985. *Trade Policies for a Better Future.* (The Leutwiler Report). Geneva.

Haberler, G. 1959. *International Trade and Economic Development.* Cairo: National Bank of Egypt.

Hudec, R. E. 1975. *The GATT Legal System and World Trade Diplomacy.* New York: Prager.

Hudec, R. E. 1987. *Developing Countries in the GATT Legal System.* London: Gower, for the Trade Policy Research Center.

Jackson, J. H. 1989. *The World Trading System: Law and Policy of International Economic Relations.* Cambridge, Mass., and London: MIT Press.

Keesing, D. B. 1976. "Outward Looking Policies and Economic Development." *Economic Journal* 77 (June): 303–20.

Kruger, A. O. 1978. *Liberalization Attempts and Consequences.* Cambridge, Mass.: Ballinger.

Little, M. D. 1982. *Economic Development: Theory, Policy and International Relations.* New York: Basic Books.

Little, I. M. D., T. Scitovsky, and M. F. Scott. 1970. *Industry and Trade in Some Developing Countries: A Comparative Study.* London and New York: Oxford University Press for the Development Centre of the Organization for Economic Cooperation and Development.

Prebisch, R. 1964. *Towards a New Trade Policy for Development.* New York: United Nations.

United Nations Conference on Trade and Development. 1968. *The Kennedy Round: Estimated Effects on Tariff Barriers.* New York: United Nations.

Viner, J. 1953, *International Trade and Economic Development.* London: Oxford University Press.

Whalley, J., coordinator. 1989. *The Uruguay Round and Beyond.* London: Macmillan.

World Bank. 1988. *Adjustment Lending: An Evaluation of Ten Years of Experience.* Policy and Research Series No. 1. Washington, D.C.

3. The Political Economy of Administered Protection

J. M. Finger, H. K. Hall, and D. R. Nelson

Trade restrictions are hardly ever voted directly by Congress. Though the threat of direct congressional action is frequently present, pressure for protection is usually applied through the major instruments for the administrative regulation of imports: the antidumping and countervailing duty procedures and the escape clause mechanism.

In this paper, we will examine these instruments for the administrative regulation of imports. The form of the paper is not novel – a theory of how these mechanisms work is developed, then operational implications of this theory are deduced and tested over the record of countervailing duty, antidumping, and escape clause cases decided from 1975 through 1979. This is the period over which the Trade Act of 1974 was in force. Because the nature of these mechanisms is relatively unfamiliar, a relatively large amount of institutional information is provided.[1]

I. ADMINISTRATIVE MECHANISMS

The distinction between "high" and "low" policy tracks is one which Richard Cooper has used in the international relations literature. The low, or technical, track is the "rules" track. Cases here are "determined," not "decided" according to criteria established by law, administrative regulations and precedent. Higher-track decisions are less circumscribed by rules and regulations and require considerable attention by government officials entrusted with discretionary authority and subject to political accountability. Political influence is applied directly in high-track cases, but comes to bear on low-track cases only indirectly, through the shaping of the laws and regulations which define their technocratic nature.

The highest, most open, decision mechanism in trade matters is, of course, Congress. Here decisions are made in the light of public awareness by decision makers directly responsible to the voters. At this level, decision criteria are very open – any industry seeking protection may present any reason which it feels will be convincing.

Both the escape clause and the less than fair value mechanism are delegations of Congress's authority to regulate trade. One might assume that the same forces which would have come to bear on Congress will influence the delegated decision.

We will, however, argue that the delegation of such decisions to a technical track will significantly affect their substance.

A. The Escape Clause

The more political of the administrative tracks created by Congress is the escape clause (Section 201 of the 1974 Trade Act). Under this clause, an industry may petition the International Trade Commission (ITC) to conduct an investigation of "injury" from imports. The ITC's investigation is limited to whether or not there has been or is likely to be injury to "the domestic industry producing an article like or directly competitive with the imported article." The ITC reports its findings to the president, and if injury to the domestic industry has been found, the report includes the ITC's recommendation as to the import restriction and/or adjustment assistance necessary to prevent or remedy the injury. The president, however, is not legally constrained by the ITC's recommendation. He may, if the ITC determines injury, decline to provide import relief or adjustment assistance, may decide to provide one when the other was recommended, or may negotiate orderly marketing agreements with exporting countries. Thus, the ITC's function is like that of a grand jury, the commissioners being charged with examining only one side of the issue which the president must decide. The ITC decides not the outcome of the case, but whether or not the case should be taken up by the president.

B. Less-than-Fair Value Cases

Countervailing duty cases are concerned with the sale of subsidized exports in the U.S. market, and antidumping cases with sales in the United States at a price below the foreign producer's long run costs, or below his home-market price. Such cases are described as "less-than-fair value (*LFV*) cases," because the trade practices they are intended to control involve, in legal terms, the sale of products at less than their "fair value." The imposition of dumping duties requires both a determination of *LFV* pricing and a determination of resulting injury to domestic producers. Over the period covered by this study, a countervailing duty case included an injury test only if the product involved was duty free in the U.S. tariff schedule. During this period, *LFV* investigations were the responsibility of the Treasury Department and injury investigations were the responsibility of ITC.[2]

The *LFV* criteria are, by law, more technically precise than escape clause criteria. Dumping, for example, is defined by 300 lines of text in the antidumping act plus 1,000 *Federal Register* lines of administrative regulations. In contrast, the only criterion the Trade Act of 1974 imposed on the president's escape clause decisions was "the national economic interest of the United States," and the criteria by which the 1974 Trade Act charged the ITC with judging injury take up only 35 lines.

Further, the injury criteria are illustrative, while the dumping criteria are limiting. The Trade Act tells the ITC to take into account "all economic factors which it considers relevant, including (but not limited to) . . . [A list follows]." The antidumping act, in defining foreign value, specifies, for example, that "the amount for general expenses shall not be less than 10 percentum of the cost as defined in paragraph . . ., and the amount of profit shall not be less than 8 percentum of the sum of such general expenses and cost. . . ."

That the technical criteria are followed is assured by the right of appeal. Any interested party can appeal a *LFV* determination into the federal courts. This right of court appeal does not apply to escape clause findings.

II. NATURE OF THE TECHNICAL TRACK

A technical track is cheaper to operate than a political process. Discretion must be vested in relatively senior government officials, while a more tightly constrained process can be administered by a technically trained, as opposed to a broadly educated and politically astute, staff which could work out a political solution for their superior's signature.

A much more important characteristic of the technical track relates to the minimization of the *political* costs of making a decision. Protection involves large transfers of income – those from consumers to producers are typically eight to ten times the net costs of protection (Dale Larson). As Lester Thurow has pointed out, it is very difficult for democratic political systems to make such nearly zero-sum transfer decisions. Losses seem always to be more identifiable than gains; hence the optimal outcome is often to avoid a political decision.

A. Positive-Sum Decision

When protection is the issue, the opposed interests are domestic producers, who want imports restricted, and domestic consumers or users, who want access to foreign sources of supply.[3] By specifying precisely how the interests of one group are to be taken into account, legal or technical criteria spare policy level officials from having to decide whose interests will be taken into account, and from having to explain why to those whose interests are left out. They provide solid reasons for the government's decision, and hence allow the government to point out to the losing side that no other decision was legally possible. This justification helps to diffuse the political costs of the decision without preventing the government from harvesting the gratitude of the winners.

In short, the technical track provides a way to decide between the course of action which would be advocated by two directly opposed interest groups without facing up to the issue which divides them, that is, without weighing in comparable terms one side's interests against the other's. In terms of the interests *effectively* represented, the technical track turns a zero-sum situation into a positive-sum decision.

B. Role of Misdirection and Obfuscation

The key to the effectiveness of a technical track is that it disenfranchises one "side" with major interest in the decisions it makes. But the mechanism itself is established through democratic processes, hence, the disenfranchised "losers" from the decisions have the same right to shape its mechanisms as the "winners" do. That they do not is a reflection of their unawareness of what is going on. This unawareness in turn depends on two elements critical to an effective democratic decision mechanism – misdirection and obfuscation.

Misdirection has to do with the difference between the *LFV* mechanism's legal purpose and its economic function. In law, the mechanism is designed to impose import restrictions only in instances of "unfair" foreign pricing, for example, subsidized exports thereby priced below cost. (The *LFV* duties offset, in theory, the effects on import prices of unfair foreign practices.) But, as will be explained below, the economics of such mechanisms suggests that they will go "too far" and protect domestic producers from "fair" foreign competition as well.

As misdirection is the basis for establishing such mechanisms, obfuscation is what keeps them going. The *LFV* mechanism is an outlet for complaints by domestic producers, not domestic users or buyers, and hence at the initiation of each case, those who benefit from the possible import restriction will be better prepared than those of a case investigation. Lower-track procedures *are* technical, and thus incomprehensible without lengthy training. This means that such material is not likely to attract news media attention, and certainly not the attention which the more comprehensible political track events will receive. Thus technical procedures, whatever their purpose, tend to be obscure and the obfuscation they create allows the government to serve the advantaged interest group without being called to task by the disadvantaged.

C. Nature of the Biases in the LFV Mechanism

Our argument suggests that a low track will not function unless it is biased in favor of one or the other interest group in conflict. The direction of the basis in the *LFV* mechanism does not follow from the fact that it is technical, but simply from the fact that it is a channel for complaints about a surfeit of import competition, not a lack. Thus by design, it weighs domestic producers' interests more heavily than domestic users – it has the capacity to impose trade restrictions but not to remove them (other than those it imposes itself).

The characteristics of the *LFV* decision process come together in such a way as to suggest that the mechanism will be protectionist in more than the obvious sense just described. Control of the technocratic apparatus is ultimately political; hence the overall bias in the mechanism depends on how the political impacts of the disadvantaged interest's losses and of the advantaged interest's gains balance each other within it.

The existence itself of the mechanism demonstrates that one side has the advantage, and the obscure nature of its proceedings assures that that advantage can (to some degree) be exploited without generating opposition. Thus along whatever scale the *LFV* mechanism operates, it will be, as a central tendency, on the advantaged group's side of zero.[4]

The scale along which the *LFV* mechanism operates is the nature of the pricing practices which foreign sellers are allowed to employ in the U.S. market. Zero on this scale – the position accepted (as fair) by both conflicting interests, domestic producers and domestic consumers – is when foreign sellers are limited to the same pricing practices available to domestic sellers.[5] On the side of zero advantageous to domestic producers, foreigners will be more tightly restricted than U.S. sellers, that is, the *LFV* laws and mechanism will take pricing practices away from foreign sellers which the equivalent "domestic" law (for example, antitrust law) does not take away from domestic sellers. Thus our model predicts that the *LFV* mechanism imposes constraints on foreign sellers not imposed on domestic ones by equivalent domestic laws.

More than that, this approach suggests that protectionist pressure will bring about qualitative changes in the *LFV* mechanism and bring it to focus more on the question of comparative costs between domestic and foreign competitors for sales in the U.S. market than on the fairness of the foreigner's trade practices.

This argument is based on two propositions from social anthropology. The first of these is that the institutionalization of a social issue will attract, or cause to form, interest groups which stand to gain from that mechanism. The second is that institutional systems change over time, and that this change is significantly influenced by the interests of those groups which come to focus on it (Shmuel Eisenstadt, pp. 419–20; Walton Hamilton).

The legal objective of the *LFV* mechanism is to police the fairness of trade practices, and it pursues that objective by restricting imports (in design, from unfair exporters only). It is therefore an economic instrument with the power to restrict imports, and it will attract those with an interest in having imports restricted. This will include not only firms and industries beset by unfair competition, but more generally, those least favorably situated vis-à-vis their foreign competitors' costs. They will, the logic of social anthropology suggests, attempt to make their needs fit its scope, and its scope fit their needs. These tendencies, particularly the latter, suggest a convergence of the *economic* subject matter of *LFV* and escape clause (*EC*) cases – suggest that the *LFV* rules will tend toward protecting against the sort of injury from import competition which the escape clause goes at "officially."

III. EMPIRICAL EXAMINATION OF LFV DETERMINATIONS

A. Empirical Questions

In the most general sense, the purpose of our empirical examination of *LFV* and *EC* decisions is to demonstrate that the *LFV* system displays the characteristics of a technical track, and the *EC* mechanism those of a more political track. Several questions derived from the high-track, low-track model will be valuated. The first and most obvious of these is that technical, not political, factors determine the outcome of cases on the lower track, and vice versa on the higher track.

The second point we want to make is that it is the relaxing of technical criteria rather than the direct specification of political criteria which allows political factors to influence a case outcome.

The difference between the *LFV* pricing and *LFV* injury determination provide almost a controlled experiment for testing this hypothesis. Under the 1974 Trade Act, each dumping case and each countervailing duty case involving a duty-free product on which the Treasury Department's preliminary determination was affirmative then went to the ITC for an injury investigation. The decision environment of an injury investigation differed from that of a pricing determination in two important respects. First (as explained above), the technical criteria defining *LFV* pricing. Second, the pricing, but not the injury determination, could be appealed in federal court – the pricing, but not the injury decision, is subject to a technical review which has the force of law behind it.

There is no formal political review of either determination. In form, the only difference is the relatively ambiguous technical definition of injury.

The third area we will examine is the nature of the bias in the *LFV* mechanism. We will take up two overlapping hypotheses. The first is that the technical rules which calibrate the mechanism not only prevent foreign sellers from using practices considered unfair (for all sellers) in the U.S. market, but spill over to protect U.S. producers against fair competition from foreigners. The second is that comparative costs have a major influence on *LFV pricing* decisions.

B. Statistical Model

The statistical objective of our data analysis is to determine the influence of political and economic variables on the likelihood of an affirmative determination in an *LFV* case. The dependent variable in this analysis was the case decision (affirmative or negative). The *LFV* pricing tests covered every case decided during 1975–79 for which we could develop values for the independent variables – 183 of 208 cases, or 96 percent of the value of imports covered by the 208 cases.[6] Analysis of *LFV* injury determinations covered 57 cases of 68 decided – again, all the cases for which we could assemble the relevant data.

C. Independent Variables

Political Influences: International. Two variables in our model represent international political influences. The first of these measures the proportion of total U.S. exports (1976) which are imported by the country against which the *LFV* case was filed. The hypothesis which this variable tests is that nations with which we experience a high level of economic interdependence exercise greater influence on *LFV* outcomes than nations with which we are less interdependent.

The second international political variable is a dichotomous variable which identifies those cases brought against less-developed countries (*LDCs*). The hypothesis here is that the *LFV* decision process is prejudiced against the *LDCs*. The basis for this hypothesis is the argument by some proponents of "dependency" analysis that the institutional and legal structure in the advanced capitalist countries is rigged against *LDCs*.[7] A less conspiratorial way of viewing such an expectation is that the *LDCs* are simply not as well equipped to apply political pressure on their own behalf as other more developed countries.

Political Influences: Domestic. Our model will test two hypotheses that relate to domestic political influence:

HYPOTHESIS 1: *Industry size is positively related to success in the LFV mechanism.*

HYPOTHESIS 2: *Industrial concentration is positively related to success in the LFV mechanism.*

Both of these hypotheses are based on the assumption that, at least on economic issues, industry structure translates directly into political power.

In our statistical model, we have used three alternative measures of industry size: total employment, the value of the physical capital stock, and value-added in the industry. We have also included "case size" – the value of 1978 imports of products covered by the case – as an indicator of the political influence of size.

The widely suggested relationship between industry concentration and political influence is rooted in the theory of collective goods. This theory suggests that decision-making costs are low in groups with one or a few dominant actors, allowing relatively effective political action.

A final hypothesis about political influence refers to the administrator's instinct for self-preservation. On January 1, 1980, responsibility for enforcement of the dumping and countervailing duty laws was shifted from the Treasury to the Commerce Department. According to government officials directly affected by this transfer, the movement for trade reorganization began in earnest in January 1979, as markup of the Trade Agreements Act of 1979 was completed. Behind this shift of responsibility was the presumption that the Commerce Department would find affirmatively more often than the Treasury Department. If the frequently expressed assumption that defense and expansion of "turf" are important arguments in the objective function of bureaucrats and of bureaucratic agencies, and if the *LFV* decision mechanism allowed for discretionary response to political pressure, then there should have been a detectable shift in 1979 of the *LFV* decision function toward the affirmative. We test this hypothesis by introducing a dummy variable which identifies all cases decided in 1979.

Comparative Costs. Comparative costs are virtually impossible to measure directly. We have used instead "factor proportions," which an extensive body of theoretical and empirical work argue are the determinants of comparative costs, as an indirect measure. The variables employed are the industry physical capital-labor ratio;[8] industry average wage per worker, as a proxy for human capital intensity; and the extent of economies of scale in the industry.[9] If our hypothesis about the bias in the mechanism is valid, then *LFV* decisions will be influenced toward the affirmative by the existence of a cost disadvantage for the American industry.

In addition to supporting our hypothesis about the protectionist bias of the mechanism, a significant influence for factor proportions on *LFV* decisions would be consistent with our general hypothesis that the *LFV* mechanism is a technical, not a political, track.

This interpretation is supported by logic and by fact. As to logic, the advantaged interest has two ways to get what it wants: 1) to have the rules changed (further) in its favor; 2) to have the rules relaxed, so as to allow a more open, more expensive political track procedure. The former is the more direct, less risky, and less expensive alternative. As to fact, we will cite below examples of specific rules which bring comparative costs into the *LFV* pricing determination.

Precision. Our remaining technical variable measures the number of different products covered by the case – in operational terms, the number of 7-digit TSUSA lines. The logic behind this variable is that less than fair value is a pricing concept, and thus more appropriately applied to individual products than to large aggregates. Because the rules specify precisely what *LFV* pricing is, our hypothesis is that determinations will tend toward the status quo (negative) when the technical criteria for a decision are less clearly met. Thus the technical work hypothesis suggests a negative relation between the number of products covered by a case and the likelihood of an affirmative determination.

D. Evaluation of Results

LFV Pricing. The technical nature of the *LFV* pricing determinations is most directly illustrated by the language of the law and the related administrative regulations – the sort of information presented in Section I above. Our statistical results, presented in Table 1, are also consistent with this hypothesis. In our examination of the influences on *LFV* pricing determinations, we found each technical factor to be statistically influential. And as we hypothesized, the significant test on each political variable is inconsistent with the political track hypothesis.

Most soundly rejected is the hypothesis of international political influence. The *t*-statistics on these two variables are much below unit (in absolute value) and the coefficient on the *LDC* variable has the wrong sign. Further, when these variables are removed from the equation (from col. 2 to col. 3), the coefficients and the *t*-statistics on the significant variables are virtually unaffected.

The domestic political influence variables fare only slightly better. Of the four size variables, only employment has the expected sign, and even it is a long way from statistically significant. The closest thing to a valid domestic political influence hypothesis seems to be the "turf defending" hypothesis about the administering agency. The coefficient on the administrative reorganization threat variable has the hypothesized sign, and though insignificant at the 95 percent confidence level, has a larger *t*-statistic than the other domestic political influence variables.

On the technical track side, there is not much to add to the message in the table. Each technical track variable has the expected sign and is significant, at the 99 percent level of confidence.

LFV Injury. When we deal with injury, where the technical rules are less precise, we expect political factors to be more influential. As tests of the impacts of the various factors, we expect the same signs on the coefficients as in the analysis of the *LFV* decision, with one exception. An affirmative *LFV injury* determination will become *more* likely as the number of products covered by the case increases. While price is a concept most readily made operational on an individual product basis, injury is more appropriately (for example, in the Escape

TABLE 1 *Logit Analysis of Influences on Less-than-Fair Value Pricing Determinations, 1975–79*

Hypothesis and Variable	Hypothesized Sign	Results – Estimated Coefficient (*t*-Statistic) (1)	(2)	(3)	(4)	(5)	(6)
Political Track Hypothesis							
International Political Influences							
Proportion of U.S. Exports to Country	–	–9.1	76.2				
		(–0.03)	(0.25)				
Against a Developing Country	+	–28.	–.30				
		(–.61)	(–0.66)				
Domestic Political Influences							
Administrative Reorganization Threat	+	.69	.81.	.80	.80		
		(1.27)	(1.53)	(1.52)	(1.52)		
Industry Concentration	+	–1.8	–2.3	–2.4	–2.4	–2.3	
		(–2.28)	(–3.07)	(–3.14)	(–3.16)	(–3.08)	
Case size	+	–.13					
		(–0.71)					
Industry Size							
Employment	+	2.9	–.13	–0.4			
		(1.05)	(–0.14)	(–0.04)			
Capital Stock	+	–0.3					
		(0.52)					
Value-Added	+	–.11					
		(–0.80)					
Technical Track Hypothesis							
Comparative Costs							
Capital-Labor Ratio	+	1.8	1.8	1.7	1.7	1.8	1.6
		(2.20)[a]	(2.36)[b]	(2.33)[b]	(2.37)[b]	(2.39)[b]	(2.28)[b]
Average Wage	–	–.19	–.29	–.28	–.28	–.28	–.31
		(–1.90)[a]	(–3.56)[b]	(–3.53)[b]	(–3.77)[b]	(–3.77)[b]	(–4.47)[b]
Scale Economies	–	–4.6	–5.2	–5.1	–5.1	–4.8	–3.5
		(–2.67)[b]	(–3.05)[b]	(–3.11)[b]	(–3.12)[b]	(–3.00)[b]	(–2.40)[b]
Technical Precision							
Number of Products	–	–.90	–.88	–1.0	–1.0	–1.0	–0.8
		(–1.54)	(–2.11)[a]	(–2.39)[b]	(–2.99)[b]	(–3.11)[b]	(–2.74)[b]
Constant		2.8	4.1	3.9	3.9	4.0	3.2
		(2.75)[b]	(4.57)[b]	(4.97)[b]	(5.11)[b]	(5.20)[b]	(4.75)[b]
Proportion of Outcomes Successfully Predicted		69	71	71	71	71	68
Chi-Squared		168[b]	172[b]	171[b]	171[b]	172[b]	178[b]
Number of Observations		183	183	183	183	183	183

[a]Indicates *rejection* of the null hypothesis that the sign is not the expected one, at the 95 percent level of confidence (one-tail test).

[b]Same as fn. a, but at the 99 percent level of confidence (one-tail test).

Clause of the Trade Act) expressed in terms of capacity utilization, employment, or profits – concepts more readily made operational at the firm or industry level.

The results (Table 2) are consistent with our expectations. The political variables are much more significant here than they were in Table 1, and the technical variables much less. The hypothesized influence of the threat of administrative reorganization is supported by our data, as is the hypothesized influence of the size of the petitioning industry's labor force.

International political influences again are not significant – it is domestic politics which counts.

John Odell obtained similar results in a study of twenty-five bilateral trade disputes between the United States and Latin American countries. He found that when the foreign country worked with common economic interests within the United States, the proportion of outcomes favorable to the foreign country was higher. But mobilizing the State Department or the National Security Council staff to make "foreign policy" arguments was not effective. Thus he found that foreign interests, to get what they want, must work through allied domestic interests.

Protectionist Bias and Comparative Costs. In form, a *LFV* pricing investigation consists of observing the prices a foreign firm charges on home market sales and on sales in the United States, and then comparing the two. The details of the law and of the administrative regulations specify how the observations are to be made, and how one or the other is to be adjusted for different terms of sale (for example, lot size, payment terms, etc.), so as to make them comparable. William Dickey explains several ways in which these rules are more restrictive of foreign firms than is comparable "domestic" law of domestic firms' sales practices in the U.S. market. For example, sales below full cost during periods of slack demand (i.e., sales which cover only variable costs) are normally not considered an unfair trade practice under the antitrust laws. But the antidumping law specifies that in determining the home market price charged by a foreign firm, observations of home market sales *below cost* must be disregarded.[10]

There are other, more direct illustrations that the *LFV* process now compares foreign and domestic costs. The administrative regulations for antidumping cases state that "Petitioners unable to furnish information on foreign sales or costs may present information concerning US domestic producers' costs adjusted for differences in the foreign country in question. . . ."[11]

Our own analysis provides corroborating evidence. Each of the determinants of comparative advantage has the hypothesized sign and is significant at the 99 percent level of confidence.[12]

E. Anomalies

The coefficients on several variables do not have the signs we expected. For example, we interpreted the concentration ratio as a reflection of political influence, and expected it to have a positive coefficient in Tables 1 and 2. It is, however, negative in both cases.

TABLE 2 *Logit Analysis of Influences on ITC Injury Determinations in Less-than-Fair Value Cases*

Hypothesis and Variable	Expected Sign	Results–Estimated Coefficient (*t*-statistics) (1)	(2)	(3)	(4)	(5)	(6)	(7)
Political Track Hypothesis								
International Political Influences								
Proportion of U.S. Exports to Country	–	–1276	–1205	–967	–922	–604		
		(–1.64)	(–1.57)	(–1.41)	(–1.44)	(–0.96)		
Against a Developing Country	+	–.5						
		(–0.44)						
Domestic Political Influences								
Administrative Reorganization Threat	+	2.5	2.6		2.8	2.7	3.0	2.9
		(1.90)	(2.07)[a]		(2.30)[a]	(2.20)[a]	(2.49)[b]	(2.43)
Industry Concentration	+	–5.9	–6.1	–5.6	–3.9	–5.5	–5.6	–5.6
		(–2.22)	(–2.44)	(–2.39)	(–2.05)	(–2.34)	(–2.35)	(–2.34)
Case Size	+	2.3	2.5	2.2	1.7		1.0	
		(1.25)	(1.37)	(1.29)	(1.17)		(0.87)	
Industry Size								
Employment	+	36.1	36.0	27.5	22.3	27.9	27.9	28.4
		(1.85)[a]	(1.98)[a]	(2.22)[a]	(2.00)[a]	(2.22)[a]	(2.07)[s]	(2.14)[a]
Capital Stock	+	–.57	–.60	–.47	–.37	–.42	–.45	–.43
		(–1.87)	(–2.10)	(–2.45)	(–2.19)	(–2.27)	(–2.24)	(–2.19)
Value-Added	+	–0.7						
		(–0.12)						
Technical Track Hypothesis								
Comparative Costs								
Capital-Labor Ratio	+	1.5	1.5					
		(0.73)	(0.78)					
Average Wage	–	.35	.34	.39	.24	.38	3.7	.37
		(1.25)	(1.48)	(1.83)	(1.39)	(1.75)	(1.67)	(1.68)
Scale Economies	–	–2.2	–2.2					
		(–0.64)	(0.73)					
Technical Precision								
Number of Products	+	–55.6	–54.3	–49.8		–46.7	–50.0	–48.3
		(–1.86)	(–1.82)	(–1.84)		(–1.73)	(–1.80)	(–1.76)
Constant		–.75	–.71	–1.2	–1.2	–1.2	–1.4	–1.4
		(–0.28)	(–0.34)	(–0.61)	(–0.67)	(–0.63)	(–0.70)	(–0.72)
Proportion of Outcomes Successfully Predicted		84	81	81	79	79	83	83
Chi-Squared		127	126	130	84	129	149	145
Number of Observations		57	57	57	57	57	57	57

[a,b]See Table 1.

This result might be consistent with a technical interpretation of the variable. According to the technical track hypothesis, the outcome of a case, once it is filed, depends on technical factors not affected by the petitioner's lobbying. Protection, from a successful petition, will add to the profitability of each domestic sale by the industry – not just to those sales by the petitioning firm or firms. But in a concentrated industry, a larger share of the benefits from a successful petition will be captured by the petitioner and a smaller share will spill over to firms which did not help finance it. Hence, a firm's filing a petition will make economic sense at a lower likelihood of success if the industry is concentrated.

As this paper examines influences on the *outcomes* of *LFV* cases (once they are filed), the negative coefficient on concentration can be consistent with the positive (but insignificant) cross-section relation Finger (forthcoming) found between concentration and the industry incidence of *LFV* complaints, and Robert Baldwin (1980) found between concentration and the depth of the tariff cut made by the United States at the Tokyo Round. The Finger and the Baldwin results may indicate that the concentration ratio is not a reliable indicator of how well an industry is organized to take advantage of the avenues the government provides. And if the firms in concentrated industries tend to be multinational in scope, this weak result may simply indicate that restrictions on imports are not what they want from the government.

Several readers have suggested that the statistical significance of the wage variable might also be interpreted as evidence of political influence on *LFV* pricing decisions. One such interpretation is simply that the decision makers have sympathy for poor people, and will use the discretion the technical rules allow to protect them. A more cynical interpretation is that the politically sensitive decision makers "buy them off" by providing trade protection.

Serious questions can be raised about the analytical soundness of the latter proposition and about the validity of both.

If we accept the buy-them-off interpretation, then we are assuming that it is the votes of the poor, not their well-being, which is the politician's concern. If so, the critical variable is how *many* there are, not how *poor* they are. If so, the *number* of workers, not their wage rate, is the better representation.

Furthermore, higher-wage workers will more likely be able to afford political action and are more likely to be organized in such a way as to be politically effective. This would make the political association between affirmative decisions and the wage rate positive, not negative.

As to the evidence, if one looks at the entire pattern of statistical results, and not just at one t-statistic, a political interpretation of the average wage variable becomes untenable. All *three* comparative cost proxies are significant, and it is difficult to explain the other two in political terms. Economies of scale might lead to size and/or concentration, which would produce political power, but scale economies itself is not a political influence. Similarly, the number of workers in an industry or the industry's wealth (capital stock) might measure political power, but not the ratio of one to the other.

Even more to the point, the political interpretation of the average wage variable cannot assume that the law or the administrative regulations specify that the income or need of the affected workers be taken into account. They simply do not. Political influence slips in (if it slips in) because the technical specifications are ambiguous and allow it. If so, the more obvious and direct political influences represented by our list of political variables should be significant. They are not.

Finally, the technical criteria for injury *are* less precise than those of *LFV* pricing. The hypothesized influence of sympathy for the poor should therefore have a stronger influence on the injury determination. This is not the case. Results in Table 2 show that the domestic political factors *are* significant influences in *LFV* injury determinations, but the average wage variable's coefficient does not even have the sign which a political influences interpretation suggests.

IV. THE ESCAPE CLAUSE (*EC*) DECISION

A. Determinants of where Cases will be Resolved

From the petitioner's point of view, the distinction between the *LFV* case and an *EC* case is not a technical one. The technical criteria for demonstrating injury are not precise, hence a petitioner who feels that he has sufficient *political* influence to win has considerable latitude in putting together his supporting case. The technical criteria on *LFV* pricing are much more precise, but as our model suggests and our data demonstrate, they overlap considerably with comparative disadvantage, or the likelihood of injury from import competition. The other part of an *LFV* case *is* the ITC injury test, hence the *technical* criteria for good *LFV* cases and for good escape clause cases are much the same and do not serve to restrict a complaint to one track or the other.

The functional characteristic which separates the low from the high track is the political significance of the cases it handles. This characteristic will be closely related to the degree of public awareness of the cases being processed. If the public is unaware of a petition to the government for protection, then (as outlined in Table 3) the scope of the decision on the case can be limited to the interests of the petitioner, and a decision can be reached with dispatch. The technical criteria of the lower track will serve both to control the decision process and to keep it from becoming a public issue. They can therefore be designed to evaluate only the petitioner's interests. The decision then is easy. Those who will lose are not aware that the decision is being made.

A high degree of public awareness changes the game. It is impossible, in a democratic country, to define out of a public decision parties who are aware that their interests are at stake. Thus such a decision cannot be bounded by technical constraints, and it cannot be limited to considerations only of the petitioner's interests. Among the participants in such a decision, there will be losers as well as winners and, as Lester Thurow suggests, such decisions will be hard to achieve.

Within limits, the high track can create public awareness and the low track obscure it, but public awareness is more an exogenous factor than an endogenous one. This factor has no obvious quantitative measure, but is likely closely related to case size. Case size thus should serve to distinguish between cases which the low track can and cannot process effectively. Table 4 shows that the average case filed in the *Ec* mechanism was three times as large as the average *LFV* case. If

TABLE 3 *Characteristics of High and Low Administrative Decision Tracks*

Track	Functional Criterion	Scope of Decision	Decision Criteria	Decision Type
Low	Public Unawareness (political insignificance)	Parochial–Petitioner's Interests	Precise and Limiting	Positive Sum (easy)
High	Public Awareness (political significance)	National Interest	Open	Zero Sum (hard)

we exclude antidumping petitions for steel and autos (disputes which we shall argue below did not "belong" in this mechanism and were not resolved there), *EC* cases were more than eleven times as large as *LFV* cases.

B. The Presidential Decision

Protection cases decided in the spotlight of national attention are close to zero-sum decisions. The political net gain (or minimal net loss) is not on either side of such decisions, but in avoiding them. This has two implications for the presidential decision. First, it will push the president toward saying no. Negative decisions will discourage further petitions and hence reduce the number of times the president will have to say anything. A minimal political gain from saying yes on one case may be undone by the loss from having to decide the four others this yes encourages. Second, it will push a presidential affirmative decision as far toward a non-decision as his legally defined options allow. The president cannot avoid public scrutiny or political accountability by ordering the negotiation of an orderly marketing arrangement (*OMA*), but he can cloud the public's view and diffuse accountability somewhat. The details of an *OMA* can be made quite complex, or put off to be worked out in the future, when they will be announced at a high, but lower than presidential level (for example, the Special Trade Representative). The other affirmative options give consumer interests a more precise dimension on which to focus – several percentage points added to price by a tariff, or taken away from supply by a quota, or the budgetary cost of adjustment assistance. As Table 4 shows, the three *EC* cases in which the president recommended an orderly marketing arrangement covered 78 percent of the imports on which affirmative decisions were returned.[13] In effect, ordering the negotiation of an *OMA* is a step toward disenfranchising domestic consumers, and hence a movement toward a positive-sum decision environment. If domestic and foreign producers are the only influences at play, a minimal amount of political craft should be needed to induce the competing producers to do what the antitrust laws attempt to prevent them from doing voluntarily.

TABLE 4 *LFV and EC Mechanisms: Number of Cases, 1975–79 and Import Coverage*

	LFV Cases		*EC Cases*	
	All Cases	*Excluding Steel and Autos*	*ITC Decision*	*Presidential Decision*
Number of cases				
Filed	245	214	43	–
Decided	208	177	40	25
Affirmative	73	73	25	8
(Percent of Decided)	35	41	62	32
Orderly Marketing Arrangements	–	–	–	3
(Percent of Affirmative)	–	–	–	38
Import Coverage of Cases ($ million)[a]				
Filed	$25,948	£5,991	$14,224	–
Decided	$25,085	$5,079	$13,016	$8,968
Affirmative	$2,860	$2,860	$8,968	$4,992
(Percent of Decided)	11	56	69	56
Orderly Marketing Arrangements	–	–	–	$3,888
(Percent of Affirmative)	–	–	–	78
Average Case Size ($ million)[a]				
Filed	$106	$28	$331	–
Decided	$121	$29	$325	$359
Affirmative	$39	$39	$359	$624
Orderly Marketing Arrangements	–	–	–	$1,296

[a]In terms of 1978 import values.

On the high track, the clearest pressures are away from a decision, not toward either a yes or a no. Accepting this, and looking deeper for some political or economic basis of forecasting the president's decision when he must make one, we note that both the degree of injury to the domestic producer of import replacements and the "gains from trade" to domestic consumers will concentrate on those sectors in which the United States has comparative disadvantage. Hence, *net* losses to the national economic interest should not vary much between industries (see Larson, Table 1), and in cases which are big enough to overcome the relative dispersion of consumers and/or public enough so that consumers as well as producers will be aware of their stake in them, there is no basis for predicting that comparative costs will consistently push the decision in one direction or the other. As protection, except in unlikely "optimum tariff" situations, is a negative sum proposition, the "national economic interest" will always push toward a negative decision. But as this net loss to the economy comes to only 10 percent of the gross gain for protected producers (see Larson, Table 1), the net national interest is not likely to be a powerful influence.

The president's decision is made, therefore, at the razor's edge. The economic gains to those who want protection are only marginally smaller than its costs to those who oppose it, and this margin will not vary much from case to case. Because of the level at which the decision is made, consumers (potential losers from protection) will not be in the dark, but if there is a marginal difference in the degree of public awareness of a case and of its implications, it should favor the producer's side. Thus, the economics and the politics of the decision will each favor one side or the other only marginally, with economics tipped toward one side and politics toward the other.

The ITC's findings will not be definitive. Their role in the decision process will be more political than technical or economic, and more facilitating than decisive. Their major functions are to make sure a politically significant petitioner gets his day before the president; to occupy time during which resolution of the case may be achieved by less focused means than a presidential decision; to provide a focal point so that the president may observe how the sides are drawn before the mechanism focuses on him.

We thus find it difficult to say what will define operationally the "clout" needed to win an affirmative decision from the president. Baldwin, as we predict, did not find the ITC decision a significant factor. Our own *Logit* analysis was plagued by convergence problems, due in part, we suspect, to the smallness of the number of presidential decisions – this smallness being consistent with our predictions. The obvious, though gross measure of political clout behaved in the obvious way. On eight "Big Cases" (over $400 million of imports), the president said yes five times (three *OMAs*). On seventeen "Small Cases," he said yes only three times (no *OMA*s).

Our and Baldwin's generally poor results with statistical decision rules illustrate perhaps the nature of the presidency. Those things which can be reduced to rules will be decided at a lower level.

V. CONCLUSIONS

We have presented and tested an interpretation of how the administrative import-restraint mechanisms function. This interpretation differs in some respects from more or less "official" interpretations, but this difference is not an indictment of the mechanisms. Their function is to resolve our diffuse complaints about import competition, and all in all they seem to serve this function efficiently.

A major difference between our view and others' has to do with what the *LFV* and *EC* mechanisms actually do. In law, the escape clause deals with injury to U.S. producers from import competition and the *LFV* mechanism with the fairness of business practices used in the U.S. market by foreigners. But in economics we find that they both deal with the same thing – injury from imports and the associated gains from trade. The functional difference between the cases which belong on one track or the other is the size and perhaps the degree of public awareness of the interests at stake, not the nature of those interests. Antidumping and countervailing duties are, functionally, the poor (or small) man's escape clause.[14]

TABLE 5 *Percentage of Imports of Manufactured Goods Covered by LFV and EC Cases, 1975–79*

	Antidumping and Countervailing Duty Cases		Escape Clause Cases	
Year[a]	Filed	Affirmative	Filed	Affirmative
1975	15.4	0.3	4.1	0.0
1976	0.8	0.9	2.3	0.5
1977	4.1	0.6	2.6	2.8
1978	0.6	0.4	1.0	0.4
1979	0.4	0.1	0.5	0.0
1975–79	21.3	2.2	10.4	3.8

[a]The trade coverage of each case was measured by 1978 imports of the products covered by case, for example, *LFV* cases filed in 1975 covered products which in 1978 accounted for 15.4 percent of manufactured imports. The 1975–79 figures measure the percentage of 1978 manufactured imports covered by cases filed (or affirmatively decided) in the five-year period.

The administrative mechanism is in part self-policing, but its effective function depends in part on the good citizenship of its users. It is not likely that a politically obscure case will be filed on the high track. It is less costly to provide data for technocrats to fit into their formulae than to establish the political basis for a presidential decision. Besides, the lower-track decision weighs the petitioner's interests more heavily than does the higher. In short, if you are politically obscure, the lower track will work *for* you. But if you are politically prominent, the lower track will not work. Highly visible petitions will attract political opposition which the technical rules of the track will not be able to depose, or even effectively express. Because they have no technical outlet, buyers must press their interests at the political level, hence such cases will escalate into political issues.

The antidumping mechanism did not resolve the steel and auto cases. Though these antidumping cases were terminated, the conflicts they represented went on – autos became an escape clause case and finally an *OMA* with Japan, and the steel issue has led to high level administrative protection through the Trigger Price Mechanism. This is not to argue that the petitioner will not gain from such a filing. He will, through the news generated by such a petition and the opportunities it will create to complain about the ineffectiveness of the government and the bureaucracy, publicize his complaints about the "unfairness" of foreign competition. In so doing, he will be building the broad base of public support needed to win a favorable political decision at the national level.[15]

But using the mechanism to publicize a particular case will create public awareness of the mechanism, and hence reduce its capacity to process efficiently those cases for which it would have been appropriate. The recent trade reorganization act not only transferred administration of *LFV* cases from Treasury to Commerce, but made its procedures considerably more Byzantine – so much so that its drafters describe it as a "Lawyer's Relief Act." The motive behind this might have been to restore the degree of obscurity (and therefore effectiveness)[16] which use of the mechanism by the steel and auto industries took away.

Table 5 is presented to assure the reader that a cynical or despondent interpretation of the institutions we have described is not warranted. We have argued that in their central tendency these mechanisms are biased toward protectionism. But this bias is not large. In the five years, 1975–79, only 2.2 percent of U.S. manufactured imports have been granted relief under the *LFV* statutes, and only 3.8 percent under the escape clause.[17] The costs of gathering and disseminating information needed to reduce this bias would probably exceed the benefits. The dark side of the force is more protectionist than the light, that is, it is the openness of the system which keeps the bias as small as it is.

NOTES

The original draft of this paper was completed while we were with the U.S. Treasury Department, Office of Trade Research. The positions taken and opinions expressed in this paper are our sole responsibility.

1 Various sorts of information have gone into the development of this theory, much of it derived from firsthand observation of how things are done. The reaction of several readers to earlier drafts suggests that trained economists find "institutional information" (such as what the antidumping law actually says) repugnant, and that they are unwilling to admit such information as evidence in the testing of theories. Their position, it would seem, is that reading what the law *says* will not help one understand what it *means*. This meaning they seem to assume can only be grasped by interpreting regression results.

2 Since January 1, 1980, *LFV* investigations (in dumping and in countervailing duty cases) are done by the Commerce Department, and all countervailing duty cases include an injury test. Injury tests remain the responsibility of the ITC.

3 This exposition assumes that the foreign exporter and/or government is not a major interest effectively involved in such decision mechanisms. This hypothesis will be tested below.

4 The logic of this paragraph applies to any delegation of authority to an administering agency. Hence OSHA is a good idea but we get too much of it. Likewise for Ralph Nader and factor-proportions model trade papers in this *Review*.

5 The antitrust laws and enforcement mechanisms take up the general question of what trade practices are fair. Against this background, the *LFV* mechanisms deal only with the trade practices in the U.S. market of foreign sellers. The institutional basis for this separation may be that the mechanisms used to enforce the antitrust laws cannot be applied to foreign firms.

6 The product coverage of each *case* is defined in terms of the TSUSA seven-digit import categories covered by the petition. The *industry* affected by a case is the four-digit SIC category into which the relevant TSUSA categories are mapped by the U.S. Bureau of the Census classifications.

7 See, for example, Andre Frank.

8 The physical capital stock was estimated, for 1975, by the Branson-Monoyios method; as the gross book value of plant and equipment, plus the capitalized value of supply

and materials inventories. Data for all industry variables are from the *U.S. Census of Manufactures*.

9 Estimated by Hufbauer's method. His measure of economies of scale is the coefficient a in the regression equation $log\ v = k + a$ times $log\ n + e$, where v is the ratio between value-added per man in plants employing n persons and value-added per man for the entire four-digit industry, and k is a constant. We used 1972 data.

10 See Dickey, p. 245. He provides several other, more complicated, examples.

11 *Federal Register*, No. 26, p. 8199, col. 1. This evolution continues. Matthew Marks (p. 432) points out that the shorter time limits put into effect by the Trade Agreements Act of 1979 will make the administering agency more dependent on such cost information supplied by the petitioner.

12 We assume that scale economies and human capital intensity are positively related and physical capital intensity negatively related to U.S. comparative advantage. Virtually all relevant empirical work supports the assumed signs on the first two variables. As to our "Leontief paradox" assumption on the third variable, Robert Stern (pp. 86–90), reviewing recent cross-section studies of the trade position of U.S. industries, indicates that in each of them only when "resource intensive" industries are excluded does the relation between physical capital intensity and U.S. comparative advantage become positive. Our analysis included the resource intensive industries, and in this analysis, capital intensity is used only as a *forecaster* of comparative advantage. Correlation between physical capital and natural resource intensity, which muddles the analysis of *cause* of comparative advantage, is of no consequence to our analysis.

13 Virtually every line in the U.S. tariff has been "conceded" under the GATT. Import relief would therefore involve nullification or impairment of a GATT concession for which the countries to whom the concession had been made could demand compensation. Negotiation of an *OMA* with these trading partners would incorporate the question of compensation and thus avoid its becoming a separate issue.

14 And seems, in a way, to define having comparative advantage as an unfair trade practice.

15 The uncertainty of the case outcome might slow foreign development of a market in the United States. For details and empirical tests, see Finger.

16 Which suggests that the social value of lawyers lies in the confusion they create, not in that they dissolve.

17 Of the imports subject to relief under the escape clause, 68 percent are covered by the *OMA*s for footwear and television receivers. Larson argues that these *OMA*s have had no effect on the trends of U.S. imports of footwear and television sets.

REFERENCES

Baldwin, Robert E., "U.S. Political Pressures Against Adjustment to Greater Imports," paper presented at the Eleventh Pacific Trade and Development Conference, Korean Development Institute, Seoul, September 1–5, 1980.

Branson, William H. and Monoyios, Nikalaos "Factor Inputs in U.S. Trade," *Journal of International Economics*, 7, May 1977, 111–31.

Cooper, Richard N., "Trade Policy is Foreign Policy," *Foreign Policy*, No. 9, Winter 1972–73, 18–36.

Dickey, William L., "The Pricing of Imports into the United States," *Journal of World Trade Law*, May–June 1979, *13*, 238–56.

Eisenstadt, Shmuel N., "Social Institutions" in *International Encyclopaedia of the Social Sciences*, New York: Macmillan and the Free Press, 1968, *14*, 409–29.

Finger, J. M., "The Industry-Country Incidence of 'Less Than Fair Value' Cases in the

United States Import Trade," in Malcolm Gillis and Werner Baer, eds, *Export Diversification and the New Protectionism*, National Bureau of Economic Research, forthcoming.

Frank, Andre G., *Capitalism and Underdevelopment in Latin America*, New York: Monthly Review Press, 1967.

Hamilton, Walton H., "Institution", in *Encyclopaedia of the Social Sciences*, Vol. 8, New York: Macmillan, 1937, 84–89.

Hufbauer, Gary C., "The Impact of National Characteristics and Technology on the Commodity Composition of Trade in Manufactured Goods," in Raymond Vernon, ed., *The Technology Factor* in *International Trade*, National Bureau of Economic Research, New York: Columbia University Press, 1970.

Larson, Dale W., 'The Cost of Import Protection in the United States," U.S. Treasury Department, processed, 1979.

Marks, Matthew, J., "Recent Changes in American Law on Regulatory Trade Measures," *The World Economy*, July 1980, 2, 427–40.

Odell, John S., "Latin American Trade Negotiations with the United States, *International Organization*, Spring 1980, 34, 207–28.

Stern, Robert M., "Changes in U.S. Comparative Advantage: Issues for Research and Policy", in National Science Foundation *International Economic Policy Research*, papers and proceedings of a colloquium held in Washington, D.C., October 3 and 4, 1980.

Thurow, Lester C., *The Zero Sum Society*, New York: Basic Books, 1980.

Federal Register, No. 26, Vol. 45.

U.S. Bureau of the Census, *Census of Manufactures*, Washington, various years.

4. What Can the WTO Do for Developing Countries?

J. M. Finger and L. A. Winters

We begin from the widely accepted premise that the integration of many developing countries into the world economy has been an important source of their recent success. This integration has ensued from two factors: (1) the access to international markets that was available to them, and (2) reforms of developing countries' policies that integrated their industries into international markets. The criterion then for answering the question that is the title of our paper is obvious: how can the WTO continue to help developing countries to integrate themselves into the international economy? We deal minimally with access to international markets for products of export interest to developing countries, however, and focus instead on how the WTO supports reform of developing countries' own policies. Given that access to major markets does not vary substantially across developing countries, while trade performance and integration do, we infer that the latter plays a fundamental if not a predominant role.

The WTO assists the process of reform of developing countries' policies in several ways. GATT/WTO sponsors multilateral negotiations through which countries agree to reduce and to bind their restrictions, particularly tariffs, against unilateral increases. It provides rules that specify what restrictions are not allowed, what restrictions a country may retain or newly put in place (safeguards, antidumping, etc.), and how trade restrictions are to be administered (e.g., customs valuation).

Our emphasis is on the WTO and GATT rules, particularly on how these rules influence *unilateral* trade policy decisions by developing countries. While post-World War II liberalization among the industrialized countries has been mostly reciprocal, liberalization by the developing countries has been much more a matter of unilateral decisions by individual countries.

In the context of multilateral, reciprocal liberalization, GATT rules such as those that condition when a safeguard, antidumping, or other trade-remedy decision can be applied can be reasonably viewed as pressure valves designed to let off a bit of protectionist steam from time to time, while the engine of reciprocal liberalization keeps rolling on. In the context of unilateral liberalization, however, the GATT's policy rules have a different meaning. They become guidelines for determining which trade restrictions to impose or retain, and which to avoid. Particularly for countries whose small economies make it impossible for them to integrate the domestic politics of liberalization into the reciprocal GATT process,[1] GATT rules that relate to unilateral actions are the most influential part of the agreement. Governments will interpret these rules as guidelines for good policy.[2] Perhaps more important, international rules provide a basis for a government to resist domestic pressures for protection, and in this way that the GATT/WTO rules allow or disallow serves as a mold for unilateral policy choices.

Section 14.1 reviews developing-country participation in the reciprocal tariff negotiations of the Uruguay Round. We go on in later sections to examine three important sets of GATT/WTO rules. We argue that antidumping and other rules that specify when a country may unilaterally restrict troublesome imports are not good policy advice – they do not separate those interventions that will augment the national economic interest of the country that intervenes from those that will not. In the case of regional arrangements – currently popular among developing countries – we argue that the GATT/WTO requirements are less incorrect than incomplete. We also examine the good deal of special and differential treatment that remains in the GATT/WTO system. On market access, GATT/WTO rules ask the developing countries to meet the same standards as the industrialized countries – reciprocity in the tariff negotiations and the elimination of quantitative restrictions to defend the balance of payments are examples. In other areas such as customs valuation procedures or technical standards, areas shaded by their technical nature from the spotlight of political accountability, special and differential treatment remains substantive. Section 14.4 presents our conclusions and recommendations.

14.1 TARIFF NEGOTIATIONS AND THE DEVELOPING COUNTRIES

From the perspective of an individual country, the multilateral negotiation of tariff reductions provides opportunities of different sorts:

* to bargain for lower tariffs in markets of interest,
* to use the multilateral negotiation as leverage against domestic interests that resist tariff reductions, and
* to negotiate bindings that will provide defenses against future domestic pressures to increase rates or to provide protection by other means.

Binding has the effect not only of putting a cap on unilateral increase of tariffs; it also remains a government from providing protection through other means that could be interpreted as nullification or impairment of that tariff binding.

In this section we examine how extensively developing countries agreed at the Uruguay Round to reduce their tariffs. We also examine how extensively they agreed to bind their tariffs, and to what extent those bound rates are above presently applied rates. Finally, for a sample of developing countries that introduced extensive unilateral tariff reductions during the 1980s and early 1990s, we examine the extent to which they have bound these unilateral reductions at the Uruguay Round.

Table 14.1 provides summary results from a tabulation of the concessions agreed on at the Uruguay Round. This tabulation covers only those countries

TABLE 14.1 *Bindings of MFN Tariff Rates before and after the Uruguay Round, and Uruguay Round Tariff Reductions for Selected Countries and Country Groups*

	Percentage of Imports GATT Bound				Average Uruguay Round Tariff Reduction[a]	
		Post-Uruguay Round				
Country or Group	Pre-Uruguay Round	Total	At Applied Rate	Below Applied Rate	Across Reduced Items Only	Across All Imports
High-income countries[b]	80	89	38	30	3.2	1.0
European Union	98	100	43	39	3.1	1.5
Japan	73	83	42	38	2.7	1.0
United States	92	93	41	37	2.9	1.4
Hong Kong	1	28	28	0	–	–
Lower- and middle-income countries[c]	31	81	13	29	8.1	2.3
South Asia[d]	11	52	10	23	16.5	3.9
East Asia[e]	16	77	14	40	9.4	3.8
Korea	21	83	13	64	8.5	5.5
Philippines	9	61	27	17	7.9	1.3
Eastern Europe[f]	55	96	28	41	2.4	1.00
Latin America[g]	50	100	3	1	2.4	0.02
Argentina	17	100	0.2	0	4.2	0.001
Brazil	16	100	6.0	1	1.1	0.007
Mexico	100	100	2.0	0	0.9	0.004
Senegal and Zimbabwe[h]	26	40	22.0	1	5.8	0.05

Source: Finger, Ingco, and Reincke 1996.
[a]Weights are based on 1988 import values.
[b]Australia, Austria, Canada, European Union, Finland, Hong Kong, Ireland, Japan, New Zealand, Norway, Singapore, Sweden, Switzerland, and the United States.
[c]All countries covered below plus Tunisia and Turkey.
[d]India and Sri Lanka.
[e]Indonesia, Korea, Macao, Malaysia, Philippines, and Thailand.
[f]Czech and Slovak Customs Union, Hungary, Poland, and Romania.
[g]Argentina, Brazil, Chile, Colombia, El Salvador, Jamaica, Mexico, Peru, Uruguay, and Venezuela.
[h]Senegal and Zimbabwe are the only sub-Saharan African countries that have submitted tariff data to the WTO IDB.

that have supplied data to the WTO Integrated Data Base (IDB).[3] According to the WTO Secretariat, the IDB covers all industrial and transition economies that participated in the Uruguay Round, plus twenty-six of ninety-four developing-economy participants. The countries covered are listed in the notes to table 14.1. This data base provides post- and pre-Uruguay Round bound rates, as reported by the member countries.

Measuring applied rates was more complicated. From several alternative measures[4] we chose the best proxy for the applied rate that reflected unilateral changes made just before or during the Uruguay Round, but excluded any changes that were the results of the round. We then measured the post-Uruguay Round applied rate (tariff line by tariff line) as the lower of this applied rate and the Uruguay Round bound rate. The figures provided in the tables are averages across all merchandise imports, including agricultural products. For all sectors, including agriculture, where the Uruguay Round requires the conversion of all nontariff barriers (NTBs) to tariffs, our data do not include tariff equivalents of NTBs.[5]

14.1.1 Tariff Reductions

The right-hand columns in table 14.1 report the degree of tariff reduction agreed on at the Uruguay Round. In interpreting these numbers, the reader should be aware that we have measured tariff change as the reduction of the ad valorem rate (or ad valorem equivalent rate) divided by unity plus and ad valorem rate, as $dT/(1 + T)$, expressed as a percentage. For a country whose imports do not affect world prices, $dT/(1 + T)$ measures the percentage by which the domestic price of imports will fall as a result of the tariff cut. In this way, we take into account that halving a 20 percent rate will have a larger effect on imports, other things given, than halving a 2 percent rate. The second-to-last column in table 14.1 provides an average over only those tariff lines on which the tariff was reduced. The last column measures the overall tariff cut, an average cut across all tariff lines. Zero reductions are included in the second average, but not in the first.[6]

Our tabulations of Uruguay Road tariff reductions and bindings are presented in detail in Finger, Ingco, and Reincke 1996. Here we highlight only a few of our findings.

Looking first at the amounts by which tariffs were reduced, the table reports that the developing and transition economies agreed at the Uruguay Round to reduce their tariffs by an average 8 percent on 29 percent of their imports. These reductions come to a 2.3 percent reduction of their overall tariff. By comparison the industrial and other high-income countries agreed to reduce their tariffs by an average 3.2 percent on 30 percent of their imports, for an average reduction of 1 percent across all tariff lines. Among developing countries, the Asian countries agreed to relatively large reductions. Tariff reductions agreed on at the Uruguay Round by Latin American countries were quite small, but as we shall see below, the Latin American countries introduced large unilateral reductions in the 1980s and 1990s. For them, the relevant issue is the extent to which they bound these reductions at the round.

14.1.2 Tariff Bindings

Until the Uruguay Round, insistence on special and differential treatment was an important part of many developing countries' policy toward the multilateral

TABLE 14.2 *Average Tariffs, Post-Uruguay Round Applied and Bound Rates for Selected Countries and Country Groups*

Country or Group	Applied Rates	Bound Rates
High-income countries[a]	2.6	3.7
European Union	2.8	3.2
Japan	2.8	3.7
United States	2.8	3.3
Hong Kong	0.0	0.0
Lower- and middle-income countries[b]	13.3	25.2
South Asia[c]	30.4	50.8
East Asia[d]	11.9	21.0
Korea	7.7	16.4
Philippines	19.0	21.9
Eastern Europe[d]	6.7	13.3
Latin America[f]	11.7	32.7
Argentina	10.3	31.0
Brazil	11.7	29.0
Mexico	10.4	34.1
Senegal and Zimbabwe[g]	9.0	19.4

Source: Authors' calculations based on UNCTAD TRAINS data base.
Note: Weights are based on 1988 import values.
[a]Australia, Austria, Canada, European Union, Finland, Hong Kong, Ireland, Japan, New Zealand, Norway, Singapore, Sweden, Switzerland, and the United States.
[b]All countries covered below plus Tunisia and Turkey.
[c]India and Sri Lanka.
[d]Indonesia, Korea, Macao, Malaysia, Philippines, and Thailand.
[e]Czech and Slovak Customs Union, Hungary, Poland, and Romania.
[f]Argentina, Brazil, Chile, Colombia, El Salvador, Jamaica, Mexico, Peru, Uruguay, and Venezuela.
[g]Senegal and Zimbabwe are the only sub-Saharan African countries that have submitted tariff data to the WTO IDB.

negotiations. One result was that few developing-country tariffs were bound – in table 14.1, less than one-third of imports were under bound rates. Note, however, that at the Uruguay Round the developing and transition economies agreed to significant bindings. The major Latin American countries have agreed to bind all of their tariffs; the extent of bindings is as high now in many developing and transition economies as in the industrialized countries.

Table 14.2, which compares post-Uruguay Round applied and bound rates, focuses on this point.[7] While developing countries' tariff reductions, as we have measured them, have been rather large, their tariff rates are still high, as compared with those of the industrialized countries. Many developing-country bindings are at ceiling rates, above applied rates. India's post-Uruguay Round average bound rate is 52 percent; its average applied rate is 31 percent. Latin American countries' bound rates average around 30 percent (with minimal dispersion, most rates are near 30 percent); their applied rates average 10 to 12 percent.

TABLE 14.3 *Percentages of Unilateral Tariff Reductions by Selected Countries that were Bound at the Uruguay Round*

Country	Total Reduction[a]	Bound Reduction[b]	Percentage of Total Reduction Bound[c]
Argentina	16	9	57
Brazil	25	12	47
Chile	19	8	39
Mexico	27	8	30
Peru	20	9	46
Uruguay	6	3	41
Venezuela	19	2	12
India	27	22	82
Average, weighted by import value			39

Source: Authors' calculations based on the WTO's Integrated Database.
[a]Import weighted average of changes calculated by tariff line. The change is from the rate before unilateral reductions and before reciprocal (Uruguay Round) reductions to the rate after both. Reduction is defined as $dT/(1 + T)$.
[b]Import weighted average of changes calculated by tariff line from the rate before unilateral reductions and before reciprocal reductions to the post-Uruguay Round bound rate. Reduction is defined as $dT/(1 + T)$. In calculating the averages, in those tariff lines for which the bound rate was above the initial rate, the bound reduction was set equal to zero.
[c]Bound reduction as a percentage of total reduction.

As noted above, a ceiling binding provided a government a basis for resisting pressures to backslide on the liberalizations it had already made. Non-tariff measures other than the kind of restrictions allowed under the "rules" part of the GATT would likely be considered nullification or impairment of the tariff binding. Any restriction other than a tariff increase or a GATT-legal "trade remedy" would open the possibility of complaints through GATT enforcement processes from trading partners.

14.1.3 Binding of Unilateral Concessions

The Uruguay Round also provided countries that had unilaterally liberalized the opportunity to bind these concessions. Such binding might be useful in two ways: as "coin" for buying concessions from trading partners and as a basis for resisting domestic pressures to raise the rates again.

Table 14.3 reports calculations for selected countries of the percentage of recent tariff reductions that have been bound. (The sample is limited to the countries for which suitable data are available.) In these calculations we used the IDB

"Uruguay Round base rate" – as of 1986 – as our measure of tariff rates pre-Uruguay Round and pre-unilateral concessions. We measured the "total reduction" as the change from this base rate to the lower of the 1992 applied rate[8] or the IDB post-Uruguay Round bound rate. The "bound reduction" is the change from the base rate to the post-Uruguay Round bound rate.

Overall, our calculations indicate that the countries in the group have bound somewhat less than half of the unilateral concessions that they have implemented since 1986. Measured as we have measured tariff cuts, that comes to a bound cut of 8 to 12 percent for a number of Latin American countries and 22 percent for India. Comparing these figures with those in the last two columns of table 14.1, we find that, except for India, these countries have added little to their tariff reductions through the reciprocal negotiations. At the Uruguay Round Latin American countries agreed to reciprocal reductions that averaged only 0.02 percent across all of their imports.[9] Even so, the 5 to 6 percent bound cut compares favorably with the 1 to 2 percent reduction agreed to by the higher-income countries at the round.[10]

14.2 GATT RULES

Some eleven of the GATT's twenty-five functional articles provide rules about what trade restrictions a country can and cannot impose – nine of the eleven providing for the application of certain kinds of measures – safeguards, antidumping, general exceptions, national security exceptions, and so forth.[11]

The historical reason that the many provisions allowing trade restrictions are in the GATT is most likely that protectionist interests have been strong enough to insist that such restrictions be provided for. To those seeking to create an open international trading system, the provisions are part of their losses, not of their victories. The familiar rationale for the provisions is that, had they not been included, protectionist interests would have prevented the tariff reductions that have been the core of the GATT. In figurative language, allowing for a possible step backward was part of the price of achieving two steps forward. A related and more forward-looking version of the latter rationale is that any government that maintains a liberal trade policy must have ways to deal with constituent pressures for exceptions – pressures for protection of particular domestic sectors. We build our evaluation of such provisions on that view.

14.2.1 GATT Pressure-valve Provisions

Any government that strives to maintain an open trade regime must have mechanisms for managing domestic pressures for protection. In a system such as the GATT/WTO system, part of the discipline built into such domestic mechanisms is the international commitment not to impose new trade restrictions. Within the international system, the latitude the domestic mechanisms have to acquiesce to domestic pressures are in the rules the GATT/WTO provides as to when new restrictions may be imposed.

In reviewing the criteria that underlie the pressure valve provided by the GATT, we will evaluate them against two standards. (1) Good trade restrictions versus bad: Do the criteria make economic sense? Do they isolate actions that have greater economic benefits than costs for the country that takes the action, or for the world economy? Do these rules provide a basis for a developing-country government to resist domestic pressures for actions that would not serve the national economic interest? (2) Less trade restrictions versus more: Do the criteria provide an objective basis for saying no? On the presumption that most trade restrictions would not pass the economic sense criteria, fewer trade restrictions would make more economic sense than more.

Emergency Actions under Article XIX. GATT article XIX begins: "If, as a result of unforeseen developments and of the effect of the obligations incurred . . . under this Agreement, including tariff concessions, any product is being imported . . . as to cause or threaten serious injury to domestic producers . . . of like or directly competitive products . . . the contracting party shall be free . . . to suspend the obligation . . . or to withdraw or modify the concession." This sentence obviously authorizes import-restricting actions, but what limits are there on such actions? The following two subsections discuss two possible sources of constraint: the article's statement of the conditions under which pressure-valve actions can be taken, and the relation between this article and the notion of reciprocity that underlies the GATT tariff-cutting process.

Conditions. As the quoted sentence states, emergency action is conditioned on (1) injury from imports that results from (2) a concession (liberalization) *and* from (3) "unforeseen developments". The intent of conditioning import relief on "unforeseen developments" seems obvious: without this qualification relief would be available each time a liberalization had its probable effect – to increase imports – and the emergency-action provision would provide for the undoing of all the liberalization negotiated.

Early on in the GATT's history, in the hatters' fur case of 1950, a GATT working party interpreted "unforeseen developments" in a way that eliminated it as a constraint on emergency actions. As Gary Sampson concludes (1987, 143): "What this [interpretation] meant in practical terms was that any increase in imports, even if through normal changes in international competitiveness, could therefore be considered actionable under Article XIX."

Other interpretations further weakened article XIX as discipline against emergency actions. The hatters' fur working party also concluded that the country taking emergency action is entitled to the benefit of the doubt in determining injury: the exporting country has to actively disprove injury (to importing country producers) in order to overturn an action. Near the same time as the hatters' fur case, another working party concluded that a determination of serious injury from imports does not require even that imports be *increasing* before injury can be determined (Sampson 1987, 143).

The import of these decisions is that condition "unforeseen developments" was nullified as a constraint on article XIX actions to restrict imports. At the same time, the capacity of the condition "injury" to constrain was weakened by allowing the importing country the benefit of the doubt in determining its operational meaning.

Reciprocity. While article XIX's conditionality has not restrained its use, the other constraint, reciprocity, has provided discipline. Article XIX explicitly calls for consultations with exporters and explicitly provides for retaliation – suspension of "substantially equivalent concessions or other obligations." Compensation (to buy off retaliations) is implicit in these provisions.

In the early years of its application, most invocations of article XIX were accompanied by either mutually agreed compensation or retaliation. Of the twenty-five actions taken under the escape clause between 1948 and 1962, compensation was offered in fourteen cases and retaliation took place four times, including three cases in which compensation had been offered (GATT 1994, 500–516).

The Uruguay Round Safeguard Agreement. The major elements of the Uruguay Round on an agreement on safeguards are described below.

Phase out of voluntary export restraints (VERs) must be completed within four years, until the exception that each member may retain one VER until 31 December 1999. Only the European Union has notified an exception, its VER on Japanese cars and trucks. Likewise, existing article XIX measures (GATT-legal measures) must be phased out eight years after application or by 31 December 1999, whichever comes later. Quantitative restrictions are explicitly recognized, however, and after a formal determination of injury, an import quota applied as a safeguard measure may, by mutual agreement, be administered by the exporting country.

Actions under article XIX are subject to several limits. The key ones are progressive liberalization and limits on the duration of safeguard measures.

Two major changes that make article XIX more usable by interests seeking protection are the explicit allowance of discretionary quantitative restrictions and the removal of the exporting country's right to retaliate against a safeguard measure for the first three years. The latter change removes the burden to negotiated compensation, that is, it allows an article XIX action to be unilateral, disciplined only by the condition that injury must be determined.

The 1994 agreement contains many explicit procedural requirements for transparency and openness that were not in the original article XIX. First, a member may apply a safeguard measure only after an investigation and a determination of injury.[12] The investigation must be carried out according to procedures previously established and made public; it must include public notices to all interested parties and public hearings for the presentation of evidence, views, and comments from all sides.[13] The determination must demonstrate a causal link between imports and injury.[14] The agency that conducts the investigation and makes the determination must publish a detailed analysis, setting out its findings and conclusions, and how these relate to the facts developed and to the applicable laws.[15]

The economic criteria that conditions when an import restriction may be imposed is *serious injury* to domestic procedures of like or competing products.

Injury is more or less a translation into administrative terms of the economic concept of comparative disadvantage; hence it is not a criterion that will isolate those restrictions that serve the national economic interest. Indeed, the gains from trade are likely to be larger when the cost advantage of imports over domestic production is large, and injury is of significant magnitude. Injury, simple or serious, fails the economic sense criterion.

Likewise, unless there is injury (i.e., displaced domestic production) from imports, there will be little motive for petitions for import restrictions. Hence "injury" will not provide a basis for rejecting a significant share of petitions for relief. For the criterion to provide a basis to reject some petitions (i.e., provide less import restrictions rather than more) will depend on there being a politically convincing basis for separating serious injury from less serious. In practice, this has not been the case.[16]

The public notice and transparency requirements the Uruguay Round safeguards agreement adds to article XIX procedures – like similar requirements for antidumping procedures – are laudable on their own terms, but they do not correct the bad economics of article XIX. To do the wrong thing the right way is still to do the wrong thing. Because the requirements do nothing to bring out the costs of protection or to enfranchise those interests that will bear these costs, they are not likely to change the domestic political balance in favor of fewer restrictions.

Restrictions to Protect the Balance of Payments. GATT article XVIII permits developing countries to introduce trade restrictions either to support infant industries or to protect their balance of payments. Neither makes economic sense. In practice, developing countries' use of the balance-of-payments exception has far exceeded their use of the infant-industry exception. Table 14.4 reports almost 3,500 restrictions declared under the balance-of-payments exception, less than 100 under the infant-industry exception.[17]

Why have there been so few actions under the infant-industry provision? The procedural requirements of the balance-of-payments provision are easier – developing countries find it easier to obtain GATT "cover" for infant-industry protection under the guise of "balance-of-payments" reasons.

The facts of usage bear out this interpretation. Anjaria (1987, 680) reports that in almost three-fourths of the developing countries that declared article XVIII:B measures, the measures covered less than half of import categories. If these restrictions were truly for balance-of-payments purposes, they would cover all import categories.

Before the Uruguay Round began, the increased commercial presence of developing countries had provoked industrial countries to press for market-opening actions by the developing countries. The industrial countries applied this pressure both through the GATT Committee on Balance-of-Payments Restrictions and the Trade Committee of the Organization for Economic Cooperation and Development (OECD). One of its focal points was reduced use by developing countries of article XVIII:B restrictions.

At the same time, the demonstration effect of the Asian model of export-led development changed developing countries' view of trade policy. Realistic

TABLE 14.4 *Number of Customs Cooperation Council Nomenclature Items on Which Developing Countries Notified Quantitative Restrictions under Different GATT Articles, 1974–87*

GATT Article Cited as Justification		Number
VIII	Fees and formalities connected with importation and exportation	316
XI:2	Restrictions in order to apply standards or classifications, to manage short supplies, or to complement agricultural or fisheries support programs	108
XVII	State trading enterprises	15
XVIII:B	Balance-of-payments measures for developing countries	3,437
XVIII:C	Industrial development	91
XX	General exceptions	131
XXI	National security	4

Source: OECD 1992, 100.

exchange rates had been an important element in this experience, and there was a growing realization that an unrealistic exchange rate buttressed by trade control was bad development policy. Hence developing countries were more willing to give in on use of article XVIII:B. As of June 1996, only three developing countries (Tunisia, India, and Pakistan) maintained import restrictions declared under GATT article XVIII:B that are of major concern to potential exporters.

Uruguay Round Balance-of-Payments Understanding. During the Uruguay Round, OECD countries – the United States and Canada in particular – were strong proponents of strengthening GATT balance-of-payments provisions to more accurately reflect changes in economic ideas about the interrelation of trade and development. The Uruguay Round understanding has added statements to encourage use of price-based measures rather than quantitative restrictions, and to encourage phasing-out of balance-of-payments measures. The understanding also adds detailed documentation requirements.

The Uruguay Round understanding thus earns high marks as a guide to sensible economic policy – it reflects the growing realization that an unrealistic exchange rate that must be buttressed by trade control is bad development policy.

Antidumping. Antidumping was a minor instrument when the GATT was negotiated, and provision for antidumping regulations was included with little controversy. Since then, antidumping has become the industrial countries' major safeguard instrument, and is gaining increasing popularity among developing countries. As of July 1996, fifty-eight developing and transition-economy countries have notified antidumping laws or regulations to the WTO, and sixteen had notified antidumping actions to the WTO.[18]

Several features of antidumping explain its popularity.

* Discriminatory action is permitted.
* In national practice, the injury test for antidumping action tends to be softer than the injury test for action under article XIX.
* The rhetoric of foreign unfairness provides a vehicle for building a political case for protection.
* Antidumping and VERs have proved to be effective complements; that is, the threat of formal action under the antidumping law provides leverage to force an exporter to accept a VER.[19]
* Suspension agreements are provided for in the 1989 Tokyo Round antidumping code and in the Uruguay Round agreement.[20]
* The investigation process itself tends to curb imports. This is because exporters bear significant legal and administrative costs, importers face the uncertainty of having to pay, once an investigation is completed, backdated antidumping duties (Finger 1981; Staiger and Wolak 1994).

The Uruguay Round Agreement. The negotiations were a pitched battle between victims and users of antidumping. The only clear victory for the victims was the introduction of a sunset clause requiring that all antidumping actions be terminated after no more than five years – unless a review determines that termination would lead to continuation of recurrence of dumping and injury. The agreement considerably increases documentation requirements, but they do not change its economics.[21]

The Economics of Antidumping. National regulations allow antidumping action in a broad range of circumstances. This point, supported by considerable research, is stated by different authors in different ways, for example, that such regulations are biased toward finding dumping and toward overstating dumping margins (Bierwagen 1991; Litan and Boltuck 1991) or that antidumping is ordinary protection with a good public relations program (Finger 1993a).

An important detail of these findings is that, in practice, the criteria of what constitutes dumping are so broad that the dumping standard is met in virtually every case.[22] Without the injury standard, all antidumping cases would reach affirmative outcomes; that is, the criterion that distinguishes an affirmative antidumping finding from a negative one is the same as the criterion of an article XIX safeguard action: injury to competing domestic producers.

Its rhetoric aside, neither legal nor economic analysis finds a link between antidumping investigations and the detection of anticompetitive practices. An OECD study, for example, has found that imports posed no threat to the existence competition in more than 90 percent of the cases in which the U.S. and EU imposed antidumping duties in the 1980s (de Jonquieres 1995, 5).

As economics, antidumping is an injury test, nothing more. Thus the economic evaluation presented above of article XIX actions as a pressure valve applies equally to antidumping. Its sorting of restrictions that are authorized from those that are not makes no economic sense, and it serves minimally as an influence for fewer restrictions than for more. While antidumping may not score a zero by the criterion "fewer restrictions rather than more," the inflamatory rhetoric that antidumping supports and the weaker injury test that it embodies suggest that it should receive a lower score than article XIX. This, as noted above, is why the protectionist prefer it.

14.2.2 Conclusions about GATT Pressure Valves

This brief review of pressure valves allowed by the GATT leads to the following conclusions.

1. GATT pressure valves make no economic sense. The conditions under which the GATT allows a country to take emergency actions or antidumping actions, or to impose trade restrictions to protect the balance of payments are not the conditions under which such action would serve the national economic interest of the country. In economics, pressure valves are just ordinary protection, with sufficient political influence that antiprotection forces cannot overcome it.

The rationale for these mechanisms remains political. Their nonsense economics raises the following question, however: might there be processes that served as a pressure valve for protectionist pressures and at the same time make economic sense? One of the major disappointments of the Uruguay Round is that this question was never addressed.

2. GATT rules provide little discipline over use of pressure valves. This proposition follows that from the following two.

3. Trade restrictions are fungible. The GATT provides a long list of apparently special-purpose restrictions, but the type of restriction that a country imposes is not determined by the nature of the "problem" that the country faces. It is determined by the relative ease of qualifying for one or another type of GATT coverage for the restriction. In the GATT's first decade, article XIX actions, renegotiations, and negotiations were impossible to distinguish from each other. At present, antidumping is the instrument of choice of protection-seeking interests. In the 1970s and 1980s, VERs were the favorite form of protection of the industrial countries, article XVIII:B balance-of-payments actions the favorite GATT cover for developing countries' import restrictions.

4. Safeguard action is always possible under the rules. "Injury" is the economic concept that underlies article XIX actions and antidumping. Each of these pressure valves includes a second factor, "dumping" for antidumping and "unforeseen developments" for article XIX action. But in practice, the meaning of "dumping" is so broad that the injury test is the only constraint on antidumping action. And the "unforeseen developments" condition on article XIX action was rendered ineffective the first time it was challenged. Thus, "injury" is the sole condition that restraints article XIX or antidumping action, and "injury," as economics, is identical with comparative disadvantage. Any time imports displace or threaten to displace domestic production, pressure-valve action is GATT-legal. The GATT chain is as strong as its weakest link, and antidumping is at present the protectionists' favorite means.

5. GATT pressure-valve processes make little political sense. Only in the cheap sense of bowing to political reality are the GATT's pressure valves defensible. They do nothing, however, to empower the good guys – the interests that would be hurt by the imposition of an import restriction.

Worse, the GATT's pressure valves empower the bad guys. An investigation of injury – on which pressure-valve actions are premised – provides a tribune from which the interests that will benefit from an import restriction can make their case. An antidumping investigation adds the opportunity to accuse exporters of unfairness. Given the proprotection logic and structure of the pressure-valve process, reasons to refuse protection are arbitrary[23] – free trade, not protection, depends on exploiting the loopholes in trade law.

14.2.3 Customs Unions and Free Trade Areas

Article XXIV of the GATT seeks to specify circumstances under which countries may violate the most-favored-nation (MFN) clause by forming free trade areas or custom unions. It imposes three principal restrictions, that the free trade area or customs union (1) cover "substantially all trade" (par. 8); (2) reduce internal tariffs to zero and remove internal quantitative restrictions other than those justified by other GATT articles (par. 8); and (3) not raise the average level of protection against excluded countries (par. 5).

Mercantilist Sense. The provisions were written in a pre-Vinerian world which did not recognize the concepts of trade diversion and trade creation, and which held that liberalizing trade with a subset of partners was a good thing.[24] They are also, of course, part of a document whose primary focus is the mercantilist one on the rights of trading partners rather than the economist's one on the benefits of policy for the member country itself. From these perspectives there is some logic to conditions 2 and 3. Condition 3 may be viewed as preserving the sanctity of tariff bindings by ensuring that forming a customs union does not provide that compensation is due to individual partners (in terms of other tariff reductions) for increases induced by the customs union if the corresponding reductions to keep the average constant are not adequate. Together, these provisions offer reasonable assurances about the barriers facing nonmembers.

Condition 2 is best seen as a means of defending the MFN clause by making it subject to an "all-or-nothing" exception. If countries were free to negotiate different levels of preference with each trading partner, binding and non-discrimination would be fatally undermined – no member could be sure that it was receiving the benefits it expected from a bound tariff negotiation. Moreover, one might view customs unions as a first step toward deeper integration – ultimately nation building – and feel it inappropriate that an international trade treaty should stand in the way of such progress. If so, internal free trade, such as one (usually) achieves within a single country, would be an acceptable derogation of MFN, whereas preferences would not be. Condition 1 does not lie within the GATT tradition of tariff-line by tariff-line negotiation, but does reinforce 2 by requiring a serious degree of commitment to a free trade area or customs union before sanctioning it under the GATT.

Economic Sense. The conditions of article XXIV also make some, albeit incomplete, sense when viewed from a more modern and economic perspective. The requirement not to raise barriers against nonmembers not only honors the latters' market-access rights under the GATT but also heads off one otherwise available route to increased protectionism. This is desirable on any account, but in the context of free trade areas and customs unions the danger and costs of trade diversion will be greater if the members can increase their external tariffs. It is also useful that the Uruguay Round Understanding on the Interpretation of Article XXIV offers instruction on how to assess whether this condition has been met.[25]

Condition 2 is, from an economic point of view, unnecessary. Trade theory is now quite clear that, from the point of view of the free trade area or customs union, a small tariff on trade between members is better than free trade if there are positive tariffs on nonmember countries (Ethier and Horn 1984). However, its rationale in defending MFN seems sufficiently strong both systematically and individually to create a net benefit overall. The benefit to an individual country of preserving the condition is that, if partial preferences as permissible, governments may come under increased pressures internally or externally to use them, and could have to expend considerable effort resisting proposals for degrees of preference that did not generate Ethier-Horn-type benefits.

Political Sense. Condition 1 does have an important role from a welfare point of view. Recent advances in political-economy modeling – for example, Grossman and Helpman 1995 – have suggested that, if governments are susceptible to lobbying by sectoral producer groups, political pressures will tend to favor trade-diverting regional arrangements. Trade diversion unambiguously generates gains for partner exporters, so when two countries swap trade-diverting concessions, both sets of producers gain. On the other hand, if they swap trade-creating concessions, producers lose some sales in their home markets and may or may not gain overall. Lobbies increase the weight of producer gains and losses in overall decision making, so that it is perfectly possible that trade diversion is politically more powerful than trade creation and that the option of regional liberalization undermines the incentives for first-best non-discriminatory liberalization (Krishna 1994; Levy 1994). Condition 1 means that governments cannot select only commodities that are likely to feature trade diversion, and this in turn seems likely to encourage more efficient free trade areas and customs unions.

This argument makes obvious the case that the GATT/WTO generates welfare less through disciplining a country's trading partners than through bolstering the country's government against pressures to pursue inappropriate policies at home. Not only does condition 1 constrain the government's response to such pressures, but it also, one hopes, reduces the frequency with which such pressure is applied.

Does Article XXIV Ensure Good Policy? The previous paragraphs suggest that article XXIV is generally an aid to rational policymaking. However, they do not suggest that it is sufficient for good policy. The rules prevent a given group of countries from limiting a free trade agreement to those products on which trade will be diverted, but they do not prevent a free trade agreement among countries for which elimination of internal barriers will be entirely or predominantly trade-diverting.

In fact, article XXIV has not provided as much discipline as it might have, for it has been notoriously weakly enforced. WTO (1995) reports that of sixty-nine working parties reporting up to and including 1994, only six had been able to agree that a free trade area or customs union met the requirements of article XXIV. However, the remainder did not conclude that the agreement under review was not in conformity, but merely left the matter undetermined.

The reluctance of the GATT as an institution to decide on the consistency of regional agreements with the rules does not mean that the rules have had no effect – we do not know which potential arrangements they discouraged – but it is not an encouraging record. There have been clear breaches of condition 1 (e.g., the European Coal and Steel Community), breaches of condition 2 (e.g., the European Economic Cooperation's monetary compensatory amounts on intra-EEC agricultural trade), and, on some interpretations, breaches of condition 3 (e.g., the EEC, of which the GATT executive secretary[26] expressed "the view, with which he thought there was no disagreement, that the incidence of the Common Tariff was higher than that of the rates actually applied by the Member States at the time of entry into force of the Treaty of Rome" [GATT Document C/M/8, 6; cited in GATT 1984, 750]).

The Enabling Clause. A further complication for developing countries is the enabling clause – the Decision on Differential and More Favorable Treatment, Reciprocity, and Fuller Participation of Developing Countries of 1979 (see GATT 1994). This significantly relaxes the conditions for creating free trade areas or customs unions that include only developing countries. It drops condition 1, on the coverage of trade, and dramatically relaxes condition 2, allowing developing countries to reduce tariffs on mutual trade in any way they wish and NTBs "in accordance with criteria which may be prescribed by the CONTRACTING PARTIES." It then supplements condition 3 by requiring that the arrangement not constitute a barrier to MFN tariff reductions or cause "undue difficulties" for other contracting parties.

In practice, developing countries have had virtual carte blanche. Twelve preferential arrangements have been notified under the enabling clause, including the Latin American Integration Association (LAIA), the Association of Southeast Asian Nations (ASEAN), and the Gulf Cooperation Council (GCC). These have made liberal use of the scope allowed by the enabling clause. Internal preferences of 25 percent and 50 percent figured in ASEAN's trading plans and in many of the arrangements concluded in the LAIA and the GCC. There is little sign that internal preferences have undermined MFN agreements with other trading partners in the sense of causing a reversal of previous conditions. Until the late 1980s, however, the Latin American countries' frequency use of regional arrangements and weak participation in the multilateral rounds might suggest a substitution of one form of liberalization for the other. Probably more pernicious have been the sector agreements that have abounded in Latin America. For example, Argentina and Brazil signed seventeen such agreements in 1986; there was little doubt that they generated a fair measure of trade diversion (Nogués and Quintanilla 1993). Similarly, ASEAN's trading arrangements were, for some time, partial in their coverage of products, although they are probably better categorized as ineffective than as harmful (De Rosa 1995).

Overall, the enabling clause serves to dilute even the weak discipline that article XXIV imposes. Even if article XXIV does not actually stop many harmful practices, at least it does not give them the respectability of legal cover as a matter of course. Thus, as Finger (1993b) notes, while the GATT knowingly and willingly permitted the earlier manifestations of the LAIA (the Latin American Free Trade Agreement, 1960) and the initial notification of ASEAN (in 1977) to violate article XXIV, it at least left open the possibility of challenge in the dispute settlement process.

14.3 SPECIAL AND DIFFERENTIAL TREATMENT

One of the most profound institutional changes that the conclusion of the Uruguay Round induced in the world trading system was the advent of the so-called single undertaking. This entailed that all members of the WTO should adhere to nearly the same set of agreements on trading rules, in contrast to the situation prior to the round, in which members adhered to the GATT plus whatever subset of codes on trading rules that they chose. However, while the Uruguay Round agreements reduced the scope of the special and differential treatment that the GATT system had offered the developing countries, they did not eliminate such treatment completely. In many instances, the agreements common to all members permit or prescribe different treatment for developing countries. This section considers how much special and differential treatment has slipped through into the post-Uruguay Round trading system.

Hindley (1987) suggests five areas in which developing countries received special and differential treatment prior to the Uruguay Round: one from the 1947 GATT (article XVIII, the right to infant-industry and balance-of-payments trade restrictions); one from part IV of the 1964 GATT (exemption from making reciprocal tariff concessions); and three stemming from the enabling clause (the right not to sign the Tokyo Round codes, exemption from article XXIV, and the legitimization of the Generalized System of Preferences [GSP]). We have already dealt with articles XVIII and XXIV above. The remainder of this section comprises subsections on special and differential treatment for developing countries as perpetrators of trade policy, and some conclusions.

14.3.1 Special and Differential Treatment for "Victims"

The Generalized System of Preferences. Perhaps the developing countries' most significant exceptions from other countries' trade policy arise from the GSP, which permits industrial countries to exempt some of their exports from MFN duties. These exemptions are autonomous policies (i.e., granted unilaterally by the industrial countries), which continue quite independently of the outcome of the Uruguay Round, under the cover of the enabling clause. The reductions in tariffs in the Uruguay Round agreements eroded GSP margins of preference, but, with a few exceptions, not very significantly. For example, the average reduction in margin was below two percentage points for sub-Saharan Africa (Amjadi, Reincke, and Yeats 1996).

At first sight, there seems little to object to in the notion that industrial countries should exempt imports from developing countries from tariffs. Even if the exceptions are not much of a basis for industrial development – because many are subject to quantitative limits and all are unbound and hence reversible – at least they transfer some tariff revenue to developing-country producers. Moreover, it might be argued that, since developing countries have little bargaining power in reciprocal negotiations, this is the only way they will obtain relatively free access to the world's major markets.

There are four problems with these arguments. First, preferences essentially transmit to developing countries the production distortions inherent in developed countries' tariff structures. That is, they permit – perhaps encourage – producers to have costs above those in nonpreferred countries. Second, and closely related, current GSP schemes are so hedged with exclusions, quantitive limits, and rules of origin that they have only limited coverage.[27] The excluded imports are typically the most important from the point of view of development (e.g., clothing, footwear, leather) and the effect of the scheme is to divert resources away from them.

Third, the fact that the preferences might be withdrawn at any time encourages a degree of short-termism on the part of entrepreneurs. Their decisions are likely to be biased toward the quick fix rather than the long haul. Fourth, both for entrepreneurs and for their governments the desire to keep and exploit the rents inherent in preferences distract from longer-term and ultimately more productive activities. For example, the wish to maintain preferences could undermine developing countries' willingness to invest in rounds of negotiated trade liberalization, or even devalue their stake in the world trading system itself.

Special Treatment under the Rules. Developing countries also formally receive a measure of special and differential treatment in the ways in which they are treated by other countries' trading rules. In the case of countervailing duties and safeguards this is explicit and mandated. A developing country's exports to a market cannot be countervailed if its share of total imports of the product is 4 percent or less and if the sum of all such small suppliers' shares is 9 percent or less. Similarly, developing countries are exempt from safeguards actions if their share is 3 percent or less. There are no such limits for developed suppliers. Also, in the countervailing-duty agreement, whereas the *de minimis* limit is 1 percent for developed suppliers, it is 2 percent for developing countries (and 3 percent for least-developed countries until 2003).

In addition to these concessions, the WTO texts are handsomely endowed with exhortatory rather than mandated suggestions of special and differential treatment. For example, for antidumping, active countries are urged to seek "constructive remedies" when "essential interests of developing countries" are at stake and generally to pay regard to the "special situation" of the developing countries. In import licensing, members are asked to give "special consideration to . . . developing country members" in allocating new licenses. The Agreement on Technical Barriers to Trade (TBT) and the Agreement on the Application of Sanitary and Phytosanitary Measures have several special and differential treatment clauses urging, inter alia, special recognition of the needs of developing countries and their difficulties in formulating, implementing, and testing standards. Whether such exhortations amount to anything concrete remains to be seen.

14.3.2 Special and Differential Treatment for Perpetrators

Of much greater significance to their economic performance is the special and differential treatment that developing countries receive as perpetrators of trade policy. While the advent of the single understanding removes some aspects of special treatment, several instances remain in which general obligations under the GATT are relaxed for developing countries. If the relaxed obligations are constraining and harmful, this is indeed the "more favorable treatment" that the formal terminology for special and differential treatment implies, but if the obligations have the effect of encouraging countries' progress toward better economic policy, the exemptions are harmful. We quote those specific examples here.

Part IV. Superficially among the most important aspects of special and differential treatment is part IV of the GATT. Its article XXXVI:8 states baldly that the developed countries do not expect reciprocity from the developing countries. This exemption took quite concrete form for the former colonies of member countries, which could use it to avoid providing schedules of tariff concessions (bindings) when they assumed membership (see Hoekman and Kostecki 1995). This privilege no longer pertains: every WTO member has to submit schedules of bindings in goods and services.

The broader form of nonreciprocity embodied in part IV – the absence of need to negotiate and offer concessions in order to win them – was modified but not revoked by the Uruguay Round. Part IV was exhortatory rather than binding and has been replaced by equally nonoperational language. The Punta del Este declaration stated that developing countries were not expected to make concessions inconsistent with their "development, financial and trade needs" and the Marrakesh Decision on Measures in Favor of Least-Developed Countries continued this for least-developed countries.

Practice was quite different from these exhortations. In the Uruguay Round, developing and industrialized countries each agreed to cut their tariffs on about 30 percent of their imports. The cuts by the industrialized countries will reduce the prices of those imports by an average of 3 percent, those by the developing countries by an average of 8 percent.[28] Thus, many developing countries made significant concessions. But the Marrakesh agreement provides at least legal cover for those who wish to be left out as a matter of principle.

Technical Barriers to Trade. The TBT agreement offers special and differential treatment to developing countries on both their exports and their imports. On the latter, they are not expected to "use international standards as a basis for technical regulations or standards, including test methods, which are not appropriate to their . . . needs." This concession is intended to allow the preservation of indigenous technology and technologies appropriate to countries' development needs. While the general terms of the TBT agreement restrict the use of standards for protectionist purposes, and developing countries are not exempt from its provisions, this particular piece of language seems to grant the right to use idiosyncratic standards. If so, it could put a substantial brake on the modernization and competitiveness of developing-country industry.

Subsidy/Countervailing Measures. The Uruguay Round Agreement on Subsidies and Countervailing Measures substantially revised the corresponding Tokyo Round code, linking together for the first time the concepts used in the two parts of the agreement. The agreement imposes significant discipline on specific subsidies, identifying prohibited, actionable, and nonactionable classes and providing far readier action against the first class than against the second. Unfortunately it then goes on to use special and differential treatment to dilute the disciplines significantly for developing countries and even further for least-developed countries (defined as the UN list plus countries with per capita income below $1,000). For example, whereas export subsidies are banned almost immediately for developed countries, they are banned in eight years for developing countries and never (subject to a condition on quantities) for least-developed countries. Similar differentials impose tighter conditions on WTO members before they can take action against developing-country exports, and give more generous definitions of "de minimis" for the latter. The overall impression is that subsidies do not matter much for least-developed countries so long as they do not disrupt other countries' markets, and this view is significantly enhanced by the statement that "subsidies may play an important role in the economic development programs of developing country members" (article XXVII:1 of the Agreement on Subsidies and Countervailing Measures). In sum, the agreement offers governments of least-developed countries virtually no cover against lobbies seeking subsidies (Winters 1994).

Among other areas in which special and differential treatment dilutes developing countries' obligations to liberalize are customs valuation (longer transition periods), agriculture (smaller tariff cuts), safeguards (longer-lasting restrictions), trade-related investment measures (restrictions available for balance-of-payments purposes), and services (similar special and differential rules as for goods).

14.3.3 Conclusions on Special and Differential Treatment

It is impossible to make a simple quantitative assessment of the extent of special and differential treatment, but some qualitative conclusions are possible. In terms of market access for developing countries' exports, special and differential treatment is quite extensive – if not very effective economically – in offering tariff reductions on a wide variety of exports. In terms of market access to their own markets, developing countries have successfully managed to avoid the obligation to make tariff concessions, but have, at least in industrial products, frequently made them anyway. In the area of rules, special and differential treatment is de facto no longer very extensive in the visible high-profile cases. Thus, for example, balance-of-payments restrictions are coming under increasing pressure in the WTO Balance of Payments Committee and are fading away quite rapidly, and antidumping and countervailing-duty rules are the same for developed and developing countries. In the lower visibility areas, however, shrouded in technicality, special and differential treatment appears to continue unchecked. Least-developed countries have virtually free rein to subsidize exports, and, apparently, a great deal of latitude in both standards and, for several years, in customs valuation. Arguably, the least-developed countries need the most, not the least, support of the multilateral system in devising satisfactory policies.

14.4 WHAT THE WTO CAN DO FOR DEVELOPING COUNTRIES

We second, but have not repeated, important points about market access, such as assuring that liberalization of agricultural trade and trade in clothing and textiles and other products of export interest maintain the schedules agreed on at the Uruguay Round.

Our focus instead has been on the GATT/WTO system as a guide for unilateral decisions. From this perspective we offer two broad guidelines: Pay attention that its guidelines make economic sense; they often do not.[29] Avoid the temptation to view immunity from rules that make sense as a benefit.[30]

We provide below more specific recommendations in three issue areas.

14.4.1 A Better Pressure Valve

Some may comment that a pressure valve cannot make economic and political sense that the same time. Not true. A pressure valve or trade-remedy process that truly enfranchised all the economic interests affected by a proposed import restriction would be more honest and more transparent politics than the obfuscation and misdirection politics of the present antidumping system.

Here are some of the general guidelines on how a government might meet its need for a means to evaluate requests for exceptions to a basically liberal trade policy.

Identify the costs and the losers. Procedures should bring out the costs of the requested exception, and the identities of the persons or groups who will bear these costs. More expensive imports will cost somebody money and – if the imports are needed materials – eliminate somebody's job. These costs, and the people in the domestic economy who will bear them, should have the same standing in law and in administrative practice as the other side already enjoys. The process of considering the request for an exception should be used to help fortify the politics of not granting it.

Be clear that the action is an exception. Procedures should establish that the requested action would be an exception to the principles that underlie the liberalization program. Admitting to political weakness is better than admitting that the exception is a good idea.

Don't sanctify the criteria for the action. Procedures should not presume that there is some good reason for granting an exception – procedures that compare the situations of the petitioner with preestablished criteria for granting an exception should be avoided. Procedures should stress that the function of the review is to identify the benefits and the costs – and the domestic winners and domestic losers – for the requested action.

The last guideline is more important than it might seem. The history of antidumping and other trade remedies shows that clever people will always be able to present their situation exactly as the criteria describe. If you start out to find just the few exporters who are being unfair to Australia or the United States or Mexico, you will soon be swamped by evidence that everyone is.

At the technical level, useful concepts for review procedures – such as transparency and automatic expiration for any exception that is granted (a sunset clause) – can be gleaned from procedural changes made at the safeguards negotiations of the Uruguay Round.

14.4.2 Regional Arrangements

The guidelines presently provided suffer more from incompleteness than from error. Indeed, given their necessarily sui generis nature, it may be impossible to write GATT-style rules to cover all of the dimensions that distinguish an economically beneficial regional arrangement from a bad one. The WTO and, perhaps, other international organizations should sponsor economic analyses of regional arrangements – as was done by the European Commission for the European Union's Single Market initiative – but taking pains *not* to limit the review to criteria provided in article XXIV. As we have pointed out, the latter was written even before the basic concepts of trade creation and trade diversion were widely available to guide thinking.

Such reviews should be useful for the partners to a potential regional arrangement to identify their own interests. They should also identify effects on excluded countries – an obvious area of concern to the WTO – but not just in terms of the potential changes in their exports to the integrating countries. As we have argued elsewhere (Winters 1997), this is an inappropriate yardstick and must be supplemented at least by information on excluded countries' imports and their terms of trade. Moreover, such reviews should be done ex ante and used as a guide to the renegotiation of the free trade area's or customs union's instruments of trade policy. There is no virtue to McMillan's suggestion (1993) that ex post adjustments be made to maintain excluded countries' exports at preintegration levels: this is both the wrong criterion and redolent of managed trade.

14.4.3 Special and Differential Treatment

Special and differential treatment as commonly interpreted in the WTO agreements does not do much for developing countries. Special access to developed-country markets transfers revenue to them but at the expense of discouraging effective efforts to integrate into the world economy. Exemptions from WTO rules – inadequate as some of these are – and exemption from the need for reciprocal trade liberalization merely exacerbate the difficulties of pursuing satisfactory policies at home. They should be phased out as soon as possible.

The one element of special differential treatment that does seem to us potentially beneficial is to offer assistance in the business of being a WTO member. Meeting the full procedural requirements of the WTO is very burdensome and can absorb disproportionate amounts of human capital. To the extent that they can be implemented without compromising substance or transparency, the elements of special and differential treatment that permit developing countries to use streamlined procedures and/or lighter notification burdens seem, to us, desirable. By the same token, the actual delivery of the technical assistance referred to so frequently in the Uruguay Round agreements would be beneficial, especially if it can be devoted to training and capacity building rather than just to producing a product.

NOTES

The authors are grateful to Alan Hirsch, their official discussant, conference participants, and sone anonymous referees for comments on an earlier draft of this paper. The authors gratefully acknowledge skilful assistance from Ulrich Reincke and Francis Ng. The views expressed here are those of the authors alone. They do not necessarily represent those of the World Bank or any of its member governments.

1 In a negotiation in which all foreign liberalization is most-favored-nation (MFN), the government of a small country will have trouble convincing exporters that their access to foreign markets depends on their convincing local producers to allow foreign access to the domestic market.

2 In governments' dealings with other multilateral institutions, e.g., the World Bank and the International Monetary Fund (IMF), the objective, if not always the result, of the relationship is to determine policies that best serve the national economic interest of the country.

3 The IDB includes countries that account for 100 percent of nonpetroleum imports of North America, western Europe, and WTO members (at the time of the Uruguay Round) in central and eastern Europe. The IDB covers 90 percent of Asia's nonpetroleum imports, 80 percent of Latin America's nonpetroleum imports, but only two sub-Saharan African countries (Senegal and Zimbabwe), which together account for 30 percent of sub-Saharan Africa's nonpetroleum imports.

4 Various of the countries whose applied rates are below their bound rates provided different measures of applied rates. Some of these are labeled in the IDB as the "MFN applied rate," "the MFN Uruguay Round base rate," or the "MFN statutory rate". As our proxy for MFN applied rates before the Uruguay Round cuts, we used the MFN applied rate whenever it was available. If the MFN applied rate was not available, we used the lower of the MFN base rate and the MFN statutory rate. A number of countries, particularly in Latin America, introduced substantial unilateral reductions of their tariff rates before or during the years of the Uruguay Round. These unilateral changes were in some cases not reflected in the MFN applied rate. In those cases we updated the MFN applied rate with data from the United Nations Conference on Trade and Development (UNCTAD) TRAINS data base.

5 We measure a reduction of tariffs on agricultural products only when the post-Uruguay Round bound rate is below the pre-Uruguay Round applied tariff rate. Likewise, elimination of voluntary export restraints under the safeguards and clothing-textiles agreements are not taken into account by these figures.

6 The last column is arithmetically the product of the two immediately preceding, divided by 100.

7 Generally, Uruguay Round agreed rates will be effective no later than 1 January 1999,

but some countries have, for some commodities, negotiated later deadlines. The bound rates we report are final rates, after all stages are completed. We measure the post-Uruguay Round applied rate, tariff line by tariff line, as the lower of the current applied rate and the post-Uruguay Round bound rate. Average applied rates cover all tariff lines, but average bound rates cover only those tariff lines that are bound.

8 These data were taken from the UNCTAD TRAINS data base.

9 It is tempting to think that the bound reduction plus the reciprocal reduction equal the total reduction, but they do not. The bound reduction plus the "unbound reduction" (not presented) would equal the total reduction; the reciprocal reduction is a part of the bound reduction.

10 The results indicate that on the whole countries' bound rates are about halfway between their initial applied rates and the rates to which their unilateral reforms have brought them. For only a few tariff lines is the Uruguay Round bound rate below this unilateral rate. Since the Latin American countries' bindings are more or less uniform at 30 percent, these few tariff lines are likely the ones for which the unilateral rates are relatively high, above 30 percent.

11 Finger (1996) lists these articles and reports the frequency with which GATT members have used them.

12 The familiar details of article XIX are retained, e.g., "serious" injury, "cause or threaten."

13 Information and views may be presented to show the safeguards measure is in the public interest.

14 The "unforeseen circumstances" requirement of article XIX has been removed.

15 Extension of a safeguard measure has the same requirements as the initial action.

16 Administratively operational criteria for distinguishing degree of injury have often been arbitrary. Finger (1992) examines the same. Note that a negative finding is described in news releases and in political rhetoric as a finding of "no injury," not as a finding of "not serious" injury.

17 Article XVIII:A and D also provide in slightly different ways for import restrictions to support industry development. As of March, article XVIII:A had been invoked nine times, while section D had not been invoked at all. For details on the use of section A, see GATT 1994, 465.

18 Since 1985, GATT member countries have notified over 150 antidumping cases per year. Article XIX notifications have been less than 3 per year.

19 Finger and Murray 1993 report that over 1980–88, 348 of 774 U.S. antidumping cases were superseded by VERs.

20 Stegemann (1992, 8) reports that from July 1980 through June 1989, of 384 antidumping actions taken by the European Community, 184 were price undertakings. Though the Tokyo Round code does not explicitly provide for such settlement, both U.S. and EC antidumping regulations allow for suspension through acceptance by the exporter of a quantity limit (Jackson and Vermulst 1989, 52, 116).

21 The agreement is examined in some detail by Finger (1996), who points out that the victims were in large not successful only in adding documentation requirements to the practices that they wanted removed.

22 Quantitative evidence for this conclusion is based on U.S. experience only, the United States being the only country that separately publishes outcomes of dumping and of injury determinations. Finger 1993a, chap. 3, reviews the evidence.

23 For example, antiprotectionists oppose "cumulation," the adding-up of injury from each of many exporters, no one of which is large enough to cause "serious" injury. But it is reasonable to provide protection to an industry that has been devoured by a shark, while denying protection to an industry nibbled to death by piranhas? Finger (1992) takes up in detail the point that the constraints on safeguards actions are arbitrary.

24 In fact, Viner first defined the concepts in 1931 – in Swedish – but they were not widely known. We are grateful to Richard Snape for this observation.

25 It is worth noting that this instruction refers to the applied rates of duty, not the bound rates. The exact impact of this is not clear yet. On the one hand it may be seen as effectively binding an average of the previously applied rates – at least for so long as the conditions applicable to the *creation*, as opposed to the operation, of a customs union remain in force. On the other hand, it may imply a lack of discipline on the relationship between the preintegration bound rates of the members and those of the customs union.

26 Before 1965, the director general of the GATT was called the executive secretary.

27 UNCTAD (1994) reports that in the European Union only 68 percent of dutiable imports from beneficiary countries qualify for preferences under the Generalized System of Preferences, of which only 33 percent (slightly below half) actually take them up. The corresponding figures for Japan are 35 percent and 16 percent and for the United States 36 percent and 18 percent.

28 Abreu (1996) and Finger, Ingco, and Reincke (1996) provide details of developing country concessions.

29 "But our policies are GATT-legal" is an argument we often hear against our recommendations for reform.

30 Hudec (1987) shows why this view is a snare and a delusion.

REFERENCES

Abreu, M. 1996. Trade in Manufactures: The Outcome of the Uruguay Round and Developing Country Interests. In *The Uruguay Round and the Developing Countries*, ed. W. Martin and L. A. Winters, chap. 3. Cambridge: Cambridge University Press.

Amjadi, A., U. Reincke, and A. Yeats. 1996. Did External Barriers Cause the Marginalization of Sub-Saharan Africa in World Trade? Policy Research Working Paper no. 1586. Washington, DC: World Bank.

Anjaria, S. J. 1987. Balance of Payments and Related Issues in the Uruguay Round of Trade Negotiations. *World Bank Economic Review* 1, no. 4: 669–88.

Bierwagen, R. M. 1991. *GATT Article VI and the Protectionist Bias in Antidumping Law*. Kluwer Studies in Transnational Law, vol. 7. Deventer: Kluwer.

de Jonquiers, Guy. 1995. Report Counts Cost of Antidumping. *Financial Times*, 2 September, p. 5.

DeRosa, Dean A. 1995. Regional Trading Arrangements among Developing Countries: The ASEAN Example. Research Report no. 103. Washington, DC: International Food Policy Research Institute.

Ethier, W. J. and H. Horn, 1984. A New Look at Economic Integration. In *Monopolistic Competition and International Trade*, ed. H. Kierzkowski, 207–29. Oxford: Clarendon Press.

Finger, J. M. 1981. Policy Research. *Journal of Political Economy* 89:1270–71.

——. 1992. The Meaning of "Unfair" in United States Import Policy. *Minnesota Journal of Global Trade* 1, no. 1:35–56.

——, ed. 1993a. *Antidumping: How It Works and Who Gets Hurt*. Ann Arbor: University of Michigan Press.

——. 1993b. GATT's Influence on Regional Arrangements. In *New Dimensions in Regional Integration*, ed. J. de Melo, and A. Panagariya, 128–48. Cambridge: Cambridge University Press.

——. 1996. Legalized Backsliding: Safeguard Provisions in the GATT. In *The Uruguay*

Round and the Developing Countries, ed. W. Martin and L. A. Winters, chap. 8. Cambridge: Cambridge University Press.

Finger, J. M., M. D. Ingco, and U. Reincke, 1996. *The Uruguay Round: Statistics on Tariff Concessions Given and Received*. Washington, DC: World Bank.

Finger, J. M. and T. Murray. 1993. Antidumping and Countervailing Duty Enforcement in the United States. In *Antidumping: How it Works and Who Gets Hurt*, ed. J. M. Finger, 241–54. Ann Arbor: University of Michigan Press.

General Agreement on Tariffs and Trade. 1994. *Analytical Index: Guide to GATT Law and Practice*. 6th edition. Geneva: GATT.

Grossman, G., and E. Helpman. 1995. The Politics of Free-Trade Agreements. *American Economic Review* 85:667–90.

Hindley, B. 1987. Different and More Favorable Treatment – and Graduation. In *The Uruguay Round*, ed. J. M. Finger and A. Olechowski, 67–74. Washington, DC: World Bank.

Hoekman, B., and M. Kostecki. 1995. *The Political Economy of the World Trading System: From GATT to WTO*. Oxford: Oxford University Press.

Hudec, R. E. 1987. *Developing Countries in the GATT Legal System*. Aldershot: Gower.

Jackson, J. H., and E. A. Vermulst. 1989. *Antidumping Law and Practice: A Comparative Study*. Ann Arbor: University of Michigan Press.

Krishna, P. 1994. Regionalism and Multilateralism: A Political Economy Approach. Brown University. Photocopy.

Levy, P. I. 1994. A Political Economy Analysis of Free Trade Agreements. Economic Growth Centre Discussion Paper no. 718. New Haven: Yale University.

Litan, R. E., and R. Boltuck, eds. 1991. *Down in the Dumps: Administration of the Unfair Trade Laws*. Washington, DC: Brookings Institution.

McMillan, J. 1993. Does Regional Integration Foster Open Trade? Economic Theory and GATT's Article XXIV. In *Regional Integration and the Global Trading System*, ed. K. Anderson and R. Blackhurst, 292–309. New York: Harvester Wheatsheaf.

Nogués, J., and R. Quintanilla. 1993. Latin America's Integration and the Multilateral Trading System. In *New Dimensions in Regional Integration*, ed. J. de Melo and A. Pangariya, 278–313. Cambridge: Cambridge University Press.

Organisation for Economic Cooperation and Development. 1992. *Integration of the Developing Countries into the International Trading System*. Paris: OECD.

Sampson, G. 1987. Safeguards. In *The Uruguay Round*, ed. J. M. Finger and A. Olechowski, 143–52. Washington, DC: World Bank.

Staiger, R. W., and F. Wolak. 1994. The Trade Effects of Antidumping Investigations: Theory and Evidence. In *Analytical and Negotiating Issues in the Global Trading System*, ed. A. V. Deardorff and R. M. Stern, 231–61. Ann Arbor: University of Michigan Press.

Stegermann, K. 1992. *Price Undertakings to Settle Antidumping Cases*. Ottawa: Institute for Research on Public Policy.

United Nations Conference on Trade and Development. 1994. *Review of the Implementation, Maintenance, Improvement, and Utilization of the Generalized System of Preferences*. Geneva: UNCTAD.

Winters, L. A. 1994. Subsidies. In Organization for Economic Cooperation and Development, *The New World Trading System*, 129–34. Paris: OECD.

——. 1997. Regionalism and the Rest of the World: The Irrelevance of the Kemp-Wan Theorem. Oxford Economic Papers.

World Trade Organisation, 1995. *Regionalism and the World Trading System*, Geneva: WTO.

5. Middle Power Leadership and Coalition Building: Australia, the Cairns Group, and the Uruguay Round of Trade Negotiations

R. A. Higgott and A. F. Cooper

A central debate in international political economy turns on the question of the manner in which cooperation can be secured in the global political economy "after hegemony." This question, which was posed by Robert Keohane[1] and is important not only for scholars but also for practitioners of international relations, can be examined in any number of theoretical and methodological ways and with regard to a variety of different issue-areas in the contemporary global economic order. A second broad question of interest to the wider international relations academy is the manner in which weaker states (be they so-called small or middle powers) attempt to influence stronger ones. The relationships between these two broad questions have not been extensively explored. To date, there are few studies that are sensitive to the weaker states' use of coalitions as vehicles for cooperation and regime building in the global political economy. The major works that do discuss coalitions have, quite properly, focused principally on coalitions that involve a narrowly defined membership – usually predicated on and circumscribed by a similarity of attributes and location in the international order – and are engaged in activities designed to secure a fundamental and wide-ranging change in the existing global structures of power.[2]

There is, therefore, considerable space within our existing corpus of knowledge for studies which are more specifically and narrowly focused but which may nevertheless provide us with insight into broader theoretical questions about how to build cooperation in the global economic order on the one hand and the potential role of what we might, for effect, call "non-hegemonic" actors in that process on the other. It is the purpose of this article to make a small contribution to our understanding of these processes. Its focus is on what we see as an atypical coalition, a single-issue driven, cross-cutting coalition attempting to bring about change in one major area of the international trade regime.

We offer a case study of the Cairns Group of Fair Trading Nations, a group which is probably little known to most scholars of international political economy but which has, we argue, established itself as an actor with considerable influence in the eighth round of multilateral trade negotiations (MTNs), the Uruguay Round.[3] Formed in Cairns, Australia, in August 1986 with the aim of securing major reform in international agricultural trade and made up of economically diverse countries from the four quadrants of the globe, the Cairns Group is difficult to classify in terms of the traditional geopolitical criteria of North, South,

East, and West. While we acknowledge the dangers of writing about the Uruguay Round prior to its completion and are somewhat pessimistic regarding its outcome, it is our contention that both the emergence of the Cairns Group and its role in the round to date, whether trade reform in general and agricultural reform in particular are secured or not and notwithstanding the problematic future of the Group, are of considerable interest for students of international relations in general and students of international political economy in particular. The Group's emergence, we argue, has added a new dimension to the process of bargaining in MTNs under the auspices of the General Agreement on Tariffs and Trade (GATT).

The Uruguay Round negotiating structure is headed by the Trade Negotiations Committee, which has overall responsibility for fourteen separate groups negotiating on goods and an additional group negotiating on services. There are ninety-six members of GATT, and while not all are active participants in the Uruguay negotiations, the number of active states in this round is greater than in any previous round. In addition, many states are members of a variety of informal groups, such as the De La Paix Group, with its interests in GATT dispute settlement, safeguards, antidumping, tariff and nontariff measures, and the functioning of the GATT system; the Canadian Informal Resource Exporters Group; the Morges Group on agriculture; the Pacific Group on safeguards; the "Victims" Group on antidumping; the "Friends" Group on trade-related aspects of intellectual property and trade-related investment measures; and the Rolle Group on negotiations about services. Although none of these groups warrant the consideration we give in this article to the Cairns Group, they are nevertheless symptomatic of the inherent complexity of the negotiating process.

Above all, however, we argue that this institutional complexity in particular and the changing configuration of power in the global political economy in general have diminished the ability of the major actors – the United States and the European Community (EC) – to set the agenda and direct the negotiations in the Uruguay Round by themselves.[4] As Gilbert Winham, an astute observer of GATT negotiations, has noted, a "pyramidal structure" of decision making prevailed in previous rounds and allowed these major actors to establish the negotiating agenda: "Once a tentative trade-off was established, the negotiation process was progressively expanded to include other countries. In this way, cooperation between the United States and the EC served to direct the negotiation."[5] The essence of the pre-negotiation process and, by extension, the negotiation process for Winham was the "power" and "leadership" of major actors in the complex and uncertain context of multilateral economic negotiations.[6]

One purpose of our article, in focusing on the Cairns Group, is to argue the need for a modification of this heretofore prevailing model. While the pyramidal model still largely pertains, neither the consensus agreement for a new round of negotiations that emanated from the 1986 Punte del Este meeting nor the progression of the Uruguay Round beyond the midpoint of the Geneva meeting of April 1989 can be explained simply in terms of the brute power of the two major actors alone. Progress in agenda setting and in the negotiating process, we argue, has been significantly facilitated by the activities of the Cairns Group as a constructive bridge builder and consensus seeker in the tense and sometimes conflictual relationship not only between the major actors but also between the major actors and some of the more antagonistic developing countries.

Our methodological approach is modest. Its priority is to describe the role of the Cairns Group within the current round of MTNs with the goal of clarifying some of the linkages between the major theoretical questions we have outlined. More speculatively, we implicitly suggest that the activities of the Cairns Group form the basis for a model of group activity that smaller states can, under certain circumstances, utilize to help foster change in single issue-areas of import to them in a global economic order in which the decision-making process is increasingly more fragmented and complex and in which the major actors need both support and coercion in moving toward a more cooperative form of global economic management in the final stages of the twentieth century.

In the first two sections of this article, we offer a general and necessarily brief analysis of the pattern of change in the international trading system in the 1970s and 1980s and examine the pattern of tensions in agricultural trade during this period. In the third section, we discuss in detail the factors shaping the formation of the Cairns Group and the leadership role of Australia within the coalition. In the fourth section, we focus on the Cairns Group as an actor in the international political economy of agriculture, giving special attention to its agenda for reform and its role as a political coalition and intellectual leadership group in pursuit of more liberal agricultural trade in the Uruguay Round. We then consider the prospects for the success of this multimeter, single-issue coalition of weaker states as a vehicle for sponsoring change in an international trade regime no longer underwritten by a hegemonic actor.

TRANSFORMATION IN THE INTERNATIONAL POLITICAL ECONOMY

This article cannot and need not join the broad-ranging contemporary debate over the issue of posthegemonic change in the international political economy – other than as the necessary context for locating our study of agricultural trade in the extant international trading system. In this regard, perhaps only three general points need to be made. First, the post-1970 period has seen a serious erosion in the principles and norms that were established at Bretton Woods and in the articles of GATT that formed the basis of the post-World War II liberal international economic order.[7]

Second, the chief characteristic of change in the international economic order has been a shift from hegemony to multipolarity. This is not to say that American preponderance has been supplanted, nor that we have a system of advanced multipolar management of the global economy. Rather, the United States has been joined by other major – although still lesser – economic powers such as Japan and the EC, and this has complicated the power-sharing arrangements in the international political economy, the governance of which is no longer possible under the principles established in the second half of the 1940s.[8] It is, of course, possible to present empirical evidence that there has been no measurable decrease in the rate of trade to gross national product[9] and that, by logical extension, the real impact of nontariff barriers is in fact limited. The point of concern for us, however, is the degree to which *perceptions* both of a major shift from an earlier liberal ethos and of the pervasiveness of nontariff barriers are having a deleterious effect on the wider commitment to liberalism in many quarters of the global system.

Third, a major victim of these broad changes in the international economic order would appear to be the more specific principles and norms that are enshrined in GATT and guided the international trading system until the 1970s: multilateralism, nondiscrimination, and a legal or codified approach to regulation, rather than a negotiated approach preserving the sovereign administrative discretion of states. The codified approach represented a preferred American position to that of its European allies in the post-World War II decades.[10] These principles and norms, however, came under increasing pressure in the 1970s and 1980s. Not only has the rise to major actor status of the EC and Japan undermined the U.S. ability to set the politico-philosophical agenda, but it would appear that there is no longer the same *belief* in the United States that the principles that served it well as hegemon still serve the national interest in the way they once did.[11] In recent years, the major debate within policymaking communities concerning the international trading system has been driven much more by the ideological-cum-philosophical questions about the relative merits of liberalism and mercantilism. While GATT has been successful in lowering tariffs, it has been unable to discourage the use of nontariff instruments, which have become the major reflection of "illiberality" in the trading system. With the emergence of the new protectionism,[12] a panoply of government-sponsored measures described variously as strategic trade policy or industry policy[13] have become the norm, and the control of these measures can only be brought about by complex political processes of decision making.

THE POLITICS OF AGRICULTURE IN THE 1970s AND 1980s

It is in this broad context of change that the politics of agriculture have to be understood. In the immediate post-World War II period, the United States was the dominant actor in the international agricultural trading system. By virtue of its willingness to take on the burdens of stockholder of last resort in grains, both in respect to commercial transactions and in respect to concessional transactions, the United States may be said to have performed the role of manager of the international agricultural trading system. Indeed, the norms and rules of the post-1945 food regime may be said to have reflected the liberal economic values championed (although not always practiced) by the United States, values which included comparative advantage, specialization, and the free and open exchange of goods and technology.[14] Under such conditions, U.S. policymakers argued that economic growth and efficiency would be maximized on a global level. To make such an assertion is not, however, to deny a history of protectionism in early post-World War II U.S. agricultural policy which in part explains the weakness of GATT on the issue of agriculture. After all, within the first few years of GATT's existence, it was the United States which secured the still extant "temporary waiver" of certain quantitative import restrictions that conflicted with the interests of its own agricultural markets. The issue of U.S. protectionism in the post-World War II era is one of degree rather than substance. While the United States was less protectionist than the European countries in agricultural trade in the 1950s, it was, nevertheless, restrictionist. It became more liberal throughout the 1960s as its agricultural industry became more efficient and as its exchange rate for the dollar became more favorable and increased in its competitive edge.[15]

But a U.S.-directed regime had a number of benefits for its allies among the advanced industrialized countries. Above all, the liberal flow of foodstuffs allowed Western Europe and Japan to secure cheap and plentiful supplies of agricultural goods and thereby enabled them to concentrate on restructuring their industrial plants and infrastructures. Furthermore, it allowed them to benefit from the positive effects of technological transfer, with the import of U.S. stock, equipment, machinery, and expertise facilitating the development of new agro-industries in Japan and the EC countries.

Despite these benefits, suspicions about the principles of economic liberalism and about the leadership of the United States remained in place within the advanced industrialized world. The EC's establishment and extension of the Common Agricultural Policy (CAP) and Japan's use of the Basic Agricultural Law to retain import quotas and other protective devices on a wide range of items even after the 1961 liberalization of foreign trade controls are reflections of these suspicions and of the strength of the belief that agriculture has a unique status, serving as a basis of security and a way of life. This resistance to the imposition of liberal economic principles was also evidence of the political clout of the protectionist-oriented farm lobbies. Certainly, in both the EC and Japan, agricultural interest groups were not only vociferous in their defense of specific interests but were also bulwarks of support for conservative governing parties.

What eventually undercut the stability of the international agricultural trading system was not the internal illiberal practices of Japan and the EC. Rather, erosion came about because of a number of exogenous shocks in the early 1970s. The most dramatic of these were natural in form and included the failure of crops due to drought in Asia, the Soviet Union, North America, and Africa and the impact of other changes in the environment. This type of shock was preceded, nevertheless, by signals that the United States was withdrawing from its commitment to the orderly international marketing of grains and that it was also attempting to redefine the terms of trade with its allies in order to promote U.S. exports. Through its new emphasis on national self-interest, as opposed to international obligations, the United States helped redirect attention away from the anomalies and defects of the EC's CAP and Japan's import restrictions and toward its own declining will and capacity to maintain and defend the system.

To these indirect shocks were added the more direct shocks associated with the food crisis of 1972–74. The most publicized of these was the sudden decision of the Nixon administration to place an embargo on the export of soybeans and soybean products. The embargo itself was extremely short-lived, lasting only from 27 June to 2 July 1973, when it was replaced by export controls that continued through the rest of the summer. The decision to impose the embargo could be explained retrospectively as an action designed to defend the interests of both domestic and foreign consumers during a time of reduced supplies (due largely to the vagaries of nature) and higher prices for protein. Nevertheless, the economic as well as the psychological impact of the embargo on the EC countries and Japan was profound, given the emphasis that they have traditionally placed on "food security." Whether the U.S. decision to impose the embargo without consulting other countries was interpreted as a sign of poor crisis management, an indication of the dominance of domestic interests, or a blatant attempt to use American "food power" in the commodity sector, the credibility of the United States as a reliable supplier of foodstuffs was seriously damaged.

The ultimate effect of these shocks, compounded by the subsequent actions of the Organization of Petroleum Producing Countries (OPEC), was to place the issues of autonomy and self-sufficiency with respect to foodstuffs at the top of the political agenda in Japan and the EC. Now that dependence on the United States for specific imports had become equated in the minds of European and Japanese opinion leaders with vulnerability and the loss of independent decision making, far less emphasis was given to the idea of reform of illiberal trading practices and far more emphasis was placed on building and maintaining food security in keeping with a narrowly defined self-interest. If the United States was unwilling or unable to continue to provide adequate protection in terms of international food security, the industrialized countries would have to immunize themselves against unreliability of supplies. In other words, self-help was legitimized and encouraged at the expense of economic liberalism. As a leading U.S. proponent of a market-oriented agricultural trade approach noted, "Americans must admit that our temporary embargo . . . gave support to arguments for protectionism . . . [and created] a climate that continues to be deleterious to our efforts to ensure reductions in barriers to trade in agricultural products."[16]

The EC and Japan had a number of options available to them as part of an overall strategy of ensuring supplies of foodstuffs. The first and foremost of these options was simply to raise internal support prices for basic crops while relying less on agricultural imports. To a considerable extent, this path was followed by Japan, especially with regard to the establishment of a two-million ton rice emergency fund and restrictions on the import of meat through such measures as the 1975 beef price stabilization scheme. Such an inward-looking approach had the inevitable consequence of generating new sources of conflict with the United States and other exporting countries over access to the Japanese market. As the president of the Brookings Institution suggested with respect to the U.S. embargo and Japan's response, "It is not difficult to see how a pattern of thrust and parry could thus be established in U.S.–Japanese agricultural relations, which have hitherto been relatively free of tension."[17]

Similarly, in products covered by the CAP, the EC concentrated on increasing its internal farm production through the continuation of high prices and the expansion of open-ended intervention guarantees. While the food crisis continued, the financial cost of this approach seemed to be well justified. Even as dogmatic a critic of the CAP as *The Economist* could admit in 1974 that "instead of the ogre it once appeared to be, the CAP is protecting the community from some of the unstabilising effects of the price spiral."[18] The longer-term implications arising from this food security approach were only realized when the crisis receded in the late 1970s, for this inward-looking expansionist strategy had pushed the EC's overall agricultural production (as indeed it pushed the U.S. production) well beyond the requirements of its own immediate food security needs. By 1983, the degree of EC self-sufficiency in percentage terms was higher than 100 in sugar (144), wheat (125), butter (123), poultry (110), cheese (108), beef (104), veal (104), and pork (101).[19]

The move of the EC from a position of being a net-deficit to a net-surplus actor in a wide variety of agricultural products introduced new sources of tension into the international agricultural trading system. As massive "mountains" of agricultural produce accumulated in the postcrisis environment, the CAP was gradually globalized and a new EC agricultural export strategy, based on export subsidies and restitutions, emerged. The EC justified this new strategy on pragmatic grounds, arguing that it was better to subsidize consumers outside the community (especially those in the Third World) at a low cost than to subsidize the storage and preservation of stockpiles inside the EC at a high cost. Still, to the traditional defenders of the CAP, an explicit export strategy also had the significant advantage of institutionalizing the surpluses.

The EC's efforts to "export" the CAP's problems posed a direct challenge to U.S. leadership in international agricultural transactions. In overall commercial transactions, the United States continued to lead, with $41.7 billion of produce sold abroad in 1982, representing 70 percent more than in 1976.[26] But the EC vaulted into second place, with agricultural exports valued at $27 billion in 1982, representing a 156 percent rise during the same six-year period. In terms of major agricultural commodities, the EC had by the early 1980s become the world's largest exporter of poultry, the largest market-economy exporter of sugar, the supplier of three-fifths of the international market in butter and dried milk, the second largest exporter of beef (after Australia), and a major exporter of grain and flour.

The impact of this challenge was felt in a variety of ways. At the level of values, there continued to be fundamental differences between the rhetorical weight placed by the United States on a "free market" and the emphasis placed by the EC on "sovereignty" and the "management" of international transactions. At the level of action, the increasingly aggressive export approach prompted a backlash from the United States. During the Carter administration and during the early part of the Reagan administration (particularly prior to the November 1983 GATT ministerial meeting), this response entered on a concerted attempt to win recourse through a revamped subsidy code of international trade under GATT. Dissatisfaction with the slow pace involved in changing the formal rules governing export subsidies, however, shifted U.S. agricultural diplomacy toward "fighting fire with fire." One of the first expressions of American dissatisfaction with international dispute-settlement procedures was the largely ad hoc decision of the United States in January 1983 to openly subsidize the sale of one million tons of surplus wheat flour to Egypt, which had traditionally been supplied by the European market. With the introduction of the Export Enhancement Profram (EEP), however, subsidies became not only more institutionalized but also globalized in that the program targeted traditional markets of other agricultural exporters. Through its shift in approach, the United States signaled to the other actors involved in food and agricultural trade that it was willing to resort to explicitly neomercantilist practices in order to defend economic liberal values.

In short, while agricultural trade has always been seen as an exception by the major producers, it has in most nations also come to exhibit all the worst elements of the new protectionism and occupy a position of peculiar political sensitivity that makes it distinct from, although not unconnected to, the other sectors of global trade. Government policy in most countries – developed and developing nations, market-oriented and command economies, and major and minor powers – has been geared to defending the agricultural sector, and international trade rules have been molded accordingly. This was the case in the post-World War II period until the 1970s. Since that time, agricultural policy, especially of the major powers, has been pursued in an increasingly aggressive and nationalistic manner – indeed, as an arm of foreign policy. The manner in which this has led to strain and tension in relationships between the United States and Japan, the United States and the EC, and the EC and Japan is sufficiently well documented to be simply asserted here.[21]

Given the problems that agriculture has generated over the last decade, it comes as no surprise that its reform is extremely complex. There are three basic areas in which reform is needed: reform must be achieved in the domestic structures of agricultural production around the globe; reform must be secured within the international trading system generally; and reform must be secured in the GATT system to cope with agricultural trade specifically. These areas of reform are, of course, interlinked, and an acceptable set of new rules cannot be secured without reform in all three. To reiterate, reform of the international system of agricultural trade will not be achieved without domestic restructuring. It is, however, the international context generally and GATT and the actors in the Uruguay Round specifically which are the focus of the remainder of this article.

THE FORMATION OF THE CAIRNS GROUP: MIDDLE POWER LEADERSHIP IN A SINGLE-ISSUE COALITION

From the outset of this section, let us note the degree to which we are extremely sensitive to the problematic and often contested nature of the notion of middle powers and what the late doyen of Canadian foreign policy studies, John W. Holmes, ironically refers to as "middlepowermanship."[22] The definition of a middle power, invariably nonsystematic and intuitive, has usually commenced from a ranking that draws on the aggregation of various attributes of brute national power: size, gross domestic product (GDP), gross national product (GNP), population, estimated military capability, and so on. Alternatively, it can be a category drawn from status measurement, geostrategic location, or an amalgam of these and related characteristics. "Middlepowermanship" was seen by Holmes as a specific approach to diplomacy, an approach geared in the Canadian context to "mitigating political tensions and military conflicts Ottawa feared would spark a Third World War."[23] It emphasized the reduction of tensions between the two politico-strategic combatants of a bipolar cold war world.

If we are looking for a working definition of middle power for this article, it is one which draws on what we might call a Holmesian approach, emphasizing *process* but applied to international conflict and cooperation in the economic domain rather than in the politico-strategic domain. The behavior of the Cairns Group in the Uruguay Round is one geared to securing its desired aims of substantial agricultural reform via the mitigation of tensions and conflict between the major actors. For us, then, notwithstanding the arcane langauge of "middlepowermanship" and the danger of overstating the role of the Cairns Group as a go-between and consensus seeker in the Uruguay Round, it is the *activity* of middle power diplomacy built on the strength of the Group and the intellectual and entrepreneurial leadership of Australia that we see as innovative and interesting in the present period. Before examining the role played by Australia, however, some detailed characteristics of the Group in general need to be outlined.

The Cairns Group: a Profile of Strange Bedfellows

By no definitional criteria do all members of the Cairns Group have the status of middle powers. The purpose of this section, taking its cue from its heading, is to examine middle power *leadership* within the Cairns Group as a single-issue coalition playing an important role in the current MTNs. Prominent within the Group are Australia and Canada, two countries which have long been listed as the quintessential representatives of this category of states[24] but which, unlike most states in the category, have been characterized of late by a high degree of activism in their foreign policies, especially as reflected in their role in the Cairns Group since its formation. The Group, led by Australia, has sought to influence not only the international agricultural regime but also the domestic policies of other countries. In a paradoxical but noncontradictory fashion, this activism has been accompanied by an emphasis on the politics of constraint. Having a high sensitivity to the actions of the strong, the fundamental goal of the Cairns Group has remained that of restraining and modifying the behavior of larger, more powerful actors through the strengthening of order in the world economy. Also in common with middle power diplomatic endeavours of the past, the Cairns Group has concentrated its efforts on a specific, discrete issue-area in which the interests and expertise of its member states can be concentrated.

In the discussion that follows, we will, however, contrast the Group's strong, if not always exclusive, commonality of interest and homogeneity of policy in the Uruguay Round with its substantial heterogeneity of structure, levels of development, and interests in most other domains. It is because of these contractions that we see the Cairns Group as precedent setting. It is, in short, a heterogeneous group of states bound together in the pursuit of a specific single interest. This dysfunction in the pattern of association can be seen most clearly when the Group's activities are contrasted, for example, with middle power diplomacy featured in the Law of the Sea negotiations. In these negotiations, Australia,

Canada, and New Zealand (also a member of the Cairns Group) joined with the like-minded smaller Western European democracies of Austria, Denmark, Finland, Iceland, Ireland, the Netherlands, Norway, Sweden, and Switzerland to form the Group of 12.[25] The Cairns initiative, in terms of membership, is a completely different phenomenon. Although the Cairns Group includes several countries besides Australia and Canada which may be labeled as middle powers on the basis of their economic capabilities or diplomatic stature (for example, Brazil, Hungary, and Indonesia), these countries remain quite dissimilar from their coalition partners with respect to their comparative levels of economic development (see Table 1) and the nature of their political system. Additionally, the Group contains a relatively large number of countries not generally recognized as middle powers. These include Argentina, Chile, Columbia, Fiji, Malaysia, the Philippines, Thailand, and Uruguay. By its mixed or cross-cutting composition alone, then, the Cairns Group may be regarded as a coalition unlike any other in the contemporary international political economy. Members are, in simple terms, from both sides of the East-West and North-South divides in the international order. It is in the context of the Group's operation – its attempts to reform global agricultural trade – that the collective strengths and individual and common interests of its members become apparent.

Notwithstanding the central role of Australia and Canada, the Cairns group is primarily made up of developing countries and quite specifically the principal agricultural exporting ones. In this respect, the Cairns Group represents but one major developing country perspective on global agricultural trade, an alternative to which is the perspective of the Food Importers Group, another coalition of developing countries which also has an active, if somewhat ineffectual, voice in the current MTNs.[26] In addition to this division, there are considerable manifestations of diversity among the developing countries within the Cairns Group. Along an economic axis, Argentina, Brazil, Chile, Malaysia, and Uruguay fall into the World Bank's upper middle income category, while Colombia, Fiji, Indonesia, the Philippines, and Thailand fall into the lower middle and low income categories. Along a regional axis, developing country members come from Latin America, Southeast Asia, and the South Pacific.

Cairns Group states do have important commonalities, however. Each has a highly competitive export-oriented agricultural sector, with agricultural exports representing from 18 percent to as high as 73 percent of total exports, as shown in Table 1. The high percentages of the Group members can be contrasted with the figures of 17 percent for the United States, 1 percent for Japan, 7 percent for West Germany, 8 percent for Great Britain, 9 percent for Italy, and 19 percent for France. In addition, all of the Cairns Group states play an important role individually or collectively in a large proportion of the world's agricultural markets. Table 2 shows the wide range of agricultural commodities in which the Group is a significant actor, providing from 21.4 to 91.8 percent of the world market in thirteen different commodities.

The collective weight of the Cairns Group entitles it to be considered a "third force" in the context of the GATT negotiations. The combined GDP of the Group at close to $1.06 trillion is not much less than that of Japan at $1.3 trillion; and as Figure 1 shows, the Group's share of world agricultural exports is

TABLE 1 *The Cairns Group: Population, Gross National and Domestic Product (GNP and GDP), and Select Data on Agriculture*[a]

Group member[b]	Population (in millions)	GNP (per capita in US$)	GDP (in US$ millions)	Agriculture as a percentage of GDP	Agriculture as a percentage of exports	Percentage of labor force employed in agriculture
Argentina	31.0	2.350	69.220	13	73	13
Australia	16.0	11.920	184,940	5	39	7
Brazil	138.4	1.810	*206,750*	*11*	*41*	31
Canada	25.6	14.120	323,790	3	18	5
Chile	12.2	1.320	16,820	–	25	17
Colombia	29.0	1.230	*29,660*	*20*	*67*	34
Fiji	–	–	–	–	–	–
Hungary	10.6	2.020	23,660	17	23	18
Indonesia	166.4	490	75,230	26	21	57
Malaysia	16.1	1.830	27,580	–	38	42
New Zealand	3.3	7.460	26,630	11	68	11
Philippines	57.3	560	30,540	26	26	52
Thailand	52.6	810	41,780	17	54	71
Uruguay	3.0	1,650	5,320	12	58	16

[a]Figures in italics are for data prior to 1986. All other data are for 1986.
[b]Comparable data for Fiji are not available.
Source: World Bank, *World Development Report 1988* (Oxford: Oxford University Press, 1988), pp. 222–23, 226–27, 244–45, and 282–83.

TABLE 2 *The Cairns Group: Percentage of Total World Trade in Selected Agricultural Commodities (with global ranking shown in parentheses)*[a]

Group member[a]	*Animal feedstuffs*	*Barley*	*Cereals and prepara-tions*	*Cocoa*	*Coffee*	*Meat (chilled and frozen)*	*Oilseeds*	*Rice*	*Rubber*	*Sugar and honey*	*Vegetable oils*	*Wheat*	*Wool*
Argentina	6.0(5)	–	23.5(2)	–	–	1.9(14)	9.8(2)	–	–	–	14.1(3)	5.7(5)	4.0(6)
Australia	–	15.4(3)	3.4(10)	–	–	7.9(4)	–	3.0(6)	–	4.9(4)	–	13.5(3)	37.8(1)
Brazil	27.7(1)	–	–	23.4(1)	39.7(1)	7.4(8)	8.8(3)	–	–	9.9(2)	16.9(2)	–	1.9(12)
Canada	–	14.5(4)	3.8(7)	–	–	4.1(11)	5.7(4)	–	–	–	–	21.6(2)	–
Chile	4.4(7)	–	–	–	–	–	–	–	–	–	–	–	–
Colombia	–	–	–	–	12.2(2)	–	–	–	–	0.4	–	–	–
Fiji	–	–	–	–	–	–	–	–	–	1.0(17)	0.3	–	–
Hungary	–	–	–	–	–	–	–	–	–	–	–	–	–
Indonesia	–	–	–	–	3.8(4)	–	–	–	21.3(3)	–	2.0(10)	–	–
Malaysia	0.5	–	–	4.3(6)	–	–	3.7(6)	–	35.0(1)	–	47.0(1)	–	–
New Zealand	–	–	6.5(5)	–	–	7.8(7)	–	–	–	–	–	–	16.4(2)
Philippines	–	–	–	–	0.5	–	–	–	–	2.9(6)	11.5(4)	–	–
Thailand	–	–	7.4(4)	1.9(7)	–	–	–	33.1(1)	12.3(4)	2.3(8)	–	–	–
Uruguay	–	0.9(12)	1.3(14)	–	–	2.1(13)	–	2.2(7)	–	–	–	–	3.9(7)
Total	38.6	30.8	45.9	29.6	56.2	31.2	28.0	38.3	68.6	21.4	91.8	40.8	64.0

[a]The table excludes agricultural commodities that are only prominent in the economy of a single member of the Group, such as tobacco in Brazil, dairy produce in New Zealand, and tea in Indonesia.
[b]Comparable data for Hungary are not available.
Source. United Nations, *UN International Trade Statistics*, vols. 1 and 2 (New York: United Nations, 1988).

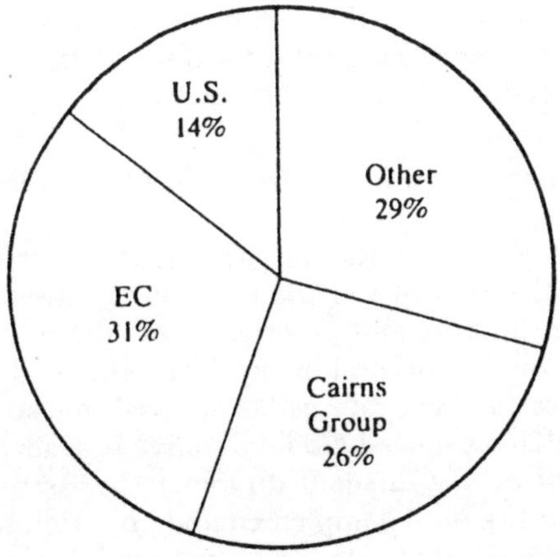

FIGURE 1 World agricultural exports by country or group, with the total representing about $273 billion in U.S. dollars

considerably larger than that of the United States and second only to that of the EC. Moreover, the amount of manufactured goods imported by the Cairns Group is roughly equal to the amount of manufactured goods exported by Japan.

Above all, and notwithstanding the competitiveness of their agricultural sectors, all members of the Group have identified the 1980s as a period in which they have been adversely affected by the growth of illiberality in agricultural trade in general and the policies of the United States and the EC in particular. While the problem of access to the markets of the major industrialized countries is important, the worst problem for the competitive status of Cairns Group members has been the growth of the EEP and, for want of a better expression, the perceived "globalization" of the CAP. Subsidized European expansion into "nontraditional markets" and subsequent U.S. retaliation adversely affected the ability of Cairns Group countries to hold their own in these markets in a way that had throughout the first part of the 1980s in part compensated for the access difficulties presented by developed country markets.

The middle-sized and smaller agricultural trading countries, therefore, increasingly perceived themselves as the real victims of the tensions between the EC and the United States. With many of their leading exports, including wheat, animal feedstuffs, rice, and meat, hard hit by the EEP and without the financial resources to engage in a protracted campaign of agricultural subsidization themselves, these countries had considerable motivation to band together in a coalition of "fair traders." The need to take collective action, it may be added, was especially felt by the Latin American debtor countries, since the servicing of their debts required, among other things, an expansion of sales of agricultural goods.

It is against this background that the members of the Cairns Group, led by Australia, have come to emphasize reforms in the global agricultural system that would reward efficiency and free market forces.

Australia and Canada: Changing Roles in Middle Power Behavior

A distinctive feature of the Cairns initiative relates to the nature of leadership within the Group. It has been Canada that has traditionally been out in front with respect to the thinking and practice of middle powers.[27] As one student of Canadian and Australian diplomacy has described the role of the two countries in the post-1945 era, "Canada appeared to lead the way in directions along which Australia has moved."[28] This source of leadership was particularly evident in the abilities of Canadian diplomats to assemble coalitions and to work with other counties on the implementation of proposals. Against this background, the transformation of roles by Canada and Australia within the Cairns Group is novel enough to merit attention. In a sharp departure from past behavior, Australia has assumed the pivotal intellectual and leadership position in the process of coalition building and maintenance, while Canada's commitment to the Cairns Group has been markedly nuanced and, at times, positively ambivalent.

The coalition behavior associated with the Cairns Group emerged as a response to the increasingly intense form of competition in the international agricultural trading system previously outlined. Faced with a rising threat not only in terms of a denial of access to the markets of the major industrialized countries but also in terms of the intensification of competitive subsidization by the United States and the EC, and lacking the financial resources to compete with these stronger actors, the middle-sized and smaller actors sought to win a commitment in the MTNs to agricultural reform, especially a standstill and rollback in reference to subsidization and a break in the nexus between production and administered internal pricing. To give momentum to this drive, some form of collective action directed toward improved rules of the game was thought necessary. Indeed, for the weak, the alternative to seeking safety in numbers was to continue to be victimized individually.

The role of Australia and Canada, from a political and historical viewpoint, is of particular interest with regard to the formation of the Cairns Group. These two countries, it could be argued, were the "first followers" of the post-1945 agricultural trade regime. More even than the hegemon, Australia and Canada remained committed to the maintenance of the rules, principles, and institutions of the regime and were willing and able to make the diplomatic effort to defend it against erosion. In the late 1960s, when the U.S. actions to increase the sales of American produce threatened to destabilize the pricing agreement established under the International Grains Agreement, for instance, both Canada and Australia took on a greater burden of responsibility in an attempt to ward off total collapse of the system. Jean-Luc Pepin, the Canadian Industry, Trade and Commerce Minister, told Parliament that even if "we may have lost a number of sales" in the process of trying to save the International Grains Agreement, it was "worth the effort."[29] Likewise, Australia showed restraint in the face of increasingly cutthroat competition during the same episode. As one Australian journalist wrote in regard to the situation, "International co-operation was only maintained by a virtual waiving of the price provisions and agreement by some exporters, such as Australia, to compete a little less aggressively so as to allow other nations to maintain their traditional share of the world market."[30]

Canadian and Australian perspectives and interests with respect to the agricultural order also help give more precise shape to the concept of "middle powers." The different diplomatic displayed by these countries in this issue-area reflect certain variations on the theme which should be examined more closely. In defending the post-1945 order, Canada always placed a greater emphasis than Australia on mediation and compromise. Though Canada was a significant actor, its diplomatic initiatives tended to be of a reactive nature in that they usually came in response to the actions of other countries, particularly the United States. In contrast, Australian diplomacy was more proactive, even to the point of being labeled "overzealous" with respect to agricultural trade issues, and Australia was inclined to actively challenge the major actors if their policies appeared to be at odds with the norms of the regime, rather than play the role of the low-key "helpful fixer" in multilateral forums.[31]

This is not to say that Canada was reluctant to criticize the actions of the United States or the EC. When it did make diplomatic protests, though, it did so either privately or in concert with other countries. Canada also paid a great deal of attention to confidence-building measures, especially with reference to the building up of consultative or dispute-resolution forums and mechanisms. The highly contentious issue of U.S. techniques to dispose of agricultural surpluses, for example, triggered the establishment of the Joint U.S.-Canadian Committee on Trade and Economic Affairs.[32] Similarly, Canada joined with the United States in various early attempts to mediate the fundamental differences on the question of restricted access to the EC market due to the implementation of the CAP. Initiatives along these lines included the formation of a special committee of the Organization for European Economic Cooperation to examine the problem and the arrangement for consultations in May 1960 between the EC and representatives of the major exporting nations.

These differences in diplomatic style highlight the important structural differences between Canada and Australia with respect to their relative positions in the international political economy.[33] Canada has a far greater dependence on a single trading partner than Australia does, since approximately 80 percent of Canada's trade is with United States. On the other hand, in relative terms, Canada remains in a far stronger overall position economically than Australia. As Table 3 shows, Canada has a higher GNP per capita as well as a more diversified overall economy. When the role of agriculture in the international political economy is looked at specifically, in turn, the exposure of Canada to trade tensions is seen to be far less marked than that of Australia. The profile of Canadian farm exports is a concentrated one, with grains and oilseeds dominating as the competitive sector and with dairy and poultry products remaining relatively uncompetitive and domestic-oriented sectors.

The Australian position is rather different. Although Australia has more diversified trading partners, it does not have the economic strengths of Canada.

TABLE 3 *The Structure of Trade in Australia and Canada*

			Percentage share of merchandise exports							
	GNP (per capita in US$)	*Average percentage of annual growth*	*Fuels, minerals, and metals*		*Other primary commodities*		*Machinery and transport*		*Other manu-factured exports*	
Country	*1986*	*1965–86*	*1965*	*1986*	*1965*	*1986*	*1965*	*1986*	*1965*	*1986*
Australia	11,920	1.7	13	40	73	39	5	6	10	16
Canada	14,120	2.6	28	18	35	18	15	42	22	22

Source. World Bank, *World Development Report 1988* (Oxford: Oxford University Press, 1988), pp. 222–23 and 246–47.

Not only has Australia remained more dependent on its export of resources, but its vulnerability to the denial of market access and to the competitive subsidization of agricultural commodities is far greater, given the wide range of agricultural produce its exports (rice and sugar as well as grains, dairy produce, and meat). Indeed, for the so-called Lucky Country, the 1980s were a sober period because agricultural prices fell and Australia no longer had the cushion of strong mineral and energy exports. From 1973 to 1983, Australia slipped from being the twelfth largest trading nation to bring the twenty-second largest in the international league, and its share of the world export market dropped from 2.6 percent to 1.2 percent. This downturn was starkly reflected in the rise in capital debt, the fall in the currency level, and the increase in the balance-of-payment deficit on the current account. Australia has, in short, undergone a process of "marginalization" in the post-World War II global economy.[35]

The changing positions of Canada and Australia in the international political economy have fundamentally shaped the foreign economic policy options available to the two countries.[36] Canada is fortunate in having a number of global, regional, and unilateral options available to it. It can take advantage of the maneuverability that its economic capabilities allow, particularly with respect to its presence in the G–7 and other exclusive forums, while placing a high emphasis on winning political and economic concessions vis-à-vis the United States (albeit, it could be argued, not without trade-offs on questions of sovereignty). Australia's options, in contrast, are much more limited. As one Australian official has bluntly put it, GATT represents the only game in town: "Despite its shortcomings, the GATT is the *only* rule of law applying to world trade. . . . Warts and all, [it] represents the best available political commitment . . . in an imperfect world."[37]

Yet, far from being successful in this global approach, Australia seemed by the mid-1980s to be increasingly isolated from its traditional political-ideological allies. In this respect, the emotional response by Australia at the 1982 ministerial meeting of GATT over the inability to get agriculture on the agenda served as a crucial learning experience and exposed the futility of pursuing an abrasive diplomatic approach. When Deputy Prime Minister Doug Anthony stormed out of the meeting, calling it a "fiasco," the action did not earn diplomatic kudos but instead was greeting with "loathing and disrespect" from some of the key actors in the issue-area.[38]

The coalition-building behavior that eventually led to the formation of the Cairns Group, then, was part of a serious process of self-criticism and re-evaluation for Australia. Frustrated in its efforts to reform the agricultural trading system head on, Australian policymakers embarked on a more indirect, step-by-step approach to achieve the same end. Reform, it was realized, could only come by collective action. The Labor government of Bob Hawke, moreover, not only had an economic imperative for "doing something" about the agricultural trade situation, but it also had a domestic imperative for action which related specifically to the rapidly escalating "rural crisis." An externally oriented campaign against the illiberal practices of the United States and the EC, while not a complete answer to the Labor government's political problems at home, certainly proved a useful political palliative.

Despite its unsuccessful performance in respect to agricultural trade diplomacy in the early 1980s, Australia had certain advantages in its efforts to mobilize a broad-based international coalition for the purpose of agricultural trade reform. On one side, Australia benefited from a long-established sense of mutuality of interest and purpose with several like-minded countries on agricultural issues. The most important of these was Canada. Between 1979 and 1981, Australia and Canada (along with Argentina) made several attempts to revive the idea of an international wheat agreement as a means to halt the cutthroat competition in that sector. Later, the two countries even talked of plans for a "joint defense" with respect to the U.S.–E.C. wheat trade war. Australia's relations with New Zealand were also good, symbolized by the Closer Economic Relationship (CER).[39]

On the other side, Australia could capitalize on an accumulated store of good will from the less developed countries (LDCs) for championing their causes in the past.[40] Australia's long-standing sympathy for the position of raw material exporting nations was exemplified by the country's repeated attempts in the 1950s and 1960s to introduce more equity into the international political economy. At the 1958 Commonwealth Trade and Economic Conference, Australian Trade Minister John McEwen suggested a plan for a worldwide agreement on commodities designed to stabilize prices. The idea was then discussed in a number of forums, including a meeting of Commonwealth trade ministers in London in May 1963, a GATT ministerial meeting a few weeks later, and a United Nations Conference on Trade and Development (UNCTAD) meeting in 1964. In 1965, Australia formally applied to GATT for an exemption allowing it to accord preferential treatment to some LDCs with respect to import duties for a range of products of special interest to them. By extending an offer of this nature despite the deeply embedded internal support for industrial protection, the Australian government stated that it hoped to "demonstrate by positive action

Australia's willingness to help overcome the trade problems of the less developed countries."[41] Australian policy remained consistent on this score, and the country continued its support of the common fund until the early 1980s.

The harmonious connection between Australia and the South was reinforced by the links that both the Fraser and the Hawke governments developed with many of the major agriculture-exporting LDCs in the late 1970s and the early 1980s. Functionally, the contacts with these countries were made through bodies such as the Southern Hemisphere Temperate Zone Agricultural Producers, the Wheat Exporting Group, the Association of Iron Ore Exporting Countries, and the International Bauxite Association, as well as UNCTAD and GATT. Geographically, the prime focus of the Australian foreign economic strategy was on the Asian Pacific countries. Building on the institutional base established through the South Pacific Area Regional Trade and Economic Cooperation AGreement (SPARTECA), the Economic and Social Commission of Asia and the Pacific (ESCAP), the Association of Southeast Asian Nations (ASEAN), and the ASEAN Australia Economic Cooperation Program, the Australians launched a diplomatic offensive in 1983–84 to make sure that the region had a coherent and integrated approach to present in the MTNs.

In acting as the driving force behind the formation of a broad-based coalition with which to make a push for the reform of agricultural trade, Australia tempered its hitherto hard line with a deft and sophisticated diplomatic approach. In the 1980s, Australia's Bureau of Agricultural Economics took the lead not only in compiling and analyzing the technical details of the costs of subsidies and protection in agriculture but also in widely publicizing this information to marshal the arguments against the supposed short-term gains of protectionist policies as opposed to the long-term goal of a fairer trading system.[42] Indeed, the research was utilized explicitly as a diplomatic tool both in the bilateral context and in the multilateral arena. Following the Australian initiative, the Organization for Economic Cooperation and Development (OECD) took steps to institutionalize the concept of producer subsidy equivalents and use it as the index of government support for agriculture.[43]

Furthermore, in "pre-negotiations" regarding the agenda for the Uruguay Round, Australia effectively used the escalating nature of the trade situation to transform the issue of agriculture from a low-level bureaucratic question to a high-level political question that could no longer be ignored. Specifically, the Australian policymakers used the U.S. decision to globalize the EEP in mid-1986 (a move highlighted by the Reagan administration's decision to negotiate sales of subsidized wheat to the Soviet Union) as a catalyst to quicken the pace of building a coalition of the smaller, "nonsubsidizing" agriculture-exporting nations in the four quadrants of the world, all of which were hard hit by the U.S. actions.

Vital to this mobilization process was the decisive leadership displayed by Australia. The declaratory statements made by Prime Minister Hawke and other Australian policymakers on the theme that it was time to call a halt to the "ridiculous world trade war" and "subsidy madness" served as a rallying call for collective action, and the Australian government buttressed this rhetoric by constructive efforts at agenda setting, coalition building, and confidence building.

Moving beyond the stage of informal discussions held in small groups or in telephone conversations between leaders (for example, between Hawke and Prime Minister Mulroney during the U.S.–Soviet subsidized wheat sale episode), Australia took the crucial step of formally initiating the "creation of a group . . . with common interests . . . for the long term" by inviting ministerial-level representatives of fourteen carefully selected nations to a meeting at Cairns in the last week of August 1986.[44] Justifying this step, the Australians argued that the external environment had become so threatening that it was only through the development of a "co-ordinated approach to such impositions" that these targeted middle and small actors might prevent "our shared interests and concerns" from being "bypassed."[45]

THE AGENDA AND STRATEGY OF THE CAIRNS GROUP

Having outlined the context of the evolution of the Cairns Group and provided some insight into the differences and common interests of its membership and the role of Australia as the intellectual driving force of the Group, we turn now to a description and analysis of the Group's agenda and strategies in the Uruguay Round. Our approach is both thematic and chronological. We first outline the central elements of the Group's demands and approaches and then discuss its participation in the specific stages of the Uruguay Round that have occurred to date.

The Aims of the Cairns Group

The aims of the Group are encapsulated in two major documents: the *Declaration of the Ministerial Meeting of Fair Traders in Agriculture*, adopted by the Group at its 26 August 1986 meeting in Cairns, and the *Comprehensive Proposal for the Reform of Agriculture*, adopted by the Group at its 21–23 November 1989 meeting in Thailand and tabled at the GATT agricultural negotiation group meeting four days later. The 1986 declaration, which was more exhortatory and less detailed than the 1989 proposal, called for the full integration of agricultural trade in a GATT process that over ten years or less would ensure a stronger market-oriented agricultural system with strengthened and operationally effective rules and disciplines.

The Group's longer-term reform package for the Uruguay Round is intended to secure four major reforms: (1) the reduction of existing tariffs and the conversion of nontariff barriers into tariffs that will be progressively reduced; (2) the reduction of distorting internal support measures; (3) the phasing out of existing export subsidies and the prohibition of new ones; and (4) the special and differential treatment of LDCs in accordance with their individual development needs and also in recognition of the particular concerns of the net food-importing countries.[46] As can be seen, central for the Group is not just the question of curbing the impact of major power subsidy policies on the agricultural system; issues of market access are also fundamental.

The above longer-term goals of the Cairns Group have been supported by a series of short-term recommendations geared toward confidence building in the relationship between the major players. In particular, the Group has attempted to come up with remedies which assuage EC preoccupations with "rebalancing" (such as withdrawing Dillon Round concessions on zero-bindings for various commodities) and which also assuage U.S. preoccupations with "tariffication" as a way of placing an easily identifiable ceiling on variable levies. The Group's short-term proposals have included the following: (1) a freeze on all new access barriers; (2) immediate across-the-board cuts in subsidies by agreed percentages; (3) fixed-percentage increases to improve market access; (4) the establishment of targets for reducing support and protection over a ten-year period; and (5) a ban on the introduction of any new nontariff barriers and trade-distorting subsidies.

While the combined status of the Cairns Group members in global agricultural trade has placed them in a formidable "third force" position in the negotiations, they have been careful to offer positive initiatives that build confidence in the major players with regard to the prospects for success in the Uruguay Round. Without such confidence, the chances for reform are slight. And as the Cairns Group negotiators and especially the central figures in the Australian trade negotiations bureaucracy are also well aware, without such initiatives the ever-present prospect for a U.S.–EC imposed solution geared only toward resolving their own specific differences as the round draws to a close will be so much the greater.

The term "confidence building," which has been widely used in both academic and policymaking circles involved in arms control, is defined as the regulation of the negotiating environment designed to improve communication and understanding, offer reassurance about the intentions of the participants, and thereby reduce the prospects for conflict.[47] Confidence-building measures are thus intended to generate predictability and monitor deviations from the norm in state behavior. A major problem throughout the Uruguay Round and indeed in the years of waning faith in the GATT system of the early 1980s has been that the major actors have increasingly lacked confidence in their ability to understand the intentions of others and in their ability to compete successfully in the absence of protectionist support mechanisms. In this regard, confidence-building measures are not a substitute for a new trade agreement but, rather, are simply a tool to smooth the way toward a new agreement.

The paths to building a climate of confidence are many and varied, and as the chronological discussion that follows illustrate, the activities of the Cairns Group in general and Australia in particular have been multifaceted. Three components of Group policy are worth noting prior to this discussion: first, a commitment to a gradual, step-by-step approach to edge the major actors over potential stumbling blocks: second, a commitment to the technical improvement of the methods of transparency,[48] since transparency (like verification in arms control agreements) is assumed to enhance mutual understanding and trust; and third, in cases in which deadlock appears likely, a commitment to the extensive use of shuttle diplomacy and brokerage by senior Australian trade negotiators.

From Punte del Este to Montreal (the Midterm Review)

The Cairns meeting accomplished a great deal with respect to the establishment of an informal working relationship among Group members, the identification of principles, and the development of tactics to maximize the Group's influence within the international political economy. Although the individual members may have been unclear about what they were committing themselves to at this stage, the momentum generated from the meeting and the negotiating demands issued at it allowed the Cairns Group to quickly move to the point where it could be considered an emergent "third force" in agricultural trade issues.[49]

In the declaration issued by the Cairns Group, primacy was given to the need for agriculture to be adequately addressed in the MTNs, with ministers seriously questioning "the value of a new Round which failed to solve the longstanding problems in agricultural trade." To ensure that "their concerns regarding the negotiating objectives on agriculture" were "adequately met," the Cairns Group agreed to consider ongoing cooperative efforts at the bilateral, regional, and joint level. These efforts would include "pressure to secure early changes in current domestic farm support policies of those countries whose policies adversely affect international trade in agricultural products."[50]

Crucial to the campaign for agricultural trade reform and liberalization was the move toward a division of labor among Cairns Group members, with each country concentrating on what it was most involved with, was best equipped to do, or found the least sensitive to domestic political concerns. The LDCs concentrated on ensuring that the problem of agricultural trade remained high on the agenda of forums such as the Food and Agriculture Organization (FAO) and UNCTAD, while Canada focused on presenting the Cairns position at the G-7 meeting in Venice and Toronto and at the Quadilateral meetings.

Australia, for its part, focused on institution building, leadership, and policy innovation within the Cairns Group. As a diverse agricultural exporter and also as a reputation builder within the international system,[51] Australia was willing to devote a considerable amount of time and resources to building up the profile and capabilities of the Group. Indeed, it is not an overstatement to say that Australia took on the functions as well as the burdens of being the manager of the Group with relish. To push the coalition forward, the Australians paid particular attention to consolidating and giving coherence to the activities of the Group's diverse members through the establishment of a loose coordinating mechanism. As John Dawkins, Australia's Minister of Trade and the Group's first acting chairman, informed the Australian House of Representatives in October 1986, "My department will provide the necessary secretariat to facilitate continued co-operation and liaison both within its membership and in its dealings with the major trading economies."[52]

Australia also came increasingly to play the role of intellectual leader of the Group. More than any of its partners, Australia was willing to continue to invest heavily in the MTNs – putting everything it had on the negotiating table – even though this approach was detrimental to certain domestic sectoral interests in the short run. The perception that GATT continued to be the "only game in town" for Australia was well captured by Prime Minister Hawke in a speech given to the GATT Contracting Parties in October 1987 and committing Australia to an ambitious ten-year internal reform program as part of a broad-based multilateral strategy.

Australia is one of the few countries, other than the major players in the Uruguay Round, with a sufficiently substantial and skilled multilateral trade bureaucracy capable of understanding the complexities of the GATT negotiation process not only in the specific negotiating panel on agriculture but also *in toto*. As Jeffrey Schott has recently noted, there is a tendency to overestimate the actual proportion of GATT's ninety-six signatory states, other than the major states, that are capable of comprehending and contributing to all facets of the negotiating processes in a given round.[53] Australia is one; Canada is another.

With respect to the delicate negotiation process with the United States, the EC, and other actors, Australia was instrumental in shaping the incremental, step-by-step approach of the Cairns Group. The key to this approach was, as indicated above, the adoption of confidence-building techniques (techniques traditionally associated in the multilateral context with Canada) which would clear the air of animosity and bilateral recriminations, convince all actors of the usefulness of the negotiations, and gain a collective commitment to a "standstill and rollback." The group recognized that without such a "litmus test of the good faith of all countries," confidence and trust between the parties would be difficult to achieve.[54]

By the date of the Punte del Este meeting, the nationalist protectionist tendencies in international trade had grown to severe proportions. Agricultural markets were suffering from oversupply and depressed prices; there was an increasing tendency toward dumping and subsidization; and the need to stabilize the agricultural markets was widely accepted in both the United States and Europe.[55] The timing for the Cairns Group's activities was, therefore, propitious. Facilitated by the Group's collective share of world agricultural exports (Figure 1), as well as the emotional and practical appeal of its declaration, the Cairns Group was able at the Punte del Este meeting in September 1986 to secure a central place for agriculture on the GATT agenda. There were to be no exclusion clauses or qualifications concerning the "special" nature of agriculture. The support of the United States (which, with the Cairns Group making the running, could offer its "moderation" at the appropriate time) and the reluctance of the EC to stand against the proposals were, of course, crucial. In some analyses, this interpretation would almost certainly be seen as inverted. Gilbert Winham's discussion of the Punte del Este meeting, for example, makes no mention of the Cairns Group.[56] Yet even allowing for a degree of antipodean licence in our interpretation of the meeting (based on extensive interview and media reports), there is no gainsaying the judgment of the U.S. *Journal of Commerce*, which argued that it was the whip of the Cairns Group that secured the agenda: "The Mighty Cairns . . . succeeded in embarrassing both the European Community and the United States into serious negotiations on farm talks."[57]

The Cairns Group nevertheless faced serious constraints in translating this procedural victory into substantive success in securing major reform as the MTNs proceeded. Most crucially, the incremental and flexible approach of the Group remained at odds with the rigid U.S. proposal for agricultural negotiations,[58] which notwithstanding its status as a negotiating tool, called for the complete phase-out of all barriers to import access and subsidies over a ten-year period. Until these long-term demands were met by the EC and other actors, the United States declared itself unwilling to address issues in relation to short-term relief.

Significant also was the rise to the surface of tensions within the Cairns Group itself. Although the members had common objectives, they continued to have differing priorities. This was certainly the case with respect to many of the LDCs. While "signing on," they were reluctant to identify themselves too explicitly with a mixed coalition of developed and developing countries. The overriding concern for most was "special and differential" treatment for their agricultural economies. Some, such as Brazil (a member of the hardline G–10) and Argentina, went even further in their demands, hard-pressed as they were to come up with the funds needed to cope with their enormous debt problems. But Argentina, it should be noted, has nevertheless been one of the most steadfast supporters of Group unity throughout the Uruguay Round.[59]

Pressure on unity in the Cairns Group emanated from a need to assuage the concerns of the members of the Food Importers Group, as discussed earlier. Egypt, Jamaica, Mexico, and Nigeria, for example, believed that the Cairns Group had a "temperate" producers' bias and that acceptance of its proposals would bring about an increase in prices, which would have a negative impact on their own balances of payments as well as on their efforts to increase food self-sufficiency. Under these circumstances, the LDCs in the Cairns Group were extremely sensitive about maintaining G-77 solidarity. Indeed, the Food Importers Group members were able to secure assurances from the Latin American members of the Cairns Group that they would be consulted about initiatives on agricultural trade policy.[60] As these communications linkages increased, through, liaison between the Cairns Group members themselves became more difficult and the overall relationship more tense. Contrary to the assurances received at the initial Cairns meeting, for instance, Brazil on several occasions failed to keep the other members of the Group informed of its activities in terms of agricultural policy. To overcome these problems and ensure group unity, Australia took a stand consistent with its overall foreign policies toward LDCs and argued the case for differential treatment of LDCs vis-à-vis external markets and domestic support systems. This approach was subsequently incorporated in the Group's proposal.

From the perspective of international credibility, however, it was the Canadian position within the Cairns Group, rather than the division between developed and less developed countries, which caused the most problems. As was the case with some other important trade-related issues, the perceptual gap between Canadian rhetoric and Canadian practice was growing.[61] Canadian policymakers persisted in talking about Canada's leadership within the Group. The Minister of State for the Canadian Wheat Board, for instance, claimed that "we have been taking the lead internationally in seeking a lasting solution to these problems."[62] Yet, because of Canada's apparent unwillingness to accept its burden of costs for the internationalist campaign, the country was increasingly viewed by its partners as a free rider within the coalition. Members of the Group were also concerned about Canada's defection from the principle of "standstill and rollback." Canada did not keep strictly to the guidelines of this central confidence-building measure and moved instead to higher levels of subsidization of the domestic grain and oilseeds industry.[63] Most significant, of course, was the Group's concern about the U.S.–Canadian negotiations on a free trade agreement, a bilateral arrangement at odds with the spirit of the MTNs. At the very least, the agreement would undermine the principle of nondiscrimination, giving Canada differential status from its Cairns Group partners with regard to U.S. import laws. Indeed, in late 1989, Australia registered its objections to Canada's failure to grant some of its products the same access rights as those applied to U.S. products under the free trade agreement.

In contrast to Canada, Australia at that stage had reviewed and rejected the idea of seeking a free trade agreement with the United States,[64] thereby highlighting the differences between the two major members of the Cairns Group. Australia was thus to become not only the driving force behind the Cairns Group's negotiating demands but also the mediator and stabilizer of the coalition. Above all, to preserve unity within the Group, Australia had to continue to find compromise solutions acceptable to the more assertive LDCs and to the cautious and recalcitrant Canadians. This was possible with regard to a number of issues. On the one hand, Australia was able to persuade a skeptical Canada that the idea of special and differential treatment for the LDCs should be entrenched in the policy statements of the Cairns Group.[65] On the other hand, Australia was able to preserve the single-issue orientation of the coalition by defusing Brazilian pressures to broaden the Group's agenda and include nonagricultural issues. Of particular relevance here was the issue of linkages between agriculture and the services and intellectual property negotiations in the Uruguay Round, a theme picked up again by Brazil and other Latin American countries at the December 1988 GATT midterm review.

As the Uruguay Round has progressed, the issue of linkage has become much more difficult to manage. Yet on both a theoretical and practical level, it has attained increased importance.[66] It appears that on "new issues" such as services and trade in intellectual property, major agreements between their keenest supporters in the developed world and their opponents in the developing world will not be reached without significant reform of the international system of agricultural exchange and especially the protectionist polices of the developed countries. This cross-issue linkage has, since the period prior to the midterm review, caused some problems for the unity of the Cairns Group, given that some of its members strongly oppose substantial codification of trade in services and intellectual property, whereas others strongly support it. For example, an antagonistic Brazil and a protagonistic Australia that is keen to support U.S. initiatives in these domains have continued to be at odds on the issue.

Perhaps an even more contentious issue for Australia to manage has been its step-by-step approach to the GATT negotiations. The delicate nature of this process can be best illustrated by the Australian proposal, put forward at the Bariloche meeting of the Cairns Group in February 1988, for a freeze on all farm subsidies and new import barriers to commence in 1989. The practical arguments for a freeze were strong, and the proposal was well timed to coincide with the midterm review of the current GATT round. Representing a "down payment" or "advance" on a longer-term agreement on agriculture, the proposal was to be yet another step in the process of confidence building. However, the political constraints on the implementation of this "down payment" proposal was formidable. As Michael Aho has pointed out, "Trade negotiations are as much domestic negotiations as they are negotiations among countries,"[67] and this was certainly true in the case of Canada, which had to take into account the domestic-oriented sectors. This profile of dual interests accounts for Canada's ambiguous role in the Cairns Group. As long as the Cairns initiative was directed at the competitive sectors, the sectors in which Canadian farmers had been victimized by a high degree of subsidization by the stronger countries, Canada showed some enthusiasm for the internationalist approach of the Cairns Group, especially since that initiative was fully consistent with the long-standing tradition of Canadian multilateralism. When uncompetitive sectors such as the dairy industry were targeted, however, this enthusiasm was dampened, and Canada increasingly appeared to be at odds with other members of the coalition because it was unwilling to accept measures that involved significant political and economic costs to itself.

Contrary to the Australian expectation that all the members would be willing and capable of making the necessary "advance" in 1989 and 1990, Canada argued persistently that because of its internal difficulties in making structural adjustments, these "adjustments should be phased-in progressively over time and governments should retain some flexibility in the choice of policy instruments."[68] In the defense of its own long-term agricultural programs, Canada tried hard to establish a criterion for differentiating between government support measures per se and trade-distorting measures. In this regard, if favored the substitution of consumer subsidy equivalents for producer subsidy equivalents.

The firmness of the Canadian resistance to the "down payment" proposal was in part due to questions of timing. When the Australian proposal was introduced at Bariloche, the U.S.–Canada negotiations for a free trade agreement were at a critical point, and bilateral negotiations were highly sensitive in terms of the future of the marketing boards, the Canadian Wheat Board, and other institutions held sacrosanct by substantial elements of the Canadian farming community. Furthermore, the Mulroney Progressive Conservative government was beginning to campaign for the Autumn 1988 general election, an election in which the support of regional economic interest groups such as the Western grain farmers and Eastern dairy and poultry producers was considered vital for success. This resistance on the part of Canada was exacerbated by the buildup of tensions within the Cairns Group resulting from the ascendancy of Australian leadership and the increasingly ambivalent Canadian attitude toward membership in the coalition.

These differences ultimately led to serious questions about the stability of the Cairns Group. Speculation along these lines was fueled, in turn, by a number of public controversies. In mid-1988, stories in the *Australian Financial Review* suggested that Canada was about to leave the coalition altogether because of the ambit nature of the Australian proposal.[69] Although these stories were denied by Australian and Canadian policymakers, the crisis management techniques adopted by both countries indicated the seriousness of the problem. In fact, agricultural trade policy dominated the discussions when Canadian Deputy Prime Minister Don Mazankowski traveled to Australia in early June 1988. Despite high-level diplomatic efforts, the rift between Canada and Australia about how the freeze was to be implemented resurfaced later in the same month over the submission of a Cairns Group proposal to a GATT agricultural committee session in Geneva. Canada, although willing to agree to a freeze on further trade-distorting initiatives and prepared to accept an overall reduction of 10 percent in subsidies over the next two years, remained adamantly opposed to any commodity-specific measures, particularly those directed toward the domestic-oriented sectors. As John Crosbie, Canadian Minister for International Trade, bluntly put it, "We're not going to accept any settlement in GATT that would endanger our farmers. . . . They're not part of the problem."[70]

Confronted by this threat to its image as a progressive force in the international political economy, Australia was determined to push forward with the proposal – but not at the expense of the long-term stability of the coalition. The awkward compromise Australia subsequently settled upon was to delete the specifics with respect to the "down payment" in the Cairns Group's "Time for Action" proposal but to hand in a separate proposal of its own with detailed recommendations.[71] The Group approached the mid-term review of the Uruguay Round at the end of 1988 somewhat uneasily. that it did so as a unified force was in large part due to Australian diplomatic efforts.

From Montreal to Geneva and Beyond

Notwithstanding the diplomatic duty on the part of smaller players such as Australia and Cairns Group, the Montreal midterm review meeting demonstrated the degree to which big player intransigence could jeopardize progress in the Uruguay Round. The much-touted review appeared set to founder on the U.S. insistence on securing a commitment to its "zero-option" on all forms of agricultural subsidy and the equally strong European refusal to countenance such an approach rather than a gradual, step-by-step method. The deadlock saw eleven Latin American GATT contracting parties, led by Argentina and including four other Cairns Group members, threaten to block progress in eleven of the other fourteen areas of negotiation in the round if there was no progress on agriculture. This action indicated to all contracting parties the degree to which success in agriculture was the central element in any successful outcome for the Uruguay Round. As noted earlier, many of the developing countries, especially India and Brazil, linked a favorable outcome on agriculture with progress on trade in intellectual property and services – agenda items becoming increasingly central to the goals of the United States. In order to overcome the Montreal deadlock, the midterm review was set in abeyance until April 1989.

The Montreal meeting shook the contracting parties and appeared to engender a new spirit of compromise in the agricultural negotiations. While the softening of the U.S. and EC positions was the essential component of this newfound spirit, the Cairns Group played a crucial role in nudging the Uruguay Round over the barrier. The United States moved from an "all or nothing" position on trade-distorting subsidies to a position of accepting a "ratcheting down of support," and the EC joined the United States in agreeing to the Cairns Group's demands for a minimum 10 percent reduction in 1990 and "substantial progressive reductions in agricultural support and protection . . . sustained over an agreed period of time."[72] Contracting parties were to reach agreement on the nature of "long-term reform" by the end of 1990. The modus operandi for achieving the reform was disputed, with the EC wanting an aggregate approach and the United States wanting a direct approach to specific measures. The freeze over the remainder of the Uruguay Round was to be by either approach, thereby giving concessions to both the EC and the United States.

We do have to keep the role of the Cairns Group in proportion. It was, of course, an important force for compromise between the major protagonists in the movement from deadlock in Montreal to breakthrough in Geneva. Also of considerable significance, however, was the arrival of a new administration in Washington during the interval between meetings. The electorally induced paralysis that had hung over Clayton Yeutter as the U.S. Trade Representative in Montreal was removed by the time he took over as Secretary for Agriculture and Carla Hills replaced him at the Geneva meeting.

Yet our justification for stressing the importance of the Cairns Group activities is more than circumstantial. It was the Cairns Group proposal for itemized progressive reductions which offered the opportunity for the required U.S. movement away from the "zero option." The U.S. movement was possible because the Group's proposal also offered a way to bring pressure on the EC to move. Cairns Group involvement in the pre-Geneva meetings was also much greater than is commonly appreciated. While welcoming the U.S.–EC bilateral talks prior to the meetings, the Group let it be known that agreement at Geneva required real overall progress and was not simply a case of the two major conflicting parties reaching an accommodation of them own. This point was articulated at the March ministerial meeting of Group members in New Zealand and in letters from Australian Prime Minister Hawke to President Bush and the European leaders in which they were encouraged to adopt greater flexibility. Cairns Group positions were also articulated by the Australian Minister for Trade Negotiations, Michael Duffy, in a bout of transatlantic shuttle diplomacy with Clayton Yeutter, Willy de Clerg, and Frans Andreissen, as well as by GATT's chief executive officer, Arthur Dunkel, during informal trilateral meetings with American, European, and Australian officials representing the Cairns Group.[73] These meetings in effect gave the Group de facto status as the "third force" in the agricultural negotiations.

Above all, of course, concrete evidence of the importance of the Group is found in the adoption by the major players of its proposals, especially the freeze on the existing support levels, the early cutback in 1990, and the formulation of a longer-term package by the end of 1990. The U.S. proposals for the November 1989 agricultural negotiations group meeting in Geneva drew extensively on the Cairns Group's initiatives, especially on its commitment to "tariffication" of nontariff import access barriers and a ten-year timetable for the total prohibition of subsidies and other trade-distorting measures.[74] This major softening of the initial U.S. negotiating position brought the United States much closer to the Cairns Group and provided what Michael Duffy has called a "circuit breaker" in the agricultural negotiations.[75]

The position of the EC, however, continues to differ sharply from that of the United States and the Cairns Group. As outlined in its negotiating paper, the EC still defends price support intervention to prevent abrupt adjustments of agricultural production in cyclical crises. This position leaves the CAP mechanisms largely unchanged and continues agricultural surpluses through price support. The EC also adheres to its proposal for the reduction program based on aggregation of all internal support mechanisms, a proposal that remains much too imprecise for either the United States or the Cairns Group.

A situation in which the position of one of the major players – in this case, the United States – moves toward that of the Cairns Group leaves open the prospect for some change in the Group's negotiating strategy. After functioning as an "honest broker" and keeping the agenda moving along in the early stages of the Uruguay Round, the Group may in the final stages move to throw its weight behind the U.S. position and keep pressure on the EC to accept more substantial reform than it has to date accepted in the negotiations. But a negotiating shift such as this is not necessarily inevitable, given the willingness of the EC to adopt the "tariffication" proposals and to be move flexible. Because of the differences of opinion between the United States and the EC, the Cairns Group has established a procedure for monitoring the compliance levels of participants to the freeze and cutback measures. While Cairns Group members, especially Australian negotiators, would argue that any initiatives which create a greater transparency in contracting party behavior are good things in their own right, the short-term issue of compliance throughout 1990 is clearly an important consideration in securing a favorable outcome in the Uruguay Round. Goodwill and trust in the bona fide intentions of the major actors is becoming an increasingly important question for smaller players cognizant of the growing recourse that major players have to economically nationalist activity in other domains, including the U.S.–Canada Free Trade Agreement and Europe 1992.

Although this section of our article has concentrated on the process of negotiation in the current round, care must be taken not to lose sight of the larger context and of the factors that constrain the prospects for reform. Analysis cannot be quantified in a simple debit-credit fashion, since many of the factors that should dictate the imperative for successful agricultural reform are also the chief reasons why reform is so difficult to secure. For example, while the high cost of EC and U.S. farm support programs – representing over 60 percent of the EC budget and costing the United States $30 billion in 1985[76] – generates considerable political hostility toward them and thus generates some desire for change, their very size nevertheless militates against action. The size of the U.S. budget deficit in fact undermines the leadership role of the United States in the MTNs in a number of ways. Since it requires more and has less to give, it cannot in this round make the kind of concessions it made in previous rounds.[77] Its major negotiating asset is not the distribution of largesse but, rather, the prospect for the negative sanction of increased protectionism in industrial trade if liberalization in agricultural trade is not forthcoming.[78] Further, the fact that attempts to "manage" trade outside the norms and principles of multilateralism – via specific reciprocity, subsidy, or other measures – may have their own pitfalls for the United States does not mean the measures are without considerable domestic support and, as a consequence, influence over the conduct of negotiations in the current round. It has, however, been the impact of the Cairns Group within the negotiating process, rather than the impact of exogenous variables on that process, which has been the focus of our analysis in this section.

CONCLUSION

At our boldest, we have argued that the Cairns Group has been a major force, indeed the "third force," in the Uruguay Round. Its role in setting the agenda and providing an important "middle way" for progress when negotiations between the United States and the EC have appeared to be heading for deadlock has been of the utmost significance. But two caveats in our analysis should be noted. First, the Uruguay Round is still in progress and will conclude at the end of 1990 if it keeps within its current time frame.[79] It thus remains to be seen whether the Cairns Group will be successful in securing its desired outcome of a freer, nondiscriminatory, and more open trade regime for agriculture. Second, our emphasis on the Cairns Group as a "third force" in the negotiations has inevitably been at the expense of a more detailed analysis of the negotiating positions and actions of the other major players. Our justification for this is twofold. Not only are the positions of the major players better understood, but the Cairns Group is also, we have argued, a sufficiently novel coalition of states to be of considerable interest in its own right to students of international political economy and to practitioners of multilateral economic negotiations. Thus, by viewing the Uruguay Round through the lenses of the Group, we are in fact providing a corrective to other MTN analyses, which have tended to focus on the major powers.

In our article, we have attempted to show that notwithstanding the heterogeneity of the Cairns Group's membership, the Group's aims and policy approach to the Uruguay Round have demonstrated a surprising degree of homogeneity and solidarity. This is because areas of potential conflict in the Group's various interests (regarding services and intellectual property, for example) have been kept firmly in a secondary position behind the goal of agricultural reform. The Group has not overplayed its hand or tried to push negotiating parties beyond what their own domestic political constraints or action would permit. Moreover, by keeping its aims sharply focused on the single issue of agricultural reform, the Group has avoided ideological conflict and the dissipation of its energies in pursuit of wider nontangible goals.

The Group's approach has been firmly anchored in the understanding that agricultural reform is not simply a technical or market-specific process but a political process and, as Henry Nau notes, primarily a domestic political process at that.[80] While informal groups in general and commodity groups in particular have existed before in GATT, these have largely been groups of officials concerned with activities related to a specific commodity, such as sugar. The Cairns Group has gone considerably beyond this approach. Its efforts to reform agricultural trade have been underpinned by a greater recourse than in previous rounds to the ministerial decision-making process as a way of overcoming the potential for bureaucratic inertia in the negotiating process. Australian negotiators were especially aware of the degree to which political action at various stages, but especially in the pre-negotiation phase at Punte del Este,[81] would be needed to break technical and other deadlocks. Small players acting individually would have no role in the negotiations as a political process. The formation of the Cairns Group was designed to overcome this disadvantage.

The preparation and research underpinning the Group's negotiating position have been important to its performance. Instrumental here, we have argued, has been the role of Australia as intellectual leader, provider of technical support, and political convener of the Group. In arguing that Australia has been innovative both in its refinements of the analytic abilities of states to measure and identify liberality in the trading system and in its consistency of intellectual commitment to free trade, we are not unaware of the long history of protection in Australia, especially protection of the manufacturing sector. Indeed, it is this history that makes the intellectual sea change in Australia in the 1980s so very interesting.[82] In addition, the valuable role of the Australian multilateral trade bureaucracy in providing supporting documentation and argumentation for the Cairns Group positions in the Uruguay Round has been widely recognized. The technical competence of Australia has been of considerable importance in establishing the Group's credibility and its need to be taken seriously in the negotiations.

At the political level, Australia's acceptability to a variety of competing political and ideological interests in the current MTNs is important. Its economic profile as a commodity exporter, its regional location in the Southern Hemisphere, and its stand on various North–South issues over the last decade have placed it in good stead with the LDCs. At the same time, however, Australia's membership in the Western alliance in general and in the Australia–New Zealand–U.S. (ANZUS) alliance in particular and its close economic relationship with Japan have helped convince the other major actors in the Uruguay Round of the Group's moderation and earnestness of intent.

Our emphasis on Australian leadership within the Cairns Group is not without wider analytic insight for more general efforts to secure global economic reform. As Oran Young noted in a recent discussion of regime formation in this journal, leadership is not simply a function of hegemony. It is also a question of entrepreneurship involving "a combination of imagination in inventing institutional options and skill in brokering the interests of numerous actors to line up support for such options."[83] Our case study of Australian activity in the Cairns Group would, we hope, provide some empirical support not only for this argument but also for Young's more general observation that the two principal models or explanations for regime formation – regimes are formed either by rational utility maximizing or by power maximizing – are inadequate when treated as mutually exclusive. Following Young, we would argue that elements of both of these and additional models are necessary to understand the formation and approach of the Cairns Group. Australia and the other members of the Group are clearly egoistic actors seeking to maximize the prospects for securing the economic benefits of a freer and more open agricultural regime, prospects that are unlikely to come about in the absence of major institutional reform. To this end, they are evidently utility maximizers. But this is not a sufficient explanation. The Cairns Group is also engaged in power maximizing by the assertion of its aggregate strength in a variety of major agricultural markets. Yet the success of the Group is still inadequately explained by these two sets of factors. We have offered the role of Australian entrepreneurial and technical leadership as the vital added dimension that explains why the group has managed to hang together in the face of both external and internal pressures.

In explaining Australia's incentives for taking on the leadership role, we must look beyond the self-interest of an egoistic actor engaged in economic welfare maximization. Here the self-perception of Australia's role in the contemporary international order is important. It is not simply that Australia, in Young's words, is "an ethically motivated actor . . . [seeking] to fashion a workable institutional arrangement as a contribution to the common good."[84] It is also that Australia has a central component of its foreign policy under the Hawke Labor government the goal of being a "good international citizen," the essence of which is "strengthening the machinery of multilateralism" as part of a process of what Gareth Evans, Minister of Foreign Affairs and Trade, calls "enlightened self-interest."[85]

A sophisticated commitment to leadership on the part of Australia, a significant aggregate share of global agricultural trade, and a common interest in reform are three of the factors accounting for the Cairns Group's strength as a coalition. A fourth factor is the innovativeness of the Group's ideas and the persuasiveness with which these ideas have been introduced in the negotiations. It has been this factor that has cemented the Group's strategically significant position in the negotiations and has gained it the reputation of being not only an "agenda moving coalition" but also a "proposal making coalition."[86] As we have demonstrated, the Group's ideas and initiatives have been successful in at least two ways. First, they have provided a "middle way" between the two major protagonists without simply being exercises in "difference splitting." Specifically, they have recognized the degree to which procedure is a central factor in the success of any reform process. The Group's initiatives have thus been geared toward generating confidence in the procedures. Second, the ideas of the Group have represented a substantive contribution to the debate, in both its technical and political guises, over how to advance the process of agricultural reform. The Group has not only offered proposals geared toward securing immediate short-term relief but has also given suggestions for longer-term goals that would, if adopted, provide for rational and significant reform in international trade in agriculture. No other body, coalition, group, or individual actor in the Uruguay Round has provided such a significant contribution to the amelioration of differences between the major actors or offered such concrete proposals for reform.

The power of the Cairns Group has stemmed less from the fact that it has bargained away concessions to the other negotiating parties in return for support for its position than from the fact that it has provided a genuine alternative middle ground upon which the major actors could meet. To date, the Group has used the threat of sanction sparingly. It has not acted as a "blocking coalition." The closest it has come to such activity was at the midterm review. As we suggested in our earlier discussion of the midterm review, the threat of blocking progress in other negotiating panels if reform on agriculture was not forthcoming (a threat brought on by the Latin American members of the Group) was, despite the uncoordinated nature of the action, not without success. The action would have been unlikely to have had the influence it did, however, if it had not been for the Group's record of constructive action in the earlier stages of the Uruguay Round. While the behavior of the Latin Americans and the Australians in the Group at the midterm review was not, if it is fair to say, unlike the well-worn "hard cop/ soft cop routine, it is difficult to gauge the degree to which such an approach would be successful in the final stages of the round. For example, initiatives to free up trade in services and protect intellectual property have emerged as high-priority concerns for both the United States and the EC in the closing stages of the round. Although the Cairns Group to date has not explicitly linked success in these areas to success in agricultural reform, it is unlikely that the more radical members of the Group, with mixed feelings about the direct benefits to them of an agreement on services and intellectual property, will resist the temptation to use what leverage they have to block this agreement in the absence of major reform in agriculture. While such an approach would clearly test the Group's unity, given the interests of Australia, Canada, and a few other members of the Group in a services and intellectual property agreement, its possibility remains a strong factor inhibiting the prospect for an imposed U.S.–EC agricultural agreement. The Group's potential to forestall any such bilaterally imposed deal is seen by Secretary-General Dunkel as the great strength of the Cairns Group and a major contribution to the negotiating process.

Lest the posture and the performance of the Cairns Group appear overstated in our analysis, we can compare them briefly with those of the coalition of smaller states that attempted to secure a new international economic order (NIEO) in the 1970s. The coalition's conceptual framework for an NIEO was broad and poorly defined, with its aims appearing to be more a "wish list" than a set of specific and tightly articulated proposals, and the research and preparation leading to the call for an NIEO was far weaker than that of the Cairns Group. In addition, the coalition's tactics to secure NIEO reforms outstripped what could realistically be regarded as likely to secure negotiating success in any North–South standoff. Not only was political conflict within the Southern camp frequently ideological in nature and invariably not constrained, but the political commitment required from member states was greater than the control of their own domestic polities would allow them.[87] While we have not tried to gloss over the conflicts that exist within the Cairns Group or the degree to which domestic political pressures run counter to Group policy and posture (notably in Canada), we have demonstrated the degree to which these conflicts and difficulties have been contained by skilful and judicious processes of compromise and mediation.

If the Cairns Group ultimately fails to secure major reform in agricultural trade, it will not be for want of purpose or direction, lack of an appropriate bargaining strategy, or inability to maintain unity among Group members. Rather, the failure to secure a new agricultural regime will be conditioned by constraints generated within and between the other major actors. The history of GATT in particular and the international trade regime in general over the last few decades illustrates the degree to which major actors are able to stall negotiations by adopting positions of considerable rigidity. In this regard, the importance of the Cairns Group to date is attributable less to the fact that it has tried to impel the major protagonists to accept its positions either by the force of its collective economic weight or by the force of rational argument – strong as both may be – than to the fact that it has tried to build confidence and provide a "middle way" for the major players to move beyond positions of intransigence when they decide for whatever reason (such as a change of domestic leadership or administration) that the timing is right. As such, the activities of the Cairns Group are an important contribution to our general understanding of efforts are confidence building in international economic relations, efforts that have been the focus of little analysis to date.

That there is a dearth of studies regarding confidence building in the international economy is perhaps not altogether surprising. It is only of late that research on the matter has become significant. Confidence building is a definitionally illusive concept and is often not an activity explicitly articulated by those engaged in its practice. Indeed, the psychology of international economic relations has not been subjected to the same sophisticated scrutiny as has the psychology of international security, which has been analyzed by Robert Jervis and other scholars.[88] Yet it must be apparent to all who monitor economic relations between the major economic actors, especially U.S.–EC and U.S.–Japan relations, that *perceptions* of mistrust and misunderstanding are every bit as significant in the potential for conflict between states as is the *reality* of fiercer economic competition in a more globally interdependent era. It is certainly evident to the smaller players in global economic relations that stand to be adversely affected by enhanced conflict. In its attempts to bridge gaps and build confidence in the relationship between the major players in the Uruguay Round, the Cairns Group represents a concerted response by the smaller, but collectively not insignificant, powers to their inherent individual inability to influence large-scale multilateral economic negotiations.

The immediate future of the Uruguay Round is, therefore, of considerable interest. It is, in effect, a laboratory in which to observe the degree to which the Cairns Group of Fair Trading Nations can support and enhance an environment that minimizes the proclivities for rigidity and conflict and maximizes the prospect for greater collaboration toward the goal of agricultural reform. The Cairns Group demonstrates both the strengths and the weaknesses of coalitions in the transformation of international regimes. It would appear that it cannot, of its own accord, make or break a regime. On the other hand, if the role of the Cairns Group is to be our yardstick, a well-organized and for the most part united coalition practicing the politics of brokerage and constraint can play a major role in providing intellectual leadership, diplomacy, and strategically weighted assistance to the other principal actors in specific cases of regime support or regime transformation.

Although clearly unable to substitute for the role of a hegemon that is no longer willing or able to make the preponderant contribution to maintaining cooperation in what is now popularly called the posthegemonic era, a purposive issue-oriented coalition such as the Cairns Group can play an important secondary role in the process of securing cooperation between the waning hegemon and the other major actors. The policymakers driving the Cairns Group's strategy in the Uruguay Round may not have read Robert Keohane's *After Hegemony*, but in keeping with his analysis, their behavior is clearly egoistic and realist in the pursuit of state-defined interests and consistent with the recognition that if there is to be cooperation "it will be cooperation without hegemony." Further, as Keohane also notes, like many other international institutions, GATT was created "under conditions of American hegemony."[89] While we make no normative judgments on the nature of that hegemony, we will conclude by noting that the degree to which it will continue to ensure openness and liberality in the international trading system may be conditioned by the constructive, reform-minded, cooperation-inducing activities of coalitions such as the Cairns Group.

We have been at pains to stress that the longer-term significance of the Cairns Group as a subject of study is not constrained simply by the outcome of the Uruguay Round. Rather, we see it as a pointer to the need for a renewed interest, at both the scholarly and policy level, in forms of leadership in the international order that differ from those to which we had become almost instinctively responsive "under hegemony." In this regard, the Cairns Group provides an initial locus for at least two wider avenues of theoretical investigation in the 1990s. The first, following the work of Oran Young, is the complex and evolving nature of leadership in international cooperation in general and in regime building in particular. The activities of the Group provide a fertile environment for examining Young's threefold classification of structural, entrepreneurial, and technical leadership.[90] The second avenue of investigation that needs more attention in the 1990s than it received in the previous decade is the role of coalition building by smaller players in the global order. While the decline of studies in this regard may have been understandable in the wake of the failed attempts by the developing countries to bring about reform through collective pressure in the late 1970s, the 1990s may offer a set of circumstances and opportunities conducive to renewed exercises in coalition building. As Stanley Hoffman has noted, the 1990s will be a period when "games of skill must replace tests of will."[91] If the activities of the Cairns Group demonstrate nothing else, they show that the prospect for innovation and variety in coalition building is much greater than the earlier literature on the subject led us to believe. Further, recent literature would suggest that the Group offers but one example of emerging "middle power," "like-minded," and "North–South" coalition building[92] across a variety of issue-areas in which innovative entrepreneurial and technical leadership might provide a substantial counterweight to and support system for more traditional structural or power-driven forms of leadership.

NOTES

This article is the first enterprise in our larger project involving the comparison of Australian and Canadian foreign policy. It is a jointly authored article in which we have chosen to ignore the alphabet for naming purposes. We thank Stuart Harris, Richard Leaver, and Jim Richardson of the Australian National University, Peter Field and Peter Gallagher of the Australian Department of Foreign Affairs and Trade, Kim Richard Nossal of McMaster University, T. K. Warley of Guelph University, and the editor and two anonymous referees of *International Organization* for their helpful and constructive comments on earlier drafts of this article. We also thank Lynne Payne for all her efforts in the final preparation of the article. We are grateful to the Social Sciences and Humanities Research Council of Canada for the financial support of Andrew Cooper's work. Richard Higgott has, for the last two years, been a member of the Australian Minister for Trade Negotiations Advisory Group. Needless to say, the views expressed in this article are our own and do not represent the views of the groups, institutions, or individuals acknowledged above.

1 Robert O. Keohane, *After Hegemony: Cooperation and Discord in the World Political Economy* (Princeton, N.J.: Princeton University Press, 1984).

2 For a discussion of strategies that less developed countries have used through bodies such as the Group of 77 to secure a new international economic order (NIEO), see, for example, Stephen D. Krasner, *Structural Conflict: The Third World Against Global Liberation* (Los Angeles: University of California Press, 1985); Robert L. Rothstein, *Global Bargaining: UNCTAD and the Quest for an NIEO* (Princeton, N.J.: Princeton University Press, 1979); and Robert L. Rothstein, *The Weak in the World of the Strong* (New York: Columbia University Press, 1977).

3 Even two of the most recent works on the Uruguay Round make only passing mention of the role of the Cairns Group in the negotiations. See Henry Nau, ed., *Domestic Trade Policy and the Uruguay Round* (New York: Columbia University Press, 1989); and Gilbert Winham, "The Pre-Negotiation Phase of the Uruguay Round," *International Journal* 44 (Spring 1989), pp. 280–303. It is for this reason and even at the risk of overstating the role of the Cairns Group that we feel our corrective case study is necessary.

4 Krasner has persuasively argued that a change in the configuration of power was in fact under way in the Tokyo Round. See Stephen D. Krasner, "The Tokyo Round: Particularistic Interests and Prospects for Stability in the Global Trading System," *International Studies Quarterly* 23 (December 1979), pp. 491–531.

5 Winham, "The Pre-Negotiation Phase of the Uruguay Round," p. 290.

6 Ibid., pp. 286–87.

7 The nature of this change is, of course, much contested, but it cannot be reviewed here. For examples of competing interpretations, see Robert Keohane, "The World Political Economy: The Crisis of Embedded Liberalism," in John Goldthorpe, ed., *Order and Conflict in Contemporary Capitalism* (Oxford: Clarendon Press, 1984), pp. 15–38; Robert Gilpin, *The Political Economy of International Relations* (Princeton, N.J.: Princeton University Press 1987); Robert Cox, *Power, Production and World Order* (New York: Columbia University Press, 1987); Stephen Gill and David Law, *Global Political Economy* (Baltimore, Md.: Johns Hopkins University Press, 1988); Bruce Russett, "The Mysterious Case of Vanishing Hegemony," *International Organization* 39 (Spring 1985), pp. 207–31; Susan Strange, "The Persistent Myth of Lost Hegemony," *International Organization* 41 (Autumn 1987), pp. 551–74; and Walter Russell-Mead, "The United States and the World Economy," *World Policy* 6 (Winter 1988), pp. 1–47.

8 See John Odell, *U.S. International Monetary Policy* (Princeton, N.J.: Princeton University Press, 1982); and Fred Block, *The Origins of International Economic Disorder* (Berkeley: University of California Press, 1977).

9 See Michael C. Webb and Stephen D. Krasner, "Hegemonic Stability Theory: An Empirical Assessment," *Review of International Studies* 15 (Spring 1989), pp. 183–98.

10 See Gilbert R. Winham, *International Trade and the Tokyo Round Negotiation* (Princeton, N.J.: Princeton University Press, 1986). See also Jock A. Finlayson and Mark W. Zacher, "The GATT and the Regulation of Trade Barriers: Regime Dynamics and Functions," in Stephen D. Krasner, ed., *International Regimes* (Ithaca, N.Y.: Cornell University Press, 1983), pp. 273–314.

11 For a discussion about the early period, see Gerald Maier, "The Politics of Productivity: Foundations of American International Economic Policy After World War II," *International Organization* 31 (Summer 1977), pp. 607–34.
12 Gilpin, *The Political Economy of International Relations.*
13 See, for example, Paul Krugman, ed., *Strategic Trade Policy and the New International Economics* (Cambridge, Mass.: MIT Press, 1986); Jagdish Bhagwati, *Protectionism* (Cambridge, Mass.: MIT Press, 1988); and R. Pomfret, *Unequal Trade: The Economics of Discriminatory International Trade Policies* (Oxford: Basil Blackwell, 1988).
14 Raymond Hopkins and Donald J. Puchala, eds., *The Global Political Economy of Food*, special issue of *International Organization* 32 (Spring 1978), pp. 581–880.
15 For an excellent discussion of American agricultural policy in this period, see Ivan Roberts et al., *U.S. Grain Policies and the World Market* (Canberra: Australian Bureau of Agricultural and Resource Economics, 1989), pp. 17–27.
16 See D. G. Johnson, "Food Reserves and International Trade Policy," in J. S. Hillman and A. Schmitz, eds., *International Trade and Agriculture: Theory and Policy* (Boulder, Colo.: Lynne Reinner, 1979), p. 247. See also, however, Andrew F. Cooper, "The Protein Link: Complexity in the US–EC AGricultural Trade Relationship," *Journal of European Integration* 11 (Winter 1987), pp. 29–45.
17 Fred H. Sanderson, *Japan's Food Prospects and Policies* (Washington, D.C.: Brookings Institution, 1978).
18 *The Economist*, 28 December 1974, p. 44.
19 D. G. Johnson, K. Hemmi, and P. Lardinois, *Agricultural Policy and Trade: Adjusting Domestic Programs in an International Framework – A Report to the Trilateral Commission* (New York: New York University Press, 1985).
20 Paul Lewis, "Europe's Farm Policies Clash with American Export Goals," *The New York Times*, 22 February 1983, pp. 1 and 5.
21 See, for example, Elaine Frost, *For Richer, For Poorer: The New U.S.–Japan Relationship* (New York: Council on Foreign Relations, 1987); Benjamin J. Cohen, "An Explosion in the Kitchen? Economic Relations with Other Advanced Countries," in Kenneth Oye, Robert J. Leiber, and Donald Rothchild, eds., *Eagle Defiant: United States Foreign Policy in the 1980s* (Boston: Little, Brown, 1983), pp. 105–30; and Stephen D. Krasner, *Asymmetries in Japanese–American Trade: The Case for Specific Reciprocity* (Berkeley: University California, Institute of International Studies, 1987).
22 For a good discussion of Holmes' work and the question of middle powers in general, see Kim Richard Nossal, *The Politics of Canadian Foreign Policy*, 2d ed. (Scarborough, Ontario: Prentice-Hall, 1989), pp. 46–52.
23 Ibid., p. 50.
24 See Carsten Holbraad, *Middle Powers in International Polities* (London: Macmillan, 1984), p. 57; Annette Fox, *The Politics of Attraction: Four Middle Powers and the United States* (New York: Columbia University Press, 1977); Annette Fox, "The Range of Choice for Middle Powers: Australia and Canada Compared," *Australian Journal of Politics and History* 26 (Spring 1980), pp. 193–203; and Forschungsinsitut der Deutschen Gesellschaft fur Answartige Politik, *The Rule of Middle Powers in World Politics*, Bonn, 1969.
25 Clyde Sanger, *Ordering the Oceans: The Making of the Law of the Sea* (Toronto: University of Toronto Press, 1987), pp. 52–53 and 55.
26 For a discussion of the diversion between food-exporting and food-importing developing countries, see Andrew F. Cooper, "Exporters Versus Importers: LDCs, Agricultural Trade and the Uruguay Round," *Intereconomics* 25 (Winter 1990), pp. 13–17.
27 See John Holmes, *The Shaping of Peace: Canada and the Search for World Order, 1943–1957*, vol. 1 (Toronto: University of Toronto Press, 1976); and Escott Reid, *On Duty:*

A Canadian at the Making of the United Nations, 1945–1946 (Kent, Ohio: Kent State University Press, 1983).

28 Fox, "The Range of Choice for Middle Powers," p. 194.

29 Canadian House of Commons, *Debates*, 21 July 1969, p. 11398.

30 Tom Connors, *The Australian Wheat Industry: Its Economics and Politics* (Armidale, Australia: Gill, 1972), pp. 120–21.

31 Alan Renouf, *The Frightened Country* (Melbourne: Macmillan, 1979).

32 "Canada Assured on Crop Disposal," The *New York Times*, 17 March 1954, p. 21.

33 Keohane, "The World Political Economy."

34 See Michael East, "National Attributes and Foreign Policy," in Charles Herman et al., eds, *Why Nations Act* (Beverly Hills, Calif.: Sage, 1978) pp. 121ff.

35 See the following works by Richard A. Higott: *The World Economic Order and the Trade Crisis: Implications for Australia* (Canberra: Australian Institute of International Affairs 1987); and "Australia and the New International Division of Labor in the Asia Pacific Region," in J. Caporaso, ed., *A Changing International Division of Labor* (Boulder, Colo.: Lynne Reiner, 1987), pp. 147–85.

36 For a discussion of Canada's position, see David B. Dewitt and John Kirton, *Canada as a Principal Power* (Toronto: John Wiley, 1983); and Nossal, *The Politics of Canadian Foreign Policy*. For a discussion of Australia's position, see the following works by Richard A. Higott: "The Ascendency of the Economic Dimension in Australian–American Relations," in J. Ravenhill, ed., *No Longer an American Lake: U.S. Policy in the Pacific in the 1980s* (Berkeley: University of California, Institute of International Studies, 1988), pp. 132–68; and *The Evolving World Economy: Some Alternative Security Questions for Australia* (Canberra: Strategic and Defence Studies Centre, Australian National University, 1989).

37 Peter Field, "Without the GATT Round: What Else?" in *Recent Trends in World Trade: Implications for Australia* (Sydney: Australian Institute of International Affairs, 1987), pp. 1–6.

38 Anthony Hoy, "Australia Must Attack in Farm War," *The Australian*, 28 May 1986, p. 9.

39 See *The Toronto Globe and Mail*, 28 December 1981; and *The Australian*, 6 April 1983, p. 7.

40 See Paul Hasluck, *Diplomatic Witness: Australian Foreign Affairs, 1941–1947* (Melbourne: Melbourne University Press, 1980); and Reid, *On Duty*.

41 John McEwen, Australian House of Representatives, *Debates*, 10 May 1965, p. 1635.

42 See, for example, Bureau of Agricultural Economics, *Japanese Agricultural Policies: Their Origins, Nature and Effects on Production and Trade* (Canberra; Australian Government Publishing Service, 1981); Bureau of Agricultural Economics, *Agricultural Policies in the European Community: Their Origins, Nature and Effects on Production and Trade* (Canberra: Australian Government Publishing Service, 1985); G. Miller, *The Political Economy of International Agricultural Policy Reform* (Canberra: Department of Primary Industry, 1986); Centre for International Economics, *The Game Plan: Successful Strategies for Australian Trade* (Canberra: Centre for International Economics, 1987); A. Stoeckel, *Intersectoral Effects of the CAP: Growth, Trade and Unemployment* (Canberra: Australian Government Publishing Service, 1985); and Bureau of Agricultural and Resource Economics, *Japanese Beef Policies: Implications for Trade, Prices and Market Sahres* (Canberra: Australian Government Publishing Service, 1988).

43 OECD, *National Policies and Agricultural Trade* (Paris: OECD, 1987).

44 See Amanda Buckley, "Aust Hopes to Help Found Group to Counter Protectionist Traders," *Australian Financial Review*, 25 August 1986, p. 10.

45 See *The Weekend Australian*, 16–17 August 1986, p. 1; and Barry Critchley, "Fair

Traders Taking Aim at Agricultural Subsidies," *Financial Post* (Toronto), 23 August 1986, p. 7.

46 Cairns Group, *Comprehensive Proposal for the Reform of Agriculture*, Chiang Mai, Thailand, 21–23 November 1989.

47 For a good introduction to the issue of confidence building, see R. A. Byers, Stephen F. Larrabee, and A. Lynch, eds, *Confidence Building Measures and International Security* (New York: East–West Security Studies Center, 1987). See also, however, J. Alford, "The Usefulness and Limitations of CBMs" and H. B. Brauch, "Confidence Building and Disarmament-Supporting Measures," both in W. Epstein and B. Feld, eds, *New Dimensions in Disarmament* (New York: Praeger, 1981), pp. 133–60.

48 See, for example, two important documents produced by the Australian Department of Foreign Affairs and Trade and published in Canberra in 1989; *Measuring the Impact of Trade Protection* and *Using the Effective Rate of Assistance in Trade Negotiations.*

49 See *The Age* (Melbourne), 26 August 1986, p. 1. For a fuller discussion, see P. Gallagher, "Setting the Agenda for Trade Negotiations: Australia and the Cairns Group," *Australian Outlook: The Australian Journal of International Affairs* 44 (April 1988), pp. 3–8.

50 Cairns Group, *Declaration of the Ministerial Meeting of Fair Traders in Agriculture*, Cairns, Australia, 26 August 1986.

51 Although Australia's role in the international system cannot be discussed in detail here, we should note that Australian foreign policy through the 1980s was characterized by a high degree of initiative and activity in a number of forums and on a number of issues other than trade regime reform. In the late 1980s, for example, Australia set forth major initiatives on Asia–Pacific economic cooperation, confidence building in North Pacific security, conservation in the Antarctic, resolution of the Cambodian question, and the control of chemical weapons.

52 See Australian House of Representatives, *Debates*, 10 October 1986. See also Department of Trade, *Transforming Australia's Trade: Annual Report, 1986–87* (Canberra: Australian Government Publishing Service, 1987), pp. 17–20.

53 Jeffrey J. Schott, ed., *Free Trade Areas and U.S. Trade Policy* (Washington, D.C. Institute for International Economics, 1989).

54 Cairns Group, *Declaration of the Ministerial Meeting of Fair Traders in Agriculture.*

55 Dale F. Hathaway, *Agriculture and the GATT: Rewriting the Rules* (Washington, D.C., Institute for International Economics, 1988).

56 Winham, "The Pre-Negotiation Phase of the Uruguay Round."

57 See *Journal of Commerce*, 27 May 1987, p. 10A. See also "Cairns Group Brings Sanity to GATT," *Agra Europe*, 23 October 1987, p. 1.

58 Compare the two proposals: Cairns Group, "Proposal to the Uruguay Round Negotiating Group on Agriculture," no. UR-87-0322, GATT, 10 December 1987; and United States, "Proposal for Negotiations on Agriculture," no. UR-87-0186. GATT, 7 July 1987.

59 Personal correspondence to Richard Higgott from Peter Field, deputy secretary of the Australian Department of Foreign Affairs and Trade and Australia's chief negotiator at the Uruguay Round, 22 September 1989.

60 *Australian Financial Review*, 14 January 1988, p. 10.

61 See Crawford Pratt, ed., *Internationalism Under Strain: The North–South Policies of Canada, the Netherlands, Norway, and Sweden* (Toronto: University of Toronto Press, 1989), pp. 45–49.

62 Canadian House of Commons, *Debates*, 28 April 1987, p. 5357.

63 Peter Benesh, "Canada Breaks Free Trade Solidarity with Subsidies," *The Age* (Melbourne), 18 December 1987, p. 9.

64 Richard H. Snape, "Should Australia Seek a Trade Agreement with the United States?"

discussion paper no. 86/01, Australian Economic Planning Advisory Council and Department of Trade, 1986.

65 See Cairns Group, "Time for Action: A Proposal for a Framework Approach for Agriculture," no. MTN.GNG/NG5/W/69, GATT, 13 July 1988, p. 5, which explicitly stated that the LDCs "should be exempted from contributing to the first steps to long-term reform." See also "Australia Will Recognise Exceptions to Free Trade for Developing Countries," *Australian Financial Review*, 22 May 1978, p. 6.

66 See Bernard Hockman, "Determining the Need for Issue Linkages in Multilateral Trade Negotiations," *International Organization* 43 (Autumn 1989), pp. 693–714.

67 See Michael Aho, "Foreword," in Robert L. Paarlberg, *Fixing Farm Trade: Options for the United States* (Cambridge, Mass.: Ballinger, 1988), p. viii. See also, however, Nau, *Domestic Trade Politics and the Uruguay Round.*

68 Canada, "Proposal by Canada Regarding the Multilateral Trade Negotiations in Agriculture," no. MTN.GNG/NG5/W19. GATT, 20 October 1987, p. 1.

69 See, for example, Sarah Sargent, "Cairns Group May Lose Canada," *Australian Financial Review*, 7 July 1988, p. 5.

70 See Peter Dockrill, "Aussies Pressed to Cut Subsidies," *Calgary Herald*, 8 July 1988; and *Winnipeg Free Press*, 23 July 1988, p. 41.

71 Australia, "Illustrative Elements of Commitments to Reduce Support as Part of First Steps to Long-Term Reform," no. MTN.GNG/NG5/W/70/Rev. 1, GATT, 13 July 1988.

72 Trade Negotiations Committee, "Meeting at the Level of High Officials," no. UR-89-0029, NTN-TNC/9, GATT, 11 April 1989, pp. 3–7.

73 Field, personal correspondence, 22 September 1989.

74 United States, "Submission of the United States on Comprehensive Long-Term Agricultural Reform," no. MTN.GNG/NG5/W/118, GATT, 28 October 1989.

75 See *Australian Financial Review*, 23 October 1989, p. 12.

76 Miller, *The Political Economy of International Agricultural Policy Reform*, p. 12.

77 Paarlberg, *Fixing Farm Trade.*

78 One U.S. observer has recently gone as far as to describe the United States as the bully boy of world trade. See William Niskanen, "The Bully of World Trade," *Orbis* 33 (Autumn 1989), pp. 531–38.

79 We should perhaps note here the manner in which the rounds have progressively increased in duration, with the Kennedy Round and Tokyo Round taking five and six years, respectively.

80 Henry Nau, "Preface," in Nau, *Domestic Trade Politics*, p. xiii.

81 See Kym Anderson and Ross Garnaut, *Australian Protectionism: Extent: Causes and Effect* (Sydney: Allen & Unwin, 1986).

82 Gallagher, "Setting the Agenda for Trade Negotiations," p. 5.

83 Oran Young, "The Politics of International Regime Formation: Managing Natural Resources and the Environment," *International Organization* 41 (Summer 1989), p. 335.

84 Ibid., p. 373.

85 See Gareth Evans, "Australian Foreign Policy: Priorities in a Changing World," *Australian Outlook: The Australian Journal of International Affairs* 43 (August 1989), p. 13. See also Gareth Evans, *Australia's Regional Security* (Canberra: Department of Foreign Affairs and Trade, 1989), in which similar themes are confirmed.

86 Colleen Hamilton and John Whalley, "Coalitions in the Uruguay Round," *Weltwirtschaftliches Archiv* 125 (Winter 1989), pp. 547–62.

87 For a discussion of the NIEO, see R. L. Rothstein, "Regime Creation by a Coalition of the Weak: Lessons for the NIEO and the Integrated Program for Commodities," *International Studies Quarterly* 28 (Summer 1984), pp. 307–28.

88 See, for example, Robert Jervis, Richard Ned Lebow, and Janice Gross Stein, *Psychology and Deterrence* (Baltimore, Md.: Hopkins University Press, 1985); and Robert Jervis, *The Meaning of Nuclear Revolution: Statecraft and the Prospect of Armageddon* (Ithaca, N.Y.: Cornell University Press, 1989), especially chap. 5.
89 Keohane, *After Hegemony*, pp. 244–46.
90 Oran Young, "Political Leadership and Regime Formation: The Emergence of Institutions in International Society," paper presented at a meeting of the International Studies Association, 10–14 April 1990, Washington, D.C.
91 See Stanley Hoffman, "What Should We Do in the World?" *The Atlantic*, October 1989, p. 91. For a fuller exposition of this line of argument, see Richard Higgott, "Towards a Non-Hegemonic International Political Economy," in Craig Murphy and Roger Tooze, eds, *The New International Political Economy* (Boulder, Colo.: Lynne Reinner, forthcoming).
92 See Cranford Pratt, ed., *Middle-Power Internationalism: The North–South Dimension* (Montreal: McGill University Press, 1990); Fen Osler Hampson, "Climate Change: Building Coalitions of the Like-Minded," *International Journal* 45 (Winter 1990), pp. 36–74; and Bernard Wood, "Towards North–South Middle Power Coalitions," in Pratt, *Middle-Power Internationalism*.

6. Assessing the General Agreement on Trade in Services

B. Hoekman

One of the major results of the Uruguay Round was the creation of a General Agreement on Trade in Services. GATS establishes rules and disciplines for policies affecting access to service markets, greatly extending the coverage of the multilateral trading system. In some respects it is a landmark achievement. In other respects it can be considered a failure. It is a landmark in terms of creating multilateral disciplines in virgin territory; a failure in terms of generating liberalization. Commitments made in the Uruguay Round on services are best described as bound standstill agreements for policies pertaining to specific sectors. Abstracting from ongoing talks on financial services, liberalization awaits future rounds of negotiations. This suggests there are two key issues that must be addressed in evaluating GATS. First, what does it do to bind current policies? Second, has it established a mechanism that is likely to induce significant liberalization in the future? The primary objective of this chapter is to provide answers to these questions.

The chapter begins with a brief overview of global trade flows in services and a discussion of the implications of the lack of information on trade barriers for multilateral negotiations. Next, it provides a summary of the main elements of GATS and analyzes the sector coverage of the commitments made by the ninety-seven members that had presented their services schedules to the GATT Secretariat as of mid-1994.[1] The chapter discusses possible implications of the scheduling approach that was chosen, and asks whether future negotiations in the GATS context are likely to lead toward a fully nondiscriminatory trade regime (as opposed to managed trade). The final section of the chapter examines options for addressing the architectural weaknesses of GATS.

TRADE FLOWS, MARKET ACCESS BARRIERS, AND DATA ISSUES

Driven by innovations in information technology, increasing specialization, and product differentiation, as well as government policies such as deregulation and liberalization, trade in services grew faster than trade in merchandise throughout the last decade. In 1992 global-services trade (nonfactor services in the balance of payments, minus government transactions) stood at some US $930 billion (table 4.1). This was equal to 22.7 percent of global trade (goods plus services), compared with 18.8 percent in 1980. Such trade occurs across borders by way

TABLE 4.1 *Global services trade flows, 1980 and 1992*

Services	1980	1992	Average annual change
Total trade in services (US$ billion)	358	931	8.3
OECD	283	765	8.6
Rest of world	75	166	6.8
Services as share of goods and services (percent)	17.0	22.0	2.2
OECD	18.8	22.7	1.6
Rest of world	12.7	19.2	3.5

Note: data pertain only to countries reporting to the International Monetary Fund.
Source: World Bank.

of telecommunications, travel abroad by consumers (for example, tourism), or temporary entry of service providers into the territory of a consumer (for example, consulting). Over the last decade, the average annual growth rate of services trade was 8.3 percent. Both industrialized and developing countries have seen the relative importance of trade in services increase, although services account for a larger share of the total trade of OECD countries. In 1992 OECD countries accounted for 82 percent of global exports of commercial services, up from 79 percent in 1982.

Many services are not tradable, in the sense that cross-border interaction through telecommunication networks or temporary physical movement of providers and consumers is not enough to make an exchange feasible (Bhagwati 1984). Producers of such services can contest foreign markets only by establishing a long-term physical presence in terms, that is, engaging in FDI. Not surprisingly, such investment in services accounts for a large share of the total stock of inward FDI in most host countries. As of the early 1990s, some 50 percent of global stock of FDI was in service activities. The share of the annual flow to many countries has been over 60 percent in recent years.[2] The relative importance of trade in services (registered in a country's balance of payments) as opposed to sales of services by affiliates is not known. Conventional wisdom holds that FDI is the dominant "mode of supply" for many services, but that it is being eroded by technological developments. Data compiled by the United States – the only country that currently collects detailed data on both trade in services and sales of services by firms active in its market – suggest that trade and sales are of roughly the same importance.[3] Not too much can be inferred from this, however, as both trade and sales via FDI will in part reflect barriers to the provision of services imposed by partner countries. Quantitative measures of these barriers do not exist.

Available data on trade in services are weak compared with those on merchandise (box 4.1). Only a limited number of industrialized countries collect and report statistics on trade services at a relatively disaggregated level (ten categories or more). More non-OECD countries only report data on trade in commercial services, broken down into transport (largely freight and passenger transport by sea and air), travel (expenditures by nonresidents, mostly tourists, while staying in a foreign country),[4] and "other services." The last category includes items such as brokerage, insurance, communications, leasing and rental of equipment, technical and professional services, income generated by the temporary movement of labor, as well as property income (royalties).

In aggregate value, the OECD dominates global trade in services (table 4.2). This does not imply that developing countries have little interest in services trade. To the contrary, many developing countries are relatively specialized in exporting services, especially tourism. As RCA indices suggest,[5] small countries (defined as those with less than 1 million people) are the most specialized in this area. Moreover, their relative specialization increased significantly during the last decade. These countries have higher-than-average export intensives for all three services categories but are clearly most specialized in tourism. The relative importance of tourism receipts was about twice the world average in 1980, rising to over three times in 1992.

Cross-country data on the magnitude of barriers to trade in services do not exist. Because services tend to be intangible, barriers to trade do not take the form of import tariffs. Instead, trade barriers take the form of prohibitions, quantitative restrictions, and government regulation. Quantitative restrictions may limit the quantity or value of imports of specific products for a given time, or the number or market share of foreign service providers. Such discriminatory restrictions go hand in hand with measures that apply to both foreign and domestic service providers, usually limitations on the number of firms allowed to contest a market or on the nature of their operations. Frequently, this involves either a monopoly such as basic telecommunications services or an oligopolistic market structure (often the case in financial services or self-regulating professional services). Often such market structures are tolerated because of the information problems involved in the exchange of services. Considerations relating to consumer protection, prudential supervision, and regulatory oversight often induce governments to require establishment by foreign providers, such as financial or professional services, or to reserve activities for government-owned or -regulated entities.

The nonexistence of tariffs as a restraint to trade greatly complicates analysis of or negotiations on incremental reductions in barriers to services trade. Analysis requires an estimation of the tariff equivalent of a given set of measures and regulations pertaining to a service activity. Little work has been done in this connection.[6] Negotiators require a focal point, some tangible variable enabling parties to set objectives, evaluate the position of others, and assess negotiating progress. In past merchandise-trade negotiations, the focus of negotiators was on the value of bilateral trade flows and the matching vector of applied tariffs. It was a measure that took into account the relative size of different countries (trade volume) and was simple to calculate. The complexity of identifying and quantifying barriers to trade in services focused the attention of negotiators on rules. Thus, a substantial amount of time and resources was devoted to deter-

Box 4.1 Services data needs and weaknesses

The main source of data on trade in services is the balance of payments. Balance-of-payments data have many weaknesses:

Consistency and coverage. For example, a user of such statistics cannot be certain that reported exports of port services by country A consist of the same items as reported exports of port services by country B. Moreover, at virtually any level of aggregation, some nations may not report information on a certain item. Examples include maritime shipment exports and air transport services as well as many business and professional services. The result is biased figures when data are added across countries to arrive at regional totals, and discrepancies when comparing world imports and exports for a given category.

Trade by origin and destination. This information is not available on a comparable and detailed basis. While some countries report information on the direction of trade by geographic region or by major trading partner, most do not.

Disaggregation. The amount of detail or disaggregation of data on trade in services is limited.

Data on trade by volume. Balance-of-payments data on services trade refer only to value, not volume or quality. This makes it difficult to determine what proportion of growth in a given category in a given year is due to inflation as opposed to improvements in quality.

Comparability across time. Another problem when comparing developments in trade in services over time at both the country and global level, is that methodologies and definitions may vary from year to year. When countries improve the sectoral coverage of their data collection, it can be difficult to determine how much of an increase in recorded trade in services for a specific period is "real," as opposed to deriving from improvements in data collection.

Concordances. It is difficult, if not impossible, to relate services-trade statistics to domestic production and employment data. This is partly because different countries include different items in various components of the current account. More important is that trade data are too aggregated, so that concordances have little meaning. Even if there were consistent disaggregated trade data across countries, trade statistics would include items that do not appear in national accounts. An example is expenditure by travelers.

Data on sales by foreign affiliates. Balance-of-payments conventions imply that if factors of production move to another country for more than one year, a change in residency status has occurred. The output generated by such factors and sold in the host market will no longer be registered as trade in the balance of payments. Data are rarely collected on the magnitude of sales by affiliates and natural persons who have established themselves in a host country. The United States is a notable exception.

Note: for a more detailed discussed of the shortcomings of services data, see Hoekman and Stern 1991.

TABLE 4.2 *Shares in global service exports and revealed comparative advantage, 1980 and 1992*

	Tourism		Transport		All other	
	1980	1992	1980	1992	1980	1992
Share in global trade (percent)						
OECD member countries	75.0	79.1	79.8	80.5	81.4	85.2
Developing countries	25.0	20.9	20.2	19.5	18.6	14.8
RCA						
OECD member countries	1.01	0.96	1.10	1.02	1.13	1.06
Developing countries	0.93	1.12	0.65	0.82	0.65	0.74
Small developing countries (1 million people or less)	2.19	3.45	1.19	1.85	0.39	1.11

Source: World Bank

mining whether and how GATT-like concepts such as national treatment and the MFN principle could be applied to service sectors. Indeed, discussions rapidly became sector-specific. But rather than focusing on the identification, quantification, and reduction of barriers, absolute sectoral reciprocity was emphasized. This contrasts with the "first-difference" approach to reciprocity used in GATT tariff negotiations (Bhagwati 1988).[7]

A SYNOPSIS OF GATS DISCIPLINES

GATS consists of two main elements: general concepts, principles, and rules that apply across the board to measures affecting trade in services; and specific commitments on national treatment and market access.[8] The agreement includes a provision for periodic negotiations that will progressively liberalize trade in services. It also carries a set of attachments and annexes that take into account sectoral specificities and ministerial decisions relating to implementation.

GATS applies to "measures by Members affecting trade in services" (Article I) and covers four modes of supply: cross-border supply of a service (that is, not requiring the physical movement of supplier or consumer); provision involving movement of the consumer to the country of the supplier; services sold in the territory of a member by (legal) entities that have established a commercial presence there but originate in the territory of another member; and provision of services requiring the temporary movement of natural persons.[9] The agreement does not apply to services supplied in the exercise of governmental functions.

Nondiscrimination and Market Access

GATT's core principle is nondiscrimination, as reflected in the MFN and national treatment rules. These apply generally to all trade flows except where explicit allowance is made for their violation, for instance, in the context of regional integration. MFN and national treatment are also key provisions of GATS, albeit less all-encompassing than in the GATT. MFN coverage for each GATS member is subject to a negative list – it applies to all services except those listed by each member. The coverage of national treatment is determined by a "conditional" positive-list approach – it only applies to sectors listed in a country's schedule, and then only to measures not exempted. In addition to MFN and national treatment rules, GATS introduces a commitment not found in GATT: a market access obligation. Its reach is also determined by a positive listing of sectors by each GATS member.

Although MFN is a general obligation, GATS contains an annex allowing countries to invoke an exemption to it. MFN exemptions may only be made upon the agreement's entry into force. Once a country becomes a member, further exemptions can only be sought by requesting the Ministerial Conference on the WTO for a waiver, which must be approved by three-quarters of the members. MFN exemptions are in principle to last no longer than ten years and are subject to negotiation in future trade-liberalization rounds, the first of which must take place within five years of the agreements' entry into force. The need for an annex on MFN exemptions largely reflects a concern on the part of some industries that MFN may allow competitors located in countries with relatively restrictive policies to benefit from their sheltered markets while enjoying a free ride in less restrictive export markets. This concern was expressed vividly in GATS discussions on financial services and telecommunications, prompting industry representatives in relatively open countries to lobby for exemptions as a way to force sectoral reciprocity.[10] In the closing days of the Uruguay Round, it became clear that a number of participants were ready to invoke the annex on MFN exemptions for financial services, basic telecommunications, maritime transport, or audiovisual services. Rather than allowing countries to withdraw commitments in these areas or to exempt them from the MFN obligation, a compromise solution was reached under which negotiations on a number of these sectors were to continue without endangering the establishment of GATS (and the WTO).

Negotiations on financial services, basic telecommunications, and maritime transport were restarted in the spring of 1994. Those on financial services were concluded in July 1995. Negotiations on basic telecommunications and maritime transport are to be concluded by the end of April and the end of June 1996, respectively. Until then, neither the MFN requirement nor the possibility of invoking an exemption will enter into force unless a member has made a specific commitment for sector.

More than sixty GATS members had submitted MFN exemptions as of mid-1994. Three sectors in particular are affected: audiovisual services, transportation (road, air, and maritime) and financial services. Exemptions in the audiovisual area tend to be justified on the basis of cultural objectives, allowing for preferential coproduction or distribution arrangements with a limited number of countries. Exemptions in the transport area often are motivated by the Liner Code of UNCTAD, a concern for many African countries in particular, or the existence of bilateral or regional agreements. Exemptions for financial services were usually made by countries seeking the flexibility to retaliate against members that did not offer reciprocal access to financial-service markets.[11] In the end, most governments decided not to invoke these exemptions for a two-year period (until November 1, 1997). The exception to this was the United States, which concluded in June 1995 that the offers made by a number of countries were inadequate in terms of guaranteeing access to financial services markets, and therefore took an MFN exemption for the whole financial service sector. It is noteworthy – and cause for some optimism – that the US decision did not cause a domino effect. Instead, all other countries will apply their commitments on financial services, many of which had been improved during the six-month additional negotiation period, on an MFN basis. The question of modifying commitments in this area and taking MFN exemptions will be addressed again in November 1997.

Many MFN exemptions relate to existing regional-integration agreements, even though GATs makes explicit allowance for economic-integration agreements involving members. Such preferential arrangements are subject to three conditions. First, they must have "substantial sectoral coverage." Second, they must either eliminate existing discriminatory measures or prohibit the introduction of new ones. Third, the overall level of barriers to trade in services against other GATS members within the respective sectors or subsectors must not rise above the level previously applicable. There is no requirement that integration agreements be open in principle to the accession of third countries.[12] These three conditions are weaker than those applying in the GATT context (Hoekman and Sauvé 1994), the second in particular (a mere standstill agreement may be sufficient). The weakness of the disciplines on regional economic integration imply only a limited constraint on strategic violations of the MFN obligation. Many countries have nonetheless felt the need to invoke MFN exemptions for existing integration agreements.

As mentioned earlier, market access and national treatment are specific commitments. These obligations apply only to services included in the members' schedules and then are only subject to listed qualifications or conditions. In principle, six types of market access restrictions are prohibited: limitations on the number of service suppliers allowed, on the value of transactions or assets, on the total quantity of service output, on the number of employees, on the type of legal entity through which a service supplier is permitted to operate (for example, branches vs. subsidiaries for banking), and on the participation of foreign capital (a limit on the percentage of foreign shareholding or on the absolute value of foreign investment). *National treatment* is defined as treatment no less favorable than that accorded to like domestic services and service providers. However, such treatment may not be identical to that applying to domestic firms, because identical treatment could actually worsen the conditions of competition for foreign-based firms (for example, a requirement for insurance firms that reserves be held locally).

The introduction of a market access commitment reflects one of the distinguishing characteristics of service markets: their contestability is frequently restricted by nondiscriminatory measures. The market access article explicitly covers six such measures that were felt to be of particular importance. However, it overlaps with the national treatment requirement, for prohibited market access measures may be discriminatory as well as nondiscriminatory. The overlap creates the potential for confusion and disputes. Because national treatment and market access are not general obligations, in the GATS context the schedules of commitments are crucial to determining the extent of market access opportunities resulting from the agreement. As discussed below, schedules are constructed in such a manner at the liberalization dynamics of GATS may turn out to be weaker than those of GATT.

Other Obligations and Disciplines

Other GATS obligations address issues such as transparency, recognition of licenses and certification, payments and transfers, domestic regulation, and the behavior of public monopolies. Article III (Transparency) requires that all members establish inquiry points to provide specific information on any laws, regulations, and administrative practices affecting services covered by the agreement. Article VI (Domestic Regulation) requires members to establish disciplines guaranteeing that qualification requirements, technical standards, and licensing procedures are based on objective and transparent criteria, are no more burdensome than necessary, and do not constitute a restriction on supply (thereby possibly circumventing a specific commitment). Article XI (Transfers and Payments) prohibits members from applying restrictions on international transfers and payments for current transactions relating to activities for which specific commitments have been made. Article VII (Recognition) allows the establishment of procedures for (mutual) recognition of licenses, education, or experience granted by a particular member. It is noteworthy in requiring members to "afford adequate opportunity" for other members to negotiate their accession to an existing bilateral or plurilateral recognition agreement. Monopoly or oligopoly supply of services do not abuse their market power to nullify specific commitments relating to activities that fall outside the scope of their exclusive rights (Article VIII).

As mentioned earlier, many of the framework's rules and disciplines apply only where specific commitments are made. This serious shortcoming is a consequence of the positive-list approach taken for scheduling commitments. Clearly one would want – and expect – disciplines regarding payments and transfers to be general. To the extent that other parties are willing to allow a country to maintain restrictions, a negative-list approach would allow for exemptions. But at least the principle would be general, not specific. Similarly, the requirement in Article VI (Domestic Regulation) that "all measures of *general application affecting trade in services*" be "administered in a reasonable, objective and impartial manner" applies only "in sectors where specific commitments are undertaken" (GATT 1994, p. 333, emphasis added).

GATS' MFN, national treatment, and market access obligations do not extend to government procurement of services. Negotiations on this issue are to be initiated within two years of the WTO's entry into force.[13] This greatly reduces the coverage of GATS, as procurement typically represents a significant share of total demand for many services, for instance, consulting engineering and construction. GATS does not impose general disciplines on subsidies either, only subjecting them to general obligations (transparency, MFN, and dispute settlement). The time frame for negotiations on this topic will be determined by a future work program. Article IX (Business Practices) recognizes that business practices of service suppliers that have *not* been granted monopoly or exclusive rights may restrain competition and thus trade in services, but no obligations are imposed regarding the scope and enforcement of competition policy. Members are only obliged to supply nonconfidential information of relevance to a competition-related matter if so requested by another member.

GATS has a number of safeguards, including Article X (Emergency Safeguard Measures), Article XII (Restrictions to Safeguard the Balance of Payments), Article XIV (Exceptions), and Article XXI (Modification of Schedules). Article X, which allows for possible industry-specific safeguard actions, is largely a shell calling for further negotiations on this topic within three years of the WTO's entry into force. The balance-of-payments provision only applies to those services for which specific commitments have been made. It requires that such measures be nondiscriminatory and phased out progressively as the invoking member's balance of payments improves.[14] Article XIV on exceptions is similar to what is found in GATT, providing members with the legal cover to take measures safeguarding public morals, order, health, security, consumer protection, and privacy. It also allows measures that violate national treatment if they are used to ensure equitable or effective collection of direct taxes, or that violate MFN if they result from a bilateral double-taxation agreement.[15] Article XXI on modification of schedules allows concessions (specific commitments) to be withdrawn subject to negotiation and compensation. Arbitration is anticipated in the event that bilateral negotiations on compensation are unsuccessful. Retaliation will only be authorized when a member does not comply with arbitration. Finally, the WTO's Dispute Settlement Body will be responsible for addressing disputes relating to GATS, as well as those pertaining to GATT and the agreement on TRIPS. Retaliation from goods to services and vice versa is possible.

Developing Country-specific Provisions

GATS Article XIX allows developing countries to make fewer specific commitments than industrialized nations. Other provisions addressing developing country concerns include Articles IV (Increasing Participation of Developing Countries), III (Transparency), and XV (Subsidies).[16] Article IV states that increased participation of developing countries in world trade in services is to be encouraged through negotiated specific commitments relating to: access to technology on a commercial basis; improved access to distribution channels and information networks; and the liberalization of market access in sectors of export interest to developing countries. On transparency, industrialized nations are to establish contact points to give developing country service suppliers more information on the commercial and technical aspects of specific services; requirements for registration, recognition, and obtaining professional qualifications; and the availability of services technology.[17] Although the negotiation of substantive disciplines on subsidies was left open (see above), Article XV recognizes the role of subsidies in the development programs of developing countries.

SPECIFIC COMMITMENTS UNDER GATS

The specific commitments are the core of GATS. To a large extent its impact depends on the commitments made by members. Negotiators chose to pursue a hybrid positive-negative list for scheduling specific commitments. It is positive in determining sectoral coverage of market access and national treatment commitments, negative with regard to identifying measures that violate either national treatment or market access disciplines. Each member first decides (negotiates) which service sectors will be subject to these disciplines. It then decides, for each such sector, what measures will be kept in place that violate market access or national treatment. Limitations and exceptions must be specified by mode of supply. With four modes of supply, there are eight opportunities for GATS members to avoid full application of market access or national treatment. In addition to specific commitments, countries also make horizontal commitments. These are usually laws and policies that restrict the use of a mode of supply by foreign suppliers, independently of the sector involved. A policy that is often scheduled is an "economic needs" test, that is, laws or regulations stipulating that foreign service providers may contest a market only if domestic providers do not exist, or are unable to satisfy demand. Another example is a general licensing or approval requirement. In many instances such horizontal "headnotes" involve a restriction on the inward movement of natural persons. The format of a schedule of specific commitments is illustrated in table 4.3. An entry of "none" means that a member binds itself to not having any measures that violate market access or national treatment for a specific sector-mode of supply combination; "unbound" implies that no commitments are made for a particular mode of supply.[18]

Quantifying the Specific Commitments: Conceptual Issues

Assessing the contents of country schedules requires a quantitative measure that allows for cross-country comparisons. Ideally, one would have information on the size (total output) of service activities across countries and would determine the level of restrictions facing foreign suppliers (a tariff-equivalent analogue of some kind) before and after negotiations. Unfortunately, although a common list of services has been used by members in scheduling commitments, inadequate information exists on the economic variables of interest. With the exception of communication and financial services, to which a GATS-specific breakdown of activities is applied (see Hoekman 1995), the list derives from the United Nations' Central Product Classification. No countries collect or report disaggregated data on the basis of this classification system, as it was only developed in the early 1990s. Obtaining output data for all GATS members, even for the eleven major service categories distinguished in the GATS list, would be a major endeavor. It has not been undertaken here, in large part because sector-specific information does not exist on the restrictiveness of measures relating to national treatment and market access.

TABLE 4.3 *Example of a schedule of specific commitments*

	Mode of supply	Conditions and limitations on market access	Conditions and qualifications on national treatment
Horizontal commitments (across all sectors)	Cross-border supply	None	None other than tax measures that result in differences in treatment with respect to R&D services
	Consumption abroad	None	Unbound for subsidies, tax incentives, and tax credits.
	Commercial presence (FDI)	Maximum foreign equity stake is 49 percent	Unbound for subsidies, under law *x*. Approval is required for equity stakes over 25 percent; new investment that exceeds *y* million
	Temporary entry of natural persons	Unbound except for the following: intra-corporate transferees of executives and senior managers: specialist personnel for up to one year; specialist personnel subject to economic-needs test for stays longer than one year, service seller (sales people) for up to three months	Unbound except for categories of natural persons mentioned referred to in the market-across column
Specific commitments (e.g. legal services)	Cross-border supply	Commercial presence required	Unbound
	Consumption abroad	None	None
	Commercial presence (FDI)	25 percent of senior management should be nationals	Unbound
	Temporary entry of natural persons	Unbound, except as indicated in horizontal commitments	Unbound, except as indicated in horizontal commitments

Source: GATS schedules of commitments.

The absence of such data is a major problem in evaluating GATS. To compare schedules, commitments listing measures that violate national treatment and market access obligations must be somehow discounted. In most cases there is no information regarding the restrictiveness of policies maintained or the relative importance of modes of supply on a sector-by-sector basis. Some modes may be irrelevant because of technological factors. For example, there is little value in offering zero restrictions on cross-border delivery or consumer movement in the context of retail banking services, as selling such products usually requires a commercial presence. A commercial presence in retail banking in turn requires some movement of personnel (management, technical support staff for data processing and information technology, for example). If there are no limitations on commercial presence, but if there are restrictions on the movement of personnel, market access may be severely limited. Similarly, there may be restrictions on an activity (for example, no deposit taking allowed) but no limitations on movement of personnel. Establishing mode-of-supply weights on a sector-by-sector basis is another monumental task.[19] A final problem concerns quantifying the restrictiveness of horizontal commitments, which though they apply to particular modes of supply across all sectors will affect particular sectors differently.

Clearly, a significant amount of conceptual and empirical work remains to be done. No attempt is made here to determine the change in restrictiveness of policies affecting either scheduled or nonscheduled services.[20] Instead, the focus is on scaling the sector commitments of GATS members and thereby "quantifying" two things: the extent to which policy measures have been bound; and the share of sectors where such binding relates to the absence of any policy violating market access or national treatment. Lack of information on the economic impact of policies applied to services makes it impossible to have even a qualitative assessment of the liberalization implied by specific commitments. Unfortunately, schedules do not reveal to what extent they imply liberalization, if at all. It *appears* that virtually all commitments are standstill, that is, a binding of (part of) the status quo. This is the perception of negotiators, and in what follows it is assumed.[21] Because liberalization in the sense of reducing discrimination and enhancing market access did not occur, the relevance of weighted sectoral-coverage indicators increased; the key issue became one of determining the extent to which members were willing to bind the status quo.

For purposes of evaluation, each member's specific commitments were entered into a spreadsheet (commitments made as of April 1994 were considered in this exercise). With 155 nonoverlapping service sectors in the GATS classification list and four modes of supply, there is a maximum of 620 possible commitments (table 4.4).[22] As commitments apply to national treatment and market access separately, there are 1,240 data cells for each member. Schedules were submitted by ninety-seven members. Two country groups were created for comparison, one for low- and middle-income countries, one for high-income countries. Country groups follow World Bank classifications. The high-income group includes all OECD member countries except Mexico and Turkey, as well as Brunei, Cyprus, Hong Kong, Israel, Kuwait, and Singapore. The European Union is counted as one member. The low- and middle-income group includes

TABLE 4.4 *GATS members: number of commitments schedules*

Developing countries	
Algeria	4
Antigua and Barbuda	68
Antilles (Netherlands)	144
Argentina	208
Aruba	140
Bahrain	16
Bangladesh	4
Barbados	24
Belize	8
Benin	44
Bolivia	24
Brazil	156
Burkina Faso	8
Cameroon	12
Chile	140
China	196
Colombia	164
Congo	16
Costa Rica	52
Côte d'Ivoire	56
Cuba	120
Czech Republic	304
Dominica	20
Dominican Republic	264
Egypt	104
El Salvador	92
Fiji Islands	4
Gabon	44
Ghana	100
Grenada	20
Guatemala	40
Guyana	72
Honduras	64
Hungary	336
India	132
Indonesia	140
Jamaica	128
Kenya	84
Korea	311
Macao	76
Madagascar	8
Malaysia	256
Malta	28
Mauritius	43
Mexico	252
Morocco	144
Mozambique	48
Myanmar	12
Namibia	12
New Caledonia	24
Nicaragua	196
Niger	20
Nigeria	96
Pakistan	108
Paraguay	36
Peru	96
Philippines	160
Poland	212
Romania	176
St Lucia	32
St Vincent and the Grenadines	32
Senegal	104
Slovak Republic	308
South Africa	288
Sri Lanka	8
Surinam	16
Swaziland	36
Tanzania	4
Thailand	260
Trinidad and Tobago	68
Tunisia	52
Turkey	276
Uganda	8
Uruguay	96
Venezuela	156
Zambia	64
Zimbabwe	72
High-income countries	
Australia	360
Austria	412
Brunei	76
Canada	352
Cyprus	36
European Union	392
Finland	328
Hong Kong	200
Iceland	372
Israel	180
Japan	408
Kuwait	176
New Zealand	276
Norway	360
Singapore	232
Sweden	320
Switzerland	400
Liechtenstein	312
United States	384

Note: the maximum number of commitments is 620 – 155 activities multiplied by 4 modes of supply.

countries with a wide range of per capital income and substantial variation in service-market size (GDP).

Commitments were classified as "none" (no restrictions applied on either market access or national treatment for a given mode of supply or sector), "unbound" (no policies bound for a given mode of supply or sector), and "other" (restrictions are listed and thus bound for a mode of supply or sector). These limitations (policies) are bound. To calculate the sectoral coverage of commitments, one of three numerical indicators (weights) was allocated to each element of a member's schedule: a 1 in all instances where "none" was stated for a sector-mode of supply; a 0 in all instances where members list "unbound" for a sector-mode of supply; and 0.5 in all instances where specific restrictions or limitations are listed for a sector-mode of supply.[23] These values were chosen to allow aggregation across sectors and countries. The higher the number, the greater the implied extent of openness-cum-binding.[24] Assigning 0 to unbound commitments and 0.5 to commitments implying maintenance of measures violating national treatment or market access reflects the perception that scheduling and binding have value, no matter how restrictive the policies being maintained.

Tariff bindings (schedules) are critical to the function of GATT because they establish a benchmark for the conditions of market access to which a country commits itself. Any measure taken or supported by a government that nullifies or impairs the "concession" implied by the tariff binding may give rise to a complaint to GATT. That is, the binding limits the possibility not only of raising tariffs but also of using measures that have an equivalent effect. However, this constraint only bites if tariffs are bound at applied rates. In practice, many developing countries have bound their tariffs at levels substantially higher than currently applied rates. This greatly reduces the relevance of binding but does not reduce it to 0. Martin and Francois (1995) argue that a binding above the applied rate is valuable because it reduces the expected mean tariff.

Under GATS, services policy bindings are less powerful than GATT tariff bindings because the market access article applies only to some policy measures. Some market access barriers are not "caught" by the scheduling exercise. Examples include labor legislation, tax regimes, restrictions on land availability, ownership or use, licensing and related fees, the existence and reach of competition policies, regulation of monopolies, and judicial enforceability of contracts. Such measures can satisfy national treatment and are not captured by the market access article, but they can restrict the contestability of markets. Nonetheless, binding policies that violate national treatment or market access has value because the introduction of new measures violating these commitments is no longer possible. Moreover, if a member schedules a sector and later introduces policies that are not prohibited but have the effect of nullifying its specific commitments, it can face a nonviolation complaint. If the measure is determined by the Dispute Settlement Body to have nullified or impaired a specific commitment, the affected member is entitled to compensation, and if agreement cannot be reached, to retaliation (Article XXIII, GATS).[25]

Sectoral shares can be used as an indicator of the openness of countries if attention is limited to those sectors where GATS members offer free market access and full national treatment. The sectoral coverage of such no-restriction commitments in the country schedules is perhaps the most obvious quantifiable focal point available to negotiators. It also lends itself to a formula-type approach. Negotiators might have agreed that all offers should include at least *x* percent of their service sector (weighted by output) for which no restrictions on market access or national treatment would be maintained. This would have provided a clear benchmark and a minimum threshold against which country offers could be objectively compared. Adoption of such a criterion, while still allowing countries substantial flexibility in their choice of sectors, would have ensured that the minimum acceptable offer was proportional to country size. In the event, quantitative targets were not used in the scheduling exercise, leaving it to bilateral negotiations to determine the minimum acceptable level of participation. Thus, instead of pursuing a formula-based approach, service negotiators resorted to the classic bid-offer approach to liberalization.

Measures of Sectoral Coverage of Specific Commitments

For both market access and national treatment, three indicators were calculated (table 4.5): the number of sector-mode of supply combinations (cells) where a commitment was made relative to the maximum possible; the "average coverage" of the schedule defined as the arithmetic weighted mean of the scale factors allocated to each cell (0 for unbound, 0.5 for bound restrictions, and 1 for no restrictions); and the share of no-restriction commitments in a member's total commitments, and relative to the 155 possible sectors of the GATS classification list. The higher the number, the more liberal the country. The first of these ratios is conceptually similar to nontariff-barrier-frequency ratios, the second to a nontariff-barrier coverage ratio (see, for example, Nogues, Olechowski, and Winters 1986).

High-income members made commitments of some kind for 47 percent of the GATS list, compared with 16 percent for developing countries. Commitments made by large developing countries, arbitrarily defined as those with GDPs of US$40 billion or more, were substantially higher than the low- and middle-income country average, accounting for 38.6 percent of the GATS list. Generally, this reflects the fact that many developing countries made very limited commitments. One quarter of the low- and middle-income group scheduled less than 3 percent of the GATS list. Four countries scheduled only 1 of the 155 service sectors; five others made commitments on only 2 subsectors. Countries in the low- and middle-income group with the highest number of specific commitments include the Czech Republic, Hungary, Korea, and the Slovak Republic, each with more than 300 sectors/modes of supply scheduled (Hoekman 1995, p. 344).

The weighted average coverage of market access commitments is 35.9 percent for high-income countries, 10 percent for low- and middle-income countries, and 22.9 percent for large developing countries. If these figures are related to the simple count of the number of sectors where commitments were made, high-income countries appear to be more liberal, since the proportion of commitments registering a 1 or a 0.5 is higher than for low- and middle-income countries (table 4.5). The ratio achieved by dividing the average coverage of commitments by the count is some 15 percentage points lower for low- and middle-income countries than for high-income countries. Almost 60 percent of commitments for the high-income group imply no restrictions, as compared to 45 percent for low- and middle-income countries. Thus, although many developing countries made only a few specific commitments, many of them involve free access. Relative to the GATS list, no-restriction commitments account for 27 percent of the maximum possible for high-income members, 7 percent for low- and middle-income countries, and 15 percent of the large developing country group.

Identical ratios were calculated for national treatment commitments. A comparison of commitments on national treatment and market access reveals that all countries tend to be more liberal with regard to the former, and that the difference between country groups narrows somewhat. There is a high correlation between commitments in these two areas. The proportion of commitments where the value of a market access cell is equal to the corresponding national treatment cell exceeds 90 percent for both groups (Hoekman 1995). What about the magnitude of commitments where no restrictions apply to both market access and national treatment for a given sector-mode of supply? The figure for high-income countries is 25 percent, for low- and middle-income countries 7 percent. These numbers vividly illustrate how far away GATS members are from attaining free trade in services, and the magnitude of the task that remains.

The data reported in table 4.5 do not take into account the relative importance of different service activities in GDP (that is, the size of the various service markets), or the relative importance of countries in the world economy (that is, the size of the different GATS members). Table 4.6 reports coverage indicators that incorporate an attempt to take these factors into account. Table 4.6 pertains to market access commitments only, given that these tend to be more restrictive than those on national treatment. For ease of comparison, the first row repeats the unweighted average sectoral coverage ratios reported in table 4.5. The second row illustrates the importance of taking into account the relative importance (size) of individual service activities (see Hoekman 1995, pp. 352–33 for the output weights used; the same weights were employed for all countries). Sectoral coverage indicators rise substantially for high-income countries: increasing by 10 percentage points to 45 percent. The coverage ratio for low- and middle-income countries rises by 2 percentage points. This indicates that commitments were made in activities that are of above average importance in GDP terms. The third row in table 4.6 relates the specific commitments, weighted by sectoral contributions to GDP, to the global market for services, as measured by country shares in global GDP. Commitments for high-income countries cover about half of the global services market. Those by low- and middle-income countries represent only 5 percent of the world market, reflecting their much smaller share in global GDP (estimated at 16.4 percent).[26] Adjusting for the relative importance of modes of supply across service sectors suggest that this has little impact on the magnitude of coverage ratios (Hoekman 1995).

Again, sectoral coverage indices are of limited use from an economic perspective, as no account can be taken of the actual restrictiveness of policy stances maintained by different countries by sector-mode of supply. The least ambiguous measure in this respect is the no-restrictions coverage ratio.[27] This is

TABLE 4.5 *Sectoral coverage of specific commitments (percent)*

	High-income countries	Low- and middle-income countries	Large developing nations
Market access			
Unweighted average count (sectors-modes listed as a share of maximum possible)	47.3	16.2	38.6
Average coverage (sectors-modes listed as a share of maximum possible, weighted by openness or binding factors)	35.9	10.3	22.9
Coverage/count (average coverage as a share of the average count)	75.9	63.6	59.3
No restrictions as a share of total offer (unweighted count)	57.3	45.5	38.7
No restrictions as a share of maximum possible	27.1	7.3	14.9
National treatment			
Unweighted average count (sectors-modes listed as a share of maximum possible)	47.3	16.2	38.8
Average coverage (sectors-model listed as a share of maximum possible, weighted by openness or binding factors)	37.2	11.2	25.5
Coverage/count (average coverage as a share of average count)	78.6	69.1	66.1
No restrictions as a share of total offer (unweighted count)	65.1	58.0	52.3
No restrictions as a share of maximum possible	30.8	9.4	20.2
Memo item			
No restrictions on market access and national treatment as a share of maximum possible	24.8	6.9	14.3

Source: Author's calculations based on WTO and World Bank data

TABLE 4.6 *Sectoral average of specific commitments on market access, weighted by sectoral contributions to GDP and country shares in global GDP*

	High-income countries	Low- and middle-income countries
Weighted by restrictiveness	35.9	10.3
Weighted by restrictiveness and GDP	45.4	12.2
Weighted by restrictiveness, sectoral contributions to GDP, and country share in world GDP	48.4	5.2
GDP weight in world	78.9	16.4

Note: weights do not add to 1, as GATS members do not include all countries in the world.
Source: author's calculations based on GATS schedules and World Bank data.

25 percent on average for the high-income group, 7 percent on average for other GATS members. Because it is reasonable to assume that countries scheduled the "easiest" sectors, these relatively low coverage indicators suggest that in the foreseeable future most trade in services will remain subject to market access or national treatment restrictions. Of course, the average coverage of sectoral commitments is greater than the no-restriction measure. Weighted by sectoral contributions to GDP, it is about 45 percent for high-income countries and 12 percent for low- and middle-income countries. The average sectoral-coverage ratio of the bottom fifty developing countries (which account for over 60 percent of the group in number) falls substantially below the group average, only 3 percent. Many of these countries are small and have very low per capita incomes, reducing pressure from trading partners to schedule more sectors. However, this by no means justifies such a passive stance.

Although a number of poor countries scheduled a significant number of sectors, many did not (figure 4.1). It is unclear why coverage ratios (unweighted) are not close to 100 percent for all members. The mere fact that so much of the service sector was not scheduled must be counted against GATS. The cost of making specific commitments is, after all, modest, even for those countries that do not favor liberalization, for any measure violating national treatment or market access may be scheduled. This argument applies *a fortiori* to those countries that either desire to liberalize access to their service markets or that already maintain a liberal policy stance.

There is a fair amount of variance in the sectoral coverage of specific commitments (table 4.7). The fewest commitments were made by high-income countries in sectors such as land, water and air transport, postal services, basic telecoms, research and development, education, health, and recreation and social services. Of these "sensitive" sectors, developing countries have a potential export interest in the last three. But the coverage of business services, computer-related services,

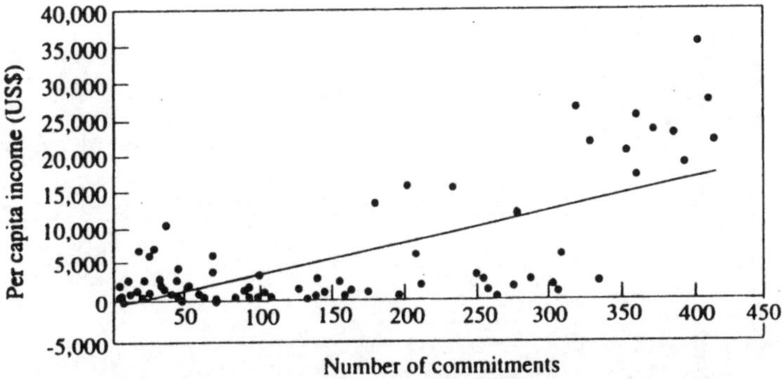

FIGURE 4.1 Relationship between per capita income and specific commitments

and construction is quite high. These sectors cover many activities where developing countries have an export potential.

Although market access commitments by high-income countries tend to be restrictive with respect to activities where developing countries have a comparative advantage – both low- and high-skill labor-intensive activities that require either temporary entry or establishment or work permits – nothing is to be gained from a retaliatory policy. Most countries are too small to influence the market access policies of large traders. Nonliberalization by trading partners restricts the potential gains from liberalization but by no means eliminates them. The annex on the movement of natural persons – currently the only mode-of-supply-specific part of GATS – requires simply that natural persons who are service suppliers or employed by the service supplier of a member be allowed to provide services in accordance with the terms of specific commitments relating to their entry and temporary stay. The extent to which labor movement is allowed is therefore completely dependent on what is specified in the schedules. Specific restrictions on labor movement may be horizontal or sector-specific. Most members only allow for entry of specialists and higher-level management staff, significantly curtailing the scope for cross-border (nonestablishment related) trade in services. Similarly, a lack of general disciplines on discriminatory licensing practices involving citizenship or permanent residency requirements can be expected to weaken the impact of GATS on trade in professional services.[28]

For developing countries the potential gains of GATS membership will result primarily from liberalizing access to their own markets. There is substantial evidence that many constraints reducing the economic efficiency of service industries are home grown (UNCTAD and World Bank 1994). Government policy measures should focus on such concerns as augmenting domestic productive capacity, increasing the quality of services and establishing a reputation for reliable supply. The availability of higher-quality or lower-cost services will often increase the output of goods and make them more competitive on world markets. The level of specific commitments under GATS suggests that governments did not grasp the opportunity to bind the status quo, let alone liberalize access to service markets.

TABLE 4.7 *Commitments by sector*

ISIC	Number of GATS sectors and modes of supply	Average number of commitments		Commitments/GATS items (percent)	
		High-income countries	Low- and middle-income countries	High-income countries	Low- and middle-income countries
Construction	20	11.2	3.3	56.0	16.5
Motor vehicle repair	4	1.8	0.3	45.0	7.5
Wholesale trade	8	4.6	0.5	57.5	6.3
Retail trade	8	4.4	0.8	55.0	10.0
Hotels, restaurants	4	2.8	2.8	70.0	70.0
Land transport	40	9.4	2.3	23.5	5.8
Water transport	48	4.4	3.0	9.2	6.3
Air transport	20	3.7	1.5	18.5	7.5
Auxiliary transport	20	5.1	1.3	25.5	6.5
Postal	4	1.3	0.6	32.5	15.0
Basic telecom	28	1.5	1.3	5.4	4.6
Value-added telecom	28	18.7	5.0	66.8	17.8
Financial	60	31.3	12.4	52.2	20.6
Real estate	8	3.5	0.3	43.8	3.8
Rental activities	20	9.5	1.3	47.5	6.5
Computer-related	20	15.5	4.2	77.5	21.0
Research and development	12	4.1	1.0	34.2	8.3
Business	108	56.5	12.2	47.9	11.3
Refuse disposal	16	8.8	1.0	55.0	6.3
Education	20	4.7	1.3	23.5	6.5
Health and social	24	5.0	1.9	20.8	7.9
Recreation, culture	48	13.3	4.6	27.9	9.6

THE FRAMEWORK'S POSSIBLE INCENTIVE EFFECTS

Progressive liberalization is a central objective of GATS. How successful will the current structure be in expanding the coverage of bindings and inducing substantial liberalization of access to service markets? Concerns can be expressed regarding both dimensions. Problems include the lack of transparency, sector-specificity, the modalities of scheduling, and the limited number of generic rules. All of these reflect the structural weaknesses of GATS.

GATS does not do nearly enough to further the goal of transparency, which should be a fundamental objective of any multilateral agreement. No information is generated on sectors, subsectors, and activities for which no commitments are scheduled – most often sensitive areas where restrictions and discriminatory practices abound. A commitment consisting of the single word "unbound" conveys nothing but the government's unwillingness to have its hands tied, in which case the regulatory stance is likely to be restrictive. Lack of transparency is a serious shortcoming considering the nature of impediments to trade in services (regulatory barriers at both the national and subnational levels). A negative list would have significantly enhanced transparency, even if it did result in country-specific "phone books' of nonconforming measures. Service providers have no comprehensive cross-country source of information on regulatory regimes. If members remain firmly committed to the positive-list approach, all should agree to compile and publish this information on a sector-by-sector basis within a given time. Article III (Transparency) may provide the justification for such a compilation. Without such transparency, negotiations will remain difficult, driven primarily by powerful export interests.

There is also a great deal of variance across countries regarding the transparency of the commitments themselves. Some members have invested substantial effort in listing all relevant laws and regulations that may limit access. Others simply make reference to a limitation, without specifying applicable laws. Limitations mentioned in a schedule may be vague and therefore open to interpretation (indeed, require it).[29] Dispute settlement in GATS is likely to revolve around interpretation of country schedules. Because of the ambiguity of the schedules, disputes may be frequent. Overlap and inconsistency between national treatment and market access obligations may prove particularly problematic, as any market access restriction will violate national treatment if it applies only to foreign service providers. For example, a member may have made a no-restriction commitment under national treatment but scheduled a limitation on the maximum equity share held by an established foreign supplier. Greater care should have been taken to ensure that the two commitments are distinct.

GATS' structure reflects the fact that negotiations in the services area were (and will be) sectoral. They can be expected to be driven by the concerns of major players in each industry. At some level a sectoral approach is probably unavoidable, given the widely differing regulatory regimes across countries and sectors. But to foster MFN-based liberalization, sectoral agreements should be firmly embedded in a framework of general rules and disciplines. GATS' emphasis on sectoral reciprocity may prove especially troublesome if incremental liberalization becomes less feasible and the scope for cross-issue tradeoffs is reduced. Turf fights between regulatory agencies might ensue, curbing chances for an economy-wide perspective and tradeoffs across issues. The positive-list approach may also make it more difficult for a government to add sectors to its schedule. Those industries affected could argue against their inclusion. With a negative list, each industry seeking special treatment has to justify why the rules should not apply to it, even though they apply to everyone else; with a positive list the government must be ready to confront each industry that it seeks to subject to multilateral disciplines. As mentioned, the "easy" sectors will probably be included first, leaving the more sensitive sectors to be dealt with in the future.

The scheduling of commitments by modes of supply may further distort incentives and resource allocation by creating the opportunity for biasing incentives toward a particular mode of supply. Ironically, given the early resistance of many developing countries to discussing establishment-related matters in the negotiations, their commitments lodged under the commercial-presence supply mode tend to be the least restrictive. But this is perhaps not surprising, commercial presence being the mode that appears to generate the most in terms of local content-domestic value added. However, more stringent controls on other modes may give firms an incentive to engage in tariff-hopping investment. Indeed, commitments on commercial presence may amount to disguised trade-related investment measures, in so far as foreign service providers are compelled to use this mode and, in the process, are subjected to measures that violate either market access or national treatment. At the same time, commitments relating to commercial presence may be subject to the right to maintain or impose authorization or screening procedures (horizontal restrictions), and the criteria or measures underpinning such procedures may not be clearly defined in the schedule.

There is another potentially perverse incentive created by the combination of specific commitments and the positive-list approach: members may be induced to adopt policies that are in the principle prohibited, then seek to negotiate these away over time. Policies in many countries may be consistent with market access and national treatment obligations. Rather than locking this in, GATS allows for the future imposition of restrictions. GATS' impact would have been substantially greater if the status quo had been bound for all sectors. The market access article is a step in the right direction, but it should have been a general obligation subject to a negative list of exemptions. Moreover, it is too weak. Instead of defining market access, GATS includes a finite list of measures prohibited in principle, leaving others that have similar effects untouched. The article would have been strengthened, and dispute settlement facilitated, if the words "or measures with equivalent effect" had been added. Such language would have allowed violation complaints; its absence puts all the weight on nonviolation, a much weaker mechanism.

To the extent that market access restrictions are maintained, their impact on the MFN obligation must be considered. With the market access restrictions being quantitative in nature – limits on the number of firms, their assets, or their turnover – there appears to be a natural incentive to negotiate quantitative increases in market access as well. Suppose that currently there are only three foreign firms established, and that they are restricted to four lines of activity. Trade negotiators might seek to increase the number of firms or lines or permitted activity. That is, GATS' approach to liberalization as a built-in incentive for the reciprocal negotiation of voluntary import-investment expansion. If a country permits a few additional firms into a sector, incentives may exist to ensure that firms from certain countries obtain access. Market access/share criteria could result in managed trade, as voluntary import-investment expansion agreements can easily be inconsistent with MFN.

Implications for Developing Countries

GATS imposes few limitations on national policy, only requiring that no discrimination occurs across alternative sources of supply. It allows members to implement policies that are detrimental to – or inconsistent with – economic efficiency. A good example is the article specifying the conditions under which measures to safeguard balance of payments may be taken, such measures rarely being efficient. Furthermore, GATS does not require a participating country to alter regulatory structures or to pursue an active antitrust or competition policy. Liberalization of trade and investment may need to be augmented by regulatory change (frequently deregulation) and an effective competition policy to increase the efficiency of service sectors such as finance, transportation, and telecommunications. If simply equated with increased market access for (certain) foreign suppliers, liberalization may have little effect in noncompetitive markets. The main result will be to redistribute rents across firms.

Many developing countries were able to accede to GATS with minimal commitments. The adoption of a positive-list approach was partly due to arguments by developing countries that a negative list was too resource intensive to be feasible within the time frame originally envisaged (completion of the Round by the end of 1990). Acceptance of this argument, willingness to accept little in the way of scheduled specific commitments, and the fact that a number of the framework's rules apply only if specific commitments are made, mean that GATS will have little impact on most developing countries. Indeed, the impact may be negative. Nongenerality of national treatment and sector-specific market access commitments limit the value of GATS to governments seeking to liberalize. Lobbies that oppose liberalization cannot be told that GATS membership requires national treatment for all sectors. Instead, the government must explicitly list each and every sector to guarantee that national treatment and market access obligations will apply.

GATS does not emulate GATT by embodying special and differential treatment provisions, but it continues the GATT tradition of putting little pressure on small and poor developing countries to participate fully, as these have little to offer in the multilateral mercantile game of give and take. However, these countries, largely left to pursue liberalization unilaterally, are arguably the ones for which a liberal policy stance is crucial. GATS allows them to lock in liberalization if so desired, but does not do much to nourish a liberal policy environment.

OPTIONS FOR FIXING THE FRAMEWORK

There are many challenges that negotiators need to address if GATS is to become an effective and therefore credible instrument of multilateral liberalization. Agreement on disciplines in the areas of subsidies, procurement, and safeguards must be reached. Sectoral coverage of GATS must be greatly extended through binding all measures violating national treatment and market access. The set of generally applicable rules and disciplines must be expanded, and the weight of specific commitments reduced. And the approach taken toward scheduling commitments in the Uruguay Round needs to be critically assessed to determine whether it will encourage significant liberalization of service markets.

The first order of business should be to explore whether a more general approach – similar to that of the European Union, NAFTA, or the Australia–New Zealand Closer Economic Relations Trade Agreement – might be feasible.[30] Given that negotiators were well aware of the approaches taken toward liberalizing service markets in regional contexts, presumably this is not an option. But it should be possible to come closer to this model. Deardorff (1994) and Snape (1994) have argued that the key requirement is to make national treatment a general obligation, the former proposing a *quid pro quo* whereby each country would be allowed to levy taxes, perhaps prohibitive, on foreign providers. Scheduled, these taxes would become the focal point for future liberalization efforts. Snape (1994) proposes the adoption of general obligations prohibiting all forms of discrimination against foreign suppliers, but rather than tariffication suggests a negotiated set of foreign suppliers. Future negotiations could focus on these measures.

The current wording of GATS implies that tariffication would have to pertain to existing market access restrictions as well as limitations on national treatment. Both Deardorff and Snape focus on classic national treatment, that is, discrimination against *foreign* suppliers. In principle, tariffication of discriminatory measures appears straightforward, because each government can simply set a tax rate. In practice, however, it may be difficult to determine the nationality of firms and to curb opportunistic behavior. Member schedules suggest that tariffs are likely to be lower on establishment than on cross-border trade, thus fostering establishment. Because origin rules will invariably exempt ventures with some degree of local ownership, policies can be expected to favor joint venture-based establishment. This is not much of a problem; the current incentive structure does it already. However, it is important that tariffication not make the policy stance more restrictive. This may easily happen, as no one knows what the tariff equivalent of the status quo is. In many instances current policy toward foreign providers is consistent with national treatment, but countries have avoided scheduling (binding) this state of affairs. To the extent that entry is in principle free (the applied policy is liberal), this should not be supplanted by discriminatory taxation of foreign providers. A relatively liberal status quo should be reflected in tax rates that are imposed. Thus, established foreign firms should be grandfathered from tariffication if they are presently granted national treatment, and no tariffication should be permitted in such sectors. Otherwise, the argument for tariffication is greatly weakened. The main rationale is harnessing the mercantilistic approaches developed in GATT to liberalizing service markets. If conditions are already liberal, tariffication is counterproductive and may be captured by – or create – vested interests that will oppose future reductions.[31]

Therefore it may be preferable to pursue Snape's proposal (1994) to seek a limited set of policies and could be applied by GATS members to discriminate against foreign suppliers. What those measures might be is unclear, however, as lengthy discussions during the Uruguay Round indicated.

The tariffication proposal might be more readily applied to nondiscriminatory market access restrictions. There is no reason potential domestic entrances would not be willing to pay an entry fee to contest a market currently subject to quota restrictions. One tariffication option could be to periodically auction off such restrictions. This would appear most appropriate for regulated monopolies and for self-regulated industries where there is a *numerus fixus* constraint on new entry. Determining origin is not a problem if the measures are applied on a nondiscriminatory basis and the focus can be on all potential entrants. Another possibility for regulated activities is to exchange price-reduction commitments based on price comparisons of several of the lowest-cost suppliers of a service. This would require substantial information and may not be feasible for some sectors. However, if there were multilateral scrutiny of pricing policies, and if the WTO's dispute-settlement mechanism were extended to cover the pricing practices of monopolies, it could help GATS get around existing legal constraints on competition in many jurisdictions.

Realistically, proposals for improving GATS should build upon the existing structure and involve the following steps: adopting a negative-list approach to scheduling for the purpose of transparency, with a transition period that gives members sufficient time to do this;[32] eliminating all overlap between national treatment and market access, ensuring that the latter applies only to nondiscriminatory measures; agreeing to horizontal disciplines on modes of supply, and eliminating mode-of-supply-specific limitation in schedules; expanding the reach of the market access article by including the term "or measures with equivalent effect"; exploring the feasibility of converting quota-like market access restrictions to price-based equivalent measures by auctioning them off, guaranteeing that MFN and national treatment are satisfied; making all framework disciplines generally applicable by eliminating all instances where rules are conditional upon the scheduling of specific commitments; and agreeing to a formula-based approach for future liberalization and expansion of the sectoral coverage of GATS. GATT experience suggests that progress is made when negotiators use a quantifiable focal point. A formula approach could help negotiations on services by establishing a target for the share of each member's service sector that should be scheduled with no restrictions, and for the share of the GATS list of services that should be bound.

So far, many GATS discussions have tended to be sector-specific. In principle, it makes sense to take into account the idiosyncrasies of particular sectors. But the current format of the schedules allows for too much discretion. Sectoral agreements should be annexes that extend or complement generally applicable rules. Such general disciplines should also pertain to modes of supply. Elimination of the mode-of-supply criterion in specific commitments may be relatively straightforward. Nothing in GATS compels members to schedule commitments by mode of supply.[33] Horizontal commitments already pertain to the four modes of supply, independent of sector. What is required is that horizontal commitments no longer consist of a positive list of bound policies, but that they be transformed into a negative list of policies that are inconsistent with generally applicable rules and disciplines. A model that could be emulated in this connection is NAFTA's, where generic disciplines were negotiated for modes of supply. This is ambitious, of course, and may be feasible only if goods and services are treated symmetrically (as they are in NAFTA). Developing common WTO disciplines on investment in goods and services should therefore be a matter of some urgency.

Outstanding Issues: Subsidies, Safeguards, and Procurement

Space constraints prohibit a detailed discussion of subsidies, safeguards, and procurement, the outstanding issues that remain on the immediate negotiating agenda.[34] All three are important, and the disciplines that emerge will influence the effectiveness of GATS as an instrument for binding policies and promoting liberalization. Without subsidy disciplines, the scope for contesting scheduled markets may be limited. Similarly, if safeguard actions are relatively easy to implement, specific commitments may lose much of their impact. Expanding the reach of GATS to government procurement is critical, as the rules and procedures that are established will help determine the potential for developing countries to expand exports of services. A key issue here will be to ensure consistency with the GPA, which was extended to services in the Uruguay Round. Noteworthy in this regard is that the GPA makes no distinctions between modes of supply. Indeed, it requires signatories not to discriminate on the basis of mode of supply. This is one more reason to eliminate the mode-of-supply distinction in specific commitments.

CONCLUSION

GATS is the first multilateral agreement on policies affecting trade in services. As such, it is not surprising that minimal liberalization was achieved. More worrisome is that GATS' structure allows members not to bind the status quo in many sectors. Much work remains if GATS' coverage is ever to be universal. The fundamental question is whether GATS will induce members to go further in future negotiating rounds. Although doubts have been expressed in this connection, any structural shortcomings can be addressed relatively easily, while others are probably best handled by expanding disciplines to apply to both goods and services. Priorities were argued to be the scheduling, or binding, of all sectors – preferably as part of the shift to a negative-list approach – and the elimination of modes of supply in schedules. The credibility of GATS as a multilateral instrument of liberalization greatly depends on the political will of members to open their markets in the future and to make changes to GATS' structure (Sauvé 1995).

The need for greater transparency cannot be overemphasized. Reference to the GATT experience in agreeing to the TPRM is appropriate here. Although most countries did not have much desire to subject themselves to a transparency-based review of their trade policies, the benefit of obtaining information on trading partners outweighed the perceived cost of being subjected to review. The agreement to create a mechanism for trade policy review has given domestic groups (and the Ministry of Finance) access to a substantial amount of information regarding trade policies applied by various countries. Better information will help analysis determine the costs and benefits of current policy in service sectors. A dearth of objective data impedes analysis and the formation of interest groups favoring liberalization.[35] Tariffication and calculation of price-cost margins, even if not used as explicit focal points for negotiations, can do much to expand information on market opportunities and the relative restrictiveness of regulatory regimes. The WTO Secretariat or the OECD could undertake efforts to calculate price-cost margins and tariff equivalents of services policies.

It is important to recognize that the problems involved in fixing GATS extend beyond services. Future multilateral efforts must center on eliminating the artificial goods-services distinction and on developing generic disciplines for foreign direct investment and labor movement. In this context, attention could also be given to whether and how market access commitments might be replaced with competition disciplines. Market access restrictions as defined in GATS are, of course, not limited to services, although competition is often more restricted in these industries than in goods-producing sectors. The subject of competition policy has been actively discussed as a likely topic for future multilateral negotiations under WTO auspices. The same applies to policies affecting investment. Attention should be devoted to both goods and services in this connection, and the same rules should apply to both. The probable expansion of the multilateral trading system to include rules on policies affecting investment is another important reason for developing horizontal, generally applicable disciplines on mode of supply. It would be most unfortunate if, in investment-related matters, GATS' approach of scheduling by mode of supply and with a positive list were extended to GATT.

NOTES

The views expressed in this chapter are the author's and should not be attributed to the World Bank. I am grateful to Julian Arkell, Carlos Braga, Alan Deardorff, Brian Hindley, Guy Karsenty, Patrick Low, Will Martin, Petros Mavroidis, Pierre Sauvé, Richard Snape, and Alan Winters for helpful comments and discussions. My thanks as well to Faten Hatab and Ying Lin for computational assistance, and to David Hartridge for providing the GATS schedules.

1 The term "member" denotes that signatories of GATS are members of the WTO and not simply contracting parties (signatories) to a treaty.

2 See UNCTAD and World Bank (1994) for data on foreign direct investment in services.

3 In 1987 foreign sales by US majority-owned affiliates were 15 percent lower than service exports; in 1992 they had grown to be 20 percent larger (World Bank 1995).

4 Note that part of tourist expenditures will be on goods such as souvenirs or artifacts.

5 These are defined as the ratio of exports of a given product to a country's total exports of goods and services, divided by the same ratio for the world: RCA = $[X_{ij}/Y_j]/[X_{iw}/Y_w]$, where X_{ij} are exports of product i by country j, Y_j are total exports of goods and services by country j, and w stands for the world. The value of this index may range

from zero to a very large number. If the index is greater than one, it implies that the country is relatively specialized in that product.

6 As discussed in greater detail in Hoekman (1994), research has focused on theoretical issues, not empirical analyses. While perhaps not surprising given the difficulty of generating data on barriers to trade, this has left negotiators without much guidance regarding the costs and benefits of alternative negotiating strategies/policy stances. It is beyond the scope of this chapter to discuss the myriad issues that complicate estimate of tariff equivalents or price-cost margins in the services context. In addition to standard problems that arise in modelling the effect of nontariff measures (see, for example, Deardorff and Stern 1985), analysts must take account of nondiscriminatory market access restrictions; the importance of natural barriers to trade (distance, language, climate, etc.); the fact that establishment is often required; complementarities between modes of supply; the prevalence of joint production (such as the need for the consumer/provider to cooperate); and the role of reputation and non-price competition in many service industries. See, for example, Hindley (1988), Messerlin and Sauvant (1990), Sapir (1993), Sapir and Winter (1994), and UNCTAD and World Bank (1994).

7 See, for example, Brock (1982), Bhagwati (1987a, b), Drake and Nicolaidis (1992), Feketekuty (1988), Giersch (1989), Grey (1985), Helleiner (1988), Hindley (1990), Richardson (1987), Sampson and Snape (1985), Sapir (1985), and Snape (1990).

8 For the complete text, see GATT (1994).

9 This follows the typology suggested in the academic literature, especially Bhagwati (1984) and Sampson and Snape (1985). "Trade in Services" in the GATS context therefore covers both trade in the balance-of-payments sense and local sales by foreign affiliates.

10 The issue mainly concerned industries in relatively open markets seeking to obtain access to more closed markets. It was not that the *demandeur* industries feared cross-subsidized competition. This implied that the carrot being offered – MFN – was unlikely to induce much pressure on countries being asked to open up.

11 Interestingly, the European Union made an exemption for distribution of audiovisual works and audiovisual services more generally, allowing it to impose "redressive duties . . . to respond to unfair pricing practices" by third-country distributors, and to "prevent, correct or counterbalance adverse, unfair, or unreasonable conditions or actions affecting EC [European Community] audiovisual services, products, or service providers, in response to corresponding or comparable actions taken by other members."

12 In contrast to Article VII on recognition (see below).

13 The GATT GPA was revised to include services. However, this is a plurilateral agreement that binds only signatories. The new agreement has eleven members, mostly OECD countries (Israel and Korea are the only non OECD parties). Coverage of procurement of services is subject to a double positive list: only the procurement by covered entities of services explicitly scheduled in annexes are subject to the agreement's rules, and then only insofar as no qualifications or limitations are maintained in the relevant annexes. A number of countries made derogations to commitments on services specifying that offered services are covered only if other parties to the agreement provide reciprocal access to those services. The approach taken in GATS regarding sectoral reciprocity was therefore also pursued in the procurement context. The new GPA is discussed in Hoekman and Mavroidis (1995).

14 As in the GATT context, import restrictions are not recognized to be second-best instruments to deal with balance-of-payments difficulties.

15 A ministerial decision included in the Final Act states that "since measures necessary to protect the environment typically have as their objective the protection of human,

animal, or plant life or health, it is not clear that there is a need to provide for" an explicit "environmental" exception. The Committee on Trade and Environment is given the tasks of determining whether there is such a need and of examining the relationship between trade in services and the environment.

16 For a more detailed discussion, see UNCTAD and World Bank (1994, pp. 144–46).

17 This provision goes beyond the requirement to establish inquiry points contained in Article III (transparency), which simply relate to laws, regulations, decisions, etc., that effect the supply of services. The contact points for developing countries also cover technical matters.

18 Most members do not list horizontal restrictions on cross-border supply or consumer movement. It is not clear whether this implies that they have bound themselves. GATS allows additional commitments to be made going beyond national treatment/market access. Virtually no use has been made of this option.

19 Hoekman (1995) uses a subjective weighing scheme to determine the possible impact of (sensitivity to) incorporating this into the analysis.

20 The GATS schedules can be used to generate some information on the *relative* restrictiveness of the policy regimes maintained by members (see Hoekman 1995, annex 2; and Brown, Deardorff, Fox, and Stern, chapter 10 in this volume).

21 The only area where some liberalization occurred is in financial services, where a number of countries improved market access conditions.

22 The GATS list has four levels of aggregation. This chapter uses the 155 "three-digit" level of aggregation. The 155 activities include various categories of other services that are not strictly comparable across countries. There is little difference between the three- and four-digit levels – the latter only differs from the former in that item 7.B.f of the list (trading in financial instruments) is disaggregated into six types of instruments.

23 If countries made commitments on sectors not individually mentioned in the GATS classification list, only one sector is recorded. The economic significance of the activities mentioned in such cases tend to be minor. Members sometimes specify that a commitment applies only to a subset of a disaggregated item. A common example is under legal services, where foreign providers are often limited to the practice of – advice on—home country law. In these cases, it is assumed that the commitment applies to the whole subsector, biasing sectoral coverage indicators upward. Some GATS members may schedule commitments for an aggregated item instead of all five of the relevant subsectors. In such cases it is assumed that the commitment applies to all respective subsectors. In a number of cases a mode of supply is not technically feasible. A good example is cross-border provision of building assembly and installation services. Most schedules note this fact, stating that the mode of supply is 'unbound due to lack of technical feasibility." Such cases are allocated the value 1 for coverage calculation purposes, if other modes of supply are unrestricted. In the case of nations with a federal structure, a limitation on a mode of supply may only apply for one of the subfederal entities. No account of this is taken in the calculations here; it is assumed that the limitation applies to the whole nation. This results in a downward bias of coverage. Affected members include Canada, the European Union, and the United States.

24 A value of 1 for a sector/mode supply does not necessarily imply that foreign service providers can freely contest a specific market through a given mode of supply. This depends on applicable horizontal commitments, which tend to focus on labor mobility. In all cases where a reference is made under the temporary entry mode of supply to a horizontal commitment (restriction), a value of 0.5 is entered.

25 See Hoekman and Mavroidis (1994) for a discussion of the nonviolation option.

26 Sources for GDP data are the World Development Report and the World Bank STARS data base.

27 The complement of the no-restrictions ratio – with services weighted by shares in GDP – is an indicator of the extent to which policy affects access to service markets. This indicator can be seen as a direct analogue of the standard non-tariff barrier frequency indicator if unweighted by GDP shares, and of the nontariff barrier coverage ratio if weighted.

28 A ministerial decision taken in Marrakesh established a negotiating group to pursue talks on further liberalization of the movement of natural persons for the purpose of supplying services. This group was to conclude its talks within six months of the WTO's entry into force. The developing country objective to improve access to markets for independent professionals was met to only a limited extent.

29 Sometimes it is not even clear that limitations apply to what sector or subsector. Some schedules fail to mention a specific mode of supply for a given sector. Members at times also diverge from the positive-negative-list approach to scheduling, instead opting for a positive-positive-list approach. That is, the sectors to which the market access article and national treatment principle apply are listed, and then what is offered for each mode of supply is specified (as opposed to listing the limitations on national treatment or market access). This reduces transparency further, by not identifying all the policies that conflict with market access and/or national treatment. As noted previously, it is also not clear whether nonlisting of horizontal measures on modes of supply implies a binding of no restrictions.

30 See Hoekman and Sauvé (1994) for a description of these arrangements.

31 Thus the difference with agriculture, where stratographic bindings were considered an acceptable price to pay to get this sector back into the GATT, is that the current policy regime in many service sectors may be much less distorted.

32 The offer of official grant-based financial assistance for low-income countries would be a great boost.

33 Article XX of GATS (Schedules of Specific Commitments) states that separate commitments must be made for national treatment and for market access, but does not require that this be by mode of supply.

34 See Hoekman (1993) and Hoekman and Mavroidis (1995) for discussion on safeguards and government procurement.

35 A negative-list approach to scheduling, while important and necessary, is not sufficient to allow analysis. An additional requirement is that comparable production, consumption and trade data are available. Members should be required to report such data for at least the eleven major GATS service sectors, and preferably on a "2-digit" basis.

REFERENCES

Bhagwati, J. 1984. "Splintering and Disembodiment of Services and Developing Nations." *The World Economy* 7:133–44.

1987a. "Trade in Services and Developing Countries." In O. Giarini, ed., *The Emerging Service Economy*. New York: Praeger.

1987b. "Trade in Services and the Multilateral Trade Negotiations." *The World Bank Economic Review* 1:549–69.

Brock, W. 1982. "A Simple Plan for Negotiating on Trade in Services." *The World Economy* 5:229–40.

Deardoff, A. 1994. "Market Access." In *The New World Trading System: Readings*. Paris: OECD.

Deardorff, A., and R. Stern 1985. *Methods of Measurement of Non-Tariff Barriers*. Geneva: UNCTAD.

Drake, W., and K. Nicolaidis 1992. "Ideas, Interests, and Institutions: Trade in Services and the Uruguay Round." *International Organization* 46:37–100.

Feketekuty, G. 1988. *International Trade in Services: An Overview and Blueprint for Negotiations*. Cambridge, Mass.: Ballinger.

GATT 1994. *The Results of the Uruguay Round of Multilateral Negotiations: The Legal Texts*. Geneva: GATT, Secretariat.

Giersch, H., ed. 1989. *Services in World Economic Growth*. Tubingen: J. C. B. Mohr.

Grey, R. 1985. "Negotiating about Trade and Investment in Services." In R. Stern, ed., *Trade and Investment in Services: Canada / U.S. Perspectives*. Toronto: Ontario Economic Council.

Helleiner, G. 1988. "Trade in Services and the Developing Countries: Negotiating Approaches." In K. Haq, ed., *Linking the World: Trade Policies for the Future*. Islamabad: North South Roundtable.

Hindley, B. 1988. "Service Sector Protection: Considerations for Developing Countries." *World Bank Economic Review* 2:205–24.

1990. "Services." In Jeffrey Schott, ed., *Completing the Uruguay Round*. Washington DC: Institute for International Economics.

Hoekman, B. 1993. "Safeguard Provisions and International Agreements Involving Trade in Services." *The World Economy* 176:29–49.

1994. "Conceptual and Political Economy Issues in Liberalizing International Transactions in Services." In A. Deardorff and R. Stern, eds, *Analytical and Negotiating Issues in the Global Trading System*. Ann Arbor: University of Michigan Press.

1995. "Tentative First Steps: An Assessment of the Uruguay Round Agreement on Services." In W. Martin and L. A. Winters, eds. *The Uruguay Round and the Developing Economies*. World Bank Discussion Paper 307. Washington, DC: World Bank.

Hoekman, B., and P. C. Mavroidis 1994. "Competition, Competition Policy, and the GATT." *The World Economy* 17:121–50.

1995. "The WTO's Agreement on Government Procurement: Expanding Disciplines, Declining Membership?" *Public Procurement Law Review* 4: 63–79.

Hoekman, B., and P. Sauvé 1994. *Liberalizing Trade in Services*. World Bank Discussion Paper 243, Washington DC: World Bank.

Hoekman, B., and R. Stern 1991. "Evolving Patterns of Trade and Investment in Services." In P. Hooper and J. D. Richardson, eds, *International Economic Transactions: Issues in Measurement and Empirical Research*. Chicago: University of Chicago Press.

Martin, W., and J. Francois 1995. "Bindings and Rules as Trade Liberalization." In K. Maskus *et al.*, *Quiet Pioneering: Robert M. Stern and his International Legacy*. Ann Arbor: University of Michigan Press.

Messerlin, P., and K. Sauvant 1990. *The Uruguay Round: Services in the World Economy*. Washington, DC: World Bank.

Nogues, J., A. Olechowski, and A. Winters 1986. "The Extent of Nontariff Barriers to Industrial Countries Exports." *World Bank Economic Review* 1:181–99.

Richardson, J. 1987. "A Subsectoral Approach to Services Trade Theory." In O. Giarini, ed., *The Emerging Service Economy*. New York: Praeger.

Sampson, G., and R. Snape 1985. "Identifying the Issues in Trade in Services." *The World Economy* 8:171–81.

Sapir, A. 1985. "North-South Issues in Trade in Services." *The World Economy* 8: 27–42.

1993. "The Structure of Services in Europe: A Conceptual Framework." *European Economy* 3:83–99.

Sapir, A. and C. Winter 1994. "Services Trade." In D. Greenaway and L. A. Winters, eds, *Surveys in International Trade*. Oxford: Basil Blackwell.

Sauvé, P. 1995. "The General Agreement on Trade in Services: Much Ado About What?" In D. Schwanen, ed., *Trains, Grains and Automobiles: Canada and the Uruguay Round*. Toronto: C. D. Howe Institute.

Snape, R. 1990. "Principles in Trade in Services." In P. Messerlin and K. Sauvant, eds, *The Uruguay Round: Services in the World Economy*. Washington, DC: World Bank.

1994. "Services and the Uruguay Round." In *The New World Trading System: Readings*. Paris: OECD.

UNCTAD and World Bank 1994. *Liberalizing International Transactions in Services: A Handbook*. Geneva: United Nations.

World Bank 1995. *Global Economic Prospects*. Washington DC: World Bank.

7. Tariffication in the Uruguay Round: How Much Liberalisation?

M. D. Ingco

1. INTRODUCTION

A MAJOR ACHIEVEMENT IN THE Uruguay Round (UR) was the agreement to convert all agricultural trade barriers[1] into tariffs subject to agreed bindings (maximum rates). Tariffication and the adoption of tariff bindings is an important advance given the fact that before the UR, a mass of complex non-tariff measures was being used to provide the sector with high and variable rates of protection in virtually every country in the world. Exports from developing countries faced significant non-tariff measures (NTMs) in industrial countries. Estimates by Low and Yeats (1995) show that almost one-fifth of all agricultural imports (based on 1992 imports) from developing countries was subject to NTMs in industrial country markets, while the corresponding share for trade among industrial countries was about one-tenth. In OECD as a whole, the average nominal protection for agriculture rose from 41 per cent in 1979–81 to 74 per cent in 1992 – about fifteen times as high as tariffs in manufacturing.

Tariffication not only simplifies the treatment of existing trade barriers within the GATT/WTO, but it will also facilitate more straightforward negotiations in future rounds. Tariffs have clear advantages over other import barriers. Tariffs are transparent, more predictable, non-discriminatory, easier to bind or reduce, and less susceptible to corruption. They also facilitate competition in internal markets and help to ensure trade adjustments by importing countries to world market changes. However, measuring the tariff equivalents of NTMs is faced with a host of difficulties well discussed in the literature.[2]

Recent studies (IATRC, 1994; and GATT, 1994) have provided broad evaluations of the final Agreement of the UR, but to date, no systematic comparison of pre- and post-UR border protection has been made on a wide range of agricultural commodities and countries. Most countries, particularly in the OECD, converted their NTMs into specific tariffs, preventing an easy assessment of protection rates. This paper provides estimates of post-UR ad-valorem tariff equivalents of border measures based on the detailed results of final concessions on tariffication commitments on major commodities.[3]

The extent of agricultural trade liberalisation as a result of the Round is evaluated by comparing post-UR protection measures with historical estimates and a hypothesised future rate of protection without the UR agreement. Participating countries subject to tariffication agreed to establish their initial base tariffs based on tariff equivalents of non-tariff barriers applied in the base period, 1986–88. These required that the base tariff equal the level of nominal protection prevailing in the base period. A significant difference between these two measures could be considered a form of 'dirty' tariffication: this is also evaluated in this paper.[4] The remainder of the paper is organised into five sections. Section 2 describes the methods used in estimating pre- and post-UR border protection. The results of tariffication and the changes in border protection before and after the UR are discussed in Sections 3. The extent of trade liberalisation and conclusions are discussed in Sections 4 and 5, respectively.

a. Tariffication in the Uruguay Round

The modalities in establishing tariff equivalents provide a range of alternatives in establishing the tariff equivalents depending on the level of development of the participating country and the nature of the tariff and import restrictions at the beginning of the Round: whether or not the tariff was already bound at the beginning of the Round and/or whether NTMs were applied. For commodities subject to bound tariffs at the beginning of the Round, participating countries were required either (i) to apply tariffication if NTMs existed, or (ii) to establish the base tariffs at the current bound rate. In commodities subject only to unbound duties (i.e., no NTMs apply) at the beginning of the Round, participating countries were required to set their 1995 base tariffs and apply tariff reductions based on the level in September, 1986. If unbound duties and NTMs existed at the beginning of the Round, tariffication was required. Many developing countries were allowed to offer new base and bound tariffs and tariff ceiling bindings in commodities with previously bound tariffs.

The effectiveness of tariffication is reduced if the tariff bindings are set at very high levels such that post-UR applied rates could remain prohibitive or if there is substantial variation in the actual duty charged in the range below the bound level. Countries can charge tariffs at varying levels within the margin of the binding, and these can be linked to an internal price. Thus, the duty can be set as the difference between a given domestic price and the import price, as long as the tariff charged does not exceed the binding. With the possible exception of who gets the revenue, such variable tariffs could work similarly to a variable levy or a minimum price, despite the fact that the agreement states that variable levies, minimum report prices and similar measures are forbidden and should be converted to tariffs (Article 4, para. 2).

The market access provisions did not result in "unconditional" tariffication in all cases. A Special Treatment clause is provided (Annex 5) which, under specific conditions, allows certain countries to delay tariffication of their rice markets for several years (e.g. Japan, the Republic of Korea and the Philippines). Safeguard Provisions were also included (Article 5) for importers in the cases of import surges and/or low world prices. Hence, in addition to the new tariffs in commodities subject to tariffication, additional duties can be charged if either imports increase above a specified base level, or border prices for imports decline below specified trigger prices. If imports exceed a certain percentage of the preceding three-year average, called the trigger level, or import prices decline below a trigger price, additional duties (up to one-third of the normal applicable duty) could be imposed.[5] The trigger levels are relatively low and can be invoked without requiring proof of injury. It is difficult to assess the likely frequency and impact of the special safeguards, but they are a potential source of additional protection.

Exporting countries obtained so-called 'minimum access commitments,' in commodities subject to tariffication. The minimum access provisions were designed to deal with continued high levels of border protection by ensuring access of a minimum quantity of imports. These require countries to maintain current market access opportunities based on the volume of imports during 1986–88 for individual commodities. Secondly, if a country's imports of a specific commodity were not already above five per cent of domestic consumption between 1986–88, countries were required to increase access up to the minimum access opportunity of three per cent of the base period domestic consumption starting in 1995, rising to five per cent by the year 2000. This access was to be achieved by the use of tariff quotas whereby countries impose lower tariffs for quantities of imports up to their minimum access commitments. In most cases, the final access provided is no more than the base period imports.

Despite the most-favoured-nation equipment, countries were allowed to count existing bilateral arrangements towards their minimum access commitments. For example, the US sugar import quota system was included by applying a new tariff quota system to the same quota from the same countries. In the same way, the US Meat Import Law was translated into a tariff quota system with the quotas given to the same countries which held previous quota rights (e.g. Australia and New Zealand). In these cases, the minimum access provisions of the UR agreement will not open markets significantly and will provide very little trade expansion beyond previous or current levels. Even in other commodities, an evaluation of the minimum access commitments for major importing countries relative to their recent import levels indicates that the additional trade likely to occur as a result of the minimum access provisions will be very small relative to current world trade levels. The only major exception is in rice, where the minimum access commitment of Japan and the Republic of Korea will result in increased trade of about one million tons annually, nearly seven per cent of 1991/92 world trade. Finally, of course, the need for quota allocations brings back the non-transparency of import protection.

2. ESTIMATES OF PRE- AND POST-UR PROTECTION

How will the new UR rules and disciplines affect border protection in agriculture? This section outlines the methods used in estimating pre- and post-UR border protection measures. Agricultural protection as a result of the Round will be disciplined primarily by the outcome of tariffication and the reduction commitments on export subsidies and domestic support. In general, the results of final concessions on tariffication will affect the post-UR nominal protection on imported goods, while the export subsidy commitments will define the rate of nominal protection on exportables. In cases where exporting countries are providing export subsidies and also maintaining import barriers on homogenous goods, arbitrage implies that in general, a country cannot set an export subsidy higher than the level of the tariff. Hence, the level of the tariff equivalent sets a ceiling on the level of the export subsidy and would also be indicative of the maximum nominal protection rate.

To be consistent with the tariffication provisions, I have represented past trade restrictions with a measure equivalent to the nominal rate of protection. This measures the magnitude of the historical price distortion or price wedge induced by non-tariff measures. The post-UR levels of protection are estimated based on the tariffication and export subsidy commitments in the UR schedules.

a. Pre-UR Border Protection

Any evaluation of the liberalising effect of the Round must begin with an assessment of the protective effects of the measures which preceded it and which would have occurred without it. Had the UR not concluded, presumably these policies, or some variant of them, would have generated the counterfactual future rate of protection against which the UR should be evaluated. The protective effects of pre-UR trade distortions in a particular market are measured in terms of their tariff equivalents defined in price terms – i.e., the change in price due to the non-tariff measures.[6] The UR tariffication procedures were outlined in a negotiating document entitled 'Modalities for the Establishment of Specific Binding Commitments under the Reform Programme' (referred to below as the Modalities). The Modalities required the establishment of initial base tariffs to afford the same level of nominal protection as the prevailing NTBs in 1986–88. That is, the post-UR base tariff, to be set at either specific or *ad-valorem* rates, would be based on the protected domestic and world prices of the relevant commodity in 1986–88. The difference between these prices would be the 'price gap' which defines the specific tariff and the percentage difference between them would be the *ad-valorem* tariff equivalent that would replace the non-tariff barrier.

The exact measure of a non-tariff barrier in terms of its effect on prices is one which compares the domestic price that would prevail without the non-tariff barrier with that which would prevail with it. However, since these prices are usually not observable, actual measures of non-tariff barriers are usually based on a comparison of domestic and world prices in the presence of non-tariff barriers. To apply this method, we have to identify the appropriate prices. This is difficult because products of a particular industry that are imported into a country usually differ from those that are produced domestically, and they may also differ from products which are produced and traded abroad. In general, the appropriate prices to use in measuring the price impact of a non-tariff barrier are the domestic (i.e. the price of imports domestically) and invoice price of the imported product. Since available domestic prices do not usually distinguish domestically produced goods from imported goods, the price of the product in the domestic market is used instead.

Let P_d represent the price of the product in the domestic market and Pw be the invoice price of imports inclusive of tariffs and transport costs (e.i.f.). The price comparisons are usually expressed as a percentage difference between the prices expressed as follows: $\tau = 100^* (P_d - P\omega]P\omega$. The latter is referred to as the *ad-valorem* tariff equivalent or the implicit protection associated with the non-tariff barrier. The *ad-valorem* tariff equivalents of border protection are estimated for each year depending on data availability – from 1982–93 in developing countries and from 1979–93 in OECD countries.

Data on world and domestic prices use were derived from several sources including the Organisation for Economic Cooperation and Development (OECD), US Department of Agriculture (USDA), FAO, and the World Bank. These sources are complemented by the information on internal and reference prices in 1986–88 reported in the supplementary tables in the country Schedules. The OECD provides estimates of producer subsidy equivalents (PSE) beginning in 1979 for 12 OECD trading blocs and up to 22 commodities or commodity groups. The USDA has extended this coverage to 34 countries and 48 commodities or commodity groups, for the period 1982–93.[7] Four types of measures are included in the OECD and USDA/ERS producer subsidy equivalent calculations, namely, market price support, direct income support, indirect income support and other assistance. Price support programmes, tariffs, and quotas are examples of the first set of measures, while deficiency payments enter the second group. Indirect income supports and other assistance include input subsidies, capital grants, research etc. To estimate the tariff equivalent of border protection based on the PSE estimates, I consider only the effects of market price support measures (price support, tariffs, quotas, and other NTMs) and exclude the direct and indirect income transfers and other assistance.

For purposes of comparison, I also estimate a pre-UR tariff equivalent based on the reported internal and reference prices in the country Schedules for the base period, 1986–88. The Modalities defined internal prices at the wholesale level. However, not all countries used wholesale prices in defining their tariff equivalent (e.g. EU's tariff equivalent are based on intervention or threshold prices). Where the wholesale prices are not available, I use producer prices to measure internal prices. This will result in some underestimation of protection by the amount of the producer-to-wholesale marketing margin.

b. Post-UR Border Protection

This section briefly reviews the rules on tariffication provided in the Modalities. The methods used in estimating the post-UR tariff equivalents are then discussed. Tariff equivalents were required to be established at the four-digit level or at the six-digit or more detailed level of the Harmonised System (HS) wherever appropriate, as in the case of certain fruits and vegetables. The Modalities also required that 'actual prices, rather than constructed ones be the basis for tariff equivalents' (e.g. the threshold price in the EU). For transformed and processed agricultural products, tariff equivalents were required to be established by multiplying the specific tariff equivalent(s) for the agricultural input(s) by the proportion(s) in value terms or in physical terms as appropriate of the agricultural inputs(s) in the transformed processed agricultural products.

The Modalities also specified the external prices to be used in tariffication as the actual average c.i.f. import unit values for the importing country. Where average c.i.f. unit values are not available or appropriate, external prices are defined as the appropriate average c.i.f. import unit values of a near country or the estimated f.o.b. unit values of (an) appropriate major export(s) adjusted by adding an estimate of insurance, freight, and other relevant costs to the importing country. External prices are converted to domestic currencies using the annual average market exchange rate for the same period as the price data. Internal prices are defined in the Modalities as the representative wholesale price ruling in the domestic market or an estimate of that price where adequate data are not available. The initial tariff equivalents have to be adjusted to take account of differences in quality or variety and applied to tariff lines which are frequently defined at 8, 10 or 12 digit levels. Where a tariff equivalent resulting from these guidelines is negative or lower than the current bound rate, countries were allowed to establish the initial base tariff equivalent at the current bound rate or on the basis of national offers for that product. The level of tariff equivalents resulting from tariffication using 1986–88 data, supplemented by the rules as stated above are specified as the base level (i.e. to be applied in 1995) for the implementation of the reduction commitments on market access.

The post-UR nominal border protection rates are derived from the tariffication commitments. In this paper, the specific tariffs in the Schedule, assumed to reflect the difference between internal and border prices as defined in the Modalities, $[T = (P_d - P\omega)]$, are translated into *ad-valorem* tariff equivalents simply by dividing the specific tariff by the appropriate border price as defined in the Modalities. The average border prices in 1986–88 used in estimating the pre-UR tariff equivalents of NTMs are now used to convert the post-UR base specific tariffs in the Schedules into *ad-valorem* rates in the base period. To translate the final or bound specific tariffs in the schedules (tariffs to apply at the end of the implementation period) into final *ad-valorem* rates, I use alternatively (a) constant world prices at the level during the base period, 1986–88 or (b) World Bank projections of world prices for the year 2000.

Since our estimated pre-UR tariff equivalents of NTMs are based on data on world and domestic prices, which are usually not available at the tariff line level, in post-UR specific tariffs which are at 10–12 digit tariff line level in the Schedules must be aggregated to attempt to match the pre-UR measures. An average specific tariff corresponding to the commodity defined at the 4-digit HS code is calculated by taking a simple unweighted average of the tariffs for the group under consideration. Unweighted tariffs are preferred in this case because trade weighted tariffs may be biased downward because imports that are highly taxed cost more and are, therefore, imported less. In the extreme, a tariff set at sufficiently high level as to eliminate imports would receive no weight in the aggregation.

In the case of commodities where the historical estimates of protection (based on the OECD and USDA data) are defined at the farmgate/first stage of trade, the specific tariffs of the processed items are transformed using appropriate conversion factors.[8] This is not an issue for commodities such as grains (wheat, maize, barley, oats, rye and sorghum) or white sugar which are reasonably homogenous and where comparable post-UR tariff equivalents are specified in the Schedules. The tariffs specified for 'within access' commitments in the tariff quota are assumed to be infra-marginal and only to represent an income transfer, hence they are not included in the estimations.

For exportables, the post-UR border protection will be determined by the export subsidy commitments. The commitments on export subsidies are in terms of maximum volume and budget outlays defined for a major group of commodities. A 36 per cent reduction in the value of export subsidies by a particular country would typically require a less than 36 per cent reduction in the *ad-valorem* equivalent of the export subsidy since the decline in value would result from changes in both the rate of assistance and in the quantity exported. In the context of multilateral reforms under the Round, reductions in export subsidies are likely to raise world prices, offsetting the reduction in export volumes implied by the reductions in export subsidies. Thus, treating the export subsidy reductions in terms of reductions in export subsidy rates could be used as an approximation to the effects of the commitments. The per unit export subsidy rates at the base period is determined as follows: $S_s = \frac{B_3}{\psi_3 X_3}$ where s is the subsidy rate, B is the total value of export refunds, X is the total volume of exports, and ψ is the share of exports which is subsidised. The subscript s denotes the goods which are net exports and use export subsidies. The per unit subsidy rates during the base period are translated to *ad-valorem* rates using border prices in 1986–88. There are goods which are treated as net exportables in estimating historical protection based on the OECD and USDA databases but do not have export subsidy commitments in the Round. In these commodities, some imports occur and the post-UR border protection are estimated based on the tariffication commitments.[9] In most of these commodities, import restrictions are an essential backstop for export subsidy programmes. The tariff equivalent based on the tariffication commitments defines the maximum post-UR border protection.

3. HOW 'DIRTY' WAS TARIFFICATION?

a. Industrial Countries

To examine 'dirty' tariffication, the estimated tariff equivalents based on the country Schedules are compared with the estimated tariff equivalent of border measures in 1986–88. The results for several major commodities in selected countries are summarised in Tables 1A and 1B. The chosen base period of tariffication was a period of relatively high agricultural support and protection in the industrial countries because world prices were at their lowest level in recent decades during the period. Hence, the tariff equivalent based on the 1986–88 period would result in high levels of protection compared with any representative period. The estimates indicate that the specific and *ad-valorem* tariffs which many countries have set in their schedules are significantly higher than the wedge between actual domestic and world market prices in the base period, hence affording higher protection than prevailed in 1986–88.

TABLE 1A *Comparison of Estimated Ad-valorem Tariff Equivalent, 1986–88 and Tariffs Declared in Country Schedules (Percent)**

Countries	Rice			Wheat			Coarse Grains			Sugar		
	Estimate 1986–88 (1)	UR Base (2)	Difference (2)–(1)	Estimate 1986–88 (7)	UR Base (8)	Difference (8)–(7)	Estimate 1986–88 (9)	UR Base (10)	Difference (10–(9)	Estimate 1986–88 (3)	UR Base (4)	Difference (4)–(3)
Industrial												
Australia	13.5	0.0	–13.5	0.7	0.0	–0.7	0.0	0.4	0.4	11.8	52.4	40.6
Canada	na	0.9	na	30.0	57.7	27.7	39.0	34.7	–4.3	349.0	34.7	–4.3
United States	1.0	5.0	4.0	20.0	6.0	–14.0	4.0	8.0	4.0	131.0	197.0	66.0
European Union	153.0	360.5	207.5	103.0	155.6	52.6	133.0	134.4	1.4	234.0	297.0	63.0
Japan	500.0	na[1]	na	651.0	239.6	–411.4	679.0	233.1	–445.9	184.0	126.1	–57.9
New Zealand	0.0	0.0	0.0	0.0	0.0	0.0	0.0	7.2	7.2	0.0	2.9	2.9
Austria	0.0	0.0	0.0	188.0	400.0	212.0	108.0	241.0	133.0	183.0	178.0	–5.0
Finland	na	10.0	na	239.0	352.0	113.0	342.0	204.0	–138.0	265.0	493.0	228.0
Norway	na	454.0	na	266.0	495.0	229.0	361.0	394.0	33.0	0.0	na	na
Switzerland	0.0	67.0	na	245.0	179.0	–66.0	226.0	242.0	16.0	277.0	273.0	–4.0
Turkey	na	50.0	na	36.0	200.0	164.0	35.0	200.0	165.0	12.0	150.0	138.0
Developing Countries												
Mexico	6.8	50.0	43.2	–1.0	74.0	75.0	73.0	174.0	101.0	–57.7	173.0	230.7
Colombia	4.0	210.0	206.0	20.0	138.0	118.0	14.0	221.0	207.0	25.3	130.0	104.7
Venezuela	174.9	135.0	–39.9	na	130.0	na	293.0	123.0	–170.0	47.0	100.0	53.0
Thailand	1.0	58.0	57.0	na	64.0	na	na	81.0	na	na	104.0	na
South Africa	na	5.0	na	10.3	74.5	64.2	47.8	68.0	20.2	98.0	124.0	26.0
Indonesia	8.8	180.0[2]	171.2	na	30.0	na	6.0	70.0[2]	64.0	87.0	110.0[2]	23.0
Rep. of Korea	213.8	na[1]	na	na	10.9		421.3	450.0	28.7	na	23.7	na
Mexico	6.8	50.0	43.2	–1.0	74.0	75.0	73.0	174.0	101.0	–57.7	173.0	230.7
Morocco	na	233.5	na	14.0	224.0	210.0	8.0	150.0	142.0	58.3	221.0	162.7
Czech Rep.	14.0	70.0	56.0	–38.0	16.0	54.0	–8.0	20.0	28.0	14.0	70.0	56.0

Notes:
[1] Delayed Tariffication.
[2] Ceiling Binding
* Selected commodities where tariffication was applied and are subject to Safeguards.

TABLE 1B *Comparison of Estimated Tariff Equivalent, 1986–88 and Tariffs Declared in Country Schedules (Percent)**

Countries	Beef & Veal Estimate 1986–88 (1)	Beef & Veal UR Base 1995 (2)	Beef & Veal Difference (2)–(1)	Pork Estimate 1986–88 (3)	Pork UR Base 1995 (4)	Pork Difference (4)–(3)	Poultry Estimate 1986–88 (5)	Poultry UR Base 1995 (6)	Poultry Difference (6)–(5)	Dairy Estimate 1986–88 (5)	Dairy UR Base (6)	Dairy Difference (6)–(5)
Industrial												
Australia	0.0	0.0	0.0	0.0	0.0	0.0	0.0	0.0	0.0	49.3	6.7	–42.6
Canada	2.0	38.0	36.0	0.0	0.0	0.0	19.0	226.0	207.0	187.0	288.4	101.4
United States	3.0	31.0	28.0	0.0	0.0	0.0	15.0	7.0	–8.0	132.0	144.0	12.0
European Union	83.0	125.4	42.4	40.0	51.7	11.7	51.0	44.5	–6.5	177.0	288.5	111.5
Japan	87.0	38.5	–48.5	99.0	87.3	–11.7	13.0	14.0	1.0	501.0	489.4	–11.6
New Zealand	0.0	0.0	0.0	1.7	20.0	18.3	100.7	28.5	–72.2	0.0	19.6	19.6
Austria	79.0	239.0	160.0	72.0	178.0	106.0	41.0	38.0	–3.0	196.0	463.0	267.0
Finland	193.3	394.0	200.7	227.0	320.0	93.0	206.6	264.0	57.4	387.0	389.0	2.0
Norway	145.0	405.0	260.0	255.0	428.0	173.0	614.0	379.0	–235.0	148.0	435.0	287.0
Switzerland	236.0	479.0	243.0	157.0	227.0	70.0	585.0	767.0	182.0	321.0	795.0	474.0
Turkey	–4.4	250.0	254.4	na	250.0	na	11.5	30.0	na	35.0	200.0	165.0
Developing												
Mexico	41.6	50.0	8.4	na	50.0	na	na	217.7	na	–3.0	75.0	78.0
Colombia	na	120.0	na	na	120.0	na	na	126.0	na	na	150.0	na
Venezuela	na	50.0	na	na	53.0	na	na	150.0	na	na	96.0	na
Thailand	na	60.0	na	na	60.0	na	na	60.0	na	na	63.0	na
South Africa	na	210.0	na	na	50.0	na	30.0	116.7	86.7	30.0	189.0	159.0
Indonesia	na	70.0	na	na	70.0	na	na	70.0	na	na	154.0	na
Rep. of Korea	95.5	44.5	–51.0	38.7	33.3	–5.4	2.2	26.3	24.1	103.4	220.0	116.6
Mexico	41.6	50.0	8.4	na	50.0	na	na	217.7	na	–3.0	75.0	78.0
Morocco	na	315.0		na	45.0	na	na	132.5	na	na	115.0	na
Czech Rep.	134.0	43.0	–91.0	15.0	46.0	31.0	na	36.0	na	–20.0	64.0	84.0

Notes:
[1] Delayed Tariffication.
[2] Ceiling Binding.

The extent of 'dirty' tariffication varied widely among countries and commodities. In many countries, it appears to have occurred in the 'sensitive' commodities such as dairy, sugar, and grains. Among the industrial countries, the magnitude appears largest in the European Union and EFTA.

During the UR negotiations, the EU had begun to reform its Common Agricultural Policy by reducing the level of price support and providing direct income compensation payments to farmers instead. Combined with increases in world prices, these reforms resulted in a decline in the rate of border protection in most commodities since the base period (1986–88). The rates agreed for bound tariffs in the Round allow scope to reverse this trend.

The EU provided an additional commitment on its tariff for grains in the form of a maximum duty-paid price linked to the intervention price. That is, for major grains the duty-paid import price shall not exceed a domestic intervention price plus 55 per cent, and for husked rice it shall be no greater than the intervention price plus 80–88 per cent. The 55 per cent and the 80–88 per cent appears to represent the mark-up between the threshold price and the intervention prices for major grains and rice, respectively, under CAP reform. Hence, this provision allows the EU to charge tariffs at levels necessary to defend its already set threshold prices under CAP reform, as long as the duty charged does not exceed the binding. In practice, this can work similarly to a variable levy or a minimum price. The actual import tariff levied on c.i.f. prices would be up to the difference between the domestic mark-up and the world price (c.i.f.). Hence, in periods of particularly low world prices, the EU will probably charge a high tariff so as to maintain the agreed 'Community preference' but at a level not exceeding the tariff binding. If world prices are high, the EU border regime may not in practice be much different from what it would have been under CAP reform. That is, when world prices are high, the EU will charge a lower tariff so as not to exceed the commitment on 'maximum duty-paid import price' to maintain the level of threshold prices already set under CAP reform policies. The determination of the actual tariff on grains would, however, apparently be shipment specific, in contrast to the pre-UR regime where the levy, calculated as the difference between the threshold price and a world price determined by the Commission, is charged on all imports irrespective of the actual price of the shipment. Under the GATT commitment, the actual tariff will be calculated based on the price of the specific grain shipment to ensure that the duty-paid price for each shipment will not exceed 155 per cent of the intervention price.

Based on World Bank world price projections, the *ad-valorem* equivalents of the bound specific tariffs for major agricultural commodities are shown in Table 2. As evident in Table 2, protection levels in most commodities are estimated to decline quite substantially from the high levels of 1995. The decline is a consequence of the scheduled agreed reductions in the level of specific tariffs and the likely gradual increase in nominal prices of agricultural commodities over time. With the high levels of post-UR base tariffs, most tariffs in 2000/2004 will still be above the average applied rates prior to the Round.

In the European Union, the post-UR base and final tariff equivalents are significantly higher in most commodities relative to average protection levels in recent years and in the base period (1986–88). The difference is even larger when compared with the average during 1979–93. If the EU applied the maximum specific tariffs committed in the UR, the estimated post-UR *ad-valorem* tariff equivalents in 1995 and 2000 indicate significant increases in protection in major commodities relative to recent levels and relative to the average protection over the last fifteen years.

The estimates also provide evidence of uneven reductions in tariffs among commodities, with the smallest percentage reduction in 'sensitive' commodities. To offset these minimal cuts, the tariffs on products that already had low tariffs were cut significantly more in percentage terms. Thus, to make an unweighted average cut of 36 per cent, a 100 per cent cut in a two or five per cent tariff could compensate in the average for 15 percent cuts in two highly protected products. The combination of 'dirty' tariffication and the unequal distribution of tariff reductions for many commodities previously protected by NTMs have allowed for continued high protection at the end of the implementation period. For example, the results indicate that the bindings for border protection for sugar and dairy products were maintained or even increased in some countries, whereas protection on products such as coffee, cocoa and oilseeds was generally reduced from an already low level. In this case, the approach of tariff reductions employed may lead to even more distortions in agricultural trade in some cases.

Although the conversion of non-tariff measures to tariffs would bring agriculture closely in line with the rules of the GATT for other products, the tariffication process has eroded the extent of the anticipated liberalisation in major commodities in many countries. In addition, the tariff bindings in the base period are high relative to the rates of protection resulting under current policies. Even after the agreed reductions over 1995–2000, the tariff equivalents in many commodities remain higher than the average level of protection in 1979–93.

In Japan, a complex system of fixed and variable levies has kept internal prices well above world prices. Protection for all major commodities in Japan is provided largely through administered prices maintained by tariffs and import restrictions. Japanese raw sugar prices, for instance, were eight times the world price in 1985–86, while rice and wheat prices were more than six times the world price during the same period. Border protection has fallen in recent years, but remains very high in rice, dairy products, wheat, barley and sugar. In contrast, protection in the Japanese beef sector has declined from 70 per cent to 60 per cent in 1992 and to 50 per cent in 1993. Japan committed to further reduce the *ad-valorem* tariff on beef to 38.5 per cent. However, the post-UR tariff equivalents for milk, sugar and wheat remain prohibitive. Japan agreed to convert all NTMs to tariffs, except for rice, where tariffication was delayed but a higher minimum access commitment (four to eight per cent of domestic consumption over the implementation period) is provided.

In the United States, tariffication has a direct effect on the policies for beef, sugar and dairy products. Both sugar and milk are assisted through administered prices, which are supported by tariffs and import quotas. The Meat Import Law and associated voluntary export restraint arrangements (VERs) have been the main source of protection for the US beef industry. On main export products, the Export Enhancement Programme (EEP) provides a discretionary authority

Table 2 *Border Protection for Selected Agricultural Goods, 1979–93 and 1995 and 2000 (Per Cent)*

Country/ Region	Wheat				Sugar				Dairy				Meat			
	Actual Protection		As bound in the Uruguay Round		Actual Protection		As bound in the Uruguay Round		Actual Protection		As bound in the Uruguay Round		Actual Protection		As bound in the Uruguay Round	
	1979–93	1986–88	1995	2000	1979–93	1986–88	1995	2000	1979–93	1986–88	1995	2000	1979–93	1986–88	1995	2000
EU	57	106	170	82	150	234	297	152	128	177	289	178	93	96	96	76
United States	20	20	6	4	126	131	197	91	92	132	144	93	2	3	31	26
Japan	308	651	240	152	126	184	126	58	207	501	489	326	30	87	93	50
Brazil	56	98	45	45	–	–	55	35	–21	–21	53	46	–40	–52	25	25
Mexico	27	–1	74	67	–42	–58	173	156	–4	–3	66	54	39	42	50	45
Other Latin America	–25	–17	34	34	35	41	85	80	–	–	75	69	–	–	51	47
Nigeria	190	249	..	150	29	32	..	150	–	–	..	150	–	–	..	150
South Africa	7	10	75	47	50	98	124	105	30	30	189	89	40	40	150	81
Sub-Saharan Africa	–1	10	..	133	16	44	..	100	–	–	..	100	–	–	..	100
Maghreb[a]	32	36	196	151	41	64	220	165	50	50	113	87	–	–	303	213
Mediterranean[b]	12	25	169	152	0	–13	107	93	–	–	166	150	–	–	166	149

Notes:

– Not available; .. no tariff bindings for the period in question.
[a] Includes Algeria, Morocco and Tunisia.
[b] Includes Cyprus, Egypt, Israel, Jordan, Lebanon, Libya, Malta, Syria and Turkey.

Source: Author's calculations.

to provide export subsidies. The post-UR base *ad-valorem* tariff equivalents of import quotas indicate higher level of protection than those applying in the base period, 1986–88. In addition, sugar and dairy products will remain highly protected with very high tariffs charged at the end of the implementation period.

b. Developing Countries

The UR negotiations provided the opportunity for developing countries to increase their integration into the international trading system. For the first time, many countries participated in the negotiations and increased the extent to which their protection will be subject to tariff bindings. Developing countries as a whole increased the proportion of agricultural product lines subject to tariff bindings from 18 per cent to 100 per cent (GATT, 1994). However, the extent to which developing countries chose to use tariff bindings and the extent of liberalization achieved varied considerably by commodity and by country. Some countries used the Round to lock in and consolidate recent unilateral and/or bilateral liberalisations while others, particularly the least-developed ones, made no substantial liberalization commitments.

Developing countries were allowed to offer tariff ceiling bindings (arbitrarily chosen maximum levels) in commodities with previous unbound tariffs, and were permitted to commit lower reduction obligations (two-thirds the level in industrial countries) to be implemented over a longer transition period (ten years). Agricultural subsidies for food security, investment, input, transport and marketing were exempted from reductions. In addition, the most prevalent trade distortions in developing countries, namely import subsidies, export taxes, and state trading import monopolies are not disciplined in the Round.

The results indicate large variations in patterns of pre-UR protection and post-UR agricultural tariff bindings. As in the industrial countries, many developing countries offered very high base tariffs in several major commodities. In most cases, these bindings were set at levels way above historical protection. Several countries (i.e., Egypt, Pakistan and Zimbabwe), which have maintained import subsidies or export taxes (indicated by negative historical tariff equivalents) in major food crops also established high maximum ceiling bindings.

In the case of wheat, a major importable in developing countries, significantly higher base tariff equivalents than actual pre-UR levels were established in several countries, including India (+98 per cent), Pakistan (+171 per cent), Colombia (+118 per cent), and Morocco (+210 per cent). In the case of rice, several net importing countries also offered higher base nominal protection than actual levels in the base period, with the largest differences occurring in Bangladesh, Colombia, and Mexico. In the case of coarse grains, similar patterns occurred in Indonesia, the Republic of Korea, Colombia, Jamaica, Mexico, and Morocco. Bangladesh offered a uniform ceiling binding of 200 per cent, Pakistan the range 100–150 per cent, Nigeria 230 per cent, Zimbabwe 150 per cent and Kenya, 100 per cent. It is interesting to note, however, that these levels of allowable protection are below those historically applied in the industrial countries. In rice, for example, increased allowable base protection is shown in Nigeria, Bangladesh,

Pakistan, Indonesia, Thailand, Colombia, Mexico, Egypt and the Czech Republic, but only at levels slightly above one-third of the rates applied in Japan.

(i) Latin America. Most countries in Latin America began unilateral trade reforms in the late 1980s or early 1990s and have overtaken the UR process in reducing tariffs and NTMs. Tariff reductions have been significant in Argentina, Brazil, Chile, Colombia, Mexico, Peru and Venezuela since the mid-1980s.[10] These countries consolidated recent liberalisation in the UR and have tariffied remaining NTMs in several commodities. However, some countries have set their post-UR bound rates above current applied rates, potentially resulting in increased applied border protection after the Round. For instance, Colombia established bound tariffs which are significantly higher than historical protection levels for durum wheat (124 per cent), barley (144 per cent), maize (194 per cent), sorghum (132 per cent), soybeans (125 per cent) and sugar (117 per cent). The average tariff equivalent of nominal border protection for these commodities, ranged between three and twenty per cent in 1982–92. In contrast, Venezuela committed tariff bindings which are significantly lower than those applying in the base period for the commodities considered, while Chile appears to have committed final bindings at or below the previous bound rates.[11] Other Latin American countries committed nearly uniform tariff bindings in most agricultural commodities: Bolivia (40 per cent), Paraguay (35 per cent), Honduras (35 per cent), Dominican Republic (40 per cent), Peru (30 per cent, except in wheat, milk, and butter set at 68 per cent). Argentina, Brazil, and Chile generally offered lower base tariff equivalents in most commodities (ranging from 25 per cent to 55 per cent in 1995) than other Latin American countries.

(ii) Asia. The extent of agricultural liberalisation in Asian countries as a result of the UR varied among commodities and countries. In general, however, the reductions in border protection as a result of the UR will be modest. The results indicate that several countries in Upper-Income Asia committed to further reduce border protection in some major commodities while others, particularly South Asian countries, will not liberalise agriculture under the Round. On the contrary, the Round may potentially increase protection in agriculture if applied rates are increased from current levels towards bound levels. The tariff commitments in low-income Asian countries do not represent any meaningful liberalisations and are unlikely to address the key distortions in trade policies.

Most countries in the region, as in other least-developed regions, were given the flexibility to establish general or specific tariff bindings (which defines maximum protection levels over the next ten years) at levels significantly above historical protection rates. In some countries, the effect of the high tariffs on domestic resource allocation are neutralised by government controlled prices, which in many cases are kept below world prices. This negative protection or taxation in some countries was not disciplined in the Round.

Several countries introduced ceiling tariff bindings at levels far above the pre-UR levels of protection. For instance, the ceiling bindings in most commodities were set at very high levels in Bangladesh (200 per cent), Pakistan (100–150 per cent), India (100–150 per cent) and Myanmar (168 per cent). India has bound most agricultural tariffs at prohibitive levels. For instance, the UR base protection for sugar was set at 75 per cent, meats and tree crops at 140 per cent, and dairy products at 45 per cent. Wheat, which was taxed at –13 per cent in 1982–93 received a tariff binding of 100 per cent, while oilseeds, cotton, tobacco, and jute received a tariff binding at 100 per cent. For other food grains (corn, rice and sorghum), protection rates shifted from small positive levels in 1986–88 to negative levels since 1989, as hikes in world prices were not transmitted to domestic producers. Interestingly, the post-UR tariffs for these commodities were bound to zero, possibly to avoid having to make a minimum access commitment.

(iii) Africa and the Middle East. The level of the tariff bindings in Africa and Middle Eastern countries is at prohibitive levels (100–300 per cent) and set way above pre-UR levels of protection in most food crops. The highest level of uniform ceiling bindings, excluding other duties and charges[12] are in Cameroon (80 per cent), Gabon (60 per cent), Ghana (99 per cent), Kenya (100 per cent), Mauritius (122 per cent), Nigeria (150 per cent) and Zimbabwe (150 per cent). In contrast, relatively lower uniform tariff ceiling bindings (less than 50 per cent) for all agricultural commodities were committed by other countries such as Congo and by the South African Customs Union (South Africa, Swaziland and Namibia).

In South Africa, duties will decline by more than 40 per cent on average, from more than 70 per cent to 40 per cent over six years. Very few of the African countries offered reductions in their ceiling bindings, with only Cote d'Ivoire, Ghana and Zimbabwe offering minimal reductions on several commodities. In some countries with previously bound tariffs, reduction commitments were made on their previous bound rates, but other duties and charges are then added. For example, the bound tariff for fluid milk in Cote d'Ivoire was reduced from seven per cent to six per cent, but more than 200 per cent on the possibility of adding other duties and charges. Other countries did not offer to cut previous bindings, with additional duties and charges listed in their schedules. If these other duties and charges are applied, the result will be a substantial increase in protection on these products. Other countries, such as Tunisia, established tariff bindings in the range of 90 per cent to 190 per cent. In the case of cash crops, where the pre-UK trade policy regime effectively taxed the sector, the UR did not provide direct disciplines.

4. HOW MUCH AGRICULTURAL LIBERALISATION WILL BE ACHIEVED?

As indicated above, any evaluation of the liberalising effect of the Round requires an assessment of the protective effects of the measures which preceded it and which would have occurred without it. Had the UR not concluded, then presumably these policies, or some variant of them, would have generated the counterfactual rate of protection against which the UR should be evaluated. To measure the extent of liberalisation, the estimated post-UR border protection is compared with two hypothesised counterfactual rates of future protection without the Round. The first is based on the average of the longest available sample,

1982-93 in developing countries and 1979–93 in OECD countries. This is based on the argument that border protection in agriculture is inherently unstable, reflecting variations in world prices and stable (politically fixed) internal prices and therefore a long-run average is most informative. This also assumes that there has been no underlying upward trend in the level of protection and that the distribution of protection during 1995–2000 would be the same as in the historical sample.

The second baseline is based on the average protection in recent years (1989–93). This is based on the argument that the recent decade has seen structural shifts in trade policies with many developing countries and some industrial countries undergoing unilateral and/or bilateral reforms, while others, particularly most industrial countries, have shown the tendency to maintain or increase protection in agriculture.

The choice of whether to base the counterfactual on the longest sample or more recent sample has important implications for the estimates of liberalisation from the Round. In countries where protection levels have increased over time, such as in several OECD countries (e.g. the EU, Japan and EFTA) and some East Asian developing countries (e.g. Republic of Korea), the long-run average protection is below more recent levels. Hence, lower estimates of liberalisation result when the post-UR rate is compared with long-run average than when a more recent average is used as a benchmark.

The *ad-valorem* equivalents of post-UR specific tariffs will be influenced by future world price changes. The estimates presented in this section are based on current World Bank world price projections. Annual estimates of post-UR border protection for the period 1996 to 2002 are constructed using the benchmark and final offers and interpolating over the phase-in period, assuming equal annual reduction.[13] Liberalisation is recorded only in those cases where the bound rate is below the benchmark rate of protection, otherwise no change is assumed.

Tables 3A and 3B show the associated price reductions for imports of major commodities in 2002 (estimated as the change in the protection rate divided by one plus the initial protection rate) as a result of the changes in protection relative to the baseline levels based on the long-run average and the average in recent years. A zero reduction (marked –) indicates that the benchmark protection rate is at or below the bound rate for all components of the aggregate.[14] The results indicate that very little or no liberalisation appears to be achieved for most commodities in most countries. For most industrial countries, the extent of trade liberalisation in agriculture as a result of the Round appears to be modest or zero. An important exception is Japan, where a significant reduction in import prices relative to the baseline levels is estimated in two major imported gains, wheat and coarse grains. Japan established very large reductions, although the final tariff levels remain relatively high.

In the case of majority of least-developed countries, where the tariff ceiling bindings were significantly higher than the historical rate of protection, no liberalisation is predicted to occur. This is true in the case of South Asia (Low-Income Asia) and Sub-Saharan Africa, where most countries were committed only to very high tariff ceiling bindings. Relative to the benchmark levels of protection, no liberalisation is estimated to occur in most Low-Income Asian

TABLE 3A *Estimates of Average Import Price Reductions Relative to Long-run Average (Per Cent, 1982–93)*[1]

Country/Region	Wheat	Rice	Coarse Grains	Sugar	Meat	Oilseeds	Dairy
European Union	–	–	–	–	-9	–	–
United States	-9	–	–	–	–	–	-8
Japan[2]	-47		-55	-35	-6	–	–
Australia	-1	-9	–	–	–	-1	-16
Canada	–	–	–	–	–	–	–
EFTA	–	-8	–	-11	–	–	–
Upper-Income Asia	-109	–	-78	-7	-33	-3	–
Indonesia	–	–	–	–	–	-33	–
India	–	–	–	–	–	-18	–
Low-income Asia	–	–	–	–	–	–	–
Brazil	-7	–	–	–	–	–	–
Mexico	–	–	–	–	–	–	–
Other Latin America	–	–	–	–	–	–	–
Nigeria	-15	–	-75	–	–	–	–
Mediterranean	–	–	–	–	–	–	–
Other Africa	–	–	–	–	–	–	–
South Africa	–	–	–	–	–	–	–
Maghreb	–	–	–	–	–	–	–

Notes:
[1] Estimates as $(t(f)-t(a))/(1+(0.5*(t(f)+t(a)))$ where $t(f)$ and $t(a)$ are the final and historical average protection, respectively. Where the calculated figure is positive, indicating a potential increase in protection, the table shows no reduction in prices (–).
[2] Japan delayed tariffication in rice.

countries, including China, under the UR. This is because these countries have generally taxed, rather than protected agriculture. Most of these countries established very high tariff ceiling bindings in the Uruguay Round. Among other developing countries, the largest reduction in border protection relative to the long-run average benchmark levels is estimated in Upper-Income Asia. Significant liberalisation appears to be achieved in wheat, coarse grains, meats, and other non-food (mainly tobacco and jute).

As shown above, most countries in Sub-Saharan Africa generally tax agricultural production in aggregate. Given the maximum ceiling bindings established in the UR, no major changes in policies and trade liberalisation is estimated in this region. Nigeria, on the other hand, provides significant protection in major gains, such as wheat and coarse grains. Import prices in wheat are estimated to decline by 15 percentage points in 2002, and coarse grains by 75 per cent relative to the baseline. No liberalisation is recorded in the Mediterranean and Gulf countries. In South Africa, tariffs are relatively low, and they have established

TABLE 3B *Estimates of Average Import Price Reductions Relative to Recent Period Average (Per Cent, 1989–93)*[1]

Country/Region	Wheat	Rice	Coarse Grains	Sugar	Meat	Oilseeds	Dairy
European Union	–	–	–	–	-12	–	–
United States	-15	–	–	–	–	–	–
Japan[2]	-81		-91	-47	-33	–	-14
Australia	–	-4	–	–	–	-1	-19
Canada	–	–	–	–	–	–	–
EFTA	–	–	0	-14	–	-18	–
Upper-Income Asia	-106	–	-76	-7	-44	-5	–
Indonesia	–	–	–	–	–	-33	–
India	–	–	–	–	–	-3	–
Low-Income Asia	–	–	–	–	–	–	–
Brazil	-31	–	–	–	–	–	–
Mexico	–	–	–	–	–	-1	–
Other Latin America	–	–	–	–	–	–	–
Nigeria	-12	–	-16	–	–	–	–
Mediterranean	–	–	–	–	–	–	–
Other Africa	–	–	–	–	–	–	–
South Africa	–	–	–	–	–	–	–
Maghreb	–	–	–	–	–	–	–

Notes:
[1] Calculated as the change in tariff rate divided by the power of the initial tariff rate. Where the calculated figure is positive, indicating a potential increase in protection, the table shows no reduction in prices (–).
[2] Japan delayed tariffication in rice.

relatively little change in post-UR protection levels (most reductions in the range of less than five per cent in absolute terms). Very little change in protection is estimated for the Latin American region. Brazil will reduce border protection slightly in wheat, but otherwise, no liberalisation in other commodities is estimated. Similarly, Mexico will reduce protection only in poultry and pork (other meat), but offered no change in the important grain sectors.

5. SUMMARY AND CONCLUSIONS

This paper provides an evaluation of the Uruguay Round agreement on agriculture and its impact on border protection over the next decade. The agreement went beyond traditional GATT rules by covering not only import restrictions but also export subsidies and domestic support programmes. The rules represent a radical and fundamental departure from the previous way agriculture was treated in GATT. Based on the final commitments on tariffication and tariff reductions, the extent of liberalisation in major commodities is assessed in major countries. The paper concludes that while there was significant reform in the rules, particularly the conversion of non-tariff barriers into tariffs and the reduction and binding of all tariffs, the extent of liberalisation that will be achieved will probably be significantly less than might have been expected from the agreed rules for liberalisation. The objective of the Round to 'reverse protectionism and remove trade distortions' (1986 Punta del Este declaration) may not be achieved in practice, at least not until further reductions are carried out in future rounds of negotiations. The goal was undermined in several ways including the choice of the base period, 'dirty tariffication", the use of unweighted averages to define reductions in bound tariffs, the use of tariff 'ceiling' bindings in developing countries and lower reduction requirements in developing countries.

While it is uncertain that countries will actually seek to apply the high level of bound tariffs they have reserved for themselves in the Round, their provision at very high levels provides a negative signal toward liberalisation. If the high tariff bindings are actually applied, it will harm developing countries' access to developed countries' markets and undermine the development of efficient agriculture in developing countries with adverse impact on their growth potential. Moreover, the Round left many of the worst distortions in developing countries outside of its scope such as import subsidies, export taxes, state trading monopolies, or domestic policies that implicitly tax agriculture. Overtly, therefore while the Round appears to have achieved new transparency in import protection, this came at the cost of a lost opportunity for significant liberalisation in most countries.

NOTES

Merlinda D. Ingco is very grateful to L. Alan Winters, Garry Pursell and Will Martin for helpful comments and reviews of earlier drafts of this paper. Any errors and omissions remain the sole responsibility of the author.

1 This includes quantitative import restrictions, variable levies, minimum import prices, discretionary import licensing, non-tariff measures maintained through state trading enterprises, voluntary export restraints and all similar measures.

2 The 'non-equivalence' of tariffs and NTMs and their effects are discussed in Deardorff and Stern (1984) and Baldwin (1988).

3 The concessions are based on the published Schedules appended to the Final Act. There are also bilateral arrangements which were not in the country Schedules. These side agreements are considered in the cases of grains for the EU and the United States and for beef and veal between the United States and Japan, and between the United States and the Republic of Korea.

4 Josling, et al., (1994) and Josling and Tangermann (1994) had briefly mentioned the way countries took advantage of tariffication to raise the level of their tariff bindings.

5 The trigger level on quantities is defined as 105 per cent of base period imports for commodities where imports are more than 30 per cent of domestic consumption; 110 per cent of base imports where imports are between 10 per cent and 30 per cent of consumption; and 125 per cent if imports account for less than 10 per cent of domestic sales. The trigger level is adjusted by the change in domestic consumption between

the two most recent years, but cannot be below 105 per cent of the preceding three-year average of imports.

6 It is well known that this measure does not guarantee equivalence in quantities except under special circumstances. See Bhagwati (1965).

7 I am grateful to Susan Leetmaa and Donna Roberts for providing the as yet unpublished data on ERS/USDA updates on PSE estimates.

8 For instance, milk is assessed as liquid milk plus fluid equivalent of butter and milk powder in the OECD and USDA calculations of PSSE. The same conversion factors for butter and milk are used in this paper to estimate the average specific tariff for the milk industry.

9 The estimates will be slightly biased by the amount of the margin between f.o.b. and c.i.f. prices which in most primary agricultural products is usually not more than 20 per cent.

10 In addition, there has been increased free-trade arrangements among countries in the region, for instance, in the southern cone common market (MERCOSUR) and Caribbean Community (CARICOM).

11 Chile sets an annual price-band to protect wheat, sugar and vegetable oils from imports. Domestic prices are maintained within the band by either adding an additional tariff to the uniform tariff level or by lowering the uniform tariff. Chile's uniform import tariff since June 1991 is 11 per cent, with preferential rates set for member countries of ALADI (Latin American Integration Association).

12 The other duties and charges listed in the schedules as part of the new bindings should be equivalent to the actual applied rates on 15 April, 1994 (Article II: 1(b)). Trading partners can challenge the applied rates during a three-year period after the enforcement of the commitment or the entry into force of the WTO. The rates of other duties and charges are as follows: Cameroon (230 per cent), Cote d'Ivoire (200 per cent), Gabbon (200 per cent), Ghana (15 per cent), Madagascar (250 per cent), Nigeria (80 per cent), Senegal (150 per cent) and Zimbabwe (15 per cent).

13 The phase-in period is between 1995 to 2000 for industrial countries and between 1995–2004 for developing countries.

14 This method does not consider reductions in average protection rates as a result of the introduction of tariff bindings above current applied rates. However, it over-estimates the marginal reduction in protection due to a binding which reduces protection below the historical average levels (Martin and Francois, 1994). For future work, different benchmarks and alternative approximations of the distribution of future protection given the new tariff bindings based on the methodology developed by Martin and Francois (1994) will be used.

REFERENCES

Baldwin, R. E. (1989), 'Measuring Nontariff Trade Policies," NBER Working Paper No. 292 (May).

Bhagwati, J. N. (1965), 'On the Equivalence of Tariffs and Quotas' in R. E. Baldwin et al. (ed.) Trade, Growth, and the Balance of Payments: Essays in Honour of Charles P. Kindleberg, North Holland, Amsterdam.

Deardorff, A. V. and R. M. Stern (1984), 'Methods of Measurement of Nontariff Barriers,' Institute of Public Policy Studies Discussion Paper No. 203 (University of Michigan, June).

GATT Secretariat (1994), The Results of the Uruguay Round of Multilateral Trade Negotiations: The Legal Text (Geneva).

Josling, T., et al. (1994), 'The Uruguay Round Agreement on Agriculture: An Evaluation:' International Agricultural Trade Research Consortium, Commissioned Paper No. 9 (July).
Martin, W. and J. Francois (1994), 'Bindings and Rules as Trade Liberalization,' paper presented to the Festschrift conference for Professor R. Stern, 'Quiet Pioneering: Robert M. Stern and 'Its International Economic Legacy' (Ann Arbor, 18–20 November).
OECD (1993), Agricultural Policies, Markets and Trade: Monitoring and Outlook (OECD, Paris).

8. Developing Country Coalition-Building and International Trade Negotiations

M. Kahler and J. Odell

For much of the post-war era, the stance of developing countries towards international trade negotiations has encompassed two somewhat contradictory strategies: on the one hand, considerable energy in maintaining the unity of a developing country bloc that vocally expressed concern over the existing trading system and demanded changes in it; on the other, a relatively passive attitude toward the negotiation rounds themselves.[1] This strategy has long been criticized by Northern sceptics, and preparations for the Uruguay Round demonstrated discontent among some of the developing countries themselves. Arguments for a more active participation by developing countries in trade negotiations have seldom dealt specifically with the other strategies that could be pursued more successfully, however. Our examination of possible coalition strategies for the developing countries in the Uruguay Round and other international economic negotiations is motivated by an awareness of both the existing criticisms of the bloc strategy previously endorsed by G-77 and the underlying logic of that strategy: individually, the developing countries are not major powers in the international trading system. For those with less power, skilful strategies of coalition formation are a major implement for increasing success in such negotiations.

In examining coalition formation, a coalition is defined as two or more actors with shared interests that influence their bargaining behaviour toward other actors. This 'loose' definition of a coalition recognizes that in trade and other international economic negotiations, coalitions are often fleeting and not exclusive. A coalition partner on one issue may not remain a partner on others. The level of organization of coalitions will also vary: few of the potential coalitions described below are likely to approach the level of institutionalization found in military alliances, for example. Finally, the coalitions that have been prominent to date in the Uruguay Round of trade negotiations have often been directed towards agenda setting; their success at the much more difficult task of formulating a common negotiating position remains to be seen.

Each developing country will need to weigh the opportunities and risks presented by possible coalitions that it could join. This study is meant primarily to illuminate both the opportunities and obstacles to a more activist and innovative attitude toward coalition formation.

SOUTHERN BLOC ON THE SIDELINES: TRADE NEGOTIATIONS BEFORE THE URUGUAY ROUND

As Gilbert Winham describes in his account of the Tokyo Round negotiations, the developing countries played a somewhat larger role in those negotiations as compared to their "wholly marginal" participation in the Kennedy Round. Their efforts were concentrated on such exercises as the framework negotiation, however, which was designed to embed preferential status within the GATT regime. Efforts to construct developing country coalitions on more concrete measures, such as tariff reductions, foundered on divisions within the group.[2]

Three principal explanations can be offered for the peripheral role of the developing countries in past GATT negotiations. First the structure of the negotiations themselves suggested that a relatively passive stance made sense. Trade negotiations, particularly tariff negotiations on a reciprocal basis, do not offer many incentives for smaller economies to participate actively: they have little to offer, since they are not principal suppliers or large markets and, given the extension of MFN status, they could obtain the resulting benefits in any case.[3] Since the developing countries did not accept the principle of reciprocity, incentives for active participation were further diminished. Alternative fora for negotiations also beckoned to the Third World. Instead of negotiating for benefits with the existing post-war regimes, the G-77 sought extensive changes in those regimes through negotiations that included a broad spectrum of issue areas. Those negotiations, and the North–South cleavage that they presupposed, also hardened the dominant, Southern bloc model of coalition formation. Finally, and related to the appeal of the NIEO, the benefits of liberalization and non-discrimination in the trading system, (two key norms of the GATT regime), were reduced by the strategy of economic development endorsed by many developing countries, particularly the largest ones (China, India and Brazil). Until the 1980s, international trade was viewed at best as an ancillary regime of growth by many developing countries. If trade and exports were not critical to economic development, then negotiations within the existing trade regime would receive less attention.

Each of these obstacles to enlarged participation by the developing countries has been lowered, if not removed, during the 1980s. In contrast to the Kennedy and Tokyo Rounds, developing countries were actively involved in the discussions that led to the Uruguay Round; the large number of accessions or requests for accession to GATT (including such major trading countries as Mexico and China) indicate that the issues on the table are regarded as important by the developing countries. Heightened interest in the latest round of trade negotiations has also been stimulated by the decline of global negotiations and the agenda of the NIEO. The GATT Round is one of the few games in town, in large measure because of the hostility of the USA regarding the global negotiations arena. Finally, the economic circumstances of the 1980s have also moved the elites of the developing countries towards greater interest in export expansion and hence the international trade regime. The debt crisis has had a mixed impact (discussed below), forcing import contraction far more than export expansion and lowering the perceived ability of many developing countries to liberalize their commercial policies. The successive shocks of the last decade and pressure from the North have produced an acceptance, sometimes grudging, of more outward-oriented policies. (Such policies need not include import liberalization, however.)

In shaping the agenda for the Uruguay Round, the new importance of developing country actors was clear, as was the erosion of the previous bloc model of interaction. The coalition model that will dominate during the Uruguay Round remains uncertain, however. There are four basic options (or some of these could be combined)

1. In the event that the trade negotiations stall or fail, an accentuation of bilateralism or minilateralism within (or outside) the multilateral GATT framework is likely.
2. A pattern of coalitions across the North–South divide could develop in the Uruguay Round.
3. A looser Southern coalition could develop in which the first- and second-generation NICs would take a leadership role.
4. The previous pattern of a broad developing country bloc could be re-established, concentrating its negotiations on questions of regime change and pursuing a joint programme with linkages to other issue areas, such as international finance.

These patterns are dependent not only on perceived developing country interests, but also on the strategies of the major industrialized country participants. They are also highly dependent on the agenda issues in question: as described below, certain issues (such as agriculture) point towards coalition formation across the North–South divide, while others (safeguards) are more likely to produce a predominantly Southern coalition. Each strategy has certain benefits and costs for particular groups of developing countries as a result; what follows is an analysis of the clusters and coalition building blocks that might result.

BILATERALISM AND MINILATERALISM: A LIKELY SECOND-BEST?

Given the circumstances of the 1980s, and particularly the absence of a dominant economic power, bilateral or minilateral approaches to trade negotiations may be more successful than multilateral negotiations at the Uruguay Round.[4] Certainly such options could grow in importance if current trade negotiations stall or fail. These less-than-multilateral outcomes describe two distinct scenarios, however. Bilateral or minilateral fragmentation of the GATT system could grow from an accentuation of the trend towards managed trade, following such existing models as the MFA, or 'grey area' measures of voluntary export restraint. Rather than organized protectionsim, a second scenario views these possibilities as a means of preserving and extending islands of liberalization in a global system tending toward greater closure. The arrangements might be discriminatory, but between partners greater liberalization would result. It is worth examining each of these scenarios for its impact on developing countries.

A system of managed trade is usually held up as a commercial nightmare for developing economies: confronting their far larger industrialized partners in an unequal contest with little or no international surveillance. The pronounced interest of many developing countries in strengthening certain norms of the GATT multilateral system (at least as applied to OECD countries) suggests that they have dreamed this nightmare. Yet one could also point to certain sectors – textiles and apparel in particular – that are already intensively managed on a bilateral basis, with little GATT oversight, which represent considerable successes for developing country exports.

The textiles and apparel case offers substantiation for minority arguments that managed trade between North and South is inevitable and that it need not be disastrous. Considerable evidence exists that any 'new protectionism' directed against the dynamic exporters of the developing world has been ineffectual in restraining the growth of their exports.[5] For the NIC, managed trade affords some of the same benefits perceived by the OECD countries – a stable market share protected from more competitive suppliers – as well as offering a substantial portion of the rents. By forcing suppliers into more sophisticated lines of production, it could be argued that such arrangements also provide a beneficial industrial policy for adaptable developing countries.[6] Finally, some of the NICs do have bargaining strengths: either a security relationship with a major industrialized market (for example, Korea or Yugoslavia) or a large potential market that can be used in retaliation for protectionist measures (for example, Brazil or China).

These short-term advantages for some of the NICs may have implications for coalition-building in such sectors as textiles, since the impact of liberalization in the textiles and apparel sector may be uneven in its benefits.[7] Nevertheless, most developing countries are not convinced of the advantages of a more managed system of trade, with the possible exception of commodities. Even the skilful Asian NICs have discovered that the import-competing industries in their major markets are capable of learning as well, and that bilateral regimes can be tightened. For the second and later generation industrializers, market sharing agreements may temporarily stimulate 'quota seeking' manufacturing exports but, in general, they are particularly damaging for new and more competitive suppliers.

Should the trading environment deteriorate, particularly because of failure at Geneva, another variant of bilateralism and minilateralism could beckon. Developing countries could seek liberalizing agreements with industrialized countries or, in an effort to expand South-South trade, with other developing countries. Such arrangements have become a theme of American commercial diplomacy in recent years – for instance, the Caribbean Basin initiative, or proposed free trade agreements with Canada and Israel – but have also been employed by other countries, most notably Australia and New Zealand in their closer Economic Relations Agreement, negotiated in 1983. The Lomé Convention is an earlier example with roots in colonial ties between European states and the ACP group of developing countries. Developing country preferential trading arrangements have a different lineage. Strongly backed by UNCTAD in the 1960s and 1970s, they have been seen as a means not only of benefiting from economies of scale, but also of increasing the bargaining leverage of developing economies with both the industrialized world and multinational corporations. Few have been very successful at increasing intra-regional trade; even ASEAN, which has had the goal of a free trade arrangement for ten years, still remains mired in highly resistant domestic politics of protection.[8] Most Northern observers are sceptical of their benefits, but many developing countries remain impressed by their prospects for market expansion, particularly as a liberalization 'half-way house' for relatively inefficient manufacturers.[9] Such arrangements pose risks for both the global trading system and for individual developing countries. They could serve as building blocks for a larger, liberalizing multilateral system, but preferential agreements could easily become inward-looking rather than outward-looking. External liberalization may fail to keep pace with internal freeing of trade; indeed, the latter may distract attention from the importance of the former. In addition, this 'à la carte' approach to trade negotiations and liberalization produces even greater fragmentation in the world trading system and both a psychological and a real undermining of the MFN principle.[10]

Individual developing countries would have to calculate their long-term bargaining advantages within such a bilateral or minilateral relationship and, given the availability of government attention and personnel, the opportunity costs for participation in the global trading arena. Larger developing countries that are highly dependent on particular industrial country markets and that have attractive internal markets to use as a bargaining resource may find bilateral arrangements attractive; Mexico is a possible case in point. For smaller and less diversified economies, even collective bargaining may not yield significant gains: the experience of the ACP states in their bargaining with the EEC provides a caution to other, similar economies.[11]

The popularity of bilateralism and minilateralism as liberalizing (rather than management) strategies is likely to be affected by the success or failure of the GATT negotiations. Some fraction of developing country interest in the new trade round derives from a certain disenchantment with South-South regional trading arrangements. In pursuing an activist course at the multilateral level, however, choice among alternative strategies remains.

NORTH–SOUTH COALITIONS WITH MULTILATERAL NEGOTIATIONS: COMMON INTEREST OR COOPTATION?

In the wake of failed efforts at global North–South negotiations, many Northern observers have suggested that developing countries must form coalitions across the North–South divide if their negotiating goals are to be achieved. Sewell and Zartman (1984), for example, argue that: 'perhaps the most important single innovation needed in North–South relations is ways and means to develop coalitions between Northern and Southern countries on various specific issues without undermining the unity of the Third World'.[12] Arguing the benefits of such coalitions does not produce them, however; embarking on this strategy requires an analysis of latent coalitions that the developing countries might bring into being and a clear assessment of the risks to Southern interests that such a course poses.

In analysing this alternative and the succeeding NIC-led model, economic interests of the developing countries are assumed to determine their behaviour

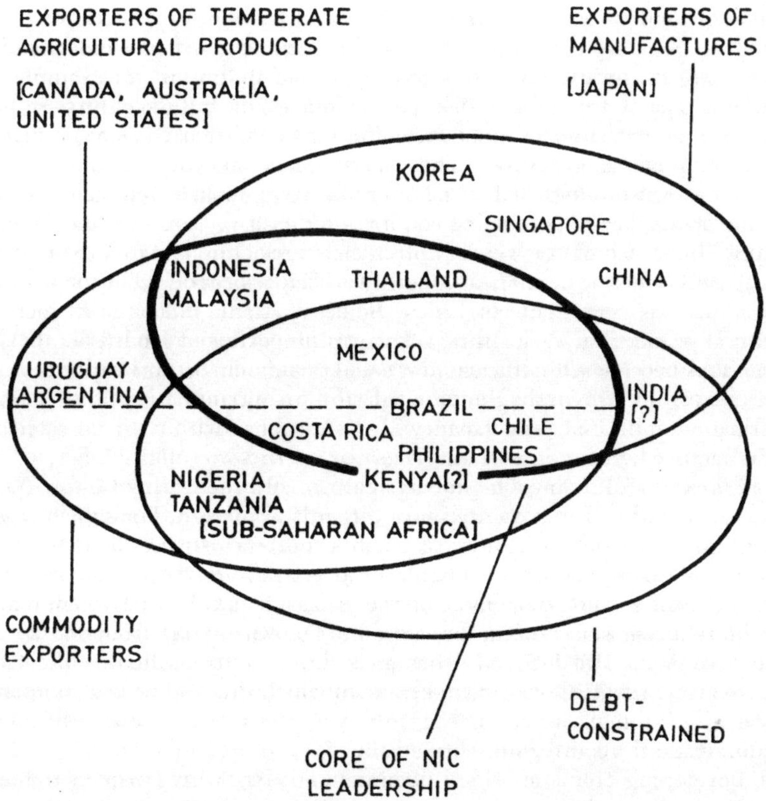

FIGURE 8.1 Developing countries' interests in international trade negotiations

in trade negotiations. As noted below, ideological or political goals could incline the Third World to a resurrection of the bloc strategy, but here economic aims are awarded dominance. In examining the heterogeneous interests of the developing economies in trade negotiations, several overlapping issue clusters emerge, as illustrated in Figure 8.1. The principal groups are competitive exporters of manufactures (the NICs, the ASEAN countries, and other second-generation industrializers); exporters of temperate agricultural products; exporters of other commodities; and those countries with serious international debt repayments constraints (indicated by rescheduling).[13] These clusters may not capture all the divisions within the developing group, but they highlight certain features that have already determined the coalition behaviour of some developing countries.

Certain likely alliances across the North–South line become apparent using these criteria for divisions. Agriculture has already witnessed an incipient coalition in the Cairns Group, formed in response to the damaging European–American agricultural subsidies war. The group is notable in that it includes not only exporters of foodstuffs, North and South, but also current exporters of tropical commodities who are concerned over indirect damage to their exports and also have hopes of future diversification (Malaysia and Indonesia, for example).

Two risks emerge from North–South collaboration on this issue. First, although the EEC agreed to the inclusion of agriculture in the Uruguay Round, it promises to be an issue of major conflict. The experience of the Tokyo Round, in which stalemate over agriculture stalled the talks for four years, could be repeated.[14] A second risk is the opposition of developing countries which have depended on imports of foodstuffs (India, China) or which protect their agricultural sectors (Korea). This potential conflict among developing countries is likely to be reduced by the substantial progress that has been made in China, South Asia and Indonesia in increasing agricultural production. From being substantial importers of foodstuffs, they have in some cases become self-sufficient and could potentially become exporters.

The power of a North–South coalition in agriculture should not be overestimated. The EEC and Japan will not dispense with their cosseted agricultural sectors lightly; despite the free-market rhetoric of the USA, its farm lobby is as powerful as any. Outside agriculture and the Cairns Group, North–South coalitions-in-formation are more difficult to discern. For selfish reasons, the USA may support developing country exporters of manufactures in their push for less managed trade, particularly in restraining the use of safeguards: the United States sees an opening of the Japanese and European markets as a means of relieving some of the pressure on its own market from the dynamic exporters of Asia. The USA also has an interest in strengthening the GATT system to avoid a system of managed trade in which it would be at a comparative political disadvantage: as compared to Japan, the USA is relatively inept at managing trade to secure competitive gain.

The developing countries share common interests with Japan in tightening the use of CVDs and the definition of subsidies, in circumscribing the use of safeguards, and in strengthening the GATT system, since Japan remains the subject of discriminatory NTBs at the hands of the USA and the Europeans. (Smaller industrialized countries, such as Canada and the Nordic countries, would also be interested in this issue.) Should resolution of the debt problems of the developing countries be linked to the trade negotiations, Japan could well smooth a resolution through contributing to its financing. With the Europeans there may also be a joint interest in resolving the debt crisis, but, given their lack of enthusiasm so far, it is not clear on what issues the developing countries might form a firm coalition with the EEC. Given Europe's interests in Sub-Saharan Africa, commodities might be one such issue but, in general, the African states may be the least involved of the participant developing countries.

Overall, a strategy of seeking alliances and coalitions across the North–South divide could offer gains on particular issues, but the risk in this strategy is that the developing countries would find themselves confronting their giant trading counterparts in asymmetric bargaining situations within the coalitions or joining battles, in agriculture for example, that may serve the interests of one or another industrialized country but not their own. Most important, the value of concessions made by the developing countries increases if they are made in a coordinated fashion by at least the largest country exporters. This positive value in coordination (and the fact that the more industrialized developing countries have the most to offer in bargaining with the industrialized countries) points to a third strategy.

LEADERSHIP BY THE NICS, FOR THE NICS?

A strategy in which the NICs, the developing countries with the greatest stake in a liberalized trading system, took the active lead in bargaining on behalf of a looser Southern coalition is the strategy of choice for most Northern observers.[15] This approach concentrates on the common interest of those developing countries seeking more secure access for their manufactures in Northern markets, using their own combined internal markets as an inducement.[16] NIC leadership in making a constructive proposal to the OECD would at least put Northern protection on the defensive and could achieve reductions in barriers that would benefit less-industrialized developing countries as well.

The strategy is appealing, but it immediately confronts an important question: which NICs? In fact, two leadership groups emerged in the negotiations preceding the Punte del Este meetings: those resisting the new agenda proposed by the USA, especially Brazil and India, and a group (with ASEAN at its core) that was willing to break with the traditional Southern stance and support the new round. (The latter group was apparently supported by several smaller Latin American states and by the Francophone African states.) In examining Figure 8.1, it is clear that two groups – the largest Latin American exporters (Brazil and Mexico) and ASEAN – are the hinges of any Southern bloc and the likeliest candidates for leadership, given their exporting records, their diversified interests in the negotiations and the size of their domestic markets. Since Brazil opposed the agenda and has been sceptical of the talks, the question of how the principal exporting countries could unify to lead is a pressing one.

A second issue is the outline of a NIC-led strategy. The answer is complicated by the fact that how the developing countries bargain – whether by reciprocal bargaining or not – is one of the issues on the table. Once again, a chorus of Northern observers has argued that S&D treatment has meant little of benefit in economic terms (though the benefits have disproportionately accrued to the NICs) and has had the more important political and legal effect of undermining the GATT regime, to the detriment of developing country interests.[17] Although uniform in their assessment, these critics are not in agreement on whether a move toward greater reciprocity or 'graduation' will result in significant gains for the developing countries.

At least three 'NIC-led' bargains seem possible: these are strategies which focus on the constitutional, the instrumental and the substantive. At the constitutional level – dealing with the structure of the trade regime – the NICs could trade a 'reasonably specific program for integrating their trade regimes into the GATT system of open trade and non-discrimination',[18] including graduation from the provisions of Part IV, for a strengthening of the GATT regime in ways desired by the developing countries, particularly in restraining CVDs, AD penalties and safeguard measures, and in strengthening procedures for dispute settlement. S&D treatment would be reserved for the poorest developing countries (although they too could be encouraged to liberalize their trade regimes), which does pose problems of definition (perhaps those countries eligible for IDA lending from the World Bank).

Such a bargain displays symmetry; at other levels of bargaining the knotty question of reciprocity might be circumvented by the same concept or by using the idea of 'unequal reciprocity'. A second bargain – the instrumental one – would focus on exchanging concessions on QRs affecting trade in manufactures. For North and South, QRs are perhaps the most salient trade barriers, and certainly are squarely within the existing GATT regime. The NICs could propose that the OECD states commit themselves to a phased elimination of existing quantitative restrictions affecting manufactures, perhaps including 'grey area' measures. (Such a bargain could be coordinated with safeguards negotiations to improve control over the emergence of new, equally restrictive barriers.) In return the NICs could offer to bargain over their own QRs on the basis of unequal reciprocity, making concessions clearly smaller in magnitude than those they would receive. For example, they could offer a code that would place some limits on their future use of GATT exceptions permitting the use of QRs or BOP reasons, infant industry promotion and development needs. The proposed limits could be quite loose, but OECD governments might value an agreement that did little more in the short run than establish principles covering NIC markets. NIC governments that would reap most of the benefits of great market access could consider side deals with neighbors and others in the G77 to obtain their political support.

A third, substantive bargain concerns the sectoral scope of GATT and would probably be the most controversial. The NICs and the other developing countries have been highly sceptical of America's strenuous efforts to bring services into the new round. (All participants seem to have some difficulty estimating their interests in this diffuse set of industries and sectors.) While the specific outlines of a services agreement or code remain obscure, the NICs could certainly demand that sectors of interest to them be brought within GATT once again, particularly textiles and apparel. This prospective trade has been rejected by some of the NICs as asymmetric, equating existing violations of GATT rules with the expansion of GATT into uncharted territory highly favourable to the OECD countries. The bargain could be made more attractive for the NICs, however, by emphasizing labour-intensive services of interest to the developing countries and by designing a graduated (unequally reciprocal) code that would impose few immediate constraints on the NICs.[19] Given the political interests of either side of this goods-for-services bargain, it would be very difficult to negotiate. NIC unity might be difficult to achieve, given their own mixed interests in the MFA regime and in any future services code.

While NIC leadership may result in bargains that benefit them more than the rest of the developing countries (particularly those whose exports are still overwhelmingly based on a small number of commodities), enough common interests exist between the NICs and these other countries to expect their interests would not be harmed by such bargaining. (Figure 8.1 demonstrates that many exporters of manufactures remain significant commodity exporters, for example.) The poorest and least industrialized developing countries are not likely to gain very much from reciprocal bargaining, indeed, their gains from the trade negotiations are likely to be small. Phasing out the MFA might help (though it would probably benefit China and India most of all), negotiations to end tariff escalation on processed raw materials have been on the agenda for some time, and linkage to issues of debt and development assistance, considered below, could well be of more interest than commercial issues *per se*. The NICs, in reserving S&D treatment for these economies and attempting to win certain concessions that would benefit them, would be exercising leadership in the strict sense, giving the less industrialized developing countries the chance of a free ride on their bargaining strengths. But the bargain between the NICs and the other developing countries might not be so one-sided: Southern unity may still produce benefits in bargaining with the North.

A UNIFIED AND PRAGMATIC SOUTH

If Northern critics are uniform in their scepticism concerning the gains derived from S&D treatment, they are even more unanimous in their disregard for the bloc strategy that has sought that goal. Robert Rothstein has offered a detailed account of the way in which the developing countries, throughout the NIEO negotiations, maintained a high degree of unity at the cost of bargaining inflexibility and ultimate lack of success.[20] The heterogeneity of the South produced a unity based on ideological principles and the simple addition of one group's demands to those of the others; as Rothstein observes, 'procedural unity without substantive unity diminishes the possibility of achieving viable settlements'.[21]

The bloc strategy was not irrational, however: it grew out of a particular perception of Southern economic weakness, and a belief that only through Southern unity could negotiating concessions be obtained from the Northern countries. That fundamental perception remains to be disproven by the critics; as Hudec declares, the main obstacle to improved market access is lack of economic power on the part of the developing countries: opposition to demands for protection 'requires having enough economic power to create, or threaten, equally important economic interests, in an equally sharp and immediate manner'.[22]

A NIC-led strategy may not amass enough economic power to force concessions from the industrialized countries. Would retaining a framework for coordinating developing country actions add substantially to developing country leverage? The non-NIC developing countries are likely to add little in a process of reciprocal bargaining, but they do add legitimacy, in the form of universality, to the norms of the trading system and to the claims of the NICs to represent the developing countries. While legitimacy has a value that is hard to assess, it does have value. It is that increment that the NICs should seek to retain in their bargaining on behalf of the other developing countries, one additional barrier to wholly self-interested deal-making.

ISSUE LINKAGE: DEBT AND COMMODITIES

The strategies of coalition formation outlined here have been limited to the arena of trade negotiations. For many developing countries in the 1980s, however, other international economic issues have been of equal or greater importance. One of the principal causes of import compression by the developing countries during the 1980s has been persistent BOP crises, aggravated by debt servicing obligations and a decline in external finance. The links between trade and finance have been underlined by the IMF and the World Bank in their calls for open markets in the OECD countries for developing country exports. There are also more specific links to trade negotiations in the phasing of any agreed liberalization in accord with BOP considerations and the possibility of developing country 'credit' for liberalization already undertaken in the course of an adjustment programme.

A broader linkage has also been suggested: connecting developing country participation in the Uruguay Round with negotiations directed toward a resolution of the debt crisis. As Figure 8.1 demonstrates, another division between prospective developing country leaders is that of the debt constraint: Latin America has been deeply affected by the debt crisis since 1982, while Asia, with the major exception of the Philippines, has largely been spared.

That division suggests a major shortcoming in any attempt at linkage between trade and debt: it would serve to fragment the developing countries further. The major Latin American debtors themselves have been unable to agree on a joint strategy *vis-à-vis* their creditors; linkage is not likely to solve the problem of coordination. Also, it is not clear that linkage in this case would strengthen the position of the developing countries: the debt 'weapon' could prove as short-lived and illusory as the oil 'weapon' of the 1980s. The reverse linkage – from trade to debt – overestimates the bargaining leverage of the developing countries within the trade negotiations.

Although a global negotiation linking debt and trade seems of dubious benefit to the developing countries, two more limited connections between the two issue areas could be put on the table during trade negotiations. First, developing countries could ask that unilateral trade liberalization undertaken during adjustment programmes be accepted as part of their concessions during the trade round. In addition, for those countries under a very tight BOP constraint, international financial assistance could be earmarked (as it has been in the past) to support liberalization measures that are negotiated.

A second issue area that is more closely tied in its substance to trade is that of commodities. Despite more than a decade of negotiation, the situation confronting commodity producers among the developing countries is as bleak as it has been in any time since the 1930s. Despite the recent upturn in certain commodity prices and the agreement of the Soviet Union to join the CFC, no solution to the plight of commodity producers is in sight. The trade round can deal directly with such barriers to processing as tariff escalation and can remove the remaining trade barriers (relatively minor) to commodity exports, but additional efforts would be required to link these negotiations to a broader attempt to assist the commodity producers, through the expanded CFS and diversification for markets and products. Here once again, it is not clear that the developing countries, following any of the strategies outlined above, can reopen the issue on more favourable terms.

CONCLUSION

While the past experience of the developing countries in trade negotiations provides some hint of their future behaviour, the choices in coalition formation, international and domestic, remain wide and possibilities for surprise, especially for academic observers, is great. Nevertheless, this review does suggest certain practical conclusions for the developing countries as they confront the Uruguay Round.

Two particular problems stare out at those who advocate a more activist stance in trade negotiations. The first is achieving substantive unity, at least among the key trading states (and we have noted the large Latin American economies and ASEAN as focal groups). The possibilities for division on issues such as services or debt is great, and the other options – disaggregated deal-making or a return to an ideological and unprofitable bloc strategy – are likely to offer fewer rewards in bargaining with the industrialized countries. Equally important is the question of representation: although the largest traders must lead, much of the leadership to this point has come from smaller economies, North and South, which perceive strong national interests in a strengthened multilateral system (Colombia is a case in point). How to couple the realities of economic power with the need for adequate representation is far more difficult for the developing countries than for the industrialized countries, where three trading powers so clearly outweigh the others. In part, the problem can be resolved by existing groups, such as ASEAN, but additional innovation may be required.

In general, among the coalition strategies examined, the NIC-led strategy appears potentially the most rewarding for the developing countries and one that seems to fit best within the existing pattern of (unequal) reciprocal bargaining within GATT. Coalition-building across the North–South divide appears promising in certain sectors, but problems of coordination in formulating a common negotiating position would probably be greater, and the shared interests outside those sectors weaker. Various bilateral and minilateral alternatives outside the multilateral bargaining could provide the arena for focused bargaining between key trading partners, but the advantages appear limited for smaller developing countries, which could offer neither a large internal market nor some strategic benefit to their Northern partners. Finally, this menu of coalitional strategies should not exclude maintenance of Southern unity on certain issues in which legitimacy provides an additional bargaining resource for the South.

NOTES

1 Hamilton and Whalley (1987), p. 8.
2 Winham (1986), pp. 272–7. While the Latin American countries pushed for preferential tariff cuts, they were opposed by the African states, which resisted a reduction in the preferences that they already received from the EEC.
3 The position of the developing countries resembled that of smaller industrial economies such as Canada in this regard (Winham, 1986, pp. 272–3).
4 This argument is made in Yarbrough and Yarbrough (1987).

5 A review of this literature is given in Anjaria, Kirmani and Petersen (1985), pp. 23–4 and 81–2. On the key question of whether exports would have been significantly higher in the absence of bilateral management, the evidence is mixed.
6 Perhaps the strongest argument of the beneficial side-effects of such protectionism, and the abilities of the developing countries to circumvent the restraints, is Yoffie (1983), especially pp. 167–8, 196–7, 234. See also Nau (1985), p. 72.
7 One estimate of the effects is given by Vincent Cable in Finger and Olechowski (1987), p. 185.
8 A recent analysis of intra-ASEAN trade suggests a substantial increase over ten years, but closer analysis reveals its dependence on trade in petroleum products among Indonesia, Malaysia and Singapore (Rieger, 1985).
9 For one harsh judgement, see Wolf (1984), pp. 214–5. A sceptical view of African efforts at economic integration is given in Mazzeo (1984). Nevertheless, a large number of authors in Whalley (1987) award a large place to such regional arrangements in their national commercial policies.
10 On these risks, see Hufbauer and Schott (1985), pp. 92–4.
11 See the conclusions of Ravenhill (1985), pp. 309–40.
12 Sewell and Zartman (1984), p. 115. They argue this point particularly in the area of trade.
13 The countries that are part of this trade project have been used to represent certain groups (Costa Rica is a proxy for other Central American countries); certain other significant participants have also been added.
14 On the treatment of agriculture in the Tokyo Round, see Winham (1986), Chapter 4.
15 For example, see Wolf (1984, p. 222) and Nau (1985, p. 78) who argues that 'NIC diplomacy seeks a fluid pattern of alignments with other developing countries that avoids NIC isolation from the "Group of 77" developing countries yet discards for good the rigid, lowest-common denominator solidarity with the South that in the 1970s sacrifices real NIC interests to ideological symbols.'
16 For example, in 1985, combined imports of South Korea, Hong Kong, Singapore, Taiwan, India, Brazil, Mexico and Malaysia amounted to US$162 billion, or 8 per cent of world imports. Even if some of this list did not join the group, other smaller traders probably would. For reference, imports of West Germany and Japan in that year totalled US$158 and US$128 billion respectively (GATT, 1985–6).
17 See, for example, Wolf (1984), pp. 212–5; Behrman (1984), p. 248; Hamilton and Whalley (1987), pp. 12–13; Hudec (1987), Part II.
18 Preeg (1985), p. 13.
19 In arguing for Southern participation in negotiations over services, Jagdish Bhagwati notes in Finger and Olechowski (1987, p. 214) that the Uruguay Round 'is unlikely to yield anything more concrete than a code or an agreement of principles'.
20 Rothstein (1979), pp. 121–2, 150.
21 Rothstein (1979), p. 196.
22 Hudec (1987), p. 215.

REFERENCES

Anjaria, S. J., Kirmani, N. and Peterson, A. B. (1985) *Trade Policy Issues and Developments*, IMF Occasional Paper No. 38 (Washington, DC: IMF).

Behrman, J. R. (1984) 'Rethinking Global Negotiations: Trade', in J. N. Bhagwati and J. G. Ruggie (eds) *Power, Passions and Purpose* (Cambridge, Mass.: MIT Press).

Finger, M. J. and Olechowski, A. (eds) (1987) *The Uruguay Round* (Washington, DC: World Bank).

GATT (1985–6) *International Trade* (Geneva: GATT).
Hamilton, C. and Whalley, J. (1987) 'A View from the Developed World', in J. Whalley (ed.), *Dealing with the North: Developing Countries and the Global Trading System* (London, Canada: CSIER, University of Western Ontario).
Hudec, R. E. (1987) *Developing Countries in the GATT Legal System* (London: Macmillan, for TPRC).
Hufbauer, G. and Schott, J. J. (1985) *Trading for Growth: The Next Round of Trade Negotiations* (Washington, DC: IIE).
Mazzeo, D. (ed.) (1984) *African Regional Organizations* (Cambridge University Press).
Nau, H. (1985) 'The NICs in a New Trade Round', in Preeg (1985).
Preeg, E. H. (1985) 'An Agenda for US Trade Policy', in E. H. Preeg (ed.), *Hard Bargaining Ahead* (New Brunswick, NJ: Transaction Books).
Ravenhill, J. (1985) *Collective Clientelism: The Lomé Conventions and North-South Relations* (New York: Columbia University Press).
Rieger, H. C. (1985) 'ASEAN Cooperation and Intra-ASEAN Trade', ISEAS/ASEAN Economic Research Unit, Research Notes and Discussion Paper No. 57 (Singapore: Institute of Southeast Asian Studies).
Rothstein, R. L. (1979) *Global Bargaining: UNCTAD and the Quest for a New International Economic Order* (Princeton University Press).
Sewell, J. W. and Zartman, I. W. (1984) 'Global Negotiations: Path to the Future or Dead-End Street?', in J. N. Bhagwati and J. G. Ruggie (eds), *Power, Passions and Purpose*, (Cambridge, Mass: MIT Press).
Whalley, J. (ed.) (1987) *Dealing with the North: Developing Countries and the Global Trading System* (London, Canada: CSIER, University of Western Ontario).
Winham, G. R. (1986) *International Trade and the Tokyo Round* (Princeton University Press).
Wolf, M. (1984) "Two-Edged Sword: Demands of Developing Countries and the Trading System', in J. N. Bhagwati and J. G. Ruggie (eds), *Power, Passions and Purpose* (Cambridge, Mass.: MIT Press).
Yarbrough, B. V. and Yarbrough, R. M. (1987) 'Cooperation in the Liberalization of International Trade: After Hegemony, What?', *International Organization* 41, 1 (Winter), pp. 1–26.
Yoffie, D. (1983) *Power and Protectionism* (New York: Columbia University Press).

9. The EC Antidumping Regulations: A First Economic Appraisal 1980–85

P. A. Messerlin

I. INTRODUCTION

Should the Uruguay Round negotiators on the Antidumping Code take the approach of the Tokyo Round and concentrate on a still more systematic interpretation of the existing notions embodied in current GATT texts on antidumping? Or should they adopt a wider approach to improve the basic notions on which GATT antidumping rules are based or to introduce new ones? So far, the proposals received by the Negotiating Group on antidumping rules have followed the first approach. They aim at tightening the interpretation of the basic notions embodied in GATT texts such as export price, normal and constructed values, comparison of normal value and export price, threat of injury, price undercutting, and undertaking. They do not introduce fundamentally new notions.

This paper argues that the Uruguay Round negotiators should not feel limited to the first approach, which is based on a too narrow conception of "codification".[1] They should not hesitate to improve the basic notions on which GATT antidumping rules are based. Looking at the experience of the Tokyo Antidumping Code applied by the EC Regulations, the paper provides systematic evidence showing that negotiations limited to a strict interpretation of the existing rules would bring short-term benefits, but long-term costs. Short-term benefits would come from easier international relationships around the negotiating table after agreement on a new Code.[2] But such benefits would be rapidly eroded if the intrinsic bias of GATT rules in favor of the "injured industry" were preserved, as was the case under the Tokyo Antidumping Code. GATT rules are biased because they condemn dumping if "it causes or threatens material injury to an established industry". They do not mention other domestic interests which, from an economic point of view, may be far more important than the "injured industry" for the welfare of the domestic economy.

This paper presents the evidence supporting the argument of the long-term costs of antidumping laws by looking at the EC Regulations, one of the most GATT-consistent laws. It is organized as follows:

- Section II shows that, contrary to what is frequently suggested, antidumping actions have little to do with short or medium-term macroeconomic fluctuations.
- Section III provides evidence on the protectionist impact of antidumping actions on trade flows.
- Section IV examines the price-fixing effect of antidumping actions.

TABLE 1 *Cases Intitiated by Selected Countries, 1980–1987*

	1980	1981	1982	1983	1984	1985	1986	1987	Total	1986	1987	Total
A. Total number of cases initiated[a]												
against	by the European Community[b]									by Korea[c]		
All Countries	25	47	55	43	42	35	31	34	305	3	1	4
	by the United States									by Mexico[d]		
All Countries	46	14	61	47	70	64	70	17	389	1	19	20
B. Percentage breakdown by selected countries (100 = all Countries)												
	European Community[b]									Korea[c]		
Ind'd Countries	56.0	17.0	30.9	23.3	16.7	20.0	9.7	38.2	25.2	66.7	100.0	75.0
EC[b]	–	–	–	–	–	–	–	–	–			
Japan	4.0	2.1	5.5	9.3	9.5	5.7	3.2	29.4	8.5	66.7	100.0	75.0
USA	32.0	12.8	12.7	2.3	2.4		3.2	2.9	7.9			
Developing Ctries	8.0	4.3	10.9	11.6	4.8	8.6	19.4	2.9	8.9			
China	4.0	4.3	10.9	7.3	4.7	2.9	6.5		4.6			
Newly-Ind'd Ctries	28.0	8.5	23.6	25.6	33.3	45.7	38.7	52.9	30.5	33.3		25.0
Asian Four	8.0	2.1		4.7	2.4	5.7	6.5	20.6	5.6	33.3		25.0
Korea		2.1				2.9	3.2	11.8	2.3	–	–	–
Asian NICs	4.0			2.3		2.9	3.2		1.0			
Latin NICs	8.0		12.7	2.3	2.4	14.3	12.9	11.8	7.5			
Mexico						2.9	3.2	8.8	1.6			
Mediter, NICs	8.0	6.4	10.9	18.6	28.6	31.4	16.1	17.6	17.4			
Non-Market Ctries	8.0	70.2	34.5	39.5	45.2	25.7	32.2	5.9	35.4			
	United States									Mexico[d]		
Ind'd Countries	91.3	50.0	77.0	53.2	35.7	31.3	41.4	76.5	53.5	100.0	84.2	85.0
EC[b]	76.1	21.4	67.2	27.7	5.7	12.5	21.4	17.6	31.4		36.8	35.0
Japan	6.5	21.4	4.9	12.8	7.1	7.8	12.9	47.1	10.8			
USA	–	–	–	–	–	–	–	–	–	100.0	42.1	45.0
Developing Ctries	6.5	7.1	8.2	10.6		14.1	14.3		8.5			
China	2.2		4.9	8.5		9.4	1.4		3.9			
Newly-Ind'd Ctries		28.6	13.1	34.0	40.0	50.0	37.1	23.3	30.3		15.8	15.0
Asian Four		21.4	6.6	19.1	7.1	21.9	12.9	11.8	11.3			
Korea		7.1	3.3	12.8	4.3	7.8	5.7		5.4			
Asian NICs						3.1	1.4		0.8			
Latin NICs			8.2	10.6	18.6	18.8	15.7	5.9	11.8		10.5	10.0
Mexico				2.1	1.4	3.1	2.9		1.5	–	–	–
Mediter. NICs		7.1		4.3	14.3	6.3	10.0	5.9	6.2		5.3	5.0
Non-Market Ctries	2.2	14.3	1.6	2.1	24.3	4.7	7.1		7.7			

[a]Cases are defined by the goods and exporting countries concerned – [b]EC with ten Member States (i.e., excluding Portugal and Spain). – [c] From January to June (inclusive) 1987 [Source: GATT]. – [d]All countries mentioned in the notices of initiation.

Source: EC Official Journal, various issues; Mexican "Diario Official", various issues; US TAMS, various issues and years; GATT Report on Antidumping Actions for Korea, various issues.

- Section V shows the complex relationships between the size of the coalitions of EC firms involved in antidumping actions, the market shares of the coalitions, the antidumping measures taken and the economic outcomes of these measures, in terms of trade restrictions, rent creating and price maintenance.

The conclusion suggests that countries willing to protect their import-competing industries may prefer antidumping actions to "voluntary export restraints", despite the "procartel" bias of antidumping procedures and the corresponding cost for the country imposing antidumping measures.

II. THE INCREASING IMPORTANCE OF ANTIDUMPING ACTIONS: A TRANSITORY OR A LONG-TERM PHENOMENON?

Table 1 shows the recent evolution of antidumping cases initiated by the EC, the US and two Developing Countries (hereafter LDCs), namely Korea and Mexico. This evolution suggests the following question: are antidumping actions a transitory or a long-term phenomenon?[3] The answer to the question depends on what triggers dumping. If macroeconomic forces determine dumping, the answer might be a transitory phenomenon. If dumping is determined by microeconomic forces – market structures and pricing strategies – then antidumping actions are protectionist devices, and are likely to last for a long time. This Section examines the arguments which are the most frequently presented when it is suggested that macroeconomic factors matter in dumping cases, i.e., exchange-rate variations and debt constraints.

1. Exchange-Rate Variations

Exchange-rate variations may matter in antidumping matters by revealing latent imperfect competition and inducing "pricing-to-market" behavior [Krugman, 1985]. Pricing-to-market occurs when firms do not pass through nominal exchange-rate changes into their export prices. When the exporting country's currency is appreciating, GATT rules induce the importing country to interpret pricing-to-market by foreign firms as dumping, since foreign export prices expressed in foreign currency are then lower than in their domestic markets. For instance, US exporters may not have increased the prices of their exports to the EC to the degree that one might have expected looking at exchange-rate variations, during the period of the strong appreciation of the dollar vis-à-vis the ECU. As a result, EC export prices may have become lower than US domestic prices of similar goods.

Using the EC case, the existence of a significantly positive coefficient between foreign nominal exchange-rate appreciations and antidumping cases initiated was tested. The results do not support such a relationship.[4]

This negative result fits well with the fact that most of the antidumping cases initiated by the EC – and by the other countries as well – concerned intermediate goods, e.g., basic chemical, pulp, paper and steel products, basic motors or electronic components. These products are characterized by a relatively high degree of standardization. This concentration on relatively standardized goods is indeed a logical consequence of GATT rules emphasizing the necessity to compare "like products". With little room for product differentiation, a major source for imperfect competition, pricing-to-market is not likely to occur significantly.[5]

2. Debt Constraints

Macroeconomic forces may matter more directly. For instance, it is often said that debt constraints may induce countries to implement policies designed to favor export sales at prices lower than domestic ones in order to get the external revenues necessary for servicing the debt. However, evidence – focusing on LDC debt – does not support the hypothesis of close relationship between antidumping actions and debt constraints.

Firstly, are antidumping cases concentrated on the most indebted LDCs for a given period of time? Tests performed for four different periods (1970–87, 1977–87, 1977–81 and 1982–87) do not show any significant relationship.[6]

Secondly, do LDCs with increasing debts face increasingly numerous antidumping cases? Exposure ratios in antidumping cases against highly indebted LDCs give a first hint of this possible relationship. Five LDCs (Argentina, Brazil, Mexico, Venezuela and Yugoslavia) have faced EC antidumping actions, three of them before as well as after 1982. The average exposure ratio of these countries increases from 1.6 for 1977–81 to 5.0 for 1982–87, which seems to substantiate the alleged relationship. But on the other hand, the ten other highly indebted countries on the Baker list did not face any antidumping action before or after 1982; Brazil's exposure ratio remained stable – roughly 3.0 for both periods; the average ratio for four other indebted countries (Egypt, Korea, Malaysia, Turkey) increased only slightly, from 1.6 for 1977–81 to 2.1 for 1982–87; and the average ratio of three indebted East European countries (Hungary, Poland and Romania) decreased from 7.1 to 5.3 between these two periods. These figures do not suggest any systematic relationship between antidumping actions and debt constraints.

Tests using pooled cross-section and time-series data were performed in order to get a more systematic view. Results do not suggest any significant relationship between debt levels or variations and antidumping actions.[7]

III. THE IMPACT OF ANTIDUMPING ACTIONS ON IMPORTED QUANTITIES

The negative results of Section II imply that antidumping actions are mainly driven by the traditional – economic and political – determinants for protection.[8] This Section provides evidence on three crucial points illustrating the protectionist content of antidumping laws: firstly, the wide range of the measures taken and the bias towards price-fixing agreements; secondly, the magnitude of the measures; thirdly, the sharp decline of imported quantities under antidumping actions.

Table 2 *Breakdown of the EC Antidumping Measures by Group of Trade Partners*

Trade partners	Total number of cases[a]	Measures taken (as a % of total number of cases)							Ad valorem equivalent of the protective measures taken (%)		
		"possibly" protective measures[b]	ad valorem duties	other duties[c]	undertakings		mixed measures		prelimi-nary[h]	definitive	
					dumping[d]	injury[e]	#1[f]	#2[g]		#1[h]	#2[i]
Ind'd Countries	64	21.9	14.1			20.3	32.8	10.9	16.5	12.1	15.2
USA	25	24.0	8.0			20.0	24.0	24.0	16.8	10.8	13.6
Japan	17	17.6	35.3			5.9	35.3	5.9	17.3	14.3	17.2
EFTA	12	25.0				33.3	41.7		8.0	3.0	6.7
Others	10	20.0	10.0			30.0	40.0		16.0	13.8	17.3
Newly-Ind'd Ctries	76	42.1	5.3	5.3	6.6	25.0	9.2	6.6	21.7	10.1	19.2
Asian NICs	9	54.5	9.1		9.1			27.3	35.5	19.2	32.0
Latin NICs	19	26.3		10.5	5.3	31.6	26.3		20.2	12.5	20.4
Medit. NICs	46	45.7	6.5	4.3	6.5	28.3	4.3	4.3	21.0	6.2	13.9
Developing Ctries	18	44.4	5.6	5.6	5.6	33.3	5.6		26.5	17.6	35.2
China	13	30.8	7.7	7.7	7.7	38.5	7.7		26.5	28.2	35.2
Other LDCs	5	80.0				20.0			–	–[j]	–[j]
Non-Market Ctries	103	26.2	1.0	5.8	11.7	46.6	5.8	2.9	34.7	20.8	32.5
All countries	261	30.5	5.8	4.2	6.9	33.2	13.5	5.7	22.3	14.5	22.7

[a]Cases initiated between 1980 and 1985. In a few cases, investigations led to determination by sub-products: this explains why there are 261 cases (and not 247 as in Table 1). – [b]Cases terminated by no or de minimis dumping or no injury. – [c] Specific or variable duties. – [d]Undertakings accepted by the Commission and based on the margin of dumping. – [e]Undertakings accepted by the Commission and based on the margin of injury. – [f]All measures terminating these cases are of a protective nature. – [g]Measures terminating these cases are of a protective or "possibly" protective nature. – [h]Unweighted averages of ad valorem duties and ad valorem equivalents of other duties and undertakings based on the margin of dumping. Cases with no or de minimis dumping and no injury receive ad valorem equivalents of 0%. Cases terminated by undertakings based on the margin of injury are not included. – [i]As footnote h, except that cases with no or de minimis dumping and no injury are excluded. – [j]No estimates available (all cases are terminated by undertakings based on the margin of injury).

Source: EC Official Journal, various issues; own computations.

1. The Measures: A Bias towards Price-Fixing Agreements

Table 2 presents antidumping measures in five main categories – ad valorem duties, "other" duties, undertakings, "mixed" measures, and "possibly" protective measures. "Other" duties refer to specific or variable duties, both de facto based on reference prices. "Undertakings" which are unilateral commitments offered by exporting firms to the EC Commission with respect to minimum import prices or maximum export quantities are de facto private price or quantity agreements between foreign and EC firms. They may aim at eliminating either the margin of "dumping" – the difference between the export price and the overseas price – or the margin of "injury", generally defined as the difference between the EC price of the "dumped" good and the price in the EC markets which would eliminate the "injury" to the EC firms. "Mixed" measures correspond to cases terminated by a mix of measures taken against the various firms and/or countries involved in the same antidumping action. Lastly, "possibly" protective measures correspond to investigations terminated by no dumping, or de minimis dumping or no-injury findings.[9]

The bulk of the protective measures taken consist of price-fixing mechanisms: specific and variable duties, price or quantity agreements – undertakings – between foreign and domestic firms. All together, these price-fixing measures represent half of all measures taken, i.e., including cases terminated by "possibly" protective measures.[10] This figure should be compared to the use of ad valorem duties – less than 6 percent of all measures taken.

The breakdown of measures by different countries shows striking contrasts. Cases against Industrialized Countries exhibit a low proportion of "possibly" protective measures, a high proportion of ad valorem duties – particularly in cases against Japan – and a high proportion of mixed measures, suggesting a high degree of complexity and differentiation in terms of decisions taken. Cases against the NICs and the LDCs are dominated by a high proportion of "possibly" protective measures and of price-fixing measures – specific and variable duties, undertakings – although interestingly, the Asian NICs are more subject to ad valorem duties. Lastly, cases against Non-Market Countries (NMCs) are dominated by price-fixing measures, i.e., undertakings based on the margin of injury.

2. The Magnitude of the Measures

The average of ad valorem equivalent of the antidumping protective measures taken by the EC against all countries (excluding "possibly" protective measures) is roughly 23 percent. This is a high figure, to be compared to the 7 percent EC average post-Tokyo most-favoured-nation tariff in manufactures or 4.2 percent in chemicals. Table 2 provides detailed estimates of the ad valorem equivalents of the measures taken by group of countries.[11] It suggests two main results, both related to LDCs and NICs.

Ad valorem equivalents are the highest for the LDCs, the Asian NICs and the NMCs. Cases against the LDCs and the Asian NICs thus exhibit both the highest rates of "possibly" protective measures and the highest rates of protection when protective measures are taken. This pattern suggests possible biases against newcomers or against countries with a weaker bargaining position. If antidumping cases are procartel devices, one should indeed expect newcomers to be kept in a situation as marginal as possible.

The ad valorem equivalent of the measures imposed and the estimated margins of dumping are related in a way which concerns the countries under investigation. The two are similar in cases against the USA, the Asian NICs and China.[12] In cases against the Mediterranean NICs, the ad valorem equivalent of the measures imposed is 60 percent lower than the estimated dumping margins. In cases against the other countries, the measures taken are 30 to 40 percent less than the dumping margins. Section V will examine this point in more detail.

3. Antidumping Actions Sharply Reduce Imported Quantities

The decline of imported quantities of goods subject to EC antidumping actions, terminated by protective or "possibly" protective measures, is shown by Table 3A.[13] The first year after the initiation of the investigation, i.e., at a time when generally definitive measures are still unknown, imported quantities decreased by 18 percent on the (unweighted) average. Three or four years after the initiation of the antidumping actions, quantities still imported represented only two thirds of the imports of the initiation year. Five years later, they were reduced to one half of the initial imports, which suggests an implicit tariff elasticity of approximately –2. A breakdown of all the cases by year shows a very similar pattern of decline for every year.[14]

The various types of protection devices have very different impacts, as shown by Table 3B. Five years after the initiation, imported quantities decline on the average by two thirds for all cases terminated by protective measures. Imports facing ad valorem tariffs declined more than imports facing mixed measures (which included some duties) and much more than imports facing undertakings. This is because most undertakings are based on injury margins lower than dumping margins, while most ad valorem duties are based on injury margins close to the dumping margins. Moreover, some undertakings may be difficult to monitor and less restrictive than expected. Table 3C shows that imports in cases with "possibly" protective measures are stable during the three years following the initiation of the cases, which is consistent with a protectionist "chilling" effect of these measures.[15]

The breakdown of the import decline by exporting countries illustrated in Table 3D shows that imports coming from the Industrialized Countries declined more than imports coming from NMCs, the NICs and the LDCs.[16] These differences perfectly match the breakdown of protective devices by group of countries illustrated in Table 2: exports of countries facing more ad valorem duties than undertakings are hurt more than exports of countries mainly facing undertakings.

Lastly, Table 3 shows that the mere threat of initiating antidumping actions may have some effect: imports decline by 5 percent on the average between the year before the initiation and the year of the initiation. "Possibly" protective

TABLE 3 *The Decline in Imported Quantities under the EC Antidumping Actions before and after the Initiation year t*

	t–3	t–2	t–1	t	t+1	t+2	t+3	t+4	t+5	Ad valorem equivalents of measures (%)
					A. All cases with all outcomes[a]					
All years	70.1	80.7	96.6	100.0	82.3	72.3	64.1	61.5	49.2	14.5
1980 cases	48.2	51.6	80.3	100.0	74.0	64.2	51.5	57.8	49.2	10.1
1981 cases	71.4	87.3	101.9	100.0	72.8	61.0	65.4	65.6		16.5
1982 cases	73.2	85.0	83.9	100.0	78.9	68.4	72.1			25.2
1983 cases	73.7	80.5	100.5	100.0	95.2	92.9				10.5
1984 cases	79.4	88.7	98.5	100.0	88.7					15.4
1985 cases	72.5	90.1	121.6	100.0						12.6[b]
					B. All cases with protective measures, by type of measures[c]					
All measures	66.1	75.2	92.3	100.0	79.8	66.4	55.5	59.6	42.1	22.7[d]
Ad valor. duties	47.6	66.1	75.7	100.0	58.4	44.9	20.5	–[d]	–[d]	20.8
Undertakings	82.4	86.1	99.4	100.0	84.2	72.6	69.4	87.2	–[d]	22.0[a]
Mixed measures	59.4	70.4	91.4	100.0	80.9	64.5	51.9	45.4	34.8	23.2[a]
					C. All cases with "possibly" protective measures					
All cases	85.6	100.4	104.3	100.0	90.6	91.6	99.7	68.2	65.0	0.0
					D. Cases with protective measures, by group of countries[a,c,f]					
All countries	62.0	72.6	87.3	100.0	75.8	63.8	49.0	58.1	42.1	14.5
Ind'd Ctries	52.5	65.5	85.6	100.0	67.1	54.0	21.9	20.9	21.0	12.1
Developing Ctries	44.0	63.8	104.9	100.0	59.2	73.7	78.3	–[d]	–[d]	17.6
Newly-Ind'd Ctries	52.1	66.2	76.4	100.0	86.8	72.9	71.5	–[d]	–[e]	10.1
Non-Market Ctries	88.0	92.4	98.6	100.0	79.5	65.5	63.6	70.6	75.0	20.8

[a]Including cases terminated by "possibly" protective measures (for details, see Table 2, footnotes b and g). – [b]According to the most plausible estimates for undertakings based on the margin of injury. – [c]Excluding, when possible, cases terminated with "possibly" protective measures. – [d]Insufficient cases. – [e]Excluding cases involving more than one group of countries. – [f]Including cases terminated with "possibly" protective measures.

Source: EC Official Journal, various issues; Eurostat trade data, various issues; own computations.

measures are associated with a minimal average decline of 15 percent (between the prior and subsequent year of the initiation) of imported quantities. These results are consistent with the classification adopted which records no or de minimis dumping and no-injury findings as "possibly" protective measures.[17]

IV. TRADE DIVERSION, RENT CREATION AND PRICE MAINTENANCE

Antidumping actions are discriminatory in the sense that they deal only with a portion of the imports of the considered products. Therefore, the drastic decrease in imported quantities of "dumped" goods can have a straightforward impact on prices only if there are no alternative sources for these goods, i.e., only if there is no trade diversion. The effects of trade diversion on prices, in turn, are related to market structures, i.e., both the market power that foreign firms had before antidumping actions were initiated and the market power that the EC firms had after the antidumping measures were taken.

1. Antidumping Actions Create Trade Diversion

The order of magnitude of trade diversion triggered by antidumping actions is presented in Table 4. Both increases of extra-EC imports coming from "nondumping" countries and increases in intra-EC trade are quite substantial. It is interesting to note that even cases terminated with "possibly" protective measures show trade diversion which may be explained by two possible factors: either "dumped" imports were not competitive, or the threat of antidumping actions was sufficient to trigger a relative contraction of the imports under investigations. Additional computations show that exports coming from the "nondumping" countries increase more when "dumping" sources are LDCs than when they are Industrialized Countries and that trade diversion favors more intra-EC trade when "dumping" countries are Industrialized Countries.

As a result of the trade diversion, the share of the "dumped" imports in the total extra-EC imports decreases strongly after the initiation year, as shown in Table 4. Interestingly, the decreased NIC share is more pronounced than the decreased LDC share. This fits well with the types and magnitudes of protection: LDC exports benefit from more "possibly" protective measures than NIC exports and from a structure of protection more dominated by undertakings based on injury margins.

These massive trade diversions suggest that total trade – i.e., the sum of "dumped", "nondumped" and intra-EC imports – of goods under antidumping actions may have expanded after the antidumping measures. Table 4 confirms that this is indeed the case.[18] This observation strongly suggests that it is not convincing to relate "dumped" import declines to domestic EC consumption declines, as sometimes suggested.[19]

2. Selectivity in Antidumping Actions: The "Foreign Rent" Effect

Trade diversion may be shaped by the degree of selectivity with which antidumping actions are used. To target the right countries and firms at the right time may determine substitutions between alternative sources of imports. The higher the selectivity is, the more likely "dumped" imports may be seriously restricted.

TABLE 4 *The Trade Diversion Effect of the EC Antidumping Measures before and after the Initiation Year t*

	t–3	t–2	t–1	t	t+1	t+2	t+3	t+4	t+5
	A. Evolution of intra-EC trade[a]								
	(i) all cases with all outcomes								
All years	112.6	108.7	102.0	100.0	108.9	113.4	116.1	120.7	124.0
	(ii) all cases with protective measures, by type of measures								
All measures	99.9	102.4	102.2	100.0	108.8	115.2	122.0	128.9	122.7
Ad valorem duties	94.8	89.8	103.4	100.0	111.0	128.1	149.3	–[b]	–[b]
Undertakings	98.4	100.8	102.6	100.0	107.4	114.1	101.5	117.6	–[b]
Mixed measures[c]	99.4	99.9	100.9	100.0	106.0	115.8	104.3	122.3	100.8
	(iii) all cases with "possibly" protective measures								
All cases	156.5	130.4	101.3	100.0	109.5	106.4	95.1	97.3	126.7
	B. Evolution of extra-EC imports[d]								
	(i) all cases with all outcomes								
All years	122.8	119.1	110.9	100.0	119.4	134.6	136.5	148.4	198.6
	(ii) all cases with protective measures, by type of measures								
All measures	114.8	113.7	114.6	100.0	119.8	136.7	147.4	161.3	218.2
Ad valor. duties	96.5	92.9	87.4	100.0	97.4	105.6	75.7	–[b]	–[b]
Undertakings	97.5	95.7	123.2	100.0	115.5	116.7	124.5	127.5	–[b]
Mixed measures	130.8	131.1	114.2	100.0	127.7	152.9	166.6	191.6	261.4
	(iii) all cases with "possibly" protective measures								
All cases	151.4	137.9	98.4	100.0	117.8	126.6	102.2	114.5	163.4
	C. Share of "dumped" imports in total extra-EC imports[e]								
All Countries	42.7	45.4	49.4	49.3	44.5	40.1	38.4	32.3	26.5
Ind'd Ctries	52.3	53.8	59.1	60.7	52.4	48.5	41.8	29.2	25.0
Developing Ctries	20.5	23.5	28 0	26.8	16.9	22.3	20.8	–[b]	–[b]
Newly-Ind'd Ctries	28.8	30.6	28.6	29.9	25.0	18.0	10.9	–[b]	–[b]
Non-Market Ctries	38.1	40.4	42.3	39.3	26.7	31.8	20.9	28.9	15.2
	D. Evolution of total EC trade[f]								
All cases with protective measures	93.5	97.1	99.9	100.0	100.7	104.3	107.0	109.8	104.0

[a]Quantities traded between the 10 Member States. – [b]Insufficient cases. – [c]Including cases with "possibly" protective measures. – [d]Imported quantities coming from "non-dumping" countries. – [e]Excluding cases involving more than one group of countries. – [f]"Dumped", "non-dumped" and intra-EC imports for all cases with protective measures.

Source: EC Official Journal, various issues; Eurostat trade data, various issues; own computations.

A crude measure of selectivity is the ratio of "dumped" imports over extra-EC total imports during the year of initiation and the three prior years: the lower the ratio is, the higher the selectivity is. Table 4 shows a significant average level of selectivity since "dumped" imports represent less than 50 percent of all extra-EC imports for the goods under investigation. This figure is an average, the individual ratios going from a maximum of 98.9 percent to a minimum of 0.3 percent at the initiation year.

Interestingly, Table 4 shows that selectivity is more pronounced in anti-dumping actions against LDCs and NICs: "dumped" exports represent only one fourth of the total extra-EC imports during the three years before the initiation, and one third during the year of initiation. Market shares of the aggregated LDC and NIC exports in terms of total EC consumption of the goods considered are correspondingly low – approximately 19 and 11 percent respectively – two or three years before the initiation, and not much higher – 22 and 16 percent respectively – at the year of initiation.

This capacity to trigger antidumping actions against LDC and NIC exports before these exports represent a substantial percentage of the total EC markets suggests that, when antidumping actions are initiated, LDCs and NICs are less likely to have strong market power in the EC markets than other exporters, particularly those from Industrialized Countries.

The evolution of the import prices under antidumping actions given in Table 5 confirms this hypothesis. Firstly, the prices (deflated unit values in ECUs) of "dumped" goods increased steadily after the year of initiation, when all the cases are considered together. This global result looks ironical: antidumping actions appear to do what "predatory pricing" – an argument often presented for justifying antidumping laws – is supposed to do, i.e., a decrease in prices is followed by price increases in what now are, as a result of the antidumping actions, more monopolistic markets. Secondly, results by groups of countries confirm that exports from NICS – and to a lesser extent, those from LDCs – do not enjoy the same price increases as exports from Industrialized Countries, when facing antidumping measures. In other words, rents are accruing to foreign exporters because of antidumping actions are lower in the case of LDC and NIC exporters than in the case of Industrialized Country exporters.

Results by type of protective measures are also striking. Prices under ad valorem duties tend to be moderately depressed, as might be expected since this form of protection does not trigger indirect effects including price increases (such as upgrading quality) and does not generate foreign rents. Prices under the other forms of protection are increasing, suggesting that foreign firms obtain rents. However, there is an interesting difference in price behaviour between cases terminated by undertakings and cases terminated by mixed measures, i.e., by a mix of undertakings and duties for the same cases. Prices under mixed measures increase during the five years after the initiation, while prices under undertakings tend to decrease after the third year. Two factors may be combined to explain this divergence. Firstly, the EC Regulations include a "sunset" clause, i.e., antidumping measures are provided for five years only. Secondly, mixed measures which incorporate some public price monitoring by the EC authorities through antidumping duties offer stronger price-maintenance mechanisms than pure undertakings. As a result, competition tends to surface again with under-

TABLE 5 *The "Foreign Rent" Effect of the EC Antidumping Measures*

	t–3	t–2	t–1	t	t+1	t+2	t+3	t+4	t+5
	A. Evolution of "dumped" prices[a]								
	(i) all cases with all outcomes								
All years	106.7	104.2	104.2	100.0	106.6	111.6	114.5	117.3	124.4
	(ii) all cases with protective measures, by type of measures								
All measures	104.6	103.1	103.9	100.0	105.9	109.2	118.7	120.0	129.6
Ad valorem duties	111.4	103.1	99.1	100.0	102.3	99.3	93.6	–[b]	–[b]
Undertakings	101.8	106.0	100.8	100.0	106.9	109.3	105.2	100.8	–[b]
Mixed measures[c]	105.0	101.0	107.0	100.0	105.8	110.1	127.0	135.9	138.1
	(iii) all cases with "possibly" protective measures								
All cases	113.6	108.1	105.2	100.0	109.6	120.6	98.6	109.5	110.1
	(iv) cases with protective measures, by group of countries[d]								
All countries	103.2	101.4	103.9	100.0	106.7	109.2	120.2	123.9	129.6
Ind'd Ctries	103.7	101.6	101.9	100.0	111.9	114.6	143.2	147.6	138.7
Developing Ctries	96.5	101.4	105.1	100.0	126.2	126.5	102.7	–[b]	–[b]
Newly-Ind'd Ctries	103.2	97.6	108.9	100.0	98.1	100.4	101.1	–[b]	–[b]
Non-Market Ctries	103.5	104.8	101.8	100.0	104.4	105.6	103.6	100.2	62.4
	B. Evolution of extra-EC "non-dumped" prices[e]								
	(i) all cases with all outcomes								
All years	110.0	99.9	97.1	100.0	104.0	102.2	105.1	102.8	100.7
	(ii) all cases with protective measures, by type of measures								
All measures	110.0	98.7	94.7	100.0	104.7	102.3	98.2	101.8	96.3
Ad valorem duties	89.3	91.1	90.9	100.0	108.4	97.4	99.9	–[b]	–[b]
Undertakings	132.3	107.3	96.7	100.0	109.0	110.4	108.6	101.4	–[b]
Mixed measures[c]	99.0	94.4	94.1	100.0	101.0	97.7	93.0	102.8	95.8
	(iii) all cases with "possibly" protective measures								
All cases	110.1	103.9	105.7	100.0	101.2	102.0	129.4	105.8	110.3
	(iv) cases with protective measures, by group of countries[d]								
All countries	114.2	97.4	94.7	100.0	107.9	104.1	98.0	101.5	96.3
Ind'd Ctries	105.2	89.8	92.0	100.0	108.0	98.0	94.7	98.9	96.6
Developing Ctries	121.4	98.1	96.4	100.0	124.2	158.2	101.9	–[b]	–[b]
Newly-Ind'd Ctries	141.3	101.7	95.0	100.0	100.2	97.6	94.8	–[b]	–[b]
Non-Market Ctries	99.0	104.5	98.1	100.0	111.9	105.1	104.0	107.4	101.4

[a]Deflated unit values (in ECUs) of the "dumped" imports. – [b]Insufficient cases. – [c]Including cases with "possibly" protective measures. – [d]Excluding cases involving more than one group of countries. – [e]Deflated unit values (in ECUs) of the "non-dumped" imports.

Source: EC Official Journal, various issues; Eurostat trade data, various issues; own computations.

takings, when the "sunset" year is approaching. Better price disciplines embodied in mixed cases rule out this potential renewal of competition.

3. Antidumping Measures as Procartel Actions: The "Price Maintenance" Effect

Existing domestic market structures combined with the price-fixing bias of the antidumping measures are mirrored by the price evolutions of the substitutes of the "dumped" goods, i.e., both goods produced by the Member States and traded between them and goods imported from the Rest of the World which are not subject to antidumping measures.

Table 6 shows that intra-EC trade prices (in constant ECUs) decrease in the years preceding the initiation, and stabilized subsequently. This stabilization is more pronounced in the cases with protective measures than in the cases with "possibly" protective measures, and in the case with undertakings and mixed measures than in the case with ad valorem duties. This last case is particularly striking: it illustrates how ad valorem duties do not protect Member Countries from price variations in the Rest of the World and how they can be borne by efficient foreign producers. The previously-observed divergence in terms of price behavior between cases terminated by undertakings and cases terminated by mixed measures also exists in the case of intra-EC prices, although less clearly.

Table 6 illustrates the relative prices of "dumped" to intra-EC imports. It provides three additional interesting pieces of information. Firstly, ad valorem duties have a clear impact on relative prices: after three years, "dumped" prices increase relatively to intra-EC prices by 16 percent, i.e., approximately by the average amount of the duties given by Table 3. Secondly, although they increase much less, relative prices under undertakings confirm the general price increase made possible by the cartelization process. Thirdly, the evolution of the relative prices by group of countries confirms that LDC and NIC exporters are less able to increase their relative prices than exporters from the Industrialized Countries or NMCs.

Moreover, the evolution of extra-EC "nondumped" import prices illustrates the general drift to more monopolistic markets. As shown in Table 5, competition from the "dumping" countries before the initiation of antidumping actions obliged the "nondumping" foreign exporters to decrease their prices. In the first few years after the imposition of antidumping measures, the "nondumping" exporters tend to align their prices, i.e., to increase them. In the case of undertakings, they are interested in joining possible cartels. In the case of specific duties, domestic firms have an additional interest in price increases by foreign competitors.[20] In the case of variable duties, they align to the reference prices implicitly introduced.

In sum, the cartelization process – at least in terms of price competition – is under way, except for the minor part of the cases terminated by ad valorem duties.

V. COALITIONS OF FIRMS, ANTIDUMPING MEASURES AND MARKET STRUCTURES

Antidumping actions are lodged by coalitions of domestic firms. The characteristics

TABLE 6 *The "Price Maintenance" Effect of the EC Antidumping Measures before and after Initiation Year t*

	t–3	t–2	t–1	t	t+1	t+2	t+3	t+4	t+5
				A. Evolution of the intra-EC prices[a]					
				(i) all cases with all outcomes					
All years	104.5	103.0	100.8	100.0	100.8	101.7	100.3	97.4	99.9
				(ii) all cases with protective measures, by type of measures					
All measures	103.1	102.3	100.9	100.0	100.6	102.3	101.4	98.4	100.2
Ad valorem duties	111.2	107.6	100.2	100.0	95.8	91.1	82.3	–[b]	–[b]
Undertakings	105.9	107.3	102.9	100.0	99.8	102.9	107.0	96.2	–[b]
Mixed measures[c]	99.5	97.8	99.8	100.0	102.2	103.0	99.9	102.7	106.7
				(iii) all cases with "possibly" protective measures					
All cases	109.3	105.6	100.2	100.0	101.3	99.1	95.9	94.5	99.3
				(iv) cases with protective measures, by group of countries[d]					
All countries	103.8	102.2	100.7	100.0	100.4	100.0	97.8	94.9	98.8
Ind'd Ctries	107.0	100.6	100.9	100.0	102.6	103.5	99.4	102.7	108.3
Developing Ctries	90.7	108.3	106.2	100.0	90.5	120.5	131.1	–[b]	–[b]
Newly-Ind'd Ctries	104.5	100.8	97.1	100.0	98.0	95.5	90.5	–[b]	–[b]
Non-Market Ctries	98.9	105.7	103.2	100.0	101.3	93.9	92.6	85.5	55.2
				B. Evolution of "dumped" prices relatively to intra-EC prices					
				(i) all cases with all outcomes					
All Years	103.9	102.1	105.2	100.0	106.1	107.0	112.6	118.9	123.0
				(ii) all cases with protective measures, by type of measures					
All measures	102.5	101.3	103.8	100.0	105.6	107.7	117.3	121.9	128.5
Ad valorem duties	100.7	96.2	99.1	100.0	106.7	109.6	116.2	–[b]	–[b]
Undertakings	98.2	99.6	99.3	100.0	107.6	106.6	102.1	105.3	–[b]
Mixed measures[c]	105.8	103.6	107.8	100.0	103.9	108.2	124.7	131.1	129.0
				(iii) all cases with "possibly" protective measures					
All cases	108.5	104.7	109.9	100.0	108.3	104.0	94.9	109.8	107.9
				(iv) cases with protective measures, by group of countries[d]					
All countries	101.7	100.7	103.8	100.0	106.1	108.8	121.1	127.2	128.5
Ind'd Ctries	101.0	104.0	100.8	100.0	108.6	110.4	141.7	141.4	129.1
Developing Ctries	100.7	97.7	102.1	100.0	136.9	105.7	80.5	–[b]	–[b]
Newly-Ind'd Ctries	102.2	98.0	112.9	100.0	100.2	107.7	109.6	–[b]	–[b]
Non-Market Ctries	102.4	99.2	99.2	100.0	102.4	108.5	108.1	113.5	110.6

[a]Deflated unit values (in ECUs) of intra-EC trade. – [b]Insufficient cases. – [c]Including cases with "possibly" protective measures. – [d]Excluding cases involving more than one group of countries.

Source: EC Official Journal, various issues; Eurostat trade data, various issues; own computations.

of the coalitions would play a minor role if EC oligopolies were to remain under the pressure of imports coming from perfectly competitive sources. However, in the case of trade diversion between imperfectly competitive sources, the coalition characteristics are expected to play a role in the design of the measures taken and in the corresponding potential changes in market structures.

This section starts by a brief overall description of the size of the coalitions (measured by the number of EC firms) involved in the 1980–85 cases. Then, it presents the measures taken in terms of the size of the coalitions and the market shares held by them. Lastly, it presents the economic outcomes – i.e., the restrictive impact on trade, the importance of rent creating and price maintenance – of the measures taken in terms of the coalition size.

1. The Number of EC Firms Involved in Antidumping Cases

Roughly 500 EC firms were involved in cases initiated between 1980 and 1985.[21] This represents an average of four EC complaining firms per case – when cases are defined in terms of the product concerned – to be compared to an average of 4.5 foreign firms on the defendant side. In one fifth of the cases, there is only one EC complaining firm. In one third of the cases, there are only one or two EC firms involved. These figures show that many antidumping cases are the domain of few firms.

The number of foreign countries involved varies significantly with the number of complaining firms and suggests that the larger the coalition is, the more countries it targets. Cases initiated by one EC firm concern around 1.7 countries on average. This figure rises to 2.7 countries for cases initiated by coalitions of two to four EC firms, and to 3.8 countries for cases lodged by coalitions of four to eight EC firms. However, cases with coalitions grouping more than eight firms involve an average of only 2.6 countries. Interestingly enough, Asian-NIC exporters face exclusively coalitions of few firms, while exporters from all the other countries face coalitions of all sizes.[22]

2. The Lobbying Activity and the Design of the Measures Taken

As shown above, antidumping measures differ widely: they offer different levels of protection with various combinations of rent creation and price maintenance. One may expect that some basic characteristics of the coalitions determine the different pattern of measures taken. Table 7 presents the average profiles of the measures taken by size of coalitions.

Table 7 suggests four main observations. Firstly, coalitions close in terms of size mostly enjoy similar measures. Indeed, the observed coalitions may be classified in four main relatively homogeneous categories: coalitions with only one firm, coalitions of two to four firms, coalitions of five to eight firms and coalitions involving more than eight firms.

Secondly, there are interesting and substantial differences in the structure of measures granted to each of the four main categories of coalitions. One-firm coalitions are characterized by the use of all the types of measures available,

Table 7 *Breakdown of the EC Antidumping Measures by Number of Firms*

Number of firms	Total number of cases[a]	Measures taken (as a % of total number of cases) "possibly" protective measures[b]	ad valorem duties	other duties[c]	undertakings: dumping[d]	undertakings: injury[e]	mixed measures #1[f]	mixed measures #2[g]	Ad valorem equivalent of the protective measures taken (%) preliminary[h]	definitive #1[h]	definitive #2[i]	"Lobbying power" indexes
1	39	10.3	10.3	12.8	7.7	43.6	12.8	2.6	24.3	19.2	19.2	52.0
2	25	40.0	4.0		8.0	20.0	12.0		18.8	10.2	21.7	25.5
3	28	42.9	7.1	3.6	17.9	17.9	10.7		34.2	16.6	25.6	58.1
4	36	52.8			2.8	33.3	2.8	8.3	17.5	2.9	13.5	12.1
5	15		13.3		13.3	53.3			45.4	48.7	48.7	100.0
6	35	25.7			14.3	25.7	25.7	5.7	24.5	14.3	21.5	66.1
7	24	16.7				66.7		16.7	14.2	4.5	9.0	15.0
8	3					66.7	33.3		12.1	10.1	10.1	18.1
>8	50	40.0	12.0	4.0		34.0	4.0	6.0	16.0	9.4	15.7	35.0
1	39	10.3	10.3	12.8	7.7	43.6	12.8	2.6	24.3	19.2	19.2	52.0
2 to 4	89	46.1	3.4	1.1	9.0	24.7	7.9	7.9	24.7	10.3	22.5	34.1
5 to 8	77	16.9	2.6	5.2	9.1	45.5	13.0	7.8	29.1	22.1	29.4	75.2
>8	50	40.0	12.0	4.0		34.0	4.0	6.0	16.0	9.4	15.7	35.0
All	255	30.6	5.9	4.7	7.1	35.7	9.4	6.7	24.3	14.5	22.5	47.6

[a]Cases initiated between 1980 and 1985. In a few cases, the number of firms is not known and investigations led to determinations by sub-products. That explains why there are only 255 cases. – [b]Cases terminated by no or de minimis dumping or no injury. – [c]Specific or variable duties. – [d]Undertakings accepted by the Commission and based on the margin of dumping. – [e]Undertakings accepted by the Commission and based on the margin of injury. – [f]All measures terminating these cases are of protective nature. – [g]Measures terminating these cases are of protective and "possibly" protective nature. – [h]Unweighted averages of ad valorem duties and ad valorem equivalents of other duties and undertakings based on the margin of dumping. Cases with de minimis dumping and no injury receive ad valorem equivalents of 0%. Cases terminated by undertakings based on the margin of injury are not included. – [i]As footnote h, except that cases with no or de minimis dumping and no injury are excluded. – [j]Defined as the ratio of ad valorem equivalent duties to the estimated margins of dumping.

Source: EC Official Journal, various issues; own computations.

very few "possibly" protective measures, and a high percentage of undertakings based on the margin of injury. As a result, protectionist measures look quasi-certain, but protection tends to be granted at the lower level of the injury margin.[23] Coalitions of two to four firms differ markedly from the previous ones by the high number of cases terminated by "possibly" protectionist devices and by the lower number of cases terminated by tariffs. As a result, the level of protection granted appears lower. Coalitions of five to eight firms show a pattern of measures closer to the pattern observed in the one EC firm case: the main differences being the lower use of tariffs and the higher use of undertakings. Coalitions involving more than eight firms show a pattern not far from the structure granted to the coalitions of two to four firms, with some differences concerning ad valorem tariffs, undertakings and mixed measures.

Thirdly, Table 7 suggests a relation between ad valorem equivalents of the measures taken and the size of the coalitions. Ad valorem rates of protection tend to increase with the size of the coalitions, to achieve a maximum for coalitions with a handful of firms, and then to decrease. This evolution is noticeable for the preliminary duties and the final duties as well, and is more marked when no-dumping and no-injury cases are omitted.

Fourthly, Table 7 presents indexes which provide some measure of the "lobbying power" of the coalition observed. The indexes are defined by the ratios of the ad valorem equivalents of the measures over the margins of dumping estimated by the EC Commission. Dumping margins may be considered as an "objective" measure of price differentials.[24] Although based on dumping margins, protective measures are also influenced by other factors, including the pressures of the EC and foreign lobbies involved in the cases. As a result, the ratios of ad valorem equivalents to margins of dumping may be interpreted as mirroring the ability of coalitions to transform the evidence gathered during the investigations into protective actions. One-firm coalitions show a higher index than coalitions of two to four firms. Coalitions of five and six firms obtain remarkably high indexes. For coalitions of more than six firms, the lobbying power indexes are significantly lower.

That the coalitions of five to eight firms and, to a lesser extent, the one-firm coalitions seem to be more "efficient" in obtaining a wider range of measures, higher lobbying power indexes and ad valorem rates of protection than other coalitions suggest that the coalition size has to be combined to other characteristics of the coalitions in order to explain the pattern of the measures taken.

An obvious candidate for such characteristics is the EC market share held by the coalitions. The hypothesis is that there is a trade-off between the size of the coalitions and the market shares held by them. The first variable captures the costs of creating a lobby, the second one the capacity of the other actors involved in the decision to resist to the lobby pressures. According to this hypothesis, small coalitions can create lobbies at a low cost, but they represent relatively small market shares so that the EC Commission can resist their pressures more easily. On the contrary, large coalitions face higher lobbing costs, but their large market shares leave less degree of freedom to the EC Commission.

The hypothesis seems to fit with available evidence. Information on market shares is available only for a subset – a little more than one third – of the antidumping cases initiated between 1980 and 1985. The average market share in terms of the total EC consumption of the product concerned which is held by one-firm coalitions is approximately 48.9 percent. This figure remains stable – around 47.2 percent – for coalitions of two to four firms. It goes up to 57.7 percent for coalitions of five to eight firms, and to 71.4 percent for the fourth category of coalitions.[25]

3. Coalitions and Economic Outcomes

Coalitions are expected to mold protective measures in order to get their "desired" economic outcomes, i.e., trade restriction, rent creation and price maintenance. If rational and well informed, only coalitions which expect to have some control over the conversion of measures into desired economic outcomes should be ready to initiate antidumping actions.

Table 8 presents the necessary information in terms of the ratios of the average indexes prior and after the year of initiation. It provides three main observations. Firstly, all the coalitions get close performance in terms of price maintenance in intra-EC trade. Secondly, some coalitions are able to get price maintenance accompanied by a massive intra-EC trade expansion, while other coalitions get price maintenance accompanied by a relatively modest change in intra-EC trade coupled with a substantial extra-EC trade expansion. Thirdly, rents for foreign "dumping" exporters are determined by the generated changes in intra-EC and by the threat that existing coalitions represent in the future.

As a result, each of the four different categories of coalitions has a different touch. One-firm coalitions show marked intra-EC trade diversions, upsurges in competition from "dumping" exporters a few years after the year of initiation, and foreign price increases by "dumping" foreign exporters.[26] Coalitions of two to four firms exhibit low trade restrictiveness, a relatively strong extra-EC trade diversion which more or less compensates the trade-restriction effect on "dumped" imports and small changes in foreign prices from the "dumping" foreign exporters. Coalitions of five to eight firms present strong price maintenance coupled with intra-EC trade diversion and moderate price increases from foreign "dumping" exporters.[27] Coalitions of more than eight firms show a structure of economic outcomes close to the coalitions of two to four firms, with more marked extra-EC trade diversion and rent creation.

VI. CONCLUSION

This paper provides evidence that current GATT-consistent antidumping laws such as the EC Regulations have a strong protectionist drift, and as such, endanger the international trade system based on GATT rules.

The evidence follows from six results. Firstly, three years after the initiation of the investigations, antidumping measures reduced imported quantities by 40 percent. Secondly, the measures taken are severe, with an average ad valorem

TABLE 8 *Coalitions and Economic Outcomes, 1980–1985*

No. of firms	t–3	t–2	t–1	t	t+1	t+2	t+3	t+4	Average indexes prior t [A]	Average indexes after t [B]	Ratio B:A (%)
	Periods prior and after year of initiation t[a]										
	A. "Dumped" imported quantities: trade restrictiveness										
1	53.9	67.5	82.9	100.0	61.1	50.8	49.1	69.7	68.1	57.7	84.6
2 to 4	71.7	82.1	87.4	100.0	99.9	80.5	69.6	70.5	80.4	80.1	99.7
5 to 8	74.4	77.8	107.9	100.0	67.7	55.7	43.9	49.7	86.7	54.2	62.5
>8	60.2	69.8	89.2	100.0	81.8	70.4	53.9	46.3	73.1	63.1	86.4
all[b]	66.1	75.2	92.3	100.0	79.8	66.4	55.5	59.6	77.8	60.7	78.0
	B. Intra-EC unit values: price maintenance										
1	103.2	103.2	100.0	100.0	97.8	100.9	104.5	89.2	102.1	98.1	96.0
2 to 4	107.5	105.7	103.5	100.0	102.8	103.2	101.8	103.0	105.6	102.7	97.3
5 to 8	99.4	99.0	98.6	100.0	101.4	101.5	98.2	93.5	99.0	98.6	99.6
>8	100.8	100.2	101.2	100.0	99.3	103.3	101.3	104.1	100.7	102.0	101.3
all[b]	103.1	102.3	100.9	100.0	100.6	102.3	101.4	98.4	102.1	100.6	98.5
	C. Intra-EC traded quantities: internal trade diversion										
1	102.1	98.7	104.5	100.0	110.0	114.1	146.6	141.7	101.8	128.1	125.9
2 to 4	92.8	93.5	96.0	100.0	104.3	108.2	97.8	106.1	94.1	104.1	110.6
5 to 8	102.7	106.6	103.7	100.0	113.0	124.7	129.2	148.7	104.4	128.9	123.5
>8	104.6	115.3	107.3	100.0	110.0	115.4	123.9	127.0	109.1	119.1	109.2
all[b]	99.9	102.4	102.2	100.0	108.8	115.2	122.0	128.9	101.5	119.5	117.8
	D. Total extra-EC imported quantities[c]: external trade diversion										
1	92.3	95.5	142.1	100.0	83.6	78.0	69.6	81.7	110.0	78.2	71.1
2 to 4	94.9	100.4	101.7	100.0	106.0	97.1	103.7	96.5	99.0	100.8	101.9
5 to 8	98.2	95.6	101.3	100.0	92.9	87.8	69.8	62.5	98.4	78.2	79.5
>8	79.9	88.8	92.3	100.0	91.9	105.4	101.0	121.5	87.0	104.9	120.6
all[b]	92.3	95.8	109.0	100.0	95.0	92.9	95.6	91.6	99.0	91.9	92.8
	E. Unit values of "dumped" imports: foreign rents										
1	102.9	104.3	99.2	100.0	108.2	120.6	112.2	111.9	102.1	113.2	110.9
2 to 4	107.8	106.4	110.7	100.0	103.2	105.8	112.2	120.9	108.3	110.5	102.1
5 to 8	99.5	99.5	100.5	100.0	105.7	106.8	102.4	102.4	99.8	104.3	104.5
>8	108.1	101.0	102.8	100.0	108.1	107.4	119.3	135.9	104.0	117.7	113.2
all[b]	104.6	103.1	103.9	100.0	105.9	109.2	111.4	120.0	103.9	115.2	110.9

[a]For the period t+5, there were more of the time insufficient cases. – [b]Slightly different figures because of missing information for few cases. – [c]"Dumped" and "non-dumped" extra-EC imports.

Source: EC Official Journal, various issues; Eurostat, various issues; own computations.

equivalent of roughly 23 percent, i.e., three times (five for chemicals) the average post-Tokyo most-favoured-nation tariffs. Thirdly, they seem to have a strong bias in favor of price-fixing agreements. Fourthly, antidumping actions create trade diversion, particularly in the case of LDC and NIC exports. Fifthly, rents created by antidumping protection accrue to foreign firms: these rents appear to be substantial for Industrialized Countries, less important for LDCs and quasi-null for NICs. Finally, some coalitions of EC firms – those characterized by an optimal trade-off between the number of firms involved and the market share held – appear much more "efficient" at obtaining protectionist measures and molding market structures.

These results suggest that countries willing to protect their import-competing industries may prefer to use antidumping actions rather than "voluntary export restraints". There is a legal reason: antidumping actions are GATT-consistent. More importantly, there are economic reasons. Antidumping actions can be more selective than VERs: they are generally initiated against firms and different protective measures can be taken against every foreign exporter. They can be preventive: antidumping complaints can be initiated against small exporters or even exporters "threatening" domestic markets. They allow a wide range of measures, from tariffs to quantitative restrictions: domestic firms can use this opportunity to increase their bargaining power vis-à-vis the foreign firms.

Further research should access the cost of antidumping laws for the country implementing them. This cost is the sum of the traditional cost of protection and of the cost due to the procartel impact of antidumping laws. This second point appears crucial, according to the results presented in this paper.

NOTES

I would like to thank J. M. Finger for many discussions on this topic, B. Balassa, L. A. Winters, J. Martin, C. Mann, P. Meo, and an anonymous referee for their comments on an earlier version. I would also like to thank Azia Amjadi for her patient research assistance. The views expressed here are those of the author and should not be attributed to the World Bank.

1 According to *Webster's Dictionary*, to codify is "to reduce to a code". It might be argued that the Tokyo Code reduced the scope of some of Article VI's most basic concepts. For instance, "material" never qualified injury in the Code, except in one footnote. This illustrates short-term benefits and long-term costs. In the short run, this US–EC compromise eased the introduction of this provision in the US law. Long-term costs came from the lax enforcement of "material injury" in the EC and US cases.

2 This argument may be debatable for the Uruguay Round case. Codification can be expected to face decreasing returns to scale, more codification being more costly to introduce and less effective in easing international politics when there are more negotiating partners.

3 For simplicity's sake, Table 1 does not give long-term perspectives. Until 1976, there were fewer than 6 EC new cases per year. After a peak of 83 new cases in 1978 due to the implementation of the EC steel trade policy, 30 to 50 cases were implemented each year. The increasing complexity of the cases means there is an increasing trend in resources allocated to antidumping actions. The US cases roughly follow the same pattern, except that the 1978 peak is not so marked. The current Korean and Mexican antidumping laws have been implemented only since 1986.

4 The basic equation tested is: $a_{t,k} = \alpha + \beta e_{t,k} + \gamma T$, where $a_{t,k}$ is the number of antidumping actions initiated by the EC against country K (or alternatively the exposure ratios, defined by the Korean and Mexican share of an exporting country in the number of cases initiated by an importing country divided by the share of the exports of the exporting country in the total imports of the importing country), $e_{t,k}$ the nominal exchange rate (in terms of ECU), and T the time trend. For the period 1970–1986, the result is: In $(a) = -108.7$ (19.1) + 0.004e (0.009) + 0.055T (0.009),

with R^2=0.06, F=17.4 and DW=1.03, and standard errors in parentheses. Correction for first-order autocorrelation does not significantly modify the results.

5 With relatively standardized products, product differentiation can only be a function of the period at which a good is available. Many antidumping cases deal with this problem when they consider the impact of short-term contracts on long-term contracts.

6 The equation tested is $a_{P,k} = \alpha + \beta d_{P,k}$ where P stands for the various periods defined in the text, and d the increases in debt during period P. For 1970–87, the result is: ln(a) = 0.67 (18.1) + 0.94d(1.9), with R^2 = 0.02, F = 0.24, DW = 2.48, and standard errors in parentheses. Lags (one period) do not significantly modify the results.

7 The basic equation tested is $a_{t,k} = \alpha + \beta d_{t,k} + \gamma T$ where d is the long-term debt outstanding disbursed (alternatively debt-export ratio). The 1982-86 results is: ln(a) = –14.4(189.1)–0.08d(0.11) + 0.008T(0.09), with R^2=0.008, F=0.27, DW = 0.91, and standard errors in parentheses. F-tests between tests for different periods or groups of countries are not significant at the 5 percent level.

8 Finger et al. [1982] examined the impact of these factors on US cases. Norall [1986] gave examples in EC cases. Compare also Dixit [1988].

9 No or de minis dumping and no-injury findings follow explicit threats of actions – in the complaint and initiation – and detailed investigations. To assume they have no "possibly" protectionist content is a legalistic fiction.

10 Roughly 30 percent of antidumping actions are terminated by "possibly" protective measures.

11 The estimates are based on the following measures: ad valorem duties, ad valorem equivalents of specific and variable duties and of the undertakings when these undertakings are based on the dumping margins. The highest ad valorem equivalents generally concern cases with specific duties imposed on NMC exports.

12 This may be also observed for the EFTA countries. However, the low magnitude of the measures taken against these countries suggests leaving them aside.

13 Tables 3–8 are based on import data at a very disaggregated level (NIMEXE 6 digit). They present unweighted averages of indexes calculated on a case-by-case basis. When less than five observations are available, no results are shown. The years (t+4) and (t+5) are, by construction, based on fewer observations than the other years. Moreover, they correspond to cases initiated in 1980 and 1981 exclusively. The interpretation of the results for these two years should therefore be more cautious than the interpretation of the results of the other years.

14 It is sometimes suggested that this sharp decline in imports may be due to the fact that imports during the year of initiation (or the two years before) are in "excessive" supply since they are "dumped". Observed decreases would thus be a statistical artifact mirroring the "inflated" (by the dumping) figures of the year of initiation, and changes in the base year would modify the results. However, computation of alternative unweighted indexes based on each of the prior three years confirms the pattern of decline.

15 The decrease afterwards is due to a drastic evolution of the imports in only two of the observed cases, and seems to correspond to very specific conditions.

16 This result is based on the cases initiated between 1980 and 1985. It would be interesting to see whether the relative increase in terms of cases initiated against LDCs and NICs since 1985 is mirrored by the relative import declines.

17 Both cases with protective measures and cases with "possibly" protective measures show increases of imports before initiation. However, cases with "possibly" protective measures exhibit lower growth rates of imports and a first decline of imports in the year preceding the initiation.

18 Interestingly, this feature is not observed for cases terminated by ad valorem duties and for cases involving NMCs. The latter point may be explained by the fact the

NMC exports under antidumping actions mainly seem to be traditional inputs the NMC firms produce for EC firms.

19 It is true that many antidumping cases involve products characterized by decreasing consumption. However, the crucial point is to determine in which direction the relation goes: it may be that a decrease in demand induces dumping practices; or, it may be that the global domestic consumption before antidumping actions declines because price stickiness imposed by dominant domestic producers depresses the demand more than price decreases from foreign exporters can increase it. The evolution of total trade after the initiation of antidumping actions – i.e., although prices were maintained or increased in the EC markets because of the protection granted – makes the second explanation the most plausible one.

20 In the case of a specific duty, the higher the "world" price is, the larger the surplus transfer from consumers to producers, and the larger the proportion of the producer surplus vis-à-vis the tariff revenue is. The first motive is common with ad valorem duty. The second motive is an additional one.

21 This is the highest possible figure since some of these firms were involved in several cases or were subsidiaries of common parent companies. Antidumping investigations mention the foreign and EC firms investigated by the EC Commission. These figures give a good estimate of the firms actively involved in the cases because these firms have agreed to provide confidential data to the Commission.

22 No pattern is noticeable in terms of industries (ISIC-four digit).

23 "Lower" here refers to the antidumping procedures and has no economic meaning, since the costs or the "reasonable" rate of profit which serve as a basis for the injury margins are function of the EC market structures.

24 They are "objective" in the sense they are based on technical defined by the Antidumping Code and the EC Regulations. It remains that EC firms lobby to favor some interpretations of the technical elements, as exemplified by some proposals in the Uruguay Round negotiations.

25 These market shares are those at the year of the initiation. Market shares prevailing in the few years prior the initiation – respectively 67.0; 54.6; 66.0 and 76.3 percent – are also consistent with our hypothesis.

26 The return of foreign competitors may reflect the fact that EC monopolies have a relatively low market share on the average and that they are by definition located in only a subset of member states, so that foreign competitors may penetrate the other EC markets relatively easily.

27 A plausible explanation for this difference from the one-firm cases is the continuous threat that a coalition of a size still manageable and representing a relatively large market share of the EC consumption imposes on the pricing behavior of foreign producers.

REFERENCES

Dixit, Avinash, "Antidumping and Countervailing Duties under Oligopoly". *European Economic Review*, Col. 23, 1988, pp. 55–68.

Finger, J. Michael, H. Keith Hall, Douglas Nelson, "The Political Economy of Administered Protection". *The American Economic Review*, Vol. 72, 1982, pp. 452–466.

GATT, *Antidumping and Countervailing Measures Legislation*. Geneva 1987.

Karsenty, Guy, Samuel Laird, "The GSP: Policy Options and the New Round". *Weltwirschaftliches Archiv*, Vol. 123, 1987, pp. 262–296.

Krugman, Paul, *Pricing to Market When the Exchange Rate Changes*. Cambridge, Mass., 1985, mimeo.

Messerlin, Patrick A. [1988a], *Antidumping and Competition Laws: the EC Experience*. Washington 1988, mimeo.
——[1988b], "The Developing Countries and the Uruguay Round Negotiations on the Antidumping Code". In: Detlev Dickie, Ernst-Ulrich Petersmann (eds), *Foreign Trade in the Present and a New International Economic Order*. Fribourg 1988, pp. 163–186.
Norall, Christopher, "New Trends in Antidumping Practice in Brussels". *The World Economy*, Vol. 9, 1986, pp. 97–111.
Official Journal of the European Communities, various issues.

10. Developing Countries' Participation in the WTO

C. Michalopoulos

I. INTRODUCTION

Throughout the 1960s and 1970s, developing countries viewed UNCTAD rather than GATT as the main institution through which they could promote their interests in international trade. Their representation in GATT reflected these priorities: many developing countries were not members, and of those that were, a large number did not maintain official representatives resident in Geneva, but instead used representatives in other European capitals to cover GATT matters – for ACP countries usually their Mission to the EU in Brussels. Moreover, their participation in GATT negotiations prior to the Uruguay Round was "passive" in that they did not engage in a significant way in the mutual exchange of concessions on a reciprocal basis (Whalley, 1987).

Beginning with the Uruguay Round, developing countries' attitude towards participation in the GATT and, subsequently, in the WTO changed significantly: many developing countries played a very active role in the Uruguay Round negotiations; and a large number decided to become members of WTO. This attitude change reflects a number of complex and inter-related developments: developing countries, in general, have become more effectively integrated in the international trading system, and several have become major exporters of manufactures. Trade policies in many countries have been liberalized, favouring an outward orientation and lower protection. And, there has been a growing appreciation of the importance of observing international rules in the conduct of trade as well as the need to safeguard trading interests through effective participation in the activities of the new organization.

The establishment of the WTO has resulted in further changes which place additional demands on developing countries for their effective participation: first, the WTO covers a variety of new areas, such as services, standards, intellectual property rights, all of which require additional institutional capacity in member governments both for more effective representation in Geneva and in their home capitals. Second, the WTO, unlike GATT, has been engaging in a number of on-going negotiations in the liberalization of different sectors which require continuous active involvement by member countries. Three such negotiations, on Basic Telecommunications, Information Technology Products and Financial Services were concluded in 1997 and more are in store starting in 1999, as part of the built-in agenda of the Uruguay Round.[1]

A key question that arises at present is whether developing countries' representation at the WTO is adequate for the pursuit of their effective participation in the activities of the Organization and, through it, the proportion of their interests in the expanding range of issues being addressed. This issue is of special importance because the WTO, like the GATT before it, is a member-driven organization, meaning that the bulk of the analytical work, the development of proposals as well as the negotiation of agreements falls on the member countries and their representatives.

This paper analyses participation of developing countries at the WTO as of mid-1997. The focus is on three main issues: (a) representation, as reflected in the existence or not of a Mission of adequate size dealing with WTO matters located in Geneva; (b) participation in the affairs of the new Organization, as reflected in the allocation of formal chairmanships in the various WTO councils and subsidiary bodies and in the informal processes that characterize WTO governance and decision making; and (c) institutional capacity in home capitals, which is necessary for both effective representation and participation. Based on this analysis, the last part of the paper draws a number of conclusions and recommendations for the more effective participation of developing countries in the WTO.

II. THE DATA

The basic information used for the analysis of representation was provided by the WTO/GATT Directories issued in 1982 and in August of 1987 and 1997. These Directories have a listing of all staff working in each member country Mission dealing with WTO/GATT matters as well as the location of the Mission. The listings contain only professional staff – secretarial and support staff (drivers etc.) are excluded; and are usually headed by an Ambassador, permanent representative of the country to the WTO/GATT. As noted above, the representation may be from a Mission in Geneva, from a Mission elsewhere in Europe or in a few cases from a Ministry in the capital of the country itself. They are all listed in the WTO/GATT Directories – whose format has changed little over the years; they have just become thicker.

The period covered is of interest because it looks at the WTO/GATT representation at three different points in time, each associated with a distinct period in the organization's activity: 1982 is before the beginning of the Uruguay Round, 1987 is a year after the Uruguay Round was launched, and 1997 is the present – ten years later, when the WTO has been established and the implementation of the Round is in full swing.

The Directories also contain a listing of the officers of the Organization and all subsidiary bodies, committees, working groups etc. as well as their country affiliation which is used in the discussion of participation in WTO activities. Chairmen have traditionally played a relatively active role in the GATT and the WTO – their role has not been purely cosmetic. An organization like the WTO – and previously the GATT – which works with consensus despite the fact that the countries represented are very different in their economic size, presents complex challenges in designing decision making structures that result in an equitable representation of the interests of all participants. Chairmanships play a role in this effort to maintain a reasonable balance of interests. Thus, the share of chairmanships and other offices held by the developing countries could shed some light on their involvement and potential influence in the organization, especially over time.

Both measures – committee chairmanships and location and size of mission staffing obviously by themselves do not necessarily imply effectiveness. The quality and effectiveness of committee chairmen and staff varies and there is no way to take account of such differences in a systematic fashion.

There is also a concern as to whether staff, listed in the Directories as working on WTO/GATT matters, actually work only on these matters, or have responsibilities regarding other Geneva-based international organizations as well, dealing with unrelated issues, such as for example ILO. Practice regarding who gets listed in the Directories relative to what they actually do tends to vary: A majority of both developed and developing countries operate joint Missions – i.e. Missions housing representatives to all international agencies in Geneva whose formal head is the Ambassador accredited to the UN. In these cases most of the staff listed in the WTO Directory also appear in the UN Directory – usually, but not always, with an explicit WTO designation. But there is a significant group of both developing and developed countries operating separate WTO Missions headed by a different Ambassador and often reporting to a different Ministry in their capitals. The establishment of separate WTO Missions increased noticeably following the establishment of the WTO and may have been partly the result of the setting up of a separate WTO headquarters agreement with the Swiss authorities.[2] Thus, there appears to be no systematic bias as between developing and developed countries concerning a divergence between their formal designation in the WTO Directories and what they actually work on or on the basis of whether there is a separate WTO Mission or not.

On the other hand, to the extent that a large number of developing countries are represented in Geneva by very small Missions, then the greater the likelihood that staff in these missions, whatever their formal designation, would have to deal with other matters as well and hence their capacity to deal with WTO matters diluted. However, the use of the measure itself, counting heads, tends to introduce an offsetting, small country bias; At the limit, each country represented has no less than one representative. A very small country with a minute proportion of world trade would still have a representative – and an influence disproportionate to its trade share – while a country like the US or a group of countries like that of the EC whose trade or GNP may be many hundreds or even thousands of times larger would not be expected to have Missions of proportionate size.[3]

But of course, numbers and formal representation and chairmanships do not tell the whole story. Informal arrangements work along with and sometime supersede the formal committee structure and arrangements. Information on these informal processes of developing consensus is hard to document. In some cases, the groups involved and their membership is a matter of public record. In other cases, they are not, and the analysis presented here has had to rely on personal interviews with the information provided on condition of no attribution.

Finally, it was not possible to undertake a systematic analysis of institutional constraints and requirements for effective representation and participation in the WTO for all developing countries. The main new data presented on this issue are based on the "Trade Related Technical Assistance Needs Assessments" prepared by a number of Least Developed Countries in the context of the High Level Meeting on Integrated Initiatives for Least Developed Countries' Trade Development held in Geneva in October 1997.

III. MEMBERSHIP

The first point to note is the familiar one that developing countries now account for 74% of WTO membership compared to 66% in 1982 (Table 1). Only one new member, Liechtenstein, was added over the period that could be considered a developed economy. The overwhelming majority of the 43 new members added, the bulk since 1987, have been developing countries and, most recently, a number of transition economies. Membership increased slightly – by seven countries in the period 1982–1987, notably with the inclusion of such large developing countries as Mexico; and exploded with the addition of 36 new members hence (see Table 1).[4] At present, total WTO membership accounts for over 90% of world exports, compared to slightly more than 75% in 1982. The largest exporting countries/territories currently not members are China, Chinese Taipei, Russia and Saudi Arabia.[5]

Over the same period, the proportion of world exports accounted by developing country members of the WTO increased even more, from 11% in 1982 to 19% in 1966 (Table 1). This was both because of an increase in developing country membership, and because of the rapid expansion of developing country exports in the 1990s. Overall however, developing countries continue to represent a much larger proportion of WTO membership than their share of international trade.

The data on membership nonetheless disguise the fact that a large number of developing countries have been at any point in time formally "inactive" for not having paid their WTO dues for more than three years.[6] At the beginning of 1997, 23 developing countries/territories were so designated. Such a designation implies that they are not able to receive technical assistance from the organization, not have their representatives chair WTO bodies, and the withholding of a number of other privileges, such as the distribution of documents etc.[7] Another seven developing countries were more than one or two years in arrears and were therefore barred from chairing WTO bodies. Thus, thirty developing countries i.e. about a third of the total membership, was barred from chairmanships. Twenty of these were least developed countries. Fifteen had no Missions in Geneva and many others had only token representation.

IV. REPRESENTATION

Location of Missions

Today, while 64 developing countries members maintain WTO Missions in

TABLE 1 *GATT/WTO Membership and World Trade 1982–1997*

Countries/Territories	GATT/WTO Membership Number			Per cent			World Exports Value in US $ Billion			Per cent of World Exports		
	1982	1987	1997	1982	1987	1997	1982	1987	1997	1982	1987	1997
Developed	24	24	25	27.3	25.3	19.1	1,168	1,734	3,554	62.5	69.7	69.4
Developing	58	65	97	65.9	68.4	74.0	211	348	972	11.3	14.0	19.0
Others	6	6	9	6.8	6.3	6.9	57	84	97	3.0	3.4	1.9
Total GATT/WTO Members	88	95	131	100.0	100.0	100.0	1,436	2,166	4,623	76.8	87.1	90.3
Non-Members							434	322	495	23.2	12.9	9.7
Total World							1,870	2,488	5,118	100.0	100.0	100.0

Source: WTO *Statistical Yearbook* 1997; WTO *Directory*, 1982, 1987, 1997.

Geneva, 26 others continue to be represented by Missions or Embassies elsewhere in Europe and seven more list as their representatives people located in Ministries at their own capitals (see Table 2a and Annex). Two thirds of those with representation from other capitals in Europe used their Brussels mission; while the remainder were spread between Bonn, London and Paris (see Annex). The proportion of developing countries members of the WTO or GATT actually represented in Geneva declined slightly between 1982 and 1997 from 69% to 66% respectively, despite the fact that a number of countries such as Uganda, Zambia and Zimbabwe, moved their representation from elsewhere in Europe to Geneva (see Annex). By contrast, all developed country members of the WTO, with the except of Liechtenstein, and all transition economies have a Mission in Geneva. The decline in the proportion of developing countries with Geneva representation is to a considerable extent due to the inclusion as WTO members at its establishment, based on simplified procedures, of a large number of smaller developing countries whose governments had previously been applying the GATT on a *de facto* basis.

There are two main reasons for the continued representation of many developing countries from outside Geneva: (a) many of the smaller ACP countries consider their main international trade policy issues to involve relations with the EC rather than the WTO and thus locate their representatives in Brussels, from where they also are supposed to follow WTO issues; (b) in addition, a number of the new members are very small island economies that have very few representatives abroad and simply can not afford separate Missions in Geneva. Of the 29 least developed countries members of the WTO, only 12 had representation in Geneva. Similarly, practically all of the small island economies were represented from missions in Europe or from capitals.

There is little doubt that representation from Brussels or another Mission in Europe can cause difficulties, delays and sometimes confusion in the participation of the activities of WTO in Geneva. The limitations and constraints to effective participation in the WTO that derive from lack of representation in Geneva have been noted many times (Blackhurst 1997, UNCTAD 1997); and they have been recently documented in the case of Sierra Leone, a least developed country with representation to the WTO from Brussels.[8]

Size of Missions

At present, the total staff of missions working on WTO matters in Geneva as well as developing countries representatives working in European capitals numbers 540, of whom 347 represent developing countries, 168 developed countries and 25 other, mostly transition economies. This is more than double the number that worked on GATT issues in 1982, with most of the increase occurring since 1987.[9]

The increase in the total head count is in smaller part due to the increase in WTO membership and in larger part due to an increase in the average size of Missions dealing with WTO matters. The average size of Mission increased from 2.9 persons per mission in 1982 to 3.3 persons in 1987 and to 4.1 persons in 1997, an increase of over 40%, with most of the changes occurring in the decade since 1987.[10]

TABLE 2A *Country Membership and Representation GATT/WTO 1982–1997*
By Location and Number of Mission Staff

Countries/ Territories	1982 Geneva		1982 Europe		1982 Capitals		1987 Geneva		1987 Europe		1987 Capitals		1997 Geneva		1997 Europe		1997 Capitals	
	No.	Staff	No.	Staff	No.	Staff	No.	Staff	No.	Staff	No.	Staff	No.	Staff	No.	Staff	No.	Staff
Developed	24	99					24	120					24	166	1		1	2
Developing	40	120	14	15	4	5	45	147	15	21	5	5	64	277	26	60	7	7
Others	6	16					6	18					9	25				
Total	70	235	14	15	4	5	75	285	15	21	5	5	97	468	26	61	8	9

TABLE 2B

Countries/ Territories	1982 No. of Countries	1982 Staff	1982 Staff/ Country	1987 No. of Countries	1987 Staff	1987 Staff/ Country	1997 No. of Countries	1997 Staff	1997 Staff/ Country
Developed	24	99	4.1	24	120	5.0	25	169	6.8
Developing	58	140	2.4	65	173	2.7	97	344	3.5
Others	6	16	2.7	6	18	3.0	9.	25	2.8
Total	88	255	2.9	95	311	3.3	131	538	4.1
Developing (Geneva)	40	120	3.0	45	147	3.3	64	280	4.4

Source: GATT/WTO *Directory* 1982, 1987, 1997.

The average size of Mission increased both for developed and developing countries. The average size Mission for developed countries increased from 4.1 persons in 1982 to 6.8 persons in 1997 or more than 50%. For developing countries the average rose exactly by 50% from 2.4 to 3.5 persons per Mission (see Table 2b).[11] Thus, the difference in the average size of Mission actually increased over the past fifteen years.[12]

The fact that the average Mission for the developing countries continued to be substantially lower and the difference with developed countries is increasing, should not necessarily be interpreted as an indicator of relative capacity for effective representation on issues of interest at the WTO for the developing countries as a whole. This is because in this, as in so many areas, the average for developing countries is quite misleading as it disguises very large variations.

At the one extreme is a group of LDCs or small, low income countries as well as a large number of small island economies (for example, St Christopher and Nevis, St Lucia, St Vincent and Grenadines etc) with little trade and basically only nominal representation. The average size of Mission for these countries was only 1.2 persons.

At the other extreme are the ASEAN countries and Korea whose average size of WTO Mission in Geneva is in excess of 8 persons (headed by Korea and Thailand with more than fifteen each) and thus substantially greater than the average Mission from developed countries. Representation from Latin American countries averages about 5.5 persons per Mission – i.e. close to developed countries, and similarly for other developing countries like India and Egypt.

Discussions with representatives of Missions from both developed and developing countries suggested that they are all hard pressed to cope with the increased number of meetings and activities of the WTO. According to one estimate (Blackhurst 1997a), there were approximately 40–45 scheduled WTO meetings in the average working week in 1995–1996. To this one must add all the other informal gatherings for consultations that occur among delegations outside formal settings to develop consensus.

Based on informal estimates developed in consultation with a number of Missions, just to follow the topics of the various WTO bodies and attend their meetings requires a staff of at least 4–5 people, and the average is increasing.[13] If one uses this yardstick, it is clear that, as of mid 1997, a very large number of developing countries did not meet it. Assuming for example, that effective representation in the WTO requires a Mission in Geneva of a size of at least three staff (including the head of the Mission) – which is actually smaller than the minimal range judged as adequate, 33 developing countries and territories did not meet it because they did not have a Mission in Geneva; another 17 had a Mission, almost always as part of a joint UN mission, but with less than three staff (including the head of Mission) assigned to WTO tasks. In addition, there were another six countries, which while having a nominally adequately sized Mission in Geneva, (in all cases, joint with the UN and thus harder to judge on the division of responsibilities) had arrears problems, as a consequence of which either they were formally "inactive" or could not have their representatives elected to WTO bodies. This gives a total of 56, or close to 60% of the total developing countries members of the WTO being in some fashion handicapped in being effectively represented.

At the same time, there are perhaps 30–35 developing countries including those already noted and several others which by virtue of their interest in the WTO, the staffing of their Missions and the leadership of their representatives, play a very active role in the affairs of the organization. They are the ones which provide the bulk of the formal leadership structure of the WTO and they are the ones that are being consulted when informal consultations to develop a consensus take place.

V. PARTICIPATION

Chairmanships

The analysis of chairmanships includes not only chairmen but also vice-chairmen who had been appointed to a number of the main bodies of the organization and subsidiary committees, often in order to maintain a balance between developing and developed countries.

The analysis distinguishes between chairmanships (including vice-chairmen) of two main groups: The first group of "important" chairmanships includes those of the main constituent bodies, such as the Chairman and Vice Chairman of the GATT Council and later the WTO Council on Goods, Services etc as well as chairmanships of the permanent organs of the GATT and later of the Committee structure of the WTO.[14] The second group of "less important" chairmanships, includes those of various ad hoc working groups and other entities established under lesser "authority" – i.e. those under the multilateral codes of the GATT, under plurilateral agreements of the WTO, working parties for accession etc. The distinction is somewhat arbitrary: Under the reorganization following the establishment of the WTO, a number of groups that functioned before under a "lower authority" of a multilateral code, such as the anti-dumping committee or customs valuation were incorporated into the more formal committee structure of the WTO. But the breakdown is helpful in bringing out some interesting points about developing country representation and is used primarily for this purpose.

The main findings are presented in Table 3. The Table shows that over the fifteen years covered, developing countries increased substantially the absolute number of "important" chairmanships they hold. Indeed, both in 1987 and in 1997 they held in absolute terms more important chairmanships than the developed countries (but not by a large margin). In all cases their proportion of chairmanships is lower than their share of the total membership of the institution but higher than their share of international trade.

The distribution of the very top leadership positions of the GATT (Chairman and three Vice Chairmen of the Council) in 1982 and 1987 seems to have been very carefully balanced: In each instance the Chairman was either from a developed or developing country (rotating on an annual basis) and the three vice-chairmen, one each of a developing country, developed one and a country in transition (though they were not called that then!).

Similar balance exists at the very top of the WTO leadership positions at present involving the positions of the Chairman of the General Council (Brazil)

TABLE 3 *Country Composition of Chairmen/Vice-Chairmen*

Countries/Territories	GATT 1982–1987 Permanent Committees & Organs				GATT 1982–1987 All other Committees under certain Arrangements, MTN Codes, Panels and Groups				WTO 1997 General Council and Subsidiary Bodies, Committees and WPs, DSB, TPRB		WTO 1997 All Other Working Parties and Committees (Plurilateral Agreements, Accessories, etc.)	
	1982		1987		1982		1987		1997			
	No.	Per Cent	No.	Per Cent	No.	Per Cent	No.	Per Cent	No.	Per Cent	No.	Per Cent
Developed	7	46.6	4	33.3	19	70.4	20	61	18	45.0	22	66.5
Developing	7	46.6	7	58.3	7	26.9	12	39	20	50.0	11	33.5
Others	1	6.8	1	8.4	1	3.7	0		2	5.0		
Total	15	100.0	12	100.0	27	100.0	32	100.0	40	100.0	33	100.0

Source: GATT/WTO *Directory* 1982, 1987, 1997

the Chairmen of the Councils of Goods (Norway), Services (Korea) and TRIPS (Chile), the Dispute Settlement Body (New Zealand), the Trade Policy Review Body (Pakistan) and key Committees. Indeed, there is a pattern of informal rotation for the top positions, with the understanding that Chairmanships – which are for one year – previously held by a developed country would be succeeded by a developing country and vice-versa.[15]

The picture that emerges from looking at the other, lesser chairmanships however, is entirely different. Both in 1982 and 1987, very few chairmanships went to developing countries. This is in part due to the fact that most of the groups involved focused on the activities of the implementation of the multilateral codes in which developing country participation was very limited. Developing countries focused their interest then on – and maintained the chairmanships of – such groups as the Trade and Development Committee, relations with ITC and similar entities which had been created to address primarily the interests of the developing countries – not the institution as a whole.

The situation has changed little in the WTO where the developing countries again hold proportionately few of the leadership positions in bodies dealing with the implementation of two remaining plurilateral agreements but also very few of the chairmanships of the many working parties set up for accession of new members. A number of the accession working parties have been in place for several years and their chairmen, mostly from developed countries, continue even after they have left their positions in Geneva. At the same time, there is proliferation of committees and working groups relative to the number of available high level, experienced developing country representatives that have time to devote to the expanding range of WTO tasks. If one judges that there are about 30–35 developing countries active in WTO affairs, their Ambassadors or senior WTO representatives hold the chairmanships of 31 WTO bodies or other Committees. This is not a bad score, given that several of these Ambassadors also have to represent their countries at other international organizations in Geneva.

The implications of the findings on chairmanships should not be exaggerated. They do suggest that the WTO as an institution is formally flexible enough to accommodate an increasing interest on the part of developing countries. Whether this translates into moving forward issues of importance to the agenda of the developing countries is a somewhat more complex issue, however. Preparation and presentation of issues does not hinge primarily on the holding of chairmanships or leadership positions. It is based on a lot of preparatory work and institutional capability in capitals; it is also based on the development of points of common interest with similarly minded countries and delegations.

Informal Consultations

Any institution such as the WTO, and the GATT before it, which is based on consensus must develop a variety of processes both formal and informal, in order to reach decisions. In principle, any single member of the institution can block a decision by casting a negative vote. It was clear, even in the context of the GATT where the developing countries had a majority of the votes but played a decidedly lesser role, that it would be futile to attempt to exercise voting strength either to block major progress or to force developed countries to implement obligations not freely accepted (Evans 1968). In practice there is rarely, if ever, any voting. This puts a premium on consultation, both formal and informal, that builds consensus.

As the WTO now has more than 130 members, it is very difficult to conduct consultations, or for that matter any kind of business activity, when everybody has to be consulted about everything. Thus, while the General Council, the ultimate decision making body where all members are represented, as well as all the various subsidiary bodies and committees meet frequently, informal consultations take place even more often. When issues of importance to the Organization as a whole require consultations, these usually involve the Director General and a smaller group of members, that include the major trading countries, both developed and developing, and others who are judged to be representative of the views of the remaining membership. The actual composition of this group (called the "Green Room Group" because it meets in the Director General's green conference room) tends to vary by issue. But on issues of general importance to the organization it could consist of upwards of thirty members. Given that in such meetings, the representative of the European Commission speaks on behalf of the fifteen members of the European Communities, developing countries typically form the majority of "voices" in such consultations.[16]

Developing countries often do not have a common position on major issues before the WTO. There is a Developing Country Group in the WTO that holds consultations from time to time; and the developing countries consult on trade policies issues of importance to them in the context of the G-77 in UNCTAD. However, the establishment of common positions, that will encompass all the developing countries members of the WTO as a group, is becoming more of a challenge as there are growing disparities in their income levels, their trading interests, their integration in the international economy, their institutional capacities and their participation in WTO affairs. Some of these countries, e.g. Korea, Mexico and Turkey, are also members of the OECD and on some issues share the outlook of the developed countries members of that group. Others, find that, on some issues, their interests tend to coincide with developed country members and hence participate in groups with mixed developed-developing country memberships.

Agriculture is one such issue. The "Cairns Group", perhaps the most well known and formal of these groups, consists of a mixed membership of exporters of agricultural products, and includes such countries as Australia, but also Argentina, Hungary and Thailand. The interests of these exporters may at times be quite different from those of a large number of developing countries which are net importers of foodstuffs.

Two other informal groups of mixed membership are worth noting: The so-called "Invisible Group" consists of officials from trade ministries of major trading countries, balanced between both developed and developing countries (including the so-called "quad" group of Canada, the EC, Japan and the US, but also such developing countries as Brazil, India and Korea). It meets in Geneva, perhaps twice a year, with the participation of the Director General to discuss, usually in general terms, upcoming issues of importance to the WTO. The other is the so called "Beau-Rivage Group", which includes the Geneva-based representatives of a number of smaller countries both developed and developing, that share an active participation in WTO affairs and a commitment to the multilateral trading system.[17]

In addition to these groups, the development of a consensus involves numerous other meetings in formal or informal settings. For example, developing countries consult in regional groupings, such as the Africa group or ASEAN as well as in context of groups with a wider agenda such the G-15, or in the context of sectorally oriented bodies such as International Textiles and Clothing Bureau or in smaller caucuses among like-minded countries whose composition sometimes includes both developed and developing countries. The 30–35 developing countries with an active representation at the WTO are usually important participants in these consultations. One of the problems that some developing countries have voiced is that they lack an institutional structure such as the one provided by OECD for the developed countries in which to undertake research and analyses as well as develop proposals of interest to a large group of developing countries, which can the be presented at the WTO for consideration by its full membership.[18]

The Agenda, New Issues and Agreements

Partly because of the lack of such a forum and partly because of their own institutional weaknesses, many developing countries feel handicapped in contributing to setting the WTO agenda. As in other fields, the largest number of participants in the recently concluded agreements on Telecommunications, Information Technology and Financial Services reached by the WTO during 1997 are developing countries. However, the initiative for all three agreements, as well as for the "new issues" that have emerged on the WTO agenda following the Singapore Ministerial, came in large measure from the developed countries, which also account for the bulk of world trade in the goods and services involved. At the same time, it is quite clear that none of the agreements could have been put in place without the active support provided by a number of developing countries from East Asia and Latin America.

VI. INSTITUTIONAL CAPACITY

Effective participation in the WTO and representation of developing country interests depends critically on the development of an adequate institutional capacity in the developing countries themselves. The increasing range and complexity of issues handled by the WTO, some of which are becoming very technical, implies that the capacity of developing countries to participate effectively in the work of the WTO will depend very heavily on the analytical capacity and strength of the governmental and other institutions handling the range of WTO issues in capitals. This is all the more so in the WTO, a member-driven organization, with a very small secretariat, where a great deal of the analysis of issues and development of positions is done by the members, usually in capitals.

Institutional weaknesses of developing countries have received formal recognition in the Uruguay Round agreements which contain provisions for special and differential treatment of developing countries in a number of areas especially in Sanitary and Phytosanitary, Standards and TRIPS, permitting longer implementation periods and/or the provision of technical assistance to strengthen their institutional capacity to meet their obligations under the agreements. Developing countries face a variety of challenges in this regard: the drafting of appropriate legislation and regulations, the meeting of procedural notification requirements, the staffing of government institutions with technical personnel able to implement the policies and commitments undertaken and the monitoring of trading partners' implementation of WTO obligations to assess whether market access has been unfairly denied or trade rights infringed – as well as to prepare an appropriate response (UNCTAD and WTO, 1996).

These weaknesses have been clear for some time, especially in the context of Africa (Oyejide, 1997). They are frequently glaring for the more than 50 developing countries with weak representation at the WTO – and some others as well; and they were amply documented in the recent assessments of technical assistance needs prepared by least developed countries in connection with the High Level Meeting on Integrated Initiatives for Least Developed Countries' Trade Development (HLMLDCTD), which took place in Geneva in October 1997. All eleven needs assessments completed so far requested assistance in strengthening domestic institutions that support international trade including, for example, through staff training of Trade Ministers and Customs Offices, preparation of legislation and regulations, and the development of a local capacity to enable countries to participate more effectively in future discussions and negotiations especially in the "new issues" handled by the WTO (see WT/COMTD/IF/1–11).

Given these weaknesses, it is often very difficult for countries to undertake the analytical work required for the development of new initiatives or for response to proposals prepared by others. As Oyejide notes, as long as "particular countries were willing to subordinate their interests to those generally articulated by and broadly acceptable to all developing countries, their participation was not particularly resource intensive at the individual country level. Because interests were not extensively differentiated, it was not necessary to be adequately represented at every meeting, nor was it required for such representatives to be supported by full documentation and background information on each issue being discussed and for the negotiators to receive prompt and adequate instructions from their home capitals. The more differential nature of their participation has called for support of the types which have never systematically built up over the years" (Oyejide, 1990, p. 442).

In the absence of institutional capacity in the government, countries have had also to rely on outside consultants to represent them at meetings in the WTO. When this is done without a presence in Geneva, it can lead to confusion and misunderstandings as the Sierra Leone experience of representation at the WTO Committee on Trade and Environment suggests (Chaytor and Hindley, 1997). Unless these weaknesses start to be addressed, merely strengthening these countries' representation in Geneva will not go very far in enhancing their participation in the WTO.

The main burden for strengthening institutional capacity has to be borne by the developing countries themselves. However, as Jan Pronk, Chairman of the HLMLDCTD, stated in his opening statement to the meeting ". . . foreign assistance can help, but often did not. Too often supply driven assistance and incoherent diagnoses from a wide range of development agencies, undercut the domestic will to reform: too much technical assistance and proliferation of donor schemes overtaxed the domestic capacity to reform and led to confusion and duplication."[19]

A systematic review of the assistance efforts of the international community in support of trade development in developing countries is beyond the scope of this paper. Some of the themes and conclusions drawn from the HLMLDCTD however, are worth noting both because of their relevance to the LDCs whose problems of effective participation in the WTO are most acute and because of their wider applicability to other developing countries.

An important conclusion of the meeting is that it is not the lack of assistance as such that is the problem, but rather that it has been supply driven, not effectively coordinated and the reforms supported are not "owned" by the recipient countries. In recent periods, assistance in the trade field has declined significantly from some donor agencies, e.g. UNDP. In the case of the World Bank, the focus on trade development in general has declined by comparison to the late 1980s and early 1990s. The World Bank shut down its Geneva office in the early 1990s and the share of its trade related operations relative to the total operations approved in the 1996 fiscal year was half of what it was in fiscal year 1991 (Nogues, 1997).[20] The WTO on the other hand, has increased its technical co-operation activities. But the bulk of the financing for these activities, perhaps as much as three quarters in any given year, is funded by trust funds provided by bilateral donors, while the WTO itself typically allocates for technical co-operation activities less than one per cent of its total annual budget.

In order to help address some of the problems faced by the Least Developed Countries the HLMLDCTD adopted an Integrated Framework for trade related technical assistance to support LDCs. The framework envisages the preparation of needs assessments for technical assistance by the LDCs themselves which are then discussed at Roundtables with the six agencies involved in the effort (IMF, ITC, UNDP, UNCTAD, World Bank and WTO) plus other interested donors, in order to develop an integrated program of technical assistance activities which focus primarily on institution building.

Beyond the Integrated Framework, deliberations at the HLMLDCTD raised two other issues: That helping LDCs strengthen their institutional capacity may require not only technical assistance, but also financial assistance *inter alia* for human resource development and trade finance; and that problems of the LDCs are shared by other low income developing countries, and that the differences are primarily a matter of degree.

VII. CONCLUSIONS AND RECOMMENDATIONS

The analysis suggests the emergence of a duality in the representation and participation of developing countries in the WTO: On the one hand there are many developing countries which have increased significantly their capacity to participate in WTO activities in the aftermath of the Uruguay Round and whose representatives are playing an active role in the decisions of the organization. Their participation in formal and informal decision making processes is substantial, although they frequently do not speak with one voice as their interests, depending on the issue, may diverge and result in the forming of different coalitions. This is very much consistent with had been anticipated at the time of the Uruguay Round (Whalley, 1987).

This does not imply that the consultation process always results in the development of a consensus that reflects the interests of the majority of the developing countries. For example, many developing countries felt that in advance of the Singapore Ministerial, their views on some issues, for example the future work of the WTO on investment, were not fully taken into account. But, if there was a problem in that regard, it could not be traced to the absence of effective representation.

On the other hand, there is an even larger group of primarily smaller and lower income developing countries, which account for more than 50% of total WTO developing country membership, for which effective representation and participation in the Organization's activities is still a serious problem. Their situation has changed little since the early 1980s. Most are not represented in Geneva and hence can not effectively participate in the consultations leading to the development of consensus on which the WTO is based. Their staffing has not increased significantly, while the complexity of the issues and the number of meetings and obligations in the WTO has multiplied significantly.

The fact that the average size of Mission increased both for developed and developing countries reflects the increasing complexity and range of issues handled by the WTO. This is probably the main reason for these increases in staffing during a period of explosive improvements in telecommunications and hence in the ability of governments to increase their Missions' capacity to communicate rapidly with capitals – and thereby reduce the needs for stationing staff abroad.

For many developing countries and especially for the least developed and some of the smaller island economies, institutional weaknesses are the major constraints in both meeting their obligations under the WTO and in effective participation in the Organization and representation of their interests. But, it must be recognized that institutional development is a complex process, that takes a great deal of time. As a consequence, the solution of the problems of representation of the developing countries in the WTO is not going to be easy and is not often amenable to quick, stroke-of-the-pen changes in policies or rules. This being said there are a number of things that can be done, some of which should start now, although their payoff may be long term.

First, developing countries which are not members of the WTO, should apply to accede. There is little to be gained by not being members and the potential that membership offers easily outweighs the costs, especially if one were to consider the risks of adverse discrimination resulting from staying outside the organization that sets the rules by which world trade is conducted. Perhaps the main benefits from participation derive from agreeing to and being legally bound by rules and procedures which post obstacles to increasing protection in the future as well as access to a dispute settlement body which treats all members equally, irrespective of trading power. For these reasons, membership is beneficial even for countries or territories which are unable to develop in the short run the institutional capacity and the requirements for effective participation discussed earlier.

Second, developing countries which are already members, need to ensure that the effectiveness of their participation is not impaired by such matters as not paying their membership dues. The amounts involved are typically very small; falling in arrears in their payments cannot be a cost effective policy even in circumstances of countries facing serious budget constraints.

Third, the matter of effective participation through Geneva Missions of the appropriate size is a complex issue for which there are no general solutions. For some countries with very small international representation in general, it may not be optimal use of scarce human and material resources to set up such Missions. In such cases, the main objective should be twofold: (a) to ensure that they have adequate information flow on the issues handled by the WTO and how they affect their interests; and (b) to identify like-minded countries or groups which do have effective representation, develop a process of consultation with them and thereby obtain some assurance that their interests are reflected on an ongoing basis. Some of the alternatives that countries need to explore in this connection are first, whether they can pool their resources and representation in Geneva in the context of regional groupings to which they belong; and second, to determine whether they can second one or more staff to already established Missions in Geneva of like-minded countries.[21]

For other countries, measures to increase effective representation in Geneva should be taken *pari passu* with measures to strengthen their institutional capacity at home, as part of a broader decision to become more effectively integrated in the international trading system. For these countries as well, adequate information flow to the appropriate ministries or other decision making bodies in capitals is essential and should be addressed at the earliest. At the same time, they need to initiate efforts to strengthen the policy making and implementation capacity of these institutions as well as to seek assistance for this purpose from international donors and the WTO itself.

The Integrated Framework of Trade Related Technical Assistance for the Least Developed Countries should be of help to this group of countries. These countries may also benefit from assistance provided by the Swiss authorities in setting up a physical presence in Geneva. But institutional weaknesses are not limited to the least developed countries; nor should technical and other assistance to strengthen these capacities. Indeed, the Uruguay Round agreements call for the provision of technical assistance to all developing countries in a number of areas, such as SPS and standards. Yet, few developing countries have sought such assistance so far.

Fourth, the WTO should undertake a review of its internal rules and procedures to ensure that they do not inadvertently prejudice the effective participation of developing countries. An example of one such rule is the provision that delegations of countries presenting cases before the Dispute Settlement Body (DSB) include only government employees. This implies that developing countries with very limited government legal staff could not include in their delegations foreign lawyers hired to advise them on their cases. While the appellate body and one of the panels have ruled in recent cases to permit such lawyers to participate, this is one example of a rule that inadvertently may prejudice developing country participation in the WTO. There may be others which should be reviewed, especially in the context of the forthcoming review of the DSB.

Fifth, the international community should place higher priority on the more effective integration of the developing countries in the international trading system and their participation in the WTO. While many developing countries have made great strides in this connection, institutional weaknesses are glaring and impose serious constraints in many others. Donors in general, and the Bretton Woods institutions, UNDP, WTO, UNCTAD and the ITC in particular, should increase their support and assistance to well co-ordinated programs of institutional development that enhance the capacity of developing countries – whether in the Least Developed country list or not – to participate effectively in the international trading system, and to permit them to meet their obligations in the WTO. Such an institutional strengthening is a *sine qua non* for effective representation of developing country interests in the WTO, as well as for the accession to the WTO of countries which are not yet members.

Finally, keeping in mind that the WTO is not a development assistance institution, it would still appear desirable that WTO review the resources it allocates from its own budget to: (a) staffing of analyses on issues of interest to developing country members, (b) technical assistance to developing countries to enable them to discharge the obligations entailed by membership in the Organization and (c) support of the accession process of others. Developing country members can promote their interests in such a review through active participation in the WTO Committee on Budget, Finance and Administration.

Issues of interest to developing countries and strengthening their institutional capacity involve many parts of the Organization and its Secretariat. It is important that the Secretariat be adequately staffed to handle these matters, while preserving the character of the WTO as a member-driven institution.[22] Also, ensuring adequate resources to provide technical assistance does not necessarily mean that the WTO should increase its own staffing for undertaking technical assistance activities. It does mean that the WTO should allocate an appropriate amount of resources from its budget to the tasks of supporting effective participation of all its membership in its activities and assisting needy non-members in their accession process, so as to become a truly global institution.

ANNEX

Country Membership and Representation GATT/WTO 1982–1997
By Location and Number of Mission Staff

	Geneva			Europe			Capitals		
	1982	1987	1997	1982	1987	1997	1982	1987	1997
Antigua-Barbuda					IL[1]	2L			
Angola			1						
Argentina	4	3	7						
Australia	3	5	8						
Austria	2	3	6						
Bahrain			2						
Bangladesh	3	3	4						
Barbados				IBr[2]	IBr	3Br			
Belgium	2	3	8						
Belize						1Br		1	
Benin		6		1Br		3Br			
Bolivia			3						
Botswana									1
Brazil	4	6	11						
Brunei			3						
Bulgaria			1						
Burkina Faso				1Br	1Br	6Br			
Burundi	3	3	1						
Cameroon	1	3	3						
Canada	5	6	9						
Central African Republic	1							1	1
Chad				1Br	1P[3]	3Br			
Chile	3	3	7						
Colombia	3	2	5						
Congo			1	1Br	3Br				
Costa Rica			4						
Cote d'Ivoire	2	2	3						
Cuba	3	3	5						
Cyprus	2	2	2						
Czech Republic	2	2	3						
Denmark	3	3	4						
Dominica			2						
Dominican Republic	2	2	3						
Djibuti			1						
EC	9	13	18						
Egypt	6	5	10						
El Salvador			5						
Equador			2						
Fiji			1						

	Geneva			Europe			Capitals		
	1982	1987	1997	1982	1987	1997	1982	1987	1997
Finland	4	3	5						
France	4	6	6						
Gabon	6	1	2						
Gambia						1Br	1	1	
Germany	5	9	8						
Ghana	3	4	3						
Greece	2	2	5						
Grenada						1Br			
Guatemala			2						
Guyana				IL	IL	IL			
Guinea									1
Guinea-Bissau						1Br			
Haiti	1	1	2						
Honduras			2						
Hong Kong	(3)[4]	5	6						
Hungary	4	5	4						
India	3	3	5						
Indonesia	5	6	7						
Ireland	2	2	4						
Iceland	2	2	4						
Israel	3	3	3						
Italy	3	4	5						
Jamaica	3	3	3						
Japan	12	15	22						
Kenya	1	2	3						
Korea	5	7	17						
Kuwait	1	2	2						
Lesotho						3Br			
Lichtenstein						1Be			2
Luxemburg	2	2	2						
Macau						5Br			
Madagascar	3	2	3						
Malaysia	4	3	3						
Malawi				1Bo[5]	1Bo	1Bo			
Maldives								1	1
Mali						4Bo			
Malta	2	1	3						
Morocco		2	5						
Mauritius			4	1Br	1Br				
Mauritania				1Br	1Br	2Br			
Mexico		7	8						
Mongolia			2						
Mozambique									1
Myanmar	3	2	3						
Namibia						3Br			
Netherlands	3	3	4						

	Geneva			Europe			Capitals		
	1982	1987	1997	1982	1987	1997	1982	1987	1997
New Zealand	3	5	5						
Nicaragua	3	3	3						
Niger				1Br	3Br	3Br			
Nigeria	4	1	7						
Norway	3	3	6						
Pakistan	2	2	4						
Papua New Guinea						1Br			
Paraguay			4						
Peru	4	4	6						
Philippines	3	3	7						
Poland	2	2	4						
Portugal	3	2	2						
Qatar			1						
Romania	3	2	3						
Rwanda				1Bo	3Bo	1Bo			
St Christ. & Nevis						IL			
St Lucia						4Br			
St Vincent & Grenadines								1	
Senegal	2	2	2						
Sierra Leone				2R[7]	1Br	2Br			
Singapore	3	3	5						
Slovakia			2						
Slovenia			2						
Solomon Islands						2Br			
South Africa	3	5	6						
Spain	6	7	10						
Sri Lanka	1	1	3						
Swaziland									1
Sweden	3	5	4						
Switzerland	3	3	5						
Surinam				1H[8]	1H	5Br			
Tanzania	2	7	5						
Thailand		5	18						
Togo				1P	1P	1P			
Trinidad	4	5	5						
Tunisia			3						
Turkey	6	4	7						
Uganda			5						
United Arab Emirates			2						
United Kingdom	4	4	5						
United States	8	10	10						
Uruguay	2	4	7						
Venezuela			6						
Yugoslavia			6						

	Geneva			Europe			Capitals		
	1982	1987	1997	1982	1987	1997	1982	1987	1997
Yugoslavia	2	4							
Zaire (Dem.Rep. of Congo)	4	3	1						
Zambia			4		IL		2		
Zimbabwe		5	4				1		

[1]L = London
[2]Br = Brussels
[3]P = Paris
[4]Listed separately in UK mission in 1982
[5]Bo = Bonn
[6]Be = Berne
[7]R = Rome
[8]H = Hague

NOTES

The views expressed in this paper are entirely those of the author and should in no way be attributed to the World Trade Organization or the World Bank. The author wishes to thank the large number of WTO colleagues and staff members of WTO Missions in Geneva who contributed information and insights on the participation of developing countries in the WTO and the GATT and without which this paper would not have been possible. He is especially grateful to Ambassadors Munir Akram, Eveline Herfkens, and Anthony Hill, Permanent Representatives to the WTO of Pakistan, the Netherlands, and Jamaica, respectively, and John Croome, formerly of the WTO/GATT and currently consultant to the World Bank, for their comments on an earlier draft of this paper.

1 The participation of the developing countries in these negotiations will be only noted in passing rather than analyzed in depth. The participation of the developing countries in the Uruguay Round has been discussed extensively elsewhere (see especially Croome 1995, Martin and Winters 1996, and UNCTAD and WTO, 1996), and is not going to be addressed in this paper.

2 Although in these cases as well, the Ambassador accredited to the UN is typically senior in rank. See UN Directory, Geneva, 1997.

3 It was also thought that Mission size would also be affected by a country's geographical proximity to Geneva. Were this to be an important factor, it would tend to bias downward the Mission size of developed, European countries. It turns out, that if that bias exists, it does not show in the statistics, as the European countries are substantially represented in Geneva – both through their national missions and, for EC matters, through the EC. On the other hand, the distance of most developing countries from Geneva means that participation in the activities of the organization by representatives from their capitals is quite costly and raises the importance of having effective representation located in Geneva.

4 The following countries or groups are defined as "developed" and "other" for the purposes of this paper: "Developed" include the fifteen members of the European

Communities, the representative of the European Commission, the four EFTA countries (Liechtenstein, Iceland, Norway, Switzerland), Australia, Canada, Japan, New Zealand, the United States; "Other" include Bulgaria, the Czech Republic, Hungary, Israel, Mongolia, Poland, Romania, Slovakia, Slovenia and Yugoslavia (not a WOT member); all remaining countries and territories are classified as "developing".

5 WTO members can be countries or customs territories, such as e.g. Hong Kong, which has been a member while formally a colony of the UK and now a part of China. Similarly, the European Communities are a member with a separate delegation from those of the 15 constituent states. For purposes of simplicity, the paper uses the term "country" whatever the legal status of the member may be.

6 These rules are contained in GATT/PC/7, L/7578

7 According to a recent WTO Council decision, Least Developed countries in arrears are no longer being barred from receiving technical assistance from the Organization.

8 See Beatrice Chaytor and Michael Hindley, *A Case Study of Sierra Leone's Participation in the World Trade Organization*, Cameron: 1997.

9 This is much larger than the expansion of WTO Secretariat staff over the same period – which went from 340 in 1982 to 383 in 1987 and 515 in 1997, using the Directory as the basis. The two listings are not comparable, however, because the Secretariat list includes support staff. As the professional staff in the Secretariat – excluding interpreters and translators, does not exceed 200, both the absolute and the relative of WTO professional Secretariat staff over the period is likely to have been much smaller than the expansion of Mission staff.

10 Only five countries (Burundi, Gabon, Malaysia, Portugal and Congo) had less Mission staff working on WTO/GATT issues in 1997 than in 1982 – and in only a few of these cases it would appear that the reductions were policy driven.

11 The average size of Mission in the "other" category, mostly transition economies, did not change.

12 Recall that "Mission" is defined to include representatives to the WTO/GATT listed in the Directories irrespective of whether located in Geneva or elsewhere. The differences are actually somewhat smaller if one compares only the countries with Missions in Geneva.

13 This is consistent with the estimate for a minimum size Mission presented in Blackhurst 1997b).

14 The Chairman and Vice-Chairman of the GATT Contracting Parties have been included in the list of "important" chairmanships although their functions were mostly ceremonial. According to GATT practice these positions were held by representatives of countries which the previous year held the same positions in the GATT General Council.

15 Interestingly enough, very few of these top leadership positions are held by representatives of the EC, the US or Japan. At the same time the Chair of the Committee on Trade and Development which deals exclusively with developing country issues, has traditionally been held by somebody from a developing country.

16 For a period in the late 1970s and early 1980s an effort was made to formalize the establishment of a smaller group of countries which would be used as a vehicle for regular consultations in the GATT. This so called "Consultative Group of Eight" included 10 developing countries. Although from time to time there have been suggestions to revive such a group in the context of the WTO, it has not been possible to reconstitute such a group, in part because of difficulties in accommodating all the various countries who would want to participate, because they would not feel that other members would adequately represent their interests. As a consequence the present loose and flexible consultation formula has remained in place. It is interesting in this

regard that neither the weighted voting nor the related representation formula, whereby one country represents a number of others (frequently of vastly different level of development) present in the decision making bodies of the IMF and the World Bank, has been at all in favour in the WTO. It is also interesting to note that despite the disparity between trade weights and voting strength, both the GATT and the WTO have been able to function perhaps for the reasons discussed by Evans (1968).

17 This is similar in composition and orientation with the "De la Paix Group" active during the Uruguay Round.

18 On some issues, e.g. investment, developing countries continue to look to UNCTAD as an institution in which such analyses and positions can be developed. UNCTAD has also provided a forum for discussion of broader aspects of a trade policy agenda for developing countries (see e.g. UNCTAD 1997).

19 WTO High Level Meeting on Integrated Initiatives for Least-Developed Countries' Trade Development, Chairman's Opening Statement, Geneva, October 27, 1997.

20 Nogues notes in this connection that, "It would be a historical error of major proportions for the Bank to conclude that because so much has been achieved (in trade reform), there remains no significant progress to be expected from investing additional intellectual and financial resources in this area." (Nogues, 1997, p. 94.)

21 Blackhurst (1997b) recommends that a minimum number of representatives of each WTO mission be funded through the budget of the WTO, much as the Executive Directors and their staff are funded by the budgets of the World Bank and the IMF. While on the face of it such a proposal may seem to have merit, it is not feasible without a major redefinition of the WTO as an institution. The reason is that, unlike the WTO, the Executive Directors of the Bretton Woods institutions play a dual role; they are both representatives of their governments and officers of the two institutions.

22 The Development Division (with only about two and one half professional staff, excluding the Director working on strictly development issues) is only one of several Divisions working on issues of actual or potential importance to developing countries; others include Trade Policies Review, Trade and Environment, Agriculture and Textiles. Many developing countries also believe that greater progress is needed in staffing the WTO Secretariat with developing country nationals in order to improve the staff's understanding of developing country problems.

REFERENCES

Blackhurst, Richard, "The Capacity of the WTO to Fulfil its Mandate" in A. O. Krueger ed. *The WTO as an International Organization*, The University of Chicago Press: Chicago, 1997.

Blackhurst, Richard, "The WTO and the Global Economy", *World Economy*, Vol. 20#5, August 1997, pp. 527–544.

Chaytor, Beatrice and Michael Hindley, *A Case Study of Sierra Leone's Participation in the World Trade Organization*, Cameron: 1997.

Croome, John, *Reshaping the World Trade System*, WTO, 1995.

Evans, John, "The General Agreement on Tariffs and Trade", *International Organization*, Vol. XXII, No. 1, 1968, pp. 72–98.

GATT, *Directory*, 1982, 1987.

GATT, "Measures to Deal with Members in Category IV of the Administrative Arrangements on Arrears", December 13, 1994, PC/7, L/7578.

Martin, Will and L. Alan Winters, *The Uruguay Round and the Developing Countries*, World Bank, 1996.

Nogues, Julio, "The Linkages of The World Bank with the GATT/WTO", in A. O. Krueger ed. *The WTO as an International Organization*, The University of Chicago Press: Chicago, 1997.

Oyejide, Ademola T. "Africa and the Uruguay Round", *The World Economy* Vol. 13, No. 3, September 1990.

Pronk, Jan, "Chairman's Opening Statement", WTO, High Level Meeting on Integrated Initiatives for Least Developed Countries' Trade Development", WTO, Geneva, October 27, 1997.

United Nations, *Directory of Geneva Agencies*, United Nations, Geneva, 1997.

UNCTAD, *The Uruguay Round and Its Follow-up: Building a Positive Development Agenda*, United Nations, Geneva, 1997.

UNCTAD and WTO, "Strengthening the Participation of Developing Countries in World Trade and the Multilateral Trading System", UNCTAD, TD/375, May 23, 1996.

Whalley, John, *Dealing with the North: Developing Countries and the Global Trading System*, CSIER Research Monograph, The University of Western Ontario, London, Ontario: 197.

WTO, *Annual Report, 1997.*

WTO, *Directory*, 1997.

WTO, *Trade-Related Technical Assistance Needs Assessment and Integrated Responses by IMF, ITC, UNCTAD, World Bank and WTO*, WT/COMTD/IF/1–11, November–December 1997.

11. Identifying the Issues in Trade in Services

G. P. Sampson and R. H. Snape

Interest in the nature and extent of government intervention in trade in services has grown rapidly in recent years.[1] From the *domestic* perspective the focus has been on the effects of government regulation on the distribution of resources and on consumer choice. From the *international* perspective the focus has been on government restrictions of market access and barriers to trade in services. Because of the impact of government regulation of internationally-traded services, there have been proposals for the liberalisation of restrictions on service transactions, with strong pressure from the United States and some other developed countries, for the subject to be on the agenda of a new round of multilateral trade negotiations. But it is apparent that a conceptual framework for such negotiations is lacking and those engaged in discussion of services *as a sector* are not always working from a common base.

In the absence of a developed "theory" of trade in services, the theory of trade in goods has often been applied on an *ad hoc* basis. This follows from the suggestions by some economists that international trade in services is the same, from an analytical point of view, as trade in goods.

But a host of very different types of services are traded internationally, ranging over computing services, shipping, insurance, medical services, tourism, construction, building design and banking. In order to examine the extent to which trade in services is 'the same' as trade in goods, a simple classification of traded services is developed in this article. It becomes clear that some services are very similar to goods; others are not. Policies relating to the movement of factors of production and to the movement of the receivers of services may distort trade in some services more than in the case of goods. Such policies may be of more importance to trade in services than restrictions on trade in the services themselves.

Thus one purpose of this article is to identify the characteristics of international transactions in services which may distinguish them from international transactions in goods. Unlike previous classifications we have seen, the classification is based on how and where the services are produced and traded, rather than on the physical characteristics of the services themselves. It would appear that adopting classifications based on the nature of the service may have clouded some of the issues in attempts to negotiate internationally the regulation of trade in services.

It is desirable to start from the basics. First, what are international transactions? In this article a 'residential' concept of national income is adopted. Thus an international transaction is a transaction between the resident of one country and a resident of another. The transaction may take place entirely within one country, geographically defined. If a geographical basis were to be adopted, a whole range of what are normally regarded as international service transactions would be excluded – tourism, for example.[2]

Next it is perhaps wise to recall that goods and services are both produced by factors of production. It is the 'services' of these factor services while 'services' are more directly supplied by the owners of factors of production to their *clientèle*.

In a greater number of cases, services require the supplier of the service and the receivers to be in physical proximity. The concept of 'receiver' is referred to frequently in this article. Receivers of services could be persons (as in medical services), commodities (as in painting or transport) or resources (as in ploughing). But the physical proximity of provider and receiver is not an ubiquitous requirement. As pointed out by Jagdish Bhagwati, of Columbia University in New York, the electronic transfer of information and some forms of entertainment is enabling the separation of provider and receiver to develop rapidly.[3] For some services such separation has existed for many years. Bridges, for example, can be designed in countries other than those where they are built. For many purposes the distinction between those services which require the physical proximity of the supplier of the service and the receiver of it and those services (like goods) which do not is unimportant. In trade across national frontiers, however, it can carry major policy implications.

A CLASSIFICATION OF TRADED SERVICES

International trade in services may be divided into four categories. The first category comprises services transacted without the physical proximity of factors and receiver. For the other three categories there is physical proximity.

(a) Transactions may occur *without* the movement of factors of production or of the receiver of the service. Such services are produced in the exporting country and then traded internationally. Like goods, they cross the border of the importing and exporting countries. Examples include consulting services, life-assurance business and architectural design which are handled through correspondence and produced in the exporting country. These can be referred to as 'separated' services, for they are separated from both factors of production and receivers. Separated services may become incorporated into goods and may be identified as goods rather than services. The demarcation of 'goods' from 'services' along a spectrum including books, floppy disks full of retrievable data, drawings of the plans of a bridge and data transmitted telegraphically is not at all clear. Are disks full of data and construction plans 'goods' or 'services'?

(b) Transactions may occur as a consequence of the movement of the factors of production, but not of the receiver of the service. Examples of such services are the product of guest workers, including imported construction teams, and the services of imported financial capital. An essential part of international trade in these services is that part or all of the means to produce the services in the country of consumption crosses the borders of the importing and exporting countries. In other words, there is an international flow of the factors of production – labour and/or capital.

(c) Transactions may occur with the movement of the receiver of the service, but not of the provider. A patient may move to a foreign country to be treated by a surgeon. A further example is the provision of services for international tourists. The Rocky Mountains, the Taj Mahal and the Eiffel Tower cannot be shifted. A foreign consumer of these tourist services has to travel to the United States, India and France. Foreign students travel to Australian universities to be educated. Likewise, doctors do not usually move to Upper Volta to carry out heart-transplant operations. (If university lecturers or a medical team moved internationally, then these services would be in category 'b' above). Again, some services may be incorporated into goods and there is a question of demarcation of goods from services. When a product is sent abroad for processing and then re-imported, is there trade in goods or in services?

(d) Transactions may occur with the movement of both factors of production and the receiver of the service. Here the transaction would take place in a third country. A surgeon and a patient may meet in a third country where the patient is treated. Three countries will now be transacting, with the host country selling the service of clinics.

All services may thus be classified into those which are traded with the movement of the factors of production and/or the movement of the receivers of the service and those for which there are no such movements. Policies *restricting* trade in services may then be divided conveniently into (i) those that restrict the service transactions *per se*, (ii) those that restrict the movement of factors producing the service and (iii) those that restrict the movement of the receivers of services.

In many cases alternatives among the four categories of transaction face transactors. Choice between the categories may depend on transport and other transaction costs; it also depends on various impediments at national frontiers – impediments not only to the movement of goods or animals but also to the movement of 'separated' services, persons and assets and liabilities. Visa and guest-worker policy, as well as foreign investment policy, may be involved. These policies may affect not only the form in which transactions take place but also whether transactions occur or not. They may also determine whether services are 'splintered' or 'disembodied' or not;[4] that is, whether trade takes place in goods incorporating the service or whether the service is traded separately from the relevant goods.

Some examples of these 'trading' choices are as follows:

> one, the choice between trade in computing services or bridge design – by having computer programmes written, or bridges designed, abroad – and allowing the foreign programmers or designers to work in the purchasing country;
>
> two, the choice between the movement of medical patients or students abroad and the movement of the providers of the services to the receivers; and,
>
> three, the choice between the movement of a commodity to be serviced and the movement of the servicer to the commodity.

This framework can assist in considering whether trade in services is similar to trade in goods, so that the standard theories of international trade and of commercial policy can be applied. For separated services, those that fall into category 'a' above, the standard theories of international trade, which assume international immobility of factors of production, apply.[5] But those services that fall into the other three categories are not addressed by theories which assume the immobility of factors of production of receivers between countries.[6] This 'non-separation' is the essential difference between trade in goods and trade in some services.

Some services that are non-tradeable without the proximity of producer and receiver become tradeable with the movement of factors of production or receivers. The same applies to some goods, although for a different reason. Roads and construed buildings are two examples of 'goods' that are not tradeable between countries, not because of the requirement of proximity of producer and consumer but because they cannot easily be transported. But construction teams can, and do, move between countries. This implies that visa and work-permit policy as well as, perhaps, foreign investment policy not only may determine whether services are traded but also may be relevant in determining the extent of effective protection received by activities which produce non-tradeable goods.

In the next section, those services associated with movements of factors of production (category 'b') are addressed, while the following section focuses on services associated with movement of the receiver of the service (category 'c'). Considerations relevant to category 'd', in which there is movement of both factors of production and the receiver, embrace those in both categories 'b' and 'c'.

SERVICES ASSOCIATED WITH FACTOR MOVEMENTS

Category 'b' above includes those services for which the factors of production shift from one country to another. Are we concerned with factor movements themselves or with what the factors produce? What is produced – be it surgery, insurance, road construction, motor vehicles, banking or household services – is associated with characteristics of the factors themselves. For present purposes, it appears to be useful to look at the characteristics of the factor services and the contribution of those characteristics, rather than the various goods and services which they produce.

Factors of production which many move internationally are physical capital, labour and financial capital.

Physical capital comprises goods and its movement internationally can generally be dealt with under merchandise trade. With leasing, however, there is a hiring of the 'services' of capital equipment without change of ownership and policy provisions other than those which apply to normal trade in goods may be involved.

Turning to the international movement of *labour* as a factor of production, this could take the form of temporary migration – for example, as a guest worker – or it could even be a business trip, examining a site, giving lectures or entertaining. Permanent migration is not relevant here since change in the country of residence is involved. The movement of labour may be unskilled labour, as with

South Korean or Philippine construction teams, or it could involve the movement of substantial knowledge and expertise. Surgeons, architects, financiers, opera singers and ballet dancers are examples. Visa and work-permit policy and registration of professions may affect the manner in which labour-related services are transacted between countries. Payments for the labour may incorporate payment for substantial accumulated skill.

As far as the services which may be attributed to *financial capital* are concerned, the payments for the capital will incorporate payments for the current rather than future use of goods and services (inter-temporal substitution), for knowledge and for risk sharing. Much has been written on the 'unpackaging' of the bundle of services associated with capital and on the extent to which these services can be separated from the international movement of capital. Looking at the three characteristics which can be associated with the services of financial capital, namely inter-temporal substitution, risk sharing and the transfer of knowledge, the major points are as follows.

Inter-temporal substitution: The sale of the service of inter-temporal substitution (that is, being able to acquire goods and services now rather than later) is the essence of the capital transactions and is therefore inextricably linked to them. But this service is not linked to equity participation or control. It is equally provided through debt. Restrictions on capital flows thus necessarily inhibit the international trading of inter-temporal choice.

Risk: Many risks can be shared internationally – that is, there is trade in the service 'risk bearing' – without there being foreign investment. Some examples are contractual arrangements in which the contract price depends on movements in wages or in other prices and insurance and futures contracts. But international movements of capital provide the possibility of other ways to spread risk internationally – for example, by borrowing in the same currency as that in which contract prices are denominated and through equity participation, where the return payable on foreign investments depends on the rate of return on the activities for which the funds are used. Thus restrictions on capital flows between countries will not inhibit all trading in risk bearing, but they will prevent some forms of it.

Knowledge: Knowledge can be transferred internationally in a variety of ways. Some forms of knowledge may require the movement of labour. Other forms appear to be closely related to the ownership of the enterprise.[7] Skills in hotel management, construction techniques, banking and merchant-banking facilities and credit-card operation are possible examples, although in all these cases it seems that, on occasion, much of this expertise has been transferred internationally without the movement of capital. The possessors of some forms of expertise, however, do seem reluctant to supply it without equity participation. This reluctance could be attributable to (i) it being less costly to transfer knowledge internationally within the corporate empire than outside it and/or (ii) retaining knowledge within the corporate empire limits competition. This being so, restrictions on capital flows may prevent the international dissemination of knowledge, although such restrictions could in some situations be warranted on economic criteria if they constrain the monopoly power associated with the possession of knowledge.

INTERNATIONAL MOVEMENT OF SERVICE RECEIVERS

Some services involve the receiver moving to the provider (category 'c' above). Tourism is an example in which there is no full substitute for movement of the receiver: viewing films of the Amazon is not a perfect substitute for seeing the real thing. Other examples in which there may be a choice between the movement of the provider and that of the receiver are education and medical services and repairs of many types of equipment, particularly transport equipment. Restrictions on the international trading of such services may be imposed as restrictions on the departure of residents through government decrees or through high departure taxes. (The flow of Indonesians to purchase services in Singapore has been reduced by the latter.) Other restrictions may be imposed by quarantine regulations, in the case of animals, or by the system of import taxes and regulations, in the case of items sent abroad for repairs and then re-imported. Restrictions may also be imposed by the country which could provide the service. Not all countries allow the unrestricted access of foreigners to their educational or medical services, particularly when these services are subsidised.

INTERACTION OF TRADE, VISA AND INVESTMENT POLICIES

What comprises 'free trade in services'? What has been said so far leads to the conclusion that free trade in services would require freedom of movement of factors of production, of 'separated' services and of service receivers. What, then, are the consequences of concentrating on those services which can be separated, in the sense that movement of neither the factors of production nor the receivers of the service is required? For these services, freedom of international trade is similar to freedom of international trade in goods.[8] It requires the absence of barriers to international contracting and to sending and receiving mail and electronic and telegraphic transmissions. Freedom of movement of factors of production or receivers of the services would not be required.

The theory of second-best teaches us that liberalising trade in some commodities, while trade in other commodities continues to be restrained, will not necessarily improve the allocation of resources. Thus, for example, a reduction of protection for some goods or services could result in a reduced price for a factor of production. If a highly protected good or service also uses this factor, the lower price of the factor could lead to increased output to this highly protected product. The allocation of resources would be worsened. Applied to services, this seems to imply that liberalising trade in 'separated' services, for example, will not necessarily improve the allocation of resources, while trade remains restricted in other services – by direct restriction, by visa or foreign investment policy or by restrictions on receivers – which can be produced by the same factors of production. Liberalising trade in, say, insurance services by reducing the domestic demand for clerks could lead to increased employment of clerks, and other factors of production, in a highly protected service (for example, until recently, foreign-exchange dealing in Australia).

Does this imply that it would be unwise to pursue a policy of free movement of services, as such, without it being accompanied by free movement of factors of production and receivers? (Note that this does not require free migration on a long-term basis, for that implies change of country of residence.) As a general proposition, the broader the front across which the liberalisation of trade operates, the more likely that the allocation of resources will be improved. Thus it is more likely – again as a general proposition to which there can be exceptions – that liberalising trade in goods *and* separated services will be more likely to improve the allocation of resources than liberalising trade in goods alone. It is also most likely that reductions in the highest trade barriers to services, as well as to goods, will improve the allocation of resources. But, in looking at the effects of such liberalisation, an eye should be kept on the effects on industries which remain protected.

In the case of services for which physical proximity of factors of production and receivers is required, a problem arises when taking the line that liberalisation is most likely to be beneficial when it is across the broadest possible front. One is then forced to define the absence of protection or an efficient allocation of resources as complete freedom of international movement of factors of production and service receivers that are resident in a country. More usually, however, factors and receivers are assumed to be immobile and goods and services separable from them. The standard argument for free trade is then that it will maximise real national income *subject to the constraints of the supplies of factors of production and of receivers with which a country is endowed.*

As soon as trade is introduced that requires the physical proximity of the receiver of a service and the factor supplying it and the possibility of factors or receivers moving, the standard reference point breaks down. No longer are the factor endowments and receivers which are resident in a country a binding constraint. In such circumstances a new reference point to specify 'efficient trade' has to be defined. Complete freedom of movement of factors (and of receivers) appears to be the obvious candidate. (Note, again, that this does not imply unrestricted long-term migration.) Other specifications may be made for one reason or another, but it is important that the constraints are specified. Otherwise one will not know what are the optimal policies – that is, those that maximise real national income subject to constraints. And for whom is 'national' income being maximised?

TRADE AS A SUBSTITUTE FOR FACTOR MOVEMENTS

It is a well-known proposition that international trade can have the same effect on the prices of factors of production as the international movement of factors of production. The import of unskilled labour-intensive products may tend to reduce the real wages of the unskilled, just like the inward migration of such labour. The full flowering of this analysis is the theorem of factor price equalisation in which factor prices are equalised internationally by international trade, even though factors are immobile internationally, for one reason or another. Such factor-price equalisation can occur on special assumptions, as is well recognised in the literature. The starting point is a separation of trade in goods from trade in factor services. It could be expected, however, that trade in factors of production would increase the likelihood of factor-price equalisation.

Holding the discussion to goods for the moment, it has been seen already how in some situations, rather than trade being a substitute for the movement of factors of production, the movement of factors may act as a substitute for trade. This may occur where trade is not possible because of transport costs. Thus construction teams can build roads in foreign countries.

Turning to trade in services, it is apparent from the discussion above that not all services may be traded separately from the factors of production which create them. In such cases, trade cannot be a substitute for factor movements, for movement of factors (or of receivers) is required to accomplish the trade. Restricting the movements of factors (or of receivers of services) will inhibit (i) the international movement of the services, (ii) the equalisation of the prices of these services internationally and (iii) the tendency to narrow the international differences in the prices of factors of production. Barriers to the movement of factors or receivers will thus provide protection to some factors of production, even if there are no barriers to trade in goods or 'separated' services.

INTERNATIONAL TRANSACTIONS AS A CONSTRAINT ON MONOPOLY

In the literature on multinational enterprises much has been written on foreign investment as a means to extend market power. Similarly, a considerable body of writing has focused on the restraint to domestic monopoly power that is provided by the availability of foreign substitutes. The theoretical trade literature on constraining domestic monopoly has focused on goods, but it also applies to separated services. It can also be extended to those services which require the physical proximity of the receivers of the service and the factors supplying them. Thus Australia is opening her doors to investment by foreign banks in order to improve competition, the Government apparently being confident that it, and/or competition in general, will be able to restrain the anti-competitive or other disruptive actions which are often attributed to multinational enterprises.

ISSUES IN SERVICES

Separated services, those in category 'a' above, are those which can be 'separated' from the receivers of the service and the factors of production that provide the service. In the case of these services, particularly when traded internationally, many of the issues, *in principle*, resemble those relating to goods. In particular, barriers to trade in separated services can take the form of impediments to trade in the service as it crosses the frontier. There could, for example, be a tax on the transmission of data as it crosses the frontier. *In practice*, however, there are many important differences. Unlike goods, many internationally traded (separated) services do not pass through customs houses. Taxing and transferral of electronically-transmitted data must be difficult. Information may move via satellites or along telephone lines – so, too, for international news transmission and various entertainment services. But it is not beyond the wit and power of some governments to inhibit trade in all such services.

Some services may be best (or only) exported if there is a presence of the factors of production in the importing country. (Such transactions are in categories 'b' or 'd' above.) In these instances the issue may be related to the right to 'establish' in the country purchasing the service and/or the right to import foreign labour. In such cases the link between the attitude of the host government to foreign investment and the granting of work permits is crucial. Thus the 'barrier' to imports of services may well be the rules applying to foreign investment and work permits.

Government regulations relating to the provision of factor services may be general in nature (applying to all foreign investment or all foreign labour) or sector specific (for example, no foreign investment in domestic banks). Sector-specific policies often take the form of measures relating both to initial establishment and to operations after establishment. Thus it is not surprising that the focus of discussions on trade liberalisation in services has been on the issues of not only 'rights of establishment' but also 'national treatment' for foreign firms once established.

The attitude of governments to foreign investment and work permits may be important for services that can be produced either in the country from which the service is exported or in the country in which the service is consumed. There are cases where a domestic presence may be desirable, but not always crucial. An example is construction-engineering consultancy. Plans for a new bridge to be built in Sydney could be drawn up in Los Angeles after visits to Sydney. Alternatively, an agency of the parent engineering company could be established in Sydney. The same is true for legal services, the provision of life assurance, shipping services, air transport and so on. Once again, the attitude to foreign investment and work permits (including business trips) is important. In these instances the restriction on movements of factors of production may not be a total barrier to trade in services, but it may distort it and make it difficult to provide a service satisfactorily.

Government measures affecting services are often imposed for reasons unrelated to trade and are not directed to the maintenance of internationally uncompetitive industries. This is mainly due to the nature of many service activities. For example, although national banking laws may directly affect a foreign bank's operation within a host country, the laws exist primarily for domestic reasons, such as protection of the consumer, protection against monopolies and control over monetary policy. Regulations concerning the operations of insurance companies and investment-management companies, for example, specifying the areas where they can invest their funds, are also for the purpose of protecting the consumer from undue risk or for attempting to guarantee a market for some types of securities. These regulations are of concern in the context of international trade and investment only when they treat foreign operations differently from domestic ones.

Clearly foreign investment is central to the discussion and the issues embrace matters of national sovereignty. Indeed, some countries suspect that the services issue in the General Agreement on Tariffs and Trade (GATT) is principally about de-regulation of foreign investment. This suspicion is strengthened by the fact that the United States, the prime mover behind the attempts to liberalise trade in services, is by far the world's largest gross earner of foreign investment income. But work-permit policy is also crucial in many areas of trade in services. Some countries may not wish to discuss 'separated' services and investment-related services without also discussing labour-related services.

Finally, it may be recalled that restrictions on the movement of service receivers may also comprise important barriers to trade in services. (Relevant transactions fell into categories 'c' and 'd' in the classification above.) These barriers may be imposed by either the producing country or the receiving country. Restriction on access to subsidised medical services is an example of the former while restrictive exit visas, punitive departure taxes and exchange controls are examples of the latter.

NOTES

1 This article was originally prepared for the Industries Assistance Commission in Canberra, Australia. The authors are grateful for perceptive comments from officers of the Commission and from Peter Lloyd, Martin Wof, Jan Tumlir and Roger Kerr.

2 Statistics of international transactions do not always consistently follow the 'residential' definition. An international 'service' transaction occurs when an enterprise engages a guest worker, and an international 'goods' transaction, when the guest worker buys a beer. In practice, these transactions are not recorded in the international accounts; what is recorded is the transmission of funds home by the guest worker – a transaction which is not in fact international, it being between residents of the same country.

3 Jagdish N. Bhagwati, 'Splintering and Disembodiment of Services and Developing Nations', *The World Economy*, June 1984, pp. 139 *et seq.*

4 *Ibid.*

5 See, for example, Brian Hindley and Alasdair Smith, 'Comparative Advantage and Trade in Services', *The World Economy*, December 1984.

6 In categories 'c' and 'd' above where 'receivers' are commodities or animals rather than people, the standard theories can be applied easily.

7 See, for example, Harry G. Johnson, 'The Efficiency and Welfare Implications of the International Corporation', in I. A. McDougall and R. H. Snape (eds), *Studies in International Economics* (Amsterdam: North-Holland, 1970).

8 Bhagwati, *loc. cit.*, p. 143.

12. International Regulation of Subsidies

R. H. Snape

1. INTRODUCTION

SUBSIDIES HAVE BEEN VERY HIGH on the agenda of international trade negotiations over the past fifteen years of so. 'Fair trade', a term much in vogue in Britain in the late nineteenth century as that country experienced competition for its manufactures on the international market, has returned to be important in the vocabulary of those who determine the pace and outcome of international trade negotiations (Bhagwati and Irwin, 1987). Subsidisation of exports is commonly regarded as an unfair trading policy, as is the 'dumping' of exports.

Import tariffs designed to countervail export subsidies have a long history. In 1890, the United States passed legislation to countervail foreign subsidies on sugar (Hufbauer and Shelton Erb, 1984, p. 45), while rules governing the use of export subsidies and countervailing import tariffs have been part of the General Agreement on Tariffs and Trade (GATT) since its inception in 1947. But it has only been since the United States started to feel severe competition on world markets that the question of subsidies has been moved to the centre of the international stage. The United States is by far the largest imposer of countervailing import duties (CVDs).

One of the main products of the Tokyo Round of multilateral trade negotiations, which concluded in 1979, was a 'Code' which interpreted and extended the GATT provisions relating to subsidies and countervailing duties. The provisions of this Code relate mainly to manufactured products – the Code, and the GATT itself, contain relatively weak restrictions on subsidies of agriculture. More recently, and in particular in relation to the Uruguay Round of multilateral trade negotiations, subsidies affecting agriculture have been receiving rather more attention – efficient agricultural exporting countries have long complained about loss of markets due to agricultural subsidies in Europe, Japan, and elsewhere.

This paper addresses the questions of what is a subsidy, which subsidies affect international trade, and why countries may wish to subsidise industries, particularly exporting industries. It considers the effects of these subsidies on other countries and the reasons why trading partners may wish to outlaw or countervail such export-promoting subsidies. The paper then outlines the provisions of the GATT and the Subsidies Code as they relate to subsidies; this is followed by some data on the extent to which these provisions have been used, and by a consideration of the purposes for which they appear, in fact, to have been used. The question is then raised as to whether or not the proscribing/countervailing approach is in fact the best way to constrain subsidies and whether, if such control is desired, other approaches may be preferable and feasible. To anticipate, it is suggested that there is not, and there cannot be, any completely common ground on what is and is not a subsidy, or even an export-promoting subsidy. It is suggested that the grounds for imposing countervailing duties are so arbitrary and therefore so open to abuse in practice, that beyond a very limited range of subsidies, the proscribing/countervailing approach is likely to be counter-productive. Further, it is pointed out that to provide assistance to producers while limiting the demands on the public purse, most subsidies of consequence to international trade are buttressed by barriers to imports into the countries granting the subsidies. Reducing these barriers while maintaining the same level of price support to major industries would be very costly to many national treasuries. This fiscal cost is likely to increase the political cost of price supports and thus constrain them. It is thus suggested that reducing the barriers to imports may, in fact, be an efficient way to reduce the effects of many price-supporting subsidies.

2. WHAT IS A SUBSIDY?

a. Level Playing Fields

In recent years there has been a great deal of talk by politicians and others regarding 'level playing fields'. Such a field appears to be viewed as one in which firms compete for markets without assistance from their governments – that is, without subsidies in one form or another. But in considering which government actions may be regarded as providing subsidies, the term subsidy can be all-embracing. Virtually *every* government action can be regarded as a subsidy for someone, and virtually all such actions can affect international trade. Even a requirement that domestically manufactured flags be flown on government building provides assistance for flag makers. By giving a secure home market and promoting economies of scale, such a regulation may assist potential exporters. Is it to be regarded as an export promoting subsidy?

Confirming the concept of a subsidy to where there is a direct transfer of goods, services or money from the government limits the field but does not solve all the problems. Such a definition would exclude exemptions from taxes or environmental regulations, etc. which may provide just as much assistance as a direct payment. Furthermore, how specific does the transfer have to be to count as a subsidy? Paving a suburban road out of public fund assists all business firms that use the road, and so does the building of a road to a remote mining site. To calculate whether subsidies are involved in each case involves complicated calculations of cost, use, and taxes paid by the users. Also there is no general agreement as to what constitutes a 'proper' role of government in many forms of economic activity – education, for example. Is 'free' education for electronic wizards a subsidy for the electronics industry? But what if education is free for all professions and skills? Does it involve a subsidy only if it is free for some skills and not for others?

There are however, other more subtle problems. There are many other forms of assistance in an economy that have effects very similar to those of direct subsidies. For example, taxing the imports of cars assists the domestic car manufacturing industry just as surely as does a direct subsidy to that industry. What is the logic of regarding one as fair assistance and the other as unfair? Then there are the very indirect effects: subsidising imports of some products will, through its indirect effects on the exchange rate for example, assist exporters of other products (in the same country) much as would a subsidy paid directly to them. But who would argue that subsidies to imports of manufactured goods provides unfair assistance to, say, agricultural exporters of the same country?

All this may be counted as no more than sophistry were it not for the pressure emanating from the United States in particular, regarding 'level playing fields' in international commerce. Given this pressure, is it then possible to attempt to limit the scope of attention by defining types of subsidies that are of particular concern to international trade? Enough has been said already to indicate that deciding what is and is not a trade-affecting subsidy has a substantial arbitrary ingredient to it. Attempts to control or neutralise such subsidies therefore must also have a substantial arbitrary element, and therefore will tend to cause friction between those with different interpretations of 'level playing fields'. Nevertheless, attempts continue to improve and expand the rules for the international control and neutralisation of subsidies, and in formulating these rules the international negotiating community has concentrated mainly on those actions that promote exports. But the beast is a Hydra, and Hercules has not yet arrives.

b. Export and Domestic Subsidies

With the attention narrowed to export-promoting subsidies, another distinction is of importance. This is between those subsidies that promote exports directly and those which do so incidentally. The contrast is between a subsidy on *exports per se*, and a subsidy that assists the *production* of particular industries but which affects exports when some of the output is exported. The attempt to provide specific rules in an international forum to control the use of the latter, domestic, form of subsidy is relatively new.

In principle, it is easy to distinguish between an export subsidy and a domestic subsidy. An export subsidy is any government action that discriminates between sales for the domestic and foreign markets, and favours the latter. A domestic subsidy, on the other hand, relates to all production whatever its destination. Discrimination according to destination is the core of the matter. But even this relatively clear and simple concept runs into problems. The following are some of them.

1. When a country has a system of value added taxation, is the exemption of exports from such taxation to be regarded as an export subsidy? The generally accepted answer to this is that countries choose between origin and destination forms of value added taxation. A destination based tax, which is the common

form of the tax, applies the tax to imports and not to exports. Such treatment is generally not regarded as an export subsidy.

2. A country may have a plethora of import restrictions and export taxes and subsidies. An export subsidy for product X may be doing nothing more than partially negating the adverse effects on X of all the other taxes on trade. Is such a subsidy *really* a subsidy? What if product X itself bears export taxes as well as export subsidies? Should they be netted out to calculate a net tax or subsidy? (The answer to this may seem obvious, but such netting out is not allowed under the United States' countervailing duty law.)
3. Is a production subsidy to be regarded as an export subsidy when there are no, or few, domestic sales? If so, what is the dividing line?
4. Is exemption for a particular product from an export tax that other exported products must bear to be regarded as an export subsidy?
5. If different products are exported at different exchange rates, how is one to calculate whether one product's exchange rate is to be regarded as a subsidising or taxing exchange rate?
6. A favourable interest rate on credit for exports is clearly a form of subsidy. But what if credit in general is rationed and exporters (or exporters of some products) are able to get credit more readily than others, though at the same interest rate? Is this a subsidy: How could the subsidy element of such treatment be calculated?
7. Is the refund of import duty on the imported content of exports to be regarded as an export subsidy? If not, then how many stages back in the production process does one allow for such import duty refunds? (For example, does one allow refunds of duty paid on imports used by a domestic supplier to the exporter, or by a supplier to the supplier? And what of imported capital equipment used by the exporter, or imported capital equipment used by a domestic supplier of components to the exporter, or by the supplier's supplier?)
8. How does one treat the special favours that are sometimes given to export processing zones with respect to labour laws, infrastructure, tax treatment etc.?
9. How is one to determine whether exports are subsidised in non-market economies?

These questions are the bread and butter of trade lawyers. Many are complex, but at least the answers can be related to a clear principle – differential treatment according to destination. In the case of domestic subsidies that may affect exports, however, even the principle is not clear. Here a fundamental problem revolves around what is, and is not, a normal or proper function of government. Much blood has been split over this issue, and the attempt by one country's government to take actions through countervailing duties against other countries' exports according to what it deems to be the appropriate role of government (which may differ from the view of the next government in the same country), or to obtain a ruling from a multilateral body regarding this role, is doomed to irritate. The more generally available is a particular form of government assistance the less likely it is to be judged a subsidy for a particular industry, and specificity is often used as a criterion. But between generality and specificity there is a continuous but blurred range of positions and placement of policies on this scale is difficult. Demarcation is arbitrary.

To illustrate the point, the following are some of the questions that have arisen in relation to foreign challenges to domestic subsidies (Mundheim and Ehrenhaft, 1984, pp. 95–107).

1. While free general education may not be regarded as being a subsidy, does the subsidisation of the education of horticulturalists give an unfair advantage to flower exporters?
2. Does apartheid in South Africa give an unfair advantage to South African steel exporters?
3. Does the building of a wharf by a government provide a subsidy for fish producers and exporters?
4. Is the amount charged by the government to exploiters of a resource on public land relevant in determining whether exports of this resource are subsidised, even when the charge is the same whether or not the resource is exported?

With all these problems of defining and measuring subsidies and the arbitrary nature of it all, one is driven to wonder whether the attempt to control them is not more trouble, and more of a problem for international trade, than the subsidies themselves. Disputes arise frequently regarding quite small subsidies that have little effect on exports. The existence of the countervailing duty machinery provides considerable opportunity for import-competing industries to harass their foreign competitors. Many observers argue that it may be better not to try to address most subsidies directly. We return to this in Section 9. We now turn to consider why governments may choose consciously to subsidise particular activities, and particularly when the subsidies are perceived to affect international trade.

3. WHY SUBSIDISE?

Like all forms of government favours, subsidies may be granted for a number of reasons, many of which are more of a political than an economic nature. We focus here on those reasons which may be termed economic, in that the intent of the government is to affect the structure of the economy in a manner that it deems to be of general benefit to the country's citizens. Before turning to export-promoting subsidies, the point should be made that if a government wishes to encourage a particular activity, a subsidy for that activity, funded from general taxation, will usually be the most economically efficient way in which to do it (Corden, 1974, Chapters 2–4). That is, if a government wishes to encourage production of product X, it could do so by means of a direct subsidy to production, by imposing barriers to imports of import-competing goods, or by subsidising exports. A production subsidy will tend to be the most efficient means of assistance because it does not raise the price of product X to domestic users of X – it does not discourage the domestic use of the product the production of which it is designed to encourage. In some instances, complications in administering a production subsidy or in raising the taxes to pay for it, may shift the efficient choice towards an import tariff. However, there is a *prima facie* case for direct subsidies for the production of X, if increased production of X is the objective.

Perhaps the main reasons for governments seeking to promote exports are not too dissimilar from the ideas associated with the so-called mercantilist, the intellectual foundations of which were attacked so successfully by Adam Smith two hundred years ago. Very often the concepts are dressed up in new and sometimes sophisticated clothing, for the idea that exports are of special value to a country is particularly durable. The idea has been fostered by the success of export-oriented countries, for example Japan and the Republic of Korea, by the pressing demands of the servicing of debts in many countries, and by the need, in countries adopting an inward-oriented development strategy, to pay for essential imports.

For countries in which the structure of trade policy is geared to shield industries from import competition, it can be argued that exports are indeed generally of more value than other forms of production. Policies that restrict imports tend to appreciate a country's real exchange rate (that is, raise a country's price level relative to the price level abroad) and thereby make exporting less attractive as compared with producing for the home market. Export-promoting subsidies then help to offset this anti-export bias. While it would be more efficient to remove the policies that cause this bias against exports, in the absence of such removal export promotion may, within limits, improve the efficiency of resource allocation in a country. Indeed there is considerable evidence that export promotion in the Republic of Korea in the 1960s and 1970s did little more than offset the bias against exports produced by support for import-competing industries.

It is another question, of course, as to whether this policy of protection 'all round' – providing it for exporting as well as for import-competing industries – will in fact bring improved resource allocation. It can all too easily develop into a political economy in which returns to investment in influencing the government exceed the returns on investing in meeting the demands for goods and services. A more efficient policy could be to remove the barriers to imports but, given these barriers, export subsidies that are generally available will tend to improve the productive efficiency of a country.

Apart from countering the anti-export bias of other policies, what other economic reasons are there for promoting exports? As with all forms of assistance, 'external economies' may provide a rationale – that is, there may be benefits that accrue to other members of the country for which the exporter receives no compensation. Goods that tend to generate such external economies will in general tend to be under-produced unless their production is encouraged by government support. What are these beneficial external effects that may flow from exports? It is perhaps easier to state the concept than to find specific examples. One example often mentioned is the benefits that can flow to other potential exporters from the pioneering of a market. Often, however, the pioneering firm will itself be able to recoup much of the benefits from pioneering (e.g. by acting as an agent for other firms, or selling its consulting services) in which case it may be well recompensed for the benefits it gives to other firms. But because they perceive potential benefits, governments often subsidise market development, or provide trade development and information services out of the public purse.

Another reason advanced for subsidising exporters, in this case in the forms of loan subsidies or risk insurance, is that commercial insurers or lenders may not be prepared to meet the risks they perceive on export markets, or that their charges for doing so may appear to be exorbitant (Fitzgerald and Monson, 1989).

In some markets these risks may include expropriation of property with uncertain compensation, or the imposition of exchange controls that do not permit the repatriation of profits. Whether in these circumstances there is a market failure and that would warrant the government stepping in would need investigation in particular cases; it could of course simply be that commercial lenders and insurers are making a correct assessment of the risks involved.

The existence of a large external debt and the difficulty of servicing it may lead some governments to subsidise exports, although the countries that are attempting to promote exports in this way appear often to be countering the anti-export bias of other policies. Indeed debt itself does not provide a case for subsidising exports. Production that reduces imports also provides the means to service debt – what is required is an increase in the production of tradeable goods and services relative to the demand for them. So the existence of a debt servicing problem may provide a case for promoting all tradeable production (for example by attempting to depreciate the real exchange rate) rather than for subsidising exports as such.

A form of export promotion that has received much attention in recent years is that associated with strategic trade policy (Krugman, 1987; and Corden, 1990). This term is used in a variety of ways, each implying that government assistance would enable a firm to achieve an objective in international markets, of national benefit, that would not have been achievable without the assistance. The essence of the idea is to assist in a competitive strategy in what is essentially a trade war with foreign firms and/or governments. The aim of the strategy may be: to sustain or develop a leading technological edge (secure and/or large scale production being judged to be necessary for the acquisition and development of this technology) and then to obtain the returns attributable to being first with the new technology; to obtain economies of scale that would then enable unassisted survival on the world market; to drive competitors out of an oligopolistic market; or to attempt to persuade a foreign government to desist from practices deemed to be harmful to the home country. The analysis of the pursuit and benefits of these objectives is complex (Cordon, 1990; and Helpman and Krugman, 1985 and 1989). The appropriate policy is very sensitive to the assumptions made regarding the structure of markets and competitors' responses, and inappropriate policies easily do more harm than good. But the concept is becoming very popular, particularly as many commentators in the United States attempt to lay blame abroad for their country's persistent balance of trade deficits. The allegation that the export success of foreigners, particularly in 'new' products, is due to strategic assistance from their governments, is a potent political argument for like treatment.

4. EFFECTS ON OTHER COUNTRIES

In considering the impact of export-promoting subsidies on other countries, it is helpful to make a distinction between subsidies of a strategic nature, as referred to in the previous paragraph, and subsidies that are introduced for other reasons. As far as strategic subsidies are concerned, and to the extent that the strategies have a valid economic base, countries that are the targets of the strategies are likely to be harmed by the policies. The appropriate nature of the response will be determined by perceptions of the nature of the 'game' being played. (Conybeare, 1987, provides an exposition of various game plans and relates them to actual trade wars of the past.) Of course the supposed strategies of foreigners could be more in the minds of the beholders than in reality, or the strategies could be misconceived or ineffectual. But even if misconceived, trade strategies can damage other countries and may warrant policies designed to prevent their implementation or to offset their effects. It might be noted that small countries – those that cannot affect their terms of trade – have no scope for strategic trade actions.

As far as non-strategic subsidies are concerned, an important economic point is that if export-promoting subsidies lower the export prices of the subsidising countries, they improve the terms of trade of other countries, considered as a whole. This does not mean that the terms of trade of those countries that are competing with the subsidising country on export markets will be improved – on the contrary, they will be worsened. But if a country is a net exporter of a product, the rest of the world as a whole must be a net importer of it. Thus an export promoting subsidy for a product of which a country is a net exporter, must improve the terms of trade of the rest of the world as a whole. Net importers of the product thus benefit from improved terms of trade arising from countries' export subsidies.

From this point of view, then, many if not most export promoting subsidies are relatively benign forms of interference in international trade. They may be contrasted with barriers to imports which in general *worsen* the terms of trade of other countries as a whole (Snape, 1986). The export subsidies which are most harmful to other countries from this perspective, are those where an importer of a product has, by means of the subsidies, been turned into a substantial net exporter; many of these are in agriculture. Such 'trade-reversing' subsidies are almost invariably accompanied by major barriers to imports into the country granting them. As noted below, if the same prices for producers were to be maintained by subsidies but without the barriers to imports, the subsidies would be very expensive for the national treasury and in many cases it is unlikely that support prices would be maintained at such high levels. Leaving aside these trade-reversing subsidies, why should governments of countries that can benefit from improved terms of trade seek to do anything about other countries' non-strategic export promoting subsidies?

As so often occurs in economic policy, there is a conflict here between the interests of the nation as a whole and the interests of one section of it. And, also as so often happens, those whose interests may be harmed are likely to be more concentrated and to have a larger per capita loss than those who gain, even though the gainers and the total gain, respectively, may greatly exceed those who lose and the total loss. In the political race, then, the specific interests that are harmed by imports, including those imports that are subsidised as exports by foreign governments, are likely to have a lead start. And such arguments as: 'We can compete with Mexican *companies*, but we cannot compete with the Mexican *government*' (Chairman of US Steel Corporation, letter to the editor, *The*

Washington Post, December 9, 1983, p. A22) strike a chord of sympathy even when considerations of trade strategy are not involved, and of course it is a simple matter to suggest that such strategies are present.

It is curious that there appears to be widespread acceptance that it is legitimate for foreign governments to restrict access to their domestic markets, and this acceptance is reflected in international agreements (eg. GATT) that limit import barriers, rather than proscribing them across-the-board. On the other hand the view is widespread that it is illegitimate for foreign governments to assist their residents to export, particularly in competition with 'our' producers. Thus import barriers are accepted as legitimate (or at least some forms of them are) and are the subject of negotiation; export promotion is much less accepted and is often branded as unfair. From an economic perspective the asymmetry of attitudes is rather confusing, as also is the invocation of fairness. The distinction between fair and unfair trade tends to be as elusive as that other economic holy grail the 'just price'. There is no doubt that the whole concept of fairness, and the asymmetry of attitudes towards trade expanding and trade contracting actions, are heavily producer-oriented and reflect mercantilist perceptions of the role of international trade which have long been regarded by most economists as fallacious. Nevertheless, these perceptions do appear to have a powerful influence on policy.

Protection for farmers against imports has for long been regarded by governments in many countries as being in a special category. Whether it be to protect a way of life that is generally respected, to attempt to guarantee food security through self-sufficiency, to solve a problem of rural poverty, or simply because of the political power of farmers as a voting coalition, price support and other assistance for agriculture products is endemic in Europe, Japan, and the United States, in particular (OECD, 1987). On the international stage, the perceived problems associated with subsidies for manufactured products have largely been related to injury to import competing industries, and more recently to strategic trade policies. For agriculture, however, subsidies have largely been directed towards import replacement, and have led to the spilling-over of production on to export markets, there to compete with the relatively unsubsidised exports of efficient agricultural exporting countries.

5. THE RULES

The multilaterally agreed-upon rules on subsidies are to be found in the GATT, as modified after the GATT Review of 1954–55, and in the 'Interpretation and Application' of the relevant GATT Articles agreed in 1979 as part of the outcome of the Tokyo Round of multilateral trade negotiations – particularly the interpretation and application usually referred to as the Subsidies Code. The national legislation of major importing countries is generally consistent with these internationally agreed rules. As the United States has for long been a leader in interpretation, as part of its legislation is thought by some not to conform to the provisions of GATT, and as there has been a surge of countervailing duty cases there, particular attention is given in this Section to that country. Attention is also given to agriculture and to developing countries, for both of which there are special provisions.

a. The Articles of GATT

While the original GATT Articles as agreed in 1947 did not prohibit subsidies for either production or exports, the GATT Review of 1955 introduced a prohibition of those export subsidies which result in a lower price for manufactured goods on the export market than the domestic market (Article XVI:4). (In fact such pricing would conform to dumping, as defined by the GATT.) A note to this paragraph explains that the intention was to abolish 'all subsidies' (presumably all subsidies that promote exports of manufactured products, for there are separate provisions for primary products), but the Article itself incorporates the dual price test (i.e., export prices lower than domestic prices) to define the proscribed subsidies. While export subsidies for products sold competitively may be expected to cause prices on the export market to be lower than on the domestic market, production subsidies will not tend to have this effect.[1] The 1995 amendment moved the GATT closer to the Havana Charter for the stillborn International Trade Organisation but the ITO Charter did not differentiate between manufactured and other products with respect to the dual pricing test – *all* export subsidies that resulted in lower prices on the international rather than on the domestic market were to be proscribed (Jackson, 1969, p. 371). The change can only be ascribed to the growth of subsidised agriculture in industrial countries and of the political power of agricultural interests in these countries in the intervening years.

As far as primary products are concerned, the GATT (as revised in 1955) provides that 'contracting parties shall seek to avoid the use of subsidies on the export of primary products', but if they do use subsidies, they should not use them in a manner 'which results in that contracting party having more than an equitable share of world trade in that product' (Article XVI:3), a very vague prescription. Domestic subsidies for agriculture and barriers to imports of agricultural products have been virtually outside GATT control since a waiver was granted to the United States in 1955 for the import restrictions which were part of its agricultural price support program (Dam, 1970, p. 260). Nevertheless, subsidisation of agricultural *exports* is still, in principle, under GATT proscription when these subsidies result in 'more than an equitable share of world trade'. In addition, they are open to countervailing tariff action by importing countries, along with all other export promoting subsidies, as noted below. However, the inability of GATT procedures to constrain the actions of the EEC effectively following successful complaints under the GATT by Australia and Brazil regarding subsidised sugar exports, leaves little doubt that such subsidies are not under GATT proscriptive control in practice (Teese, 1982).

The GATT Articles permit the levying of countervailing duties, no greater than the amount of subsidy,[2] if the government of the importing country determines that the effects of subsidies are such as to cause or threaten 'material' injury to an industry in its country (Article VI: 6(a)). It is this provision which has been most important in practice in discouraging export-promoting subsidies.[3]

GATT also allows countervailing duties by an importer (say country A) when subsidised exports by country B are displacing the exports of country C in A's market, and this loss of exports causes material injury to an industry in C (Article VI: 6(b)). In practice country A may have no incentive to take countervailing action for the benefit of an industry in country C.

Article XVI: 1 of GATT provides that member countries must notify other members of *any* subsidy which 'operates directly or indirectly to increase exports of any product from, or to reduce imports of any product into, its territory' and also of the extent and nature of the subsidy and the estimated effects on exports or imports, but it appears that this is frequently not observed. The other main Article of the GATT that relates to subsidies is Article XXII concerning 'nullification or impairment' of any benefits accruing under the Agreement. This if a country, in the course of trade negotiations, had agreed to bind a particular tariff (that is, in GATT language, has granted a 'concession'), and another country then subsidised exports so as to get 'under' that tariff, 'nullification and impairment' could be deemed to occur. The matter could then be referred to members of GATT for multilateral resolution in accordance with the provisions of that Article. Concessions granted to the offending party could be suspended.

b. The Subsidies Code

In 1979 the Subsidies Code emerged out of the Tokyo Round of multilateral trade negotiations. There are now over 90 Contracting Parties to GATT but only about a third of these have signed the Subsidies Code. Developing countries in particular have been reluctant to sign it. The Code is an 'Agreement on Interpretation and Application' of the relevant Articles (VI, XVI, and XXII) of the GATT. Thus, the Code does not replace any of the Articles of the GATT and where particular matters are not dealt with in the Code, the provisions of the GATT must be presumed to remain. For example, although the dual pricing test (Article XVI: 4) is not referred to in the Code, it remains on the books – though it is not utilised (Hufbauer and Shelton-Erb, 1984, pp. 47–8).

An important consideration concerning the Subsidies Code (and the other Codes and Framework Agreement negotiated at the Tokyo Round) is whether the provisions of the Code should be applied only to other signatories to the Code, or whether they should apply to all contracting parties to GATT. The matter is not unimportant, for arising from a grandfather provision of the Protocol of Provisional Application of GATT, the United States is not required to apply an 'injury test' in order to levy countervailing duties against subsidies granted by other countries, whether or not they are contracting parties of GATT. (That is, the 'material injury' requirement of Article VI:6(a) of GATT does not apply to the United States to the extent that it was not consistent with the US countervailing duty legislation that existed at the time the GATT was first signed.)[4] Under the Code, however, the United States *is* required to establish that there is material injury to a domestic industry prior to imposing countervailing duties. The United States maintains that this provision applies only with respect to countries which have accepted the obligations of the Code: the Act of Congress which implemented the Tokyo Round agreements specifies this requirement (Jackson, 1989, p. 260).

Governments of some other countries argue that Article 1 of the GATT has primacy – that 'any advantage, favour, privilege or immunity granted by any contracting party to any product originating in or destined for any other country shall be accorded immediately and unconditionally to the like product originating in or destined for the territories of all other contracting parties.' What is at issue is unconditional not unconditional MFN and is an important departure from the trading principles established in the post-World War II negotiations (Hufbauer, Shelton-Erb and Starr, 1980, pp. 59–70; and Snape, 1988).

The Subsidies Code distinguishes between agricultural[5] and other products, between developed and developing countries, and between export subsidies and other types of subsidies. Though not as clear as it might be – there is a good bit of vagueness which appears to be deliberate – it also distinguishes between various levels of injury.

The Code continues the trend started in the GATT review of 1955 in attempting to distinguish between export subsidies and other subsidies, some of which may encourage exports, and in attempting to prohibit export subsidies (except on agricultural products and by developing countries). It provides an illustrative list of what are deemed to be export subsidies.[6]

As far as agriculture is concerned, export subsidies are not prohibited by the Code for either developed or developing countries. Instead, the Code attempts, rather weakly, to define what the 'more than an equitable share of world export trade' is which signatories should not capture by means of export subsidies (Article 10).

Export subsidies on manufactured products are not banned for developing countries; instead: 'Developing country signatories agree that export subsidies on their industrial products shall not be used in a manner which causes serious prejudice to the trade or production of another signatory' (Article 14:3), and they 'should endeavour to enter into a commitment to reduce or eliminate export subsidies when the use of such export subsidies is inconsistent with . . . competitive and development needs' (Article 14:5). Furthermore, when such a commitment has been entered into, counter-measures which might otherwise be authorised on a *multilateral* basis against the export subsidies, may not be undertaken by other signatories. These 'multilateral actions' from which they are excused involve consultations, reconciliation and authorisation of 'such counter-measures as may be appropriate'.

For subsidies other than export subsidies, the Code takes a somewhat more permissive and ambiguous approach, but recognises that they:

> 'may cause or threaten to cause injury to a domestic industry of another signatory or may nullify or impair benefits accruing to the interests of another signatory under the General Agreement, in particular where such subsidies would adversely affect the conditions of normal competition. Signatories shall therefore seek to avoid causing such effects through the use of subsidies' (Article 11:2).

It is even more permissive regarding such subsidies when they are granted by developing countries, in that the multilateral track for action may not be taken against them unless nullification or impairment of tariff concessions or other obligations under GATT is found to exist. While at the end of it all, there appears to be little or no differentiation between developed and developing in the action that an importing country can take through the imposition of countervailing duties against subsidies, there is a considerable 'understanding' written into the Code regarding the use of subsidies in developing countries. For example:

> Signatories recognise that subsidies are an integral part of economic development programmes of developing countries (Article 14:1);
>
> Signatories recognise that in developing countries, governments may play a large role in promoting economic growth and development (Article 14:7).

But in view of the similarity of possible countervailing action, this understanding does not appear to amount to much.

Permitted remedies under the Code are complex and, as noted, include both national action on the initiative of an importing country and multilaterally authorised actions. The latter vary according to many factors including whether they are in response to export subsidies or other subsidies, whether the subsidies are on agricultural or other products, and whether the subsidies are given by developed or developing countries. On this multilateral track, consultations between the parties are the most common form of action. More important to date and in the foreseeable future, are the provisions for countervailing duties to be imposed by an importing country, although for action against subsidies that affect another country's exports to a third market the multilateral path is likely to continue to be the only feasible one. To date, however, this track has proved to be slow and rather ineffective, as illustrated by the Brazilian and Australian experiences relating to subsidised EEC sugar exports, and by a fight spanning many years between the US and the EEC regarding pasta subsidies – the issue here hinged on whether pasta is a primary product and on the size of refunds to pasta exporters of the excess cost of wheat purchased under the EEC's Common Agricultural Policy (Stern, Jackson and Hoekman, 1986, p. 29; and Jackson, 1989, p. 102). While the extent of injury to an industry that needs to be demonstrated for multilaterally-authorised action is generally less than for countervailing duties to be imposed by national authorities after their own investigation, the wheels of the multilateral gods grind slowly, and often ineffectively.

Thus, the main source of remedy is in unilaterally determined countervailing duties. These can be imposed not only against those subsidies that are proscribed by the GATT or the Subsidies Code, but also against those which are not proscribed: material injury or threat thereof to an industry in an importing country is the crucial element. Part I of the Subsidies Code specifies the procedures which countries should follow in conducting investigations into whether material injury has (or will) occur, and principles for determining the causal link between subsidised imports and the injury. The Code provides for visible and public investigation, for consultations, and also states that it is the size of the subsidy, and not the amount of injury, that should determine the limits to the countervailing duty. The Code provides for price undertakings by exporters (that would remove the source of the injury) to be entered into, in lieu of countervailing duties. It also states that in determining injury there should be 'an objective examination of both (a) the volume of subsidised imports and their effect on prices of the domestic market for like products and (b) the consequent impact of those imports on domestic producers of such products' (Article 6:1). It lists factors to be taken into account in determining the impact on prices and on domestic producers, but the attempt is far from satisfactory, as the Code itself implies. While as far as countervailing actions are concerned, there is no differentiation between export and other subsidies, an export subsidy would normally be in breach of a signatory's obligations under the Code and therefore could attract more severe multilaterally-authorised (though nationally determined and imposed) action than other subsidies.

6. AGRICULTURE

From the beginning, agriculture has been a problem for the GATT, and much of the problem has surrounded the question of subsidies and their control. The GATT allows restrictions of imports where they are necessary to complement domestic restrictions on agricultural or fishery production. This provision was introduced to accommodate the farm price support programme of the US. The accommodation proved to be inadequate, and in 1951 the US Congress passed legislation which could require the President to take action against imports in a manner that was inconsistent with US obligations under the GATT. As a result in 1955 the US sought and obtained a waiver from the relevant GATT obligations regarding agriculture; other countries then followed. As was detailed above, much of agriculture was thus removed from the GATT coverage with respect to barriers to imports. The price supports that are buttressed by these import barriers were thereby sustained and encouraged.

With the growth of protected European agricultural production and exports, the interests of the US with respect to agriculture have changed substantially. Long having been the leading proponent of discipline on subsidies for manufactured products, the US has now joined other agricultural exporters in pressing for the discipline to be extended to agriculture. During the Tokyo Round, the US and the EEC clashed repeatedly on the attempt by the US to bring agriculture under the general rule of GATT (Winham, 1987, pp. 156–7), an irony since it was the US that led agriculture out from such coverage.

The problems of excess agricultural production received attention at the Tokyo (196) and Venice (1987) summit meetings of the heads of government of the seven leading developed nations, the 'G7'. Also the August 1986, Ministerial Meetings of the 'Cairns' group of fourteen countries that describe themselves as fair traders in agriculture 'undertook to seek the removal of market access barriers, substantial reductions of agricultural subsidies and the elimination, within an agreed period, of subsidies affecting agricultural trade' within the context of multilateral trade negotiations. The following month the Ministerial Declaration that launched the Uruguay Round of multilateral trade negotiations stated that the Contracting Parties to GATT had agreed that negotiations would seek to improve 'GATT disciplines relating to all subsidies and countervailing measures that affect international trade' and that for agriculture in particular 'negotiations shall aim to achieve greater liberalisation of trade [by] . . . increasing discipline on the use of all direct and indirect subsidies and other measures affecting directly or indirectly agricultural trade, including the phased reduction of their negative effects and dealing with their clauses'. Although it is not a member of the Cairns group, the US put on the table in the Uruguay Round negotiations proposals for the elimination of all forms of farm support. And in the US–Canada Free Trade Agreement of 1987 'The Parties have agreed that their primary goal with respect to agricultural subsidies is to achieve, on a global basis, the elimination of all subsidies which distort agricultural trade and agree to work together to achieve this goal, including through multilateral trade negotiations such as the Uruguay Round'.

In the Uruguay Round negotiations agricultural subsidies have proved to be particularly difficult, as expected. By the mid-term review in Montreal in December 1988, little had been achieved and a number of countries refused to continue negotiations in other areas until progress was made in agriculture. In the following April sufficient progress was deemed to have been made for the road block to be removed, though to many observers the agreements seemed to have at best moderate substance: '[the] long term objective is . . . for substantial progressive reductions in agricultural support and protection sustained over an agreed period of time . . . realised through negotiations on specific policies and measures [and] through the negotiation of commitments on an aggregate measurement of support . . . '. With regard to other non-agricultural subsidies, the mid-term review recorded only a framework work negotiations.

7. COUNTERVAILING DUTY ACTION

The United States has viewed the Subsidies Code as a means to bring changes in the trade policies of other countries, while other countries have feared over-enthusiastic application of CVD (and anti-dumping) procedures (Beseler and Williams, 1986, pp. 9, 16; and Stern and Hoekman, 1987, p. 61). As noted above, the US has insisted on applying the benefits of the Code only to those countries which accept the obligations of the Code, rather than to all members of the GATT. The condition is not just that a country should sign the Code, a condition which in itself is of doubtful legality (Jackson, Louis and Matsusita, 1984, p. 161). It is that the country should have adjusted its subsidy policies in a manner that the US judges to be in conformity with the Code (Hufbauer and Shelton Erb, 1984, Appendix B). The Code does provide for non-application between any two signatories at the discretion of either; only the United States appears to have used this provision as a means to secure policy adjustments.

In addition to this restriction of the benefits of the Code, the US is by far the largest initiator of CVD actions. Table 1, which is drawn from data compiled under the direction of Michael Finger at the World Bank, shows that of 460 countervailing duty cases by all countries over the first seven years of the decade, 281 of them were the United States. Chile accounted for 140, nearly all prior to

March 1983, and virtually all not sustained (Finger and Nogués, 1987, p. 713). Chile's actions followed a very rapid dismantling of other trade barriers in that country, and have been regarded by some other countries as misuse of the CVD provisions of the Code.[7]

Table 1 also shows that the major initiators of countervailing duty cases had relatively few actions taken against them. To a large extent this is due to the fact that the most subsidised exports of the United States and Europe are agricultural products that injure industries not in the importing countries, but in other exporters: the importing countries have little or no incentive to take CVD initiatives. It is also true that many non-users of CVDs adopt other forms of barriers to imports, often in a concealed form and with considerable bureaucratic discretion, instead of the highly transparent CVD procedures.

The targets of CVD actions form a much larger set of the countries than the initiators. With or without the Chilean cases, Brazil is the most frequent – indeed speaking a Romance language appears to correlate well with being a target. About 60 per cent of all cases were against developing countries, and only one per cent against non-market economies. (Finger and Olechowski, 1987, Table A 8.1; and Nam, 1987, Table 1).

A CVD action may result in a countervailing duty being imposed or in the exporter agreeing to desist from subsidising or to raise the export price. Such outcomes are successful from the point of view of the petitioner. On the other hand it may be determined that there was no subsidisation or no injury (in the relevant sense) – these outcomes would be unfavourable to the petitioner. As a third possibility the case could be withdrawn either voluntarily or under duress. Of all the products for which cases were initiated and decided over the seven-year period, and excluding Chile for which only one of its 140 cases was decided in favour of the petitioner, about 60 per cent of cases gave the petitioner a favourable outcome. The figure was 55 per cent for the US.

An unfavourable decision for the petitioner does not imply that the foreign exporter is unharmed. Unlike domestic legal cases, there is no possibility of 'costs' being awarded against the plaintiff, to be paid to an innocent defendant. Thus there is a relatively small disincentive for a firm that is suffering from import competition to petition for a CVD, particularly where, as in the US, a political climate has developed regarding the unfair trading practices of some foreigners and CVD actions are seen by the government as a disciplinary action on these foreigners. Many CVD actions, and particularly by the US, are widely viewed as a form of harassment of foreign exporters (Finger and Nogués, 1987, pp. 713–22).

8. EVALUATION OF THE SUBSIDIES CODE

There is a common view that the Subsidies Code has not worked well. Judgement should, of course, be formed on the basis of the objectives of those who sought the control of subsidies, in relation to other means of achieving the same aims, and by an assessment of the aims themselves.

The provisions of the Code for agriculture are weak and ineffective, in part reflecting the determination of the European Economic Community and some

TABLE 1 *Countervailing Duty Cases*

	Number of countervailing duty cases, 1980–86		
		Against	
	By	Total	Excluding Chilean cases
I. Countries in which at least one countervailing duty case was initiated			
United States	281	1	1
Chile	140	1	0
Australia	20	2	2
Canada	11	11	11
European Community policies[a]	7	11	6
Japan	1	2	1
Summary, Part I	460	28	21
As a percentage of all cases	100	6	7
II. Countries in which no CVD cases have been initiated			
Brazil	0	88	32
Spain	0	38	22
Argentina	0	3	6
Mexico	0	28	27
Peru	0	22	7
France	0	21	21
Korea	0	21	13
Other EEC member states[a]	0	56	54
Other countries (40)	0	126	117
Summary, Part II	0	432	299
As a percentage of all cases		94	93

Source: Annex 8, Tables 1 and 2.
a. In the EEC, the CVD instrument exists only for the Community: member states do not have CVD mechanisms. Both member states and the Community provide subsidies that have been the object of CVD investigations in other countries.
Source: Finger (1987), p. 157.

other countries to keep agricultural issues separate (Winham, 1986, Ch. 4). From the viewpoint of efficient agricultural exporting countries, the Code has failed seriously at this point. The longstanding indifference to the position of these exporters has been a source of continual frustration for them. So too was the 1982 Ministerial Meeting of the Contracting Parties of the GATT, the final declaration of which the Australian trade minister angrily refused to sign. As noted above, some action directed at agricultural subsidies is now more likely to be taken, with the formation of the Cairns Group of agricultural exporting countries, the heightened US concern regarding barriers to its exports, and the suggestion of at least some progress in the Uruguay Round.

As far as manufactured products were concerned in the negotiations of the Subsidies Code, there was a marked difference between the United States and other participants. The US was particularly concerned to secure discipline over other countries' export-promoting subsidies. Other countries were more concerned that discipline should be imposed on the use, by the US, of countervailing duties (Finger and Nogués, 1987, p. 713; and Messerlin, 1986). As the US now requires the injury test for imports from those countries it judges to have fulfilled the requirements of the Code, in this regard the Code must be judged at least a partial success by those who negotiated it.

Since the acceptance of the Subsidies Code, however, use by the US of the CVD machinery has increased greatly. It is not clear to what extent each of the following has contributed to this: (a) the change in the US trading position leading to more import competing industries seeking protection against injury; (b) active encouragement by the US Administration of actions designed to exercise discipline over the trading policies of other countries; (c) possibly increased use of subsidies by other countries; (d) reduced tariff barriers negotiated in the Tokyo Round exposing more industries to import competition; and (e) increased reliance on litigation in general as a means to alleviate economic problems. Possibly all have contributed.

Use by other countries of CVD procedures has also increased since the negotiation of the Code – European countries typically had used anti-dumping duties rather than CVDs, while until 1982 Japan had used neither (Stern, Jackson and Hoekman, 1986, p. 27). To the extent that CVD actions are a more transparent means by which to seek protection than many alternative means – this transparency being an aim of the US negotiators – this greater use of CVDs can be regarded as success for the Code, and a move towards trade liberalisation. But to the extent that these CVD actions have just added another avenue for protection, as is argued by some, the Code will have failed. The evidence is not yet clear on this issue.

What is clear however, is that considerable tension has been generated as the US has negotiated with some countries regarding the eligibility of those countries for the 'injury test' (Hufbauer and Shelton Erb, 1984, p. 122; and Winham, 1986, pp. 359–60), and as markedly different perceptions of what constitutes a subsidy have been manifest. Those few cases that have been brought under the multilateral machinery of GATT and the Code – predominantly regarding agricultural subsidies – have aired, if not accentuated, discord, and generally they have not been settled to anyone's satisfaction (Teese, 1982; Hathaway, 1987, p. 106; and Messerlin, 1986).

Are export-promoting subsidies increasing? There is a general perception that they are, both for agriculture and other products, but whether this is so or simply a perception as they come more into focus, is not evident. What is even less evident is what they would be in the absence of GATT and the Subsidies Code. However, it is apparent that neither subsidies themselves, nor CVD actions, have been constrained to the extent that those who pressed for constraints in the Tokyo Round had hoped. In addition more discord has attended the subject than they probably expected. A consideration of alternatives is appropriate.

9. ALTERNATIVES

While many economists may argue that subsidies, like other government distortions of international trade, generally do more harm to the country imposing them than to others and do less harm to all than other ways of achieving similar objectives, these are not common perceptions. To a very large extent it is the injury which subsidies may bring to particular industries in other countries that makes them of international concern, not the harm they may or may not do to the world economy as a whole. Even in the US there would be little political mileage in attacking foreign subsidies that had no impact on international trade, or on US trade for that matter. So in contemplating options for the future in the field of subsidies, one possibility that appeals to many economists (and others) is to drop the search for *causes* of international competition and to focus on the consequences. There are at least major problems with this approach: (i) the view that is widely held in the US, that foreign governments are using subsidies as an element of strategic trade policy and that they need to be tackled head-on; (ii) the idea of 'unfair' competition is useful for those seeking protection, for it is a potent political concept, and they will seek to retain it unless they can get the same assistance through other means; and (iii) while a government can deal with the consequences of foreign competition in its domestic market, its options to do so in foreign (third party) markets are limited. So before considering options for international action that involve indirect, rather than direct, attacks on export promoting subsidies, attention is given to a possible improvement more or less within the current framework.

a. Ignore Domestic Subsidies

This change would continue to admit the powerful political appeal of 'unfair' trade but would also acknowledge the particular practical problems of specifying and measuring any export promoting domestic subsidies, and the international tensions that are generated by attempting to discipline such subsidies. As under the present regime, export subsidies defined (as in the Subsidies Code) could be both proscribed and countervailable. Countervailable actions would be limited to export subsidies alone, leaving domestic subsidies untouched by countervailing actions, proscription, or exhortation. Retaining the proscription of export subsidies would enable action to be taken in a multilateral context when a country's exports are 'damaged' by the export subsidies of another country, in a third market.

The second and third proposals, which are not alternatives to each other but could be complementary, are rather more radical in that they implicitly drop the distinction between fair and unfair trade and attack export promoting subsidies indirectly rather than directly.

b. Ignore the Source of Injury

It is unlikely that countries will forsake all provisions for safeguarding industries against foreign competition. Such safeguarding could be greatly simplified if the current distinction between fair and unfair trade as a cause of injury could be dropped. From an economic point of view it would, of course, be preferable if the criteria of injury for 'safeguarding' against injury could then be amended to focus on economy-wide rather than industry-specific effects. But even without this amendment, much could be gained in simplicity by repeating the special provisions covering subsidies and dumping and relying on the general safeguard provisions of Article XIX of GATT, which cover injury from 'fair' competition, together with the nullification and impairment provision of Article XXIII (see Barcelo, 1984; and Corden, 1983, 1987). Simplification and consistency – and less protection through the 'harassment' of exporters – would be achieved by getting all injury cases on the one track with the exception of 'damage' in third markets where, as now, action can be taken under the nullification and impairment provisions (Article XXIII).

While this path has much appeal, the following points should be noted if reliance is to be placed on the existing safeguard Article XIX (Barcelo, 1977, pp. 842 ff.).

- Unlike the Subsidies and Anti-Dumping Codes, the Article provides that the country taking action should grant offsetting 'concessions', or face the possibility of retaliation.
- Action taken under Article XIX must be non-discriminatory: if applied to any, it must be applied to imports from all sources. This may appear to discriminate against those who do not subsidise (or dump), but such would be a consequence of abandoning the distinction between fair and unfair changes in the prices of imports. Allowing selectivity of Article XIX safeguard action has been sought by many countries and may be accepted in the Uruguay Round, but it would be a very high price to pay (see Tumlir, 1985).
- Actions under Article XIX are viewed as temporary, giving time for adjustment. Action against subsidies and dumping, on the other hand, has no such adjustment presumption. However, the difference in practice does not appear significant.
- Barriers under Article XIX can be raised to any extent to ameliorate the injury. Unlike countervailing or anti-dumping duties they are not limited by the cause of the trouble.
- Article XIX requires 'serious' not 'material' (or less) injury, and this is regarded as being a higher injury test.
- The United States legislation for Article XIX action requires the imports to be a 'substantial cause' of injury – less than some other cause. Countervailing or Anti-Dumping duties can be imposed when the subsidy or dumping makes a much lesser contribution to injury of the relevant industry.
- Within the US one effect of this change would be to reduce the automaticity of relief action, leaving more discretion with the President, and making action and procedure less subject to appeal through the courts.

c. Attack Trade Barriers Only

It is apparent that barriers to trade inflict more harm on trading nations as a whole than do those actions (like subsidies) that promote trade, and also that most of the subsidies that have a significant impact on international trade are buttressed by barriers to imports (Snape, 1987. All production and export subsidies raise the returns to domestic producers. They also impose a cost on national treasuries. The cost on treasuries is decreased if, for any level of price support, these subsidies are complemented by barriers to imports of competing products – these barriers enable the domestic price to be raised above world prices and thus to put part of the cost of price support on domestic buyers of the product rather than on the government's budget. Reducing the barriers to imports would thus place a greater cost on the national treasury for the same level of price support. The size of the 'subsidy equivalent' of most forms of barriers to imports – that is the cost of the price support provided by the import barriers if it were to be paid for by a direct subsidy rather than by barriers to imports – is frequently greeted by disbelief. In the EEC and Japan for example more than 60 per cent of the estimated total cost of agricultural policy over the years 1979–81 was paid directly by consumers, the increased consumer price being caused by barriers to imports (OECD, 1987, Annex III, Table 3). The cost to the EEC's budget of agricultural price support is of major concern: it would be multiplied considerably if the full cost were placed on the budget. Thus the reduction of barriers to imports is itself likely to constrain policies that support prices for producers, including those that promote exports.

Although it is an indirect attack on export promoting subsidies, there are reasons for thinking that this approach may be more successful than attempts to constrain subsidies – and particularly domestic subsidies – directly. They are as follows:

1. Barriers to imports are relatively easy to define. This is particularly true of import tariffs which are easy to measure as well as define, but it applies to most other forms of import barrier as well.
2. The major developed countries have generally shown themselves to be willing to negotiate with respect to import barriers on manufactured goods under the auspices of GATT (and within the Organisation for European Economic Cooperation, the precursor of the Organisation for Economic Cooperation and Development), and these negotiations have proved to be successful. Negotiation of frontier barriers is generally a much less sensitive issue than attempting to negotiate 'internal' policies.

10. CONCLUSION

From an economist's point of view, many export promoting subsidies have relatively benign effects on international trade. Exceptions to this are (i) strategic trade subsidies and (ii) subsidies for agriculture. The former appear to be much more frequent in public perception than in actuality and along with most other subsidies probably do more economic harm to the country granting them than to others. Those subsidies that do most harm on the international scene – mainly in agriculture – are usually buttressed by import barriers, and the reduction of these barriers would tend to constrain the extent to which prices for producers can be supported.

The definition of a subsidy, and even of a trade-affecting subsidy, is essentially arbitrary and differs according to perception and political persuasion. Attempts to control or neutralise these subsidies therefore lead to conflict; negotiated agreements paper-over the cracks of disagreement. While some of the most extreme forms of export subsidy can be limited and even reduced by such negotiations, attempts to define, detect, and counter lesser subsidies, and in particular domestic subsidies, have had a negative effect on international trading relations. Negotiating efforts is likely to be more rewarding if it focuses on barriers to international trade rather than on trade-promoting actions. But the political appeal of accusing foreigners of unfair trade makes this approach difficult in practice.

NOTES

This paper is based on work carried out under the aegis of the Trade Policy Research Centre. Publication has been delayed as a consequence of the Centre's reorganisation.

1 While export subsidies can be expected to have this effect in a competitive market structure, and indeed it may have been the intention of the framers of this test to use it to discriminate between export subsidies and other subsidies, export subsidies may not result in dual pricing when producers have some monopolistic discretion regarding the prices they charge. Indeed the threat of countervailing action in the presence of dual pricing would provide an incentive to producers not to price in that way.

2 The relevant Article refers to 'bounty or subsidy determined to have been granted, directly or indirectly, on the manufacture, production or export of such product in the country of origin or exportation, including any special subsidy to the transportation of a particular product' (Article VI:3).

3 Export stabilisation schemes for primary products are not deemed to be subsidies that can trigger countervailing actions or to result in 'more than an equitable share of world share' as long as export prices on occasion rise higher than domestic prices (Articles VI: 7 and XVI: 3, Ad).

4 This exemption from the injury test applies only with regard to products which are dutiable on import to the United States. Thus it does not apply to imports that enter duty-free: for countervailing duties to be applied against subsidised exports entering duty-free, injury has to be established (Jackson, 1989, p. 259). Also, the exemption does not apply to a small number of countries with which the US has trade agreements that provide for most-favoured-nation treatment.

5 It refers to 'certain primary products' and, unlike the GATT itself, excludes minerals from these. Neither the Articles of the GATT nor the Codes cover services, with the exception of films for the cinema.

6 In short, the list covers direct subsidies on exports, bonuses for exporting through currency retention schemes, reduced freight charges for exports, cheap inputs supplied by governments for use in exports, reduction or remission of *direct* taxes with regard to exports, excessive remission of indirect taxes (and import charges) on the products exported or any exemption or remission of indirect taxes and import charges on inputs into exports unless the inputs are physically incorporated into the export product, guarantees on export credits or insurance at premium rates that are 'manifestly

inadequate' to cover the long-term costs of the program, subsidised export credits, and any other charge on the public account having similar effects. The Code list is not intended to be exhaustive: other practices may be deemed to be export subsidies. It will be noted that the destination principle for taxation is adopted for indirect taxes (but only partly for indirect taxes on inputs) but not for direct taxes.

7 It is reported that Chile ceased to initiate countervailing duty actions following threats of retaliation (Finger and Nogués, 1987, p. 713n.).

REFERENCES

Barcelo, J. J. III (1977), 'Subsidies and Countervailing Duties – Analysis and a Proposal', *Law and Policy in International Business*, 9, 3, 779–853.

Barcelo, J. III (1984), 'An Injury-Only Regime (For Imports) and Actionable Subsidies', in Don Wallace Jr, Frank J. Loftus and Van Z. Krikorian, eds. 19–27.

Beseler, J. F. and A. N. Williams (1986), *Anti-Dumping and Anti-Subsidy Law: The European Communities* (Sweet and Maxwell and ICC, London).

Bhagwati, J. N. and D. A. Irwin (1987), 'The Return of the Reciprocitarians – US Trade Policy Today', *The World Economy*, 10, 2 (June), 109–130.

Conybeare, J. A. C. (1987), *Trade Wars: The Theory and Practice of International Commercial Rivalry* (Columbia University Press, New York).

Corden, W. M. (1974), *Trade Policy and Economic Welfare* (Oxford University Press, London).

Corden, W. M. (1983), 'Towards a Policy Synthesis: Panel Discussion 3', in William R. Cline, ed., *Trade Policy in the 1980s* (Institute for International Economics, Washington D.C., distributed by MIT Press), 739–46.

Corden, W. M. (1987), 'On Making Rules for the International Trading System', in Robert M. Stern, ed., *U.S. Trade Policies in a Changing World Economy* (MIT Press, Cambridge, Mass), 413–26.

Corden, W. M. (1990), 'Strategic Trade Policy: How New? How Sensible?', Country Economics Department, World Bank, Policy, Research and External Affairs Working Papers WPS 396 (April).

Dam, K. W. (1970), *The GATT: Law and International Economic Organization* (University of Chicago Press, Chicago and London).

Finger, J. M. (1987), 'Antidumping and Antisubsidy Measures', in J. Michael Finger and Andrzej Olechowski, eds, 153–61.

Finger, J. M. and J. Nogués (1987), 'International Control of Subsidies and Countervailing Duties', *The World Bank Economic REview*, 1, 4 (September), 707–25.

Finger, J. M. and A. Olechowski, eds. (1987), *The Uruguay Round: A Handbook on the Multilateral Trade Negotiations* (The World Bank, Washington D.C.).

Fitzgerald, B. and T. Monson (1989), 'Preferential Credit and Insurance as Means to Promote Exports', *The World Bank Research Observer*, 4, 1 (January), 89–114.

Hathaway, D. E. (1987), *Agriculture and the GATT: Rewriting the Rules* (Institute for International Economics, Policy Analysis in International Economics, No. 20, September, Washington D.C.).

Helpman, E. and P. R. Krugman (1985), *Market Structure and Foreign Trade: Increasing Returns, Imperfect Competition, and the International Economy* (MIT Press, Cambridge Mass.).

Helpman, E. and P. R. Krugman (1989), *Trade Policy and Market Structure* (MIT Press, Cambridge Mass.).

Hufbauer, G. C. and J. Shelton Erb (1984), *Subsidies in International Trade* (Institute for International Economics, Washington D.C.: Distributed by MIT Press).

Hufbauer, G. C., J. Shelton Erb and H. P. Starr (1980), 'The GATT Codes and the Unconditional Most-Favored-Nation Principle', *Law and Policy in International Business*, 12, 1, 59–93.

Jackson, J. H. (1969), *World Trade and the Law of GATT* (The Mitchie Company, Charlottesville, Va.).

Jackson, J. H. (1989), *The World Trading System: Law and Policy of International Economic Relations* (The MIT Press, Cambridge Mass.).

Jackson, J. H., J.-V. Louis and M. Matsushita (1984), *Implementing the Tokyo Round: National Constitutions and International Economic Rules* (The University of Michigan Press, Ann Arbor).

Krugman, P. R. (ed.) (1987), *Strategic Trade Policies and the New International Economics* (MIT Press, Cambridge Mass.).

Messerlin, P. A. (1986), 'Public Subsidies to Industry and Agriculture and Countervailing Duties' (Processed, The World Bank, Washington D.C.).

Mundheim, R. H. and P. D. Ehrenhaft (1984), 'What is a "Subsidy?" A Discussion Paper', in Don Wallace Jr., Frank J. Loftus, and Van Z. Krikorian, eds., 95–107.

Nam, C.-H. (1987), 'Export-Promoting Subsidies, Countervailing Threats, and the General Agreement on Tariffs and Trade', *The World Bank Economic Review*, 1, 4, 727–43.

OECD (1987), *National Policies and Agricultural Trade* (Organisation for Economic Co-Operation and Development, Paris).

Snape, R. H. (1986), 'The Impact on Exporters of Import Restrictions', in K. Tucker and C. Baden Fuller, eds, *Firms and Markets: Essays in Honour of Brazil Yamey* (Croom Helm, London and Sydney), 201–24.

Snape, R. H. (1987), 'The Importance of Frontier Barriers', in Henryk Kierzkowski, ed., *Protection and Competition in International Trade: Essays in Honor of W. M. Corden* (Basil Blackwell, London), 215–32.

Snape, R. H. (1988), 'Is Non-Discrimination Really Dead?' *The World Economy* 11, 1 (March), 1-17.

Stern, R. M. and B. Hoekman (1987), 'The Codes Approach', in Finger and Olechowski, eds., 59–66.

Stern, R. M., J. H. Jackson and B. Hoekman (1986), 'An Assessment of the Implementation and Operation of the Tokyo Round Codes' (Research Seminar in International Economics, University of Michigan, Seminar Discussion Paper No. 174, Ann Arbor, Mi.).

Teese, C. F. (1982), 'A View from the Dress Circle in the Theatre of Trade Disputes', *The World Economy*, 5, 1 (March), 43–59.

Tumlir, J. (1985), *Protectionism: Trade Policies in Democratic Societies* (American Enterprise Institute for Public Policy Research, Washington D.C.).

Wallace, D. Jr., F. J. Lofthus and V. Z. Kirkorian, eds (1984), *Interface Three: Legal Treatment of Domestic Subsidies* (The International Law Institute, Washington D.C.).

Winham, G. R. (1986), *International Trade and the Tokyo Round Negotiation* (Princeton University Press, Princeton N.J.).

13. History and Economics of GATT's Article XXIV

R. H. Snape

Article XXIV is an 'exceptions' article of the GATT, the exceptions being to the unconditional most-favored-nation (MFN) provision of Article I. In order to assess the economics of the exceptions which Article XXIV provides it is necessary to address the role of unconditional MFN.

Approaching trade policy in terms of maximizing income in a multicountry world, subject to the constraint of protecting some industries, has led many economists to criticize the application of the principle of MFN. Starting from the position in which a country has frontier barriers (as there have to be for a consideration of MFN), Harry Johnson argued that the theory of the second best, whether applied nationally or to the world as a whole, does not lead to the equal treatment of all foreign sources of supply. The principle of non-discrimination

> has absolutely nothing to recommend it on the grounds of either economic theory or the realities of international commercial diplomacy. . . . The speciousness of the principle of non-discrimination is only exceeded by the irrationality of permitting nothing less than 100 per cent discrimination in the case of customs unions and free trade areas. (Johnson, 1976, p. 30)

But he then goes on to say

> the principle has an important point and function, which can be loosely and inaccurately stated as the principle that if you pay your membership dues to a club you are entitled to decent treatment as one of the paid-up members,

and, on the basis that it is the best principle we have, argues that

> it seems the wiser course not to devise further exceptions to the principle, or re-write it, but instead to improve the framework of international economic relations within which countries receive non-discriminatory most-favoured-nation treatment. (pp. 30–1)

This chapter takes the position that it is only through the systemic and 'club' approach that one can make economic sense of the GATT principle of unconditional MFN and of the Article XXIV exceptions. Without taking into account what appear to be the motivations of governments in the implementation of their trade policies, one cannot address the question of a set of rules for a desirable co-operative outcome.

There is little evidence that national trading policies vis-à-vis other countries, jointly or severally, are related to 'optimum tariff' criteria. (OPEC may be an exception. However, a good deal of national trade activity is directed to achieving worse rather than better terms of trade, for example by persuading foreign exporters to restrain their exports.) Modeling the effects of trade blocs based on the assumption that each bloc attempts to apply the optimum tariff against the others (e.g., Krugman, 1991a) cannot be expected to shed much light on the effects of the number of trade blocs in the world on world income – as Krugman himself warns in introducing such a model. And the strategic trade literature policy propositions are so sensitive to assumptions that it would be almost impossible to apply them properly even if governments attempted to do so, although some governments' policies appear to be dressed in these clothes. Thus rather than consider the establishment of a set of rules which would just curb the tendency of each country to exercise its market power to the detriment of the system as a whole, we need to consider a framework in which national governments, unconstrained by international commitments, often take actions which appear to be contrary to their own national economic interests.

12.1 THE MOST-FAVORED-NATION CLAUSE

Most-favored-nation (MFN) clauses apparently have at least a seven-hundred-year history in trade agreements (Jackson, 1989, p. 133), but it is in the last two hundred of these years that they have been particularly important. MFN clauses in bilateral (or plurilateral) agreements assure each party that, if the other parties to their treaty enter into any other agreements with third parties which provide more favorable treatment for the exports of those third parties, these more favorable conditions will be extended to the parties to the first agreement: that is, no other countries will be treated more favorably.

Throughout Europe in the nineteenth and early twentieth centuries MFN clauses provided that these benefits should be extended unconditionally, or were interpreted in this manner; hence unconditional MFN. The United States, on the other hand, attempted until 1922 to apply the clause conditionally. (For example, concessions judged to be equivalent to those given by Belgium to the US had to be given by France to the US for France to receive the same benefits from the US as did Belgium.) Viner (1924, p. 18) reports that conditional MFN appeared in treaties of Latin American countries and Japan, and of a number of European countries between 1820 and 1860, but that conditionality seldom appeared to have been applied in practice by countries other than the United States.[1]

Of course conditional and unconditional MFN do not sit well together. A third party which has a conditional agreement with one country and an unconditional agreement with another cannot satisfy the terms of both. The situation is made worse when a country, as did the United States in the latter nineteenth century, insists on receiving unconditional MFN treatment from its trading partners while it extends only conditional treatment to them. It is not surprising that Viner judged the conditional form to have brought to the United States:

> more variations in construction, more international ill-feeling, more conflict between international obligations and municipal law, and between judicial interpretation and executive practice, more confusion and uncertainty of operation, than have developed under all the unconditional most-favored-nation pledges of all the other countries combined. (Viner, 1924, p. 25.)

While nineteenth-century Europe saw a great number of bilateral trade treaties which incorporated MFN provisions, Viner (1950, p. 14) argues that it was the MFN *principle* rather than MFN *pledges* 'that constituted the important barrier to preferential tariff arrangements in the past'. In other words, it was the interpretation of the clauses that mattered.

Following the Cobden-Chevalier Treaty in 1860, liberalizing bilateral trade agreements with unconditional MFN at their cores spread throughout Europe (United States Tariff Commission, 1919, p. 395; Irwin, 1992). While there was some retreat from liberality after 1870, it is difficult to believe that such liberal trading conditions could have spread in continental Europe under conditional rather than unconditional MFN clauses – and certainly they could not have done so under a hub-and-spoke system of trade agreements with no provisions for relating the benefits of one agreement to those of others, even if Britain had been at the hub. Intent on discriminating against Germany in particular, France embraced conditional MFN in 1922, but reverted to unconditional MFN so as to obtain access to German markets in 1927 (Tumlir, 1985, p. 24; Pomfret, 1988, p. 23).

Accepting the recommendations of its Tariff Commission (United States Tariff Commission, 1919), in 1922 the US abandoned the unconditional interpretation. Following the passage of the Smoot-Hawley tariff in 1930 and then in Reciprocal Trade Negotiations Act of 1934, the US concluded bilateral trade pacts with 28 countries over the decade from the mid-1930s. (League of Nations, 1945, p. 18). These treaties incorporated unconditional coverage, so as to minimize free riding. Since the inception of the GATT no bilateral treaty negotiated by the US has incorporated MFN clause, conditional or unconditional.

The major innovation of the GATT was to incorporate unconditional MFN into a multilateral framework. Article I requires that no contracting party can treat the trade of any other *country*[2] (whether it is or is not a contracting party to the GATT) more favorably than any other GATT contracting party: any concession which is given to any country must be passed on immediately and unconditionally to all contracting parties. The obverse of this multilateral unconditional MFN rule is that there can be no discrimination *against* any contracting party to the GATT by any other contracting party, though of course there can be discrimination against countries which are not contracting parties. The fundamental rule is one of equal treatment of members, though not of course of equal treatment of all the products traded by the members. This guarantee against discrimination has been critical in preventing discriminatory application of Article XIX safeguard actions against 'fair' trade, and provides an incentive for joining the GATT.

Multilateral unconditional MFN under GATT has not driven unconditional MFN completely out of bilateral trade agreements. Thus the bilateral Closer Economic Relations Agreement between Australia and New Zealand provides that neither country can have tariffs against the other in excess of those applied to any other country (except for developing country preferences) and that each accords the other MFN treatment with respect to services trade (Article 4.9 and 4.10 of the 1983 Agreement and Article 6 of the Protocol on Trade in Services of 1988). On the other hand, there is no such clause in the Canada–United States Free Trade Agreement, or in the free trade agreement between the United States and Israel. With respect to the Canada–US negotiations, Wonnacott (1991, p. 81) reports that Canada sought to ensure that Canada would 'automatically receive any benefits that the United States might extend to any other country such as Mexico'. The US refused. The draft North American Free Trade Agreement (NAFTA) circulated in September 1992 contains no MFN provision for goods but does for services 'in like circumstances', a term which perhaps could take a conditional MFN interpretation. Of course a truly free trade agreement would provide no opportunity for additional benefits to be extended to non-member countries.

The advantages and disadvantages of unconditional MFN have been examined many times. Prior to World War II, the question of conditional and unconditional MFN was argued largely in the context of bilateral treaties. Since the formation of the GATT it has moved much more into a plurilateral or multilateral context. In asking whether it has outlived its usefulness, Hufbauer (1986) groups the arguments for unconditional MFN into political (international), preservation of the balance of the bargain, economic efficiency, and guardian of multilateral trade. The first of these, the international political aspect, lay behind the incorporation of unconditional MFN in Woodrow Wilson's Fourteen Points for peace and post-war international order, enunciated in 1918, and was much emphasized by Cordell Hull and his followers.

Regarding maintenance of the balance of the bargain, the incorporation of an unconditional MFN clause into trade treaties provides an insurance against the erosion of benefits which have been paid for by so-called concessions. These concessions can be regarded as 'paying' not just for immediate benefits but for benefits in the future, including the unconditional receipt of favors which trading partners extend to others. A classic statement of the other side of this position – that is, against securing greater benefit than has been paid for – is that of John Jay in 1787 (cited in Viner, 1924, p. 19):

> It would certainly be inconsistent with the most obvious principles of justice and fair construction, that because France purchases, at a great price, a privilege of the United States, that therefore the Dutch shall immediately insist, not on having the like privileges at the like price, but without any price at all.

Haufbauer (1986, pp. 37–8) suggests that, in a world in which competitive conditions are changing rapidly, preservation of the bargain considerations are downgraded in comparing conditional and unconditional MFN. It is difficult to press this very far; many countries were concerned with discrimination implicit in the Canada–US Trade Free Agreement, and desire to preserve its bargain in that agreement drove Canada to join in the negotiations with the US and Mexico for the North American Free Trade Agreement.

As regards efficiency, the quote from Harry Johnson at the beginning of this chapter warns us to tread carefully. The income-maximizing structure of tariffs, subject to the constraint of retaining protective tariffs, will depend on the objectives of the protection, the extent to which terms of trade with each trading partner can be affected, and the negotiating bargains which can be secured with each country. It is unlikely that equality of tariff (and other trade measures) treatment for each trade partner would be the most efficient outcome from this calculus.

But there are at least two other ingredients in considering efficiency. One is that the form of protection and the ability to discriminate between trading partners is likely to affect the supply of and demand for protection in the country imposing the protection; that is, the supposed objectives of governments with respect to trade policy are endogenous. The possibility of discrimination may lead to the selective raising, rather than lowering, of trade barriers. Second, and not independent of the first point, is the effect on other countries' policies, whether these policies are discriminatory or not, and whether or not the policies are retaliatory. The efficiency question thus leads inevitably to the fourth category listed by Hufbauer: guardian of multilateral trade. Thus we consider the two together.

There are basically two opposing views of discrimination in the context of multilateral liberalization. Both are set in the context of domestic protectionist pressures on governments. One is that preferential discrimination permits countries to liberalize further than otherwise, by engaging in reciprocal reduction of barriers in agreement with like-minded countries. The other is that discrimination permits governments to raise, selectively, barriers against 'troublesome' exporting countries – and thus to bow to domestic protectionist pressures – in a manner in which they could not if the barriers had to be raised against all exporters, friends as well as foes.

A leading advocate of the latter view was Jan Tumlir. Tumlir (1985) argued strongly that unconditional MFN provides a firm constraint on protection. He saw the possibility of discrimination among sources as weakening a government's resolve to resist protectionist pressures, and pointed out that some forms of protection which have been growing even as tariffs have been falling over the last two or three decades (for example, country-specific import quotas and voluntary export restraints) could not be imposed in a system that was really non-discriminatory. Strong implementation of unconditional MFN would have prevented them.

On the other hand, Irwin (1992, pp. 23–4) emphasizes the futility and perhaps counter-productivity[3] of the various international conferences, many under the auspices of the League of Nations, which attempted to reinstate unconditional MFN multilaterally in Europe in the inter-war period, when economic (and political) instability had led to direct controls of international trade. Those who negotiated the post-World War II international economic institutions took economic stabilization as a sine qua non of trade liberalization, and subsequent events suggest they were correct. Unconditional MFN is only likely to constrain protectionist forces if the underlying economic conditions are relatively stable.

While it is often argued against Tumlir's position that unconditional MFN does not guarantee the development of a liberal, multilateral trading system, unconditional MFN does ensure that any liberalization is spread to other countries, providing the environment is appropriate. The liberal system in Europe started to be eroded from the early 1870s, despite unconditional MFN. French protectionists were able to claim that the Cobden-Chevalier Treaty, with its unconditional MFN provisions, was initially imposed undemocratically (by Napoleon III) and that the same provision was later part of a peace treaty imposed on them by Prussian victors in 1871 (Tumlir, 1985, p. 23). If governments wish to circumvent the constraints of unconditional MFN they can do so by multiplying tariff classifications, by not renewing bilateral treaties as they expire, or by providing notice of withdrawal under the terms of the treaties (Pomfret, 1988, p. 18). But all these actions have costs; unconditional MFN can impose a constraint.

A position opposed to that of Tumlir is presented by those who argue that unconditional MFN is a drag on trade liberalization by encouraging free riding and foot-dragging. The possibility of free riding, it is argued, discourages negotiation and curbs the selection of products to be covered. Foot-dragging from those who already benefit from unconditional MFN provisions, and who hope to secure benefits without paying the price, causes some countries not to negotiate at all, when conditionality could have brought them to the table. Conditional MFN and the discrimination implied by it then could facilitate more rapid liberalization.

It appears to me that comments on free riding and foot-dragging frequently tend to focus on the proximate and ignore the whole. It is difficult to envisage a world of criss-crossing, bilaterally negotiated, conditional MFN agreements, each designed to discourage free riding and foot-dragging and each therefore with limited coverage, leading to a stable and harmonious trading system, or even one with the degree of harmony and stability produced by that which we have. We return to this question in Section 12.4 below.

12.2 MFN AND CUSTOMS UNIONS

Under the bilateral trade agreements which proliferated in Europe and elsewhere in the nineteenth and early twentieth centuries, exceptions to the unconditional MFN rule and practice were allowed for customs unions, imperial preferences and limited 'regional' agreements. While Britain maintained that an explicit exception was required to exempt customs unions from MFN legitimately (Viner, 1950, p. 12), other countries were not so demanding. What was generally required, however, was that the customs unions be 'complete', on which more later. Imperial preferences within a common sovereignty were generally accepted, but preferences between autonomous countries of the British Commonwealth were not regarded (except by the participants) as reasonable exceptions (Viner, 1950, p. 16). US hostility to these British preferences in the negotiations which led to the GATT was intense (Gardner, 1980).

Bilateral agreements frequently provided for exemptions from MFN for countries which had close affinity or which were contiguous, but these exemptions were minor in practice, at least until after World War I. The British government, having participated in the substantial extension of preferences at the Ottawa Conference in 1932 and justified such exemption from unconditional MFN on the basis of historical association, then argued that preferential arrangements based on any other criterion were unacceptable (Viner, 1950, pp. 19–21).

The conditions which Viner saw as necessary for a perfect or complete customs union were complete elimination of tariffs between partners, a common external tariff schedule, and the sharing of customs revenue according to an agreed formula (Viner, 1950, p. 5). These criteria in fact were specified by Cavour[4] in arguing the case for Sardinia against Austria: both Prussia (on behalf of the Zollverein) and Sardinia objected to an 1857 treaty between Austria and Modena in that it compromised MFN without being a 'complete' customs union (Viner, 1950, pp. 7–9). Customs unions were acceptable because a unified customs jurisdiction was being formed;[5] such unions always had political implications and on some occasions (for example, the Zollverein) led to political union.

It is most unlikely that the formation of a federation, or the political integration of two previously separate countries, would be objected to on the basis that the new trade 'bloc' would infringe unconditional MFN or inhibit the flow of intentional trade. It is in the light of an extension of a unified customs jurisdiction and the systemic implications of this that the traditional 'exception' for a customs union can be viewed.

There is a clear distinction here between a customs union and, say, a free trade area. A free trade area does not involve the loss of an autonomous customs territory. But we should note the importance of the customs union being 'complete': without this the systemic effect of losing one or more customs territories essentially does not apply.

12.3 CUSTOMS UNIONS AND ARTICLE XXIV

With this background one can readily see why in multilateralizing unconditional MFN in the GATT, customs unions were proposed as exceptions and why, until the last moment, free trade areas were not.[6] It may be noted that Article XXIV throughout refers to customs territories and that each 'customs territory shall, exclusively for the purpose of this Agreement, be treated as though it were a contracting party' (Article XXIV, 1),[7] and that a customs territory shall be understood to mean 'territory with respect to which separate tariffs . . . [etc.] are maintained for a substantial part of the trade of such territory with other territories' (Article XXIV, 2).

On the other hand, the form in which the customs union exception is expressed and the inclusion of free trade areas indicate that the traditional concept and basis for excepting customs unions were significantly bent by the time the form of the GATT was agreed. That is, the formation of a single customs territory was no longer the major criterion for exemption from unconditional MFN. We may note that Article XXIV would not exist but for MFN being unconditional in Article I; conditional MFN would not have led to the demand for such exceptions, as preferences would have been unconstrained.

The dispute between the US and Britain regarding preferences when the GATT was being negotiated is well known, as is its resolution: existing preferences were grandfathered and beyond them Article XXIV applies. Preferences were opposed, but customs unions were favored by the United States, and the American Proposals for the Charter for the International Trade Organization (ITO) provided for customs unions (Wilcox, 1949, pp. 70–1). It was only at Havana that the Article was extended to embrace free trade areas, curiously on the motion of Lebanon and Syria.[8] It appears that the title 'free trade area' as a technical name for the trade agreement with which we associate the term may have been invented in the Havana negotiations.

It can be maintained that 'if any one person can be described as the originator of the movement for an International Trade Organization it is James Meade' (Penrose, 1953, pp. 89–90). Meade's 1942 proposal for a Commercial Union generally followed the non-discriminatory prescription of Article VII of the Mutual Aid Agreement, finally agreed earlier that year after eight months of negotiations. However, Meade did provide for an exception to unconditional MFN, not for customs unions or free trade areas but for 'preferences up to a maximum of, say, 10 per cent to the produce of another state with which it formed a special recognised geographical or political union' (Meade, 1942, para. 13). He did not address the question of 'complete' customs unions, though in view of the history of such unions as exceptions he possibly took them for granted. Meade's modest exception did not see its way through to the US Proposals which formed the basis of negotiations for the ITO.

Comparing the original US Proposals of September 1946 for an ITO, as they related to customs unions, etc., with the provisions which were finally settled in the Charter negotiated in Havana between November 1947 and March 1948, there were the following significant differences (Viner, 1950, pp. 111ff).

1. There was no preamble regarding desirability. (In the Havana Charter this appeared as 'Members recognize the desirability of increasing freedom of trade by the development, through voluntary agreements, of closer integration between the economies of the countries parties to such agreements'.)[9]
2. Free trade areas were not mentioned.
3. There was no provision for interim arrangements leading to customs unions.
4. In defining the external barrier structure of a customs union, the words 'average level' rather than 'general incidence' were used for the level, which 'shall not be higher or more restrictive' after the union than before.
5. Trade barriers had to be reduced on substantially all trade between all constituent territories; in the Havana Charter the words 'or at least with respect to substantially all the trade in products originating in the constituent territories' were added.
6. There were no provisions for retaining barriers between participants for balance of payments, agricultural stabilization, health and similar purposes.
7. There were no specific provisions for waiving the constraints on the formation of customs unions. At Havana, provision for such waiving of the main requirements was introduced 'provided that the proposals lead to the formation

of a customs union or free-trade area in the sense of this Article [Article XXIV of GATT], and if approved by two-thirds of the members of the ITO.

8. Unlike the initial US Proposals, the Havana Charter allowed for preferential arrangements (limited to not more than 15 years) in special circumstances[10] between territories which were contiguous or in the same economic region. The approval of two-thirds of the members of the ITO was required. The agreements had to be open to other 'qualifying' parties.

With the exception of (8) in the above list, all the additions were carried from the Havana Charter into the GATT.

Generally regretting the concessions to discrimination, Viner (1950, p. 127) writes:

> The provisions of the Charter with respect to customs unions, free-trade areas and new regional agreements, *taken by themselves*, do constitute what is on paper at least an appreciable removal of pre-existing barriers to official discrimination in trade barriers, and it is significant that many of these provisions are written in terms of hearty encouragement rather than of regrettable departure from an ideal made necessary by special circumstances or by the less-than-universal acceptance of the ideal.

Earlier on the same page he refers to the 'odor of sanctity' given to practices which, 'whether widely practiced or not, were hitherto not in good repute'. But immediately he says:

> It should be conceded, however, that much can be said in support of the preferability of a code, even if imperfect, enforced by the possibility of unilateral national retaliation.

12.4 THE ECONOMICS OF ARTICLE XXIV

The general thrust had been shifted from customs unions being an exception allowed by the territorial application of common customs legislation, to the modes by which liberal trade might be facilitated within a multilateral agreement. Much of the economic analysis of customs unions and free trade areas has been in terms of the resource allocation implications of specific preferential arrangements – Viner's trade creation, diversion and suppression frequently being the starting point. But for the multilateral process of liberalization for which the founders of the GATT hoped, and which to a significant extent has been achieved, the main economic consequences are to be found in the economics of the process as a whole rather than in the resource allocation effects of any particular agreement. Of course if each agreement has beneficial resource allocation effects as well as contributing to a beneficial process, so much the better. As suggested at the outset of the chapter, to illuminate the process element, a brief consideration of the economics of clubs is helpful.[11]

Clubs are formed between those who wish to share in the benefits of impure or excludable public goods, recognizing that a voluntary cooperative arrangement in the area of interest will be superior to unilateral action. In some cases the club will be formed to reinforce resolve to do what one knows is good for oneself (Alcoholics Anonymous). The GATT club comprises members who recognize that by making commitments to each other they constrain the actions of others against them and also constrain their own actions, and create a system that itself yields benefits – a public good. The entrance fee is the constraint on one's own actions, a fee that in itself may be regarded as a political cost but an economic benefit in many countries.

In clubs the questions arise as to how broad the coverage of the rules should be, whether there should be special provisions for certain classes of members, whether higher fees can purchase additional benefits, whether the membership is open or closed and, if open, whether new members will be admitted o the same conditions as the old, how much the basic rules should be bent in order to retain members (particularly important ones), how to enforce the rules, and whether there might be a network of clubs with similar but differentiated purposes with partially overlapping membership. All these questions arise with respect to the GATT club.

The objectives of GATT as stated in the Preamble to the Agreement are the raising of income, ensuring full employment, developing full use of resources, and increasing the production and exchange of goods; the means are the liberalization of trade and elimination of discrimination. Equality of treatment of members thus was regarded as a key element of club membership and the natural complement to liberalization.

As noted above, GATT club membership is defined in terms of customs territories rather than countries, so complete customs unions are not to be considered 'exceptions' from equality of treatment. The main relevant exceptions to the basic non-discrimination rule of the club then are incomplete customs unions, all free trade areas. Were these exceptions necessary to create a club membership large or important enough to generate the public good associated with the establishment of the club? Do they damage the real purpose of the club and reduce the production of the public good significantly?

The answer to the first of these questions probably is yes. The GATT is not of course just an economic agreement – it is 'an international legal document whose primary purpose is to promote or protect certain political goals of nation-states' (Baldwin, 1980, p. 138). Even before the negotiation of the ITO there were those who looked to some form of European economic integration as a political (rather than economic)[12] necessity. While the Treaty of Rome rode fairly roughshod over Article XXIV (see Dam, 1970, Chapter 16; Jackson, 1969, Chapter 24), had the Article provided only for 'complete' customs union and for no (or short) phasing-in, the Treaty would have done even more harm: it is doubtful that the GATT had much influence on the form of the Treaty. If there had been an effective enforcement mechanism in the GATT so that Article XXIV had been applied strictly, the EC-6 almost certainly would have left GATT, probably with the support of the US. Thus the exceptions (and slack enforcement) protected the club.

The second of these questions – whether the exceptions damage the real purpose of the club and reduce the production of the public good significantly – addresses the question of how important non-discrimination really is for the achievement of liberalization. It was introduced in Section 12.1 above in outlining the two sides of the unconditional/conditional MFN debate. On the one side there is the view expressed forcefully by Tumlir and others that allowing discrimination (conditional MFN or preferences) facilitates the raising of trade barriers; on the other side is the view that allowing discrimination permits negotiation of more barrier reduction.[13]

The exceptions in practice extend well beyond reasonable interpretations of Article XXIV. The Director General of GATT reports that the Working Party established to examine the Canada–US Free Trade Agreement, which was not able to reach a unanimous conclusion as to the consistency of this agreement with the provisions of Article XXIV, 'was the latest in a series of more than fifty working parties on . . . customs unions or free trade areas which have not reached definitive conclusions on the compatibility of these agreements with the GATT' (GATT, 1992, p. 20). Furthermore, under the Enabling Clause[14] negotiated in the Tokyo Round of multilateral trade negotiations, developing countries can do more or less whatever they want to do with respect to preferences for each other, unconstrained by Articles I and XXIV.

What Article XXIV still does, however, is to constrain the granting of preferences (apart from those between and for developing countries) to what at least purport to be free trade areas or customs unions, and this does appear to have a restraining influence. One might note the recent attempt by the countries of the Mercosur agreement (Argentina, Brazil, Paraguay and Uruguay) to bring this agreement to GATT under the Enabling Clause, and the insistence by the US in particular that it be examined under the provisions of Article XXIV (*Financial Times*, July 14, 1992; GATT, 1992, p. 20). Governments also do appear generally to adhere to the provisions restricting the increase in trade barriers upon the formation of preferential arrangements, though the methods by which average trade barriers are to be calculated have been much in dispute.[15]

Does (or would) Tumlir's point that discrimination is the enemy of progressive liberalization still apply when the raising of barriers against third parties is proscribed and that proscription is generally adhered to? It is difficult to sustain his argument when it is interpreted narrowly, though he does make a telling point that discriminatory non-tariff barriers have flourished even as (non-discriminatory) tariffs have been reduced. But his argument gains more substance when it is considered in the context of the development of a system. The main worry is that the less demanding are the constraints on preferences, the more preferential arrangements will develop. Each government on its own may satisfy Vinerian-type criteria for improved resource allocation, but each can lead to resistance by governments to further liberalization as existing preferences are defended,[16] each tends to make further negotiation with other parties more difficult, each tends to lead to new rules of origin[17] and dispute-settlement procedures, and each is likely to lessen the system's resistance to further implicit discrimination against some countries – a development that can easily lead to explicit discrimination. Krugman (1991b, p. 56) makes the point sharply: 'the great political advantage [to European and North Americans] of regional pacts is that they can exclude Japan'.

Viewed from this perspective, the economics of Article XXIV really concerns the public good produced by the club and the damage which discrimination can do to its production. The rules of Article XXIV attempt to limit discrimination by imposing a high (political) cost on it: strictly interpreted, they would only allow it when the parties are really serious about favoring each other (free trade among the partners for most products) and when external barriers are not raised. The high political cost of establishing such preferential arrangements acts as a deterrent to their formation. However, interpretation of Article XXIV has lowered this cost for all countries, while the Enabling Clause has reduced the cost for developing countries even further. The plethora of pseudo-free trade agreements now being implemented or proposed, and the threat which they provide to an efficient, liberalizing, multilateral system, suggest that the cost may now be too low.

To help to ensure that clubs within the GATT club were facilitating the achievement of GATT's overall objectives, one could suggest an accession clause requiring openness to new members on conditions similar to those required of the existing members (Bhagwati, 1991, p. 77; Snape *et al.*, 1992, Chapter 6).[18] But *pace* Tumlir and Krugman, if a purpose of at least some of the actual or proposed discriminatory trading arrangements of some of the major trading powers is to discriminate against particular countries, this suggestion is not likely to gain much favor where it matters.

Until one of the major trading groups of the world decides to press for adherence to the existing rules, the utility of introducing additional constraints into Article XXIV appears limited. There was no provision for accession in the Canada–US Free Trade Agreement, and the accession clause in the proposed NAFTA is very tight. Thus, the scope for a binding 'openness' requirement for preferential arrangements under the GATT appears remote.

12.5 SUMMARY

While non-discrimination among countries, or unconditional MFN, does not guarantee a liberal multilateral trading system, it still appears to be the best general principle on which to build a plurilateral or multilateral trading framework. In the nineteenth century in Europe, bilateral treaties with unconditional MFN clauses brought an era of widespread trade liberalization. Again, in the decade following 1934, and on the initiate of the US, bilateral treaties with a similar clause helped reverse the wholesale raising of trade barriers associated with the Great Depression. From the introduction of GATT in 1947, unconditional MFN within the GATT club was at the heart of the multilateral liberalization of international trade which occurred in the following decades.

A traditional exception to unconditional MFN has been for 'complete' customs unions, and effectively GATT's rules are written for customs territories rather than countries. While the initial US Proposals which led to the formation of the GATT allowed only for this exception, by the time the GATT was implemented in 1947 the relevant exceptions article (Article XXIV) had grown to include 'incomplete' customs unions and free trade areas, and interim arrangements designed to lead to free trade areas and customs unions. The enforcement of the rules constraining these exceptions has been very lax, while preferences for and among developing countries have been virtually removed from constraints.

The economics of Article XXIV are best looked at in terms of a process of developing a liberalizing trading system, or club, rather than in terms of the resource allocation implications of particular preferential agreements considered on their own. The objective of the GATT club is to provide, through cooperation, a more desirable outcome than is achievable by each country acting independently. The exceptions to non-discrimination allowed in Article XXIV are provided to attract and retain some members that might not otherwise remain in the club. But at the same time the exceptions may adversely affect the degree of liberalization among the club members. The exception rules were constructed so as to discourage all preference schemes less than (almost) full preferences, so as to discourage the proliferation of preferential agreements: the political cost of negotiating preferences thus was deliberately made high. It is argued that an abundance of partial preferential agreements is more likely to damage the development and maintenance of a liberal, multilateral trading system than is a small number of almost complete preferential agreements.

Erosion of the constraints of Article XXIV, together with forms of discrimination which evade or ignore unconditional MFN, is in fact yielding a plethora of regional integration agreements and proposals which threaten the foundations and successes of the GATT. Requiring a liberal accessions clause in free trade area and customs union agreements, as put forward in the GATT-Plus proposals, would ensure that these clubs within the GATT club would further, rather than threaten, the aims of the GATT itself. But this is not likely to find favor among countries which are using the existing arrangements to discriminate implicitly or explicitly against some other countries.

NOTES

Research by the author into the economics of the GATT has been supported, in part, by the Australian Research Council.

1 See also United States Tariff Commission (1919, pp. 393ff). The attitude of the United States in practice is shown in the following quotation from p. 41 of the US Tariff Commission Report: The experience of the United States in meeting the claim of Switzerland in 1898 affords an excellent example of the impossibility of the practice of entering into reciprocity agreements with the giving of unconditional most-favored-nation pledges . . . [In] the negotiation of the treaty of 1850 with Switzerland, the American plenipotentiary had pledged the United States to unconditional most-favored-nation treatment. The Government stood by the pledge. Switzerland was therefore given, without compensation, the benefit of concessions made to France . . . [in a treaty in 1897]. Other States at once claimed the right to the same treatment, and it became necessary [sic] to denounce the favored-nation provision in the Swiss treaty.

2 As noted below, 'country' in fact is interpreted as 'customs territory'.

3 Irwin argues that the Ouchy Convention, which was signed in 1932 between the Benelux countries but was open to others, and which agreed to staged tariff reductions of 50 per cent, could have formed the basis for more general trade liberalization. But Britain and other countries insisted that without unconditional MFN extension of the tariff reductions, the convention was unacceptable. 'In the inter-war period . . .

progressive bilateralism – the sole hope for freer trade – was extinguished in the misplaced desire to restore unconditional MFN treatment first' (Irwin, 1992, p. 27).

4 Cavour was Prime Minister of Sardinia and leader with Garibaldi in the unification of Italy. Sardinia, with France, went to war against Austria in 1859.

5 This view is expressed also by Haight (1972, p. 392), a member of the secretariat of the Geneva and Havana conferences which negotiated the charter for the ITO, and of the secretariat of the GATT from 1948 to 1970.

6 We may recall that while we are now accustomed to thinking of a customs union as a possible precursor to and facilitator of closer political association (as in the German Zollverein and the European Economic Community), or at least for the two to occur at the same time (as in the Australian Federation), in earlier days political union tended to precede customs union. Viner writes that 'it was almost a general rule until comparatively recently that the area of political unification was greater than the area of tariff unification' (1950, p. 95). From 1997 it is likely that Hong Kong, Macao and mainland China will provide new examples of the older tradition.

7 This paragraph refers to the 'metropolitan customs territories' of contracting parties and to any other customs territories on behalf of which the Agreement has been signed.

8 The proposal envisaged that the free trade area between countries of the same region, but this restriction was removed by the relevant subcommittee (Haight, 1972, p. 393).

9 Haight (1972, pp. 395–7) writes that this sentence originated from a proposal by France to write into the objectives of the ITO in Article I of the Havana Charter, to facilitate the progressive freeing of trade in increasingly extensive economic zones by promoting . . . between neighbouring countries, or countries which are closely related economically owing to the complementary nature of their economic systems, of economic units wider in character than those resulting from political frontiers. Against objections by the French the wording was changed to that in the text and the sentence was moved to the customs union Article, its location in that Article being determined by a desire not to change the existing paragraph numbering. As Haight says: 'Thus did the word "integration" creep into the GATT, and the desirability of closer economic integration was inscribed – more by accident than design – as the philosophical basis for the formation of customs unions [and free trade areas]'.

10 Not necessarily confined to reconstruction and development, though the conditions appear in an Article under this heading.

11 The book by Cornes and Sandler (1986) is a very useful reference on the theory of clubs.

12 Late in the nineteenth century there were many Europeans who saw it as necessary counter the economic might and threat of the US.

13 This is the process which (taking their position at its face value) the French appeared to be envisaging in seeking to encourage preferential arrangements at the Havana negotiations (see note 9 above). It is also the process envisaged by Kemp and Wan (1976) in their well-known paper.

14 This clause (termed 'Differential and More Favourable Treatment Reciprocity and Fuller Participation of Developing Countries') provides that 'Notwithstanding Article I of the General Agreement, contracting parties may accord differential and more favourable treatment to developing countries, without according such treatment to other countries.' As well as applying to preferences granted by developed countries to developing countries under the generalized system of preferences, they also apply (*inter alia*) to 'regional or global' arrangements among developing countries.

15 The Draft Final Act of the Uruguay Round of multilateral trade negotiations, placed on the table by the Director General of the GATT on December 20, 1991 (the 'Dunkel Draft'), provides that in calculating the before and after incidence of tariffs upon the

formation of customs unions in order to judge that the general incidence against outsiders has not been increased, a weighted average of applied tariffs is to be calculated by the GATT Secretariat. This appears to be a very useful specification. John McMillan (in Chapter 13 of this volume) makes an interesting proposal regarding the calculation of common tariffs, consistent with Kemp and Wan (1976).

16 There have been several cases in which developing countries have objected to proposed reductions of MFN tariffs by developed countries on the grounds that the reductions would erode existing preferences for developing countries.

17 There are 193 pages of rules of origin in the draft NAFTA circulated in September 1992.

18 GATT-Plus proposals have this characteristic and further the liberal, multilateral objectives of the GATT.

REFERENCES

Baldwin, R. E. (1980), 'The Economics of the GATT', in *Issues in International Economics*, edited by P. Oppenheimer, London: Oriel Press. (Reprinted in Baldwin's *Trade Policy in a Changing World Economy*, London: Harvester Wheatsheaf; page references are to the reprinted version.)

Bhagwati, J. N. (1991), *The World Trading System at Risk*, London: Harvester Wheatsheaf.

Cornes, R. and T. Sandler (1986), *The Theory of Externalities, Public Goods and Club Goods*, Cambridge: Cambridge University Press.

Dam, K. W. (1970), *The GATT, Law and International Economic Organization*, Chicago: University of Chicago Press.

Gardner, R. N. (1980), *Sterling-Dollar Diplomacy in Current Perspective: The Origins and Prospects of Our International Economic Order*, New York: Columbia University Press, revised edition.

GATT (1992), *International Trade and the Trading System: Report by the Director General, 1991–1992*, Geneva: GATT Secretariat, May.

Haight, F. A. (1972), 'Customs Unions and Free-Trade Areas under GATT: A Reappraisal', *Journal of World Trade Law* 6: 391–404.

Hufbauer, G. C. (1986), 'Should Unconditional MFN be Revived, Retired or Recast?', in *Issues in World Trade Policy: GATT at the Crossroads*, edited by R. H. Snape, London: Macmillan, and New York: St Martins Press.

Irwin, D. A. (1992), 'Multilateral and Bilateral Trade Policies in the World Trading System: An Historical Perspective', presented at the World Bank/Centre for Economic Policy Research (CEPR) Conference on New Dimensions to Regional Integration, Washington, DC, April 2–3.

Jackson, J. H. (1969), *World Trade and the Law of GATT*, Charlottesville: Michie.

Jackson, J. H. (1989), *The World Trading System: Law and Policy of International Economic Relations*, Cambridge, MA: MIT Press.

Johnson, H. G. (1976), *Trade Negotiations and the New International Monetary System*, Leiden: A. W. Sijthoff, for the Graduate Institute of International Studies, Geneva, and the Trade Policy Research Centre, London.

Kemp, M. C. and H. Y. Wan (1976), 'An Elementary Proposition Concerning the Formation of Customs Unions', *Journal of International Economics* 6: 95–7.

Krugman, P. R. (1991a), 'Is Bilateralism Bad?', in *International Trade and Trade Policy*, edited by E. Helpman and A. Razin, Cambridge, MA: MIT Press.

Krugman, P. R. (1991b), 'Regional Trade Blocs: The Good, the Bad and the Ugly', *The International Economy* 5: 54–6.

League of Nations (1945), *Commercial Policy in the Post-War World*, Report of the Economic and Financial Committees, C.31.M.31.1945.II.A, Geneva: League of Nations.

Meade, J. E. (1942), 'A Proposal for an International Commercial Union', published as an addendum to J. Culbert, 'War-time Anglo-American Talks and the Making of the GATT', *The World Economy* 10: 381–407, December 1987. (Meade's proposal is dated July 25, 1942.)

Penrose, E. F. (1952), *Economic Planning for Peace*, Princeton: Princeton University Press.

Pomfret, R. (1988), *Unequal Trade: The Economics of Discriminatory Trade Policies*, Oxford: Basil Blackwell.

Snape, R. H., J. Adams and D. Morgan (1992). *Regional Trade Agreements, Part I: Implications for Australia* (Report to the Australian Government's Department of Foreign Affairs and Trade), Monash University, Melbourne, June.

Tumlir, J. (1985), *Protectionism: Trade Policy in Democratic Societies*, Washington, DC: American Enterprise Institute.

United States Tariff Commission (1919), *Reciprocity and Commercial Treaties*, Washington, DC: Government Printing Office.

Viner, J. (1924), 'The Most-Favored-Nation Clause in American Commercial Treaties', *Journal of Political Economy* 32: 101–129. (Reprinted in his *International Economics*, Glencoe: The Free Press, 1951; page references are to the reprinted version.)

Viner, J. (1950), *The Customs Union Issue*, New York: Carnegie Endowment for International Peace. (Reprinted by Anderson Kramer Associates, Washington, DC, 1961.)

Wilcox, C. (1949), *A Charter for World Trade*, New York: Macmillan.

Wonnacott, P. and M. Lutz (1989), 'Is there a Case for Free Trade Areas?', in *Free Trade Areas and U.S. Policy*, edited by J. J. Schott, Washington, DC: Institute for International Economics.

Wonnacott, R. J. (1991), 'Canada's Role in the US-Mexican Free Trade Negotiations', *The World Economy* 14: 79–86.

14. Regionalism versus Multilateralism

L. A. Winters

1. INTRODUCTION

THE LITERATURE ON "regionalism vs. multilateralism" is burgeoning as economists and a few political scientists grapple with the question of whether regional integration arrangements (RIAs) are good or bad for the multilateral system as a whole. Are RIAs "building blocks or stumbling blocks," in Bhagwati's (1991) memorable phrase, or stepping stones towards multilateralism? As we worry about the ability of the WTO to maintain the GATT's unsteady yet distinct momentum towards liberalism, and as we contemplate the emergence of world-scale RIAs – the EU, NAFTA, FTAA, APEC and, possibly, TAFTA – this question has never been more pressing.

"Regionalism vs. multilateralism" switches the focus of research from the immediate consequences of regionalism for the economic welfare of the integrating partners to the question of whether it sets up forces which encourage or discourage evolution towards globally freer trade. The answer is "we don't know yet." One can build models that suggest either conclusion but to date these are sufficiently abstract that they should be viewed as parables rather than sources of testable predictions.

Moreover, even if we had testable predictions we have very little evidence. Arguably the European Union is the only RIA that is both big enough to affect the multilateral system and long-enough lived to have currently observable consequences. The EU allows one convincingly to reject the hypothesis that one act of regionalism necessarily leads to the collapse of the multilateral system. But it is difficult to go further: the *anti-monde* to EU creation is unknown and one does not know to what extent the EU is special. Thus any discussion of the evidence is necessarily judgmental. The majority view is, I think, that the advent of the EU aided multilateralism. While I should like to believe this – especially now that US commitment to multilateralism is diluted by other "lateralisms" (Summers, 1991) – more needs to be done before it can be considered proven beyond reasonable doubt.

This paper has three substantive sections. Section 2 tries to define some terms, which turns out to be much more complicated than I expected: any reader who can define multilateralism simply can skip Section 2.1 and let me know his or her definition. It also proposes an organizational classification for models of "regionalism vs. multilateralism." Section 3 discusses these models under five headings and Section 4 discusses some evidence. Section 5 offers some conclusions.

Survey articles are sometimes used to resolve issues of intellectual precedence. I have not sought to do this and would caution against using the dates of the papers included here as a means of doing so. In a field barely five years old, publication delays completely distort the time picture.

2. DEFINITIONS AND CLASSIFICATIONS

2.1 Definitions

"Regionalism vs. Multilateralism" is a much discussed topic among trade economists, but one which is surprisingly short on precise measures. I shall define "regionalism" loosely as any policy designed to reduce trade barriers between a subset of countries regardless of whether those countries are actually contiguous or even close to each other. I shall not define "multilateralism" precisely, however, because – to my surprise and regret – I find that I cannot easily do so.

Although multilateralism is a characteristic of the world economy or world economic system, it must ultimately reside in the behaviour of individual countries – the extent to which they behave in a multilateral fashion. For any one country I shall treat the latter as a positive function of

(a) the degree to which discrimination is absent – perhaps the proportion of trade partners that receive identical treatment; and
(b) the extent to which the country's trading regime approximates free trade.

Strictly speaking (a) would seem to be a sufficient definition of multilateralism. However, it is neither very interesting in the current context (any preferential trade arrangements with relatively few members will worsen multilateralism), nor, I infer from their writings, what most commentators have in mind when they debate the effects of regionalism on multilateralism. Criterion (b) attempts to add back the missing dimension.

The weights and functional form with which the two criteria enter the index of individual multilateralism are left vague. If, starting from a universal (mfn) tariff, a country abolished tariffs on one (small) partner, that would seem to decrease its multilateralism, but if it abolished them on all but one (small) partner that would seem to increase it.[1] Similarly I cannot pin down precisely how to combine countries into a single global index of multilateralism. Thus we need to be cautious in comparing between views of "regionalism vs. multilateralism" – maybe their bottom lines differ.

In assessing regionalism we need to recognize another complication. Shifting one partner into an FTA has a direct impact on our measure of multilateralism, but, far more important, it also potentially initiates a whole series of accommodating adjustments, as the integrating partners and countries in the rest of the world (RoW) adjust their policies to the new circumstances. We must consider multilateralism at the end of this process not just at the beginning. Moreover, in some circumstances the final outcome will not be determinate; rather, regionalism might affect the probabilities with which different outcomes occur. Several of the models surveyed below examine whether regionalism makes it more or less likely that countries within and without the RIA can strike a deal to create or maintain worldwide free trade. Such models do not forecast particular outcomes but nonetheless comment pertinently on the environment in which they might flourish.

The previous paragraph mentioned a "process." Multilateralism is sometimes referred to as a process whereby countries solve problems in an interactive and cooperative fashion (Yarbrough and Yarbrough, 1992). While such interactions could clearly be affected by regionalism, I do not use this definition here. It is a view far too closely associated with professional negotiators and international bureaucrats for my taste, and is far too vague on the question of what purpose process serves if it is not to generate outcomes.

Other commentators might focus entirely on the final outcome – the pattern of international trade. If one could determine the perfectly multilateral volume and pattern of trade, one could then easily define the index of actual multilateralism by any of several distance measures between actual and "perfect" trade. The problem is all too obvious, however: how do we determine perfectly multilateral trade? From a policy point of view I should also be uneasy about a definition that focused on outcomes rather than trade policy instruments, for such a definition might imply indifference between methods of achieving particular trade patterns. I recognize, however, that such unease should not influence us too much in the intellectual business of defining the phenomenon.

Finally, many economists explore the interactions between countries and the effects of regionalism on them by focusing on country welfare, and, usually, world welfare. These contributions are not strictly about regionalism versus multilateralism, for we surely cannot define multilateralism in terms of increasing welfare – even if, slightly less indefensibly, we sometimes equate them. Nonetheless, welfare is sufficiently basic to the business of economics that I include this class of studies in this survey.

2.2 A classification

To try to organize the rapidly growing model-based literature on "regionalism vs. multilateralism," I have classified contributions according to four characteristics of their basic approach. These concern political objectives and organization rather than economics *per se*, for, in fact, most models adopt one of two main representations of the economy: the simple competitive homogeneous good model or the monopolistically competitive model. In each there is usually a one-to-one correspondence between goods and geographical entities – each entity having comparative advantage in one good – but in the latter several entities – say, provinces – accrete into one country. The four characteristics are:

(A) Is the objective function (1) national economic welfare or (2) some other criterion deriving from political considerations? Within the latter set, (2), does the analysis explicitly treat (i) one country, (ii) two (i.e., the partners) or (iii) three-plus (the partners and the RoW)?

(B) Is the model (1) symmetric or (2) asymmetric, the former entailing that the model deals only with circumstances in which all blocs are qualitatively identical? Within the latter set, I distinguish models which consider (i) only the integrating blocs, (ii) only the non-member countries (which are candidates for accession), or (iii) both.

(C) Is the interaction between countries (1) one-off or (2) repeated? The latter is operationalized (universally, I believe) in the form of trigger strategies.

(D) Is the aggregation of preferences or behaviour in the post-integration bloc (1) implicit – by far the more common assumption – or (2) explicit? While dimension (A_2) considers the roles of groups and interests as they affect each of the governments involved in the integration, this dimension (D_2) explicitly focuses on the interactions between pressure groups and between governments within the bloc when it comes to making post-integration decisions.

It is not possible to find examples of work in each of the 64 boxes that this classification defines. Equally, many authors offer examples in several boxes, and in a survey of this length one cannot enumerate all of these explicitly. Rather I locate studies according to their principal insights or those of the stream of literature to which they belong. Section 3 is based loosely on the classification. It starts with the conceptually simple symmetric welfare-maximizing models (A_1, B_1, C_1, D_1) and then moves on to asymmetric models (A_1, B_2, C_1, D_1). Sub-section 3.3 deals with models of negotiated tariffs

(A_1, B_1 or B_2, C_2, D_1) and 3.4 with models of political economy (A_2). Finally, I consider models of the institutional structure of policy-making within an integrated bloc (D_2).

3. MODELS OF TARIFF REGIMES

3.1 Symmetric models

While the consistency of regional grading arrangements with the multilateral trading system had attracted some debate previously and had, indeed, been modeled formally, the subject took off with a seminal trade by Paul Krugman (1991a).[2] This considers a simple model of integration and trade policy in which there are N identical countries and B identical blocs. Each country produces one product; these are differential symmetrically from all others and all consumers consume all goods (Dixit & Stiglitz differentiation); there are no transport costs, but each country levies a tariff on imports from all non-partner countries. When $B=N$ each country is a bloc, but as B falls (with N/B taking integer values) the countries within each bloc offer each other free market access and levy a common tariff on all non-partners. Within each country some products are available tariff-free – domestic and partner supplies – while all others face an identical tariff, t. Tariffs are set to maximize bloc welfare given the tariffs charged elsewhere in the world – a traditional Nash optimum tariff game.

Krugman shows that as the number of blocs in the world decreases (that is, as integration occurs) each bloc's share in the other blocs' consumption rises, conferring more market power on each and raising the optimum tariff. Integration creates trade diversion but in this model it is exacerbated by raising the external tariff. Krugman (1993) shows that the effect of the latter on economic welfare is relatively weak, however, and that even if it is suppressed his main conclusion continues to hold. The latter is that the pessimum number of blocs in terms of welfare is very small – three for most of his examples.

Krugman (1993) disaggregates the causes of the welfare losses from regionalism and finds that they owe far more to trade diversion than to increases in the optimum tariff. That is, the first-order impact of what countries do to themselves through regionalism matters more than the second-order interactions between countries. This is a useful lesson when considering any trade policy, but it is particularly salutary for our discussion, reminding us that multilateralism is not the only dimension of relevance. According to the imperfect index developed above, regionalism with a fixed external tariff may or may not harm multilateralism *ceteris paribus* – see Figure A.1 – but the act of raising the external tariff certainly does.

Krugman's work stimulated a storm of criticism and extension. The most pressing theoretical criticism was that this production structure contained no element of comparative advantage, and that this led him to over-emphasize trade diversion. Srinivasan (1993) offers one counter-example and Deardorff and Stern (1994) another; the latter have equal numbers of two kinds of country in the world and show that blocs containing equal numbers of each type realize the full benefits of free trade regardless of their external trade policies. Thus the latter become irrelevant.

A more sophisticated alternative is to be found in Bond and Syropoulos (1996a), who introduce comparative advantage in an elegant way. Each country has an equal endowment of all goods plus a supplementary amount (positive and negative) of one of them; the relative size of the supplement and the regular endowment represents the degree of comparative advantage. Working with a lower elasticity of substitution than Krugman, Bond and Syropoulos find that optimum tariffs can fall as bloc size increases symmetrically. The world welfare-minimizing number of blocs is two if comparative advantage comprises having more of one good than others, but may be three or even higher if it comprises having less of only one. Thus the Krugman result, and, indeed, the effect of regionalism on multilateralism, is obviously sensitive to issues of comparative advantage.

Sinclair and Vines (1995) reproduce Bond and Syropoulos's result about the possibility of a falling optimum tariff as the number of blocs decreases, but in slightly more general circumstances – CES preferences (as in Krugman) rather than Cobb-Douglas. They also relate it to another important qualification. Krugman and most of his successors in this literature consider the creation of customs unions (CUs), which can increase tariffs above pre-integration levels because, by coordinating several countries' policies, they can exert more market power than any individual country. If the integration takes the form of free trade areas, however, countries retain control of their own tariffs on the RoW and these will fall as regionalism proceeds. As more and more partners receive tariff-free access to one country's market the smaller between the set of goods subject to the tariff and thus the more distortionary the effect of a given tariff. Thus the incentive arises to cut the tariff in order to achieve better balance in the composition of imports – through what Sinclair and Vines call the "optimal import-sourcing condition."

The optimal import-sourcing conditions also helps to explain why the optimal tariff for a CU might fall as the union enlarges. If countries have rather similar endowments,[3] they trade rather small proportions of their output and income and hence have rather little monopsony power over each other. Thus the optimal import allocation condition which promotes equal tariffs across partners (equal to zero if some tariffs are constrained by regional arrangements) can overcome the increased monopsony power arising from larger bloc size which tends to raise the tariff on the RoW. Krugman has wholly different endowments across countries and hence for him the monopsony effect always dominates.

An important extension of Krugman's model is to recognize the role of transport costs. Krugman was the first to do this, in Krugman (1991b), but the issue has been most thoroughly taken up by Frankel, Stein and Wei in a series of papers.[4] Krugman (1991b) subdivided the world into continents and observed that if inter-continental trading costs were infinite – thus precluding inter-continental trade – a series of regional blocs each covering one continent would produce a first-best outcome equivalent to global free trade.[5] Krugman inferred a notion of "natural blocs" from this – blocs for which low trade costs made regionalism a natural and beneficial policy.

Frankel, Stein and Wei (1995, 1996) and Frankel (1996) fill in the middle ground between the two Krugman views by allowing transport costs to be finite but non-zero. As might be expected they find that, as inter-continental transportation and business costs increase relative to intra-continental ones, regionalism becomes a better policy in welfare terms. For a particular parameter constellation (three continents each with two countries, tariffs of 30%, an elasticity of substitution between varieties of four, and zero intra-continental trading costs) they find that if inter-continental costs absorb above 15% of the gross value of an export, intra-continental regionalism is welfare-improving. This result is interesting, but not very robust. Frankel, Stein and Wei themselves quote contrary results and Nitsch (1996a) shows that just raising intra-continental costs to 5% in the case above, means that regional blocs are welfare-improving for all values of inter-continental costs. Inter-continental regionalism (i.e., blocs between countries in different continents) is always harmful for Frankel Stein and Wei, although as inter-continental costs rise it becomes less so because it affects less and less trade. This result has also been challenged by Nitsch (1996b) who gives examples with relatively low inter-continental transport costs in which "unnatural" integration dominates "natural" integration!

Frankel et al also consider preferential trading areas which merely reduce rather than abolish tariffs between partners. Preferential areas can always be constructed to be welfare improving – essentially because they ensure that the optimal import-sourcing condition is not too badly violated. In this sense Frankel et al argue that bloc-formation is a stepping stone towards multilateral free trade, but since there is no mechanism through which the benign path is ensured or even encouraged this does not seem a particularly powerful characterization to me. Merely referring to the welfare benefits is not sufficient, for one could equally well refer to the (greater) benefits of jumping straight to free trade.[6] I shall not pursue this (GATT-proscribed) analysis of preferential trading blocs further. It seems to me seriously flawed on the political economy grounds that potentially it completely undermines the mfn clause (which could easily prevent multilateral progress towards liberalization) and encourages too much trade activism.

A further wrinkle on the Frankel model is provided by Spillembergo and Stein (1995) who introduce trade based on comparative advantage in addition to Krugman's and Frankel's basic intra-industry variety. If inter-continental trading costs are very low Spillembergo and Stein replicate the results above – i.e., Krugman's (1991a) 'anti-bloc" result if variety effects are strong, and welfare increasing with the size of blocs (and thus their fewness) if these effects are weak. With moderate inter-continental costs, on the other hand, Spillembergo and Stein replicate Frankel, Stein and Wei. This model is the current encompassing model for CUs – all the above discussion is, at least loosely speaking, a special case of Spillembergo and Stein.

For completeness I mention one final symmetric welfare-maximizing model which suggests that regionalism can provide stepping stones to multilateralism within a somewhat unconventional framework. Collie (1995) considers countries each with a constant returns to scale sector and one differentiated good sector. The latter compete in a third market and receive export subsidies as in the traditional strategic trade policy story. Integration between these countries allows – and encourages – better coordination of export subsidies and hence reduces distortions and raises welfare. This effect continues as bloc size grows until all the (producing) countries are integrated. This is not a particularly persuasive model, however, for the CRS sectors do not change their level of integration, export subsidies are not the instrument of concern in a regionalism and there is, in this model, no incentive for any country to join a bloc. For these reasons, Collie's is not a convincing refutation of the concerns that regionalism undermines multilateralism.

3.2 Asymmetric models

A feature of all the results discussed so far is that regionalism is always symmetric in the sense that as bloc size increases countries recombine into groups of equal size. This is a useful simplification for asking what are the effects of having bloc size B_1 in the world economy and how such effects compare with those of having bloc size B_2 in an otherwise identical world. But there is no sense of evolution or expansion in such a static setup and this severely limits the light they can shed on the issue of whether regionalism might *lead to* multilateralism. I turn now, therefore, to models in which blocs grow endogenously and thus which at some stage are asymmetric.

Bond and Syropoulos (1996a) make a start in the required direction by allowing their blocs to expand asymmetrically. Starting from a symmetric equilibrium, they show that a bloc would gain by admitting new members drawn equally from each of the other blocs. The terms of trade benefits of boosting demand for the bloc's comparative advantage goods would outweigh the trade diversionary effects in this model, even if the enlarged bloc did not increase its tariff on other countries. Second, Bond and Syropoulos ask what bloc size maximizes member countries' welfare given that other countries levy optimum tariffs. The answer is large but not the whole world, for the benefits depend on terms of trade gains which are obviously missing if the bloc contains all countries.

Frankel (1996) also sheds a little light on this issue. In a world of four continents the countries of which initially practice mfn trade policy, he shows that a sequential Nash game leads to regionalism and lower welfare for all. (This does, of course, depend on parameter values.) Specifically, one continent (any one, since all are identical) can improve its welfare by creating an FTA, assuming that the other three keep their mfn tariffs. These three lose because, even absent the bloc increasing its tariff, their terms of trade decline. From here a second continent benefits itself by integrating, assuming unchanged policies elsewhere, and thence the third and fourth continents. In the end all are worse off than under mfn policies, but none has the incentive to undo the regionalism. Whether the process then continues to create two inter-continental blocs, however, Frankel does not say, but at least for a variety of parameter values this does not seem likely since inter-continental blocs have previously been shown not to be desirable.

Very similar results were derived by Goto and Hamada (1994, 1995) using a Krugman (1993)-type model with four countries.[7] They too found a scenario in which one regional bloc begat another but in which the two "superblocs" then had an incentive to combine in order to achieve global free trade. More sinisterly, however, they also showed that once *A* and *B* had continued into a bloc it would pay them to pre-empt *C* and *D*'s combining similarly, by bringing one of the latter into their own bloc. Of course, this would impose high costs on the country that was left out, but unless the other three acquiesced this country could do nothing about achieving freer trade. In detail this result just reflects an overly powerful terminal condition to an *N* country game – the last country is always powerless. In more realistic circumstances the superbloc excludes more than one country and these countries would then have an incentive to create their own bloc. The insight that integrators may veto indefinite bloc expansion is real enough, however.

Nordstrom (1995) discusses these issues in a slightly more general framework, although at the cost of having to simulate his model rather than solve it analytically. Nordstrom starts with a model very similar to that of Frankel and his collaborators – with product differentiation and finite transport costs. He starts by considering just one bloc – a customs union (CU). Its creation and expansion harm excluded countries even at constant external tariffs; but in mitigation, these countries can always raise their welfare above free trade levels by joining the bloc and "exploiting" further the remaining outsiders. As suggested by Goto and Hamada and by Bond and Syropoulos, however, this process does not lead to the so-called global coalition (all countries within the CU), because existing members will eventually lose from further growth as the set of outsiders to exploit declines. Nordstrom suggests that after about half the countries are inside the CU, further growth will be vetoed from the inside.

Nordstrom observes that if the CU chooses an optimum tariff rather than a constant one, it will increase its tariff as it grows, hitting outsiders harder than in the previous example. Then, in the absence of retaliation, the optimum size of the union is about 60% of the world economy. But, of course, the excluded countries might retaliate against such aggression. If they alter their mfn tariffs so that they are punishing each other as well as the CU, there is little they can do, but if they maintain tariffs against each other and coordinate their punishment tariff against the CU they can exercise significant market power. Such retaliation could reduce the CU's welfare below what it could achieve at a constant external tariff (and no retaliation) if it is smaller than about 75% of countries.[8] A CU of more than 75% of countries would win the tariff war even in the face of coordinated opposition.

The implication of all this for "regionalism vs. multilateralism" is ambiguous. The assumed form of retaliation effectively transforms the excluded countries into a second CU, albeit one with non-zero internal tariffs. This raises the possibility that the two blocs could gain jointly from cooperation. However, in this model there is no identified way out of their prisoner's dilemma: the issue is not addressed. The threat of retaliation if the union raises its tariffs does nothing to prevent the creation of the union, it just limits its behaviour once formed.

Nordstrom explores inter-bloc issues more formally by breaking this world into two "continents" – *A* and *B* – and allowing blocs in each – very similar to the approach taken by Frank et al. Nordstrom finds that a CU on continent *A* hurts all excluded countries, but impinges much more heavily on those in *A*, which are the CU's "natural" trading partners, than on those in *B*. The incentives are for both sets of countries to seek integration; as previously, the CU in *A* may close its doors, but nothing can stop a CU forming in *B*. However, if there is the prospect that after the formation of blocs on both continents an inter-bloc negotiation will take place, the blocs seem likely to include all the countries on their continents in order to maximize their power in this second round. Then, provided the continents are not of very disparate sizes, negotiation of inter-bloc free trade would be mutually advantageous.

If one couples the previous paragraph with an argument that countries operating independently would not be able to negotiate global free trade, and if one is lucky with the relative sizes, Nordstrom's results are very favorable to regionalism. Starting from mfn tariffs a local CU forms; it is matched elsewhere in the world; both CUs expand to increase their bargaining power and then ultimately they negotiate global free trade.

Clearly there are many points at which this rosy scenario could break down. One, noted almost *en passant* by Perroni and Whalley (1994), arises because one can interpret the anxiety of small countries to join large neighboring blocs as seeking insurance – a desire not to be left isolated if global trade war breaks out. Small countries pay for the privilege of belonging to a bloc by offering up their markets preferentially.[9] Insurance premia are higher the more uncertain the world and the costs of errors are lower if one is insured: in other words, the large powers may gain from sabre-rattling while small countries are deciding whether to join them, and after they have joined, the small countries will be less concerned to preserve a global system than previously. Since sable-rattling is effective only if there is some chance of violence, this makes the *possibility* of regionalism look quite hostile to multilateralism.

Finally, again for completeness, I note an interesting model of a quite different nature in which regionalism is benign and welfare increases monotonically with bloc size. No country has any special characteristics, but the model is asymmetric in allowing for the formation of any coalition to block global free trade. In Kowalczyk and Sjostrom (1994) countries have monopolies in their own export goods and exploit each other by charging monopoly prices. The only policy variables in use are import price ceilings, although equivalent results would arise if import subsidies were used. Integration entails agreeing to use ceilings to force firms to price exports at marginal cost in partners' markets – i.e., it entails moving from free trade to intervention (!). The details of preferences and cost functions ensure that excluded countries are quite unaffected by such integration. In this world identical or nearly identical countries that behaved rationally would find their way to global integration. If countries differed strongly, however, coalitions could arise that block this evolution, because they would find it more advantageous to exploit certain other countries. In these cases, however, a system of side payments could be devised to achieve the first-best optimum. While Kowalczyk and Sjostrom's model is very stylized, it does suggest that regionalism may not lead to multilateralism and that this may be because global institutional structure cannot support mechanisms for side-payments.

A significant criticism of the work surveyed so far is that tariffs and other forms of protection are determined not by optimal tariff considerations but rather by domestic political processes mitigated by international negotiation. This is true, but the simple models are still useful in illustrating the spillovers and interactions between countries and in identifying threat points for various negotiating games. Moreover, the apparently related criticism – the GATT's Article XXIV prevents integrating countries from raising their tariffs – is not particularly powerful. Article XXIV has been notable for its weak enforcement so far; many trade policies have been unbound under the GATT and hence free of constraint; there are several GATT-consistent policies of protection – e.g., antidumping; and in a world of trend liberalization, merely going more slowly than you otherwise would is essentially a form of increased protection. For these reasons I am not unhappy with models that take seriously the threat that blocs could raise barriers. On the other hand, the implications of strictly optimal tariffs (e.g., indifference to changes in trade volumes) are uncomfortable and generalizations would be welcome. The rest of this part of the paper therefore considers a broader set of models starting by recognizing the importance of negotiations.

3.3 Negotiated tariffs

An early and elegant step in the direction of incorporating trade agreements into the analysis of regionalism is Bond and Syropoulos (1996b). Using the same basic model as Bond and Syropoulos (1996a), they consider trigger strategies such that initially there is inter-bloc free trade supported by the threat of perpetual trade war if any party breaks the agreement. They then ask what rate of discount just leaves blocs indifferent between defecting and continuing to cooperate. (The discount rate is critical because the decision balances current benefits to defection against future costs.) If the actual discount rate is above this value blocs defect from free trade; thus, if integration (moving from smaller to larger blocs) reduces the critical discount rate, it makes cooperation less likely to be maintained.

Two countervailing forces exist as we consider larger blocs: the incentive to deviate is greater the larger are the blocs, but so too is the welfare loss in the resulting trade war. Bond and Syropoulos find that the former effect dominates, making it more difficult to maintain free trade in a bloc-ridden world. They also find that for any given discount rate the minimum supportable cooperative tariff rises as bloc size increases, also suggesting that integration increases the pressures for protectionism. Bagwell and Staiger (1993a, b) reach a similar conclusion in a somewhat similar fashion, although only in the context of a temporary transition phase.

The discount rate is crucial to the assessment of trigger strategies because it trades off the immediate benefits of defection against the eventual costs of trade war. This raises the question of the time scale over which these games are played. In terms of individual tariffs and tariff wars – e.g., the occasional EC–US spats such as the Chicken War and the tussle over public procurement in early 1993 – the period required for retaliation is so short that there are hardly gains to defection. Thus discipline seems virtually complete and the model suggests that nothing much affects the cooperative outcome. (This may change if finite rather than infinite periods of punishment were permitted, whereupon the main question would become what determines the punishment period.) If, on the other hand, we view this as a game in regimes, so that the GATT Rounds represent the natural periodicity, and policies such as Super 301, the zeal with which anti-dumping policies are applied and the use of health and technical regulations become the weapons, the periods required to recognize defection and retaliate become much more meaningful. I find the latter interpretation more plausible: namely that the important effect of integration is not on the "tactics" of trade policy, but on the "strategy," in some sense it tends to reduce the incentive to take a world view. In this regard I find the EC's concern with the volume of intra-EC trade as an indicator of the success of integration disturbing – see, for example, Jacquemin and Sapir (1988).

Campa and Sorenson (1996) apply the repeated game model of tariff-setting to something like Nordstrom's (1995) problem, and with similar results. In part they consider a hegemon facing a competitive fringe of small countries, and conclude that if the latter coordinate they might offset the former's market power and move the world towards freer trade. Of course, if the (ex-) fringe were too large it might become hegemonic in which case it would dominate the original one. In a second, symmetric, exercise they conclude that, as the number of blocs falls, the probability of free trade falls (i.e., the critical discount rate falls), but that equi-sized blocks are preferable (more likely to be liberal) than disparate-sized ones.

In a specifically EU application Bond, Syropoulos and Winters (1996) use the Bond and Syropoulos framework to consider explicitly the deepening of an existing regional arrangement. They consider a world of N symmetric provinces split initially into one large country (the United States) and two smaller ones (France and Germany); the latter have already combined into a bloc (the EU) with a common external tariff that is the result of a self-sustaining agreement between the EU and the United States. They then allow the latter pair to integrate more deeply by reducing trade frictions between them and ask whether tariff cuts within the union affect the incentive-compatibility of agreements with the outside country. It turns out that the Kemp-Wan tariff reduction – the reduction in the union's external tariff that just leaves the outside country indifferent to the internal tariff reduction – is a useful benchmark for this.

For the outside country, the reduction in the union's internal tariffs reduces the attractiveness of an initial trade agreement because its trade with the union is reduced. The Kemp-Wan reduction in the union's external tariff, however, will just restore incentive compatibility for the outside country because it restores to their initial levels both its welfare under the agreement and its incentive to violate it. For the union, a Kemp-Wan adjustment generates two conflicting forces. First, the initial trade agreement becomes more attractive to union members because the expanded volume of intra-union trade raises the welfare of member countries at the initial level of the external tariff. This suggests that the union could "live with" a lower tariff on the outside country. On the other hand, deviating from the agreement also becomes more attractive because the payoff to cheating also rises. This suggests that the external tariff needs to rise in order to keep the union in the agreement. (A higher tariff makes sticking to the agreement more attractive.) The first effect almost always dominates the second, so that incentive-compatibility is consistent with a fall in the union's external staff.

To be more precise, the two forces on the union exactly offset each other if the share of union expenditure on union goods is invariant with respect to the external tariff. In that case, since the Kemp-Wan tariff reduction is incentive-compatible for both the union and the outside country, internal liberalization plus a Kemp-Wan reduction will generate a new sustainable agreement. Of course, many other agreements will also be sustainable, so there is no guarantee that the Kemp-Wan reduction in the external tariff will actually be chosen, but at least for one simple representation of the negotiating process Bond, Syropoulos and Winters show that it will be.

If the share of union expenditure on union goods rises as the external tariff rises (heuristically, if demand is elastic) the Kemp-Wan tariff reduction is not incentive-compatible for the union: that is, if the original agreement was just sustainable, internal liberalization plus a Kemp-Wan reduction will leave the union preferring to defect than to cooperate. As a result, the union, while likely to reduce its external tariff somewhat, will not be prepared to go as far as the Kemp-Wan reduction. Since the latter is necessary to keep the outside country at its initial level of welfare, the presumption is that, under these circumstances, the outside country will suffer from the union's internal liberalization. This illustrates the dilemma of defining multilateralism starkly. By reducing all tariffs in the model we have presumably enhanced multilateralism, and yet the RoW – the intended beneficiary of multilateralism – suffers a decline in welfare.

Somewhat similarly to Bond, Syropoulos and Winters, Bagwell and Staiger (1996) analyze a three-country model in a repeated game context. They assume two countries are patient (A and B) – and hence are happy with low tariff equilibria – while the third (*C*) is very impatient. Under mfn rules *A* and *B* offer *C* lower tariffs than it reciprocates with because they wish to have low tariffs on their mutual trade. How is this affected if they sign a free trade agreement? Under such an eventuality the import sourcing condition suggests further reducing *A*'s and *B*'s tariffs on *C*, but, pushing in the opposite direction, the same condition suggests that *A* and *B* are likely to impose less harsh punishment on *C* if it defects, and *A*'s and *B*'s mutual tariffs are no longer dependent on their tariff on *C*. The net effect is ambiguous, but Bagwell and Staiger show that if *C* is very impatient and *A* and *B* very patient it could entail higher tariffs on *C*. This is more likely if and *A* and *B* form a CU rather than a free trade area because, being larger, a CU is less interested in freer trade.

Bagwell and Staiger's model is quite special because it assumes that, out of three goods, each country imports one from both partners while exporting both others, one to each partner. Its real significance, however, is to highlight the sensible proposition that if we ask "how useful is regionalism" part of the answer must be "that depends on how well the mfn rule was doing initially."

Bond and Syropoulos introduce regional blocs exogenously – e.g., for political reasons – and ask how they disturb an existing equilibrium. Ludema (1996) asks a more sophisticated question: how does the *possibility* of creating a regional bloc affect the conduct of multilateral negotiations aimed at achieving free trade. He uses welfare-maximization as his objective function and considers a three-country multi-round two-step negotiation. In each negotiating round the first step is a multilateral offer and if this is rejected a bilateral one may be made. If this is rejected a new round is initiated. A very strong assumption is that international transfers of utility are feasible. This guarantees that negotiations will always eventually end up with global free trade – the only efficient solution – and because in these games (a) time is money (the discount rate is positive) and (b) information is complete, they actually get there straight away. Thus negotiation is *only* about distribution – every offer is "global free trade plus some vector of transfers."

In this context Lydema does not help us much on "regionalism vs. multilateralism," except to the extent that his results may condition attitudes towards whether to rewrite Article XXIV to ban regional arrangements. Ludema considers two questions. First, how would a pre-existing regional bloc affect a multilateral negotiation. If it is an FTA, not very much, because an FTA does not constrain the partners' negotiations with outside countries. If it is a CU, however, the effect is stronger because a CU precludes independent negotiation. However, this effect is weakened if the partners are asymmetric because the partners' ideal policies vis-à-vis outsiders would differ. Ludema's second question is how the possibility of regionalism affects negotiations. If only FTAs are possible the multilateral outcome resembles that of three separate bilateral negotiations, whereas if only CUs are permitted the first-mover advantage for the country that can first propose a CU allows it a disproportionate share of world income. In Ludema's model this is randomly decided.

A model of negotiated tariffs in which the repeated game is only implicit is Bagwell and Staiger's (1997) contribution to this volume. This starts from the position that countries gear trade policy to their own ends – be they political, economic, or whatever – and that trade agreements (and the GATT) exist to internalize the effects that *A*'s policy has on *B* – specifically to internalize terms of trade effects. If mfn trade rules allow complete internalization, then countries can reach the efficiency frontier (defined over their own objectives, not the economics community's) and regional arrangements have nothing to add. If, on the other hand, mfn tariffs cannot yield efficiency or, say, they pose enforcement problems, regional arrangements may have a role to play. In these cases regionalism is (potentially) optimal; there is no question of building blocs or stumbling blocks unless we wish to challenge governments' objectives. This brings us neatly to the next group of models which recognize that governments are not always economic welfare maximizers.

3.4 Pressure groups and voters

I now move on to what might loosely be called political economy models of integration – those in which governments are driven by economic considerations but not merely the (unweighted) maximization of welfare/utility. In this section we take governments' objective functions as given and assume they are efficiently pursued. In the next we ask how the decision process itself – the institutions which determine government behaviour – affect the outcome. Many of the political economy models have a lot in common with the models I have already surveyed, but I collect them into one section because their focus on political economy is their main distinguishing characteristic.

Much of the political economy modeling derives from Grossman and Helpman (1994, 1995).[10] They argued persuasively that lobbying influences governments less in terms of determining which of the two polar policy stances wins an election than in terms of what policies an incumbent or newly elected government will pursue – the market for influence. In general consumers find it hard to recognize a lobby and so lobbying is dominated by producers, who organize along sector lines. This effectively gives profits additional weight in the government's objective function; they enter once in the traditional calculus of surpluses (consumer, producer and government revenue), and again as the source of lobbying funds which the government values in their own right. Thus moving into the realms of political economy effectively biases integration outcomes towards what producers desire.

Grossman and Helpman (1995) consider a negotiation between two governments that have suddenly been offered the chance of concluding a free trade area (FTA). That is they compare *staying* with mfn trade policy with creating mutual preferences. In certain circumstances they find that the latter is politically feasible, i.e., raises government "welfare" which depends on consumer and producer surpluses but with different weights. The FTA is feasible either if it enhances the profits of well-organized producers who pass some of the benefit onto the government via lobbies. The latter possibility is malign for it makes likely precisely those FTAs which generate most trade diversion. Trade creation is a mixed blessing for a negotiating government: it generates surpluses for consumers at home and for exporters in the partner country, but reduces them for domestic import-competing producers; trade diversion, on the other hand, generates no such reduction in profits, and although it correspondingly generates no (or fewer) consumer gains that matters less to governments. If two such governments can swap trade diverting concessions, trade diversion is good politics even if it is bad economics. Grossman and Helpman do not consider whether their process continues to create superblocs, although if it were driven by diversion alone it would have to stop before it achieved the global coalition, because the last step in that direction would have only trade creation.

Krishna (1994) has an elegant stripped-down three-country version of Grossman and Helpman in which policy is determined solely by its effects on profits. He assumes imperfectly competitive markets that are segmented from each other. He replicates the Grossman-Helpman result that, considering two of the countries, the more trade diverting an FTA between them, the stronger its backing and hence the more likely it is to come about. He then shows that the backing for further multilateral liberalization with the third country is reduced. Included in this is the possibility that multilateral liberalization that was feasible before the FTA would cease to be so afterwards – i.e., that, if the world attempted to achieve the multilateral free trade it desired via regionalism, progress would stop at the intermediate stage.

Very simply, let a sector's profits be π_1 under mfn tariffs, π_2 under the FTA and π_3 under global free trade. The gains from FTA $(\pi_2 - \pi_1)$ may be sufficient to allow successful lobbying for the FTA; similarly, if it were the only option, the gains from global liberalization $(\pi_3 - \pi_1)$ might also permit successful lobbying; the gains from moving from an FTA to free trade $\pi_3 - \pi_2$, however, may be insufficient to encourage lobbying for that step: they will certainly be smaller than $(\pi_3 - \pi_1)$ because $\pi_2 > \pi_1$ if the FTA was formed, and they may actually be negative. Moreover, this "suspended liberalization" outcome is more likely the more trade diverting was the initial FTA. Krishna shows that it may not even be possible for producers in the outside country to bribe those in the partners to adopt global free trade. This is because much of the benefit of the latter is "wasted" on consumers.

Kirshna's is a *very* simple model – which is one of its attractions – and clearly requires some generalization. However, it is rather convincing that regionalism may hinder multilateralism – "the good" preventing "the best"!

The second extension of Grossman and Helpman is Baldwin (1995). This model of "domino" regionalism has many countries each with a constant returns to scale (CRS) (numeraire) sector and a differential product sector with capitalists who receive the rent. Government objectives are a convex combination of worker and capitalist welfare, the latter being enhanced by their ability to lobby. Baldwin assumes that a bloc already exists and that this situation is an equilibrium in the sense that countries on the outside wish to remain so because the economic benefits of joining do not outweigh the non-economic costs. He then shocks this world by deepening integration within the bloc – "1992" – or by allowing one country's desire for integration to increase – the United States in the 1980s. Each shock would increase the incentives for new members to join – starting with those that were previously just on the margin of joining – and as they do so the costs to others of remaining outside grow. This in turn attracts others and so on.

Baldwin notes that the process of enlargement could stop as soon as all remaining non-members have high enough objections to joining. It could also, of course, do so when existing members shut the door. Baldwin deals, in fact, only with the demand for membership. As a parable for the absorption of the EFTA countries into the EC following "1992" – its intended purpose – Baldwin's explanation is admirable, but its generalization to other accessions looks less secure – think, for example, of Poland, Cyprus and Turkey. Given that deepening integration is bad for excluded countries – see above – Baldwin does not actually need political economy to generate his results, but it does help to explain some of the facts of political activity that surrounded the EFTA accession. Overall, however, the implications of all this for multilateralism are quite unclear.

An early contribution to the theory of endogenous protection and integration is Richardson (1993, 1995). Like Baldwin, Richardson's basic insight does not require a political economy dimension – welfare maximization would suffice. Suppose one country creates an FTA with a large partner (with a horizontal supply curve) and suppose that for certain imported goods the FTA is trade diverting because $p_p < p_w(1+t)$ where p_p is the partner's price, p_w is the world price and t is the mfn tariff. Domestic firms and consumers now face p_p instead of $p_w(1+t)$, but the government loses tariff revenue. A rational government would now reduce its mfn tariff to just below t', where $p_w(1+t') = p_p$. This would leave domestic residents unaffected relative to the FTA but generate tariff revenue. The main constraint on this behaviour is the reaction of the partner country which loses the rents it expected under the FTA. But if it is large and has other objectives in the integration, it might acquiesce. A reservation to this elegant model is the extent to which tariff revenues really motivate trade policy – the prevalence of VERs casts some doubt on this.

Political economy considerations support the rational outcome in Richardson's model. The initial reduction in the domestic price would probably reduce the size of the lobby for tariffs on the goods concerned,[11] and, besides, no one in the lobby has any interest in whether they are hurt by partner imports rather than non-partner imports. Richardson's results seem to require that partner and non-partner imports are perfect substitutes with fixed prices. If import supply curves slope upwards and/or the imports (and the home good) are imperfect substitutes in demand, then free access for the partner could well increase the demand for protection against non-members and this may outweigh the government's revenue concerns. The necessary condition for this to occur seems to be that imports are drawn from both sources after integration.

Two contributions offer significant generalizations of Richardson's work. Cadot, de Melo and Olarreaga (1996) have a three-country model with Grossman-Helpman lobbying for influence by the fixed factors in each of the three industries. They ask what *A*/*B* integration does to protection against *C*'s exports and focus carefully on different types of integration. They find that if *A* and *B* create an FTA without rules of origin, protection is likely to fall, essentially for the reasons identified by Richardson. If there are rules of origin, however, the protective effects of the FTA are more complex and it is possible that either *A* or *B* will increase protection above either of the pair's pre-integration tariffs. Similar outcomes are also possible under customs unions. The reason is that in this model tariffs on different goods are substitutes: if one is reduced (by FTA membership), others rise (on *C*). This is because the disprotected sector contracts, increasing the sizes and reducing the lobbying costs of the other sectors.[12] Cadot, de Melo and Olarrega do not consider how *C* reacts to integration – it always offers free trade – but the propensity of the bloc members to raise their tariffs is likely to move us away from multilateralism.

The second generalization of Richardson is Levy (1996b – preliminary) who considers many countries in a model that also includes lobbying for influence and negotiated tariffs. He focuses on two major countries negotiating with each other and asks how this negotiation is affected if each acquires (exogenously) a fringe of FTA partners. Each country has effective lobbying in one import-competing ("sensitive") sector; export interests aim to reduce the other country's tariff in its "sensitive" sector by inducing reductions in their own country's. The existence of the fringe affects the extent to which trade policy changes translate into increases in profits in the major powers. For example, suppose *A*'s fringe can supply *A*'s export good along a fairly elastic supply curve. *A* now has less interest in inducing *B* to reduce its tariff on these goods because part of the benefit spills over onto *A*'s fringe's suppliers so that *A*'s own producers get a smaller increase in price.[13] Levy shows that considering both countries' fringes these effects could go in any direction, so that giving major negotiating powers FTA fringes could either increase or reduce tariffs on their mutual trade. Thus if it is the major powers that determine the progress of multinational negotiations (e.g., the United States and EU in the Uruguay Round) Levy's model suggests we cannot necessarily be sanguine about the EU association agreements, APEC and NAFTA.

I turn now to models with slightly different pressure group technologies. Richardson and Desruelle (1994) use a model with features of both Krishna's and Baldwin's to explain the height of EC-countries' tariffs before and after integration: they have three countries and an economic specification like Baldwin's except that they explicitly consider the distribution of tariff revenues. In addition they allow both workers and capitalists (now a single group) to lobby. Richardson and Desruelle compare Nash tariffs before and after the creation of a customs union, assuming that the partners of the latter are identical.[14] Integration does not affect the relative weights of workers and capitalists in the formation of trade policy. The partners both export the differentiated good to each other and the excluded country, while the latter exports the CRS good.

It turns out that integration could push the external tariff (on imports of the CRS good) either way in Richardson and Desruelle's model. Generally it will raise it: before integration each partner moderates its desire to tax the CRS good because doing so will increase its costs in the differentiated sector with a resultant loss of sales and rents to the other partner. A customs union internalizes this spillover and hence allows a higher price. The counter-example occurs when workers determine the tariff but receive little of the revenue. Before integration they drive the tariff very high because they have no interest in the rents of the differentiated sector but do benefit from the Stolper-Samuelson effect on real wages. But this spills over to the other partners in terms of higher costs and prices of differentiated goods. Under the customs union this spillover is recognized and the tariff on the CRS good falls to the revenue-maximizing level. Overall, Richardson and Desruelle's results seem to suggest that RIAs increase trade restriction, for the starting point of their counter-case – very high tariffs on the CRS good – does not accord very closely with reality.

Levy (1994) continues (implicitly) with labor and capital and explores the stepping stones argument with a median voter model. He reaches similar conclusions to Krishna. The median voter's response to the offer of a trade policy change depends on his labor-capital ratio and the labor-capital ratio of the trading blocs to which he belongs before and after the change. An important restriction is that voters first consider autarky versus a bilateral deal and then whatever they choose first versus multilateralism. This allows Levy to show that in a simple Heckscher-Ohlin model one does not get stuck at the bilateral stage.

Suppose *A* and consider forming a bloc and that $K^{AB} < k^{AB} < K^{B}$ where k^{i} is the capital-labor ratio of country i and k^{AB} that of *A* and *B* combined. The median vector in *A* will agree to the FTA if increasing his economy's *k* is beneficial *to him* and the median voter in *B* will approve if he gains from a decrease. Suppose both approve and that we then pose the second question which would produce a world economy with ratio $k^{W} > k^{AB}$ voter *A* will favor multilateralism. Voter *B* might also if k^{w} far exceeds k^{AB}, but more likely he will reject it, leaving the world stuck in bilateral mode. But voter *A* can foresee this and would therefore veto bilateralism at the first stage relying on the second ballot – which would then become autarky vs. multilateralism – to achieve his goals. Essentially no two countries that favored multilateralism initially can create an FTA, so the world is safe!

Now Levy adds variety effects so that the median voter receives utility not just from his real income but also from increased variety. This can cause a breakdown at the intermediate stage. Suppose the median voter is only just in favor of multilateralism, balancing increased variety against disadvantageous price/wage effects. If the FTA offers disproportionate gains it could push the voter's utility above the multilateral level. For example, if *A* and *B* have identical capital-labor ratios $k^{A} = k^{AB} = k^{B}$ there are no price wage effects but there are variety effects. These could leave the median voter better off and resisting the move to multilateralism, even though the latter would have been chosen relative to autarky. It is FTAs between similar countries that pose the greatest threats to multilateralism, those between dissimilar ones that pose the least. This suggests that the current rash of North–South arrangements, such as NAFTA and the EU Association Agreements, are not likely to be very harmful. However, subsequent work – Levy (1996b), see above – rebuts this presumption.

Frankel and Wei (1996) offer a counter-example to Levy's argument that bilateralism can never increase support for multilateralism. They do so in a Ricardian world with costs of adjustment for workers changing sectors. There are three countries (*A*, *B* and *C*) each with comparative advantage in one of three goods (*a*, and *c*, respectively); in each two potential partner countries (*A* and *B*) workers are spread over the three sectors such that none has a majority. If workers focus on the costs of adjustment a majority in *A* will oppose multilateral liberalization (those in *b* and *c*) but favor bilateral liberalization (those in *a* and *c*, who will benefit from the falling price of *b*). If the bilateral bloc is formed workers will have to move – perhaps all *b*-workers move to *a*. Now there will be a majority in favor of opening up with *C* as well.

Frankel and Wei's argument relies either on workers not realizing that the multilateral vote will follow the bilateral one (otherwise *c* workers would oppose bilateralism) or on voters behaving that the following voting structure will be used regardless of outcomes: vote first on the *A*/*B* bloc and then, whatever the outcome, vote on opening up to *C*. In the latter case *c*-workers cannot avoid liberalization and so would go along with the *A*/*B* bloc. The latter seems implausible to me, but not the former given the uncertainties and glacial pace of trade diplomacy. It also seems fairly plausible that voters do focus on adjustment costs. Almost any discussion of trade liberalization with policy-makers takes about ten minutes to get around to unemployment. Thus contrary to Levy's (1996a) comments on this paper, it seems to me a plausible counter-example, albeit one which is far from categorical, for the voting weights could easily generate alternative outcomes.

General conclusions from the political economy literature are elusive. One such conclusion is that the dominance of sector-based lobbies over economy-wide ones (factor-based or consumer) makes trade diversion more attractive to policy-makers, for trade diversion shifts rents and/or activity towards producers. While one cannot be categorical, this tendency seems likely to gravitate away from multilateralism for trade diversion is possible *only* from preferential arrangements. The tendency is manifest first in the notion that integration beyond a trade-deflecting FTA may induce higher tariffs on the rest of the world, and, second, in the more interesting observation, that one might get stopped on a regional stepping stone before achieving free trade. While there are counter-examples I find the broad thrust of this argument convincing.

3.5 Institutional arrangements for regional blocs

The discussion in Section 3.4 presupposed that all the features of a regional bloc are fully determined at its outset – implicitly in the negotiation phase during which national governments, pressure groups and voter interests are identifiable and distinct. For FTAs this seems a reasonable assumption, for, other than maintaining mutual free trade, governments are quite unconstrained by an FTA. Even for an FTA, however, it would be worth asking – rather along the lines of Levy (1996b) – how the existence of an FTA conditions governments' reactions to exogenous shocks. For example, if the price of a major exportable falls will governments be more likely to resort to protection with or without an FTA? Bhagwati and Panagariya (1996) have suggested that being in NAFTA made the Mexican government's response to the 1994/5 crisis *less* liberal than if it had been unencumbered: the previous mid-80s crisis eventually led to thorough-going liberalization whereas the mid-90s crisis produced tariff increases on some non-NAFTA imports. Most other commentators have argued that since the response in the mid-80s was initially very protectionist, NAFTA appears to have constrained behaviour to be moderately liberal. While the literature surveyed so far sheds some light on these issues by asking whether an FTA increases propensities to protectionism, it does not address it directly because it does not really consider how FTA members take decisions.

If consideration of this issue is desirable for FTAs it is indispensable for customs unions and deeper forms of integration. One might determine the initial common external tariff in the negotiation phase, but thereafter one needs mechanisms for deciding how to change it either in multilateral negotiations or ad hoc via anti-dumping actions, etc. How one does this – how one aggregates preferences across members – is likely to be very important in determining the outcomes. This problem does not arise in models of welfare-maximizing governments where members are symmetric, for one maximizes the representative country's welfare. Thus it is essentially a problem of asymmetry and politics.

One interesting aspect of joint decision-making concerns how formerly national lobbies interact to bring pressure to bear on the customs union authorities. The only formal analyses of this question all suggest that interest group pressure is diluted by the customs union. The essential point is that it costs more to lobby for a 1% increase in your tariff in a customs union than in a constituent member country with the right to set its own tariffs: there is more opposition to overcome (Panagariya and Findlay, 1994, de Melo, Panagariya and Rodrik, 1993) or more representatives to influence (Richardson, 1994). Given the lower returns less lobbying occurs and the sum of the members' lobbying activity falls as a result of integration. This can equivalently be viewed as a public good problem, for a common external tariff is a public good: the lobby from *A* does not wish to devote resources to lobbying for protection for producers in country *B*. Whether the resulting tariff is lower than that which would rule in *all* member countries in the absence of integration is unclear, however, and so one might be trading less protection in some members for more in others. Whether this enhances multilateralism clearly depends on precisely how you trade off breadth against depth in the external tariff.

All these models presuppose that lobbies in different member countries will oppose each other, but it is also possible that some of them have their power enhanced through integration (Winters, 1993). For example, anti-protectionist forces might also be diluted by the free-riding problem. Alternatively each member state might initially start with a lobbying game in which industry and agriculture more or less cancel each other out, but if integration lets the agriculture lobbies cooperate (because they produce the same things) while the industry lobbies compete (because they produce different things) the union may end up with high agricultural protection. Overall, therefore, while dilution effects will undoubtedly be present, it is not proven that they will always predominate.

I turn now to the organization of government. Gatsios and Karp (1991, 1995) show that it might matter which member state "leads" negotiations with the rest of the world on a particular issue. In their model, if a more aggressive member determines the union's position, the union is able to extract a more favorable deal from RoW than if the "average" member does so. This is because the former is more credible in its threats to retaliate (with the whole of the union's resources). In this model, "passive" members could benefit from delegating power for certain policies to aggressive ones, because, although for any given RoW policy they would prefer a less aggressive union stance, the RoW is so much more accommodating under the delegation that they are better off overall. What about multilateralism? That depends on whether a more aggressive union can achieve a more liberal outcome with the RoW by virtue of its readiness to retaliate, or whether it actually needs to use its muscle. Gatsios and Karp's model deals with this essentially only by assumption.

The formal delegation of the power to settle negotiating positions is of limited relevance in real customs unions, but informal and partial delegation clearly exists. It has commonly been observed (e.g., Winter, 1993) that the EU allows countries disproportionate influence over policy in areas in which they claim vital interests, allowing them, in extremis, veto power. Given that for all the reasons noted above a country's "interest" in a sector is commonly correlated with that sector's share of its GDP, it is easy to imagine this feature enhancing further the interest of producers. What effect this has on the union's trade policy depends on whether a sector's having a high share of a member's GDP reflects its comparative advantage or past policy distortions. If the former, one might expect reactively liberal stances,[15] whereas if the latter, protection will be more strongly favored. One encouraging aspect of this is that since integration will tend to relocate union production in a sector towards relatively more efficient countries, over time this argument could lead to reduction in protectionist pressure.

Winters (1994, 1995) considers the institutional basis of decision-making more closely, and, in an EU context, observes several features that could lead to protectionist biases in the aggregation of preferences. If the union is essentially inter-governmental, rather than democratic in its own right, policy will be made by groups of bureaucrats and, eventually, ministers representing their own governments. This can be protectionist, first because, as Messerlin (1983) notes, the incentives for bureaucrats tend towards protectionism, and, second, because as Scharpf (1988) notes, adding layers of inter-governmental decision-making tends to swing influence away from voters and towards official preferences for administrative convenience and a quiet life. The secrecy that surrounds EU deliberations reinforces these tendencies because it confuses public perceptions of where the responsibility for trade policy outcomes actually lies.

Within the EU, trade policy is essentially made by committee – the so-called "113 Committee" – the members of which represent particular constituencies (countries) and none of whom is publicly accountable for the final outcome. This gives rise to at least two (related) failures of aggregation. First, the restaurant bill problem: suppose the benefits of a policy on product j to a country i are proportionate to the latter's share of union output (x_{ij}) and the costs to its share of GDP (g_i), and suppose that each country has a veto, or at least that consensus is valued very highly. If representatives sit down to decide a package of policies on $j=1 \ldots N$ products, each will press for inclusion of any good for which $x_{ij}>a\,g_i$, where $a>$ reflects the inefficiency of the conversion of costs into benefits. Since each is highly likely to have some j for which this is true and, provided the *perceived a* is not too large, the easiest package to construct will cover nearly all products even if, overall, each country would prefer no change to the final outcome.

The second failure is similar but operates in probability space – see Shepsle and Weingast (1981), who christened the phenomenon "universalism," Schattschneider (1935) on the Smoot-Hawley tariff, and Winters (1994) on the EU. Imagine that protecting footwear is being discussed and that each of three

TABLE 1 *The universalist argument: Costs and benefits for a single country if the measures passes*

Total number of countries voting 'for/in/	2	3
Cost	$-2(c+d)/3$	$-(c+d)$
This country votes 'in'		
benefit	c	c
probability of measure passing	0.5	0.25
This country votes 'out'		
probability of measure passing	0.25	0

member states is a producer of one type. If any one type is protected, the government in whose country it is produced perceives benefits of c (surplus to producers, political convenience etc.) and each member bears cost of $-(c+d)/3$, where d(>0) is the deadweight cost of transferring c through protection. Net costs are zero is the measure is rejected. The issue is to be decided by simple majority, and each member must decide how to vote; each accepts that if it votes against the measure, its type of footwear will not be protected.

Table 1 reports the costs and benefits of the proposal passing according to whether a member votes 'for/in' or 'no/out.' It also reports the probability of the proposal passing, assuming that the other countries vote randomly with probability one half each way. The expected value of voting 'for/in' is $0.5^*[c-2(c+d)/3] + 0.25^*[c-(c+d)]$ ($\gtrless 0$), while that of voting 'no/out' is $-0.25^*2(c+d)/3(<0)$. Thus a government will vote 'for/in' if $4c>5d$ – i.e., if its 'benefits' from the protection exceed the deadweight loss by 25% or more – and even if it expects negative returns to doing so!

A more sophisticated view of voting for trade policy in the EU is offered by Widgren (1995a, b) drawing on Hamilton (1991). Widgren notes that small countries have disproportionate numbers of votes; he considers voting coalitions and calculates countries' voting power in terms of the frequency with which they might command a pivotal position in the EU's qualified majority voting system. He argues that if we contrast liberals (the Netherlands, Luxembourg, Germany, Denmark, Belgium and the United Kingdom) with protectionists (Spain, Portugal, Italy and France) with Ireland and Greece as uncertain, no group has power in a deterministic sense (each has a blocking minority). The EFTA enlargement does not change this and so changes to the status quo look unlikely. However, allowing for probabilistic voting, with the probabilities being the same for each member of each group but varying by group, change is possible most probably in a protectionist direction: the power of the two groups is roughly balanced over proposals covering the whole range of restrictiveness (as measured by the probability of receiving support from the liberals), but in the more protective range the protectionists appear to muster rather greater power and thus are more likely to get their way. Widgren's work clearly depends on particular constitutional structure, but it illustrates how voting patterns may generate aggregation biases. Given that in the post-war period liberalism has required positive action, the EU system favoring the status quo is not particularly multilateral.

4. WHAT THE EVIDENCE SUGGESTS

This section briefly surveys the evidence on "regionalism vs. multilateralism." Regrettably it seems to be as ambiguous as the theory, at least so far as issues of current policy are concerned. As noted above, among current RIAs only the EU is large enough and long-lived enough to have had identifiable consequences on the world trading system itself, and it is more or less impossible to sort out what is generic and what specific among the lessons it teaches. Perhaps the only unambiguous lesson is that the creation of one regional bloc does not necessarily lead to the immediate break down of the trading system.

Several fundamental problems confront the scholar in this area. Foremost is creating an *anti-monde* – how can we know what member countries' trade policy would have been in the absence of the RIA? Second, systems evolve over long periods of time; it is not inconceivable that while post-war RIAs have been liberal so far, they are sowing the seeds of destruction, for example by reducing the number of independent middle-sized states which have an interest in maintaining the world system. Third, as noted above, trade policy responds to shocks from other areas: RIAs may be benign under one set of circumstances, but not another. How, then, do we allocate responsibility over causes. Forth, how do we define and measure multilateralism? Fifth, the rhetoric required to achieve a political objective does not necessarily reflect actual causes. Even if policy-makers say they are responding to an instance of regional integration – e.g., in raising tariff or seeking a multilateral negotiation – how do we know this is the real cause?

One solution to these difficulties is to dispense with looking at the evidence altogether on the grounds that nothing concrete can emerge. I prefer an alternative view: as long as we are frank about the degree of confidence we can have in various conclusions, it is better to consider actual cases than to ignore them.

4.1 Members' own trade policies

The evidence on whether the EU has led to higher or lower tariffs and non-tariff barriers for member states' non-partner trade continues to defy simple conclusions. Hufbauer (1990) argues that it created the conditions for France and Italy to contemplate liberalization and that Germany would not have proceeded without its continental partners. Messerlin (1992) agrees that the EEC aided French liberalization indirectly by creating the appropriate macroeconomic environment. *Prima facie* these views of France do seem plausible, for she has always appeared a reluctant liberalizer. On the other hand, crises and sudden perceptions that one is getting left behind can have dramatic effects: France's switch in the early 1980s from Keynesian expansionism to fiscal orthodoxy arose precisely because the former failed to work. A similar "road to Damascus" could also have affected a highly protectionist France in a more liberal continent – consider Mexico in the mid-1980s, for example. Hufbauer, it seems to me, may well be wrong about Germany: in each of the two years prior to the creation of the EEc, Germany undertook tariff cuts of 25% (Irwin, 1995). Thus not only did the tariff averaging attending the creation of the EEC raise German tariffs, it also possibly curtailed a liberalizing momentum.

No-one, I suspect, would argue that the EU has set external tariffs above the levels that would otherwise have ruled in at least one of its member countries, but this is quite different from arguing that it has not raised protection in some countries and sectors – e.g., footwear in Germany, agriculture in the United Kingdom, and textiles and clothing in Sweden. The trade-off between the breadth and depth of protection is not well defined and so we cannot satisfactorily rule on whether these examples constitute increases or decreases in multilateralism.

Other recent evidence on countries' own trade is equally mixed. Following NAFTA, Canada reduced tariffs on 1,500 tariff items (mostly inputs) to help her industry compete with the United States where tariffs were lower (WTO, 1995). This looks similar to Richardson's tariff competition. On the other hand Mexico increased tariffs on 500 items – see above. In Mercosur, Argentina's tariffs on capital goods' imports will be raised to Brazilian levels.

Going back further in time, the 1960s RIAs in Latin America were inward-looking and frequently maintained and even raised barriers against the RoW. The Central American Common Market, for example, generated huge growth in intra-trade behind such barriers (Nogues and Quintanilla, 1993). In all probability the import-substitution policy would have been less broad and/or foundered sooner if it had been restricted to small countries operating on an mfn basis. Even further back, in the 1930s, one also finds high external tariffs and burgeoning regionalism, but here the evidence is probably more favorable to regionalism – Oye (1992) and Irwin (1993). Trade barriers were going up anyway and regional arrangements probably served to reduce the coverage of the increases by exempting some flows.

4.2 Other countries' policies

When one thinks of the effects of regionalism on the multilateral system one is obliged to deal with interactions between countries. How does an RIA cause other countries to respond? WTO (1995) suggests three classes of response: to seek to join an existing group; to create a new group; and to seek multilateral liberalization.

The observation that regional arrangements have recently attracted new members is commonplace; one need not even list examples. However, whether this is good or bad for multilateralism is moot, for we are clearly far away from achieving a global coalition. Moreover, accretion is not inevitable and irreversible. Countries do leave groups – e.g., Chile and Peru effectively left the Andean Pact, although admittedly after it had become rather rigid. In both cases, multilateralism benefited from the defections.

The second option, of creating new RIAs, also looks popular according to the evidence. Regionalism has proceeded in waves – the 1960s and the later 1980s and 1990s – and policy makers variously refer to demonstration effects, to the need to create their own market areas in case other blocs turn inwards, and the desire to create bargaining power. Examples include the establishment of EFTA, and recent discussions surrounding AFTA (Asean Free Trade Area) and the CBI (Cross-Border Initiative in Africa). Again, of course, it is moot whether this enhances or undermines multilateralism.

Finally, most directly relevant and most contentious, many commentators argue that excluded countries will seek multilateral liberalizations in response to RIAs. This occurs mainly in the realms of super-power trade diplomacy, because only super-powers can manipulate the multilateral system but even smaller powers may warm towards multilateral talks if they perceive a fragmenting world economy. Arguments of this sort have been made about each of the last four GATT Rounds as well as in certain earlier instances.

Many commentators have argued that the creation of the EEC led directly to the Dillon and Kennedy Rounds as the United States sought to mitigate the former's trade diversionary consequences – see, for example, Lawrence (1991), Sapir (1993) and WTO (1995). I have expressed some reservations about this linkage – Winters (1993, 1994). I do not deny some connection between these events, but I am still concerned that we have not established a necessary link between them, that any such link was benign, or that it is generalizable to other instances of integration.

First, it seems implausible to argue that multilateral progress would have stopped had the EEC not been created. After all, the benefits of liberalization are not much affected by other countries' regionalism, it is just that, following the creation of an RIA, multilateral liberalization may be necessary to avoid actual harm to excluded countries. The United States still had considerable hegemonic power in the late 1950s and early 1960s and so could probably have generated enough support for a Round whenever it wanted. It is not generally maintained that the EEC made the Europeans more willing to negotiate. Thus overall, I suspect that, at most, we are talking about the timing not the existence of the next Round.

Second, the Administration played the EEC card hard in public and in Congress. But whether they actually believed they *had* to respond to its creation and whether that creation was the major factor behind the push for talks is less clear. Recent debate in the United States about trade issues has sometimes demonstrated a disconnect between rhetoric and economic reality and so the EEC could just have been a convenient handle with which to maneuver US domestic interests and the EC nations into talks.

Third, since agriculture played such an important and delicate role in its formation, it is not surprising that the EEC resisted that sector's inclusion in the negotiations. But the fact that it got away with this (because the United States refused the "*montant de soutien*" offer) reinforced agricultural protectionism throughout the world and made it doubly difficult to negotiate in future rounds. Future agricultural disarmament may have been easier in the absence of the EEC.

Fourth, suppose it were true that the creation of the EEC forced the US Congress into trade talks. That would be tantamount to the aggressive unilateralism that many currently deplore in US trade policy. "The Six" would have done something to harm their partners, at least in the partners' eyes, and then mitigated it in return for concessions. This is a dangerous game, even if a successful one, and might be playable only a few times. Indeed, if it were the case, it could explain why US policy has become more belligerent towards the latest enlargement and towards "1992". However, in fact, the United States was generally sympathetic towards EC integration and actually encouraged it by allowing the Administration to offer deeper tariff cuts to a European Customs Union than to the separate European nations – Jackson (1991).[16]

It has also been argued – although less frequently – that regionalism was behind the Tokyo Round. Winham (1986) reports both the first EEC enlargement (including free trade with EFTA) and the restrictiveness of the CAP as factors in the US view. The former observation seems no more compelling than those surrounding the creation of the EEC, while the latter is distinctly two-edged from our perspective: it requires, first, that the CAP induced negotiations and, second, that regionalism induced the CAP – i.e., that regionalism increased trade restrictions. Again, for this to be advantageous in its net effect on multilateralism requires a negotiating model in which might and countervailing power are the critical elements of liberalization, quite contrary to the hegemonic views of, say, Keohane (1984). It has also been suggested to me that enlargement finally achieved a US goal by bringing the four biggest economies of Europe into one bloc and that this required a commensurate foreign policy response. Maybe, but why this response took the form of initiating a trade negotiation in the face of European opposition is unclear.

Finally, consider the Uruguay Round. Its initiation has not been related to regionalism, but its completion has. WTO (1995) says "there is little doubt that . . . the spread of regionalism [was a] major factor in eliciting the concessions needed to conclude" the Round. Frankel (1996) reports Fred Bergsten's conversation with German policy-makers in which it was stated that the APEC meeting in Vancouver was a major jolt to the EU which prompted it to reach settlement in the Round. On the WTO's general assertion there was a perception that the failure of the Round would lead to regional fragmentation, and this certainly encouraged the spread of defensive regionalism. How much pressure this put on the two major negotiating parties is not clear, however, for they would not have been the principal casualties of fragmentation. Bergsten's interlocutor seems to me (albeit from the outside) likely to have been confusing rhetoric and substance. The EU had set up the conditions for settlement in the MacSharry farm reforms in 1991/2 and some insiders report that as early as 1990 EU negotiators recognized that they would complete the Round as soon as they had built an appropriate domestic coalition on agriculture, e.g., Hathaway and Ingco (1996).

A common theme runs through all these accounts of regionalism and GATT multilateral Rounds: the threat of (or, worse, actual) violence and response. All the accounts report countries running back to the multilateral system to counter the damage that other countries' RIAs may do them. This may be an effective way forward but it clearly relies on rather fine judgment by both (all) protagonists that folding is better than fighting. Perhaps if regionalism has raised the average de facto level of multilateralism it has done so at the expense of increasing the chances of catastrophe.

Earlier evidence on regionalism is somewhat more positive, but in different circumstances. Irwin (1993) reports how the Cobden-Chavalier Treaty spawned a rash of mfn trade treaties and so created an era of significant liberalism (if not formal multilateralism). After about 1880, however, this began slowly to erode, not in a regional fashion but with mfn rates being increased. Nonetheless, the last quarter of the nineteenth century remained a reasonably liberal period. In the inter-war period the multilateral trading system fell apart very rapidly following the imposition of the (mfn) Smoot-Hawley tariff. Both Oye (1992) and Irwin (1993) argue that whereas multilateral attempts to halt and reverse the collapse failed, regional attempts induced a measure of liberalism. Britain, France and Germany sought to protect their export markets by preferential arrangements, and in so doing did violence to US exports. This in turn induced the United States to turn to bilateral approaches in the Reciprocal Trade Agreements Act of 1934.

I draw two lessons from these historical analyses. First, regionalism/bilateralism, which entails much more obvious pay-offs for exporters (internalization) than multilateralism, can help to break down restrictive regimes. Whether it can lead all the way to multilateral liberalism is not proven, but it clearly has the ability to start the process off. This is consistent with the observation that difficult issues such as public procurement, standards and services feature more strongly in regional than in multilateral arrangements. The challenge for the policy-makers is to establish a means of switching to the multilateral horse once the rate has started.

Second, building on Oye's analysis of "shiftable externalities," potentially regionalized systems are likely to break down much more quickly than purely multilateral ones – cf the late 1800s and the 1930s. Shiftable externalities are externalities which an action creates but whose incidence can be moved between other agents according to their actions. Suppose I import equally from five partners and want to cut my total imports by 20%. An mfn tariff increase might cut those from *A*, *B*, *C*, *D* and *E* each by 20%. But suppose *A* offers me a concession to exempt itself from the cut. The others now have to bear a 25% cut if I am to make the same target. Now suppose *B* wants to negotiate. It has to offer a bigger concession because it has to claw back a bigger cut in exports. And so on. There is a clear incentive for any supplier to strike an exclusionary deal and as quickly as possible. The possibility of regionalism increases the speed of decay.

Perhaps the crucial question is "where is the world economy now?" Fairly closed, so that regionalism is necessary (efficient) to crack open widespread barriers, or fairly open, so that the danger is that regionalism could precipitate a collapse if someone made a wrong call? Perhaps the answer differs by sector, so that while regional arrangements are important in new issues, they are a potential danger in areas such as goods trade.

5. FINALE

This section collects together the principal lessons from this survey both in terms of conclusions and directions for future research. Before doing so, however, it reports one final contribution to the literature that I have been unable to fit into the schema above.

5.1 Investment Not Trade

Many commentators argue that the recent crop of North–South RIAs – e.g., NAFTA and the Europe Agreements – have been aimed at locking in the southern partner's economic reforms and stimulating inflows of foreign direct investment (FDI). Ethier (1996) offers a brilliant formalization of these ideas. Briefly, developing countries start in autarchy, and as the world grows and liberalizes they start to think about opening up themselves. If they reform successfully and attract an inflow of FDI, they gain a step increase in productivity. Their problem is that if several of them reform simultaneously, none can guarantee that it will get the FDI – maybe the inflow will go to their rivals. Regionalism, by which an industrial country offers a particular developing country small preferences on its exports, overcomes this problem by ensuring that the industrial country will invest in its partner developing country rather than any other. (Since all industrial countries are assumed to be identical, as are all developing countries, the smallest preference on return exports stemming from an FDI flow is sufficient to create this link.) Thus regionalism ensures the success of reform, not only increasing the proportion of reforming developing countries that succeed but also encouraging more to try. This is regionalism as coordination – it removes a source of uncertainty and thus encourages reform and openness.

Ethier's paper is original and important, but its model is very special. In particular, there are no conceivable costs to regionalism to the partners, and, because countries are identical within their type-class, no dangers of inefficient regional arrangements growing up within the classes. Thus coordination comes essentially for free. Additionally, small changes to the model would allow the same coordination to be achieved multilaterally. For example, if each developing country considers coming out of the closet of autarchy at a unique time (because they all differ slightly from one another in dimensions that affect the timing of their reform decision), or if the supply of FDI for the industrial world is sufficiently large or the movements of the factor prices in developing countries sufficiently strong, every developing country can be sure of getting some FDI if it opens up. Nonetheless the focus on FDI rather than trade is a powerful attraction of this approach, given the structure of and rhetoric surrounding current North–South regional arrangements.

5.2 Conclusions and Future Research

The issue of "regionalism vs. multilateralism" is new analytically and deficient of empirical evidence. It is hardly surprising, therefore, that this survey should conclude with more statements about research strategy than about the world we live in. Indeed, as I noted above, the only categorical statement that can be made in the last class is that one incident of regionalism is not sufficient to undermine a relatively multilateral system immediately.

My main conclusions from working on this fascinating literature include:

- Since we value "multilateralism," we had better work out what it means, and, if it means different things to different people, ensure that we identify the sense in which we are using the term when we do so.
- The symmetric models looking at the welfare effects of regionalism have served their purpose and probably offer rather little return to future research. Their structure is not plausible and their results seems very fragile with respect to assumed parameter values. If completely new ways of thinking about regionalism emerge, it may be worth exploring them in a symmetric framework as a way of elucidating their properties, but this is not going to resolve the positive "stepping stones" question.
- Asymmetric models are more plausible but it is important to model both the demand for and supply of bloc membership.
- Models of negotiated trade policy also take a significant step towards realism. However, it would be nice, in future, to try to move beyond the repeated game trigger strategies approach to model a richer set of objectives and disciplines. This, of course, is a challenge not only to researchers on regionalism, but also to those working on the trading system in general.
- Sector-specific lobbies are a danger if regionalism is permitted. Trade diversion is good politics even if it is bad economics. I find quite convincing the view that multilateral liberalism could stall because producers get most of what they seek from regional arrangements.
- The direct effect of regionalism on multilateralism is important, but possibly more so is the indirect effect it has by changing the ways in which (groups of) countries interact and respond to shocks in the world economy. The way in which the existence of fringes of small partners affects relations between large players seems to be a fruitful avenue, as does the structure of post-integration institutions.
- It would be useful to embed the "regionalism vs. multilateralism" question in a framework of general economic reform and/or economic growth to generate richer menus of potential benefits and chains of causation.
- Regionalism, by allowing stronger internalization of the gains from trade de-restriction, seems likely to be able to facilitate freer trade in highly restrictive circumstances or sectors.
- The possibility of regionalism probably increases the risks of catastrophe in the trade system. The incentives established by the insurance motive for joining regional arrangements and Oye's analysis of "shiftable externalities" both lead to such a conclusion. So too does the view that regionalism is a means to bring trade partners to the multilateral negotiating table, because it is essentially coercive. The latter may have been an effective strategy, but it is risky.

APPENDIX 1: AN INDEX OF MULTILATERALISM?

A country's multilateralism index is a positive function of

(a) the absence of discrimination in its trade policy
(b) the closeness its trade regime is overall to free trade.

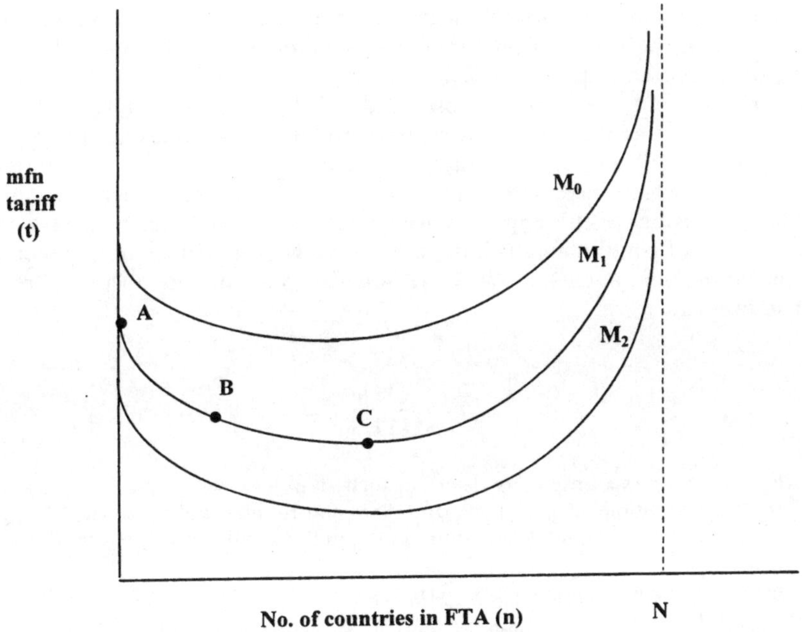

FIGURE A.1 *Iso-Multilateralism Loci (M_2>M_1>M_0)*

Assume that only one commodity is traded in the world and that our country imports it from every other country in an (N+1) country world. Assume also that initially all partners face the same (mfn) traffic at level t and that no other distortions exist. Suppose now that the country signs an FTA with some (n) partners. How do t and n enter the index of multilateralism (M)?

Figure A.1 plots contours of equal M in the space of the mfn tariff (t) and the number of FTA partners (n). Starting at, say, A, with a positive t, assume we sign an FTA with one partner. This increases discrimination and so would require a decrease in t to keep M constant; similarly if another partner entered the FTA, t would need to fall further. Thus the iso-M curve would include a point like B. Eventually, however, say, at C, enough countries would be in the FTA that increasing n would, *ceteris paribus*, increase measured multilateralism, allowing an increase in t along the iso-M curve. Now imagine the far end of the curve. When the final country gets into the FTA, our country offers everyone free trade and the mfn tariff can be infinity.

For any n, n countries pay a tariff of zero, while (N-n) pay t. Since freer trade entails higher multilateralism, if, say, m countries are "exceptional ($m<N/2$)," M will be higher if the majority ($N-m$) pay zero than if the minority (m) does. Looked at alternatively, for many values of the tariff (t), a given level of multilateralism ($\bar{M}$) could arise with two different values of n, say n_1 and n_2, $n_1 < n_2$. We require that $n_1<(N-n_2)$ as in figure A.1. Figure A.1 presents three such iso-multilateralism loci, with the degree of multilateralism increasing the closer the locus is to the $\underline{x}$-axis. In the limit the locus for perfect multilateralism runs along the $\underline{x}$-axis and up the vertical from N.

Clearly this index is quite complex and will become even more so once we recognize that more than two trade regimes might exist (in this example partners pay either t or 0) and that regimes will actually vary across commodities. It becomes even worse once we recognize that we need to aggregate across countries.

The conclusions of this appendix are twofold. First, we actually need to think what we mean by multilateralism if we think we are worried about it. Second, in the meantime our conclusions about regionalism vs. multilateralism will remain a little fuzzy.

NOTES

1 Appendix 1 offers a little more detail on such an index.

2 Earlier contributions include Reizman (1985) and Kennan and Reizman (1990).

3 Sinclair and Vines model the similarity somewhat differently from Bond and Syropoulos.

4 They refer to their discussion as "Krugman vs. Krugman," my nomination for title of the year.

5 Deardorff and Stern (1994) effectively use the same approach but pairing countries by complementary comparative advantage rather than transportation costs. Arguably, however, their results gravitate away from continental blocs rather than towards them if comparative advantage varies more across continents than within them.

6 Similar arguments surround the Kemp and Wan (1976) result that a customs union can always find a common external tariff renders it welfare improving and thus that unions can beneficially expand and combine until they arrive at global free trade. "Can," but there is no analysis of "do." This is not to criticize Kemp and Wan; their focus was not on stepping stones.

7 That is, blocs do not raise their optimum tariffs as a result of integration.

8 An alternative strategy would be for the union to *reduce* its tariff to keep non-member welfare constant – a so-called Kemp-Wan reduction. The union would prefer this to trade war if it had below about 40% of countries.

9 As Perroni and Whalley observe, in strict trade-policy terms Eastern Europe, the Mediterranean countries and Mexico gain little from their associations with larger blocs relative to unilateral mfn liberalization.

10 See also Helpman (1995) for a summary.

11 This point is also made by McCulloch and Petri (1994).

12 Similar causal channels are found in Panagariya and Findlay (1994)

13 The analysis revolves around the elasticities with which the fringe demands and supplies sensitive products, not its excess supply *per se*. Presumably the latter would enter the decision to create the FTA in the first place. The link with Richardson (1993) is best seen on the import analogue of the argument in the text. If the fringe supply curve of the sensitive import is perfectly elastic, the lobbies in A lose all interest in maintaining a higher post-tariff price on B.

14 They still gain from integration because of the differentiated goods.

15 Such a sector may prefer high EU protection, so that it can reap high rents on EU sales, but at least it could survive with lower protection.

16 Maybe this reflected US fears of the EEC – i.e., that it felt obliged to offer and to seek bigger tariff reductions if the EEC completed its integration – but publishing the fact seems a clumsy negotiating ploy if that were the case.

REFERENCES

Bagwell, K. and Staiger, R. W. 1993a. "Multilateral Tariff Cooperation During the Formation of Regional Free Trade Areas," NBER Working Paper Series 4364.

——. 1993b. "Multilateral Tariff Cooperation During the Formation of Customs Unions," Northwestern University Center for Mathematical Studies in Economics and Management Science. Discussion Paper 1070.

——. (1996) "Regionalism and Multilateralism Tariff Cooperation," Paper prepared for International Economics Association Round-Table Conference, International Trade Policy and the Pacific Rim, 15–17 July, pages 37.

——. (1997) "Preferential Agreements and the Multilateral Trading System."

Baldwin, R. E., Haaparanta, P. and Kiander, J. 1995. *Expanding Membership in the European Union*, Cambridge University Press, Cambridge.

Baldwin, R. E. 1995. "A domino theory of regionalism," Chapter 2 of Baldwin, Haaparanta and Kiander (eds), pp. 25–48.

Bhagwati, J. N. 1991. *The World Trading System at Risk*, Harvester Wheatsheaf, Hemel Hempstead.

Bhagwati, J. N. and Panagariya, A. 1996. "Preferential Trading Areas and Multilateralism: Strangers, Friends of Foes?" in Bhagwati and Panagariya (eds) *Free Trade Areas or Free Trade? The Economics of Preferential Trading Agreements*, AEI press, Washington D.C. (forthcoming).

Bond, E. W. and Syropoulos, C. 1996a. "The Size of Trading Blocs: Market Power and World Welfare Effects" (forthcoming), Journal of International Economics.

Bond, E. W. and Syropoulos, C. 1996b. "Trading Blocs and the Sustainability of Interregional Cooperation," forthcoming in Canzoneri, M., Ethier, W. and Grilli V. (eds). *The New Transatlantic Economy*, Cambridge University Press, Cambridge.

Bond, E. W., Syropoulos, C. and Winters, L. A. 1996. "Deepening of Regional Integration and External Trade Relations," CEPR Discussion Paper No. 1317.

Cadot, O., De Melo, and Olarrega, J. 1996. "Regional Integration and Lobbying for Tariffs Against Non-Members," mimeo, University of Geneva.

Campa, J. M. and Sorenson, T. L. (1996) "Are Trade Blocs Conducive to Free Trade?" *The Scandinavian Journal of Economics*, Vol. 98, pp. 263–273.

Collie, D. "Bilateralism is Good: Trade Blocs and Strategic Export Subsidies," mimeo, University College, Cardiff.

Deardorff, A. W. and Stern, R. M. 1994. "Multilateral Trade Negotiations and Preferential Trading Arrangements," in Deardorff, A. V. and Stern, R. M., *Analytical and Negotiating Issues in the Global Trading System*, Ann Abor: University of Michigan Press.

De Melo, J. and Panagariya, A. 1993. *New Dimensions in Regional Integration*, Cambridge University Press, Cambridge.

Ethier, W. J. (1996) "Regionalism in a Multilateral World," mimeo.

Eichengreen B. 1995. *Europe's Post-War Recovery*, Cambridge University Press, Cambridge.

Frankel, J. A. (1996). *Regional Trading Blocs*, forthcoming, Institute for International Economics, Washington, D.C.

Frankel, J. A., Stein, E. and Wei, S. J. 1995. "Trading Blocs and the Americas: The Natural, the Unnatural, and the Super-Natural," *Journal of Development Economics*, 47, 61–95.

Frankel, J. A., Stein, E. and Weis, S. J. 1996. "Continental Trade Blocs: Are They Natural and Super-Natural?," Chapter 4 of Frankel (ed.) *The Regionalism of the World Economy*, forthcoming, Chicago University Press.

Frankel, J. A. and Wei, S. J. 1996. "Regionalization of World Trade and Currencies: Economics and Politics," Chapter 7 of Frankel (ed.) *The Regionalization of the World Economy*, forthcoming, Chicago University Press.

Gatsios, K. and Karp, L. 1991. "Delegation Games in Customs Unions," *Review of Economic Studies*, 58(2), pp. 391–97.

Gatsios, K. and Karp, L. 1995. "Delegation in a General Equilibrium Model of Customs Unions," *European Economic Review*, 39(2), pp. 319–33.

Goto, J. and Hamada, K. 1994. "Economic Integration and the Welfare of those who are left Behind: An Asian Perspective," RIEB Kobe University, Discussion Paper No. 47.

Goto, J. and Hamada, K. 1994. "EU, NAFTA and Asian Responses: A Perspective from the Calculus of Participation," NBER Working Paper No. 5325.

Grossman, G. and Helpman, E. 1994. "Protection of Sale," *American Economic Review*, 85, 667–90.

Grossman, G. and Helpman, E. 1995, "The Politics of Free-Trade Agreements," *American Economic Review*, 84, 833–50.

Hamilton, C. B. 1991. "The Nordic EFTA Countries' Options: Community Membership or a Permanent EEA – Accord," Chapter 7 in *EFTA Countries in a Changing Europe*, EFTA, Geneva, pp. 97–128.

Hathaway, D. E. and Ingco, M. D. 1996. "Agricultural liberalization and the Uruguay Round," Chapter 2 of Martin and Winters (eds) *The Uruguay Round and the Developing Countries*, Cambridge University Press, Cambridge.

Helpman, E. 1995. "Politics and Trade Policy," CEPR Discussion Paper No. 1269.

Hufbauer, G. C. 1990. *Europe 1992: An American Perspective*, Brookings, Washington, D.C.

Irwin, D. A. 1993. "Multilateral and Bilateral Trade Policies in the World Trading System: A Historical Perspective," Chapter 4 of De Melo and Panagariya (eds), pp. 90–119.

Irwin, D. A. 1995. "The GATT's contribution to economic recovery in post-war Western Europe," Chapter 5 of Eichengreen (ed.), pp. 127–50.

Jackson, J. H. 1991. "The European Community and World Trade: The Commercial Policy Dimension," Discussion Paper No. 298, Institute for Public Policy Studies, University of Michigan, Ann Arbor.

Jacquemin, A. and Sapir, A. 1988. "European Integration or World Integration?," *Weltwirtschaftlihes Archiv*, vol. 124, pp. 127–39.

Kemp, M.C. and Wan, H., Jr. 1976. "An Elementary Proposition Concerning the Formation of Customs Union," *Journal of International Economics*, vol. 6, pp. 95–7.

Kennan, J. and Riezman, R. 1990. "Optimal Tariff Equilibria with Customs Unions," *Canadian Journal of Economics*, 23, 70–83.

Keohane, R. O. 1984. *After Hegemony: Cooperation and Discord in the World Political Economy*, Princeton University Press, Princeton, N.J.

Kowalcyzk, C. and Sjostrom, T. 1992. "Bringing GATT into the Core," *Economica*, vol. 61, pp. 301–17.

Krishna, P. 1994. "Regionalism and Multilateralism: A Political Economy Approach," mimeo, Brown University.

Krugman, P. 1991a. "Is Bilateralism Bad?," in Helpman and Razin (eds) *International Trade and Trade Policy*, Cambridge MA, MIT Press.

Krugman, P. 1991b. "The Move Towards Free Trade Zones" in "Policy Implications of Trade and Currency Zones." A symposium sponsored by the Federal Reserve Bank of Kansas City. Jackson Hole, Wyoming: 7–42.

Krugman, P. 1993. "Regionalism versus Multilateralism: Analytical Notes," in J. De Melo and A. Panagariya (eds.), *New Dimensions in Regional Integration*, op. cit., pp. 58–78.

Lawrence, R. Z. 1991. "Emerging Regional Arrangements: Building Blocs or Stumbling Blocks?" in O'Brien (ed.) *Finance and the International Economy 5*: The AMEX Bank Review Prize Essays, New York: Oxford University Press, pp. 23–35.

Levy, P. I. 1994. "A Political Economy Analysis of Free Trade Agreements," Economic Growth Centre Discussion Paper No. 718, Yale University.

Levy, P. I. 1996a. "Lobbying and International Cooperation in Tariff Setting, mimeo, Yale University.

Levy, P. I. 1996b. Comment on "Regionalization of World Trade and Currencies: Economics and Politics," Chapter 7 of Frankel (ed.) *The Regionalization of the World Economy*, forthcoming Chicago University Press.

Ludema, R. 1996. "On the Value of Preferential Trade Agreements in Multilateral Negotiations," forthcoming in *Journal of International Economics.*

Messerlin, P. A. 1983. "Bureaucracies and the Political Economy of Protection: Reflections of a Continental European," *Weltwirtschaftliches Archiv*, 117, pp. 468–96.

Nitsch, V. (1996) "Natural Trading Blocs: A Closer Look," prepared for European Economic Association Meeting, Istanbul, August.

Nitsch, V. (1996) "Do Three Trade Blocs Minimize World Welfare?," *Review of International Economics*, Vol. 4, pp. 355–363.

Nogues, J. and Quintanilla, R. 1993. "Latin America's Integration and the Multilateral Trading System," in De Melo and Panagariya (eds) *New Dimensions in Regional Integration*, pp. 278–313.

Nordstrom, H. 1995. "Customs unions, regional trading blocs and welfare," Chapter 3 of Baldwin, Haaparanta and Kiander (eds), pp. 54–78.

Oye, K. 1992. *Economic Discrimination and Political Exchange: World Political Economy in the 1930s and 1980s.* Princeton University Press: Princeton, NJ.

Paragariya, A. and Findlay, R. 1994. "A Political Economy Analysis of Free Trade Areas and Customs Unions," Policy Research Working Paper 1261, World Bank, Washington D.C.

Perroni, C. and Whalley, J. 1994. "The New Regionalism: Trade Liberalization or Insurance?" NBER Working Paper No. 4626.

Richardson, M. and Desruelle, D. 1994. "Fortress Europe: Jericho or Chateau d'If?," mimeo.

Richardson, M. 1993. "Endogenous Protection and Trade Diversion," *Journal of International Economics*, 34(3–4), 309–24.

Richardson, M. 1994. "Why a Free Trade Area? The Tariff Also Rises," *Economics and Politics*, 6(1), pp. 79–96.

Richardson, M. 1995. "Tariff Revenue Competition in a Free Trade Area," *European Economic Review*, vol. 39, pp. 1429–37.

Riezman, R. 1985. "Customs Unions and Core," *Journal of International Economics*, 19, 355–65.

Sapir, A. 1993. "Discussion of Chapter 7," De Melo and Panagariya (eds), pp. 1491–1506.

Scharpf, F. W. 1988. "The Joint-Decision Trap: Lessons from German Federalism and European Integration," *Public Administration*, vol. 66, pp. 239–278.

Schattschneider, E. E. 1935. *Politics, Pressures and the Tariff*, New York: Prentice-Hall.

Shepsle, K. A. and Weingat, B. R. 1981. "Political preferences for the pork barrel: a generalisation," *American Journal of Political Science*, 25, pp. 96–111.

Sinclair, P. and Vines, D. 1995. "Bigger Trade Blocs Need not Entail more Protection," mimeo, University of Birmingham.

Spilmbergo, A. and Stein, E. 1996. "The Welfare Implications of Trading Blocs among Countries with Different Endowments," Chapter 5 of Frankel (ed.) *The Regionalization of the World Economy*, forthcoming, Chicago University Press.

Srinivasan, T. N. 1993. "Regionalism vs. Multilateralism: Analytical Notes' Comment," in De Melo and Panagariya (eds) *New Dimension of the Regional Integration*, pp 84–89.
Summers, L. 1991. "Regionalism and the World Trading System," in "Policy Implications of Trade and Currency Zones." A symposium sponsored by the Federal Reserve Bank of Kansas City. Jackson Hole, Wyoming: 295–302.
Widgren, M. 1995a. "Voting power and control in the EU: the impact of EFTA entrants," Chapter 5 of Baldwin, Haaparanta and Kiander (eds), pp. 113–42.
Widgren, M. 1995b. "Probabilistic voting power in the EU Council: the cases of trade policy and social regulation," *Scandinavian Journal of Economics* 97 (2), pp. 345–56.
Winham, G. R. 1986. *International Trade and the Tokyo Round Negotiation*, Princeton University Press, Princeton, N.J.
Winters, L. A. 1993. "The European Community: A Case of Successful Integration," CEPR Discussion Paper No. 755.
Winters, L. A. 1994. "The EC and Protection: The Political Economy," *European Economic Review*, 38, pp. 596–603.
Winters, L. A. 1995. "Who Should Run Eastern European Trade Policy and How," Chapter 2 of Winters (ed.) *Foundations of an Open Economy: Trade Laws and Institutions for Eastern Europe*, CEPR, London, pp. 19–39.
World Trade Organization, 1995. *Regionalism and the World Trading System*, WTO, Geneva.
Yarbrough, B. V. and Yarbrough, R. M. 1992. *Cooperation and Governance in International Trade: The Strategic Organizational Approach*. Princeton University Press, Princeton, N.J.

15. How to Cut the Textile Knot: Alternative Paths to Liberalization of the MFA

M. Wolf

> The experience in the textile sphere clearly shows that it is simply an illusion to believe that one can manage trade in a particular sector in response to the exigencies of that sector without any consequence for trade policy in general. International trade policies are either based on norms or create norms. World economic relations, therefore, cannot be managed by solving each problem separately without reference to previous solutions and without prejudice to the solution of future problems. (Dunkel 1984, p. 363).

> The protectionism of the 1930s was openly adversary; the new one, however, builds on negotiation, indeed, is in a perverse way the result of international cooperation. As a result, the new protectionism is politically stronger because it accommodates a broader range of interests. Where earlier forms of protection created vested interests in the importing country only, the new protectionism has built up equally strong vested interest on the export side as well; paradoxically perhaps, discrimination has become the means of making export industries interested in continuing protection. For all these reasons the new protectionism will be much more difficult to roll back. (Tumlir 1985, pp. 38–39).

There are many ways to eliminate the Multi-Fibre Arrangement (MFA) and return trade in textiles and clothing to the normal rules of the General Agreement on Tariffs and Trade (GATT). They all share one drawback: they will harm a great many influential people.

It is for this reason, no doubt, that wise words on the need to liberalize the MFA have fallen on stormy ground. The author of the present paper has either co-authored or authored papers on the liberalization of the MFA before the negotiations of both MFAs III and IV (Curzon and others 1981, Wolf 1985). Both of them stressed that further renewal was certain if an explicit commitment to the termination of the MFA was not built into the framework of the agreement. Back in 1981, for example, the Commission of the European Communities (1981, p. 9) said of the upcoming MFA III that "it considers that this period should enable the Community's industry to make new progress in its restructuring efforts." Restructuring there may have been, but this did not make the Community a jot more willing to dispense with the MFA when the time for renewal came round in 1986. After nearly thirty years of the textile arrangements, Benjamin Franklin might conclude that there are three certainties in life: death, taxes and the MFA.

But now, we are told, all will be different. In April 1989, Ministers agreed that (GATT 1989a, p. 8):

(a) substantive negotiations will begin in April 1989 in order to reach agreement within the time frame of the Uruguay Round on modalities for the negotiation of this sector into GATT, in accordance with the negotiating objective;
(b) such modalities for the process of integration into GATT on the basis of strengthened GATT rules and disciplines should *inter alia* cover *the phasing out of restrictions under the Multi-fibre Arrangement and other restrictions on textiles and clothing not consistent with GATT rules and disciplines*, the time span for such a process of integration, and the progressive character of this process which should commence following the conclusion of the negotiations in 1990 (our emphasis).

We have been told; but should we also believe?

There are good reasons for skepticism, not merely past, bitter experience, but also the truth that dares not speak its name: almost everyone who matters has loved the MFA. Liberalization of the MFA would, in large part, be a triumph of principle over expediency,. It is wrong to assume that liberalizing principle always loses; but it is foolish to pretend it often wins.

Yet it would be wrong to be too pessimistic. The Uruguay Round offers what may well prove to be a unique opportunity to liberalize trade in textiles and clothing. But agreement to liberalize the MFA will be difficult to come by. Success will only come if the chosen approach goes some way toward dealing with the major political obstacles. This is the first criterion for evaluating any plan to liberalize the MFA.

The second is rather different: it is that the chosen means of liberalization should not itself damage the GATT. This is no small danger. The price for liberalizing the MFA that will be demanded by the major importing countries will be "strengthened rules and disciplines within GATT" (GATT 1989b, p. 1). This could prove to be a polite euphemism for the GATT's ruination, an attempt to introduce some of the most pernicious aspects of the MFA into the GATT itself.

ORIGIN OF THE MFA

If one is to assess plans for reform against such criteria one needs to start with an appreciation of why the textile arrangements exist. With the MFA gone, one might return to something close to the *status quo ante*, but a glance at history reveals that the *status quo ante* was not particularly liberal.

Origin of the Textile Arrangements

It was in Osaka in 1937 that the first "Gentlemen's Agreement" between the American and Japanese textile trade associations was negotiated. "The U.S. Government clearly favored the unofficial approach, else anti-trust law would have been used to prevent it . . . It is particularly significant that at the very beginning of the modern era of American trade policy the two prime movers in its development – Roosevelt and Hull – recognized the uniqueness of the textile import problem and arranged to handle it separately from their general trade program [as embodied in Reciprocal Trade Agreements Act of 1934]." (Brandis, 1982, pp. 7–8.)

The explanation for these governmental nods and winks to an informal, probably illegal agreement was that the United States possessed no legal authority for the introduction of import quotas, let alone discriminatory quotas. On the contrary, both were precluded not merely by existing law but by the fundamental policy of the Administration. The political itch created by "disruptive" imports from Japan could only be scratched extralegally.

What had happened before the Second World War happened again soon after, but at a time when the United States was strongly committed to nondiscrimination – the most-favored nation (MFN) principle – within the GATT, a treaty made in the image of its own prewar legislation. "Toward the end of 1955, Japan began to impose internal restrictions on some of her cotton textile exports to the United States . . . in January, 1957, Japan gave American officials details of a five-year program of 'voluntary' export controls. . . . American pressure contributed to this outcome, particularly a provision in a new law, the Agricultural Act of 1956, which empowered the President, 'whenever he determines such action appropriate,' to negotiate agreements limiting exports from other countries or imports into United States of textiles or textile products and also giving him some emergency power to restrict these imports unilaterally." (Keesing and Wolf 1980, p. 15.) What was it that persuaded the American Administration, averse to such intervention as it appeared to be, to put the required pressure on Japan?

Pressure from Congress is the answer, pressure orchestrated by the American Textile Manufacturers Institute. In 1956 the Senate only narrowly defeated an amendment to a pending foreign aid bill that would have mandated cotton textile import quotas based on the preceding three-year average import level. One reason for the defeat was that several senators were persuaded that other action would be taken to deal with the problem, as was, indeed, to be the case (Brandis 1982, p. 10). As the Finance Committee commented, "many members of the Senate may not wish to continue past support of international programs which contribute to widespread unemployment or serious injury to domestic producers." (Brandis 1982, p. 11.)

The voluntary export restraint (VER) with Japan might have been the end of the matter. But, the textile industry spread like a plague. Exports expanded rapidly from Hong Kong, Portugal, Spain, Egypt and India. Worse, Hong Kong refused to accept a VER with the United States, although it did accept VERs on exports to the United Kingdom, along with India and Pakistan (Keesing and Wolf 1980, p. 15–16). But then, being a colony, it could hardly do otherwise.

Within the United States political pressure grew to such intensity that President Kennedy committed himself to support of the textile industry during the presidential election campaign of 1960. Quite apart from this commitment, it was clear that he would have to assuage the textile industry and its supporters in Congress if the dream of a new GATT multilateral trade negotiation (MTN), subsequently the Kennedy Round, was to become a reality. Moreover, like his predecessors (and successors as well) he was determined to avoid a bill authorizing textile import quotas. Such a bill would not merely comprehensively violate the GATT, but could almost certainly not be limited to textiles either.

So the search was on for an internationally respectable figleaf to cover the abandonment of the GATT's first article in the case of this industry. That figleaf was found in "the question of the avoidance of market disruption," already placed on the GATT agenda by the United States in 1959 (Dam 1970, pp. 297–300). For, to the horror of the developed countries, the GATT appeared to commit them to trading over bound tariffs with countries that had a decisively different pattern of comparative advantage from themselves. Of no industry was this more true than textiles and clothing.

In the end, 'market disruption" was incorporated into a new international agreement, an anti-GATT for textiles: the Short-Term Arrangement Regarding International Trade in Cotton Textiles (STA) of 1961, which begat the Long-Term Arrangement (LTA) of 1962, which begat the MFA of 1974 and so forth to the present day. With an international agreement that contained an explicit clause for unilateral safeguard action in Article 3, it was no longer particularly difficult for the United States to persuade the exporters to sign up for "voluntary," bilateral agreements under Article 4. It merely required plenty of action under Article 3 (Dam 1970, pp. 307–8).

Where were the other developed countries while the United States was going through these agonies? Most of them were comfortably protected by a rampart of quantitative restrictions that had originally been allowed under the GATT's balance of payments clause (Article XII) and had since metamorphosed into illegal, but persistent "residual restrictions." An important objective of the United States in pushing for the STA and then LTA was to secure "burden sharing," namely, liberalization of the nontariff barriers maintained by other advanced countries (particularly, the six members of the European Community, the three Scandinavian countries and Austria).[1] Substantial expansion of the quotas imposed by these countries was set in motion under Article II of the LTA (Dam 1970, p. 302), though the nontariff barriers themselves were not to be eliminated until the first MFA came into effect (when many of them metamorphosed into restrictions unilaterally imposed under Article III or agreed under Article IV).

The desire to persuade other industrial countries to liberalize was one reason for the American desire to create an international textile arrangement, but the most important aim was to protect both its own trade policy and the GATT from irresistible political pressure at a time when appearances still mattered a great deal. There was a belief that the GATT's safeguard clause (Article XIX) would explode if used as a container for the pressures generated by textiles. The greatest danger was thought to be congressional legislation in violation of the international obligations of the United States, leading to disintegration of the fabric of the GATT. The solution was an arrangement authorising discriminatory protection against 'disruptive" exporters, but one that also promised liberalization, if not yet.

For the governments of the developing countries the motive for acquiesence was essentially the same as for American demands. If there were to be restrictions upon their exports, there would also be an international arrangement that ostensibly committed all industrial countries to liberalization. Developing countries also hoped the LTA would protect the GATT through a mutually-agreed exception in an area of particularly high sensitivity.[2]

Not only were they deceived in their hopes. A liberally inclined scholar like the late Gerard Curzon (1965, pp. 257–8) saw the LTA as 'an economist's dream . . . What is praiseworthy about the situation is that the protection-inclined countries [of continental Europe] should voluntarily admit that this market-conforming mechanism should come into play, asking only for some measures that will reduce the abruptness of the disappearance of old industries . . . this type of agreement is obviously going to be the answer to many of the changes in world trade that will have to take place during the next few decades."

Developing of the Textile Arrangements

The birth of the textile arrangements marked an important failure of the GATT approach to trade liberalization. The political costs of liberalization turned out to outweigh the economic gains. The subsequent history of the textile arrangements merely confirmed the strength of the initial pressures.

The MFA says that "the basic objectives shall be to achieve the expansion of trade, the reduction of barriers to such trade and the progressive liberalization of world trade in textile products, while at the same time ensuring the orderly and equitable development of this trade and avoidance of disruptive effects in individual markets and on individual lines of production in both importing and exporting countries." (GATT 1974, p. 6.) A finer bit of bureaucratic schizophrenia one could hardly find. There has been expansion of trade, but there has certainly not been reduction of barriers or progressive liberalization. Whether the development of trade has been either orderly or equitable, one may leave to those who understand these concepts. What is certain is that trade in textiles and clothing is now infested by thousands of origin-, destination- and product-specific quotas.

One episode in this long and sordid history is of particular importance to the theme of the present paper. Just as the STA and the LTA were seen by the United States as instruments for the liberalization of imports into other developed countries, so the MFA was *inter alia* viewed as an instrument for ending the "residual restrictions" of the European countries. Indeed, the general tenor of the MFA was, apart from the extension of product coverage, notably more liberal than that of the LTA. In particular, Article 2 explicitly committed the importing countries to phase out those restrictions inconsistent with either the GATT or the MFA.

Moreover, the members of the European Community went a long way in that direction. The period immediately after 1974 was one of substantial liberalization of Community restrictions as policy was shifted from the individual members to the Community level. Unfortunately, that liberalization coincided with the first oil shock. Whether the liberalization could have been maintained if fate had not intervened in this way is unclear. In any case, the Community suffered a trauma from which it has not yet recovered. Under the impact of rapid growth of imports and declining demand, political pressure built up irresistibly, resulting in the "reasonable departures" clause of MFA II's infamous protocol of renewal. Thus ended any pretense that the MFA would prove to be a liberalizing agreement.

The policy changes in the United States during the 1980s in response to the effect of the soaring dollar on the textile and clothing industries were nails in a coffin (Wolf 1987, pp. 264–66; Cline 1987, pp. 178–86 and Ch. 9). As a liberalizing agreement, the MFA was by then already a corpse.

SOURCES OF SUPPORT FOR THE MFA

The pressures that created the textile arrangements are powerful. So powerful, in fact, that the GATT proved incapable of handing them. But as time passed another element became increasingly important: the web of vested interests committed to the system. As the late Jan Tumlir remarked, the MFA is an example of cooperative protection. It provides something for everyone who has a place at the table, while keeping those it harms well away from the hallowed place.

Importing Countries

Producers in importing countries are obvious beneficiaries of any system of protection of textiles and clothing. Also important, however, are the bureaucrats who design and implement the system and the lawyers and consultants engaged within it. In some countries – the United States, in particular – these are often the same people at different stages in their careers. As young men and women fresh from law school they hone their tolls on the job and then extract rent for the remainder of their professional lives by selling their skills to the highest bidder. Not infrequently, this involves advising exports on how to take advantage of a quota system they have themselves been responsible for creating. Within the European Community, too, the relationship between the industry lobbies and the bureaucracy is intimate. Comitextil, the Community's textile lobby, for example, played an active part in the design of the system of textile and clothing categories used in MFA II and, with slight modification, thereafter.

Exporting Countries

What makes the new protectionism special is the role of exporters. As a system of discriminatory export restraints, the MFA is an international cartel policed by the importing countries. One would expect at least some members of the cartel to be happy about its existence – and so they are. One would also expect each member of the cartel to be quite happy to see his competitors under restraint. There will be differences, however, over whether it is better to be restrained oneself, along with one's principal competitors, or to operate in a world with no restraints, instead.

Normally, one would expect the chief supporters of a cartel among exporting countries to be those with large export shares, like Hong Kong or the Republic of Korea. Correspondingly, one would expect the strongest opposition to the principle of the MFA to come from latecomers, who have little prospect of gaining the favored position now enjoyed by the East Asian newly industrializing countries. Hitherto it has not worked that way in practice, the reason being the widely held presumption that the exporters with the largest shares have also been the most competitive. This somewhat unusual situation ensures that the liveliest disputes have concerned the allocation of quotas among countries, rather than the principle of quotas.

Interests within the exporting countries also have a role. Generally, quota rent is significant for the economies of exporting countries, taken as a whole. Estimates for the 1970s suggest that quota rent may have contributed 4 to 6 percent of Hong Kong's gross domestic product at that time, but the contribution was certainly much smaller by the 1980s (Wolf 1987, p. 273). Quota rents are far more important, however, for the bureaucrats, politicians and entrepreneurs directly engaged in the industry.

In exporting countries most quotas are allocated to existing firms on the basis of past performance, with a small proportion available to new or exceptionally successful firms. One consequence of these methods for allocating quotas is the extraction of rent as bribes by politicians and officials; another is the contribution of quota rent to the profits of many existing procedures. It has been estimated, for example, that quota rent may have contributed most of the profits of the Hong Kong clothing industry during the boom in exports to the United States in the early 1980s (Wolf 1987, pp. 273–74). No wonder the otherwise fiercely independent producers of Hong Kong are so attached to the MFA. Quota rent must have been equally important to established exporters in the Republic of Korea and Taiwan, and in recent years it has become valuable to established exporters in India as well (Kumar and Khanna in this volume, Table 14).

Third Countries

Often ignored in discussions of obstacles to liberalization of the MFA are the interests of exporters – principally, in the developed countries – not covered by export restraints. This is, however, an historically important feature of the system. The "gentleman's agreement" between the United States and the European Community to leave the exports of each other alone allowed both of them to evade the restraint on increased protection inherent in the GATT's MFN clause. Correspondingly, their own producers are among the important beneficiaries of the MFA. Remember that even the United States, not a significant exporter of these products, exported more clothing in 1987 (US$1.14 billion) than all the economies restrained by export quotas, except Hong Kong, the Republic of Korea, Taiwan and India.

The determination to avoid restrictions on their own exports and the corresponding evasions of GATT discipline have been quite an important element in the textile story. On a number of occasions, the United States has reacted particularly violently against decisions by other industrial countries to introduce global quotas. This demonstrates the role of the MFN principle as an obstacle to protection and how important its violation was in the creation and sustenance of the MFA.

Tyranny of the Status Quo

Quite apart from the interests actively engaged, the tyranny of the status quo should not be ignored. Arrangements of this kind change only if there are powerful forces working in that direction. For those engaged within it, the MFA is a well-loved friend. Life without it is almost unthinkable. Most important, perhaps, is fear of the unknown. Studies might suggest that all – or at least most – developing countries would benefit from liberalization in the long run, but many exporting countries wonder how well they would fare if all restraints were removed. Even if moderately optimistic in this regard, they are concerned about the sorts of trade policies that might follow termination of the MFA. A restraint in the hand has seemed more valuable than export expansion in the bush.

The Feeble Forces for Liberalization

Set against the powerful forces in favor of the MFA, the opposition has been decidedly feeble. Consumers in importing countries are the main victims, but have had little clout. Importers have a voice, but one that lacks impact. Retailers will still sell clothes even if they are not made in developing countries, while importers employ too few people to matter. Intriguingly, the main opposition has been intellectual. It has come from economists and a number of policymakers concerned about the costs of the MFA itself as well as its damaging effects as a precedent.

OPPORTUNITY FOR LIBERALIZATION

Despite all the obstacles, there is now a great opportunity to liberalize textiles and clothing. While over-optimism would be unreasonable, the window of opportunity presented by the Uruguay Round must be recognized. Only in such a Round can the broad tradeoffs be made, both across issues and between countries, that are a necessary condition for liberalizing textiles and clothing. Furthermore, the declaration on textiles and clothing at the mid-term review suggests that there is at least some intention to seize this opportunity.

Perhaps the most important reason for optimism is the declining importance of the textiles and clothing industries in developed countries, especially in the countries of northern Europe. Thus between 1972/73 and 1983 employment in textiles and clothing fell by 64 percent in France, 47 percent in the Federal Republic of Germany, 30 percent in Japan, 19 percent in the United States and 15 percent in Italy (Cline 197, Table 5.3). Correspondingly, the political clout of the industry lobbies has diminished.

In the European Community the protection of textiles and clothing has become very much a North–South issue, but the greater dynamism of the Western European economy as a whole – itself partly a result of the program to complete the internal market – has rendered the issue less fraught than the late 1970s. Furthermore, the balance of opinion on trade policy may have become more liberal, one reason being changing opinions in particular countries (notably the

United Kingdom). Partly as a reflection of these developments and partly because of the personalities involved, the present Commission has shown a markedly more liberal bent than its predecessors. One way for such a liberally inclined Commission to show that no "fortress Europe" is in the offing would be to liberalize textiles and clothing.

In the past the textiles and clothing interests in the United States have been able to hold successive MTNs hostage by making maintenance of a special protectionist regime for textiles and clothing the price of the MTN. The Uruguay Round has been an exception, since President Bush has made no formal commitment to the textile industry. This is, no doubt, a reflection of the dwindling importance of the industry. None the less, its clout in the United States should not be underestimated, partly because of its regional importance and the weight given to regional interests by the American political system. The influence of the industry in Congress was shown in 1985 by the support given to the highly protectionist textile bill introduced by Representative Edgar Jenkins (Cline 1987, pp. 208–10). To some extent, however, that support reflected the general protectionist fever of the time, a fever that should continue to decline, along with the United States trade deficit.

No less important than changes in the developed world have been changes among the developing countries. Until quite recently the MFA was seen by many exporting countries as a means of guaranteeing a secure market against the competition of the highly constrained, newly industrializing economies (Hong Kong, the Republic of Korea and Taiwan). This is true no longer. Quite a number of exporting countries – India, Indonesia, the Philippines and Thailand, for example – view the MFA as an obstacle to increased imports. They also believe the newly industrializing economies are losing their comparative advantage, particularly in clothing, because of rising wages (just as Japan did in the 1960s). Businessmen in the newly industrializing economies concur, as is shown by their increasing interest in investment abroad. Thus the MFA is now thought to be an obstacle to the natural economic evolution of trade in textiles and clothing by a growing number of businessmen and policymakers in the developing countries.

SUGGESTED PROPOSALS FOR LIBERALIZATION

Many suggestions have been made for liberalization of the textile arrangement. These ideas fall into three broad categories: liberalization within the framework of the MFA; an immediate fall-back onto a revised GATT; and hybrid schemes, such as tariff quotas and auctioned quotas, which modify the MFA, while still maintaining important features of it. It should be stressed that these are not mutually exclusive alternatives. A successful scheme might incorporate all elements.

Liberalizing the MFA

Assume that the next MFA is to be the last. Then an agreement might be reached, to take effect on 1st August 1991 and run for ten years, with an explicit commitment to liberalization within that term. Thus, by 1st August 2001 there would be no restrictions within the MFA and any surviving restrictions would be fully GATT-consistent, which means above all that they would be nondiscriminatory.

How might one get from here to there within the MFA framework? There are many possibilities.

(a) *Accelerated growth rates.* Under this proposal growth rates of individual restraint levels would increase over the period, probably more rapidly in the second five years, until all restraints ceased to be binding (Wolf 1985). Meanwhile, new restraints would not be introduced during the currency of the agreement. The main advantage of this approach is that it would be familiar to textile negotiators, embodying as it does a very simple extension of the approach of the MFA itself.

(b) *Progressive quota removal.* This scheme would follow that used by the Organisation for European Economic Cooperation during the 1950s. A count would be made of all quotas by product, by origin and by destination. Then a certain proportion would be removed every year (perhaps 10 percent of the original number). By the end of the last year the liberalization coefficient would then be 100 percent.

Under this scheme importing countries would have complete freedom in choosing which quota to liberalize first, with the liberalization valued simply by numbers of quotas or by trade affected. The disadvantage of the former is that much of the earlier liberalization is likely to be of little meaning as trivial quotas are withdrawn. The disadvantage of the latter is that the weighting of quotas by trade affected is complex, since trade weights alter over time. Under this approach it might be necessary to stipulate which quotas are to be removed, year by year, during the initial negotiating period.

(c) *Removal of quotas by product.* Yet another route to liberalization is by products, starting perhaps with the intermediate products that need the least protection. Thus, complete liberalization of all textile products might be completed within the first five years, followed by progressive liberalization of clothing restraints in the second five years. This approach could easily be combined with (a) or (b) above.

(d) *Removal of underutilized quotas.* Underutilized quotas might be eliminated. This could be part of a scheme for liberalization, but it would self-evidently be insufficient on its own.

(e) *Removal of quotas on small suppliers.* As with removal of underutilized quotas, this would be a valuable starting point for a comprehensive scheme for liberalization, but it could not be the whole of it.

The above approaches are not particularly elegant, but they would have the advantage of being simple to manage within the MFA framework, with which everyone is familiar.

Falling Back on the GATT

A second strategy is to move textiles and clothing as swiftly as possible into the GATT framework, but one amended to give higher levels of protection than afforded by the GATT at present. The GATT would be used as a transitional mechanism for liberalization.

The starting point would be a decision within the Uruguay Round not to renew the MFA, which would then disappear after July 1991. It could be replaced by one of two nondiscriminatory, unquestionably GATT-consistent alternatives.

(a) *Global quotas.* Global quotas might be introduced on textiles and clothing in accordance with Article XIX. The important implication is that those of the United States would cover exports from the European Community and *vice versa.* There would then be a powerful incentive to remove such quotas as quickly as possible, though it would also be difficult to introduce them in the first place. If introduced, they might start with the total level of existing imports. The quotas would then either be allocated to importers or auctioned (the latter being a better way of achieving the Article XIII requirement of nondiscrimination).[3] There would also be an explicit, time-bound commitment to phase out the quotas, perhaps by progressive expansion, though most of the alternative techniques, discussed above in the context of individual quotas under the MFA, could be applied to global quotas as well.

Proposals on the above lines were advanced by Gary Clyde Hufbauer and Jeffrey J. Schott (1985, pp. 56–60) when both were at the Institute for International Economics in Washington, D.C. Their proposals include an MFA element, however, in that origin-specific quotas on exports would be maintained during the transitional period.

(b) *Higher tariffs.* Bound tariffs could be raised by mutual agreement, presumably under Article XXV (which allows waivers) or Article XXVII (which permits negotiated modification of bound tariffs). The aim might be to duplicate the overall level of protection now afforded by the MFA.

Estimates of the MFA's protective effect are extremely uncertain, since the results of the many different studies of the implicit protection afforded by the restraints are inconsistent with one another. They do agree on the variability of protection over time. The uncertainty and the variability mean that the replacement of MFA restraints by tariffs can only be a very rough and ready procedure. But then protection by restraints under the MFA is itself rough and ready. For example, the protective effect of MFA restraints is pro-cyclical: the greatest protection is given when it is least needed.

To give some indication of the magnitudes, William Cline of the Institute for International Economics in Washington, D.C., estimated (1987, p. 167) that "today the tariff-equivalent of apparel quotas is probably in the range of 25 percent (beyond the tariff), and that on textiles some 15 percent. . . . [T]he (multiplicative) impact of tariff and quota protection would have risen from 31 percent in the early 1960s to 56 percent today for apparel, while that for textile fabric would have changed from 30 percent to 28 percent." The position of the European Community might not be very different, though tariffs are lower.

The upper limit for "ratification" might then be taken as a tariff of 50 percent on appeal and 25 percent on textiles. The advantage of making such an adjustment during the Uruguay Round is that it would provide the framework for a reciprocal, tariff-cutting negotiation on classic lines, which could include the main exporting developing countries as well as the industrial countries. This negotiation would then commit all concerned to a phased reduction in tariffs on textiles and apparel. There would be the additional advantage that, even though the overall level of protection might initially be similar to that under the MFA, its structure would be more rational than at present, since the MFA provides constantly varying implicit tariffs, which are highest for the least competitive production.

Both of the above approaches have the enormous advantage of representing a forthright repudiation of discrimination. The second has the still greater merit of entailing a return to the basic GATT-consistent means of protection, the tariff. This disadvantage would be that for many exporters the protective barrier could be much higher than at present. For this reason, it would be important to achieve a reduction of tariffs as well. This would have to be achieved within the Uruguay Round, since lowering of tariffs would be impossible outside an MTN.

Hybrid Approaches to Liberalization

The more complex, but intriguing, proposals are hybrids. They involve a degree of globalization and a degree of "tariffication," but they retain the discrimination inherent in the MFA. The main point of difference is whether auction quotas or tariff quotas are to be the principal instrument of protection during the period of liberalization.

(a) *Auction quotas.* In their study of the prospective MRN, published in 1985, Professor Hufbauer and Dr Schott (1985, p. 57) recommended a scheme that combines auctioned global quotas (discussed above) with the maintenance of discriminatory quotas. Under their proposal the global quota would be increased by 6 percent a year, while national quotas would be reduced by 10 percent a year.

The proposal was subsequently developed by Fred Bersten, Director of the Institute, along with a number of his colleagues (1987). The main difference from the earlier proposal was that, in their case, the so-called global quota would only cover producers under restraint. It would be a discriminatory, global quota, a notion entirely suitable to the wonderland world of the MFA.

The principal advantages of auction quotas are greater transparency, a more efficient allocation of resources through simplification of the quota structure and repatriation of quota rent. The latter is deemed particularly valuable by these authors because of their view that the federal government is unable to raise more revenue, for political reasons, and so is unable to finance desirable adjustment assistance programs without the additional revenue. Quota auctions are also justified as a step toward tariffs because of the information they would provide on the tariff equivalent of the quantitative restrictions.

It may be noted that many of the advantages of tariff auctions could be obtained, without the transfer of quota rents from exporters, by encouraging the exporting countries to auction export quotas *anywhere in the world.* While difficult to imagine in practice, nothing would make protection more unpopular in the importing countries, more quickly.

That auction quotas are superior to country-specific import quotas is unquestionable. Their superiority to export restraints is far less certain. For the exporting countries they would only be preferable as part of a strong commitment to liberalization. But this must be doubtful. If auction quotas are a way of helping the finances of a government that is inhibited about raising revenue in any other way, why should that government abandon them? Auction quotas would inevitably increase the political weight of interests in the importing country that are in favor of protection. Since these are, in any case, the most important interests, it hardly seems sensible to strengthen them further.

(b) *Tariff quota*. An alternative to auction quotas is the tariff quota, which has been recommended by Dr Cline (1987; pp. 257–60) and by Gary Sampson, now at the GATT Secretariat (1987, p. 468–68). Under Dr Cline's proposal all existing bilateral restraints would be turned into tariff quotas, with the higher tariff rate coming into effect at the existing quota level. The surcharge over the MFN tariff would be 25 percent for apparel and 15 percent for textiles. A second-tier surcharge would be imposed on "major suppliers" who increased the volume of their exports to the American market by more than 5 percent in a given year. The higher tier would bring the total tariff rate quota to 35 percent for apparel and 25 percent for textiles. Revenue from tariff quotas would be used to finance adjustment assistance.

All tariff rate quotas would be lowered at a rate of 1.5 percentage points a year until eliminated, and the volume threshold for the tariff quota would rise over time, at 1 percent a year for the major suppliers, 6 percent a year for those with less than 5 percent of total imports and 15 percent a year for those with less than 1 percent of the market and those eligible for assistance from the International Development Association (IDA).

Under Dr Cline's proposals the tariff quotas would all be exporting-country-specific, though the tariff rate itself would have only two bands for countries under restraint (and three overall, with the MFN tariff). Dr Sampson's ideas are a little different (1987, p. 464). "The current bilateral export-restraint arrangements would first be converted to category-specific quotas administered by importing countries. Imports by non-quota-holders would be permitted provided a penalty tariff was paid. To avoid disturbances . . . the penalty tariffs would be high enough to render out-of-quota imports prohibitive. . . . Likewise, the distribution of restrained imports across countries would not change, for initially each restrained country would be permitted to maintain its export entitlement."

Each year a proportion of each bilateral tariff quota would be transferred to a global pool to be auctioned by the importing-country government. Imports under the global pool would be at MFN tariffs. (This part of Dr Sampson's proposals would be very similar to that of Dr Bergsten and others, discussed above, since the "global quota" would only apply to countries under restraint.) Over time, liberalization would occur by a steady lowering of the tariff rate on out-of-quota imports.

Tariff rate quotas have attractive features. They could combine most of the existing characteristics of the MFA – discrimination and capture of rent by exporters on intra-quota exports – with a more transparent, price-conforming instrument of protection. For example, the quotas could be by value instead of by physical quantities, which would be an improvement over existing arrangements.

Tariff rate quotas have the advantage of giving a predictable margin of protection rather than the "variable levy" implicit in auction quotas. The margin of protection could also be the same for all exporters, not variable across countries as in the current MFA. They would raise some revenue as the tariffs fall (which would also provide an incentive for lowering them), while continuing to provide compensation to exporters in the form of the rent on the intra-quota amount. They are clearly more consistent with the GATT's general presumption in favor of the tariff. At the same time, they are somewhat complex and unfamiliar. There is also the important objection that acceptance of tariff quotas would legitimize discriminatory tariffs within the GATT.

KEY ISSUES IN LIBERALIZATION

If the MFA is to be liberalized it will be by exploiting such support as can be gained, while trying to assuage protectionist interests to the greatest possible extent. Account must also be taken of perhaps the most disturbing question raised by the history of the textile arrangement: can the GATT cope with textiles and clothing?

The history of the MFA offers two lessons. First, it will never be liberalized without a built-in mechanism of self-destruction. The commitment to liberalize must be irreversible. Otherwise, there is a vicious circle: unless firms are sure that protection will disappear, they will not adjust to living without it, the reason being that governments will, they believe, not remove protection unless firms have adjusted to its absence. Second, the textile interests themselves are unlikely to come up with an agreement to liberalize. Unless such a scheme is evolved in the context of a GATT Round, it never will be. The Uruguay Round probably offers the last opportunity to set a timetable for liberalization this century.

Recommendations for Liberalization

There are innumerable ways to liberalize the MFA and return trade in textiles and clothing to the GATT. The question is whether any of them would work politically. Can the interests now so effectively represented within the MFA be persuaded to prefer liberalization? This is doubtful. It is quite likely that the hostility expressed toward the MFA – even by exporting countries – is a negotiating tactic, the aim being to improve its terms rather than eliminate it.

Assume, however, that there is a real desire to eliminate the MFA. How should it be done? The broad requirements are irreversibility, simplicity and flexibility, with each importing country able to pursue a path toward the agreed end that seems best to it.

The existence of the Uruguay Round makes the termination of the MFA with the present agreement (MFA IV) and its replacement by higher tariffs, to be negotiated and then negotiated down in the course of the Round, attractive. Such a change would represent a decisive shift away from discriminatory restraints and toward a reaffirmation of basic GATT principles, which is precisely what the GATT needs. This would be the approach of Alexander the Great, who solved the Gordian knot by cutting it. Unfortunately, statesmen of that decisiveness are in short supply and, without such determination, the proposal looks infeasible.

If one is to liberalize within the framework of the current MFA, tariff quotas have attractions, largely because they can duplicate most of the features of the MFA, including extraction of rent by exporters. A possible plan is the following.

First, discriminatory restraints on minor suppliers would be removed, while the remaining export restraints would be kept as quotas to be allocated by exporting countries. A global tariff quota for all exports of the category in question from exporters under restraint would be established at the level of the average *value* of imports in the three preceding years adjusted upward by the general inflation of the prices of manufactured goods in world trade. The penal tariff would be established as 25 percent on clothing and 15 percent on textiles, with the quota itself auctioned by the government of the importing country (the advantage over the standard proposal for auctioned global quotas then being that out-of-quota exports would be possible, at the penal rate).

Liberalization would then occur in three ways. First, a given proportion of the initial discriminatory export restraints would be transferred into the global quota every year; second, the global quota would be expanded progressively; third the penal tariff on the global quota would be steadily reduced toward the MFN tariff (which might itself have been increased somewhat in the course of the Uruguay Round). The penal tariff would be eliminated altogether after ten years. Whether all discriminatory export restraint had been eliminated by that time or whether the global quota had ceased to be binding would be unimportant. One could allow importing countries some flexibility in these respects provided the reduction of the tariff continued on the present timetable.

While elegant and well worth consideration, the route via tariff quotas suffers from the disadvantages of being both fairly complex and unfamiliar to negotiators. In addition, it would provide a precedent for discriminatory tariffs. If these advantages were considered insuperable, it would always be possible to take the simplest route of all, however inelegant: liberalization within the existing MFA. A problem with this is that, at some point, there would have to be a jump from a world with quantitative restrictions to one without them. It may be difficult to persuade governments to make this jump.

Buying Out the Opposition

It would be essential to have an international agreement on the broad outlines of a plan to liberalize textiles and clothing. It would not be necessary to agree on all the details. Authors at the Institute for International Economics in Washington, D.C., have argued, for example, that adjustment assistance is a necessary condition for import liberalization in the United States. Accordingly, their proposed reforms incorporate the self-financing of such assistance, whether through tariff quotas or auctioned quotas (Haufbauer and Rosen 1986; Cline 1987; Bergsten and others 1987). A similar view is taken by Robert Lawrence and Robert Litan of the Brookings Institution (1986). A desire by the United States to have such a special program of adjustment assistance, to be financed in this way, would not seem a matter of great international moment.

It is debatable, however, whether adjustment assistance is, in fact, a viable alternative to protection, rather than a supplement to it. The protectionist interests that matter – managers, shareholders and union officials – would not be among those helped by adjustment assistance. Furthermore, the role of trade-related adjustment assistance and the need for earmarked funds are significant issues only in the United States. In the European Community, with its far more developed systems of social welfare and training, there is no role for schemes related only to trade. In addition, most European countries do not suffer from the self-inflicted fiscal wounds of the United States.

When one looks at the exporting side, the question of whether and how to buy out vested interests in the MFA is still trickier. One approach would be to start liberalization by removing restraints on exports from minor suppliers, thus splitting them off from other developing countries. It is possible that a combination of such a move with the introduction of auction quotas, which are clearly inimical to the interests of all exporting countries (unless combined with fairly immediately liberalization), would create a powerful exporting country interest in the abolition of restraints. But this would be a strategically dangerous move. While reducing the desire of interests in the relatively powerless exporting countries to preserve the MFA, it would increase the weight of those interests in the decisively important importing countries. This looks like a half-baked strategy for liberalization.

What is clear is that technocratic solutions, however ingenious, will not be enough. The MFA is a solution to a political problem. It will not be liberalized if the alternative is not politically effective.

Strengthening the GATT

The really fundamental issue is what happens to the GATT. It is already clear that the developed countries would accept the integration of textiles and clothing within the GATT and even the elimination of the MFA, but only if the GATT itself were, in the euphemistic parlance, first "strengthened."

This is not surprising. Textiles and clothing, like agriculture, were taken out of the GATT for a reason. The importing countries found themselves unable to live by their GATT commitments in these important cases. Being somewhat shame-faced about this, they have been prepared to subcontract the business of running the protection of textiles and clothing to the exporting countries. The GATT does, however, remain essentially the same agreement as the one from which the industrial countries escaped, though rather the worse for thirty years of wear. If they are to forego their special arrangement for textiles and clothing, industrial countries will wish to do something about the supposed defects of the GATT that drove them into the special arrangement in the first place.

The European Community has already revealed what changes it wishes to see (GATT 1989b, p. 6):

> Strengthening the GATT rules and disciplines should ensure:
>
> - the effective and lasting opening-up of markets, involving contributions from all the negotiating partners, particularly as regards tariffs, non-tariff measures and derogations for balance-of-payments and infant industry reasons;

- the creation of fair competitive conditions, particularly as regards subsidies, dumping, access to raw materials and the protection of intellectual property;
- improved safeguard discipline.

The important point about this agenda (which is likely to be broadly shared by the United States) is its comprehensiveness. Consider the three elements in turn.

In the first place, developing countries would be expected "according to their level of development" to assume a full range of GATT obligations and commit themselves to substantial liberalization of tariffs and non-tariff barriers affecting textiles and clothing. In so doing they would also have to agree to limit their reliance on the GATT's Article XVIII, which allows protection for balance of payments and infant industry reasons.

From the point of view of the liberalization of world trade and the economic interests of the developing countries themselves, these demands are not objectionable. Nonetheless, they create two major difficulties: first, the developing countries can rightly object that they are being asked to give up perfectly legal and long-accepted forms of protection in return for the liberalization of an illegal system of protection; second, the developing countries are also being required to accept huge changes both in their own trade policies and in their status under the GATT. One must wonder whether these are realistic demands and, still more, whether they are intended to be. They look more like conditions that cannot be met and are not expected to be met.

In the second place, the European Community is proposing to make trade more "fair" by changes in provisions of the GATT governing dumping, subsidies, cheap access to domestically produced raw materials and protection of intellectual property.[4] In these cases the aim would be to improve the ability of the Community to protect its own industry in the face of what it sees as unfair practices by its suppliers. Given the proclivities of the Community's existing antidumping policy (Hindley 1988), antidumping and countervailing duties under such revised codes might serve as a more than adequate, and less than desirable, substitute for restraints under the MFA. Once enough suits were filed, the exporters would queue at the door in their desire to offer VERs. There is the additional risk that the proposed changes would make increased protection easier across the board, which would be no very good return for liberalization of textiles and clothing.

Finally, there is the long-vexed and central issue of the GATT's treatment of safeguard protection under Article XIX. The European Community suggests a special transitional safeguard arrangement for the period of MFA liberalization. It also suggests a new safeguard code that would include "selectivity" (in other words, discrimination). There is little doubt that the MFA could, indeed, be eliminated if nonconsensual selectivity were permitted freely enough under Article XIX, as has been proposed by the European Community since the early 1970s. It is less obvious that this would be a good bargain.

In short, demands for "strengthening" the GATT by major industrial countries would appear to include changes that would make the grant of protection across the whole range of trade easier than it is already. The question is whether one can do better than this. If so, there would have to be two elements. First, the major developing country exporters would, indeed, have to accept both liberalization and more equal participation in the GATT, notwithstanding their resistance to this idea. Second, a way has to be found to make the GATT not more permissive, but both less permissive and more effective.

There are, for example, many excellent proposals for improving Article XIX of the GATT. The problem with all of them is that they would reduce the flexibility of the protecting countries. It is doubtful whether changes in a liberalizing direction would prove acceptable, while changes that would be acceptable are likely to make the position worse.

A partial escape from the dilemma might be through recently announced plans to strengthen GATT surveillance, though these changes will need to be complemented by greater domestic transparency of the costs of protection (Long and others 1989). It would only be if the absurdities of the MFA (and similar systems of protection) were to become obvious to all that their disappearance would leave trade in textiles and clothing more liberal than before.

In the end, the GATT might prove no more able to contain the political pressures generated in textiles and clothing now than thirty years ago. If so, liberalization would only be the temporary way station between two protectionist arrangements. An optimist might argue that the political leverage of the industry is declining and that we have learned our lesson about such special arrangements. Nonetheless, there is a danger that the price of liberalizing the MFA would be acceptance of some of its basic features within the GATT itself. That price would not be worth paying. There are things worse even than the MFA. One of them would be a trading system with the GATT's body and the MFA's heart.

NOTES

The experience in the textile sphere clearly shows that it is simply an illusion to believe that one can manage trade in a particular sector in response to the exigencies of that sector without any consequence for trade policy in general. International trade policies are either based on norms or create norms. World economic relations, therefore, cannot be managed by solving each problem separately without reference to previous solutions and without prejudice to the solution of future problems. (Dunkel 1984, p. 363).

The protectionism of the 1930s was openly adversary; the new one, however, builds on negotiation, indeed, is in a perverse way the result of international cooperation. As a result, the new protectionism is politically stronger because it accommodates a broader range of interests. Where earlier forms of protection created vested interests in the importing country only, the new protectionism has built up equally strong vested interest on the export side as well; paradoxically perhaps, discrimination has become the means of making export industries interested in continuing protection. For all these reasons the new protectionism will be much more difficult to roll back. (Tumlir 1985, pp. 38–39.)

1 The United Kingdom also had such restrictions, but was allowed to maintain them without offering increased market access on the grounds that it was already a large importer and that its domestic industry had made substantial adjustments as well (Dam 1970, p. 302).

2 The fact that this was a formal international agreement was of particular importance

to the Government of Hong Kong, whose policy was (and is) that it should not accept VERs. None the less, it had become convinced of the risks implicit in failure to consent to the textile arrangements.

3 Article XII.2 states that "in applying import restrictions to any product, contracting parties shall aim at a distribution of trade in such product approaching as closely as possible the shares which the various contracting parties might be expected to obtain in the absence of such restrictions." Auctioned global quotas would seem more likely to achieve this than any other form of quantitative restriction.

4. One cannot avoid observing that the European Community's high moral position on dumping is somewhat peculiar for an entity that regards the subsidized export of agricultural produce as an inalienable right.

REFERENCES

Bergsten, C. Fred, Kimberly Ann Elliott, Jeffrey J. Schott and Wendy E. Takacs. 1987. *Auction Quotas and United States Trade Policy*. Policy Analyses in International Economics no. 19. Washington, D.C.: Institute for International Economics.

Brandis, R. Buford. 1982. *The Making of Textile Trade Policy 1935–1981*. Washington, D.C.: American Textile Manufactures Association.

Cline, William R. 1987. *The Future of World Trade in Textiles and Apparel*. Washington, D.C.: Institute for International Economics.

Commission of the European Communities. 1981. "The European Community's Textile Trade." *Europe Information* 44/81. Brussels.

Curzon, Gerard. 1965. *Multilateral Commercial Diplomacy: the General Agreement on Tariffs and Trade and its Impact on National Commercial Policies and Techniques*. London: Michael Joseph.

Curzon, Gerard, Jose de la Torre, Jürgen B. Donges, Alasdair I. MacBean, Jean Waelbroeck and Martin Wolf. 1981. *MFA Forever? Future of the Arrangement for Trade in Textiles*. International Issues No. 5. London: Trade Policy Research Centre.

Dam, Kenneth W. 1970. *The GATT: Law and the International Economic Organization*. Chicago and London: University of Chicago Press.

Dunkel, Arthur. 1984. "Lessons from Textile Experience for General Trade Policy." *The World Economy 7* (4): 361–8.

GATT. (General Agreement on Tariffs and Trade). 1974. *Arrangement Regarding International Trade in Textiles.* Geneva.

——. 1989a. "Mid-Term Review Agreements." MTN.TNC/11. Geneva.

——. 1989b. "Negotiating Group on Textiles and Clothing: Communication from the European Communities." MTN.GNG/NG4/W/24. Geneva.

Hindley, Brian. 1988. "Dumping and the Far East Trade of the European Community." *The World Economy*, 11 (4) 445–63.

Hufbauer, Gary Clyde and Jeffrey J. Schott. 1985. *Trading for Growth: the Next Round of Trade Negotiations*, Policy Studies in International Trade no. 1. Washington, D.C.: Institute for International Economics.

Hufbauer, Gary Clyde and Howard F. Rosen, 1986. *Trade Policy for Troubled Industries*. Policy Analyses in International Economics no. 15. Washington, D.C.: Institute for International Economics.

Keesing, Donald B. and Martin Wolf. 1980. *Textile Quotas against Developing Countries*. Thames Essay no. 23. London: Trade Policy Research Centre.

Lawrence, Robert Z., and Robert E. Litan. 1986. *Saving Free Trade: a Pragmatic Approach*. Washington, D.C.: The Brookings Institution.

Long, Oliver and others. 1989. *Public Scrutiny of Protection: Domestic Policy Transparency and Trade Liberalization*, Special Report No. 7. London: Gower, for the Trade Policy Research Centre.

Sampson, Gary P. 1987. "Pseudo-economics of the MFA: a Proposal for Reform," *The World Economy* 10 (4), 455–68.

Tumlir, Jan. 1985. *Protectionism: Trade Policy in Democratic Societies*. AEI study no. 436. Washington, D.C.: American Enterprise Institute for Public Policy Research.

Wolf, Martin. 1985. "How to Unravel the Multi-fibre Arrangement." *The World Economy* 8 (3), 235–47.

——. 1987. "Handmaiden under Harassment: The Multi-fibre Arrangement as an Obstacle to Development." In Herbert Giersch, ed., *Free Trade in the World Economy: Toward an Opening of Markets*. Tübingen: J. C. B. Mohr (Paul Siebeck).